THE LIVING LINCOLN

THIS IS NO BOOK;
WHO TOUCHES THIS TOUCHES A MAN.
Walt Whitman

The Living Lincoln

THE MAN, HIS MIND, HIS TIMES, AND THE WAR HE FOUGHT, RECONSTRUCTED FROM HIS OWN WRITINGS

Edited by
Paul M. Angle
and
Earl Schenck Miers

BARNES
&NOBLE
BOOKS
NEW YORK

This edition published by Marboro Books Corp.,
a division of Barnes & Noble, Inc.,
by arrangement with Rutgers University Press.

1992 Barnes & Noble Books

ISBN 1-56619-043-6

Printed and bound in the United States of America

M 9 8 7 6 5 4 3

For C. H. W.

Ten years ago the Abraham Lincoln Association of Springfield, Illinois, undertook the preparation of a new edition of the writings of Abraham Lincoln. In 1953 the project was completed with the publication, by the Rutgers University Press, of *The Collected Works of Abraham Lincoln*, edited by Roy P. Basler, with Marion Dolores Pratt and Lloyd A. Dunlap as assistant editors. Eight sturdy volumes made available hundreds of letters and other writings which had not been included in any previous compilation, and offered, for the first time, accurate and fully annotated texts. Without this work, a truly monumental contribution to American historical scholarship, we would not have attempted to compile the present volume.

Our greatest debt, therefore, is to the officers of the Abraham Lincoln Association—now no longer functioning as an active organization—and to the Rutgers University Press, not only for their part in producing the whole corpus of Lincoln's writings, but also for allowing us to make such use of it as we chose. We are only less indebted to Mr. Basler, Mrs. Pratt, and Mr. Dunlap for their annotations, which lightened immeasurably our own editorial work.

For the texts of Lincoln's writings in the present volume we have followed *The Collected Works of Abraham Lincoln*, with one exception. Now and then Lincoln slipped in spelling, and sometimes he inadvertently omitted or repeated a word. We see no reason for retaining "inaugerate" when it is clear he meant "inaugurate," nor do we believe that we are committing any kind of literary sacrilege in making such minor verbal corrections as Lincoln himself would have made, had he always taken the trouble to read over what he had written. We have, of necessity, omitted parts of many speeches and other long documents. Such omissions are clearly indicated by ellipses.

PMA *and* ESM

CONTENTS

THE LIVING LINCOLN

I. New Salem

1831-1837 $\quad$ WHEN John L. Scripps, of the Chicago *Press & Tribune,* asked Lincoln for material to be used in a campaign biography, the prospective author discovered that he would have to deal with a reluctant subject. "Why, Scripps," Lincoln protested, "it is a great piece of folly to attempt to make anything out of me or my early life. It can all be condensed into a single sentence, and that sentence you will find in Gray's Elegy: 'The short and simple annals of the poor.' "

Lincoln's attitude was not a pose. Only twice before had he provided autobiographical information. In the summer of 1858 he had sent the compiler of the *Dictionary of Congress* his life-story in forty-six words. Late in 1859 Lincoln yielded, reluctantly, to the urging of Jesse W. Fell and supplied a sketch to be expanded into a newspaper biography. On the horizon Lincoln could see even then the Presidency as a possibility, yet he limited himself to two and one-half manuscript pages. In transmitting what he had written he charged Fell: "If anything be made out of it [the autobiography], I wish it to be modest, and not to go beyond the material." To Scripps, the necessities of the situation demanded that Lincoln be more expansive—he was then a nominee for the Presidency, and an accurate and reasonably detailed campaign biography was an essential political weapon—yet he satisfied the requirement in seven printed pages. Diffidently, he wrote of himself with disarming candor. This was the narrative of a boy named "A." who, from humble beginnings, now aspired to the highest office in the land.

But all the while Lincoln was disdaining formal autobiography he was creating a unique personal record. Throughout his mature life, as storekeeper, postmaster, surveyor, legislator, lawyer, and politician, he had to write letters, speeches, and other papers. In the Presidency what he wrote—and it constitutes more than half

3

the body of his writing—was distinctly his own. It might be said of many men that the written record which they create in the course of day-to-day living reveals more about their true selves than anyone else can reveal; that statement can be made with certainty of Lincoln.

On hundreds of pages in Lincoln's handwriting are delineated the characteristics for which he is known and venerated—honesty, candor, compassion, humor, humility, faith, love of family and country. Other traits less familiar—pride, impatience, testiness—may be discerned with perhaps more clarity than in the pages of his biographers; not often discerned, but often enough to bring the man within the fellowship of humanity. And of course there is the evidence of development—evolving character, deepening convictions, maturing mastery of expression.

Few great Americans have approached Lincoln's skill with words; none has surpassed it. In moments of inspiration his prose possessed the lyric quality of poetry. But even Lincoln's routine correspondence often had literary distinction. Here is spare writing, logical clarity, imagery when imagery is needed, and frequently a turn of phrase distinctively his own.

The entire body of Lincoln's writings fills eight large volumes. Inevitably, much that he wrote was repetitious, much was too routine or too brief to reveal the man. This volume is made up of those writings having, in the broadest sense, personal significance. Here Lincoln bequeathed to history his story.

In the first twenty-two years of Lincoln's life he left no revealing record. As a mature man he would write that he was born in Kentucky near Hodgen's mill—now Hodgenville—on the 12th of February, 1809. His parents were decent, honest Americans of their time and place. The cabin in which the child first saw life was a primitive and comfortless dwelling, but so were the homes of the majority of those who, like his father Thomas Lincoln, were breaking a wilderness to the plow.

After seven years in Kentucky, Lincoln recorded, the family moved across the Ohio River to southwestern Indiana, settling in a wilderness "with many bears and other wild animals still in the woods." A cabin had to be raised, trees felled, and crops planted—back-breaking labor in which the eight-year-old Lincoln had to take his full share. Within two years Nancy Hanks Lincoln, his mother, died, the victim of an epidemic. The boy's sister Sarah, only eleven years old, cared for the little family as well as she could until Thomas Lincoln brought a new wife, the widow Sarah Bush Johnston, to the backwoods cabin. Other settlers took up land nearby, and the region moved slowly toward civilization. Itinerant schoolmasters, hardly more than literate, set up subscription schools. Abraham attended for short periods, as he had in Kentucky. His total schooling, he computed later, did not exceed a year, but in that time he learned to read and write, and mastered the elements of grammar and arithmetic.

The boy grew tall and muscular, capable, beyond his years, of doing a man's work. As time passed he escaped the narrow limits of his father's farm, sometimes "hiring out" to neighbors, sometimes clerking in the store at the crossroads village of Gentryville, at still other times ferrying passengers from a boat landing on the Ohio, fifteen miles distant, to passing steamers. When, in 1828, Lincoln joined the son of a neighbor in taking a flatboat loaded with produce to New Orleans, he saw, for the first time, a world beyond the stumps and cabins and primitive habits of pioneer Indiana.

Over the years Lincoln grew mentally as he grew in height and muscle. By firelight he read such books—a few only—as he could come by; from his friends he discovered that he possessed the art of anecdote; he found that he could hold the attention of a handful of rustics when he mounted a stump to make a speech, whether in mockery or seriousness. No one else in the region had such abilities.

In fourteen years in Indiana, Thomas Lincoln's worldly circumstances, poor to begin with, became worse. His farm would never yield more than a bare living; the community promised nothing. From Illinois, relatives sent word of treeless prairies with deep black soil of fabulous fertility. Frightened by another epidemic of milk-sickness, the disease that had taken Nancy Hanks Lincoln, the family decided to move again.

In the spring of 1830 the Lincolns lumbered westward. Abraham, now twenty-one years of age, drove one of the ox teams. In ten days the settlers reached their destination—an unbroken prairie on the Sangamon River ten miles west of the new town of Decatur. Lincoln helped to plow the prairie, put in the first crop, and split rails for fences. The following spring, his filial duty done, he struck out on his own.

In the spring of 1831 Lincoln settled in the frontier hamlet of New Salem, Illinois, a straggling collection of log cabins located on a bluff above the Sangamon River twenty miles northwest of Springfield. As a hired hand on a flatboat loaded with produce destined for New Orleans, he had watched the awkward craft hang itself on the New Salem mill dam. Denton Offut, owner of the boat and Lincoln's employer, decided that the infant village offered an ideal site for the commercial empire he intended to create on the prairies of Illinois. After the voyage to New Orleans, Offut opened a store at New Salem, bought the mill that stood there, and hired Lincoln in the dual capacity of clerk and mill hand.

At this point in life Lincoln assumed the role of self-biographer. In less than a year Offut's ventures failed. Lincoln found himself at loose ends. Encouraged by his neighbors, he decided to run for election to the Illinois legislature. By publishing an announcement in the *Sangamo Journal,* of Springfield, on March 15, 1832, he plunged into an activity that would engross him for the rest of his life. Lincoln's first political effort revealed a young man who expected to see the frontier prairies grow into an empire.

To the People of Sangamo County

FELLOW-CITIZENS: Having become a candidate for the honorable office of one of your representatives in the next General Assembly of this state, in accordance with an established custom, and the principles of true republicanism, it becomes my duty to make known to you—the people whom I propose to represent—my sentiments with regard to local affairs.

Time and experience have verified to a demonstration, the public utility of internal improvements. That the poorest and most thinly populated countries would be greatly benefitted by the opening of good roads, and in the clearing of navigable streams within their limits, is what no person will deny. But yet it is folly to undertake works of this or any other kind, without first knowing that we are able to finish them—as half-finished work generally proves to be labor lost. There cannot justly be any objection to having railroads and canals, any more than to other good things, provided they cost nothing. The only objection is to paying for them; and the objection to paying arises from the want of ability to pay.

With respect to the county of Sangamo, some more easy means of communication than we now possess, for the purpose of facilitating the task of exporting the surplus products of its fertile soil, and importing necessary articles from abroad, are indispensably necessary. A meeting has been held of the citizens of Jacksonville, and the adjacent country, for the purpose of deliberating and enquiring into the expediency of constructing a railroad from some eligible point on the Illinois River, through the town of Jacksonville, in Morgan County, to the town of Springfield, in Sangamo County. This is, indeed, a very desirable object. No other improvement that reason will justify us in hoping for, can equal in utility the railroad. It is a never-failing source of communication, between places of business remotely situated from each other. Upon the railroad the regular progress of commercial intercourse is not interrupted by either high or low water, or freezing weather, which are the principal difficulties that render our future hopes of water communication precarious and uncertain. Yet, however desirable an object the construction of a railroad through our country may be; however high our imaginations may be heated at the thought of it—there is always a heart-appalling shock accompanying the account of its cost, which forces us to shrink from our pleasant anticipations. The probable cost of this contemplated railroad is estimated at $290,000;—the bare statement of which, in my opinion, is sufficient to justify the belief, that the improvement of Sangamo River is an object much better suited to our infant resources.

Respecting this view, I think I may say, without fear of being contradicted, that its navigation may be rendered completely practicable, as high as the mouth of the South Fork, or probably higher, to vessels of from 25 to 30 tons burthen, for at least one-half of all common years, and to vessels of much greater burthen a part of that time. From my peculiar circumstances, it is probable that for the last twelve months I have given as particular attention to the stage of the water in this river, as any other person in the country. In the month of March, 1831, in company with others, I commenced the building of a flatboat on the Sangamo, and finished and took her out in the course of the spring. Since that time, I have been concerned in the mill at New Salem. These circumstances are sufficient evidence, that I have not been very inattentive to the stages of the water. The time at which we crossed the mill dam, being in the last days of April, the water was lower than it had been since the breaking of winter in February, or than it was for several weeks after. The principal difficulties we encountered in descending the river, were from the drifted timber, which obstructions all know is not difficult to be removed. Knowing almost precisely the height of water at that time, I believe I am safe in saying that it has as often been higher as lower since.

From this view of the subject, it appears that my calculations with regard to the navigation of the Sangamo, cannot be unfounded in reason; but whatever may be its natural advantages, certain it is, that it never can be practically useful to any great extent, without being greatly improved by art. The drifted timber, as I have before mentioned, is the most formidable barrier to this object. Of all parts of this river, none will require so much labor in proportion, to make it navigable, as the last thirty or thirty-five miles; and going with the meanderings of the channel, when we are this distance above its mouth, we are only between twelve and eighteen miles above Beardstown, in something near a straight direction; and this route is upon such low ground as to retain water in many places during the season, and in all parts such as to draw two-thirds or three-fourths of the river water at all high stages.

This route is upon prairie land the whole distance;—so that it appears to me, by removing the turf a sufficient width and damming up the old channel, the whole river in a short time would wash its way through, thereby curtailing the distance, and increasing the velocity of the current very considerably, while there would be no timber upon the banks to obstruct its navigation in future; and being nearly straight, the timber which might float in at the head, would be apt to go clear through. There are also many places above this where the river, in its zigzag course, forms such complete peninsulas, as to be easier cut through at the necks than to remove the obstructions from the bends—which if done, would also lessen the distance.

What the cost of this work would be, I am unable to say. It is probable, however, it would not be greater than is common to streams of the same length. Finally, I believe the improvement of the Sangamo River, to be vastly important and highly desirable to the people of this county; and if elected, any measure in the legis-

8

lature having this for its object, which may appear judicious, will meet my approbation, and shall receive my support. . . .

Limitations that affected Lincoln's own life shaped the advantages for others that he now advocated.

Upon the subject of education, not presuming to dictate any plan or system respecting it, I can only say that I view it as the most important subject which we as a people can be engaged in. That every man may receive at least, a moderate education, and thereby be enabled to read the histories of his own and other countries, by which he may duly appreciate the value of our free institutions, appears to be an object of vital importance, even on this account alone, to say nothing of the advantages and satisfaction to be derived from all being able to read the scriptures and other works, both of a religious and moral nature, for themselves. For my part, I desire to see the time when education, and by its means, morality, sobriety, enterprise and industry, shall become much more general than at present, and should be gratified to have it in my power to contribute something to the advancement of any measure which might have a tendency to accelerate the happy period. . . .

But, fellow-citizens, I shall conclude. Considering the great degree of modesty which should always attend youth, it is probable I have already been more presuming than becomes me. However, upon the subjects of which I have treated, I have spoken as I thought. I may be wrong in regard to any or all of them; but holding it a sound maxim, that it is better to be only sometimes right, than at all times wrong, so soon as I discover my opinions to be erroneous, I shall be ready to renounce them.

Every man is said to have his peculiar ambition. Whether it be true or not, I can say for one that I have no other so great as that of being truly esteemed of my fellow men, by rendering myself worthy of their esteem. How far I shall succeed in gratifying this ambition, is yet to be developed. I am young and unknown to many of you. I was born and have ever remained in the most humble walks of life. I have no wealthy or popular relations to recommend me. My case is thrown exclusively upon the independent voters of this county, and if elected they will have conferred a favor upon me, for which I shall be unremitting in my labors to compensate. But if the good people in their wisdom shall see fit to keep me in the background, I have been too familiar with disappointments to be very much chagrined. Your friend and fellow-citizen,

New Salem, March 9, 1832.

A. Lincoln.

Lincoln, unsuccessful in his first bid for public office, accepted appointment as New Salem's postmaster. The position, though unimportant, offered money that he needed badly. Yet there were limits to the abuse which he would accept from his patrons.

[July 1, 1834]

Mr. Spears

At your request I send you a receipt for the postage on your paper. I am somewhat surprised at your request. I will however comply with it. The law requires newspaper postage to be paid in advance and now that I have waited a full year you choose to wound my feelings by insinuating that unless you get a receipt I will probably make you pay it again. Respectfully

A. Lincoln

Received of George Spears in full for postage on the Sangamo Journal up to the first of July 1834.

A. Lincoln, PM

Tragic to a young man in Lincoln's circumstances was the loss of one of his principal possessions.

STRAYED OR STOLEN

March 26, 1836

FROM a stable in Springfield, on Wednesday, 18th inst. a large bay horse, star in his forehead, plainly marked with harness; supposed to be eight years old; had been shod all round, but is believed to have lost some of his shoes, and trots and paces. Any person who will take up said horse, and leave information at the Journal office, or with the subscriber at New Salem, shall be liberally paid for their trouble.

A. Lincoln.

New Salem

In 1834 Lincoln ran again for the legislature, this time successfully. Two years later, a seasoned campaigner taking his politics in stride, he stood for reelection. The *Sangamo Journal* announced his candidacy.

New Salem, June 13, 1836.

To the Editor of the Journal:

In your paper of last Saturday, I see a communication over the signature of "Many Voters," in which the candidates who are announced in the Journal, are called upon to "show their hands." Agreed. Here's mine!

I go for all sharing the privileges of the government, who assist in bearing its burthens. Consequently I go for admitting all whites to the right of suffrage, who pay taxes or bear arms, (by no means excluding females).

If elected, I shall consider the whole people of Sangamon my constituents, as well those that oppose, as those that support me.

While acting as their representative, I shall be governed by their will, on all subjects upon which I have the means of knowing what their will is; and upon all others, I shall do what my own judgment teaches me will best advance their interests. Whether elected or not, I go for distributing the proceeds of the sales of the public lands to the several states, to enable our state, in common with others, to dig canals and construct railroads, without borrowing money and paying interest on it.

If alive on the first Monday in November, I shall vote for Huge L. White for President. Very respectfully,

A. Lincoln.

Every candidate for office must expect misrepresentation. Few handle themselves as deftly as Lincoln did when one of his opponents tried to ruin him by rumor.

New Salem, June 21, 1836

Dear Col.

I am told that during my absence last week, you passed through this place, and stated publicly, that you were in possession of a fact or facts, which, if known to the public, would entirely destroy the prospects of N. W. Edwards and myself at the ensuing election; but that, through favour to us, you should forbear to divulge them.

11

The Living Lincoln

No one has needed favours more than I, and generally, few have been less unwilling to accept them; but in this case, favour to me, would be injustice to the public, and therefore I must beg your pardon for declining it. That I once had the confidence of the people of Sangamon, is sufficiently evident, and if I have since done anything, either by design or misadventure, which if known, would subject me to a forfeiture of that confidence, he that knows of that thing, and conceals it, is a traitor to his country's interest.

I find myself wholly unable to form any conjecture of what fact or facts, real or supposed, you spoke; but my opinion of your veracity, will not permit me, for a moment, to doubt, that you at least believed what you said.

I am flattered with the personal regard you manifested for me, but I do hope that, on more mature reflection, you will view the public interest as a paramount consideration, and, therefore, determine to let the worst come.

I here assure you, that the candid statement of facts, on your part, however low it may sink me, shall never break the tie of personal friendship between us.

I wish an answer to this, and you are at liberty to publish both if you choose   Very Respectfully,

A. Lincoln.

Mary Owens was a Kentucky girl who came to New Salem on a visit in 1833. Brought together by a local matchmaker, she and Lincoln reached some kind of understanding. Now Lincoln, elected a second time, found Vandalia, the state capital, duller than he had remembered it. His thoughts turned to Mary Owens.

Vandalia, Decr. 13 1836

Mary

I have been sick ever since my arrival here, or I should have written sooner. It is but little difference, however, as I have very little even yet to write. And more, the longer I can avoid the mortification of looking in the post office for your letter and not finding it, the better. You see I am mad about that *old letter* yet. I don't like very well to risk you again. I'll try you once more anyhow.

The new State House is not yet finished, and consequently the legislature is doing little or nothing. The Governor delivered an inflamatory political message, and it is expected there will be some sparring between the parties about it as soon as the two houses get to business. Taylor delivered up his petitions for the *new county* to one of our members this morning. I am told that he despairs of its success on account of all the members from Morgan County opposing it. There are names enough on the petition, I think, to justify the members from our county in going for it; but if the members from Morgan oppose it, which they say they will, the chance will be bad.

Our chance to take the seat of government to Springfield is better than I expected. An internal improvement convention was held here since we met, which recommended a loan of several millions of dollars on the faith of the state to construct railroads. Some of the legislature are for it, and some against it; which has the majority I cannot tell. There is great strife and struggling for the office of U. S. Senator here at this time. It is probable we shall ease their pains in a few days. The opposition men have no candidate of their own, and consequently they smile as complacently at the angry snarls of the contending Van Buren candidates and their respective friends, as the Christian does at Satan's rage. You recollect I mentioned in the outset of this letter that I had been unwell. That is the fact, though I believe I am about well now; but that, with other things I cannot account for, have conspired and have gotten my spirits so low, that I feel that I would rather be any place in the world than here. I really cannot endure the thought of staying here ten weeks. Write back as soon as you get this, and if possible say something that will please me, for really I have not been pleased since I left you. This letter is so dry and stupid that I am ashamed to send it, but with my present feelings I cannot do any better. Give my respects to Mr. and Mrs. Abell and family. Your friend

Miss Mary S. Owens

Lincoln

Lincoln, a Whig, stood with his party in support of the State Bank, then under virulent attack by the followers of Andrew Jackson. When a Democratic leader offered a resolution providing for an investigation, Lincoln took the floor to argue with skill, and glints of humor, in the bank's defense.

January 11, 1837

There are several insinuations in the resolution, which are too silly to require any sort of notice, were it not for the fact, that they conclude by saying, *"to the great injury of the people at large."* In answer to this I would say, that it is strange enough, that the people are suffering these "great injuries," and yet are not sensible of it! Singular indeed that the people should be writhing under oppression and injury, and yet not one among them to be found, to raise the voice of complaint. If the Bank be inflicting injury upon the people, why is it, that not a single petition is presented to this body on the subject? If the Bank really be a grievance, why is it, that no one of the real people is found to ask redress of it? The truth is, no such oppression exists. If it did, our table would groan with memorials and petitions, and we would not be permitted to rest day or night, till we had put it down. The people know their rights; and they are never slow to assert and maintain them, when they are invaded. Let them call for an investigation, and I shall ever stand ready to respond to the call. But they have made no such call. I make the assertion boldly, and without fear of contradiction, that no man, who does not hold an office, or does not aspire to one, has ever found any fault of the Bank. It has doubled the prices of the products of their farms, and filled their pockets with a sound circulating medium, and they are all well pleased with its operations. No, Sir, it is the *politician* who is the first to sound the alarm, (which, by the way, is a false one). It is he, who, by these unholy means, is endeavoring to blow up a storm that he may ride upon and direct. It is he, and he alone, that here proposes to spend thousands of the people's public treasure, for no other advantage to them, than to make valueless in their pockets the reward of their industry. Mr. Chairman, this movement is exclusively the work of politicians; a set of men who have interests aside from the interests of the people, and who, to say the most of them, are, taken as a mass, at least one long step removed from honest men. I say this with the greater freedom because, being a politician myself, none can regard it as personal. . . .

I am by no means the special advocate of the Bank. I have long thought that it would be well for it to report its condition to the General Assembly, and that cases might occur, when it might be proper to make an examination of its affairs by a committee. . . . But I do not believe any such case has now occurred; and if it has, I should still be opposed to making an examination without legal authority. I am opposed to encouraging that lawless and mobocratic spirit, whether in relation to the bank or anything else,

New Salem

which is already abroad in the land; and is spreading with rapid and fearful impetuosity, to the ultimate overthrow of every institution, or even moral principle, in which persons and property have hitherto found security.

But supposing we had the authority, I would ask what good can result from the examination? Can we declare the Bank unconstitutional, and compel it to cease operations? Can we compel it to desist from the abuses of its power, provided we find such abuses to exist? Can we repair the injuries which it may have done to individuals? Most certainly we can do none of these things. Why then shall we spend the public money in such employment? O, say the examiners, we can injure the credit of the Bank, if nothing else. Please tell me, gentlemen, who will suffer most by that? You cannot injure, to any extent, the stockholders. They are men of wealth — of large capital; and consequently, beyond the power of fortune, or even the shafts of malice. But by injuring the credit of the Bank, you will depreciate the value of its paper in the hands of the honest and unsuspecting farmer and mechanic, and that is all you can do. But suppose you could effect your whole purpose; suppose you could wipe the Bank from existence, which is the grand *ultimatum* of the project, what would be the consequence? Why, sir, we should spend several thousand dollars of the public treasure in the operation, annihilate the currency of the state; render valueless in the hands of our people that reward of their former labors; and finally, be once more under the comfortable obligation of paying the Wiggins' loan, principal and interest.

The slavery question would not come to a fatal issue for almost a quarter of a century, yet it was raised in the Illinois legislative session of 1836–37. The General Assembly, consisting principally of men with strong Southern sympathies, passed resolutions asserting that "the right of property in slaves, is sacred to the slave-holding States by the Federal Constitution, and that they cannot be deprived of that right without their consent." Lincoln and a fellow-legislator filed a dissent.

March 3, 1837

Resolutions upon the subject of domestic slavery having passed both branches of the General Assembly at its present session, the undersigned hereby protest against the passage of the same.

They believe that the institution of slavery is founded on both

15

injustice and bad policy; but that the promulgation of abolition doctrines tends rather to increase than to abate its evils.

They believe that the Congress of the United States has no power, under the constitution, to interfere with the institution of slavery in the different states.

They believe that the Congress of the United States has the power, under the constitution, to abolish slavery in the District of Columbia; but that that power ought not to be exercised unless at the request of the people of said District.

The difference between these opinions and those contained in the said resolutions, is their reason for entering this protest.

Dan Stone,
A. Lincoln,
Representatives from the county of Sangamon.

II. Early Years in Springfield

1837-1842 WHILE Lincoln lived at New Salem, he studied law in the simple fashion that then prevailed. In Blackstone, Chitty and other classic texts he read until he knew enough to pass the easy examination prescribed by state law. In the spring of 1837 he was admitted to the bar.

New Salem could not support a lawyer. Never more than a village, it was fast declining in population and importance. Lincoln turned to Springfield, which, in two years, would become the state capital. John T. Stuart, a Springfield lawyer, offered Lincoln a partnership. One April day in 1837 the young man packed his meager belongings in his saddlebags, rode to Stuart's town, found lodging with a merchant named Joshua F. Speed, and began his career.

Springfield was less hospitable than Lincoln expected. Homesickness and indecision led him to write another letter to Mary Owens.

Springfield, May 7, 1837

Friend Mary

I have commenced two letters to send you before this, both of which displeased me before I got half-done, and so I tore them up. The first I thought wasn't serious enough, and the second was on the other extreme. I shall send this, turn out as it may.

This thing of living in Springfield is rather a dull business after all, at least it is so to me. I am quite as lonesome here as I ever was anywhere in my life. I have been spoken to by but one woman since I've been here, and should not have been by her, if she could have avoided it. I've never been to church yet, nor probably shall not be soon. I stay away because I am conscious I should not know how to behave myself.

17

The Living Lincoln

I am often thinking about what we said of your coming to live at Springfield. I am afraid you would not be satisfied. There is a great deal of flourishing about in carriages here, which it would be your doom to see without sharing in it. You would have to be poor without the means of hiding your poverty. Do you believe you could bear that patiently? Whatever woman may cast her lot with mine, should any ever do so, it is my intention to do all in my power to make her happy and contented; and there is nothing I can imagine, that would make me more unhappy than to fail in the effort. I know I should be much happier with you than the way I am, provided I saw no signs of discontent in you. What you have said to me may have been in jest, or I may have misunderstood it. If so, then let it be forgotten; if otherwise, I much wish you would think seriously before you decide. For my part I have already decided. What I have said I will most positively abide by, provided you wish it. My opinion is that you had better not do it. You have not been accustomed to hardship, and it may be more severe than you now imagine. I know you are capable of thinking correctly on any subject; and if you deliberate maturely upon this, before you decide, then I am willing to abide your decision.

You must write me a good long letter after you get this. You have nothing else to do, and though it might not seem interesting to you, after you had written it, it would be a good deal of company to me in this "busy wilderness." Tell your sister I don't want to hear any more about selling out and moving. That gives me the hypo * whenever I think of it.   Yours &c.

Lincoln.

Mary Owens left Lincoln troubled. After three months he wrote a last letter.

Springfield Aug. 16th 1837

Friend Mary.

You will, no doubt, think it rather strange, that I should write you a letter on the same day on which we parted; and I can only account for it by supposing, that seeing you lately makes me think of you more than usual, while at our late meeting we had but few expressions of thoughts. You must know that I cannot see you, or think of you, with entire indifference; and yet it may be, that you

* Hypochondria.

are mistaken in regard to what my real feelings towards you are. If I knew you were not, I should not trouble you with this letter. Perhaps any other man would know enough without further information; but I consider it *my* peculiar right to plead ignorance, and your bounden duty to allow the plea. I want in all cases to do right, and most particularly so, in all cases with women. I want, at this particular time, more than anything else, to do right with you, and if I *knew* it would be doing right, as I rather suspect it would, to let you alone, I would do it. And for the purpose of making the matter as plain as possible, I now say, that you can now drop the subject, dismiss your thoughts (if you ever had any) from me forever, and leave this letter unanswered, without calling forth one accusing murmur from me. And I will even go further, and say, that if it will add anything to your comfort, or peace of mind, to do so, it is my sincere wish that you should. Do not understand by this, that I wish to cut your acquaintance. I mean no such thing. What I do wish is, that our further acquaintance shall depend upon yourself. If such further acquaintance would contribute nothing to your happiness, I am sure it would not to mine. If you feel yourself in any degree bound to me, I am now willing to release you, provided you wish it; while, on the other hand, I am willing, and even anxious to bind you faster, if I can be convinced that it will, in any considerable degree, add to your happiness. This, indeed, is the whole question with me. Nothing would make me more miserable than to believe you miserable—nothing more happy, than to know you were so.

In what I have now said, I think I cannot be misunderstood; and to make myself understood, is the only object of this letter.

If it suits you best to not answer this—farewell—a long life and a merry one attend you. But if you conclude to write back, speak as plainly as I do. There can be neither harm nor danger, in saying, to me, anything you think, just in the manner you think it.

My respects to your sister. Your friend

Lincoln.

Within a few months Lincoln felt at home in Springfield. Like most thoughtful citizens of his day, he was concerned with a rising wave of mob violence. In Mississippi outraged citizens had lynched a number of gamblers, then had attacked Negroes suspected of planning a slave insurrection; in St. Louis a mob had killed a harmless mulatto on mere suspicion of wrongdoing. In Alton, Illinois, even nearer home, pro-slavery fanatics had murdered Elijah P. Lovejoy to suppress the Abolitionist newspaper which he persisted in publishing.

Asked to speak before the Young Men's Lyceum, Lincoln took the platform to voice a warning. In parts of his address omitted here, Lincoln belabored the St. Louis and Mississippi outrages. Out of shrewd deference to the prejudices of his fellow-citizens, he made only one veiled allusion to the Lovejoy murder, even though that had caused far more consternation throughout the country, and far bitterer cleavage in Illinois, than the other acts of lawlessness which he mentioned.

January 27, 1838

THE PERPETUATION OF OUR POLITICAL INSTITUTIONS

As a subject for the remarks of the evening, *the perpetuation of our political institutions,* is selected.

In the great journal of things happening under the sun, we, the American people, find our account running, under date of the nineteenth century of the Christian era. We find ourselves in the peaceful possession of the fairest portion of the earth, as regards extent of territory, fertility of soil, and salubrity of climate. We find ourselves under the government of a system of political institutions, conducing more essentially to the ends of civil and religious liberty, than any of which the history of former times tells us. We, when mounting the stage of existence, found ourselves the legal inheritors of these fundamental blessings. We toiled not in the acquirement or establishment of them—they are a legacy bequeathed us, by a *once* hardy, brave, and patriotic, but *now* lamented and departed race of ancestors. Their's was the task (and nobly they performed it) to possess themselves, and through themselves, us, of this goodly land; and to uprear upon its hills and its valleys, a political edifice of liberty and equal rights; 'tis ours only, to transmit these, the former, unprofaned by the foot of an invader; the latter, undecayed by the lapse of time, and untorn by usurpation—to the latest generation that fate shall permit the world to know. This task of gratitude to our fathers, justice to ourselves, duty to posterity, and love for our species in general, all imperatively require us faithfully to perform.

Early Years in Springfield

How, then, shall we perform it? At what point shall we expect the approach of danger? By what means shall we fortify against it? Shall we expect some transatlantic military giant, to step the ocean, and crush us at a blow? Never! All the armies of Europe, Asia and Africa combined, with all the treasure of the earth (our own excepted) in their military chest; with a Buonaparte for a commander, could not by force, take a drink from the Ohio, or make a track on the Blue Ridge, in a trial of a thousand years.

At what point then is the approach of danger to be expected? I answer, if it ever reach us, it must spring up amongst us. It cannot come from abroad. If destruction be our lot, we must ourselves be its author and finisher. As a nation of freemen, we must live through all time, or die by suicide.

I hope I am over-wary; but if I am not, there is, even now, something of ill-omen amongst us. I mean the increasing disregard for law which pervades the country; the growing disposition to substitute the wild and furious passions, in lieu of the sober judgment of courts; and the worse than savage mobs, for the executive ministers of justice. This disposition is awfully fearful in any community; and that it now exists in ours, though grating to our feelings to admit, it would be a violation of truth, and an insult to our intelligence, to deny. Accounts of outrages committed by mobs, form the everyday news of the times. They have pervaded the country, from New England to Louisiana;—they are neither peculiar to the eternal snows of the former, nor the burning suns of the latter;—they are not the creature of climate—neither are they confined to the slaveholding, or the non-slaveholding states. Alike, they spring up among the pleasure-hunting masters of Southern slaves, and the order-loving citizens of the land of steady habits. Whatever, then, their cause may be, it is common to the whole country. . . .

Now Lincoln asked: "What has this to do with the perpetuation of our political institutions?"

I answer, it has much to do with it. Its direct consequences are, comparatively speaking, but a small evil; and much of its danger consists, in the proneness of our minds, to regard its direct, as its only consequences. . . . When men take it in their heads today, to hang gamblers, or burn murderers, they should

21

recollect, that, in the confusion usually attending such transactions, they will be as likely to hang or burn some one, who is neither a gambler nor a murderer as one who is; and that, acting upon the example they set, the mob of tomorrow, may, and probably will, hang or burn some of them, by the very same mistake. And not only so; the innocent, those who have ever set their faces against violations of law in every shape, alike with the guilty, fall victims to the ravages of mob law; and thus it goes on, step by step, till all the walls erected for the defence of the persons and property of individuals, are trodden down, and disregarded. But all this even, is not the full extent of the evil. By such examples, by instances of the perpetrators of such acts going unpunished, the lawless in spirit, are encouraged to become lawless in practice; and having been used to no restraint, but dread of punishment, they thus become, absolutely unrestrained. Having ever regarded government as their deadliest bane, they make a jubilee of the suspension of its operations; and pray for nothing so much as its total annihilation. While, on the other hand, good men, men who love tranquility, who desire to abide by the laws, and enjoy their benefits, who would gladly spill their blood in the defence of their country; seeing their property destroyed; their families insulted, and their lives endangered; their persons injured; and seeing nothing in prospect that forebodes a change for the better; become tired of, and disgusted with, a government that offers them no protection; and are not much averse to a change in which they imagine they have nothing to lose. Thus, then, by the operation of this mobocratic spirit, which all must admit is now abroad in the land, the strongest bulwark of any government, and particularly of those constituted like ours, may effectually be broken down and destroyed—I mean the *attachment* of the people. Whenever this effect shall be produced among us; whenever the vicious portion of population shall be permitted to gather in bands of hundreds and thousands, and burn churches, ravage and rob provision stores, throw printing presses into rivers, shoot editors, and hang and burn obnoxious persons at pleasure, and with impunity; depend on it, this government cannot last. By such things, the feelings of the best citizens will become more or less alienated from it; and thus it will be left without friends, or with too few, and those few too weak, to make their friendship effectual. At such a time and under such circumstances, men of sufficient talent and ambition will not be wanting to seize the opportunity, strike the blow, and overturn that fair fabric, which for the last half century, has been the fondest hope, of the lovers of freedom, throughout the world.

I know the American people are *much* attached to their government;—I know they would suffer *much* for its sake;—I know they would endure evils long and patiently, before they would ever think of exchanging it for another. Yet, notwithstanding all this, if the laws be continually despised and disregarded, if their rights to be secure in their persons and property, are held by no better tenure than the caprice of a mob, the alienation of their affections from the government is the natural consequence; and to that, sooner or later, it must come.

Here then, is one point at which danger may be expected.

The question recurs "how shall we fortify against it?" The answer is simple. Let every American, every lover of liberty, every well wisher to his posterity, swear by the blood of the Revolution, never to violate in the least particular, the laws of the country; and never to tolerate their violation by others. As the patriots of Seventy-six did to the support of the Declaration of Independence, so to the support of the Constitution and laws, let every American pledge his life, his property, and his sacred honor;—let every man remember that to violate the law, is to trample on the blood of his father, and to tear the charter of his own, and his children's liberty. Let reverence for the laws, be breathed by every American mother, to the lisping babe, that prattles on her lap—let it be taught in schools, in seminaries, and in colleges;—let it be written in primers, spelling books, and in almanacs;—let it be preached from the pulpit, proclaimed in legislative halls, and enforced in courts of justice. And, in short, let it become the *political religion* of the nation; and let the old and the young, the rich and the poor, the grave and the gay, of all sexes and tongues, and colors and conditions, sacrifice unceasingly upon its altars. . . .

There is no grievance that is a fit object of redress by mob law. In any case that arises, as for instance, the promulgation of abolitionism, one of two positions is necessarily true; that is, the thing is right within itself, and therefore deserves the protection of all law and all good citizens; or, it is wrong, and therefore proper to be prohibited by legal enactments; and in neither case, is the interposition of mob law, either necessary, justifiable, or excusable. . . .

23

The Living Lincoln

Lincoln propounded these questions to his audience: "Why suppose danger to our political institutions? Have we not preserved them for more than fifty years? And why may we not for fifty times as long?"

We hope there is no *sufficient* reason. We hope all dangers may be overcome; but to conclude that no danger may ever arise, would itself be extremely dangerous. There are now, and will hereafter be, many causes, dangerous in their tendency, which have not existed heretofore; and which are not too insignificant to merit attention. That our government should have been maintained in its original form from its establishment until now, is not much to be wondered at. It had many props to support it through that period, which now are decayed, and crumbled away. Through that period, it was felt by all, to be an undecided experiment; now, it is understood to be a successful one. Then, all that sought celebrity and fame, and distinction, expected to find them in the success of that experiment. Their *all* was staked upon it: – their destiny was *inseparably* linked with it. Their ambition aspired to display before an admiring world, a practical demonstration of the truth of a proposition, which had hitherto been considered at best no better than problematical; namely, *the capability of a people to govern themselves.* If they succeeded, they were to be immortalized; their names were to be transferred to counties and cities, and rivers and mountains; and to be revered and sung, and toasted through all time. If they failed, they were to be called knaves and fools, and fanatics for a fleeting hour; then to sink and be forgotten. They succeeded. The experiment is successful; and thousands have won their deathless names in making it so. But the game is caught; and I believe it is true, that with the catching, end the pleasures of the chase. This field of glory is harvested, and the crop is already appropriated. But new reapers will arise, and *they,* too, will seek a field. It is to deny, what the history of the world tells us is true, to suppose that men of ambition and talents will not continue to spring up amongst us. And, when they do, they will as naturally seek the gratification of their ruling passion, as others have *so* done before them. The question then is, can that gratification be found in supporting and maintaining an edifice that has been erected by others? Most certainly it cannot. Many great and good men sufficiently qualified for any task they should undertake,

24

may ever be found, whose ambition would aspire to nothing beyond a seat in Congress, a gubernatorial or a presidential chair; *but such belong not to the family of the lion, or the tribe of the eagle.* What! think you these places would satisfy an Alexander, a Caesar, or a Napoleon? Never! Towering genius disdains a beaten path. It seeks regions hitherto unexplored. It sees *no distinction* in adding story to story, upon the monuments of fame, erected to the memory of others. It *denies* that it is glory enough to serve under any chief. It *scorns* to tread in the footsteps of *any* predecessor, however illustrious. It thirsts and burns for distinction; and, if possible, it will have it, whether at the expense of emancipating slaves, or enslaving freemen. Is it unreasonable then to expect, that some man possessed of the loftiest genius, coupled with ambition sufficient to push it to its utmost stretch, will at some time, spring up among us? And when such a one does, it will require the people to be united with each other, attached to the government and laws, and generally intelligent, to successfully frustrate his designs.

Distinction will be his paramount object; and although he would as willingly, perhaps more so, acquire it by doing good as harm; yet, that opportunity being past, and nothing left to be done in the way of building up, he would set boldly to the task of pulling down.

Here then, is a probable case, highly dangerous, and such a one as could not have well existed heretofore.

Another reason which *once was;* but which, to the same extent, is *now no more,* has done much in maintaining our institutions thus far. I mean the powerful influence which the interesting scenes of the Revolution had upon the *passions* of the people as distinguished from their judgment. By this influence, the jealousy, envy, and avarice, incident to our nature, and so common to a state of peace, prosperity, and conscious strength, were, for the time, in a great measure smothered and rendered inactive; while the deep rooted principles of *hate,* and the powerful motive of *revenge,* instead of being turned against each other, were directed exclusively against the British nation. And thus, from the force of circumstances, the basest principles of our nature, were either made to lie dormant, or to become the active agents in the advancement of the noblest of causes—that of establishing and maintaining civil and religious liberty.

The Living Lincoln

Lincoln sensed that the nation had concluded the first cycle of its history. He saw danger in clinging to the emotions that had dominated that era.

But this state of feeling *must fade, is fading, has faded*, with the circumstances that produced it.

I do not mean to say, that the scenes of the Revolution *are now* or *ever will be* entirely forgotten; but that like everything else, they must fade upon the memory of the world, and grow more and more dim by the lapse of time. In history, we hope, they will be read of, and recounted, so long as the Bible shall be read;—but even granting that they will, their influence *cannot be* what it heretofore has been. Even then, they *cannot be* so universally known, nor so vividly felt, as they were by the generation just gone to rest. At the close of that struggle, nearly every adult male had been a participator in some of its scenes. The consequence was, that of those scenes, in the form of a husband, a father, a son or a brother, a *living history was* to be found in every family—a history bearing the indubitable testimonies of its own authenticity, in the limbs mangled, in the scars of wounds received, in the midst of the very scenes related—a history, too, that could be read and understood alike by all, the wise and the ignorant, the learned and the unlearned. But *those* histories are gone. They *can* be read no more forever. They *were* a fortress of strength; but, what invading foemen could *never do*, the silent artillery of time *has done;* the levelling of its walls. They are gone. They *were* a forest of giant oaks; but the all-resistless hurricane has swept over them, and left only, here and there, a lonely trunk, despoiled of its verdure, shorn of its foliage; unshading and unshaded, to murmur in a few more gentle breezes, and to combat with its mutilated limbs, a few more ruder storms, then to sink, and be no more.

They *were* the pillars of the temple of liberty; and now, that they have crumbled away, that temple must fall, unless we, their descendants, supply their places with other pillars, hewn from the solid quarry of sober reason. Passion has helped us; but can do so no more. It will in future be our enemy. Reason, cold, calculating, unimpassioned reason, must furnish all the materials for our future support and defence. Let those materials be moulded into *general intelligence, sound morality* and, in particular, *a reverence for the Constitution and laws;* and, that we improved to the last; that we

26

remained free to the last; that we revered his name to the last; that, during his long sleep, we permitted no hostile foot to pass over or desecrate his resting place; shall be that which to learn the last trump shall awaken our WASHINGTON.

Upon these let the proud fabric of freedom rest, as the rock of its basis; and as truly as has been said of the only greater institution, *"the gates of hell shall not prevail against it."*

At times Lincoln was betrayed by his youthfulness and allowed his flair for ridicule to escape his sense of discretion. On All Fools' Day, 1838, recalling Mary Owens, he acted like a boy. His confidante, Mrs. Orville H. Browning, was the wife of a fellow-legislator and a very good friend.

Springfield, April 1. 1838

Dear Madam:

Without apologizing for being egotistical, I shall make the history of so much of my own life, as has elapsed since I saw you, the subject of this letter. And by the way I now discover, that, in order to give a full and intelligible account of the things I have done and suffered *since* I saw you, I shall necessarily have to relate some that happened *before*.

It was, then, in the autumn of 1836, that a married lady of my acquaintance, and who was a great friend of mine, being about to pay a visit to her father and other relatives residing in Kentucky, proposed to me, that on her return she would bring a sister of hers with her, upon condition that I would engage to become her brother-in-law with all convenient dispatch. I, of course, accepted the proposal; for you know I could not have done otherwise, had I really been averse to it; but privately between you and me, I was most confoundedly well pleased with the project. I had seen the said sister some three years before, thought her intelligent and agreeable, and saw no good objection to plodding life through hand in hand with her. Time passed on, the lady took her journey and in due time returned, sister in company sure enough. This stomached me a little; for it appeared to me, that her coming so readily showed that she was a trifle too willing; but on reflection it occurred to me, that she might have been prevailed on by her married sister to come, without anything concerning me ever having been mentioned to her; and so I concluded that if no other objection presented itself, I would consent to waive this. All this occurred upon my *hearing* of her arrival in the neighbourhood; for, be it remembered, I had not yet *seen* her, except about three years previous, as before mentioned.

In a few days we had an interview, and although I had seen her before, she did not look as my imagination had pictured her. I knew she was over-size, but she now appeared a fair match for Falstaff; I knew she was called an "old maid," and I felt no doubt of the truth of at least half of the appellation; but now, when I beheld her, I could not for my life avoid thinking of my mother; and this, not from withered features, for her skin was too full of fat, to permit its contracting into wrinkles; but from her want of teeth, weather-beaten appearance in general, and from a kind of notion that ran in my head, that *nothing* could have commenced at the size of infancy, and reached her present bulk in less than thirty-five or forty years; and, in short, I was not all pleased with her. But what could I do? I had told her sister that I would take her for better or for worse; and I made a point of honor and conscience in all things, to stick to my word, especially if others had been induced to act on it, which in this case, I doubted not they had, for I was now fairly convinced, that no other man on earth would have her, and hence the conclusion that they were bent on holding me to my bargain. Well, thought I, I have said it, and, be consequences what they may, it shall not be my fault if I fail to do it. At once I determined to consider her my wife; and this done, all my powers of discovery were put to the rack, in search of perfections in her, which might be fairly set-off against her defects. I tried to imagine she was handsome, which, but for her unfortunate corpulency, was actually true. Exclusive of this, no woman that I have seen, has a finer face. I also tried to convince myself, that the mind was much more to be valued than the person; and in this, she was not inferior, as I could discover, to any with whom I had been acquainted.

Shortly after this, without attempting to come to any positive understanding with her, I set out for Vandalia, where and when you first saw me. During my stay there, I had letters from her, which did not change my opinion of either her intellect or intention; but on the contrary, confirmed it in both.

All this while, although I was fixed "firm as the surge repelling rock" in my resolution, I found I was continually repenting the rashness, which had led me to make it. Through life I have been in no bondage, either real or imaginary from the thraldom of which I so much desired to be free.

After my return home, I saw nothing to change my opinion of her in any particular. She was the same and so was I. I now spent my time between planning how I might get along through life after my contemplated change of circumstances should have taken place; and how I might procrastinate the evil day for a time, which I really dreaded as much—perhaps more, than an Irishman does the halter.

After all my suffering upon this deeply interesting subject, here I am, wholly unexpectedly, completely out of the "scrape"; and I now want to know, if you can guess how I got out of it. Out clear in every sense of the term; no violation of word, honor or conscience. I don't believe you can guess, and so I may as well tell you at once. As the lawyers say, it was done in the manner following, to wit. After I had delayed the matter as long as I thought I could in honor do, which by the way had brought me round into the last fall, I concluded I might as well bring it to a consummation without further delay; and so I mustered my resolution, and made the proposal to her direct; but, shocking to relate, she answered, No. At first I supposed she did it through an affectation of modesty, which I thought but ill-became her, under the peculiar circumstances of her case; but on my renewal of the charge, I found she repelled it with greater firmness than before. I tried it again and again, but with the same success, or rather with the same want of success. I finally was forced to give it up, at which I very unexpectedly found myself mortified almost beyond endurance. I was mortified, it seemed to me, in a hundred different ways. My vanity was deeply wounded by the reflection, that I had so long been too stupid to discover her intentions, and at the same time never doubting that I understood them perfectly; and also, that she whom I had taught myself to believe nobody else would have, had actually rejected me with all my fancied greatness; and to cap the whole, I then, for the first time, began to suspect that I was really a little in love with her. But let it all go. I'll try and outlive it. Others have been made fools of by the girls; but this can never be with truth said of me. I most emphatically, in this instance, made a fool of myself. I have now come to the conclusion never again to think of marrying; and for this reason; I can never be satisfied with any one who would be blockhead enough to have me.

When you receive this, write me a long yarn about something

to amuse me. Give my respects to Mr. Browning. Your sincere friend

    Mrs. O. H. Browning.

A. Lincoln

To William Butler, hot-tempered political associate, Lincoln showed the conciliatory side of his nature when he refused to quarrel over the boundary lines of the new counties which the General Assembly was then creating.

Vandalia, Jany. 26– 1839

Dear Butler:

    Your letter of the 21st. inst. is just received. You were in an ill-humor when you wrote that letter, and, no doubt, intended that I should be thrown into one also; which, however, I respectfully decline being done. All you have said about our having been bought up by Taylor, Wright, Turley, enemies &c I *know you would not say, seriously, in your moments of reflection;* and therefore I do not think it worth while to attempt *seriously* to prove the contrary to you. I only now say, that I am willing to pledge myself in black and white to cut my own throat from ear to ear, if, when I meet you, you shall *seriously* say, that you believe me capable of betraying my friends for any price. . . .

    Nothing could do more credit to your heart, than the mortification you express at seeing the friends with whom you acted in getting up the remonstrance disappointed; but *surely* you ought not to blame us for being unable to accomplish impossibilities.

    My respects to Mrs. Butler & Salome. Your friend in spite of your ill-nature

Lincoln

With Butler, Lincoln continued to play the part of peacemaker, this time as intermediary rather than as principal.

Vandalia, Feb: 1. 1839

Friend Butler:

    Your letter enclosing one to Mr. Baker, was received on yesterday evening. There is no necessity for any bad feeling between Baker & yourself. Your first letter to him was written while you were in a state of high excitement, and therefore ought not to have been construed as an emanation of deliberate malice. Unfortunately however it reached Baker while he was writhing under a severe toothache, and therefore he at that time was incapable of exercising that patience and reflection which the case required. The note he sent you was written while in that state of feeling, and for that reason I think you ought not to pay any serious regard to it. It is always magnanimous to recant whatever we may have said in passion; and when you and Baker shall have done this, I am sure there will no difficulty be left between you. I write this without Baker's knowledge; and I do it because nothing would be more painful to me than to see a difficulty between two of my most particular friends. . . .

No news here now. Your friend as ever

A. Lincoln

The Springfield lawyer, already showing signs of absent-mindedness, moved to recover his belongings from the keeper of a tavern at Tremont, Illinois.

Springfield Nov. 2nd. 1839

Mr. Doughty

I understand my coat was left in your possession. Will you please get a yard or so of coarse domestic (for which I will pay you the first time I see you) and fold the coat in it and tie the card herein enclosed upon it, and hand the bundle to the stage driver on his trip towards Springfield?

You will very much oblige me by doing so. Your friend

A. Lincoln

At the congressional election of 1838 John T. Stuart, Whig, defeated the young and popular Democrat, Stephen A. Douglas. Lincoln undertook the necessary job of keeping his partner informed about what was happening in Springfield. For the time being, Lincoln's own political ambitions must take second place.

Stuart had been elected by a margin of 36 votes out of a total of 36,495. Now, in Washington more than a year later, Stuart still feared that Douglas might contest the election. Lincoln's racy report on the political situation in Sangamon County should have relieved the Congressman's anxiety.

The Living Lincoln

Springfield, Nov: 14. 1839—

Dear Stuart:

I have been to the Secretary's office within the last hour; and find things precisely as you left them—no new arrivals of returns on either side. Douglas has not been here since you left. A report is in circulation here now, that he has abandoned the idea of going to Washington; though the report does not come in a very authentic form, so far as I can learn. Though, by the way, speaking of authenticity, you know that if we had heard Douglas say that he had abandoned the contest, it would not be very authentic. There is no news here. Noah, I still think will be elected very easily. I am afraid of our race for Representative. Dr. Knapp has become a candidate; and I fear the few votes he will get will be taken from us. Also, some one has been tampering with old Esqr. Wycoff, and induced him to send in his name to be announced as a candidate. Francis refused to announce him without seeing him, and now I suppose there is to be a fuss about it. I have been so busy that I have not seen Mrs. Stuart since you left, though I understand she wrote you by today's mail, which will inform you more about her than I could. The very moment a speaker is elected write me who he is. Your friend as ever—

A. Lincoln

A second letter to Stuart dealt in unorthodox fashion with legal matters of mutual concern. The time would come when Lincoln would not dismiss the "Democratic giant"—Douglas—as lightly as he did in this communication.

Springfield, Dec: 23rd. 1839—

Dear Stuart:

Dr. Henry will write you all the political news. I write this about some little matters of business. You recollect you told me you had drawn the Chicago Musick money & sent it to the claimants. A d——d hawk-billed Yankee is here, besetting me at every turn I take, saying that Robt. Kinzie never received the $80. to which he was entitled. Can you tell anything about the matter?

Again Old Mr. Wright, who lives up South Fork somewhere, is teasing me continually about some *deeds* which he says he left with you, but which I can find nothing of. Can you tell where they are?

32

Early Years in Springfield

The legislature is in session, and has suffered the Bank to forfeit its charter without *benefit* of *clergy*. There seems to be but very little disposition to resuscitate it. Whenever a letter comes from you to Mrs. Stuart, I carry it to her, and then I see Betty. She is a tolerably nice *fellow* now. Maybe I will write again when I get more time. Your friend as ever

A. Lincoln

P.S. The Democratic giant is here; but he is not now worth talking about.   *A.L.*

At the age of thirty-one Lincoln had mastered the fundamental political principle that success at the polls depends upon the efficacy of organization at the lowest and broadest level.

[c. January, 1840]

1st. Appoint one person in each county as county captain, and take his pledge to perform promptly all the duties assigned him.

DUTIES OF THE COUNTY CAPTAIN

1st. To procure from the poll-books a separate list for each precinct of all the names of all those persons who voted the Whig ticket in August.

2nd. To appoint one person in each precinct as precinct captain, and, by a personal interview with him, procure his pledge, to perform promptly all the duties assigned him.

3rd. To deliver to each precinct captain the list of names as above, belonging to his precinct; and also a written list of his duties.

DUTIES OF THE PRECINCT CAPTAIN

1st. To divide the list of names delivered him by the county captain, into sections of ten who reside most convenient to each other.

2nd. To appoint one person of each section as section captain, and by a personal interview with him, procure his pledge to perform promptly all the duties assigned him.

3rd. To deliver to each section captain the list of names belonging to his section and also a written list of his duties.

DUTIES OF THE SECTION CAPTAIN

1st. To see each man of his section face to face, and procure his pledge that he will for no consideration (impossibilities excepted) stay from the polls on the first Monday in November; and that he will record his vote as early on the day as possible.

2nd. To add to his section the name of every person in his vicinity who did not vote with us in August, but who will vote with us in the fall, and take the same pledge of him, as from the others.

3rd. To *task* himself to procure at least such additional names to his section.

Lincoln knew that his partner in Washington would be amused by a fracas between the Little Giant and Simeon Francis, editor of the *Illinois Journal,* and heartened by the support of Joseph Smith and his Mormon followers.

Springfield, March 1, 1840.

Dear Stuart:

I have never seen the prospects of our party so bright in these parts as they are now. We shall carry this county by a larger majority than we did in 1836, when you ran against May. I do not think my prospects individually are very flattering, for I think it is probable I shall not be permitted to be a candidate; but the party ticket will succeed triumphantly. Subscriptions to the "Old Soldier" pour in without abatement. This morning I took from the post office a letter from Dubois inclosing the names of sixty subscribers; and on carrying it to Francis, I found he had received one hundred and forty more from other quarters by the same day's mail. That is but an average specimen of every day's receipts. Yesterday Douglas, having chosen to consider himself insulted by something in the "Journal," undertook to cane Francis in the street. Francis caught him by the hair and jammed him back against a market-cart, where the matter ended by Francis being pulled away from him. The whole affair was so ludicrous that Francis and everybody else

Early Years in Springfield

(Douglas excepted) have been laughing about it ever since. . . .

Speed says he wrote you what Jo. Smith said about you as he passed here. We will procure the names of some of his people here and send them to you before long. Speed also says you must not fail to send us the New York journal he wrote for some time since. Evan Butler is jealous that you never send your compliments to him. You must not neglect him next time. Your friend, as ever,

A. Lincoln.

For some time Lincoln had indicated clearly that he could not always be counted on to turn the other cheek. Campaigning for William Henry Harrison in southeastern Illinois, he offended a local Democrat, and handled himself creditably in an exchange of bristling letters.

Lawrenceville, Oct. 31st. 1840.

W. G. Anderson
Dear Sir:

Your note of yesterday is received. In the difficulty between us, of which you speak, you say you think I was the aggressor. I do not think I was. You say my "words imported insult." I meant them as a fair set-off to your own statements, and not otherwise; and in that light alone I now wish you to understand them. You ask for my "present feelings on the subject." I entertain no unkind feeling to you, and none of any sort upon the subject, except a sincere regret that I permitted myself to get into such an altercation. Yours, &c

A. Lincoln

Young, vivacious Mary Todd belonged to a prominent Southern family. In 1839 she came to Springfield to live. Lincoln's persistent courtship ended in an engagement. Then, on January 1, 1841, for reasons still obscure, the engagement was broken. Stuart, Miss Todd's cousin, heard from his despondent partner. Lincoln said nothing about the reasons for the break.

Springfield, Jany. 20th. 1841

Dear Stuart:

I have had no letter from you since you left. No matter for that. What I wish now is to speak of our post office. You know I

35

desired Dr. Henry to have that place when you left; I now desire it more than ever. I have, within the last few days, been making a most discreditable exhibition of myself in the way of hypochondriasm and thereby got an impression that Dr. Henry is necessary to my existence. Unless he gets that place he leaves Springfield. You therefore see how much I am interested in the matter.

We shall shortly forward you a petition in his favour signed by all or nearly all the Whig members of the legislature, as well as other Whigs.

This, together with what you know of the Dr.'s position and merits I sincerely hope will secure him the appointment. My heart is very much set upon it.

Pardon me for not writing more; I have not sufficient composure to write a long letter. As ever yours

A. Lincoln

Three days later Lincoln, still sorely depressed, again wrote to his partner.

Jany. 23rd. 1841– Springfield, Ills.

Dear Stuart:
Yours of the 3rd. inst. is recd. & I proceed to answer it as well as I can, tho' from the deplorable state of my mind at this time, I fear I shall give you but little satisfaction. About the matter of the congressional election, I can only tell you, that there is a bill now before the Senate adopting the general ticket system; but whether the party have fully determined on its adoption is yet uncertain. There is no sign of opposition to you among our friends, and none that I can learn among our enemies; tho', of course, there will be, if the genl. ticket be adopted. The Chicago American, Peoria Register, & Sangamo Journal, have already hoisted your flag upon their own responsibility; & the other Whig papers of the district are expected to follow immediately. On last evening there was a meeting of our friends at Butler's; and I submitted the question to them & found them unanimously in favour of having you announced as a candidate. A few of us this morning, however, concluded, that as you were already being announced in the papers, we would delay announcing you, *as by your own authority* for a week or two. We thought that to appear too keen about it might spur our opponents on about their genl. ticket project.

Early Years in Springfield

Upon the whole, I think I may say with certainty, that your re-election is sure, if it be in the power of the Whigs to make it so.

For not giving you a general summary of news, you *must* pardon me; it is not in my power to do so. I am now the most miserable man living. If what I feel were equally distributed to the whole human family, there would not be one cheerful face on the earth. Whether I shall ever be better I cannot tell; I awfully forebode I shall not. To remain as I am is impossible; I must die or be better, it appears to me. The matter you speak of on my account, you may attend to as you say, unless you shall hear of my condition forbidding it. I say this, because I fear I shall be unable to attend to any business here, and a change of scene might help me. If I could be myself, I would rather remain at home with Judge Logan. I can write no more. Your friend, as ever—

A. Lincoln

A mysterious disappearance, suggesting murder, stirred Springfield and aroused in Lincoln a degree of excitement that he sought to throw off by writing a long letter to Joshua F. Speed, now living on the family estate near Louisville, Kentucky.

Springfield, June 19th. 1841

Dear Speed:

We have had the highest state of excitement here for a week past that our community has ever witnessed; and, although the public feeling is now somewhat allayed, the curious affair which aroused it, is very far from being, even yet, cleared of mystery. It would take a quire of paper to give you anything like a full account of it; and I therefore only propose a brief outline. The chief personages in the drama, are Archibald Fisher, supposed to be murdered; and Archibald Trailor, Henry Trailor, and William Trailor, supposed to have murdered him. The three Trailors are brothers; the first, Arch: as you know, lives in town; the second, Henry, in Clary's Grove, and the third, Wm., in Warren County; and Fisher, the supposed *murderee,* being without a family, had made his home with William. On Saturday evening, being the 29th. of May, Fisher and William came to Henry's in a one-horse dearborn, and there staid over Sunday; and on Monday all three came to Springfield, Henry on horseback, and joined Archibald at Myers' the Dutch carpenter. That evening at supper Fisher was missing, and so next morning. Some ineffectual search was made for him; and on Tuesday at 1 o'clock PM. Wm. & Henry started home without him. In a day or so Henry and one or two of his Clary Grove neighbours came back and searched for him again, and advertised his disappearance in the paper. The knowledge of the matter thus far, had not been general; and here it dropped entirely till about the 10th. inst. when Keys received a letter from the post master in Warren County, stating that Wm. had arrived at home, and was telling a very mysterious and improbable story about the disappearance of Fisher, which induced the community there to suppose that he had been disposed of unfairly. Keys made this letter public, which immediately set the whole town and adjoining country agog; and so it has continued until yesterday. The mass of the people commenced a systematic search for the dead body, while Wickersham was dispatched to arrest Henry Trailor at the Grove; and Jim Maxey, to Warren to arrest William. On Monday last Henry was brought in, and showed an evident inclination to insinuate that he knew Fisher to be dead, and that Arch: & Wm. had killed him. He said he guessed the body could be found in Spring Creek between the Beardstown road bridge and Hickox's mill. Away the people swept like a herd of buffaloes, and cut down Hickox's mill dam *nolens volens,* to draw the water out of the pond; and then went up and down, and down and up the creek, fishing and raking, and ducking and diving for two days, and after all, no dead body found. In the meantime a sort of scuffling ground had been found in the brush in the angle or point where the road leading into the woods past the brewery, and the one leading in past the brickyard join. From this scuffle-ground, was the sign of something about the size of a man having been dragged to the edge of the thicket, where it joined the track of some small-wheeled carriage which was drawn by one horse, as shown by the horse tracks. The carriage track led off towards Spring Creek. Near this drag-trail, Dr. Merryman found *two hairs,* which after a long scientific examination, he pronounced to be triangular human hairs, which term, he says includes within it, the whiskers, the hairs growing under the arms and on other parts of the body; and he judged that these two were of the whiskers, because the ends were cut, showing that they had flourished in the neighbourhood of the razor's operations. On Thursday last, Jim: Maxey brought in William Trailor from Warren. On the same day Arch: was arrested and put in jail. Yesterday (Friday) William was put upon his examining trial before May and Lavely. Archibald and Henry were both present. Lamborn prosecuted, and Logan, Baker, and your humble servant, defended. A great many witnesses were introduced and examined; but I shall only mention those whose testimony seemed to be the most important. The first of these was Capt. Ransdell. He swore, that when William and Henry left Springfield for home on the Tuesday before mentioned, they did not take the direct route, which, you know, leads by the butcher shop, but that they followed the street north until they got opposite, or nearly opposite May's new house, after which he could not see them from where he stood; and it was afterwards proven that in about an hour after they started, they came into the street by the butcher's shop from towards the brickyard. Dr. Merryman & others swore to what is before stated about the scuffle-ground, drag-trail, whiskers, and carriage tracks. Henry was then introduced by the prosecution. He swore, that when they started for home, they went out north as Ransdell stated, and turned down west by the brickyard into the woods, and there met Archibald; that they proceeded a small distance further, where he was placed as a sentinel to watch for, and announce the approach of anyone that might happen that way; that William and Arch: took the dearborn out of the road a small distance to the edge of the thicket, where they stopped, and he saw them lift the body of a man into it; that they then moved off with the carriage in the direction of Hickox's mill, and he loitered about for something like an hour, when William returned with the carriage, but without Arch: and said that they had put *him* in a safe place; that they then went somehow, he did not know exactly how, into the road close to the brewery, and proceeded on to Clary's Grove. He also stated that sometime during the day, William told him, that he and Arch: had killed Fisher the evening before; that the way they did it was by him (William) knocking him down with a club, and Arch: then choking him to death. An old man from Warren, called Dr. Gilmore, was then introduced on the part of the defence. He swore that he had known Fisher for several years; that Fisher had resided at his house a long time at each of two different spells; once while he built a barn for him, and once while he was doctored for some chronic disease; that two or three years ago, Fisher had a serious hurt in his head by the bursting of a gun, since which he has been subject to continual bad health, and occasional aberations of mind. He also stated that on last Tuesday, being the same day that Maxey arrested William Trailor, he (the Dr.) was from home in the early part of the day, and on his return about 11 o'clock, found Fisher at his house in bed, and apparently very unwell; that he asked how he had come from Springfield; that Fisher said he had come by Peoria, and also told of several other places he had been at not in the direction of Peoria, which showed that he, at the time of speaking, did not know where he had been, or that he had been wandering about in a state of derangement. He further stated that in about two hours he received a note from one of William Trailor's friends, advising him of his arrest, and requesting him to go on to Springfield as a witness, to testify to the state of Fisher's health in former times; that he immediately set off, catching up two of his neighbours, as company, and riding all evening and all night, overtook Maxey & William at Lewiston in Fulton County; that Maxey refusing to discharge Trailor upon his statement, his two neighbours returned, and he came on to Springfield. Some question being made whether the doctor's story was not a fabrication, several acquaintances of his, among whom was the same post master who wrote to Keys as before mentioned, were introduced as sort of compurgators, who all swore, that they knew the doctor to be of good character for truth and veracity, and generally of good character in every way. Here the testimony ended, and the Trailors were discharged, Arch: and William expressing, both in word and manner their entire confidence that Fisher would be found alive at the doctor's by Galaway, Mallory, and Myers, who a day before had been dispatched for that purpose; while Henry still protested that no power on earth could ever show Fisher alive. Thus stands this curious affair now. When the doctor's story was first made public, it was amusing to scan and contemplate the countenances, and hear the remarks of those who had been actively engaged in the search for the dead body. Some looked quizzical, some melancholy, and some furiously angry. Porter, who had been very active, swore he always knew the man was not dead, and that *he* had not stirred an inch to hunt for him; Langford, who had taken the lead in cutting down Hickox's mill dam, and wanted to hang Hickox for objecting, looked most awfully woebegone; he seemed the *"wictim of hunrequited haffection"* as represented in the comic almanac we used to laugh over; and Hart, the little drayman that hauled Molly home once, said it was too *damned* bad, to have so much trouble, and no hanging after all.

I commenced this letter on yesterday, since which I received yours of the 13th. I stick to my promise to come to Louisville. Nothing new here except what I have written. I have not seen Sarah since my long trip, and I am going out there as soon as I mail this letter. Yours forever

Lincoln.

In the summer of 1841 Lincoln visited the Speed homestead. Returning to Springfield with his host, he saw a sight that he would never forget. His first record of the experience, which minimized the intensity of his feeling, went to Speed's younger sister.

Bloomington, Illinois, Sept. 27th. 1841

Miss Mary Speed,
Louisville, Ky.

My Friend:

Having resolved to write to some of your mother's family, and not having the express permission of any one of them to do so, I have had some little difficulty in determining on which to inflict the task of reading what I now feel must be a most dull and silly letter; but when I remembered that you and I were something of cronies while I was at Farmington, and that, while there, I once was under the necessity of shutting you up in a room to prevent your committing an assault and battery upon me, I instantly decided that you should be the devoted one.

I assume that you have not heard from Joshua & myself since we left, because I think it doubtful whether he has written.

You remember there was some uneasiness about Joshua's health when we left. That little indisposition of his turned out to be nothing serious; and it was pretty nearly forgotten when we reached Springfield. We got on board the steamboat Lebanon, in the locks of the canal about 12. o'clock. M. of the day we left, and reached St. Louis the next Monday at 8 P.M. Nothing of interest happened during the passage, except the vexatious delays occasioned by the sandbars be thought interesting. By the way, a fine example was presented on board the boat for contemplating the effect of *condition* upon human happiness. A gentleman had purchased twelve Negroes in different parts of Kentucky and was taking them to a farm in the South. They were chained six and six together. A small iron clevis was around the left wrist of each, and this fastened to the main chain by a shorter one at a convenient distance from the others; so that the Negroes were strung together precisely like so many fish upon a trot-line. In this condition they were being separated forever from the scenes of their childhood, their friends, their fathers and mothers, and brothers and sisters, and many of them, from their wives and children, and going into perpetual slavery where the lash of the master is proverbially more ruthless and unrelenting than any other where; and yet amid all these distressing circumstances, as we would think them, they were the most cheerful and apparently happy creatures on board. One, whose offence for which he had been sold was an over-fondness for his wife, played the fiddle almost continually; and the others danced, sung, cracked jokes, and played various games with cards from day to day. How true it is that "God tempers the wind to the shorn lamb," or in other words, that He renders the worst of human conditions tolerable, while He permits the best, to be nothing better than tolerable.

To return to the narrative. When we reached Springfield, I staid but one day when I started on this tedious circuit where I now am. Do you remember my going to the city while I was in Kentucky, to have a tooth extracted, and making a failure of it? Well, that same old tooth got to paining me so much, that about a week since I had it torn out, bringing with it a bit of the jawbone; the consequence of which is that my mouth is now so sore that I can neither talk, nor eat. I am literally "subsisting on savoury remembrances"—that is, being unable to eat, I am living upon the remembrance of the delicious dishes of peaches and cream we used to have at your house.

When we left, Miss Fanny Henning * was owing you a visit, as I understood. Has she paid it yet? If she has, are you not convinced that she is one of the sweetest girls in the world? There is but one thing about her, so far as I could perceive, that I would otherwise than as it is. That is something of a tendency to melancholy. This, let it be observed, is a misfortune not a fault. Give her an assurance of my very highest regard, when *you* see her.

Is little Siss Eliza Davis at your house yet? If she is kiss her "o'er and o'er again" for me.

* Speed's fiancée.

Early Years in Springfield

Tell your mother that I have not got her "present" * with me; but that I intend to read it regularly when I return home. I doubt not that it is really, as she says, the best cure for the "blues" could one but take it according to the truth.

Give my respects to all your sisters (including "Aunt Emma") and brothers. Tell Mrs. Peay, of whose happy face I shall long retain a pleasant remembrance, that I have been trying to think of a name for her homestead, but as yet, cannot satisfy myself with one. I shall be very happy to receive a line from you, soon after you receive this; and, in case you choose to favour me with one, address it to Charleston, Coles Co. Ills as I shall be there about the time to receive it. Your sincere friend

A. Lincoln

Speed returned to Kentucky, heart set on marriage, but torn by doubt. Lincoln, out of his experience with Mary Owens and Mary Todd, tried to counsel his friend.

[January 3? 1842]

My Dear Speed:

Feeling, as you know I do, the deepest solicitude for the success of the enterprize you are engaged in, I adopt this as the last method I can invent to aid you, in case (which God forbid) you shall need any aid. I do not place what I am going to say on paper, because I can say it any better in that way than I could by word of mouth; but because, were I to say it orally, before we part, most likely you would forget it at the very time when it might do you some good. As I think it reasonable that you will feel very badly some time between this and the final consummation of your purpose, it is intended that you shall read this just at such a time.

Why I say it is reasonable that you will feel very badly yet, is, because of *three special causes,* added to the *general one* which I shall mention.

The general cause is, that you are *naturally* of a *nervous temperament;* and this I say from what I have seen of you personally, and what you have told me concerning your mother at various times, and concerning your brother William at the time his wife died.

The first special cause is, *your exposure to bad weather* on

* An Oxford Bible.

your journey, which my experience clearly proves to be very severe on defective nerves.

The second is, *the absence of all business and conversation of friends,* which might divert your mind, and give it occasional rest from that *intensity* of thought, which will sometimes wear the sweetest idea thread-bare and turn it to the bitterness of death.

The third is, *the rapid and near approach of that crisis on which all your thoughts and feelings concentrate.*

If from all these causes you shall escape and go through triumphantly, without another "twinge of the soul," I shall be most happily, but most egregiously deceived.

If, on the contrary, you shall, as I expect you will at some time, be agonized and distressed, let me, who have some reason to speak with judgment on such a subject, beseech you, to ascribe it to the causes I have mentioned; and not to some false and ruinous suggestion of the Devil.

"But" you will say "do not your causes apply to everyone engaged in a like undertaking?"

By no means. *The particular causes,* to a greater or less extent, perhaps do apply in all cases; but the *general one,* nervous debility, which is the key and conductor of all the particular ones, and without which *they* would be utterly harmless, though it *does* pertain to you, *does not* pertain to one in a thousand. It is out of this, that the painful difference between you and the mass of the world springs.

I know what the painful point with you is, at all times when you are unhappy. It is an apprehension that you do not love her as you should. What nonsense!—How came you to court her? Was it because you thought she desired it; and that you had given her reason to expect it? If it was for that, why did not the same reason make you court Ann Todd, and at least twenty others of whom you can think, & to whom it would apply with greater force than to *her?* Did you court her for her wealth? Why, you knew she had none. But you say you *reasoned* yourself *into* it. What do you mean by that? Was it not, that you found yourself unable to *reason* yourself *out of* it? Did you not think, and partly form the purpose, of courting her the first time you ever saw or heard of her? What had reason to do with it, at that early stage? There was nothing *at that time* for reason to work upon. Whether she was moral, amiable, sensible, or even of good character, you did not, nor could not then know; except perhaps you might infer the last from the company you found her in. All you then did or could know of her, was her *personal appearance and deportment;* and these, if they impress at all, impress the *heart* and not the head.

Say candidly, were not those heavenly *black eyes,* the whole basis of all your early *reasoning* on the subject?

After you and I had once been at her residence, did you not go and take me all the way to Lexington and back, for no other purpose but to get to see her again, on our return, seeming to take a trip for that express object?

What earthly consideration would you take to find her scouting and despising you, and giving herself up to another? But of this you have no apprehension; and therefore you cannot bring it home to your feelings.

I shall be so anxious about you, that I want you to write me every mail. Your friend

Lincoln

A man whose fiancée is gravely ill needs the sympathy of a friend like Lincoln.

Springfield, Ills. Feby. 3– 1842–

Dear Speed:

Your letter of the 25th. Jany. came to hand today. You well know that I do not feel my own sorrows much more keenly than I do yours, when I know of them; and yet I assure you I was not much hurt by what you wrote me of your excessively bad feeling at the time you wrote. Not that I am less capable of sympathizing with you now than ever; not that I am less your friend than ever, but because I hope and believe, that your present anxiety and distress about *her* health and *her* life, must and will forever banish those horrid doubts, which I know you sometimes felt, as to the truth of your affection for her. If they can be once and forever removed, (and I almost feel a presentiment that the Almighty has sent your present affliction expressly for that object) surely, nothing can come in their stead, to fill their immeasurable measure of misery. The death scenes of those we love, are surely painful enough; but these we are prepared to, and expect to see. They happen to all, and all know they must happen. Painful as they are, they are not an unlooked-for-sorrow. Should she, as you fear, be destined to an early grave, it is indeed, a great consolation to know that she is so well prepared to meet it. Her religion, which you once disliked so much, I will venture you now prize most highly.

But I hope your melancholy bodings as to her early death, are not well founded. I even hope, that ere this reaches you, she will have returned with improved and still improving health; and that you will have met her, and forgotten the sorrows of the past, in the enjoyment of the present.

I would say more if I could; but it seems I have said enough. It really appears to me that you yourself ought to rejoice, and not sorrow, at this indubitable evidence of your undying affection for her. Why Speed, if you did not love her, although you might not wish her death, you would most calmly be resigned to it. Perhaps this point is no longer a question with you, and my pertinacious dwelling upon it, is a rude intrusion upon your feelings. If so, you must pardon me. You know the hell I have suffered on that point, and how tender I am upon it. You know I do not mean wrong.

I have been quite clear of hypo * since you left, —even better than I was along in the fall.

I have seen Sarah but once. She seemed very cheerful, and so, I said nothing to her about what we spoke of.

Old Uncle Billy Herndon is dead; and it is said this evening that Uncle Ben Ferguson will not live. This I believe is all the news, and enough at that unless it were better.

Write me immediately on the receipt of this. Your friend, as ever

Lincoln

Speed, in marrying, passed beyond the range of Lincoln's experience, but not beyond the limits of his imagination.

Springfield, Ills. Feby. 13. 1842—

Dear Speed:

Yours of the 1st. inst. came to hand three or four days ago. When this shall reach you, you will have been Fanny's husband several days. You know my desire to befriend you is everlasting— that I will never cease, while I know how to do anything.

But you will always hereafter, be on ground that I have never occupied, and consequently, if advice were needed, I might advise wrong.

* Hypochondria.

Early Years in Springfield

I do fondly hope, however, that you will never again need any comfort from abroad. But should I be mistaken in this—should excessive pleasure still be accompanied with a painful counterpart at times, still let me urge you, as I have ever done, to remember in the depth and even the agony of despondency, that very shortly you are to feel well again. I am now fully convinced, that you love her as ardently as you are capable of loving. Your ever being happy in her presence, and your intense anxiety about her health, if there were nothing else, would place this beyond all dispute in my mind. I incline to think it probable, that your nerves will fail you occasionally for awhile; but once you get them fairly graded now, that trouble is over forever.

I think if I were you, in case my mind were not exactly right, I would avoid being *idle;* I would immediately engage in some business, or go to making preparations for it, which would be the same thing.

If you went through the ceremony *calmly,* or even with sufficient composure not to excite alarm in any present, you are safe, beyond question, and in two or three months, to say the most, will be the happiest of men.

I hope with tolerable confidence, that this letter is a plaster for a place that is no longer sore. God grant it may be so.

I would desire you to give my particular respects to Fanny, but perhaps you will not wish her to know you have received this, lest she should desire to see it. Make her write me an answer to my last letter to her at any rate. I would set great value upon another letter from her.

Write me whenever you have leisure. Yours forever.

A. Lincoln

P.S. I have been quite a man ever since you left.

The Washingtonian Society, seeking to reform inebriates through the experience of reformed drunkards, was at the height of its crusading fervor when Lincoln addressed its members.

February 22, 1842

Although the temperance cause has been in progress for near twenty years, it is apparent to all, that it is, *just now,* being crowned with a degree of success, hitherto unparalleled.

The list of its friends is daily swelled by the additions of fifties, of hundreds, and of thousands. The cause itself seems suddenly transformed from a cold abstract theory, to a living, breathing, active, and powerful chieftain, going forth "conquering and to conquer." The citadels of his great adversary are daily being stormed and dismantled; his temples and his altars, where the rites of his idolatrous worship have long been performed, and where human sacrifices have long been wont to be made, are daily desecrated and deserted. The trump of the conqueror's fame is sounding from hill to hill, from sea to sea, and from land to land, and calling millions to his standard at a blast.

For this new and splendid success, we heartily rejoice. That that success is so much greater *now* than *heretofore,* is doubtless owing to rational causes; and if we would have it to continue, we shall do well to enquire what those causes are. The warfare heretofore waged against the demon of intemperance, has, somehow or other, been erroneous. Either the champions engaged, or the tactics they adopted, have not been the most proper. These champions for the most part, have been preachers, lawyers, and hired agents. Between these and the mass of mankind, there is a want of *approachability,* if the term be admissible, partially at least, fatal to their success. They are supposed to have no sympathy of feeling or interest, with those very persons whom it is their object to convince and persuade.

And again, it is so easy and so common to ascribe motives to men of these classes, other than those they profess to act upon. The *preacher,* it is said, advocates temperance because he is a fanatic, and desires a union of church and state; the *lawyer,* from his pride and vanity of hearing himself speak; and the *hired agent,* for his salary. But when one, who has long been known as a victim of intemperance, bursts the fetters that have bound him, and appears before his neighbors "clothed, and in his right mind," a redeemed specimen of long-lost humanity, and stands up with tears of joy trembling in eyes, to tell of the miseries *once* endured, *now* to be endured no more forever; of his once naked and starving children, now clad and fed comfortably; of a wife long weighed down with woe, weeping, and a broken heart, now restored to health, happiness, and renewed affection; and how easily it all is done, once it is resolved to be done; however simple his language, there is a logic, and an eloquence in it, that few, with human feelings, can resist. They cannot say that *he* desires a union of church and state, for he is not a church member; they cannot say *he* is vain of hearing himself speak, for his whole demeanor shows, he would gladly avoid speaking at all; they cannot say *he* speaks for pay for he receives none, and asks for none. Nor can his sincerity in any way be doubted; or his sympathy for those he would persuade to imitate his example, be denied.

Lincoln realized that the heavy drinker was a person before he was a problem.

In my judgment, it is to the battles of this new class of champions that our late success is greatly, perhaps chiefly, owing. But, had the old school champions themselves, been of the most wise selecting, was their *system* of tactics, the most judicious? It seems to me, it was not. Too much denunciation against dram-sellers and dram-drinkers was indulged in. This, I think, was both impolitic and unjust. It was *impolitic,* because, it is not much in the nature of man to be driven to anything; still less to be driven about that which is exclusively his own business; and least of all, where such driving is to be submitted to, at the expense of pecuniary interest, or burning appetite. When the dram-seller and drinker, were incessantly told, not in the accents of entreaty and persuasion, diffidently addressed by erring man to an erring brother; but in the thundering tones of anathema and denunciation, with which the lordly judge often groups together all the crimes of the felon's life, and thrusts them in his face just ere he passes sentence of death upon him, that *they* were the authors of all the vice and misery and crime in the land; that *they* were the manufacturers and material of all the thieves and robbers and murderers that infested the earth; that *their* houses were the workshops of the devil; and that *their* *persons* should be shunned by all the good and virtuous, as moral pestilences—I say, when they were told all this, and in this way, it is not wonderful that they were slow, *very slow,* to acknowledge the truth of such denunciations, and to join the ranks of their denouncers, in a hue and cry against themselves.

To have expected them to do otherwise than as they did—to have expected them not to meet denunciation with denunciation, crimination with crimination, and anathema with anathema, was to expect a reversal of human nature, which is God's decree, and never can be reversed. When the conduct of men is designed to be influenced, *persuasion,* kind, unassuming persuasion, should ever be adopted. It is an old and a true maxim, that a "drop of honey catches more flies than a gallon of gall." So with men. If you would win a man to your cause, *first* convince him that you are his sincere friend. Therein is a drop of honey that catches his heart, which, say what he will, is the great highroad to his reason, and which, when once gained, you will find but little trouble in convincing his judgment of the justice of your cause, if indeed that cause really be a just one. On the contrary, assume to dictate to his judgment, or to command his action, or to mark him as one to be shunned and despised, and he will retreat within himself, close all the avenues to his head and his heart; and tho' your cause be naked truth itself, transformed to the heaviest lance, harder than steel, and sharper than steel can be made, and tho' you throw it with more than Herculean force and precision, you shall no more be able to pierce him, than to penetrate the hard shell of a tortoise with a rye straw.

Such is man, and so *must* he be understood by those who would lead him, even to his own best interest.

On this point, the Washingtonians greatly excel the temperance advocates of former times. Those whom *they* desire to convince and persuade, are their old friends and companions. They know they are not demons, nor even the worst of men. *They* know that generally, they are kind, generous and charitable, even beyond the example of their more staid and sober neighbors. *They* are practical philanthropists; and *they* glow with a generous and brotherly zeal, that mere theorizers are incapable of feeling. Benevolence and charity possess *their* hearts entirely; and out of the abundance of their hearts, their tongues give utterance. "Love through all their actions runs, and all their words are mild." In this spirit they speak and act, and in the same, they are heard and regarded. And when such is the temper of the advocate, and such of the audience, no good cause can be unsuccessful. . . .

Lincoln admitted that the practice of drinking was as old as the world itself. Moreover, there was no stigma to the buying and selling of liquor.

If, then, what I have been saying be true, is it wonderful, that *some* should think and act *now*, as *all* thought and acted *twenty years ago?* And is it *just* to assail, *contemn,* or despise them, for doing so? The universal *sense* of mankind, on any subject, is an argument, or at least an *influence* not easily overcome. The success of the argument in favor of the existence of an over-ruling Providence, mainly depends upon that sense; and men ought not, in justice, to be denounced for yielding to it, in any case, or for giving it up slowly, *especially,* where they are backed by interest, fixed habits, or burning appetites.

Another error, as it seems to me, into which the old reformers fell, was, the position that all habitual drunkards were utterly incorrigible, and therefore, must be turned adrift, and damned without remedy, in order that the grace of temperance might abound to the temperate *then,* and to all mankind some hundred years *thereafter.* There is in this something so repugnant to humanity, so uncharitable, so cold-blooded and feelingless, that it never did, nor ever can enlist the enthusiasm of a popular cause. We could not love the man who taught it—we could not hear him with patience. The heart could not throw open its portals to it. The generous man could not adopt it. It could not mix with his blood. It looked so fiendishly selfish, so like throwing fathers and brothers overboard, to lighten the boat for our security—that the noble-minded shrank from the manifest meanness of the thing.

And besides this, the benefits of a reformation to be effected by such a system, were too remote in point of time, to warmly engage many in its behalf. Few can be induced to labor exclusively for posterity; and none will do it enthusiastically. Posterity has done nothing for us; and theorize on it as we may, practically we shall do very little for it, unless we are made to think, we are, at the same time, doing something for ourselves. What an ignorance of human nature does it exhibit, to ask or expect a whole community to rise up and labor for the *temporal* happiness of *others* after *themselves* shall be consigned to the dust, a majority of which community take no pains whatever to secure their own eternal welfare, at a no-greater-distant day? Great distance, in either time or space, has wonderful power to lull and render quiescent the human mind. Pleasures to be enjoyed, or pains to be endured, *after* we shall be dead and gone, are but little regarded, even in our *own* cases, and much less in the cases of others.

Still, in addition to this, there is something so ludicrous in *promises* of good, or *threats* of evil, a great way off, as to render the whole subject with which they are connected, easily turned into ridicule. "Better lay down that spade you're stealing, Paddy,— if you don't you'll pay for it at the day of judgment." "By the powers, if ye'll credit me so long, I'll take another, jist."

By the Washingtonians, this system of consigning the habitual drunkard to hopeless ruin, is repudiated. *They* adopt a more enlarged philanthropy. *They* go for present as well as future good. *They* labor for all *now* living, as well as all *hereafter* to live. *They* teach *hope* to all—*despair* to none. As applying to *their* cause, *they* deny the doctrine of unpardonable sin. As in Christianity it is taught, so in this *they* teach, that

> "While the lamp holds out to burn,
> The vilest sinner may return."

And, what is matter of the most profound gratulation, they, by experiment upon experiment, and example upon example, prove the maxim to be no less true in the one case than in the other. On every hand we behold those, who but yesterday, were the chief of sinners, now the chief apostles of the cause. Drunken devils are cast out by ones, by sevens, and by legions; and their unfortunate victims, like the poor possessed, who was redeemed from his long and lonely wanderings in the tombs, are publishing to the ends of the earth, how great things have been done for them.

To these *new champions,* and this *new* system of tactics, our late success is mainly owing; and to *them* we must chiefly look for the final consummation. The ball is now rolling gloriously on, and none are so able as *they* to increase its speed, and its bulk—to add to its momentum, and its magnitude. Even though unlearned in letters, for this task, none others are so well educated. To fit them for this work, they have been taught in the true school. *They* have been in *that* gulf, from which they would teach others the means of escape. *They* have passed that prison wall, which others have long declared impassable; and who that has not, shall dare to weigh opinions with *them,* as to the mode of passing.

To Lincoln, the problem of drinking belonged neither to any individual nor to any group of individuals: it was society's problem.

But if it be true, as I have insisted, that those who have suffered by intemperance *personally,* and have reformed, are the most powerful and efficient instruments to push the reformation to ultimate success, it does not follow, that those who have not suffered, have no part left them to perform. Whether or not the world would be vastly benefitted by a total and final banishment from it of all intoxicating drinks, seems to me not *now* to be an open question. Three-fourths of mankind confess the affirmative with their *tongues,* and, I believe, all the rest acknowledge it in their *hearts.*

Ought *any,* then, to refuse their aid in doing what the good of the *whole* demands? Shall he, who cannot do *much,* be, for that reason, excused if he do *nothing?* "But," says one, "what good can I do by signing the pledge? I never drink even without signing." This question has already been asked and answered more than millions of times. Let it be answered once more. For the man to suddenly, or in any other way, break off from the use of drams, who has indulged in them for a long course of years, and until his appetite for them has become ten or a hundred fold stronger, and more craving, than any natural appetite can be, requires a most powerful moral effort. In such an undertaking, he needs every moral support and influence, that can possibly be brought to his aid, and thrown around him. And not only so; but every moral prop, should be taken *from* whatever argument might rise in his mind to lure him to his backsliding. When he casts his eyes around him, he should be able to see, all that he respects, all that he admires, and all that he loves, kindly and anxiously pointing him onward; and none beckoning him back, to his former miserable "wallowing in the mire."

But it is said by some, that men will *think* and *act* for themselves; that none will disuse spirits or anything else, merely because his neighbors do; and that *moral influence* is not that powerful engine contended for. Let us examine this. Let me ask the man who would maintain this position most stiffly, what compensation he will accept to go to church some Sunday and sit during the sermon with his wife's bonnet upon his head? Not a trifle, I'll venture. And why not? There would be nothing irreligious in it: nothing immoral, nothing uncomfortable. Then why not? Is it not because there would be something egregiously unfashionable in it? Then it is the influence of *fashion;* and what is the influence of fashion, but the influence that *other* people's actions have on our own actions, the strong inclination each of us feels to do as we see all our neighbors do? Nor is the influence of fashion confined to any particular thing or class of things. It is just as strong on one subject as another. Let us make it as unfashionable to withhold our names from the temperance pledge as for husbands to wear their wives' bonnets to church, and instances will be just as rare in the one case as the other.

"But," say some, "we are no drunkards; and we shall not acknowledge ourselves such by joining a reformed drunkards' society, whatever our influence might be." Surely no Christian will adhere to this objection. If they believe, as they profess, that Omnipotence condescended to take on Himself the form of sinful man, and, as such, to die an ignominious death for their sakes, surely they will not refuse submission to the infinitely lesser condescension, for the temporal, and perhaps eternal salvation, of a large, erring, and unfortunate class of their own fellow-creatures. Nor is the condescension very great.

Lincoln doubted that anyone could claim much virtue in the absence of temptation.

In my judgment, such of us as have never fallen victims, have been spared more from the absence of appetite, than from any mental or moral superiority over those who have. Indeed, I believe, if we take habitual drunkards as a class, their heads and their hearts will bear an advantageous comparison with those of any other class. There seems ever to have been a proneness in the brilliant, and the warm-blooded, to fall into this vice. The demon of intemperance ever seems to have delighted in sucking the blood of genius and of generosity. What one of us but can call to mind some dear relative, more promising in youth than all his fellows, who has fallen a sacrifice to his rapacity? He ever seems to have gone forth, like the Egyptian angel of death, commissioned to slay if not the first, the fairest born of every family. Shall he now be arrested in his desolating career? In that arrest, all can give aid that will; and who shall be excused that *can,* and will not? Far around as human breath has ever blown, he keeps our fathers, our brothers, our sons, and our friends, prostrate in the chains of moral death. To all the living everywhere, we cry, "come sound the moral resurrection trump, that these may rise and stand up, an exceeding great army"—"Come from the four winds, O breath! and breathe upon these slain, that they may live."

If the relative grandeur of revolutions shall be estimated by the great amount of human misery they alleviate, and the small amount they inflict, then, indeed, will this be the grandest the world shall ever have seen. Of our political revolution of '76, we all are justly proud. It has given us a degree of political freedom, far exceeding that of any other of the nations of the earth. In it the world has found a solution of that long-mooted problem, as to the capability of man to govern himself. In it was the germ which has vegetated, and still is to grow and expand into the universal liberty of mankind.

But with all these glorious results, past, present, and to come, it had its evils too. It breathed forth famine, swam in blood and rode on fire; and long, long after, the orphan's cry, and the widow's wail, continued to break the sad silence that ensued. These were the price, the inevitable price, paid for the blessings it bought.

Turn now, to the temperance revolution. In *it,* we shall find a stronger bondage broken; a viler slavery manumitted; a greater tyrant deposed. In *it,* more of want supplied, more disease healed, more sorrow assuaged. By *it* no orphans starving, no widows weeping. By *it,* none wounded in feeling, none injured in interest. Even the dram-maker, and dram-seller, will have glided into other occupations *so* gradually, as never to have felt the shock of change; and will stand ready to join all others in the universal song of gladness.

And what a noble ally this, to the cause of political freedom. With such an aid, its march cannot fail to be on and on, till every son of earth shall drink in rich fruition, the sorrow quenching draughts of perfect liberty. Happy day, when, all appetites controlled, all passions subdued, all matters subjected, *mind,* all conquering *mind,* shall live and move the monarch of the world. Glorious consummation! Hail fall of Fury! Reign of Reason, all hail!

And when the victory shall be complete—when there shall be neither a slave nor a drunkard on the earth—how proud the title of that *Land,* which may truly claim to be the birthplace and the cradle of both those revolutions, that shall have ended in that victory. How nobly distinguished that people, who shall have planted, and nurtured to maturity, both the political and moral freedom of their species.

This is the one hundred and tenth anniversary of the birthday of Washington. We are met to celebrate this day. Washington is the mightiest name of earth—*long since* mightiest in the cause of civil liberty; *still* mightiest in moral reformation. On that name, an eulogy is expected. It cannot be. To add brightness to the sun, or glory to the name of Washington, is alike impossible. Let none attempt it. In solemn awe pronounce the name, and in its naked deathless splendor, leave it shining on.

Lincoln struggled persistently with Speed's continuing torment over his unfitness for marriage.

Springfield, Feb: 25– 1842–

Dear Speed:

I received yours of the 12th. written the day you went down to William's place, some days since; but delayed answering it, till I should receive the promised one, of the 16th., which came last night. I opened the latter, with intense anxiety and trepidation – so much, that although it turned out better than I expected, I have hardly yet, at the distance of ten hours, become calm.

I tell you, Speed, our *forebodings*, for which you and I are rather peculiar, are all the worst sort of nonsense. I fancied, from the time I received your letter of *Saturday*, that the one of *Wednesday* was never to come; and yet it *did* come, and what is more, it is perfectly clear, both from its *tone* and *handwriting*, that you were much *happier*, or, if you think the term preferable, *less miserable*, when you wrote *it*, than when you wrote the last one before. You had so obviously improved, at the very time I so much feared, you would have grown worse. You say that "something indescribably horrible and alarming still haunts you." You will not say *that* three months from now, I will venture. When your nerves once get steady now, the whole trouble will be over forever. Nor should you become impatient at their being even very slow, in becoming steady. Again; you say you much fear that that Elysium of which you have dreamed so much, is never to be realized. Well, if it shall not, I dare swear, it will not be the fault of her who is now your wife. I now have no doubt that it is the peculiar misfortune of both you and me, to dream dreams of Elysium far exceeding all that anything earthly can realize. Far short of your dreams as you may be, no woman could do more to realize them, than that same black-eyed Fanny. If you could but contemplate her through my imagination, it would appear ridiculous to you, that anyone should for a moment think of being unhappy with her. My old father used to have a saying that "If you make a bad bargain, *hug* it the tighter"; and it occurs to me, that if the bargain you have just closed can possibly be called a bad one, it is certainly the most *pleasant one* for applying that maxim to, which my fancy can, by any effort, picture.

I write another letter inclosing this, which you can show her, if she desires it. I do this, because, she would think strangely perhaps should you tell her that you receive no letters from me; or, telling her you do, should refuse to let her see them.

I close this, entertaining the confident hope, that every successive letter I shall have from you, (which I here pray may not be few, nor far between,) may show you possessing a more steady hand, and cheerful heart, than the last preceding it. As ever, your friend

Lincoln

Speed married. Lincoln had won his point.

Springfield, Feby. 25– 1842–

Dear Speed:

Yours of the 16th. inst. announcing that Miss Fanny and you "are no more twain, but one flesh," reached me this morning. I have no way of telling how much happiness I wish you both; tho' I believe you both can conceive it. I feel somewhat jealous of both of you now; you will be so exclusively concerned for one another, that I shall be forgotten entirely. My acquaintance with Miss Fanny (I call her thus, lest you should think I am speaking of your mother) was too short for me to reasonably hope to long be remembered by her; and still, I am sure, I shall not forget her soon. Try if you cannot remind her of that debt she owes me; and be sure you do not interfere to prevent her paying it.

I regret to learn that you have resolved to not return to Illinois. I shall be very lonesome without you. How miserably things seem to be arranged in this world. If we have no friends, we have no pleasure; and if we have them, we are sure to lose them, and be doubly pained by the loss. I did hope she and you would make your home here; but I own I have no right to insist. You owe obligations to her, ten thousand times more sacred than any you can owe to others; and, in that light, let them be respected and observed. It is natural that she should desire to remain with her relatives and friends. As to friends, however, *she* could not need them anywhere; she would have them in abundance here.

Give my kind remembrance to Mr. Williamson and his family,

particularly Miss Elizabeth—also to your mother, brothers, and sisters. Ask little Eliza Davis if she will ride to town with me if I come there again.

And, finally, give Fanny a double reciprocation of all the love she sent me. Write me often, and believe me Yours forever

Lincoln

Speed wrote that his marriage had given him greater happiness than he had thought possible. Now the torment was all Lincoln's. In one of the most revealing letters he ever wrote, he spoke of Mary Todd as the *"one* still unhappy."

Springfield, March 27th. 1842

Dear Speed:

Yours of the 10th. inst. was received three or four days since. You know I am sincere, when I tell you, the pleasure its contents gave me was and is inexpressible. As to your farm matter, I have no sympathy with you. *I* have no farm, nor ever expect to have; and, consequently, have not studied the subject enough to be much interested with it. I can only say that I am glad *you* are satisfied and pleased with it.

But on that other subject, to me of the most intense interest, whether in joy or sorrow, I never had the power to withhold my sympathy from you. It cannot be told, how it now thrills me with joy, to hear you say you are *"far happier than you ever expected to be."* That much I know is enough. I know you too well to suppose your expectations were not, at least sometimes, extravagant; and if the reality exceeds them all, I say, enough, dear Lord. I am not going beyond the truth, when I tell you, that the short space it took me to read your last letter, gave me more pleasure, than the total sum of all I have enjoyed since that fatal first of Jany. '41. Since then, it seems to me, I should have been entirely happy, but for the never-absent idea, that there is *one* still unhappy whom I have contributed to make so. That still kills my soul. I cannot but reproach myself, for even wishing to be happy while she is otherwise. She accompanied a large party on the railroad cars, to Jacksonville last Monday; and on her return, spoke, so that I heard of it, of having enjoyed the trip exceedingly. God be praised for that.

You know with what sleepless vigilance I have watched you, ever since the commencement of your affair; and altho' I am now almost confident it is useless, I cannot forbear once more to say that I think it is even yet possible for your spirits to flag down and leave you miserable. If they should, don't fail to remember that they cannot long remain so.

One thing I can tell you which I know you will be glad to hear; and that is, that I have seen Sarah, and scrutinized her feelings as well as I could, and am fully convinced, she is far happier now, than she has been for the last fifteen months past.

You will see by the last Sangamo Journal that I made a temperance speech on the 22. of Feb. which I claim that Fanny and you shall read as an act of charity to me; for I cannot learn that anybody else has read it, or is likely to. Fortunately, it is not very long and I shall deem it a sufficient compliance with my request, if one of you listens while the other reads it. . . .

The sweet violet you enclosed, came safely to hand, but it was so dry, and mashed so flat, that it crumbled to dust at the first attempt to handle it. The juice that mashed out of it, stained a place on the letter, which I mean to preserve and cherish for the sake of her who procured it to be sent. My renewed good wishes to her, in particular, and generally to all such of your relatives as know me. As ever

Lincoln

Irresolution had distracted Lincoln when he fancied himself in love with Mary Owens. Now, to Speed, he came close to confessing that the same doubts had caused him to break his engagement with Mary Todd.

Springfield, Ills. July 4th. 1842—

Dear Speed:

Yours of the 16th. June was received only a day or two since. It was not mailed at Louisville till the 25th. You speak of the great time that has elapsed since I wrote you. Let me explain that. Your letter reached here a day or two after I started on the circuit; I was gone five or six weeks, so that I got the letter only a few days before Butler started to your country. I thought it scarcely worth while to write you the news, which he could and would tell you more in detail. On his return, he told me you would write me soon; and so I waited for your letter. As to my having been displeased with your advice, surely you know better than that. I know you do; and therefore I will not labour to convince you. True, that subject is painful to me; but it is not your silence, or the silence of all the world that can make me forget it. I acknowledge the correctness of your advice too; but before I resolve to do the one thing or the other, I must regain my confidence in my own ability to keep my resolves when they are made. In that ability, you know, I once prided myself as the only, or at least the chief, gem of my character; that gem I lost—how, and when, you too well know. I have not yet regained it; and until I do, I cannot trust myself in any matter of much importance. I believe now that, had you understood my case at the time, as well as I understood yours afterwards, by the aid you would have given me, I should have sailed through clear; but that does not now afford me sufficient confidence, to begin that, or the like of that, again.

You make a kind acknowledgement of your obligations to me for your present happiness. I am much pleased with that acknowledgement; but a thousand times more am I pleased to know, that you enjoy a degree of happiness, worthy of an acknowledgement. The truth is, I am not sure there was any merit, with me, in the part I took in your difficulty; I was drawn to it as by fate; if I would, I could not have done less than I did. I always was superstitious; and as part of my superstition, I believe God made me one of the instruments of bringing your Fanny and you together, which union, I have no doubt He had foreordained. Whatever He designs, He will do for *me* yet. "Stand *still* and see the salvation of the Lord" is my text just now. If, as you say, you have told Fanny *all*, I should have no objection to her seeing this letter, but for its reference to our friend here. Let her seeing it, depend upon whether she has ever known anything of my affair; and if she has not, do not let her.

I do not think I can come to Kentucky this season. I am so poor, and make so little headway in the world, that I drop back in a month of idleness, as much as I gain in a year's rowing. I should like to visit you again. I should like to see that "Sis" of yours, that was absent when I was there; tho' I suppose she would run away again, if she were to hear I was coming. . . .

I have made you a subscriber to the Journal; and also sent the number containing the temperance speech. My respect and esteem to all your friends there; and, by your permission, my love to your Fanny. Ever yours—

Lincoln

Early Years in Springfield

Once more Lincoln's fondness for ridicule betrayed him. A squabble between Whigs and Democrats furnished the occasion. The rift between Lincoln and Mary Todd began to mend. A rising gayety of spirit suddenly trapped the reinstated suitor. The Whigs, Lincoln among them, were wrangling with the Democrats. The target of the Whigs was James Shields, the Democratic State Auditor, who had refused to accept the notes of the State Bank in payment of taxes. After several amateurishly satirical letters signed "Rebecca," written by Mary Todd and a friend, had appeared in the *Sangamo Journal,* Lincoln, helping them at their game, did a highly competent job on the same theme.

LETTER FROM THE LOST TOWNSHIPS

Lost Townships, Aug. 27, 1842.

Dear Mr. Printer:

I see you printed that long letter I sent you a spell ago—I'm quite encouraged by it, and can't keep from writing again. I think the printing of my letters will be a good thing all round,—it will give me the benefit of being known by the world, and give the world the advantage of knowing what's going on in the Lost Townships, and give your paper respectability besides. So here come another. Yesterday afternoon I hurried through cleaning up the dinner dishes, and stepped over to neighbor S——— to see if his wife Peggy was as well as mought be expected, and hear what they called the baby. Well, when I got there, and just turned round the corner of his log cabin, there he was setting on the door-step reading a newspaper.

"How are you Jeff," says I,—he sorter started when he heard me, for he hadn't seen me before. "Why," says he, "I'm mad as the devil, Aunt Becca."

"What about," says I, "ain't its hair the right color? None of that nonsense, Jeff—there ain't an honester woman in the Lost Township than—"

"Than who?" says he, "what the mischief are you about?"

I began to see I was running the wrong trail, and so says I, "O nothing, I guess I was mistaken a little, that's all. But what is it you're mad about?"

"Why," says he, "I've been tugging ever since harvest getting out wheat and hauling it to the river, to raise State Bank paper enough to pay my tax this year, and a little school debt I owe; and

61

now just as I've got it, here I open this infernal Extra Register, expecting to find it full of 'glorious Democratic victories,' and 'High Comb'd Cocks,' when, lo and behold, I find a set of fellows calling themselves *officers of State*, have forbidden the tax collectors and school commissioners to receive State paper at all; and so here it is, dead on my hands. I don't now believe all the plunder I've got will fetch ready cash enough to pay my taxes and that school debt."

I was a good deal thunderstruck myself; for that was the first I had heard of the proclamation, and my old man was pretty much in the same fix with Jeff. We both stood a moment, staring at one another without knowing what to say. At last says I, "Mr. S——— let me look at that paper." He handed it to me, when I read the proclamation over.

"There now," says he, "did you ever see such a piece of impudence and imposition as that?" I saw Jeff was in a good tune for saying some ill-natured things, and so I tho't I would just argue a little on the contrary side, and make him rant a spell if I could.

"Why," says I, looking as dignified and thoughtful as I could, "it seems pretty tough to be sure, to have to raise silver where there's none to be raised; but then you see *there will be danger of loss* if it ain't done."

"Loss, damnation!" says he, "I defy Daniel Webster, I defy King Solomon, I defy the world,—I defy—I defy—yes, I defy even you, Aunt Becca, to show how the people can lose anything by paying their taxes in State paper." "Well," says I, "you see what the *officers of State* say about it, and they are a desarnin set of men." "But," says I, "I guess you're mistaken about what the proclamation says; it don't say *the people* will lose anything by the paper money being taken for taxes. It only says *there will be danger of loss*, and though it is tolerable plain that the people can't lose by paying their taxes in something they can get easier than silver, instead of having to pay silver; and though it is just as plain, that the State can't lose by taking State Bank paper, however low it may be, while she owes the Bank more than the whole revenue, and can pay that paper over on her debt, dollar for dollar; still *there is danger of loss* to the *officers of State*, and you know Jeff, we can't get along without *officers of State*."

"Damn officers of State," says he, "that's what you Whigs are always hurraing for." "Now don't swear so Jeff," says I, "you know I belong to the meetin, and swearin hurts my feelins." "Beg pardon, Aunt Becca," says he, "but I do say it's enough to make Dr. Goddard swear, to have tax to pay in silver, for nothing only that Ford may get his two thousand a year, and Shields his twenty-four hundred a year, and Carpenter his sixteen hundred a year, and all without 'danger of loss' by taking it in State paper. Yes, yes, it's plain enough now what these *officers of State* mean by 'danger of loss.' Wash, I 'spose, actually lost fifteen hundred dollars out of the three thousand that two of these 'officers of State' let him steal from the Treasury, by being compelled to take it in State paper. Wonder if we don't have a proclamation before long, commanding us to make up this loss to Wash in silver."

And so he went on, till his breath run out, and he had to stop. I couldn't think of anything to say just then: and so I begun to look over the paper again. "Aye! here's another proclamation, or something like it." "Another!" says Jeff, "and whose egg is it, pray?" I looked to the bottom of it, and read aloud, "Your obedient servant, JAS SHIELDS, Auditor."

"Aha!" says Jeff, "one of them same three fellows again. Well read it, and let's hear what of it." I read on till I came to where it says, *The object of this measure is to suspend the collection of the revenue for the current year.* "Now stop, now stop," says he, "that's a lie aready, and I don't want to hear of it." "O maybe not," says I.

"I say *it—is—a—lie.*—Suspend the collection, indeed! Will the collectors that have taken their oaths to make the collection DARE to suspend it? Is there anything in the law requiring them to perjure themselves at the bidding of Jas. Shields? Will the greedy gullet of the penitentiary be satisfied with swallowing *him* instead of all *them* if they should venture to obey him? And would he not discover some 'danger of loss' and be off, about the time it came to taking their places?

"And suppose the people attempt to suspend by refusing to pay, what then? The collectors would just jerk up their horses, and cows, and the like, and sell them to the highest bidder for silver in hand, without valuation or redemption. Why, Shields didn't believe that story himself—it was never meant for the truth. If it was true, why was it not writ till five days after the proclamation?

Why didn't Carlin and Carpenter sign it as well as Shields? Answer me that, Aunt Becca. I say it's a lie, and not a well-told one at that. It grins out like a copper dollar. Shields is a fool as well as a liar. With him truth is out of the question, and as for getting a good bright passable lie out of him, you might as well try to strike fire from a cake of tallow. I stick to it, it's all an infernal Whig lie."

"A *Whig* lie,—Highty! Tighty!!"

"Yes, a *Whig* lie; and it's just like everything the cursed British Whigs do. First they'll do some devilment, and then they'll tell a lie to hide it. And they don't care how plain a lie it is; they think they can cram any sort of a one down the throats of the ignorant loco focos, as they call the Democrats."

"Why, Jeff, you're crazy—you don't mean to say Shields is a Whig."

"*Yes I do.*"

"Why, look here, the proclamation is in your own Democratic paper as you call it."

"I know it, and what of that? They only printed it to let us Democrats see the deviltry the Whigs are at."

"Well, but Shields is the Auditor of this loco—I mean this Democratic State."

"So he is, and Tyler appointed him to office."

"Tyler appointed him?"

"Yes (if you must chaw it over) Tyler appointed him, or if it wasn't him it was old granny Harrison, and that's all one. I tell you, Aunt Becca, there's no mistake about his being a Whig—why his very looks shows it—everything about him shows it—if I was deaf and blind I could tell him by the smell. I seed him when I was down in Springfield last winter. They had a sort of a gatherin there one night, among the grandees, they called a fair. All the gals about town was there, and all the handsome widows, and married women, finickin about, trying to look like gals, tied as tight in the middle, and puffed out at both ends like bundles of fodder that hadn't been stacked yet, but wanted stackin pretty bad. And then they had tables all round the house kivered over with baby caps, and pin-cushions, and ten thousand such little nicknacks, tryin to sell 'em to the fellows that were bowin and scrapin, and kungeerin about 'em. They wouldn't let no Democrats in, for fear they'd disgust the ladies, or scare the little gals, or dirty the floor. I looked in at the window, and there was this same fellow Shields floatin about on the air, without heft or earthly substance, just like a lock of cat-fur where cats had been fightin.

"He was paying his money to this one and that one, and tother one, and sufferin great loss because it wasn't silver instead of State paper; and the sweet distress he seemed to be in,—his very features; in the ecstatic agony of his soul, spoke audibly and distinctly—'Dear girls, *it is distressing,* but I cannot marry you all. Too well I know how much you suffer; but do, *do* remember, it is not my fault that I am *so* handsome and *so* interesting.'

"As this last was expressed by a most exquisite contortion of his face, he seized hold of one of their hands and squeezed, and held on to it about a quarter of an hour. O, my good fellow, says I to myself, if that was one of our Democratic gals in the Lost Township, the way you'd get a brass pin let into you, would be about up to the head. He a Democrat! Fiddle-sticks! I tell you, Aunt Becca, he's a Whig, and no mistake: nobody but a Whig could make such a conceity dunce of himself."

"Well," says I, "maybe he is, but if he is, I'm mistaken the worst sort. Maybe so; maybe so; but if I am I'll suffer by it; I'll be a Democrat if it turns out that Shields is a Whig; considerin you shall be a Whig if he turns out a Democrat."

"A bargain, by jingoes," says he, "but how will we find out."

"Why," says I, "we'll just write and ax the printer." "Agreed again," says he, "and by thunder if it does turn out that Shields is a Democrat, I never will ————"

"Jefferson,—Jefferson—"

"What do you want, Peggy."

"Do get through your everlasting clatter some time, and bring me a gourd of water; the child's been crying for a drink this livelong hour."

"Let it die then, it may as well die for water as to be taxed to death to fatten *officers of State.*"

Jeff run off to get the water though, just like he hadn't been sayin anything spiteful; for he's a rall good-hearted fellow, after all, once you get at the foundation of him.

I walked into the house, and "why Peggy," says I, "I declare, we like to forgot you altogether." "O yes," says she, "when a body can't help themselves, everybody soon forgets 'em; but thank God by day after tomorrow I shall be well enough to milk the cows and pen the calves, and wring the contrary one's tails for 'em, and no thanks to nobody." "Good evening, Peggy," says I, and so I sloped, for I seed she was mad at me, for making Jeff neglect her so long.

And now Mr. Printer, will you be sure to let us know in your next paper whether this Shields is a Whig or a Democrat? I don't care about it for myself, for I know well enough how it is already, but I want to convince Jeff. It may do some good to let him, and others like him, know *who* and *what* these *officers of State* are. It may help to send the present hypocritical set to where they belong, and to fill the places they now disgrace with men who will do more work, for less pay, and take a fewer airs while they are doing it. It ain't sensible to think that the same men who get us into trouble will change their course; and yet it's pretty plain, if some change for the better is not made, it's not long that neither Peggy, or I, or any of us, will have a cow left to milk, or a calf's tail to wring. Yours, truly,

Rebecca————.

Lincoln's raillery stung Shields. The result was a letter which fore-shadowed a challenge to a duel. In reply, Lincoln temporized.

Tremont, Sept. 17, 1842.

Jas. Shields, Esq.

Your note of today was handed me by Gen. Whiteside. In that note you say you have been informed, through the medium of the editor of the Journal, that I am the author of certain articles in that paper which you deem personally abusive of you: and without stopping to enquire whether I really am the author, or to point out what is offensive in them, you demand an unqualified retraction of all that is offensive; and then proceed to hint at consequences.

Now, sir, there is in this so much assumption of facts, and so much of menace as to consequences, that I cannot submit to answer that note any farther than I have, and to add, that the consequence to which I suppose you allude, would be matter of as great regret to me as it possibly could to you. Respectfully,

A. Lincoln.

Shields, unsatisfied, sent his second, John D. Whiteside, to Lincoln. Under the code, Lincoln had the right to select weapons and specify conditions.

Early Years in Springfield

MEMORANDUM OF DUEL INSTRUCTIONS
TO ELIAS H. MERRYMAN

[September 19, 1842]

In case Whiteside shall signify a wish to adjust this affair without further difficulty, let him know that if the present papers be withdrawn, & a note from Mr. Shields asking to know if I am the author of the articles of which he complains, and asking that I shall make him gentlemanly satisfaction, if I am the author, and this without menace, or dictation as to what that satisfaction shall be, a pledge is made, that the following answer shall be given—

"I did write the 'Lost Township' letter which appeared in the Journal of the 2nd. inst. but had no participation, in any form, in any other article alluding to you. I wrote that, wholly for political effect. I had no intention of injuring your personal or private character or standing as a man or a gentleman; and I did not then think, and do not now think that that article, could produce or has produced that effect against you, and had I anticipated such an effect I would have forborne to write it. And I will add, that your conduct towards me, so far as I knew, had always been gentlemanly; and that I had no personal pique against you, and no cause for any."

If this should be done, I leave it with you to arrange what shall & what shall not be published.

If nothing like this is done—the preliminaries of the fight are to be—

1st. Weapons—Cavalry broadswords of the largest size, precisely equal in all respects—and such as now used by the cavalry company at Jacksonville.

2nd. Position—A plank ten feet long, & from nine to twelve inches broad to be firmly fixed on edge, on the ground, as the line between us which neither is to pass his foot over upon forfeit of his life. Next a line drawn on the ground on either side of said plank & parallel with it, each at the distance of the whole length of the sword and three feet additional from the plank; and the passing of his own such line by either party during the fight shall be deemed a surrender of the contest.

3. Time—On Thursday evening at five o'clock if you can get it so; but in no case to be at a greater distance of time than Friday evening at five o'clock.

The Living Lincoln

4th. Place—Within three miles of Alton on the opposite side of the river, the particular spot to be agreed on by you.

Any preliminary details coming within the above rules, you are at liberty to make at your discretion; but you are in no case to swerve from these rules, or to pass beyond their limits.

Lincoln and Shields traveled with their seconds to an island in the Mississippi River, where they would be beyond the reach of Illinois law. On the duelling ground they patched up their differences. But, as Lincoln informed Speed, the duelling fever had not yet run its course.

Springfield, Oct. 5 1842—

Dear Speed:

You have heard of my duel with Shields, and I have now to inform you that the duelling business still rages in this city. Day-before-yesterday Shields challenged Butler, who accepted, and proposed fighting next morning at sun-rising in Bob. Allen's meadow, one hundred yards distance with rifles. To this, Whiteside, Shields' second, said "No" because of the law. Thus ended duel No. 2. Yesterday, Whiteside chose to consider himself insulted by Dr. Merryman, and so, sent him a kind of *quasi*-challenge inviting him to meet him at the Planters' House in St. Louis on the next Friday to settle their difficulty. Merryman made me his friend, and sent W. a note enquiring to know if he meant his note as a challenge, and if so, that he would, according to the law in such case made and provided, prescribe the terms of the meeting. W. returned for answer, that if M. would meet him at the Planters' House as desired, he would challenge him. M. replied in a note, that he denied W's right to dictate time and place; but that he, M, would waive the question of *time,* and meet him at Louisiana, Missouri. Upon my presenting this note to W. and stating verbally, its contents, he declined receiving it, saying he had business at St. Louis, and it was as near as Louisiana. Merryman then directed me to notify Whiteside, that he should publish the correspondence between them with such comments as he thought fit. This I did. Thus it stood at bedtime last night. This morning Whiteside, by his friend Shields, is praying for a new trial, on the ground that he was mistaken in Merryman's proposition to meet him at Louisiana, Missouri, thinking it was the State of Louisiana. This Merryman hoots at, and is preparing his publication—while

the town is in a ferment and a street fight somewhat anticipated.

But I began this letter not for what I have been writing; but to
say something on that subject which you know to be of such infinite solicitude to me. The immense suffering you endured from the
first days of September till the middle of February you never tried
to conceal from me, and I well understood. You have now been the
husband of a lovely woman nearly eight months. That you are
happier now than you were the day you married her I well know;
for without, you would not be living. But I have your word for it
too; and the returning elasticity of spirits which is manifested in
your letters. But I want to ask a closer question—"Are you now,
in *feeling* as well as *judgment,* glad you are married as you are?"
From anybody but me, this would be an impudent question not
to be tolerated; but I know you will pardon it in me. Please answer
it quickly as I feel impatient to know.

I have sent my love to your Fanny so often that I fear she is
getting tired of it; however I venture to tender it again. Yours forever

Lincoln

From affairs of honor Lincoln turned to his profession. In the fall
of 1841 he had become the partner of Stephen T. Logan, an able lawyer
and a shrewd businessman. Lincoln found occasion to educate a client
on the touchy subject of legal fees.

Springfield, Nov. 2 1842.

Jas. S. Irwin Esqr.

Owing to my absence, yours of the 22nd. ult. was not received
till this moment.

Judge Logan & myself are willing to attend to any business in
the Supreme Court you may send us. As to fees, it is impossible to
establish a rule that will apply in all, or even a great many cases.
We believe we are never accused of being very unreasonable in this
particular; and we would always be easily satisfied, provided we
could see the money—but whatever fees we earn at a distance, if
not paid *before*, we have noticed we never hear of after the work
is done. We therefore, are growing a little sensitive on that point.
Yours &c.

A. Lincoln

The Living Lincoln

On the 4th of November, 1842, the Reverend Charles Dresser, Episcopal clergyman, married Lincoln and Mary Todd. A week later the new husband wrote a curious letter to Samuel D. Marshall, a fellow-lawyer.

Springfield, Nov. 11th. 1842—

Dear Sam.

Yours of the 10th. Oct. enclosing five dollars was taken from the office in my absence by Judge Logan who neglected to hand it to me till about a week ago, and just an hour before I took a wife. Your other of the 3rd. inst. is also received. The Forbes & Hill case, of which you speak has not been brought up as yet.

I have looked into the Dorman & Lane case, till I believe I understand the facts of it; and I also believe we can reverse it. In the last I may be mistaken, but I think the case, at least worth the experiment; and if Dorman will risk the cost, I will do my best for the "biggest kind of a fee" as you say, if we succeed, and nothing if we fail. I have not had a chance to consult Logan since I read your letters, but if the case comes up, I can have the use of him if I need him.

I would advise you to procure the record and send it up immediately. Attend to the making out of the record yourself, or most likely, the clerk will not get it all together right.

Nothing new here, except my marrying, which to me, is matter of profound wonder. Yours forever

A. Lincoln

III. Prairie Politics

1843-1847   POLITICAL ambitions nibbled at Lincoln. Had a contributing cause of the dissolution of his partnership with John T. Stuart been the fact that both men coveted political careers? Again, when the partnership between Lincoln and Logan ended in 1844, was there basis for the rumor that they had separated in large part over conflicting aspirations? When next Lincoln decided on the young and untested William H. Herndon for a partner was the surprise less for those who saw in Billy's influence with the "shrewd, wild boys about town" an asset that Lincoln might turn to profit?

Whig strength in Illinois was centered in the Seventh Congressional District, comprising eleven counties in the central part of the state. The rivalry for Whig preferment was spirited, and produced promising leaders in Lincoln, in John J. Hardin from Jacksonville in Morgan County, and in Edward D. Baker of Springfield.

Lincoln now was thirty-four, one year the senior of Hardin and two years the senior of Baker. To use a popular idiom of the day, the three men were in many ways like peas in a pod: all were respected lawyers, all had served in the Black Hawk War, all had been elected to the state legislature. The British-born Baker reportedly had wept at learning that his foreign birth excluded him from the Presidency; and Hardin, who struggled with a speech impediment, was fired with a desire to emulate a father who had served in the United States Senate. Baker and Lincoln were self-educated; the Kentucky-born Hardin had graduated from Transylvania University. With the approach of the congressional election of 1844, it was understandable that three political pots should begin to bubble.

Four terms in the state legislature had brought distinctions to Lincoln. Twice he had been the Whig candidate for speaker, twice the floor

71

The Living Lincoln

leader of his party. Far from satisfied with these achievements, Lincoln wrote a confidential letter to Richard S. Thomas of Cass County.

Springfield, Ills., Feb. 14, 1843.

Friend Richard:

. . . Now if you should hear anyone say that Lincoln don't want to go to Congress, I wish you as a personal friend of mine, would tell him you have reason to believe he is mistaken. The truth is, I would like to go very much. Still, circumstances may happen which may prevent my being a candidate.

If there are any who be my friends in such an enterprise, what I now want is that they shall not throw me away just yet. Yours as ever,

A. Lincoln.

The Seventh Congressional District held its convention on March 20. The seventh ballot brought a result that Lincoln reported gloomily to Speed.

Springfield, March 24. 1843—

Dear Speed:

. . . We had a meeting of the Whigs of the county here on last Monday to appoint delegates to a district convention, and Baker beat me & got the delegation instructed to go for him. The meeting, in spite of my attempt to decline it, appointed me one of the delegates; so that in getting Baker the nomination, I shall be "fixed" a good deal like a fellow who is made groomsman to the man what has cut him out, and is marrying his own dear "gal." About the prospect of your having a namesake at our house can't say, exactly yet.

[Signature removed.]

Lincoln suspected that some degree of political skulduggery had underscored the convention. He accepted defeat, but a spark of hope flickered. A letter from Martin S. Morris, a delegate from Menard County, brought encouraging news. Lincoln replied with candor.

Springfield March 26th. 1843

Friend Morris:

Your letter of the 23rd. was received on yesterday morning, and for which (instead of an excuse which you thought proper to

72

ask) I tender you my sincere thanks. It is truly gratifying to me to
learn that while the people of Sangamon have cast me off, my old
friends of Menard who have known me longest and best of any,
still retain their confidence in me. It would astonish if not amuse,
the older citizens of your county who twelve years ago knew me a
strange, friendless, uneducated, penniless boy, working on a flatboat—at ten dollars per month to learn that I have been put down
here as the candidate of pride, wealth, and aristocratic family
distinction. Yet so chiefly it was. There was too the strangest combination of church influence against me. Baker is a Campbellite,
and therefore as I suppose, with few exceptions got all that church.
My wife has some relatives in the Presbyterian and some in the
Episcopal churches, and therefore, wherever it would tell, I was set
down as either the one or the other, whilst it was everywhere contended that no Christian ought to go for me, because I belonged to
no church, was suspected of being a deist, and had talked about
fighting a duel. With all these things Baker, of course had nothing
to do. Nor do I complain of them. As to his own church going for
him, I think that was right enough, and as to the influences I have
spoken of in the other, though they were very strong, it would be
grossly untrue and unjust to charge that they acted upon them in a
body or even very nearly so. I only mean that those influences
levied a tax of a considerable per cent. upon my strength throughout the religious community.

But enough of this. You say that in choosing a candidate for
Congress you have an equal right with Sangamon, and in this you
are undoubtedly correct. In agreeing to withdraw if the Whigs of
Sangamon should go against me I did not mean that they alone
were worth consulting; but that if she with her heavy delegation
should be against me, it would be impossible for me to succeed—
and therefore I had as well decline. And in relation to Menard having rights, permit me to fully recognize them—and to express the
opinion that if she and Mason act circumspectly they will in the
convention be able so far to enforce their rights as to decide absolutely which *one* of the candidates shall be successful. Let me
show you the reason of this. Hardin or some other Morgan candidate will get Morgan, Scott, & Cass—14. Baker has Sangamon
already, and he or he and someone else not the Morgan man will
get Putnam, Marshall, Woodford, Tazewell & Logan—which with
Sangamon make 16. Then you & Mason having three, can give the

victory to either man. You say you shall instruct your delegates to go for me unless I object. I certainly shall not object. That would be too pleasant a compliment for me to tread in the dust. And besides if anything should happen (which however is not probable) by which Baker should be thrown out of the fight, I would be at liberty to accept the nomination if I could get it. I do however feel myself bound not to hinder him in any way from getting the nomination. I should despise myself were I to attempt it. I think it would be proper for your meeting to appoint three delegates, and instruct them to go for someone as first choice, someone else as second choice, and perhaps someone as *third*—and if in those instructions I were named as the first choice, it would gratify me very much. If you wish to hold the balance of power, it is important for you to attend too, and secure the vote of Mason also. You should be sure to have men appointed delegates, that you know you can safely confide in. If yourself & James Short were appointed for your county all would be safe. But whether Jim's woman affair a year ago might not be in the way of his appointment is a question. I don't know whether you know it, but I know him to be as honorable a man as there is in the world. You have my permission and even request to show this letter to Short; but to no one else unless it be a very particular friend who you know will not speak of it. Yours as ever

A. Lincoln

P.S. Will you write me again?   *A. L—*

Lincoln guessed wrong. Hardin, rather than Baker, became the Whig candidate. In good spirit Lincoln composed a notice to run in the *Sangamo Journal*.

May 11, 1843

A PROPOSITION

We have a proposition to make to our friends of Morgan, that, in case the locos * run a candidate for Congress in that county at the August election, the majority of votes in SANGAMON COUNTY for HARDIN shall DOUBLE the number of his majority in MORGAN COUNTY. The losing county shall give a free BARBECUE to the Whigs of the other county—the said barbecue

* Locos, or loco focos—a derisive term which Whigs applied to Democrats.

to be provided at some place most convenient for the accommodation of the Whigs of the two counties.

Whigs of Morgan, will you go it?

Although Lincoln offered the resolution that made Hardin's nomination unanimous, his successful rival remained suspicious. Lincoln tried to allay Hardin's fears.

Springfield, May 11th, 1843.

Friend Hardin:

Butler informs me that he received a letter from you, in which you expressed some doubt whether the Whigs of Sangamon will support you cordially. You may, at once, dismiss all fears on that subject. We have already resolved to make a particular effort to give you the very largest majority possible in our county. From this, no Whig of the county dissents. We have many objects for doing it. We make it a matter of honor and pride to do it; we do it, because we love the Whig cause; we do it, because we like you personally; and last, we wish to convince you, that we do not bear that hatred to Morgan County, that you people have so long seemed to imagine. You will see by the Journal of this week, that we propose, upon pain of losing a barbecue, to give you twice as great a majority in this county as you shall receive in your own. I got up the proposal.

Who of the five appointed, is to write the district address? I did the labor of writing one address this year; and got thunder for my reward. Nothing new here. Yours as ever.

A. Lincoln.

P.S.—I wish you would measure one of the largest of those swords, we took to Alton, and write me the length of it, from tip of the point to tip of the hilt, in feet and inches, I have a dispute about the length.   *A. L.*

Many problems confronted Lincoln, and he was glad to confide in an old friend. The "coming events" announced the approaching birth of Robert Todd Lincoln (August 1, 1843). Dr. William S. Wallace was Mary Lincoln's brother-in-law; Ann Todd her cousin.

Springfield, May 18th, 1843—

Dear Speed:

Yours of the 9th. inst. is duly received, which I do not meet as a "bore," but as a most welcome visitor. . . .

75

In relation to our Congress matter here, you were right in supposing I would support the nominee. Neither Baker or I, however is the man; but *Hardin*. So far as I can judge from present appearances, we shall have no split or trouble about the matter; all will be harmony. In relation to the "coming events" about which Butler wrote you, I had not *heard* one word before I got your letter; but I have so much confidence in the judgment of a Butler on such a subject, that I incline to think there may be some reality in it. What *day* does Butler appoint? By the way, how do "events" of the same sort come on in your family? Are you possessing houses and lands, and oxen and asses, and men-servants and maid-servants, and begetting sons and daughters? We are not keeping house; but boarding at the Globe tavern, which is very well kept now by a widow lady of the name of Beck. Our room (the same Dr. Wallace occupied there) and boarding only costs four dollars a week. Ann Todd was married something more than a year since to a fellow by the name of Campbell, and who Mary says, is pretty much of a "dunce" though he has a little money & property. They live in Boonville, Mo; and have not been heard from lately enough, to enable me to say anything about her health. I reckon it will scarcely be in our power to visit Kentucky this year. Besides poverty, and the necessity of attending to business, those "coming events" I suspect would be somewhat in the way. I most heartily wish you and your Fanny would not fail to come. Just let us know the time a week in advance, and we will have a room provided for you at our house, and all be merry together for awhile. Be sure to give my respects to your mother and family. Assure her, that if I ever come near her I will not fail to call and see her. Mary joins in sending love to your Fanny and you. Yours as ever

A. Lincoln

Another congressional election approached, and Lincoln started early to mend political fences. The Durley brothers, Williamson and Madison, both supporters of Lincoln, lived in Putnam County at Hennepin—fertile soil for nurturing abolitionism, since here in 1838 Benjamin Lundy had published his *Genius of Emancipation*. As a result, Putnam was the least characteristic of the counties in the Seventh Congressional District, yet in a letter to Williamson Durley, Lincoln tried to make his position on slavery seem agreeable to the sentiments of the region.

Prairie Politics

Springfield, Octr. 3. 1845

Friend Durley:

When I saw you at home, it was agreed that I should write to you and your brother Madison. Until I then saw you, I was not aware of your being what is generally called an abolitionist, or, as you call yourself, a Liberty man; though I well knew there were many such in your county. I was glad to hear you say that you intend to attempt to bring about, at the next election in Putnam, a union of the Whigs proper, and such of the Liberty men, as are Whigs in principle on all questions save only that of slavery. So far as I can perceive, by such union, neither party need yield anything, on *the* point in difference between them. If the Whig abolitionists of New York had voted with us last fall, Mr. Clay would now be President, Whig principles in the ascendant, and Texas not annexed; whereas by the division, all that either had at stake in the contest, was lost. And, indeed, it was extremely probable, beforehand, that such would be the result. As I always understood, the Liberty men deprecated the annexation of Texas extremely; and, this being so, why they should refuse to so cast their votes as to prevent it, even to me, seemed wonderful. What was their process of reasoning, I can only judge from what a single one of them told me. It was this: "We are not to do *evil* that *good* may come." This general proposition is doubtless correct; but did it apply? If by your votes you could have prevented the *extension,* &c. of slavery, would it not have been *good* and not *evil* so to have used your votes, even though it involved the casting of them for a slaveholder? By the *fruit* the tree is to be known. An *evil* tree cannot bring forth *good* fruit. If the fruit of electing Mr. Clay would have been to prevent the extension of slavery, could the act of electing have been *evil?*

But I will not argue farther. I perhaps ought to say that individually I never was much interested in the Texas question. I never could see much good to come of annexation; inasmuch, as they were already a free republican people on our own model; on the other hand, I never could very clearly see how the annexation would augment the evil of slavery. It always seemed to me that slaves would be taken there in about equal numbers, with or without annexation. And if more *were* taken because of annexation, still there would be just so many the fewer left, where they were taken from. It is possibly true, to some extent, that with annexation, some slaves may be sent to Texas and continued in slavery, that otherwise might have been liberated. To whatever extent this may be true, I think annexation an evil. I hold it to be a paramount duty of us in the free states, due to the Union of the states, and perhaps to liberty itself (paradox though it may seem) to let the slavery of the other states alone; while, on the other hand, I hold it to be equally clear, that we should never knowingly lend ourselves directly or indirectly, to prevent that slavery from dying a natural death—to find new places for it to live in, when it can no longer exist in the old. Of course I am not now considering what would be our duty, in cases of insurrection among the slaves.

To recur to the Texas question, I understand the Liberty men to have viewed annexation as a much greater evil than I ever did; and I would like to convince you if I could, that they could have prevented it, without violation of principle, if they had chosen.

I intend this letter for you and Madison together; and if you and he or either shall think fit to drop me a line, I shall be pleased. Yours with respect

A. Lincoln

Beginning eight months in advance of the 1846 elections, Lincoln worked in dead earnest to capture the nomination. The Whig principle of rotation in office became his chief weapon as the race narrowed to a choice between Lincoln and Hardin. A letter to Henry E. Dummer of Beardstown revealed Lincoln's opening gambit.

Springfield, Nov: 18th. 1845

Friend Dummer:

Before Baker left, he said to me, in accordance with what had long been an understanding between him and me, that the track for the next congressional race was clear to me, so far as he was concerned; and that he would say so publicly in any manner, and at any time I might desire. I said, in reply, that as to the manner and time, I would consider a while, and write him. I understand friend Delahay to have already informed you of the substance of the above.

I now wish to say to you that if it be consistent with your feelings, you would set a few stakes for me. I do not certainly know, but I strongly suspect, that Genl. Hardin wishes to run again. I know of no argument to give me a preference over him, unless it be "Turn about is fair play."

The Pekin paper has lately nominated or suggested Hardin's name for Governor, and the Alton paper, noticing that, indirectly nominates him for Congress. I wish you would, if you can, see that, while these things are bandied about among the papers, the Beardstown paper takes no stand that may injure my chance, unless the conductor really prefers Genl. Hardin, in which case, I suppose it would be fair.

Let this be confidential, and please write me in a few days. Yours as ever

A. Lincoln

The pro-Lincoln press attempted to take Hardin out of the race for Congress by offering him the nomination for Governor. Hardin balked. A perplexed Lincoln confessed his worries to Dr. Robert Boal of Marshall County, who stoutly supported the principle of rotation in office.

Springfield Jany. 7 1846.

Dear Doctor

Since I saw you last fall, I have often thought of writing you as it was then understood I would, but on reflection I have always found that I had nothing new to tell you. All has happened as I then told you I expected it would — Baker's declining, Hardin's taking the track, and so on.

If Hardin and I stood precisely equal — that is, if *neither* of us had been to Congress, or if we *both* had — it would only accord with what I have always done, for the sake of peace, to give way to him; and I expect I should do it. That I *can* voluntarily postpone my pretentions, when they are no more than equal to those to which they are postponed, you have yourself seen. But to yield to Hardin under present circumstances, seems to me as nothing else than yielding to one who would gladly sacrifice me altogether. This, I would rather not submit to. That Hardin is talented, energetic, usually generous and magnanimous, I have, before this, affirmed to you, and do not now deny. You know that my only argument is that "turn about is fair play." This he, practically at least, denies.

If it would not be taxing you too much, I wish you would

write me, telling the aspect of things in your county, or rather your district; and also send the names of some of your Whig neighbours, to whom I might, with propriety write. Unless I can get someone to do this, Hardin, with his old franking list, will have the advantage of me. My reliance for a fair shake (and I want nothing more) in your county is chiefly on you, because of your position and standing, and because I am acquainted with so few others. Let this be strictly confidential, & any letter you may write me shall be the same if you desire. Let me hear from you soon. Yours truly

A. Lincoln

Hardin believed that an attempt had been made to trick him out of the re-nomination. Lincoln bridled. He used a review of events to prove that in every instance he had acted with scrupulous fairness.

Springfield.
Feb. 7. 1846—

Genl. J. J. Hardin:
Dear Sir:
Your second letter was duly received and, so far as it goes, it is entirely satisfactory.

I had set apart the leisure this day affords, to write you the long letter alluded to by me in my last; but on going to the post office, and seeing the communication in the Morgan Journal, I am almost discouraged of the hope of doing any good by it; especially when I reflect that most probably that communication was written with your knowledge, inasmuch as it proceeds partly on information which could only have been furnished by you.

However, as I suppose it can do no *harm,* I will proceed. Your letter, admitting my right to seek, or desire, a nomination for Congress, opens with an expression of dissatisfaction with the *manner* in which you think I have endeavoured to obtain it. Now, *if I have* sought the nomination in an *improper* manner; you have the right, to the extent, to be dissatisfied. But I deny all *impropriety* on my part, in the matter.

In the early part of your letter, you introduce the proposition made by me to you and Baker, that we should take a turn apiece; and alluding to the principle you suppose to be involved in it, in an after part of your letter, you say—"As a Whig I have constantly combatted such practices when practiced among the Locos; & I do not see that they are any more praiseworthy, or less anti-republican, when sought to be adopted by Whigs." Now, if my proposition had been that we (yourself, Baker & I) should be candidates by turns, and that we should unite our strength throughout to keep down all other candidates, I should not deny the justice of the censurable language you employ; but if you so understood it, you wholly misunderstood it. I never expressed, nor meant to express, that by such an arrangement, any one of us should be in the least restricted in his right to support any person he might choose, in the district; but only that he should not *himself,* be a candidate out of his turn. I felt then, and it seems to me I *said* then, that even with such an arrangement, should Governor Duncan be a candidate, when you were not, it would be your *privilege* and perhaps your *duty* to go for him.

In this, the true sense of my proposition, I deny that there is anything censurable in it—anything but a spirit of mutual concession, for harmony's sake.

In this same connection you say, "It is, in effect, acting upon the principle that the district is a horse which each candidate may mount and ride a two-mile heat without consulting anybody but the grooms & jockeys." Well, of course, you go the contrary of this principle; which is, in effect acting on the principle that the district is a horse which, the first jockey that can mount him, may whip and spur round and round, till jockey, or horse, or both, fall dead on the track. And upon your principle, there is a fact as fatal to your claims as mine, which is, that neither you nor I, but *Baker* is the jockey now in the stirrups.

"Without consulting anybody but the grooms & jockeys" is an implied charge that I wish, in some way to interfere with the right of the people to select their candidate. I do not understand it so. I, and my few friends say to the people that "Turn about is fair play." You and your friends do not meet this, and say "Turn about is *not* fair play"—but insist the argument itself, ought not to be used. Fair or unfair, why not trust the people to decide it?

In the early part of your letter you say "It is also true that you did come to my house early in September to know whether I desired to run, stating that you wanted to give Baker a race." In this you are mistaken. I did not state to you that I wanted to give Baker a race; but on the contrary I told you I believed I could get Baker off the track. I do not know that you attached any importance to what I am disavowing; but, on the contrary, I do not know but you mean it as the basis of an inference that I acted deceitfully with you, in pretending to expect a contest with Baker, when in fact I did not expect it.

It is true, that after Baker's interview with you in September, he did send a letter, by a messenger, to me at Tremont; in which letter he detailed what passed at the interview, and the result, precisely as you do, in substance; and in which letter he did urge me to relinquish my pretensions. He had before told me that he would not be a candidate, if I desired he should not; and he then repeated it; but at the same time argued that you, by having been in Congress, and having taken a high stand then, would in all probability beat me; so that the sacrifice he made for me, in declining, would, in the end, do me no good. And this is as near as I ever came of hearing Baker express the determination that I should beat you, if he could not; which you say you have learned he did. When he finally determined to decline, he did express the wish that I might succeed; and he has since written his letter of declension; and when *that* is told; all I know, or believe, as to him, *is told*. If he has ever, in any way, attempted to dictate to any friend of his to go for me in preference of you, it is more than I know or believe. That he has a part assigned him to act in the drama, I know to be untrue. What I here say, is not in its nature capable of very certain proof; but it may be said, that being where he is, he can only operate against you by letters. If he attempts this to any considerable extent, some of them will fall into the hands of your friends who will apprize you of them. Have you yet seen or heard of any?

I now quote from your letter again. "You well knew I would not be a candidate for Governor. Yet during the fall courts, whilst I learn you were obtaining pledges from all the Whigs you could to support you for the next candidate, my name was run up as a candidate for Governor by one of your friends under circumstances which now leave no room for doubt that the design was to keep my name out of view for Congress, so that the Whigs might be more easily influenced to commit themselves to go for you."

Now this is a direct imputation that I *procured,* or *winked at,* or in some way directly or indirectly, *had a hand in,* the nominating of you for Governor; and the imputation is, to the utmost hair-breadth of it, unjust. I never *knew,* or *believed,* or had any *suspicion,* that it *was done,* or *was to be done,* until it was out, had gone to Alton, and been commented upon in the Alton paper, and came back to Springfield, and my attention was called to it by Stuart, in our circuit court room, a few days, as I remember it, after you had been here attending to the case of Thayer vs Farrell, and had left. I went immediately to the Journal office, and told them it was my wish that they should not fall in with the nomination for Governor. They showed me a little paragraph, which they had already prepared, and which was published, and seen by you, as I suppose.

The reason I had not seen the nomination in the Tazewell paper was, as I suppose, because I did not then, as I do not now, take that paper. That I was wholly *innocent* and *ignorant* of that movement, I believe, if need be, I can prove more conclusively than is often in the power of man to prove any such thing.

Lincoln became more aggressive. His determination to set the record straight reflected the confidence of a trial lawyer who knew a jury of his peers would support him.

In the paragraph last quoted you say that the design was to keep your name out of view &c. In the general disavowal I have made, this last is, of course included; and I now go farther, and declare, that to my recollection, I have not, in a single instance, presented my name as a candidate for Congress, without, at the same time presenting yours for the same place. I have sometimes met a man who would express the opinion that you would yield the track to me; and sometimes one who believed you would be a candidate for Governor; and I invariably assured such, that you would, in my opinion, be a candidate *for Congress.* And while I have thus kept your name *in view* for Congress, I have not reproached you for being a candidate, or for anything else; on the contrary I have constantly spoken of you in the most kind and commendatory terms, as to your talents, your past services, and your goodness of heart. If I falsify in this, you can convict me. The witnesses live, and can tell.

And now tell me: If you think so harshly of me because a paper under the control of one of my friends nominated *you* for Governor, *what,* or *how,* ought I to think of you because of your paper at Jacksonville doing the same thing for *me* twice? Why, you will say you had nothing to do with it; and I shall believe you; but why am I to be judged less charitably?

In another part of your letter you attempt to convict me of giving a double account as to my motive in introducing the resolution to the convention at Pekin. You say "You then told me the object was to soothe Baker's mortified feelings, and that it did not amount to a committal of anybody. Now you say the object was to give Baker the field for the next race, so as to keep the party together." I kept no copy of my letter; but I *guess* if you will turn to it, you will find that I have not, anywhere in it, said "the object was to give Baker the field for the next race &c" and then if you will allow that you may have committed as great a mistake, as to what I told you at Pekin, you will find yourself a good deal short of the conviction you intended. What I told you at Pekin I do not precisely recollect; but I am sure of some things I did *not* tell you or anyone else. If you shall say that I told you it was *an* object with me, in introducing the resolution, to soothe Baker's feelings, I shall admit it; but if you shall say I told you that, that was *the sole* object, I deny it.

If you shall say I then told you that the passage of the resolution amounted to a committal of no one, I deny that also; but if you shall say I then told you, it amounted to a committal of no one, except the delegates, generally who voted for it, and me, particularly, who introduced it, I shall not deny it.

This much, and no more, as a committal, I always supposed it to amount to; and I guess you will be able to find nothing in my late letter to you that is inconsistent with this. And I here add, that I have not since entering this contest with you, or at any time, sought to appropriate to myself any benefit from that resolution, either as settling the succession to pass through me, or as settling a principle that shall give the succession that direction. I have said that "Turn about is fair play"; but this I have said just as I would, if that resolution had never been thought of. I should not hesitate to say publicly, that I claim nothing, in any form, through the Pekin convention, were it not that some friends have thought and spoken differently, and I dislike to rebuke them for what they have not supposed to be injustice to you, while they have meant it in kindness to me—yet, rather than be over-delicate, if you desire it, I will do it anyhow. I repeat, I desire *nothing* from the Pekin convention. If I am not, (in services done the party, and in capacity to serve in future) near enough your equal, when added to the fact of your having had a turn, to entitle me to the nomination, I scorn it on any and all other grounds. The question of capacity, I opine your Morgan Journal correspondent will find little difficulty in deciding; and probably the district may concur, with quite as little.

A good long paragraph of your letter is occupied in an argument to prove that struggles for the succession will break down the party. It is certain that struggles between candidates, do not strengthen a party; but who are most responsible for these struggles, those who are willing to live and let live, or those who are resolved, at all hazards, to take care of "number one"? Take, as an example, the very case in hand. You have (and deservedly) many devoted friends; and they have been gratified by seeing you in Congress, and taking a stand that did high credit to you and to them. I also have a few friends (I fear not enough) who, as well as your own, aided in giving you that distinction. Is it natural that they shall be greatly pleased at hearing what they helped to build up, turned into an argument, for keeping their own favourite down? Will they grow, and multiply on such grateful food? Is it by such exclusiveness that you think a party will gain strength?

In my letter to you, I reminded you that you had first at Washington, and afterwards at Pekin, said to me that if Baker succeeded he would most likely hang on as long as possible, while with you it would be different. If I am not mistaken in your having said this (and I am sure I am not) it seems you *then* thought a little more favourably of "turn about" than you seem to now. And in writing your letter you seem to have felt this; for that is about the only part of mine, that you have failed to notice.

After, by way of imputations upon me, you have used the terms "management" "manoeuvering" and "combination" quite freely, you, in your closing paragraph say: "For it is mortifying to discover that those with whom I have long acted & from whom I expected a different course, have considered it all fair to prevent my nomination to Congress." Feeling, as I do, the utter injustice of these imputations, it is somewhat difficult to be patient under them—yet I content myself with saying that if there is cause for mortification anywhere, it is in the readiness with which you believe, and make such charges, against one with whom you truly say you have long acted; and in whose conduct, you have heretofore marked nothing as dishonorable.

I believe you do not mean to be unjust, or ungenerous; and I, therefore am slow to believe that you will not yet think *better* and think *differently* of this matter. Yours truly

A. Lincoln.

While serving in the Illinois House of Representatives in 1839, Lincoln had formed a friendship with Andrew Johnston, a lawyer of Quincy, Illinois. Both men were dabblers in verse, and both embraced the melancholy romanticism that distinguished the middle decades of the nineteenth century. Lincoln sent Johnston a copy of a poem called "Mortality," which began: "Oh why should the spirit of mortal be proud?" The Quincy lawyer responded with a parody of Poe's "The Raven," one stanza of which delighted Lincoln:

> All that night I washed and scrubbed me, long with
>   soap and sand I rubbed me,
> Still next day my dear wife snubbed me, "Jeremiah!
>   how you stink!"
> Once more to the creek I hasted; scrubbed and washed,
>   prayed and fasted;
> All, alas! was labor wasted, by that fair stream's
>   flowery brink,
> Vain were soap, sand, prayer, and fasting, by that
>   fair stream's flowery brink,
> "Jeremiah! how you stink!"

Lincoln in turn sent Johnston a poem of his own composition.

Tremont, April 18, 1846.

Friend Johnston:

Your letter, written some six weeks since, was received in due course, and also the paper with the parody. It is true, as suggested it might be, that I have never seen Poe's "Raven," * and I very well know that a parody is almost entirely dependent for its interest upon the reader's acquaintance with the original. Still there is enough in the polecat, self-considered, to afford one several hearty laughs. I think four or five of the last stanzas are decidedly funny,

* The poem was first published in January, 1845.

Prairie Politics

particularly where Jeremiah "scrubbed and washed, and prayed and fasted."

I have not your letter now before me; but, from memory, I think you ask me who is the author of the piece I sent you, and that you do so ask as to indicate a slight suspicion that I myself am the author. Beyond all question, I am not the author. I would give all I am worth, and go in debt, to be able to write so fine a piece as I think that is. Neither do I know who is the author. I met it in a straggling form in a newspaper last summer, and I remember to have seen it once before, about fifteen years ago, and this is all I know about it.*

The piece of poetry of my own which I alluded to, I was led to write under the following circumstances. In the fall of 1844, thinking I might aid some to carry the state of Indiana for Mr. Clay, I went into the neighborhood in that state in which I was raised, where my mother and only sister were buried, and from which I had been absent about fifteen years. That part of the country is, within itself, as unpoetical as any spot of the earth; but still, seeing it and its objects and inhabitants aroused feelings in me which were certainly poetry; though whether my expression of those feelings is poetry is quite another question. When I got to writing, the change of subjects divided the thing into four little divisions or cantos, the first only of which I send you now and may send the others hereafter. Yours truly,

A. Lincoln.

> My childhood's home I see again,
>   And sadden with the view;
> And still, as memory crowds my brain,
>   There's pleasure in it too.
>
> O Memory! thou midway world
>   'Twixt earth and paradise,
> Where things decayed and loved ones lost
>   In dreamy shadows rise,
>
> And, freed from all that's earthly vile,
>   Seem hallowed, pure, and bright,
> Like scenes in some enchanted isle
>   All bathed in liquid light.

* The author was William Knox, a minor Scotch poet.

87

The Living Lincoln

As dusky mountains please the eye
  When twilight chases day;
As bugle notes that, passing by,
  In distance die away;

As leaving some grand waterfall,
  We, lingering, list its roar—
So memory will hallow all
  We've known, but know no more.

Near twenty years have passed away
  Since here I bid farewell
To woods and fields, and scenes of play,
  And playmates loved so well.

Where many were, but few remain
  Of old familiar things;
But seeing them, to mind again
  The lost and absent brings.

The friends I left that parting day,
  How changed, as time has sped!
Young childhood grown, strong manhood gray,
  And half of all are dead.

I hear the loved survivors tell
  How nought from death could save,
Till every sound appears a knell,
  And every spot a grave.

I range the fields with pensive tread,
  And pace the hollow rooms,
And feel (companion of the dead)
  I'm living in the tombs.

In February, Hardin withdrew from the congressional contest; and in May, Lincoln was nominated by acclamation. His Democratic opponent was the grim-faced, circuit-riding Methodist parson, Peter Cartwright, who spread an ugly rumor. Friends advised Lincoln to ignore such tactics, but he retorted in a handbill.

Prairie Politics

TO THE VOTERS OF THE SEVENTH
CONGRESSIONAL DISTRICT

Fellow-citizens:

A charge having got into circulation in some of the neighborhoods of this district, in substance that I am an open scoffer at Christianity, I have by the advice of some friends concluded to notice the subject in this form. That I am not a member of any Christian church, is true; but I have never denied the truth of the Scriptures; and I have never spoken with intentional disrespect of religion in general, or of any denomination of Christians in particular. It is true that in early life I was inclined to believe in what I understand is called the "Doctrine of Necessity"—that is, that the human mind is impelled to action, or held in rest by some power, over which the mind itself has no control; and I have sometimes (with one, two or three, but never publicly) tried to maintain this opinion in argument. The habit of arguing thus however, I have entirely left off for more than five years. And I add here, I have always understood this same opinion to be held by several of the Christian denominations. The foregoing is the whole truth, briefly stated, in relation to myself, upon this subject.

I do not think I could myself, be brought to support a man for office, whom I knew to be an open enemy of, and scoffer at, religion.Leaving the higher matter of eternal consequences, between him and his Maker, I still do not think any man has the right thus to insult the feelings, and injure the morals, of the community in which he may live. If, then, I was guilty of such conduct, I should blame no man who should condemn me for it; but I do blame those, whoever they may be, who falsely put such a charge in circulation against me.

July 31, 1846.

A. Lincoln.

Lincoln won the election on August 3, but the Cartwright charge still rankled. Said Dr. Boal: "Cartwright *sneaked* through this part of the district after Lincoln, and grossly misrepresented him." Still angry despite victory, Lincoln sent his handbill to Allen N. Ford, editor of the *Illinois Gazette* of Lacon, who reprinted Lincoln's reply in his columns on August 15.

The Living Lincoln

Springfield, August 11th, 1846.

Mr. Ford:

I see in your paper of 8th inst. a communication in relation to myself, of which it is perhaps expected of me to take some notice.

Shortly before starting on my tour through yours, and the other northern counties of the district, I was informed by letter from Jacksonville that Mr. Cartwright was whispering the charge of infidelity against me in that quarter. I at once wrote a contradiction of it, and sent it to my friends there, with the request that they should publish it or not, as in their discretion they might think proper, having in view the extent of the circulation of the charge, as also the extent of credence it might be receiving. They did not publish it. After my return from your part of the district, I was informed that he had been putting the same charge in circulation against me in some of the neighborhoods in our own, and one or two of the adjoining counties. I believe nine persons out of ten had not heard the charge at all; and, in a word, its extent of circulation was just such as to make a public notice of it appear uncalled for; while it was not entirely safe to leave it unnoticed. After some reflection, I published the little handbill, herewith enclosed, and sent it to the neighborhoods above referred to.

I have little doubt now, that to make the same charge—to slyly sow the seed in select spots—was the chief object of his mission through your part of the district, at a time when he knew I could not contradict him, either in person or by letter before the election. And, from the election returns in your county, being so different from what they are in parts where Mr. Cartwright and I are both well known, I incline to the belief that he has succeeded in deceiving some honest men there.

As to Mr. Woodward, "our worthy commissioner from Henry," spoken of by your correspondent, I must say it is a little singular that he should know so much about me, while, if I ever saw *him,* or heard of him, save in the communication in your paper, I have forgotten it. If Mr. Woodward has given such assurance of my character as your correspondent asserts, I can still suppose him to be a worthy man; he may have believed what he said; but there is, even in that charitable view of his case, one lesson in morals which he might, not without profit, learn of even me—and that is, never to add the weight of his character to a charge against his fellow-man, without *knowing* it to be true. I believe it is an established maxim in morals that he who makes an assertion without knowing whether it is true or false, is guilty of falsehood; and the accidental truth of the assertion, does not justify or excuse him. This maxim ought to be particularly held in view, when we contemplate an attack upon the reputation of our neighbor. I suspect it will turn out that Mr. Woodward got his information in relation to me, from Mr. Cartwright; and I here aver, that he, Cartwright, never heard me utter a word in any way indicating my opinions on religious matters, in his life.

It is my wish that you give this letter, together with the accompanying handbill, a place in your paper. Yours truly,

A. Lincoln.

Lincoln continued to send verses to Johnston. One poem read like a folk legend of the Indiana wilderness.

THE BEAR HUNT

[September, 1846]

A wild-bear chase, didst never see?
  Then hast thou lived in vain.
Thy richest bump of glorious glee,
  Lies desert in thy brain.

When first my father settled here,
  'Twas then the frontier line:
The panther's scream, filled night with fear
  And bears preyed on the swine.

But wo for Bruin's short-lived fun,
  When rose the squealing cry;
Now man and horse, with dog and gun,
  For vengeance, at him fly.

A sound of danger strikes his ear;
  He gives the breeze a snuff:
Away he bounds, with little fear,
  And seeks the tangled *rough*.

The Living Lincoln

On press his foes, and reach the ground,
   Where's left his half-munched meal;
The dogs, in circles, scent around,
   And find his fresh made trail.

With instant cry, away they dash,
   And men as fast pursue;
O'er logs they leap, through water splash,
   And shout the brisk halloo.

Now to elude the eager pack,
   Bear shuns the open ground;
Through matted vines, he shapes his track
   And runs it, round and round.

The tall fleet cur, with deep-mouthed voice,
   Now speeds him, as the wind;
While half-grown pup, and short-legged fice.
   Are yelping far behind.

And fresh recruits are dropping in
   To join the merry *corps:*
With yelp and yell,—a mingled din—
   The woods are in a roar.

And round, and round the chase now goes,
   The world's alive with fun;
Nick Carter's horse, his rider throws,
   And more, Hill drops his gun.

Now sorely pressed, bear glances back,
   And lolls his tired tongue;
When as, to force him from his track,
   An ambush on him sprung.

Across the glade he sweeps for flight,
   And fully is in view.
The dogs, new-fired by the sight,
   Their cry, and speed, renew.

The foremost ones, now reach his rear,
   He turns, they dash away;

Prairie Politics

And circling now, the wrathful bear,
    They have him full at bay.

At top of speed, the horsemen come,
    All screaming in a row.
"Whoop! Take him Tiger. Seize him Drum."
    Bang,—bang—the rifles go.

And furious now, the dogs he tears,
    And crushes in his ire.
Wheels right and left, and upward rears,
    With eyes of burning fire.

But leaden death is at his heart,
    Vain all the strength he plies.
And, spouting blood from every part,
    He reels, and sinks, and dies.

And now a dinsome clamor rose,
    'Bout who should have his skin;
Who first draws blood, each hunter knows,
    This prize must always win.

But who did this, and how to trace
    What's true from what's a lie,
Like lawyers, in a murder case
    They stoutly *argufy*.

Aforesaid fice, of blustering mood,
    Behind, and quite forgot,
Just now emerging from the wood,
    Arrives upon the spot.

With grinning teeth, and up-turned hair—
    Brim full of spunk and wrath,
He growls, and seizes on dead bear,
    And shakes for life and death.

And swells as if his skin would tear,
    And growls and shakes again;
And swears, as plain as dog can swear,
    That he has won the skin.

The Living Lincoln

Conceited whelp! we laugh at thee —
Nor mind, that not a few
Of pompous, two-legged dogs there be,
Conceited quite as you.

Lincoln's old friend Speed hears news that quite outstripped in importance any political success.

Springfield, Octr. 22nd. 1846

Dear Speed:

. . . Being elected to Congress, though I am very grateful to our friends, for having done it, has not pleased me as much as I expected.

We have another boy, born the 10th. of March last.* He is very much such a child as Bob † was at his age — rather of a longer order. Bob is "short and low," and, I expect, always will be. He talks very plainly — almost as plainly as anybody. He is quite smart enough. I sometimes fear he is one of the little rare-ripe sort, that are smarter at about five than ever after. He has a great deal of that sort of mischief, that is the offspring of much animal spirits. Since I began this letter a messenger came to tell me, Bob was lost; but by the time I reached the house, his mother had found him, and had him whipped — and, by now, very likely he is run away again.

Mary has read your letter, and wishes to be remembered to Mrs. S. and you, in which I most sincerely join her. As ever Yours —

A. Lincoln

The Thirtieth Congress would not convene for its first session until December, 1847. Lincoln turned to routine labors. In Quincy, Orville H. Browning heard of law suits and courts, and also an exciting prospect — Lincoln's first visit to Chicago, which now claimed 16,000 inhabitants and required a four-day journey by stagecoach.

Springfield, June 24th. 1847.

Dear Browning:

Yours of the 19th. inst. is received, and I have filed a plea for you, in the case of Moore vs Latourette.

* Edward Baker Lincoln.
† Robert Todd Lincoln.

Prairie Politics

Don't *fret* yourself about the trouble you give me; when I get tired, I'll tell you.

I am glad you sent this letter, because it reminds me to write you the result of your two cases of Moore vs Brown, & God knows who all, the charge of which you sent to Logan, and into which he drew me with him. We tried one of them, in which, after the plaintiff proved title, we offered the Auditor's deed, as the first link of connected title and seven years' possession, which was objected to, and the judges divided in opinion, which division is certified for the Supreme Court. The other case stands over to abide &c.

Indeed, *indeed,* I do not know what they are doing in the convention.* It is considered as almost settled, that they will *not* prohibit banks; that they *will* establish a poll tax; *will* restrict the number of members of both houses of the legislature to 100; *will* limit their *per diem* to $2 or 2.50– and make it still less after the first forty days of the session. So far as I have mentioned, I am pleased. Some other things I have fears for. I am not easy about the *courts.* I am satisfied with them as they are; but shall not care *much* if the judges are made elective by the people, and their terms of office limited. I fear, however, something more; and, as I think, much worse than all this, to wit "A Puppy Court" that is, a judge in each county, with civil jurisdiction in all cases up to a thousand dollars, and criminal, in all cases not capital. "A Migratory Supreme Court" and *salaries* so low as to exclude all respectable talent. From these, may God preserve us.

As to what I, Baker, and everybody else are doing, *I* am preparing to go to the Chicago River & Harbor Convention.† *Baker* has gone to Alton, as is thought, to be Colonel of the Sixth Regiment, and *everybody* is doing pretty much what everybody is always doing.

I hope this may find you well, and Mrs. Browning recovered from her hurt. I don't believe Mary & I can visit Quincy, although it would be very pleasant to do so.

My Chicago trip and *"several other gentlemen"* (Bob. & Ed) are very much in the way of it. Our love to Mrs. Browning and yourself.

A. Lincoln

* The Illinois Constitutional Convention of 1847.
† Held July 5–7. As the "lone Whig" from Illinois, Lincoln attracted some notice.

IV. Congressman Lincoln

1847-1849 IN 1847 Mrs. Sprigg's Washington boarding house stood on the present site of the Library of Congress. Since Mrs. Sprigg's home had become a favorite among Whigs, Congressman Lincoln established his residence here almost as a matter of political habit. Although Mary and the two boys accompanied him on the long journey from Springfield, life in the nation's capital quickly palled on Lincoln's wife. Her growing loneliness became a neurosis so that in time she seldom left her room except for meals. After three months she took the boys to her family home at Lexington, and Lincoln settled into the quasi-bachelorhood that the country's legislators often experienced. Nonetheless Lincoln made an agreeable member of Mrs. Sprigg's household; he enjoyed a reputation as a lively raconteur at the dinner table, occasionally went bowling in the evening with his fellow-boarders, and attended the Marine Band concerts on Wednesday and the Sunday afternoon concerts on the White House lawn.

The wings had not yet been added to the Capitol, and the improvised dome that Lincoln saw when he walked up the Hill to his day's duties was more utilitarian than aesthetic. Lincoln's seat in the House was in the back row on the Whig side. Whigs who had become national figures strolled the aisles—venerable, crusty ex-President John Quincy Adams; sickly little Alexander H. Stephens from Georgia; Joshua R. Giddings, the Ohio Abolitionist who also boarded with Mrs. Sprigg. On the Democratic side of the House sat Pennsylvania's David Wilmot, for whose "Proviso" in one form or another Lincoln would vote some forty times in the next two years; South Carolina's aristocratic, immovable Robert Barnwell Rhett; and the scowling Tennesseean, Andrew Johnson.

Lincoln supported the chip-on-shoulder attitude that Whigs carried into the Thirtieth Congress. With a presidential election imminent, Lincoln's party intended to lose no political profit from the War with Mexico, and so, while voting supplies for the war's effective prosecution, Whigs were determined that Polk and his Democratic administration must bear the guilt for the war and all the trials it produced. The Wilmot Proviso, prohibiting slavery in any territory subsequently acquired from Mexico, found sectional rather than party lines separating opponents. The great shadow of disunion was falling, and in thirteen years its principal image would be that of the tall, ungainly small town lawyer who watched and listened from a back row seat.

After a short time in Washington, Lincoln began to feel at ease. The "little speech" to which he referred concerned postal contracts. Already Herndon had raised the possibility of re-election, and Lincoln now had to face the fact that the Whig principle of rotation in office could become a double-edged sword.

Washington, January 8, 1848.

Dear William:

Your letter of December 27 was received a day or two ago. I am much obliged to you for the trouble you have taken, and promise to take in my little business there. As to speech-making, by way of getting the hang of the House I made a little speech two or three days ago on a post office question of no general interest. I find speaking here and elsewhere about the same thing. I was about as badly scared, and no worse, as I am when I speak in court. I expect to make one within a week or two, in which I hope to succeed well enough to wish you to see it.

It is very pleasant to learn from you that there are some who desire that I should be reëlected. I most heartily thank them for their kind partiality; and I can say, as Mr. Clay said of the annexation of Texas, that "personally I would not object" to a reëlection, although I thought at the time, and still think, it would be quite as well for me to return to the law at the end of a single term. I made the declaration that I would not be a candidate again, more from a wish to deal fairly with others, to keep peace among our friends, and to keep the district from going to the enemy, than for any cause personal to myself; so that, if it should so happen that nobody else wishes to be elected, I could not refuse the people the right of sending me again. But to enter myself as a competitor of others, or to authorize anyone so to enter me, is what my word and honor forbid.

The Living Lincoln

I got some letters intimating a probability of so much difficulty amongst our friends as to lose us the district; but I remember such letters were written to Baker when my own case was under consideration, and I trust there is no more ground for such apprehension now than there was then. Remember I am always glad to receive a letter from you. Most truly your friend,

A. Lincoln.

The first session of the Thirtieth Congress erupted into an intense political struggle. In a message to Congress, Polk fixed the blame on Mexico for starting the war; and a stout administration supporter from Illinois, William A. Richardson, introduced a resolution justifying the necessity of the conflict and demanding indemnity commensurate with Mexico's persistence in dragging on the struggle. Whigs rallied to defeat the resolution. Within a few weeks, and following the well-established position of the party, Lincoln made his first major speech as a Congressman.

January 12, 1848

Mr. Chairman:

Some, if not all the gentlemen on the other side of the House, who have addressed the committee within the last two days, have spoken rather complainingly, if I have rightly understood them, of the vote given a week or ten days ago, declaring that the war with Mexico was unnecessarily and unconstitutionally commenced by the President. I admit that such a vote should not be given, in mere party wantonness, and that the one given, is justly censurable, if it have no other, or better foundation. I am one of those who joined in that vote; and I did so under my best impression of the *truth* of the case. How I got this impression, and how it may possibly be removed, I will now try to show. When the war began, it was my opinion that all those who, because of knowing too *little,* or because of knowing too *much,* could not conscientiously approve the conduct of the President, in the beginning of it, should, nevertheless, as good citizens and patriots, remain silent on that point, at least till the war should be ended. Some leading Democrats, including Ex-President Van Buren, have taken this same view, as I understand them; and I adhered to it, and acted upon it, until since I took my seat here; and I think I should still adhere to it, were it not that the President and his friends will not allow it to be so.

Congressman Lincoln

Besides the continual effort of the President to argue every silent vote given for supplies, into an endorsement of the justice and wisdom of his conduct—besides that singularly candid paragraph, in his late message in which he tells us that Congress, with great unanimity, only two in the Senate and fourteen in the House dissenting, had declared that, "by the act of the Republic of Mexico, a state of war exists between that Government and the United States," when the same journals that informed him of this, also informed him, that when that declaration stood disconnected from the question of supplies, sixty-seven in the House, and not fourteen merely, voted against it—besides this open attempt to prove, by telling the *truth,* what he could not prove by telling the *whole truth* —demanding of all who will not submit to be misrepresented, in justice to themselves, to speak out—besides all this, one of my colleagues (Mr. Richardson) at a very early day in the session brought in a set of resolutions, expressly endorsing the original justice of the war on the part of the President. Upon these resolutions, when they shall be put on their passage I shall be *compelled* to vote; so that I cannot be silent, if I would.

Seeing this, I went about preparing myself to give the vote understandingly when it should come. I carefully examined the President's messages, to ascertain what he himself had said and proved upon the point. The result of this examination was to make the impression, that taking for true, all the President states as facts, he falls far short of proving his justification; and that the President would have gone farther with his proof, if it had not been for the small matter, that the *truth* would not permit him. Under the impression thus made, I gave the vote before mentioned. I propose now to give, concisely, the process of the examination I made, and how I reached the conclusion I did. The President, in his first war message of May 1846, declares that the soil was *ours* on which hostilities were commenced by Mexico; and he repeats that declaration, almost in the same language, in each successive annual message, thus showing that he esteems that point, a highly essential one. In the importance of that point, I entirely agree with the President. To my judgment, it is the *very point,* upon which he should be justified, or condemned. In his message of Decr. 1846, it seems to have occurred to him, as is certainly true, that title—ownership— to soil, or anything else, is not a simple fact; but is a conclusion following one or more simple facts; and that it was incumbent upon him, to present the facts from which he concluded the soil was ours, on which the first blood of the war was shed.

Accordingly a little below the middle of page twelve in the message last referred to, he enters upon that task; forming an issue, and introducing testimony, extending the whole, to a little below the middle of page fourteen. Now I propose to try to show, that the whole of this,—issue and evidence—is, from beginning to end, the sheerest deception. The issue, as he presents it, is in these words "But there are those who, conceding all this to be true, assume the ground that the true western boundary of Texas is the Nueces, instead of the Rio Grande; and that, therefore, in marching our army to the east bank of the latter river, we passed the Texan line, and invaded the territory of Mexico." Now this issue, is made up of two affirmatives and no negative. The main deception of it is, that it assumes as true, that *one* river or the *other* is necessarily the boundary; and cheats the superficial thinker entirely out of the idea, that *possibly* the boundary is somewhere *between* the two, and not actually at either. A further deception is, that it will let in *evidence*, which a true issue would exclude. A true issue, made by the President, would be about as follows "I say, the soil *was ours*, on which the first blood was shed; there are those who say it was not."

I now proceed to examine the President's evidence, as applicable to such an issue. When that evidence is analyzed, it is all included in the following propositions:

1. That the Rio Grande was the western boundary of Louisiana as we purchased it of France in 1803.

2. That the Republic of Texas always *claimed* the Rio Grande, as her western boundary.

3. That by various acts, she had claimed it *on paper*.

4. That Santa Anna, in his treaty with Texas, recognized the Rio Grande, as her boundary.

5. That Texas *before*, and the U. S. *after*, annexation had *exercised* jurisdiction *beyond* the Nueces—*between* the two rivers.

6. That our Congress, *understood* the boundary of Texas to extend beyond the Nueces.

Lincoln, adept at reducing complicated problems to terms of everyday experience, flayed the President.

Now for each of these in its turn.

His first item is, that the Rio Grande was the western boundary of Louisiana, as we purchased it of France in 1803; and seeming to expect this to be disputed, he argues over the amount of nearly a page, to prove it true; at the end of which he lets us know, that by the treaty of 1819, we sold to Spain the whole country from the Rio Grande eastward, to the Sabine. Now, admitting for the present, that the Rio Grande was the boundary of Louisana, what, under heaven, had that to do with the *present* boundary between us and Mexico? How, Mr. Chairman, the line, that once divided your land from mine, can *still* be the boundary between us, *after* I have sold my land to you, is, to me, beyond all comprehension. And how any man, with an honest purpose only, of proving the truth, could ever have *thought* of introducing such a fact to prove such an issue, is equally incomprehensible.

His next piece of evidence is that "The Republic of Texas always *claimed* this river (Rio Grande) as her western boundary." That is not true, in fact. Texas *has* claimed it, but she has not *always* claimed it. There is, at least, one distinguished exception. Her state constitution,—the republic's most solemn, and well considered act —that which may, without impropriety, be called her last will and testament revoking all others—makes no such claim. But suppose she had always claimed it. Has not Mexico always claimed the contrary? so that there is but *claim* against *claim,* leaving nothing proved, until we get back of the claims, and find which has the better *foundation.*

Though not in the order in which the President presents his evidence, I now consider that class of his statements, which are, in substance, nothing more than that Texas has, by various acts of her convention and congress, claimed the Rio Grande, as her boundary, *on paper.* I mean here what he says about the fixing of the Rio Grande as her boundary in her old constitution (not her state constitution) about forming congressional districts, counties &c &c. Now all of this is but naked *claim;* and what I have already said about claims is strictly applicable to this. If I should claim your land, by word of mouth, that certainly would not make it mine; and if I were to claim it by a deed which I had made myself, and with which, you had had nothing to do, the claim would be quite the same, in substance—or rather, in utter nothingness.

I next consider the President's statement that Santa Anna in his *treaty* with Texas, recognized the Rio Grande, as the western boundary of Texas. Besides the position, so often taken that Santa

Anna, while a prisoner of war—a captive—*could* not bind Mexico by a treaty, which I deem conclusive—besides this, I wish to say something in relation to this treaty, so-called by the President, with Santa Anna. If any man would like to be amused by a sight of that *little* thing, which the President calls by that *big* name, he can have it, by turning to Niles' Register, volume 50, page 336. And if anyone should suppose that Niles' Register is a curious repository of so mighty a document, as a solemn treaty between nations, I can only say that I learned, to a tolerable degree of certainty, by enquiry at the State Department, that the President himself, never saw it anywhere else.

By the way, I believe I should not err, if I were to declare, that during the first ten years of the existence of that document, it was never, by anybody, *called* a treaty—that it was never so-called, till the President, in his extremity, attempted, by so calling it, to wring something from it in justification of himself in connection with the Mexican War. It has none of the distinguishing features of a treaty. It does not call itself a treaty. Santa Anna does not therein, assume to bind Mexico; he assumes only to act as the President-Commander-in-chief of the Mexican Army and Navy; stipulates that the then present hostilities should cease, and that he would not *himself* take up arms, nor *influence* the Mexican people to take up arms, against Texas during the existence of the war of independence. He did not recognize the independence of Texas; he did not assume to put an end to the war; but clearly indicated his expectation of its continuance; he did not say one word about boundary, and, most probably, never thought of it. It *is* stipulated therein that the Mexican forces should evacuate the territory of Texas, *passing to the other side of the Rio Grande;* and in another article, it is stipulated that, to prevent collisions between the armies, the Texan army should not approach nearer than within five leagues—of *what* is not said—but clearly, from the object stated it is—of the Rio Grande. Now, if this is a treaty, recognizing the Rio Grande, as the boundary of Texas, it contains the singular feature, of stipulating, that Texas shall not go within five leagues of *her own* boundary.

Next comes the evidence of Texas before annexation, and the United States, afterwards, *exercising* jurisdiction *beyond* the Nueces, and *between* the two rivers. This actual *exercise* of jurisdiction, is the very class or quality of evidence we want. It is excellent so far as it goes; but does it go far enough? He tells us it went *beyond* the Nueces; but he does not tell us it went to the Rio Grande. He tells us, jurisdiction was exercised *between* the two rivers, but he does not tell us it was exercised over *all* the territory between them. Some simple minded people, think it is *possible,* to cross one river and go beyond it without going *all the way* to the next—that jurisdiction may be exercised *between* two rivers without covering *all* the country between them. I know a man, not very unlike myself, who exercises jurisdiction over a piece of land between the Wabash and the Mississippi; and yet so far is this from being *all* there is between those rivers, that it is just one hundred and fifty-two feet long by fifty wide, and no part of it much within a hundred miles of either. He has a neighbour between him and the Mississippi,—that is, just across the street, in that direction— whom, I am sure, he could neither *persuade* nor *force* to give up his habitation; but which nevertheless, he could certainly annex, if it were to be done, by merely standing on his own side of the street and *claiming* it, or even, sitting down, and writing a *deed* for it.

But next the President tells us, the Congress of the United States *understood* the State of Texas they admitted into the Union, to extend *beyond* the Nueces. Well, I suppose they did. *I* certainly so understood it. But how *far* beyond? That Congress did *not* understand it to extend clear to the Rio Grande, is quite certain by the fact of their joint resolutions, for admission, expressly leaving all questions of boundary to future adjustment. And it may be added, that Texas herself, is proved to have had the same understanding of it, that our Congress had, by the fact of the exact conformity of her new constitution, to those resolutions.

I am now through the whole of the President's evidence; and it is a singular fact, that if anyone should declare the President sent the army into the midst of a settlement of Mexican people, who had never submitted, by consent or by force, to the authority of Texas or of the United States, and that *there,* and *thereby,* the first blood of the war was shed, there is not one word in all the President has said, which would either admit or deny the declaration. This strange omission, it does seem to me, could not have occurred but by design. My way of living leads me to be about the courts of justice; and there, I have sometimes seen a good lawyer, struggling for his client's neck, in a desperate case, employing every artifice to work round, befog, and cover up, with many words, some point arising in the case, which he *dared* not admit, and yet *could* not deny. Party bias may help to make it appear so; but with all the allowance I can make for such bias, it still does appear to me, that just such, and from just such necessity, is the President's struggle in this case.

To Lincoln, the right of revolution was sacred. He would never abuse it for the sake of expediency.

Some time after my colleague (Mr. Richardson) introduced the resolutions I have mentioned, I introduced a preamble, resolution, and interrogatories, intended to draw the President out, if possible, on this hitherto untrodden ground. To show their relevancy, I propose to state my understanding of the true rule for ascertaining the boundary between Texas and Mexico. It is, that *wherever* Texas was *exercising* jurisdiction, was hers; and *wherever* Mexico was *exercising* jurisdiction, was hers; and that *whatever* separated the actual exercise of jurisdiction of the one, from that of the other, was the true boundary between them. If, as is probably true, Texas was exercising jurisdiction along the western bank of the Nueces, and Mexico was exercising it along the eastern bank of the Rio Grande, then *neither* river was the boundary; but the uninhabited country between the two, was.

The extent of our territory in that region depended, not on any *treaty-fixed boundary* (for no treaty had attempted it) but on revolution. Any people anywhere, being inclined and having the power, have the *right* to rise up, and shake off the existing government, and form a new one that suits them better. This is a most valuable,—a most sacred right—a right, which we hope and believe, is to liberate the world. Nor is this right confined to cases in which the whole people of an existing government, may choose to exercise it. Any portion of such people that *can, may* revolutionize, and make their *own,* of so much of the territory as they inhabit. More than this, a *majority* of any portion of such people may revolutionize, putting down a *minority,* intermingled with, or near about them, who may oppose their movement. Such minority, was precisely the case, of the Tories of our own revolution. It is a quality of revolutions not to go by *old* lines, or *old* laws; but to break up both, and make new ones. As to the country now in question, we bought it of France in 1803, and sold it to Spain in 1819, according to the President's statements. After this, all Mexico, including Texas, revolutionized against Spain; and still later, Texas revolutionized against Mexico. In my view, just so far as she carried her revolution, by obtaining the *actual,* willing or unwilling, submission of the people, *so far,* the country was hers, and no farther.

Now sir, for the purpose of obtaining the very best evidence, as to whether Texas had actually carried her revolution, to the place where the hostilities of the present war commenced, let the President answer the interrogatories, I proposed, as before mentioned, or some other similar ones. Let him answer, fully, fairly, and candidly. Let him answer with *facts,* and not with arguments. Let him remember he sits where Washington sat, and so remembering, let him answer, as Washington would answer. As a nation *should* not, and the Almighty *will* not, be evaded, so let him attempt no evasion—no equivocation. And if, so answering, he can show that the soil was ours, where the first blood of the war was shed—that it was not within an inhabited country, or, if within such, that the inhabitants had submitted themselves to the civil authority of Texas, or of the United States, and that the same is true of the site of Fort Brown, then I am with him for his justification. In that case I shall be most happy to reverse the vote I gave the other day.

I have a selfish motive for desiring that the President may do this. I expect to give some votes, in connection with the war, which, without his so doing, will be of doubtful propriety in my own judgment, but which will be free from the doubt if he does so. But if he *can* not, or *will* not do this—if on any pretence, or no pretence, he shall refuse or omit it, then I shall be fully convinced, of what I more than suspect already, that he is deeply conscious of being in the wrong—that he feels the blood of this war, like the blood of Abel, is crying to Heaven against him. That originally having some strong motive—what, I will not stop now to give my opinion concerning—to involve the two countries in a war, and trusting to escape scrutiny, by fixing the public gaze upon the exceeding brightness of military glory—that attractive rainbow, that rises in showers of blood—that serpent's eye, that charms to destroy—he plunged into it, and has swept, *on* and *on,* till, disappointed in his calculation of the ease with which Mexico might be subdued, he now finds himself, he knows not where.

How like the half-insane mumbling of a fever-dream, is the whole war part of his late message! At one time telling us that

Mexico has nothing whatever, that we can get, but territory; at another, showing us how we can support the war, by levying contributions on Mexico. At one time, urging the national honor, the security of the future, the prevention of foreign interference, and even, the good of Mexico herself, as among the objects of the war; at another, telling us, that "to reject indemnity, by refusing to accept a cession of territory, would be to abandon all our just demands, and to wage the war, bearing all its expenses, *without a purpose or definite object.*" So then, the national honor, security of the future, and everything but territorial indemnity, may be considered the *no-purposes,* and *indefinite,* objects of the war! But, having it now settled that territorial indemnity is the only object, we are urged to seize, by legislation here, all that he was content to take, a few months ago, and the whole province of Lower California to boot, and to still carry on the war—to take *all* we are fighting for, and *still* fight on. Again, the President is resolved, under all circumstances, to have full territorial indemnity for the expenses of the war; but he forgets to tell us how we are to get the *excess,* after those expenses shall have surpassed the value of the *whole* of the Mexican territory. So again, he insists that the separate national existence of Mexico, shall be maintained; but he does not tell us *how* this can be done, after we shall have taken *all* her territory.

Lest the questions I here suggest, be considered speculative merely, let me be indulged a moment in trying to show they are not. The war has gone on some twenty months; for the expenses of which, together with an inconsiderable old score, the President now claims about one-half of the Mexican territory; and that, by far the better half, so far as concerns our ability to make anything out of it. *It* is comparatively uninhabited; so that we could establish land offices in it, and raise some money in that way. But the other half is already inhabited, as I understand it, tolerably densely for the nature of the country; and all its lands, or all that are valuable, already appropriated as private property. How then are we to make anything out of these lands with this incumbrance on them? or how, remove the incumbrance? I suppose no one will say we should kill the people, or drive them out, or make slaves of them, or even confiscate their property. How then can we make much out of this part of the territory?

Congressman Lincoln

Skilfully, Lincoln defined the dilemmas into which the President had stumbled.

If the prosecution of the war has, in expenses, already equalled the *better* half of the country, how long its future prosecution, will be in equalling, the less valuable half, is not a *speculative,* but a *practical* question, pressing closely upon us. And yet it is a question which the President seems to never have thought of. As to the mode of terminating the war, and securing peace, the President is equally wandering and indefinite. First, it is to be done by a more vigorous prosecution of the war in the vital parts of the enemy's country, and, after apparently talking himself tired on this point, the President drops down into a half-despairing tone, and tells us that "with a people distracted and divided by contending factions, and a government subject to constant changes, by successive revolutions, *the continued success of our arms may fail to secure a satisfactory peace.*" Then he suggests the propriety of wheedling the Mexican people to desert the counsels of their own leaders, and trusting in our protection, to set up a government from which we can secure a satisfactory peace; telling us, that *"this may become the only mode of obtaining such a peace."* But soon he falls into doubt of this too; and then drops back on to the already half-abandoned ground of "more vigorous prosecution." All this shows that the President is, in no wise, satisfied with his own positions. First he takes up one, and in attempting to argue us *into* it, he argues himself *out* of it; then seizes another, and goes through the same process; and then, confused at being able to think of nothing new, he snatches up the old one again, which he has some time before cast off. His mind, tasked beyond its power, is running hither and thither, like some tortured creature, on a burning surface, finding no position, on which it can settle down, and be at ease.

Again, it is a singular omission in this message, that it nowhere intimates *when* the President expects the war to terminate. At its beginning, Genl. Scott was, by this same President, driven into disfavor, if not disgrace, for intimating that peace could not be conquered in less than three or four months. But now, at the end of about twenty months, during which time our arms have given us the most splendid successes—every department, and every part, land and water, officers and privates, regulars and volunteers, doing all that men *could* do, and hundreds of things which it had ever before been thought men could *not* do, — after all this, this same President gives us a long message, without showing us, that, *as to the end,* he himself, has even an imaginary conception. As I have before said, he knows not where he is. He is a bewildered, confounded, and miserably perplexed man. God grant he may be able to show, there is not something about his conscience, more painful than all his mental perplexity!

Disdainfully Polk ignored Lincoln's remarks; a suddenly excited Herndon could not. Herndon was further agitated by Lincoln's support of an amendment to a resolution, introduced by George Ashmun of Massachusetts, that characterized the war as "unconstitutionally and unnecessarily begun by the President." But Lincoln thought that he was on firm moral ground and refused to be budged.

Washington, Feb. 1–1848

Dear William:

Your letter of the 19th. ult. was received last night, and for which I am much obliged. The only thing in it that I wish to talk to you about at once, is that, because of my vote for Mr. Ashmun's amendment, you fear that you and I disagree about the war. I regret this, not because of any fear we shall remain disagreed, after you shall have read this letter, but because, if *you* misunderstand, I fear other good friends will also. That vote affirms that the war was unnecessarily and unconstitutionally commenced by the President; and I will stake my life, that if you had been in my place, you would have voted just as I did. Would you have voted what you felt you knew to be a lie? I know you would not. Would you have gone out of the House—skulked the vote? I expect not. If you had skulked one vote, you would have had to skulk many more, before the end of the session. Richardson's resolutions, introduced before I made any move, or gave any vote upon the subject, make the direct question of the justice of the war; so that no man can be silent if he would. You are compelled to speak; and your only alternative is to tell the *truth* or tell a lie. I cannot doubt which you would do.

This vote has nothing to do, in determining my votes on the questions of supplies. I have always intended, and still intend, to vote supplies; perhaps not in the precise form recommended by the President, but in a better form for all purposes, except loco-foco party purposes. It is in this particular you seem to be mistaken. The locos are untiring in their effort to make the impression that all who vote supplies, or take part in the war, do, of necessity, approve the President's conduct in the beginning of it; but the Whigs have, from the beginning, made and kept the distinction between the two. In the very first act, nearly all the Whigs voted *against* the preamble declaring that war existed by the act of Mexico, and yet nearly all of them voted *for* the supplies. As to the Whig men who have participated in the war, so far as they have spoken to my hearing, they do not hesitate to denounce, as unjust the President's conduct in the beginning of the war. They do not suppose that such denunciation, is dictated by undying hatred to them, as the Register would have it believed. There are two such Whigs on this floor, Col. Haskell, and Major Gaines. The former fought as a Col. by the side of Col. Baker at Cerro Gordo, and stands side by side with me, in the vote, that you seem to be dissatisfied with. The latter, the history of whose capture with Cassius Clay, you well know, had not arrived here when that vote was given; but as I understand, he stands ready to give just such a vote, whenever an occasion shall present. Baker too, who is now here, says the truth is undoubtedly that way, and whenever he shall speak out, he will say so. Col. Doniphan too, the favourite Whig of Missouri, and who overran all northern Mexico, on his return home in a public speech at St. Louis, condemned the administration in relation to the war as I remember. G. T. M. Davis, who has been through almost the whole war, declares in favour of Mr. Clay, from which I infer that he adopts the sentiments of Mr. Clay, generally at least. On the other hand, I have heard of but one Whig, who has been to the war, attempting to justify the President's conduct. That one is Capt. Bishop, editor of the Charleston Courier, and a very clever fellow.

I do not mean this letter for the public, but for you. Before it reaches you, you will have seen and read my pamphlet speech, and perhaps, scared anew, by it. After you get over your scare, read it over again, sentence by sentence, and tell me honestly what you think of it. I condensed all I could for fear of being cut off by the hour rule, and when I got through, I had spoke but 45 minutes. Yours forever

A. Lincoln

The Living Lincoln

Herndon remained adamant. Once more Lincoln met his partner's arguments on constitutional grounds, giving specific attention to the war-making powers of a President.

Washington, Feb. 15. 1848

Dear William:

Your letter of the 29th. Jany. was received last night. Being exclusively a constitutional argument, I wish to submit some reflections upon it in the same spirit of kindness that I know actuates you. Let me first state what I understand to be your position. It is, that if it shall become *necessary, to repel invasion,* the President may, without violation of the Constitution, cross the line, and *invade* the territory of another country; and that whether such *necessity* exists in any given case, the President is to be the *sole* judge.

Before going further, consider well whether this is, or is not your position. If it is, it is a position that neither the President himself, nor any friend of his, so far as I know, has ever taken. Their only positions are first, that the soil was *ours* where hostilities commenced, and second, that whether it was rightfully *ours* or not, *Congress had annexed it,* and the President, for that reason was bound to defend it, both of which are as clearly proved to be false in fact, as you can prove that your house is not mine. That soil was not ours; and Congress did not annex or attempt to annex it. But to return to your position: Allow the President to invade a neighboring nation, whenever *he* shall deem it necessary to repel an invasion, and you allow him to do so, *whenever he may choose to say* he deems it necessary for such purpose—and you allow him to make war at pleasure. Study to see if you can fix *any limit* to his power in this respect, after you have given him so much as you propose. If, today, he should choose to say he thinks it necessary to invade Canada, to prevent the British from invading us, how could you stop him? You may say to him, "I see no probability of the British invading us" but he will say to you "be silent; I see it, if you don't."

The provision of the Constitution giving the war-making power to Congress, was dictated, as I understand it, by the following reasons. Kings had always been involving and impoverishing their people in wars, pretending generally, if not always, that the good of the people was the object. This, our Convention understood to be the most oppressive of all kingly oppressions; and they

110

resolved to so frame the Constitution that *no one man* should hold the power of bringing this oppression upon us. But your view destroys the whole matter, and places our President where kings have always stood. Write soon again. Yours truly.

A. Lincoln

No one had hoped more fervently than Lincoln that some day Henry Clay would occupy the White House, but the war had produced a Whig hero in Zachary Taylor. To an old friend in Illinois, Usher F. Linder, Lincoln explained one of Taylor's virtues.

Washington, Feb. 20. 1848–

Dear Linder:

In law it is good policy to never *plead* what you *need* not, lest you oblige yourself to *prove* what you *can* not. Reflect on this well before you proceed. The application I mean to make of this rule is, that you should simply go for Genl. Taylor; because by this, you can take some Democrats, and lose no Whigs; but if you go also for Mr. Polk on the origin and mode of prosecuting the war, you will still take some Democrats, but you will lose more Whigs, so that in the sum of the operation you will be loser. This is at least my opinion; and if you will look round, I doubt, if you do not discover such to be the fact amongst your own neighbors. Further than this: By justifying Mr. Polk's mode of prosecuting the war, you put yourself in opposition to Genl. Taylor himself, for we all know he has declared for, and, in fact originated, the defensive line policy.

You know I mean this in kindness, and wish it to be confidential. Yours as ever

A. Lincoln

Lincoln thought of what he would do as President, and offered some advice to Taylor.

WHAT GEN. TAYLOR OUGHT TO SAY

[March, 1848]

The question of a national bank is at rest; were I President I should not urge its re-agitation upon Congress; but should Congress see fit to pass an act to establish such an institution, I should not arrest it by the veto, unless I should consider it subject to some constitutional objection, from which I believe the two former banks to have been free.

It appears to me that the national debt created by the war, renders a modification of the existing tariff indispensable; and when it shall be modified, I should be pleased to see it adjusted with a due reference to the protection of our home industry. The particulars, it appears to me, must and should be left to the untrammeled discretion of Congress.

As to the Mexican War, I still think the defensive line policy the best to terminate it. In a final treaty of peace, we shall probably be under a sort of necessity of taking some territory; but it is my desire that we shall not acquire any extending so far south, as to enlarge and aggravate the distracting question of slavery. Should I come into the Presidency before these questions shall be settled, I should act in relation to them in accordance with the views here expressed.

Finally, were I President, I should desire the legislation of the country to rest with Congress, uninfluenced by the executive in its origin or progress, and undisturbed by the veto unless in very special and clear cases.

Solomon Lincoln lived in Hingham, Massachusetts. At the time of the following correspondence Congressman Lincoln did not know that his ancestors had come from this region.

Washington,
March 6– 1848

Mr. Solomon Lincoln,
Dear Sir:
Your letter to Mr. Hale,* in which you do me the honor of making some kind enquiries concerning me, has been handed me by Mr. Hale, with the request that I should give you the desired information. I was born Feb: 12th. 1809 in Hardin County, Kentucky. My father's name is *Thomas;* my grandfather's was *Abraham,*—the same as my own. My grandfather went from Rockingham County in Virginia, to Kentucky, about the year 1782; and, two years afterwards, was killed by the Indians. We have a vague

* Artemas Hale, a Representative from Massachusetts.

tradition, that my great-grandfather went from Pennsylvania to Virginia; and that he was a Quaker. Further back than this, I have never heard anything. It may do no harm to say that "Abraham" and "Mordecai" are common names in our family; while the name "Levi" so common among the Lincolns of New England, I have not known in any instance among us.

Owing to my father being left an orphan at the age of six years, in poverty, and in a new country, he became a wholly uneducated man; which I suppose is the reason why I know so little of our family history. I believe I can say nothing more that would at all interest you. If you shall be able to trace any connection between yourself and me, or, in fact, whether you shall or not, I should be pleased to have a line from you at any time. Very respectfully

A. Lincoln

Washington,
March 24– 1848

Mr. Solomon Lincoln
Dear Sir:

Yours of the 21st. is received. I shall not be able to answer your interrogatories very fully; I will, however, do the best I can. I have mentioned that my grandfather's name was Abraham. He had, as I think I have heard, four brothers, Isaac, Jacob, Thomas, and John. He had three sons, Mordecai, Josiah, and Thomas, the last, my father. My uncle Mordecai, had three sons, Abraham, James, and Mordecai. Uncle Josiah had several daughters, and an only son, Thomas. My father has an only child, myself, of course.

This is all I know certainly on the subject of names; it is, however, my father's understanding that Abraham, Mordecai, and Thomas are old family names of ours. The reason I did not mention Thomas as a family name in my other letter was because it is so very common a name, as to prove but little, if anything, in the way of identification.

Since I wrote you, it occurred to me to enquire of Gov. McDowell, who represents the district in Virginia, including Rockingham, whether he knew persons of our name there. He informs he does; though none very intimately except one, an old man by the Christian name of David. That he is of our family I have no doubt. I now address him a letter, making such enquiries as suggest themselves; and, when I shall receive an answer, I will communicate to you, anything that may seem pertinent to your object. Very truly yours

A. Lincoln

To Lincoln's delight David Lincoln filled in some of the gaps in the family genealogy.

Washington, April 2nd. 1848

Dear Sir,

Last evening I was much gratified by receiving and reading your letter of the 30th. of March. There is no longer any doubt that your uncle Abraham, and my grandfather was the same man. His family did reside in Washington County, Kentucky, just as you say you found them in 1801 or 2. The oldest son, Uncle Mordecai, near twenty years ago, removed from Kentucky to Hancock County, Illinois, where within a year or two afterwards, he died, and where his surviving children now live. His two sons there now are Abraham & Mordecai; and their post office is "La Harpe."

Uncle Josiah, farther back than my recollection, went from Kentucky to Blue River in Indiana. I have not heard from him in a great many years, and whether he is still living I cannot say. My recollection of what I have heard is, that he has several daughters & only one son, Thomas. Their post office is "Corydon, Harrison County, Indiana."

My father, Thomas, is still living, in Coles County Illinois, being in the 71st. year of his age. His post office is Charleston, Coles Co. Ill. I am his only child. I am now in my 40th. year; and I live in Springfield, Sangamon County, Illinois. This is the outline of my grandfather's family in the West.

I think my father has told me that grandfather had four brothers, Isaac, Jacob, John and Thomas. Is that correct? and which of them was your father? Are any of them alive? I am quite sure that Isaac resided on Watauga, near a point where Virginia and Tennessee join; and that he has been dead more than twenty, perhaps thirty, years. Also, that Thomas removed to Kentucky, near Lexington, where he died a good while ago.

What was your grandfather's Christian name? Was he or not, a Quaker? About what *time* did he emigrate from Berks County, Pa. to Virginia? Do you know anything of your family (or rather I may now say, *our* family) farther back than your grandfather?

114

Congressman Lincoln

If it be not too much trouble to you, I shall be much pleased to hear from you again. Be assured I will call on you, should anything ever bring me near you. I shall give your respects to Gov. McDowell, as you desire. Very truly yours—

A. Lincoln—

The first session of the Thirtieth Congress dragged on. Lincoln missed Mary and the boys. No one can be sure of what Lincoln meant by *"gone tapila";* possibly the phrase was Eddy's way of saying "Capitol." Robert Wickliffe had married a cousin of Robert S. Todd and the two Roberts were personal and political enemies. William Strong was a Democrat from Pennsylvania; his wife, Matilda, was a distant relative of Mary Lincoln.

Washington, April 16– 1848–

Dear Mary:

In this troublesome world, we are never quite satisfied. When you were here, I thought you hindered me some in attending to business; but now, having nothing but business—no variety—it has grown exceedingly tasteless to me. I hate to sit down and direct documents, and I hate to stay in this old room by myself. You know I told you in last Sunday's letter, I was going to make a little speech during the week; but the week has passed away without my getting a chance to do so; and now my interest in the subject has passed away too. Your second and third letters have been received since I wrote before. Dear Eddy thinks father is *"gone tapila."* Has any further discovery been made as to the breaking into your grandmother's house? If I were she, I would not remain there alone. You mention that your uncle John Parker is likely to be at Lexington. Don't forget to present him my very kindest regards.

I went yesterday to hunt the little plaid stockings, as you wished; but found that McKnight has quit business, and Allen had not a single pair of the description you give, and only one plaid pair of any sort that I thought would fit "Eddy's dear little feet." I have a notion to make another trial tomorrow morning. If I could get them, I have an excellent chance of sending them. Mr. Warrick Tunstall, of St. Louis is here. He is to leave early this week, and to go by Lexington. He says he knows you, and will call to see you; and he voluntarily asked, if I had not some package to send to you.

The Living Lincoln

I wish you to enjoy yourself in every possible way; but is there no danger of wounding the feelings of your good father, by being so openly intimate with the Wickliffe family?

Mrs. Broome has not removed yet; but she thinks of doing so tomorrow. All the house—or rather, all with whom you were on decided good terms—send their love to you. The others say nothing.

Very soon after you went away, I got what I think a very pretty set of shirt-bosom studs—modest little ones, jet, set in gold, only costing 50 cents a piece, or 1.50 for the whole.

Suppose you do not prefix the "Hon" to the address on your letters to me any more. I like the letters very much, but I would rather they should not have that upon them. It is not necessary, as I suppose you have thought, to have them to come free.

And you are entirely free from headache? That is good—good —considering it is the first spring you have been free from it since we were acquainted. I am afraid you will get so well, and fat, and young, as to be wanting to marry again. Tell Louisa I want her to watch you a little for me. Get weighed, and write me how much you weigh.

I did not get rid of the impression of that foolish dream about dear Bobby till I got your letter written the same day. What did he and Eddy think of the little letters father sent them? Don't let the blessed fellows forget father.

A day or two ago Mr. Strong, here in Congress, said to me that Matilda would visit here within two or three weeks. Suppose you write her a letter, and enclose it in one of mine; and if she comes I will deliver it to her, and if she does not, I will send it to her. Most affectionately

A. Lincoln

Lincoln traveled to Philadelphia in early June to attend the Whig National Convention. The Illinois delegation split its vote four for Taylor, three for Clay, and one for Winfield Scott until the fourth ballot, when the convention went unanimously for Taylor. Returning to Washington, Lincoln still missed Mary and the children.

Washington, June 12. 1848—

My dear wife:

On my return from Philadelphia, yesterday, where, in my anxiety I had been led to attend the Whig convention I found your

116

last letter. I was so tired and sleepy, having ridden all night, that I could not answer it till today; and now I have to do so in the H.R. The leading matter in your letter, is your wish to return to this side of the mountains. Will you be a *good girl* in all things, if I consent? Then come along, and that as *soon* as possible. Having got the idea in my head, I shall be impatient till I see you. You will not have money enough to bring you; but I presume your uncle will supply you, and I will refund him here. By the way you do not mention whether you have received the fifty dollars I sent you. I do not much fear but that you got it; because the want of it would have induced you to say something in relation to it. If your uncle is already at Lexington, you might induce him to start on earlier than the first of July; he could stay in Kentucky longer on his return, and so make up for lost time. Since I began this letter, the H.R. has passed a resolution for adjourning on the 17th. July, which probably will pass the Senate. I hope this letter will not be disagreeable to you; which, together with the circumstances under which I write, I hope will excuse me for not writing a longer one. Come on just as soon as you can. I want to see you, and our dear —*dear* boys very much. Everybody here wants to see our dear Bobby. Affectionately

A. Lincoln

Lincoln's support of "Old Zach" was whole-hearted. To Herndon he forecast "a most overwhelming, glorious, triumph." Herndon remained dubious; he judged by the temper in Illinois. Lincoln could not conceal his testy feelings.

Washington, June 22. 1848—

Dear William:

Last night I was attending a sort of caucus of the Whig members held in relation to the coming presidential election. The whole field of the nation was scanned, and all is high hope and confidence. Illinois is expected to better her condition in this race. Under these circumstances, judge how heart-sickening it was to come to my room and find and read your discouraging letter of the 15th. We have made no gains, but have lost "A. R. Robinson, *Turner,* Campbell, and four or five more." Tell Arney to reconsider, if he would be saved. Baker and I used to do something, but I think you attach more importance to our absence than is just. There is another cause. In 1840, for instance, we had two Senators and five Representatives in Sangamon; now we have part of one Senator, and two Representatives. With quite one-third more people than we had then, we have only half the sort of offices which are sought by men of the speaking sort of talent. This, I think, is the chief cause. Now as to the young men. You must not wait to be brought forward by the older men. For instance do you suppose that I should ever have got into notice if I had waited to be hunted up and pushed forward by older men? You young men get together and form a Rough & Ready club, and have regular meetings and speeches. Take in everybody that you can get, Harrison Grimsley, Z. A. Enos, Lee Kimball, and C. W. Matheny will do well to begin the thing, but as you go along, gather up all the shrewd wild boys about town, whether just of age, or little under age—Chris: Logan, Reddick Ridgely, Lewis Zwizler, and hundreds such. Let everyone play the part he can play best—some speak, some sing, and all hollow. Your meetings will be of evenings; the older men, and the women will go to hear you; so that it will not only contribute to the election of "Old Zach" but will be an interesting pastime, and improving to the intellectual faculties of all engaged. Don't fail to do this.

You ask me to send you all the speeches made about "Old Zac" the war &c. &c. Now this makes me a little impatient. I have regularly sent you the Congressional Globe and Appendix, and you cannot have examined them, or you would have discovered that they contain every speech made by every man, in both Houses of Congress, on every subject, during this session. Can I send any more? Can I send speeches that nobody has made? Thinking it would be most natural that the newspapers would feel interested to give at least some of the speeches to their readers, I, at the beginning of the session made arrangement to have one copy of the Globe and Appendix regularly sent to each Whig paper of our district. And yet, with the exception of my own little speech, which was published in two only of the then five, now four Whig papers, I do not remember having seen a single speech, or even an extract from one, in any single one of those papers. With equal and full means on both sides, I will venture that the State Register has thrown before its readers more of Locofoco speeches in a month, than all the Whig papers of the district, have done of Whig speeches during the session.

If you wish a full understanding of the beginning of the war, I repeat what I believe I said to you in a letter once before, that the whole, or nearly so is to be found in the speech of Dixon of Connecticut. This I sent you in pamphlet, as well as in the Globe. Examine and study every sentence of that speech thoroughly, and you will understand the whole subject.

You ask how Congress came to declare that war existed by the act of Mexico. Is it possible you don't understand that yet? You have at least twenty speeches in your possession that fully explain it. I will, however, try it once more. The news reached Washington of the commencement of hostilities on the Rio Grande, and of the great peril of Gen: Taylor's army. Everybody, Whig and Democrat, was for sending them aid, in men and money. It was necessary to pass a bill for this. The Locos had a majority in both Houses, and they brought in a bill with a preamble, saying— *Whereas* war exists by the act of Mexico, therefore we send Gen: Taylor men and money. The Whigs moved to strike out the preamble, so that they could vote to send the men and money, without saying anything about how the war commenced; but, being in the minority they were voted down, and the preamble was retained. Then, on the passage of the bill, the question came upon them, "shall we vote *for* preamble and bill both together, or against both together." They could not vote *against* sending help to Gen: Taylor, and therefore they voted *for* both together. Is there any difficulty in understanding this? Even my little speech, shows how this was; and if you will go to the library you may get the Journals of 1845–6, in which you can find the whole for yourself.

We have nothing published yet with special reference to the Taylor race; but we soon will have, and then I will send them to everybody. I made an Internal Improvement speech day-before-yesterday, which I shall send home as soon as I can get it written out and printed, and which I suppose nobody will read. Your friend as ever

A. Lincoln

Washington settled into a typically humid summer. Lincoln wondered about his wife's bills, and about two girls and an escort with a guilty look.

Washington, July 2. 1848.

My dear wife:

Your letter of last Sunday came last night. On that day (Sunday) I wrote the principal part of a letter to you, but did not finish it, or send it till Tuesday, when I had provided a draft for $100 which I sent in it. It is now probable that on that day (Tuesday) you started to Shelbyville; so that when the money reaches Lexington, you will not be there. Before leaving, did you make any provision about letters that might come to Lexington for you? Write me whether you got the draft, if you shall not have already done so, when this reaches you. Give my kindest regards to your uncle John, and all the family. Thinking of them reminds me that I saw your acquaintance, Newton, of Arkansas, at the Philadelphia Convention. We had but a single interview, and that was so brief, and in so great a multitude of strange faces, that I am quite sure I should not recognize him, if I were to meet him again. He was a sort of Trinity, three in one, having the right, in his own person, to cast the three votes of Arkansas. Two or three days ago I sent your uncle John, and a few of our other friends each a copy of the speech I mentioned in my last letter; but I did not send any to you, thinking you would be on the road here, before it would reach you. I send you one now. Last Wednesday, P. H. Hood & Co, dunned me for a little bill of $5.38 cents, and Walter Harper & Co, another for $8.50 cents, for goods which they say you bought. I hesitated to pay them, because my recollection is that you told me when you went away, there was nothing left unpaid. Mention in your next letter whether they are right.

Mrs. Richardson is still here; and what is more, has a baby— so Richardson says, and he ought to know. I believe Mary Hewett has left here and gone to Boston. I met her on the street about fifteen or twenty days ago, and she told me she was going soon. I have seen nothing of her since.

The music in the Capitol grounds on Saturdays, or, rather, the interest in it, is dwindling down to nothing. Yesterday evening the attendance was rather thin. Our two girls, whom you remember seeing first at Carusis,* at the exhibition of the Ethiopian Serenaders, and whose peculiarities were the wearing of black fur bonnets, and never being seen in close company with other ladies, were at the music yesterday. One of them was attended by their brother, and the other had a member of Congress in tow. He went home with her; and if I were to guess, I would say, he went away a somewhat altered man—most likely in his pockets, and in some other particular. The fellow looked conscious of guilt, although I believe

* Carusi's Saloon, a theater.

120

he was unconscious that everybody around knew who it was that had caught him.

I have had no letter from home, since I wrote you before, except short business letters, which have no interest for you.

By the way, you do not intend to do without a girl, because the one you had has left you? Get another as soon as you can to take charge of the dear codgers. Father expected to see you all sooner; but let it pass; stay as long as you please, and come when you please. Kiss and love the dear rascals. Affectionately

A. Lincoln

From Springfield came Herndon's report that the young men among the Whigs resented "the stubbornness and bad judgment of the old fossils in the party." Lincoln, not yet forty, replied temperately.

Washington, July 10, 1848

Dear William:

Your letter covering the newspaper slips, was received last night. The subject of that letter is exceedingly painful to me; and I cannot but think there is some mistake in your impression of the motives of the old men. I suppose I am now one of the old men—and I declare on my veracity, which I think is good with you, that nothing could afford me more satisfaction than to learn that you and others of my young friends at home, were doing battle in the contest, and endearing themselves to the people, and taking a stand far above any I have ever been able to reach, in their admiration. I cannot conceive that other old men feel differently. Of course I cannot demonstrate what I say; but I was young once, and I am sure I was never ungenerously thrust back. I hardly know what to say. The way for a young man to rise, is to improve himself every way he can, never suspecting that anybody wishes to hinder him. Allow me to assure you, that suspicion and jealousy never did help any man in any situation. There may sometimes be ungenerous attempts to keep a young man down; and they will succeed too, if he allows his mind to be diverted from its true channel to brood over the attempted injury. Cast about, and see if this feeling has not injured every person you have ever known to fall into it.

Now, in what I have said, I am sure you will suspect nothing but sincere friendship. I would save you from a fatal error. You have been a laborious, studious young man. You are far better informed on almost all subjects than I have ever been. You cannot fail in any laudable object, unless you allow your mind to be improperly directed. I have some the advantage of you in the world's experience, merely by being older; and it is this that induces me to advise.

You still seem to be a little mistaken about the Congressional Globe and Appendix. They contain *all* of the speeches that are published in any way. My speech, and Dayton's speech, which you say you got in pamphlet form, are both, word for word, in the Appendix. I repeat again all are there. Your friend, as ever

A. Lincoln

Now thoroughly at ease as a freshman in Congress, a relaxed Lincoln, taking the floor, rallied to the support of Taylor. The sting of Lincoln's easy-flowing humor punctured the military reputation of Lewis Cass, the Democratic candidate. Lincoln also was an old soldier.

July 27, 1848

Mr. Speaker

Our Democratic friends seem to be in great distress because they think our candidate for the Presidency don't suit *us*. Most of them cannot find out that Gen: Taylor has any principles at all; some, however, have discovered that he has *one*, but that that one is entirely wrong. . . .

The gentleman from Georgia *. . . says we have deserted all our principles, and taken shelter under Gen: Taylor's military coat-tail; and he seems to think this is exceedingly degrading. Well, as his faith is, so be it unto him. But can he remember no other military coat-tail under which a certain other party have been sheltering for near a quarter of a century? Has he no acquaintance with the ample military coat-tail of Gen: Jackson? Does he not know that his own party have run the five last presidential races under that coat-tail? and that they are now running the sixth, under the same cover? Yes sir, that coat-tail was used, not only for Gen: Jackson himself; but has been clung to, with the grip of death, by every Democratic candidate since. You have never ventured, and dare not now venture, from under it. Your campaign papers have constantly been "Old Hickories" with rude likenesses of the old gen-

* Representative Alfred Iverson.

Congressman Lincoln

eral upon them; hickory poles, and hickory brooms, your never-ending emblems; Mr. Polk himself was "Young Hickory" "Little Hickory" or something so; and even now, your campaign paper here, is proclaiming that Cass and Butler are of the true "Hickory stripe." No sir, you dare not give it up.

Like a horde of hungry ticks you have stuck to the tail of the Hermitage lion to the end of his life; and you are still sticking to it, and drawing a loathsome sustenance from it, after he is dead. A fellow once advertised that he had made a discovery by which he could make a new man out of an old one, and have enough of the stuff left to make a little yellow dog. Just such a discovery has Gen: Jackson's popularity been to you. You not only twice made President of him out of it, but you have had enough of the stuff left, to make Presidents of several comparatively small men since; and it is your chief reliance now to make still another.

Mr. Speaker, old horses, and military coat-tails, or tails of any sort, are not figures of speech, such as I would be the first to introduce into discussions here; but as the gentleman from Georgia has thought fit to introduce them, he, and you, are welcome to all you have made, or can make, by them. If you have any more old horses, trot them out; any more tails, just cock them, and come at us. . . .

But in my hurry I was very near closing on the subject of military tails before I was done with it. There is one entire article of the sort I have not discussed yet; I mean the military tail you Democrats are now engaged in dovetailing onto the great Michigander. Yes sir, all his biographers (and they are legion) have him in hand, tying him to a military tail, like so many mischievous boys tying a dog to a bladder of beans. True, the material they have is very limited; but they drive at it, might and main. He *in*vaded Canada without resistance, and he *out*vaded it without pursuit. As he did both under orders, I suppose there was, to him, neither credit or discredit in them; but they are made to constitute a large part of the tail. He was not at Hull's surrender, but he was close by; he was volunteer aid to Gen: Harrison on the day of the Battle of the Thames; and, as you said in 1840, Harrison was picking whortleberries two miles off while the battle was fought, I suppose it is a just conclusion with you, to say Cass was aiding Harrison to pick whortleberries. This is about all, except the mooted question of the broken sword. Some authors say he broke it, some say he threw it away, and some others, who ought to know, say nothing about it. Perhaps it would be a fair historical compromise to say, if he did not break it, he didn't do anything else with it.

By the way, Mr. Speaker, did you know I am a military hero? Yes sir; in the days of the Black Hawk War, I fought, bled, and came away. Speaking of Gen: Cass' career, reminds me of my own. I was not at Stillman's defeat, but I was about as near it, as Cass was to Hull's surrender; and, like him, I saw the place very soon afterwards. It is quite certain I did not break my sword, for I had none to break; but I bent a musket pretty badly on one occasion. If Cass broke his sword, the idea is, he broke it in desperation; I bent the musket by accident. If Gen: Cass went in advance of me in picking whortleberries, I guess I surpassed him in charges upon the wild onions. If he saw any live, fighting Indians, it was more than I did; but I had a good many bloody struggles with the mosquitoes; and, although I never fainted from loss of blood, I can truly say I was often very hungry. Mr. Speaker, if I should ever conclude to doff whatever our Democratic friends may suppose there is of black cockade Federalism about me, and thereupon, they shall take me up as their candidate for the Presidency, I protest they shall not make fun of me, as they have of Gen: Cass, by attempting to write me into a military hero.

August brought discouraging news from Illinois; Logan, running for Congress, lost to a Democrat. To dissuade antislavery Whigs from supporting the Free Soilers, who had nominated Martin Van Buren as a third party candidate, Lincoln stumped Massachusetts. First, however, he asked advice from a shrewd politician, a newly elected Congressman from the key state of Pennsylvania.

Washington,
Sept. 3. 1848

Hon: Thaddeus Stevens
Dear Sir:

You may possibly remember seeing me at the Philadelphia convention—introduced to you as the lone Whig star of Illinois. Since the adjournment, I have remained here, so long, in the Whig document room. I am now about to start for home; and I desire the undisguised opinion of some experienced and sagacious Pennsylvania politician, as to how the vote of that state, for Governor, and President, is likely to go. In casting about for such a man, I have settled upon you; and I shall be much obliged if you will write me at Springfield, Illinois.

The news we are receiving here now, by letters from all quarters is steadily on the rise; we have none lately of a discouraging character. This is the sum, without giving particulars. Yours truly
                                                                    A. Lincoln

En route from Boston to Springfield, Lincoln visited Niagara Falls. This fragment, detailing his impressions, ends with an unfinished sentence. Later, Herndon heard the one memory that Lincoln retained: "Where in the world did all that water come from?"

[*c. September 25–30, 1848*]

Niagara Falls! By what mysterious power is it that millions and millions, are drawn from all parts of the world, to gaze upon Niagara Falls? There is no mystery about the thing itself. Every effect is just such as any intelligent man knowing the causes, would anticipate, without seeing it. If the water moving onward in a great river, reaches a point where there is a perpendicular jog, of a hundred feet in descent, in the bottom of the river,—it is plain the water will have a violent and continuous plunge at that point. It is also plain the water, thus plunging, will foam, and roar, and send up a mist, continuously, in which last, during sunshine, there will be perpetual rainbows. The mere physical of Niagara Falls is only this. Yet this is really a very small part of that world's wonder. Its power to excite reflection, and emotion, is its great charm. The geologist will demonstrate that the plunge, or fall, was once at Lake Ontario, and has worn its way back to its present position; he will ascertain how *fast* it is wearing now, and so get a basis for determining how *long* it has been wearing back from Lake Ontario, and finally demonstrate by it that this world is at least fourteen thousand years old. A philosopher of a slightly different turn will say Niagara Falls is only the lip of the basin out of which pours all the surplus water which rains down on two or three hundred thousand square miles of the earth's surface. He will estimate with approximate accuracy, that five hundred thousand tons of water, falls with its full weight, a distance of a hundred feet each minute—thus exerting a force equal to the lifting of the same weight, through the same space, in the same time. And then the further reflection comes that this vast amount of water, constantly pouring *down,* is supplied by an equal amount constantly *lifted up,* by the sun; and still he says, "If this much is lifted up, for *this one* space of two or three hundred thousand square miles, an equal amount must be lifted for every other equal space"; and he is overwhelmed in the contemplation of the vast power the sun is constantly exerting in quiet, noiseless operation of lifting water *up* to be rained *down* again.

But still there is more. It calls up the indefinite past. When Columbus first sought this continent—when Christ suffered on the cross—when Moses led Israel through the Red Sea—nay, even, when Adam first came from the hand of his Maker—then as now, Niagara was roaring here. The eyes of that species of extinct giants, whose bones fill the mounds of America, have gazed on Niagara, as ours do now. Contemporary with the whole race of men, and older than the first man, Niagara is strong, and fresh today as ten thousand years ago. The Mammoth and Mastodon—now so long dead, that fragments of their monstrous bones, alone testify, that they ever lived, have gazed on Niagara. In that long—long time, never still for a single moment. Never dried, never froze, never slept, never rested,

Relatives repeatedly dunned Lincoln for funds. To Thomas Lincoln, his father, he sent a note of skeptical irritation—and the money requested. With John D. Johnston, his shiftless stepbrother, Lincoln dealt in more hard-headed terms.

Washington, Decr. 24th. 1848—

My dear father:

Your letter of the 7th. was received night before last. I very cheerfully send you the twenty dollars, which sum you say is necessary to save your land from sale. It is singular that you should have forgotten a judgment against you; and it is more singular that the plaintiff should have let you forget it so long, particularly as I suppose you have always had property enough to satisfy a judgment of that amount. Before you pay it, it would be well to be sure you have not paid it; or, at least, that you cannot prove you have paid it. Give my love to Mother, and all the connections. Affectionately your Son

A. Lincoln

Congressman Lincoln

Dear Johnston:

Your request for eighty dollars, I do not think it best, to comply with now. At the various times when I have helped you a little, you have said to me "We can get along very well now" but in a very short time I find you in the same difficulty again. Now this can only happen by some defect in your *conduct*. What that defect is, I think I know. You are not *lazy,* and still you *are* an *idler.* I doubt whether since I saw you, you have done a good whole day's work, in any one day. You do not very much dislike to work; and still you do not work much, merely because it does not seem to you that you could get much for it. This habit of uselessly wasting time, is the whole difficulty; and it is vastly important to you, and still more so to your children that you should break this habit. It is more important to them, because they have longer to live, and can keep out of an idle habit before they are in it; easier than they can get out after they are in.

You are now in need of some ready money; and what I propose is, that you shall go to work, "tooth and nails" for somebody who will give you money for it. Let father and your boys take charge of things at home – prepare for a crop, and make the crop; and you go to work for the best money wages, or in discharge of any debt you owe, that you can get. And to secure you a fair reward for your labor, I now promise you, that for every dollar you will, between this and the first of next May, get for your own labor, either in money, or in your own indebtedness, I will then give you one other dollar. By this, if you hire yourself at ten dollars a month, from me you will get ten more, making twenty dollars a month for your work. In this, I do not mean you shall go off to St. Louis, or the lead mines, or the gold mines, in California, but I mean for you to go at it for the best wages you can get close to home in Coles County. Now if you will do this, you will soon be out of debt, and what is better, you will have a habit that will keep you from getting in debt again. But if I should now clear you out, next year you will be just as deep in as ever. You say you would almost give your place in Heaven for $70 or $80. Then you value your place in Heaven very cheaply for I am sure you can with the offer I make you get the seventy or eighty dollars for four or five months work. You say if I furnish you the money you will deed me the land, and, if you don't pay the money back, you will deliver possession. Nonsense! If you can't now live *with* the land, how will

127

you then live without it? You have always been kind to me, and I do not now mean to be unkind to you. On the contrary, if you will but follow my advice, you will find it worth more than eight times eighty dollars to you. Affectionately Your brother

A. Lincoln

Lincoln evaluates himself to a seeker of autographs.

Washington,
Jan: 5. 1849

Mr. C. U. Schlater:
Dear Sir:

Your note, requesting my "signature with a sentiment" was received, and should have been answered long since, but that it was mislaid. I am not a very sentimental man; and the best sentiment I can think of is, that if you collect the signatures of all persons who are no less distinguished than I, you will have a very undistinguishing mass of names. Very respectfully

A. Lincoln

Washington was far from an elegant city in 1849. Pigsties and privies cluttered backyards, but even more offensive to many Northern visitors was what Lincoln described as a "sort of Negro livery stable" that served as a center of the domestic slave trade. Soon after the opening of the second session of the Thirtieth Congress, Lincoln offered the following remarks and resolution on a bill prohibiting slavery in the District of Columbia. (Three days later he promised to offer a bill of his own, but never did. In 1861 Lincoln explained his position: "Finding that I was abandoned by my former backers and having little personal influence, I *dropped* the matter knowing that it was useless to prosecute the business at that time.")

January 10, 1849

MR. LINCOLN appealed to his colleague * to withdraw his motion, to enable him to read a proposition which he intended to submit, if the vote should be reconsidered.

MR. WENTWORTH again withdrew his motion for that purpose.

MR. LINCOLN said, that by the courtesy of his colleague, he would say, that if the vote on the resolution was reconsidered,

* John Wentworth, of Illinois.

128

he should make an effort to introduce an amendment, which he should now read.

And Mr. L. read as follows:

Strike out all before and after the word "Resolved" and insert the following, to wit: That the Committee on the District of Columbia be instructed to report a bill in substance as follows, to wit:

Section 1. Be it enacted by the Senate and House of Representatives of the United States of America, in Congress assembled: That no person not now within the District of Columbia, nor now owned by any person or persons now resident within it, nor hereafter born within it, shall ever be held in slavery within said District.

Section 2. That no person now within said District, or now owned by any person, or persons now resident within the same, or hereafter born within it, shall ever be held in slavery without the limits of said District: *Provided,* that officers of the government of the United States, being citizens of the slave-holding states, coming into said District on public business, and remaining only so long as may be reasonably necessary for that object, may be attended into, and out of, said District, and while there, by the necessary servants of themselves and their families, without their right to hold such servants in service, being thereby impaired.

Section 3. That all children born of slave mothers within said District on, or after the first day of January in the year of our Lord one thousand, eight hundred and fifty shall be free; but shall be reasonably supported and educated, by the respective owners of their mothers or by their heirs or representatives, and shall owe reasonable service, as apprentices, to such owners, heirs and representatives until they respectively arrive at the age of —— years when they shall be entirely free; and the municipal authorities of Washington and Georgetown, within their respective jurisdictional limits, are hereby empowered and required to make all suitable and necessary provisions for enforcing obedience to this section, on the part of both masters and apprentices.

Section 4. That all persons now within said District lawfully held as slaves, or now owned by any person or persons now resident within said District, shall remain such, at the will of their respective owners, their heirs and legal representatives: *Provided* that any such owner, or his legal representative, may at any time receive from the treasury of the United States the full value of his or her slave, of the class in this section mentioned, upon which such slave shall be forthwith and forever free: and *provided further* that the President of the United States, the Secretary of State, and the Secretary of the Treasury shall be a board for determining the value of such slaves as their owners may desire to emancipate under this section; and whose duty it shall be to hold a session for the purpose, on the first Monday of each calendar month; to receive all applications; and, on satisfactory evidence in each case, that the person presented for valuation, is a slave, and of the class in this section mentioned, and is owned by the applicant, shall value such slave at his or her full cash value, and give to the applicant an order on the treasury for the amount; and also to such slave a certificate of freedom.

Section 5. That the municipal authorities of Washington and Georgetown, within their respective jurisdictional limits, are hereby empowered and required to provide active and efficient means to arrest, and deliver up to their owners, all fugitive slaves escaping into said District.

Section 6. That the election officers within said District of Columbia, are hereby empowered and required to open polls at all the usual places of holding elections, on the first Monday of April next, and receive the vote of every free white male citizen above the age of twenty-one years, having resided within said District for the period of one year or more next preceding the time of such voting, for, or against this act; to proceed, in taking said votes, in all respects not herein specified, as at elections under the municipal laws; and, with as little delay as possible to transmit correct statements of the votes so cast to the President of the United States. And it shall be the duty of the President to canvass said votes immediately, and, if a majority of them be found to be for this act, to forthwith issue his proclamation giving notice of the fact; and this act shall only be in full force and effect on, and after the day of such proclamation.

Section 7. That involuntary servitude for the punishment of crime, whereof the party shall have been duly convicted shall in no wise be prohibited by this act.

Section 8. That for all the purposes of this act the jurisdictional limits of Washington are extended to all parts of the District of Columbia not now included within the present limits of Georgetown.

Congressman Lincoln

Mr. LINCOLN then said, that he was authorized to say, that of about fifteen of the leading citizens of the District of Columbia to whom this proposition had been submitted, there was not one but who approved of the adoption of such a proposition. He did not wish to be misunderstood. He did not know whether or not they would vote for this bill on the first Monday of April; but he repeated, that out of fifteen persons to whom it had been submitted, he had authority to say that every one of them desired that some proposition like this should pass.

Lincoln's term in Congress soon would end. Washington had been exciting; Springfield seemed remote, quiet, dull. A letter to Speed reflected Lincoln's uneasiness.

Washington, Feb: 20. 1849.

Dear Speed:

Your letter of the 13th. was received yesterday. I showed it to Baker. I did this because he knew I had written you, and was expecting an answer; and he still enquired what I had received; so that I could not well keep it a secret. Besides this, I knew the contents of the letter would not affect him as you seemed to think it would. He knows he did not make a favorable impression while in Congress, and he and I had talked it over frequently. He tells me to write you that he has too much self-esteem to be put out of humor with himself by the opinion of any man who does not know him better than Mr. Crittenden does; and that he thinks you ought to have known it. The letter will not affect him the least in regard to either Mr. Crittenden or you. He understands you to have acted the part of a discreet friend; and he intends to make Mr. Crittenden think better of him, hereafter. I am flattered to learn that Mr. Crittenden has any recollection of me which is not unfavorable; and for the manifestation of your kindness towards me, I sincerely thank you. Still there is nothing about me which would authorize me to think of a first-class office; and a second-class one would not compensate me for being snarled at by others who want it for themselves. I believe that, so far as the Whigs in Congress, are concerned, I could have the Genl. Land office almost by common consent; but then Sweet, and Don: Morrison, and Browning, and Cyrus Edwards all want it. And what is worse, while I think I could easily take it myself, I fear I shall have trouble to get it for

131

any other man in Illinois. The reason is, that McGaughey, an Indiana ex-member of Congress is here after it; and being personally known, he will be hard to beat by anyone who is not.

Baker showed me your letter, in which you make a passing allusion to the Louisville post office. I have told Garnett Duncan I am for you. I like to open a letter of yours, and I therefore hope you will write me again on the receipt of this.

Give my love, to Mrs. Speed. Yours as ever

A. Lincoln

P.S. I have not read the Frankfort papers this winter; and consequently do not know whether you have made a speech. If you have, and it has been printed send me a copy.   *A. L.*

The session of Congress ended. Lincoln remained in Washington for three weeks. He argued—and lost—his one case before the United States Supreme Court. Also he obtained a patent for a device to help vessels over shoals. Herndon said that Lincoln's one effort as an inventor grew out of his trip to Niagara Falls when the vessel on which he sailed stranded on a sand bar. Herndon thought it likely that Lincoln's mind also carried him back to the spring of 1831 when he and John Hanks had maneuvered Offut's flatboat over the dam at New Salem.

March 10, 1849

TO THE COMMISSIONER OF PATENTS

The Petition of Abraham Lincoln, of Springfield in the County of Sangamon & State of Illinois

Respectfully represents.

That your petitioner has invented a new and improved manner of combining adjustable buoyant chambers with steamboats or other vessels which has not, as he verily believes been heretofore used or known, and that he is desirous that Letters Patent of the United States may be granted to him therefor, securing to him and to his legal representatives, the exclusive right of making and using, and of vending to others the privilege to make or use, the same, agreeably to the provisions of the Acts of Congress in that case made and provided, he having paid thirty dollars into the

Treasury of the United States, and complied with other provisions of the said Acts.

And he hereby authorizes and empowers his Agent and Attorney, Z. C. ROBBINS, to alter or modify the within specification and claim as he may deem expedient, and to receive his patent; and also to receive back any moneys which he may be entitled to withdraw, and to receipt for the same.

A. Lincoln.

V. The Reflective Years

1849-1853 M ELANCHOLY dripped from him as he walked," Herndon said of the Lincoln who now settled back into his old life in Springfield. The years in Washington had left a mark, and those who knew Lincoln intimately came in time to sense the change. There were periods when he seemed almost a man who had withdrawn to some private Olympian height to watch, to wait, to listen, and to reflect. He returned to practicing law and to riding the circuit with a steadfastness of purpose that brought increased financial rewards.

Apparently Lincoln accepted the fact that his public service had ended and henceforth he would be plain A. Lincoln, Private Citizen. In this decision he seemed content, but whether at heart he felt he had somehow failed can only be conjectured.

A new Lincoln would emerge. Clarity of thought and cultivation of an ability to express his ideas in utterly simple terms would become his two ruling passions. At home and on the circuit his long nose was forever thrust between the pages of a newspaper as he brought to the problems of the day the two viewpoints he now possessed—that of Springfield and that of Washington.

So Lincoln continued to grow. The times were made for precisely the type of honest mental effort and objectivity that he had selected to develop. History is often this quiet phenomenon—a force that grows within the privacy of one man's thoughtful mind.

The break with Washington was not altogether graceful. The Commissionership of the General Land Office had been promised to an Illinois Whig, and the two candidates in the field were Cyrus Edwards of Edwardsville and J. L. D. Morrison of St. Clair County. When neither candidate would withdraw to leave the office open to the other, Lincoln was urged to break the deadlock by announcing himself as a candidate. In a letter to William B. Warren and other prominent Illinois Whigs, Lincoln explained why he felt uncomfortable at this suggestion.

Springfield, Ills. April 7. 1849

Gentlemen:

In answer to your note concerning the General Land Office I have to say that, if the office can be secured to Illinois by my consent to accept it, and not otherwise, I give that consent. Some months since I gave my word to secure the appointment to that office of Mr. Cyrus Edwards, if in my power, in case of a vacancy; and more recently I stipulated with Col. Baker that if Mr. Edwards and Col. J. L. D. Morrison could arrange with each other for one of them to withdraw, we would jointly recommend the other. In relation to these pledges, I must not only be chaste but above suspicion. If the office shall be tendered to me, I must be permitted to say "Give it to Mr. Edwards, or, if so agreed by them, to Col. Morrison, and I decline it; if not, I accept." With this understanding, you are at liberty to procure me the offer of the appointment if you can; and I shall feel complimented by your effort, and still more by its success. It should not be overlooked that Col. Baker's position entitles him to a large share of control in this matter; however, one of your number, Col. Warren, knows that Baker has at all times been ready to recommend me, if I would consent. It must also be understood that if at any time, previous to an appointment being made, I shall learn that Mr. Edwards & Col. Morrison have agreed, I shall at once carry out my stipulation with Col. Baker, as above stated. Yours truly

Col. W. B. Warren, & others.   *A. Lincoln*

A new complication arose when Thomas Ewing, Secretary of the Interior, favored the candidacy of a "dark horse" from Chicago. William B. Preston, Secretary of the Navy, heard from a thoroughly nettled Lincoln.

Springfield, Ills.
May 16. 1849

Hon: W. B. Preston:
Dear Sir:

It is a delicate matter to oppose the wishes of a friend; and consequently I address you on the subject I now do, with no little hesitation. Last night I received letters from different persons at

The Living Lincoln

Washington assuring me it was not improbable that Justin Butterfield, of Chicago, Ills, would be appointed Commissioner of the Genl. Land Office. It was to avert this very thing, that I called on you at your rooms one Sunday evening shortly after you were installed, and besought you that, so far as in your power, no man from Illinois should be appointed to any high office, without my being at least heard on the question. You were kind enough to say you thought my request a reasonable one. Mr. Butterfield is my friend, is well qualified, and, I suppose, would be faithful in the office. So far, good. But now for the objections. In 1840 we fought a fierce and laborious battle in Illinois, many of us spending almost the entire year in the contest. The general victory came, and with it, the appointment of a set of drones, including this same Butterfield, who had never spent a dollar or lifted a finger in the fight. The place he got was that of district attorney. The defection of Tyler came, and then B. played off and on, and kept the office till after Polk's election. Again, winter and spring before the last, when you and I were almost sweating blood to have Genl. Taylor nominated, this same man was ridiculing the idea, and going for Mr. Clay; and when Gen: T. was nominated, if he went out of the city of Chicago to aid in his election, it is more than I ever heard, or believe. Yet, when the election is secured, by other men's labor, and even against his effort, why, he is the first man on hand for the best office that our state lays any claim to. Shall this thing be? Our Whigs will throw down their arms, and fight no more, if the fruit of their labor is thus disposed of. If there is one man in this state who desires B's appointment to anything, I declare I have not heard of him. What influence operates for him, I cannot conceive. Your position makes it a matter of peculiar interest to you, that the administration shall be successful; and be assured, nothing can more endanger it, than making appointments through old-hawker foreign influences, which offend, rather than gratify, the people immediately interested in the offices.

Can you not find time to write me, even half as long a letter as this? I shall be much gratified if you will. Your Obt. Servt.

A. Lincoln

Ewing's support of Butterfield placed Lincoln in a ticklish position. Somehow he must bypass the Secretary of the Interior and win the support of General Taylor. Richard W. Thompson, Whig Congressman from Terre Haute, Indiana, learned of the problem.

CONFIDENTIAL

Springfield, Ills.
May 25. 1849—

Hon: R. W. Thompson:
Dear Sir.

I am about to ask a favor of you—one which, I hope, will not cost you much. I understand the General Land Office is about to be given to Illinois; and that Mr. Ewing desires Justin Butterfield of Chicago to be the man. I will not trouble you with particulars, but will assure you, that the appointment of Mr. Butterfield will be an egregious political blunder. I believe it will gratify no single Whig in the state, except it be Mr. B. himself. Now, the favor I wish of you is, that you will write Gen: Taylor at once, saying that in your opinion, either *I, or the man I recommend*, should be appointed to that office, if anyone from Illinois, shall be. I restrict my request to Illinois, because I think it probable you have already recommended someone, probably from your own state; and I do not wish to interfere with that. Yours truly

A. Lincoln

The pressure that Lincoln exerted on his Whig friends in Washington led Taylor to delay the appointment for three weeks. In a letter to Nathaniel Pope, United States Judge for the District of Illinois, Lincoln decided to put aside his scruples and fight vigorously for the office.

Springfield,
June 8. 1849

Hon: N. Pope:
Dear Sir:

I do not *know* that it would, but I can well enough conceive it *might*, embarrass you to *now* give a letter recommending me for the General Land Office. Could you not, however, without embarrassment, or any impropriety, so far vindicate the truth of history, as to briefly state to me, in a letter, what you *did* say to me last spring on my arrival here from Washington, in relation to my becoming an applicant for that office? Having at last concluded to be an applicant, I have thought it is perhaps due me, to be enabled to show the influences which brought me to the conclusion—among which influences the wishes and opinions you expressed were not the least. Your Obt. Servt.

A. Lincoln

As a further step, Lincoln endeavored, by this memorandum, to give the President of the United States a sound lesson in regional politics.

June, 1849

Nothing in my papers questions Mr. B.'s competency or honesty, and, I presume, nothing in his questions mine. Being equal so far, if it does not appear I am preferred by the Whigs of Illinois, I lay no claim to the office.

But if it does appear I am preferred, it will be argued that the whole Northwest, and not Illinois alone, should be heard. I answer I am as strongly recommended by Ohio and Indiana, as well as Illinois; and further, that when the many appointments were made for Ohio, as for the Northwest, Illinois was not consulted. When an Indianian was nominated for Governor of Minnesota, and another appointed for Commissioner of Mexican claims, as for the Northwest, Illinois was not consulted. When a citizen of Iowa was appointed Second Assistant Postmaster General and another to a land office in Minnesota, Illinois was not consulted. Of none of these have I ever complained. In each of them, the state whose citizen was appointed was allowed to control, and I think rightly. I only ask that Illinois be not cut off with less deference.

It will be argued that all the Illinois appointments, so far, have been south, and that therefore this should go north. I answer, that of the local appointments every part has had its share, and Chicago far the best share of any. Of the transitory, the marshal and attorney are all; and neither of these is within a hundred miles of me, the former being south and the latter north of west. I am in the center. Is the center nothing?—that center which alone has ever given you a Whig representative? On the score of locality, I admit the claim of the north is no worse, and I deny that it is any better than that of the center.

The Reflective Years

Ewing prevailed and the appointment went to Butterfield. The defeat threatened Lincoln with a loss that he had neither anticipated nor desired. To an old friend in Edwardsville, Joseph Gillespie, Lincoln tried to explain his disappointment and embarrassment.

Springfield, July 13. 1849.

Dear Gillespie:

Mr. Edwards is unquestionably offended with me, in connection with the matter of the General Land Office. He wrote a letter against me, which was filed at the Department. The better part of one's life consists of his friendships; and, of these, mine with Mr. Edwards was one of the most cherished. I have not been false to it. At a word, I could have had the office any time before the Department was committed to Mr. Butterfield—at least Mr. Ewing & the President say as much. That word I forebore to speak, partly for other reasons, but chiefly for Mr. Edwards' sake. Losing the office that he might gain it, I was always for; but to lose his *friendship* by the effort for him, would oppress me very much, were I not sustained by the utmost consciousness of rectitude. I first determined to be an applicant, unconditionally, on the 2nd. of June; and I did so then upon being informed by a telegraphic despatch, that the question was narrowed down to Mr. B. and myself, and that the Cabinet had postponed the appointment three weeks for my benefit. Not doubting, that Mr. Edwards was wholly out of the question, I nevertheless would not then have become an applicant, had I supposed he would thereby be brought to suspect me of treachery to him. Two or three days afterwards a conversation with Levi Davis convinced me Mr. E. was dissatisfied; but I was then too far in to get out. His own letter, written on the 25th. of April, after I had fully informed him of all that had passed up to within a few days of that time, gave assurance I had that entire confidence from him, which I felt my uniform and strong friendship for him entitled me to. Among other things it says "whatever course your judgment may dictate as proper to be pursued, shall never be excepted to by me." I also had had a letter from Washington, saying Chambers of the Republican had brought a rumor then that, Mr. E. had declined in my favor, which rumor I judged came from Mr. E. himself, as I had not then breathed of his letter, to any living creature.

In saying I had never before the 2nd. of June determined to

139

be an applicant, *unconditionally,* I mean to admit that before then, I had said substantially I would take the office rather than it should be lost to the state, or given to one in the state whom the Whigs did not want; but I aver that in every instance in which I spoke of myself, I intended to keep, and now believe I did keep, Mr. E. ahead of myself. Mr. Edwards' first suspicion was that I had allowed Baker to overreach me, as his friend, in behalf of Don: Morrison. I knew this was a mistake; and the result has proved it. I understand his view now is, that if I had gone to open war with Baker I could have ridden him down, and had the thing all my own way. I believe no such thing. With Baker & some strong men from the Military Tract, & elsewhere for Morrison; and we and some strong men from the Wabash & elsewhere for Mr. E. it was not possible for either to succeed. I *believed* this in March, and I *know* it now. The only thing which gave either any chance was the very thing Baker & I proposed – an adjustment with themselves.

You may wish to know how Butterfield finally beat me. I cannot tell you particulars now, but will, when I see you. In the meantime let it be understood I am not greatly dissatisfied. I wish the office had been so bestowed as to encourage our friends in future contests, and I regret exceedingly Mr. Edwards' feelings towards me. These two things away, I should have no regrets – at least I think I would not.

Write me soon. Your friend, as ever

A. Lincoln –

Lincoln, now safe from any charge of self-interest, reprimanded the administration for its indifferent political leadership.

Springfield, Ill., July 28, 1849.

Hon. J. M. Clayton.
Dear Sir:

It is with some hesitation I presume to address this letter – and yet I wish not only you, but the whole Cabinet, and the President too, would consider the subject matter of it. My being among the people while you and they are not, will excuse the apparent presumption. It is understood that the President at first adopted, as a general rule, to throw the responsibility of the appointments upon the respective Departments; and that such rule is adhered to and practiced upon. This course I at first thought proper; and, of course, I am not now complaining of it. Still I am disappointed with the effect of it on the public mind. It is fixing for the President the unjust and ruinous character of being a mere man of straw. This must be arrested, or it will damn us all inevitably. It is said Gen. Taylor and his officers held a council of war, at Palo Alto (I believe); and that he then fought the battle against unanimous opinion of those officers. This fact (no matter whether rightfully or wrongfully) gives him more popularity than ten thousand submissions, however really wise and magnanimous those submissions may be.

The appointments need be no better than they have been, but the public must be brought to understand, that they are the *President's* appointments. He must occasionally say, or seem to say, "by the Eternal," "I take the responsibility." Those phrases were the "Samson's locks" of Gen. Jackson, and we dare not disregard the lessons of experience. Your Ob't Sev't

A. Lincoln

The administration now sought to placate its critic.

Springfield Sept. 27th. 1849.

Hon Thomas Ewing
I respectfully decline Governorship of Oregon; I am still anxious that Simeon Francis shall be secretary of that Territory.
A. Lincoln

A disgruntled office-seeker discovered how thin Lincoln's skin had been rubbed by political frictions.

Springfield,
Decr. 15– 1849

G. W. Rives, Esq.
Dear Sir:
On my return from Kentucky, I found your letter of the 7th. of November, and have delayed answering it till now, for the reason I now briefly state. From the beginning of our acquaintance I had felt the greatest kindness for you, and had supposed it was reciprocated on your part. Last summer, under circumstances which I mentioned to you, I was painfully constrained to withhold a recommendation which you desired; and shortly afterwards I learned,

141

in such way as to believe it, that you were indulging open abuse of me. Of course my feelings were wounded. On receiving your last letter, the question occurred whether you were attempting to *use* me, at the same time you would *injure* me, or whether you might not have been misrepresented to me. If the former, I ought not to answer you; if the latter I ought, and so I have remained in suspense. I now enclose you a letter which you may use if you think fit. Yours &c.

A. Lincoln

A Baptist preacher in Petersburg, Illinois, Abram (Lincoln misspelled the name) Bale, received legal advice revealing the unfailing integrity of the Springfield lawyer.

Springfield,
Feb: 22. 1850

Mr. Abraham Bale:
Dear Sir:
I understand Mr. Hickox will go, or send to Petersburg tomorrow, for the purpose of meeting you to settle the difficulty about the wheat. I sincerely hope you will settle it. I think you *can* if you *will*, for I have always found Mr. Hickox a fair man in his dealings. If you settle, I will charge nothing for what I have done, and thank you to boot. By settling, you will most likely get your money sooner; and with much less trouble & expense. Yours truly
A. Lincoln—

To John D. Johnston, Lincoln's step-brother, went word of a family tragedy.

Springfield, Feb. 23 1850

Dear Brother
Your letter about a mail contract was received yesterday. I have made out a bid for you at $120, guaranteed it myself, got our PM here to certify it, and send it on. Your former letter, concerning some man's claim for a pension was also received. I had the claim examined by those who are practiced in such matters, & they decide he can not get a pension.
As you make no mention of it, I suppose you had not learned that we lost our little boy. He was sick fifty-two days & died the

morning of the first day of this month. It was not our *first,* but our second child. We miss him very much. Your Brother in haste
A. Lincoln

Lincoln, lawyer and family man, had found a pattern of life in which he saw no place for politics.

Springfield,
June 5, 1850.

Editors of the Illinois Journal:
Gentlemen—
  An article in the Tazewell Mirror in which my name is prominently used, makes me fear that my position, with reference to the next congressional election in this district, is misunderstood, and that such misunderstanding may work injury to the cause of our friends. I therefore take occasion to say that I neither seek, expect, or desire a nomination for a seat in the next Congress; that I prefer my name should not be brought forward in that connection; and that I would now peremptorily forbid the use of it, could I feel entirely at liberty to do so. I will add, that in my opinion, the Whigs of the district have several other men, any one of whom they *can* elect, and that too quite as *easily* as they could elect me. I therefore shall be obliged, if any such as may entertain a preference for me, will, at once turn their attention to making a choice from others. Let a convention be held at a suitable time, and in good feeling, make a nomination; and I venture the prediction we will show the district once more *right side up.* Your obd't servant,
A. Lincoln.

The man in the long, ill-fitting coat evaluated himself and the profession which now absorbed his interest. His sense of honor was his brightest armor, his dogged honesty his sharpest weapon. Prospective lawyers, then or now, could not ask for more cogent advice than Lincoln offered in these notes.

[July 1, 1850?]
  I am not an accomplished lawyer. I find quite as much material for a lecture in those points wherein I have failed, as in those wherein I have been moderately successful. The leading rule for the lawyer, as for the man of every other calling, is diligence.

Leave nothing for tomorrow which can be done today. Never let your correspondence fall behind. Whatever piece of business you have in hand, before stopping, do all the labor pertaining to it which can then be done. When you bring a common law suit, if you have the facts for doing so, write the declaration at once. If a law point be involved, examine the books, and note the authority you rely on upon the declaration itself, where you are sure to find it when wanted. The same of defenses and pleas. In business not likely to be litigated,—ordinary collection cases, foreclosures, partitions, and the like,—make all examinations of titles, and note them, and even draft orders and decrees in advance. This course has a triple advantage; it avoids omissions and neglect, saves your labor when once done, performs the labor out of court when you have leisure, rather than in court when you have not. Extemporaneous speaking should be practiced and cultivated. It is the lawyer's avenue to the public. However able and faithful he may be in other respects, people are slow to bring him business if he cannot make a speech. And yet there is not a more fatal error to young lawyers than relying too much on speech-making. If anyone, upon his rare powers of speaking, shall claim an exemption from the drudgery of the law, his case is a failure in advance.

Discourage litigation. Persuade your neighbors to compromise whenever you can. Point out to them how the nominal winner is often a real loser—in fees, expenses, and waste of time. As a peacemaker the lawyer has a superior opportunity of being a good man. There will still be business enough.

Never stir up litigation. A worse man can scarcely be found than one who does this. Who can be more nearly a fiend than he who habitually overhauls the register of deeds in search of defects in titles, whereon to stir up strife, and put money in his pocket? A moral tone ought to be infused into the profession which should drive such men out of it.

The matter of fees is important, far beyond the mere question of bread and butter involved. Properly attended to, fuller justice is done to both lawyer and client. An exorbitant fee should never be claimed. As a general rule never take your whole fee in advance, nor any more than a small retainer. When fully paid beforehand, you are more than a common mortal if you can feel the same interest in the case, as if something was still in prospect for you, as well as for your client. And when you lack interest in the case the job will very likely lack skill and diligence in the performance. Settle the amount of fee and take a note in advance. Then you will feel that you are working for something, and you are sure to do your work faithfully and well. Never sell a fee note—at least not before the consideration service is performed. It leads to negligence and dishonesty—negligence by losing interest in the case, and dishonesty in refusing to refund when you have allowed the consideration to fail.

There is a vague popular belief that lawyers are necessarily dishonest. I say vague, because when we consider to what extent confidence and honors are reposed in and conferred upon lawyers by the people, it appears improbable that their impression of dishonesty is very distinct and vivid. Yet the impression is common, almost universal. Let no young man choosing the law for a calling for a moment yield to the popular belief—resolve to be honest at all events; and if in your own judgment you cannot be an honest lawyer, resolve to be honest without being a lawyer. Choose some other occupation, rather than one in the choosing of which you do, in advance, consent to be a knave.

Thomas Lincoln was dying. Lincoln chose to stay at the bedside of a sick wife, and sent the consolations of religion to a parent with whom he had never been intimate.

Springfield, Jany. 12. 1851—

Dear Brother:

On the day before yesterday I received a letter from Harriett,* written at Greenup. She says she has just returned from your house; and that Father is very low, and will hardly recover. She also says you have written me two letters; and that although you do not expect me to come now, you wonder that I do not write. I received both your letters, and although I have not answered them, it is not because I have forgotten them, or been uninterested about them—but because it appeared to me I could write nothing which could do any good. You already know I desire that neither Father or Mother shall be in want of any comfort either in health or sickness while they live; and I feel sure you have not failed to use my name, if necessary, to procure a doctor, or anything else for Father in his present sickness. My business is such that I could hardly

* Harriett Hanks Chapman, a member of the Hanks-Lincoln clan.

leave home now, if it were not, as it is, that my own wife is sick-abed. (It is a case of baby-sickness, and I suppose is not danger-ous.) I sincerely hope Father may yet recover his health; but at all events tell him to remember to call upon, and confide in, our great, and good, and merciful Maker; who will not turn away from him in any extremity. He notes the fall of a sparrow, and numbers the hairs of our heads; and He will not forget the dying man, who puts his trust in Him. Say to him that if we could meet now, it is doubtful whether it would not be more painful than pleasant; but that if it be his lot to go now, he will soon have a joyous meeting with many loved ones gone before; and where the rest of us, through the help of God, hope ere long to join them.

Write me again when you receive this. Affectionately

A. Lincoln

Thomas Lincoln died in Coles County on January 15, 1851. The shiftless John D. Johnston was filled with schemes for running away from reality. Lincoln's love for the sweet, patient stepmother who had understood and encouraged him when Thomas Lincoln had not, was one of the precious possessions of his life. In three letters to his step-brother Lincoln revealed an almost tigerish devotion to his stepmother and her security.

Shelbyville, Novr. 4. 1851

Dear Brother:

When I came into Charleston day-before-yesterday I learned that you are anxious to sell the land where you live, and move to Missouri. I have been thinking of this ever since; and cannot but think such a notion is utterly foolish. What can you do in Missouri, better than here? Is the land any richer? Can you there, any more than here, raise corn, & wheat & oats, without work? Will anybody there, any more than here, do your work for you? If you intend to go to work, there is no better place than right where you are; if you do not intend to go to work, you cannot get along anywhere. Squirming & crawling about from place to place can do no good. You have raised no crop this year, and what you really want is to sell the land, get the money and spend it—part with the land you have, and my life upon it, you will never after, own a spot big enough to bury you in. Half you will get for the land, you spend in moving to Missouri, and the other half you will eat and drink, and wear out, & no foot of land will be bought. Now I feel it is my duty to have no hand in such a piece of foolery. I feel that it is so even on your own account; and particularly on *Mother's* account. The eastern forty acres I intend to keep for Mother while she lives—if you *will not cultivate it;* it will rent for enough to support her—at least it will rent for something. Her dower in the other two forties, she can let you have, and no thanks to me.

Now do not misunderstand this letter. I do not write it in any unkindness. I write it in order, if possible, to get you to *face* the truth—which truth is, you are destitute because you have *idled* away all your time. Your thousand pretences for not getting along better, are all nonsense—they deceive nobody but yourself. *Go to work* is the only cure for your case.

A word for Mother:

Chapman * tells me he wants you to go and live with him. If I were you I would try it awhile. If you get tired of it (as I think you will not) you can return to your own home. Chapman feels very kindly to you; and I have no doubt he will make your situation very pleasant. Sincerely your Son

> *A. Lincoln*

> *Shelbyville, Novr. 9. 1851*

Dear Brother:

When I wrote you before I had not received your letter. I still think as I did; but if the land can be sold so that I get three hundred dollars to put to interest for mother, I will not object if she does not. But before I will make a deed, the money must be had, or secured, beyond all doubt, at ten per cent.

As to Abram,† I do not want him *on my own account;* but I understand he wants to live with me so that he can go to school, and get a fair start in the world, which I very much wish him to have. When I reach home, if I can make it convenient to take him, I will take him, provided there is no mistake between us as to the object and terms of my taking him. In haste As ever

> *A. Lincoln*

> *Springfield, Novr. 25. 1851.*

Dear Brother

Your letter of the 22nd. is just received. Your proposal about selling the east forty acres of land is all that I want or could claim for *myself;* but I am not satisfied with it on *Mother's* account. I

---

* Augustus H. Chapman was the husband of Harriett Hanks Chapman.
† Johnston's thirteen-year-old son.

want her to have her living, and I feel that it is my duty, to some extent, to see that she is not wronged. She had a right of dower (that is, the use of one-third for life) in the other two forties; but, it seems, she has already let you take that, hook and line. She now has the use of the whole of the east forty, as long as she lives; and if it be sold, of course, she is entitled to the interest on *all* the money it brings, as long as she lives; but you propose to sell it for three hundred dollars, take one hundred away with you, and leave her two hundred, at 8 per cent, making her the *enormous* sum of 16 dollars a year. Now, if you are satisfied with treating her in that way, I am not. It is true, that you are to have that forty for two hundred dollars, *at* Mother's death; but you are not to have it *before*. I am confident that land can be made to produce for Mother, at least $30 a year, and I cannot, to oblige any living person, consent that she shall be put on an allowance of sixteen dollars a year. Yours &c

A. Lincoln

The presence in America of Louis Kossuth stimulated deep interest in Hungary's struggle for freedom. Lincoln helped to draft resolutions that for him expressed a political truth implicit in American history.

January 9, 1852

Whereas, in the opinion of this meeting, the arrival of Kossuth in our country, in connection with the recent events in Hungary, and with the appeal he is now making in behalf of his country, presents an occasion upon which we, the American people, cannot remain silent, without justifying an inference against our continued devotion to the principles of our free institutions, therefore,

Resolved, 1. That it is the right of any people, sufficiently numerous for national independence, to throw off, to revolutionize, their existing form of government, and to establish such other in its stead as they may choose.

2. That it is the duty of our government to neither foment, nor assist, such revolutions in other governments.

3. That, as we may not legally or warrantably interfere abroad, *to aid,* so no other government may interfere abroad, *to suppress* such revolutions; and that we should at once, announce to the world, our determination to insist upon this *mutuality* of nonintervention, as a sacred principle of the international law.

4. That the late interference of Russia in the Hungarian struggle was, in our opinion, such illegal and unwarrantable interference.

5. That to have resisted Russia in that case, or to resist any power in a like case, would be no violation of our own cherished principles of non-intervention, but, on the contrary, would be ever meritorious, in us, or any independent nation. . . .

The presidential election of 1852 found Lincoln resuming a mild interest in politics. He agreed to serve as a national committeeman for the Whigs, but shied away from the suggestion that he become their candidate for Governor. Knowing his audience and the kind of earthy humor it enjoyed, he reduced the campaign between Winfield Scott and Franklin Pierce to a joust over political windmills. This passage, from his one fully recorded speech, contained no hint of the man who, living in his own thoughts, would soon speak to the political conscience of the nation.

August 14, 26, 1852

Gentlemen:

Unlike our young friend who has just taken his seat, I do not appear before you on a flattering invitation, or on any invitation at all; but, on the contrary I am about to address you, by your permission, given me at my own special request. . . .

Judge Douglas runs a tilt at Gen. Scott as a military politician, commencing with the interrogatory "Why has the Whig party forgotten with an oblivion so complete all that it once said about military politicians?". . . We cannot help observing the fact that the Democrats . . . have themselves put a general on the track. Why is this? It must have been by *accident* or by *design;* and it could not have been by accident, because I understand the party has become very philosophical, and it would be very unphilosophical to do such a thing by *accident.* It was by design, then. Let us try to trace it. They made their nomination before we made ours; but they knew we *ought,* and therefore concluded we *would,* not nominate Gen. Scott, and they shaped their course accordingly. They said "confound these old generals, is there no way of beating them? In 1840 we thought it would be mere sport to beat Harrison. We charged that his friends kept him in a cage; that he was an abolitionist, so far as he had sense enough to be anything; and we called him a petticoat general, and an old granny; but the election showed we had not hit upon the true philosophy. Again when Taylor was put up, we did not venture to call him an old granny, but we insisted he was not a Whig; and, to help along, we put up a general against him, relying on our accustomed confidence in the capacity of the people to *not see* the difference between one who *is* a general, and one who is *called* a general, but we failed again. History is philosophy teaching by example, and if we regard the examples it has given us, we must try something new, before we can succeed in beating a general for the presidency."

Accordingly they nominated Pierce. It soon came to light that the first thing ever urged in his favor as a candidate was his having given a strange boy a cent to buy candy with. An examination of the official reports of his doings as a general in Mexico, showed him to have been the victim of a most extraordinary scene of mishap, which though it might by possibility have so happened with a brave and skillful general, left no considerable evidence that he was such. Forthwith also appears a biographical sketch of him, in which he is represented, at the age of seventeen, to have spelled "but" for his father, who was unable to spell it for himself. By the way I *do* wish Frank had not been present on that trying occasion. I have a great curiosity to know how "old dad" would have spelled that difficult word, if he had been left entirely to himself. But the biography also represents him as cutting at the enemy's flying cannon balls with his sword in the battles of Mexico, and calling out, "Boys there's a game of ball for you;" and finally that he added enough to a balance due him to raise the whole to three hundred dollars, and treated his men.

When I first saw these things I suspected they had been put forward by mischievous Whigs; but very soon I saw the biography published at length in a veritable Democratic paper, conducted by a man whose party fidelity and intelligent cooperation with his party, I know to be beyond suspicion. Then I was puzzled. But now we have a letter from Gen. Shields, in which, speaking of Pierce and himself, he says, "As we approached the enemy's position, directly under his fire, we encountered a deep ditch, or rather a deep narrow, slimy canal, which had been previously used for the purpose of irrigation. It was no time to hesitate, so we both plunged in. The horse I happened to ride that day was a light active Mexican horse. This circumstance operated in my favor, and enabled me to extricate myself and horse after considerable difficulty. Pierce, on the contrary, was mounted on a large, heavy American horse, and man and horse both sank down and rolled over in the ditch. There I was compelled to leave him . . . After struggling there, I cannot say how long, he extricated himself from his horse, and hurried on foot to join his command, &c."

Now, what right had a brigadier general, when approaching the enemy's position, and directly under his fire, to sink down and roll over in a deep slimy canal and struggle there before he got out, how long, another brigadier general cannot tell, when the whole of both their brigades got across that same "slimy canal," without any difficulty worth mentioning? I say, Judge Douglas, "Is *this* manoeuvre sanctioned by Scott's Infantry Tactics as adopted in the army?" This ludicrous scene in Gen. Pierce's career had not been told of before; and the telling of it by Gen. Shields, looks very much like a pertinacious purpose to "pile up" the ridiculous. This explains the new plan or system of tactics adopted by the democracy. It is to ridicule and burlesque the whole military character out of credit; and thus to kill Gen. Scott with vexation. Being philosophical and literary men, they have read, and remembered, how the institution of chivalry was ridiculed out of existence by its fictitious votary Don Quixote. They also remember how our own "militia trainings" have been "laughed to death" by fantastic parades and caricatures upon them. We remember one of these parades ourselves here, at the head of which, on horseback, figured our old friend Gordon Abrams, with a pine wood sword, about nine feet long, and a paste-board cocked hat, from front to rear about the length of an ox yoke, and very much the shape of one turned bottom upwards; and with spurs having rowels as large as the bottom of a teacup, and shanks a foot and a half long. That was the last militia muster here. Among the rules and regulations, no man is to wear more than five pounds of codfish for epaulets, or more than thirty yards of bologna sausages for a sash; and no two men are to dress alike, and if any two should dress alike the one that dresses most alike is to be fined, (I forget how much). Flags they had too, with devices and mottoes, one of which latter is, "We'll fight till we run, and we'll run till we die."

Now, in the language of Judge Douglas, "I submit to you gentlemen," whether there is not great cause to fear that on some occasion when Gen. Scott suspects no danger, suddenly Gen. Pierce will be discovered charging upon him, holding a huge roll of candy in one hand for a spy glass; with B U T labelled on some appropriate part of his person; with Abrams' long pine sword cutting in the air at imaginary cannon balls, and calling out "boys there's a game of ball for you," and over all streaming the flag, with the motto, "We'll fight till we faint, and I'll treat when it's over."

It is calculated that such opposition will take "Old Fuss and Feathers" by surprise. He has thought of, and prepared himself for, all the ordinary modes of assault—for over-reachings, and under-minings; for fires in front and fires in the rear; but I guess this would be a fire on the "blind side"—totally unlooked for by him. Unless the opposition should, once more sink down, and roll over, in that deep slimy canal, I cannot conceive what is to save Gen. Scott. . . .

The kindness of Lincoln shows through a letter about "Billy the Barber," a Negro in Springfield who had failed to record and then had lost the deed to his lots.

Bloomington,
Sept. 27. 1852.

C. R. Welles, Esq.
Dear Sir

I am in a little trouble here. I am trying to get a decree for our "Billy the Barber" for the conveyance of certain town lots sold to him by Allen, Gridly and Prickett. I made you a party, as administrator of Prickett, but the clerk omitted to put your name in the writ, and so you are not served. Billy will blame me, if I do not get the thing fixed up this time. If, therefore, you will be so kind as to sign the authority below, and send it to me by *return mail,* I shall be greatly obliged, and will be careful that you shall not be involved, or your rights invaded by it. Yours as ever

A. Lincoln

Lincoln the lawyer was also a man of compassion.

Springfield,
Oct. 27. 1852

L. M. Hays Esq.
Dear Sir:

Yours of Sept. 30th. just received. At our court, just past, I could have got a judgment against Turley, if I had pressed to the utmost; but I am really sorry for him—*poor* and a *cripple* as he is.

He begged time to try to find evidence to prove that the deceased on his deathbed, ordered the note to be given up to him or destroyed. I do not suppose he will get any such evidence, but I allowed him till next court to try. Yours &c

A Lincoln

A touch of tight-fistedness led Lincoln into a minor dilemma.

Springfield, March 8. 1853.

Dear Linder—

The change of circuits prevents my attending the Edgar court this spring, and perhaps generally hereafter. There is a little ejectment case from Bloomfield, in which the name of Davidson figures, but in which a couple of men by the name of Bailey are interested; and for defending which I have been paid a little fee. Now I dislike to keep their money without doing the service; & I also hate to disgorge; and I therefore request of you to defend the case for me; & I will, in due time, do as much or more for you. Write me whether you can do it. Yours as ever,

A. Lincoln

Lincoln's absorption in his profession had produced results. He had become a lawyer widely respected and sought after. In one of the most important lawsuits ever to come before an Illinois court, both parties wanted Lincoln to represent them.

Bloomington,
Sept. 12. 1853.

T. R. Webber, Esq—
My dear Sir:

On my arrival here to court, I find that McLean County has assessed the land and other property of the Central Railroad, for the purpose of county taxation. An effort is about to be made to get the question of the right to so tax the Co. before the court, & ultimately before the Supreme Court, and the Co. are offering to engage me for them. As this will be the same question I have had under consideration for you, I am somewhat trammeled by what has passed between you and me; feeling that you have the prior right to my services; if you choose to secure me a fee something near such as I can get from the other side. The question, in its magnitude, to the Co. on the one hand, and the counties in which the Co. has land, on the other, is the largest law question that can now be got up in the state; and therefore, in justice to myself, I cannot afford, if I can help it, to miss a fee altogether. If you choose to release me; say so by return mail, and there an end. If you wish to retain me, you better get authority from your court, come directly over in the stage, and make common cause with this county. Very truly your friend

A. Lincoln—

Pekin, Ills.
Oct. 3, 1853.

Mr. Brayman, Esq
Dear Sir:

Neither the county of McLean nor any one on its behalf, has yet made any engagement with me in relation to its suit with the Illinois Central Railroad, on the subject of taxation. I am now free to make an engagement for the road; and if you think fit you may "count me in." Please write me, on receipt of this. I shall be here at least ten days. Yours truly

A. Lincoln—

Lincoln had known John Marshall, an attorney of Shawneetown, for many years. The book was a novel by his daughter, Sarah Marshall Hayden, entitled *Early Engagements: and Florence (a Sequel)*, published in 1854.

Springfield,
Feby. 8. 1854.

Hon: John Marshall
Shawneetown, Ills.
My dear Sir:

Your letter of the 1st. inst. was received yesterday. I went at once to the express office, got the books, placed twenty-three of them at one bookstore; & twenty-four at another, for sale, at a commission of ten per cent, and took their receipts. Of the other three books, I took one to the Register, one to the Journal, and took one home with me. I found that the editors and booksellers had all previously seen favorable notice of the work; and one of the booksellers had sent an order to Cincinnati for some copies of it. I am not much of a reader of this sort of literature; but my wife got hold of the volume I took home, and read it half through last night, and is greatly interested in it. When the papers here shall have noticed it, I will send you copies. The charge at the express office was only $1.50; I return herewith one dollar, & hold fifty cents subject to your order.

My attention to this matter has been rather a pleasure than a trouble. Yours truly—

A. Lincoln—

Lincoln rarely read any book. He preferred a different kind of mental stimulation. Now that the reflective years approached a crisis, he began, privately, to test his beliefs by subjecting them to his own scrutiny. What should government mean to him as a private citizen?

[July, 1854]

The legitimate object of government, is to do for a community of people, whatever they need to have done, but cannot do, *at all,* or cannot, *so well do,* for themselves—in their separate, and individual capacities.

In all that the people can individually do as well for themselves, government ought not to interfere.

The desirable things which the individuals of a people cannot do, or cannot well do, for themselves, fall into two classes: those which have relation to *wrongs,* and those which have not. Each of these branch off into an infinite variety of subdivisions.

The first—that in relation to wrongs—embraces all crimes, misdemeanors, and non-performance of contracts. The other embraces all which, in its nature, and without wrong, requires combined action, as public roads and highways, public schools, charities, pauperism, orphanage, estates of the deceased, and the machinery of government itself.

From this it appears that if all men were just, there still would be *some,* though not *so much,* need of government.

If ambition for office had clouded these years, could Lincoln have approached the most explosive issue of his age with this detachment of honest thinking?

[July, 1854]

The ant, who has toiled and dragged a crumb to his nest, will furiously defend the fruit of his labor, against whatever robber assails him. So plain, that the most dumb and stupid slave that ever toiled for a master, does constantly *know* that he is wronged. So plain that no one, high or low, ever does mistake it, except in a plainly *selfish* way; for although volume upon volume is written to prove slavery a very good thing, we never hear of the man who wishes to take the good of it, *by being a slave himself.*

Most governments have been based, practically, on the denial of equal rights of men, as I have, in part, stated them; *ours* began, by *affirming* those rights. *They* said, some men are too *ignorant,* and *vicious,* to share in government. Possibly so, said we; and, by your system, you would always keep them ignorant, and vicious. We proposed to give *all* a chance; and we expected the weak to grow stronger, the ignorant, wiser; and all better, and happier together.

We made the experiment; and the fruit is before us. Look at it —think of it. Look at it, in its aggregate grandeur, of extent of country, and numbers of population—of ship, and steamboat, and rail. . . .

[July, 1854]

If A. can prove, however conclusively, that he may, of right, enslave B.—why may not B. snatch the same argument, and prove equally, that he may enslave A?—

You say A. is white, and B. is black. It is *color,* then; the lighter, having the right to enslave the darker? Take care. By this rule, you are to be slave to the first man you meet, with a fairer skin than your own.

You do not mean *color* exactly?—You mean the whites are *intellectually* the superiors of the blacks, and, therefore have the right to enslave them? Take care again. By this rule, you are to be slave to the first man you meet, with an intellect superior to your own.

But, say you, it is a question of *interest;* and, if you can make it your *interest,* you have the right to enslave another. Very well. And if he can make it his interest, he has the right to enslave you.

VI. National Emergence

1854-1858   During the first months of 1854 Lincoln's law practice filled all his time. In January and February the Illinois Supreme Court, sitting in Springfield, heard him argue eight cases. When the court adjourned the circuit courts began. After two busy weeks in his home county Lincoln followed David Davis, the corpulent judge of the eighth judicial circuit, to the town of Lincoln in Logan County, to Bloomington, and then to five other central Illinois county seats. During these five months Lincoln also wrote several legal opinions and learned, with satisfaction, of the dismissal of a lawsuit which a disgruntled brother of his wife had filed against him several months earlier.

But law suits and legal opinions by no means monopolized Lincoln's thoughts. Stephen A. Douglas had seen to that. The "Democratic giant," whom Lincoln had once dismissed as not worth talking about, was now serving his second term in the United States Senate, where he headed the powerful Committee on Territories. On January 23, 1854, Douglas introduced a bill to organize territorial governments for Kansas and Nebraska. The bill contained a provision expressly repealing the Missouri Compromise of 1820, which had prohibited slavery in the national domain north of the line of 36°30'. Since both proposed territories were north of that line, slavery could break out of the limits which had been imposed upon it for thirty-four years. In the North, millions who hated the South's "peculiar institution" had been willing to let it remain, undisturbed, where it existed; but they would resist its spread with all their strength. Among them stood Abraham Lincoln.

Ever since 1849, when Lincoln failed to obtain appointment as Commissioner of the General Land Office, he had paid little attention to politics. Now that basic human rights were involved, he could no longer remain aloof. As Douglas, backed by the full strength of the Pierce administration, overcame bitter opposition and forced his bill through Congress, Lincoln brooded. In his law office, in the inns of the county towns on the circuit, his melancholy grew as he foresaw disaster threatening the nation.

Characteristically, Lincoln said little and did nothing until the approach of the fall elections. The ballot, in his creed, was the instrument by which a citizen registered his protest.

In the central Illinois congressional district Richard Yates, a Whig with strong antislavery convictions, opposed Thomas L. Harris, Democrat and stanch supporter of Douglas. Lincoln wanted to see Yates elected. In a letter to the state senator from Macoupin County, John M. Palmer, Lincoln appealed to a man torn between party loyalty and conscience.

(CONFIDENTIAL)

Springfield,
Sept. 7. 1854

Hon. J. M. Palmer.
Dear Sir.

You know how anxious I am that this Nebraska measure shall be rebuked and condemned everywhere. Of course I hope something from your position; yet I do not expect you to do anything which may be wrong in your own judgment; nor would I have you do anything personally injurious to yourself. You are, and always have been, *honestly,* and *sincerely* a Democrat; and I know how painful it must be to an honest sincere man, to be urged by his party to the support of a measure, which on his conscience he believes to be wrong. You have had a severe struggle with yourself, and you have determined *not* to swallow the *wrong.* Is it not just to yourself that you should, in a few public speeches, state your reasons, and thus justify yourself? I wish you would; and yet I say "don't do it, if you think it will injure you." You may have given your word to vote for Major Harris, and if so, of course you will stick to it. But allow me to suggest that you should avoid speaking of this; for it probably would induce some of your friends, in like manner, to cast their votes. You understand. And now let me beg your pardon for obtruding this letter upon you, to whom I have ever been opposed in politics. Had your party omitted to make Nebraska a test of party fidelity; you probably would have been the Democratic candidate for Congress in the district. You deserved it, and I believe it would have been given you. In that case I should have been quiet, happy that Nebraska was to be rebuked at all events. I still should have voted for the Whig candidate; but I should have made no speeches, written no letters; and you would have been elected by at least a thousand majority. Yours truly

A. Lincoln—

To the editors of the *Illinois Journal*—the same newspaper which, as the *Sangamo Journal,* had published Lincoln's first political announcement—he offered an editorial in which he had reduced the Kansas-Nebraska issue to a simple parable.

THE 14TH SECTION

September 11, 1854

The following is the 14th section of the Kansas-Nebraska law. It repeals the Missouri Compromise; and then puts in a declaration that it is not intended by this repeal to legislate slavery in or exclude it therefrom, the territory.

"SEC. 14. That the Constitution, and all the laws of the United States which are not locally inapplicable, shall have the same force and effect within said territory of Nebraska as elsewhere in the United States, except the 8th section of the act preparatory to the admission of Missouri into the Union, approved March sixth, eighteen hundred and twenty, which being inconsistent with the principles of nonintervention by Congress with slavery in the states and territories as recognized by the legislation of eighteen hundred and fifty, commonly called the compromise measures, is hereby declared inoperative and void; it being the true intent and meaning of this act not to legislate slavery into any territory or state, nor to exclude it therefrom, but to leave the people thereof perfectly free to form and regulate their domestic institutions in their own way, subject only to the Constitution of the United States: Provided, that nothing herein contained shall be construed to revive or put in force any law or regulation which may have existed prior to the act of sixth of March, eighteen hundred and twenty, either protecting, establishing, prohibiting, or abolishing slavery."

The state of the case in a few words, is this: The Missouri Compromise excluded slavery from the Kansas-Nebraska territory. The repeal opened the territories to slavery. If there is any meaning to the declaration in the 14th section, that it does not mean to legislate slavery into the territories, it is this: that it does not require slaves to be sent there. The Kansas and Nebraska territories are now as open to slavery as Mississippi or Arkansas were when they were territories.

To illustrate the case: Abraham Lincoln has a fine meadow, containing beautiful springs of water, and well fenced, which John Calhoun had agreed with Abraham (originally owning the land in common) should be his, and the agreement had been consummated in the most solemn manner, regarded by both as sacred. John Calhoun, however, in the course of time, had become owner of an extensive herd of cattle—the prairie grass had become dried up and there was no convenient water to be had. John Calhoun then looks with a longing eye on Lincoln's meadow, and goes to it and throws down the fences, and exposes it to the ravages of his starving and famishing cattle. "You rascal," says Lincoln, "what have you done? what do you do this for?" "Oh," replies Calhoun, "everything is right, I have taken down your fence; but nothing more. It is my true intent and meaning not to drive my cattle into your meadow, nor to exclude them therefrom, but to leave them perfectly free to form their own notions of the feed, and to direct their movements in their own way!"

Now would not the man who committed this outrage be deemed both a knave and a fool,—a knave in removing the restrictive fence, which he had solemnly pledged himself to sustain;—and a fool in supposing that there could be one man found in the country to believe that he had not pulled down the fence for the purpose of opening the meadow for his cattle?

Lincoln also took the stump. In speeches to earnest, sun-baked crowds of farmers and storekeepers in town after town—Winchester, Carrollton, Jacksonville, Bloomington—he presented the issues with a degree of gravity and an elevation of thought that reflected his months of concern. The Illinois State Fair, held at Springfield during the first week in October, gave him more than a local audience. Douglas, under sharp attack from antislavery members of his own party, defended the Nebraska Bill at length on the afternoon of October 3. Lincoln replied twenty-four hours later.

On October 16 the two men repeated their addresses at Peoria, At Springfield, the newspapers had only summarized what they said. After Peoria, both speakers gave the full texts of their addresses to the press.

To enable his hearers to judge whether the repeal of the Missouri Compromise was right or wrong, Lincoln began with a historical review of national policy with reference to slavery in the territories. Then he proceeded to answer his own question.

Peoria, October 16, 1854

. . . I think, and shall try to show, that it is wrong; wrong in its direct effect, letting slavery into Kansas and Nebraska—and wrong in its prospective principle, allowing it to spread to every other part of the wide world, where men can be found inclined to take it.

This *declared* indifference, but as I must think, covert *real* zeal for the spread of slavery, I cannot but hate. I hate it because of the monstrous injustice of slavery itself. I hate it because it deprives our republican example of its just influence in the world—enables the enemies of free institutions, with plausibility, to taunt us as hypocrites—causes the real friends of freedom to doubt our sincerity, and especially because it forces so many really good men amongst ourselves into an open war with the very fundamental principles of civil liberty—criticising the Declaration of Independence, and insisting that there is no right principle of action but self-interest.

Before proceeding, let me say I think I have no prejudice against the Southern people. They are just what we would be in their situation. If slavery did not now exist amongst them, they would not introduce it. If it did now exist amongst us, we should not instantly give it up. This I believe of the masses north and south. Doubtless there are individuals, on both sides, who would not hold slaves under any circumstances; and others who would gladly introduce slavery anew, if it were out of existence. We know that some southern men do free their slaves, go north, and become tip-top abolitionists; while some northern ones go south, and become most cruel slave-masters.

When southern people tell us they are no more responsible for

161

the origin of slavery than we, I acknowledge the fact. When it is said that the institution exists, and that it is very difficult to get rid of it, in any satisfactory way, I can understand and appreciate the saying. I surely will not blame them for not doing what I should not know how to do myself. If all earthly power were given me, I should not know what to do, as to the existing institution. My first impulse would be to free all the slaves, and send them to Liberia,—to their own native land. But a moment's reflection would convince me, that whatever of high hope, (as I think there is) there may be in this, in the long run, its sudden execution is impossible. If they were all landed there in a day, they would all perish in the next ten days; and there are not surplus shipping and surplus money enough in the world to carry them there in many times ten days. What then? Free them all, and keep them among us as underlings? Is it quite certain that this betters their condition? I think I would not hold one in slavery, at any rate; yet the point is not clear enough for me to denounce people upon. What next? Free them, and make them politically and socially, our equals? My own feelings will not admit of this; and if mine would, we well know that those of the great mass of white people will not. Whether this feeling accords with justice and sound judgment, is not the sole question, if indeed, it is any part of it. A universal feeling, whether well or ill-founded, cannot be safely disregarded. We cannot, then, make them equals. It does seem to me that systems of gradual emancipation might be adopted; but for their tardiness in this, I will not undertake to judge our brethren of the South.

When they remind us of their constitutional rights, I acknowledge them, not grudgingly, but fully, and fairly; and I would give them any legislation for the reclaiming of their fugitives, which should not, in its stringency, be more likely to carry a free man into slavery, than our ordinary criminal laws are to hang an innocent one.

But all this, to my judgment, furnishes no more excuse for permitting slavery to go into our own free territory, than it would for reviving the African slave-trade by law. The law which forbids the bringing of slaves *from* Africa; and that which has so long forbid the taking them *to* Nebraska, can hardly be distinguished on any moral principle; and the repeal of the former could find quite as plausible excuses as that of the latter.

National Emergence

Lincoln already had explained the emotional basis of his position. Now he proceeded to intellectualize it.

The arguments by which the repeal of the Missouri Compromise is sought to be justified, are these:

First, that the Nebraska country needed a territorial government.

Second, that in various ways, the public had repudiated it, and demanded the repeal; and therefore should not now complain of it.

And lastly, that the repeal establishes a principle, which is intrinsically right.

I will attempt an answer to each of them in its turn.

First, then, if that country was in need of a territorial organization, could it not have had it as well without as with the repeal? Iowa and Minnesota, to both of which the Missouri restriction applied, had, without its repeal, each in succession, territorial organizations. And even, the year before, a bill for Nebraska itself, was within an ace of passing, without the repealing clause; and this in the hands of the same men who are now the champions of repeal. Why no necessity then for the repeal? But still later, when this very bill was first brought in, it contained no repeal. But, say they, because the public had demanded, or rather commanded the repeal, the repeal was to accompany the organization, whenever that should occur.

Now I deny that the public ever demanded any such thing— ever repudiated the Missouri Compromise—ever commanded its repeal. I deny it, and call for the proof. It is not contended, I believe, that any such command has ever been given in express terms. It is only said that it was done *in principle*. The support of the Wilmot Proviso, is the first fact mentioned, to prove that the Missouri restriction was repudiated in *principle,* and the second is, the refusal to extend the Missouri line over the country acquired from Mexico. These are near enough alike to be treated together. The one was to exclude the chances of slavery from the *whole* new acquisition by the lump; and the other was to reject a division of it, by which one *half* was to be given up to those chances. Now whether this was a repudiation of the Missouri line, in *principle,* depends upon whether the Missouri law contained any *principle* requiring the line to be extended over the country acquired from

Mexico. I contend it did not. I insist that it contained no general principle, but that it was, in every sense, specific. That its terms limit it to the country purchased from France, is undenied and undeniable. It could have no principle beyond the intention of those who made it. They did not intend to extend the line to country which they did not own. If they intended to extend it, in the event of acquiring additional territory, why did they not say so? It was just as easy to say, that "in all the country west of the Mississippi, which we now own, *or may hereafter acquire* there shall never be slavery," as to say, what they did say; and they would have said it if they had meant it. . . .

Another fact showing the *specific* character of the Missouri law —showing that it intended no more than it expressed—showing that the line was not intended as a universal dividing line between free and slave territory, present and prospective—north of which slavery could never go—is the fact that by that very law, Missouri came in as a slave state, *north* of the line. If that law contained any prospective *principle*, the whole law must be looked to in order to ascertain what the *principle* was. And by this rule, the South could fairly contend that inasmuch as they got one slave state north of the line at the inception of the law, they have the right to have another given them *north* of it occasionally—now and then in the indefinite westward extension of the line. This demonstrates the absurdity of attempting to deduce a prospective *principle* from the Missouri Compromise line.

When we voted for the Wilmot Proviso, we were voting to keep slavery *out* of the whole Mexican acquisition; and little did we think we were thereby voting, to let it *into* Nebraska, laying several hundred miles distant. When we voted against extending the Missouri line, little did we think we were voting to destroy the old line, then of near thirty years standing. To argue that we thus repudiated the Missouri Compromise is no less absurd than it would be to argue that because we have, so far, forborne to acquire Cuba, we have thereby, *in principle*, repudiated our former acquisitions, and determined to throw them out of the Union! No less absurd than it would be to say that because I may have refused to build an addition to my house, I thereby have decided to destroy the existing house! And if I catch you setting fire to my house, you will turn upon me and say I INSTRUCTED you to do it! The most conclusive argument, however, that, while voting for the Wilmot Proviso, and while voting against the EXTENSION of the Missouri line, we never thought of disturbing the original Missouri Compromise, is found in the facts, that there was then, and still is, an unorganized tract of fine country, nearly as large as the state of Missouri, lying immediately west of Arkansas, and south of the Missouri Compromise line; and that we never attempted to prohibit slavery as to it. I wish particular attention to this. It adjoins the original Missouri Compromise line, by its northern boundary; and consequently is part of the country, into which, by implication, slavery was permitted to go, by that compromise. There it has lain open ever since, and there it still lies. And yet no effort has been made at any time to wrest it from the south. In all our struggles to prohibit slavery within our Mexican acquisitions, we never so much as lifted a finger to prohibit it, as to this tract. Is not this entirely conclusive that at all times, we have held the Missouri Compromise as a sacred thing; even when against ourselves, as well as when for us?

. . . But next it is said that the compromises of '50 and the ratification of them by both political parties, in '52, established a *new principle,* which required the repeal of the Missouri Compromise. This again I deny. I deny it, and demand the proof. I have already stated fully what the compromises of '50 are. The particular part of those measures, for which the virtual repeal of the Missouri Compromise is sought to be inferred (for it is admitted they contain nothing about it, in express terms) is the provision in the Utah and New Mexico laws, which permits them when they seek admission into the Union as states, to come in with or without slavery as they shall then see fit. Now I insist this provision was made for Utah and New Mexico, and for no other place whatever. It had no more direct reference to Nebraska that it had to the territories of the moon. But, say they, it had reference to Nebraska, *in principle.* Let us see. The North consented to this provision, not because they considered it right in itself; but because they were compensated—paid for it. They, at the same time, got California into the Union as a free state. This was far the best part of all they had struggled for by the Wilmot Proviso. They also got the area of slavery somewhat narrowed in the settlement of the boundary of Texas. Also, they got the slave trade abolished in the District of Columbia. For all these desirable objects the North could afford to yield something; and they did yield to the South the Utah and New Mexico provision. I do not mean that the whole North, or even a majority, yielded, when the law passed; but enough yielded, when added to the vote of the South, to carry the measure. Now can it be pretended that the *principle* of this arrangement requires us to permit the same provision to be applied to Nebraska, *without any equivalent at all?* Give us another free state; press the boundary of Texas still further back, give us another step toward the destruction of slavery in the District, and you present us a similar case. But ask us not to repeat, for nothing, what you paid for in the first instance. If you wish the thing again, pay again. . . .

With insight into the practical motivation of political action, Lincoln propounded a series of questions.

Again, if Congress, at that time, intended that all future territories should, when admitted as states, come in with or without slavery, at their own option, why did it not say so? With such an universal provision, all know the bills could not have passed. Did they, then—could they—establish a *principle* contrary to their own intention? Still further, if they intended to establish the principle that wherever Congress had control, it should be left to the people to do as they thought fit with slavery why did they not authorize the people of the District of Columbia at their adoption to abolish slavery within these limits? I personally know that this has not been left undone, because it was unthought of. It was frequently spoken of by members of Congress and by citizens of Washington six years ago; and I heard no one express a doubt that a system of gradual emancipation, with compensation to owners, would meet the approbation of a large majority of the white people of the District. But without the action of Congress they could say nothing; and Congress said "no." In the measures of 1850 Congress had the subject of slavery in the District expressly in hand. If they were then establishing the *principle* of allowing the people to do as they please with slavery, why did they not apply the *principle* to that people?

. . . Finally, it is asked "If we did not mean to apply the Utah and New Mexico provision, to all future territories, what did we mean, when we, in 1852, endorsed the compromises of '50?"

For myself, I can answer this question most easily. I meant not to ask a repeal, or modification of the fugitive slave law. I meant not to ask for the abolition of slavery in the District of Columbia. I meant not to resist the admission of Utah and New Mexico, even should they ask to come in as slave states. I meant nothing about additional territories, because, as I understood, we then had no territory whose character as to slavery was not already settled. As to Nebraska, I regarded its character as being fixed, by the Missouri Compromise, for thirty years—as unalterably fixed as that of my own home in Illinois. As to new acquisitions I said "sufficient unto the day is the evil thereof." When we make new acquisitions we will, as heretofore, try to manage them somehow. That is my answer. That is what I meant and said; and I appeal to the people to say, each for himself, whether that was not also the universal meaning of the free states. . . .

Having demonstrated that the people had never demanded the repeal of the Missouri Compromise, Lincoln grappled with the fundamental question of right and wrong.

I now come to consider whether the repeal, with its avowed principle, is intrinsically right. I insist that it is not. Take the particular case. A controversy had arisen between the advocates and opponents of slavery, in relation to its establishment within the country we had purchased of France. The southern, and then best part of the purchase, was already in as a slave state. The controversy was settled by also letting Missouri in as a slave state; but with the agreement that within all the remaining part of the purchase, north of a certain line, there should never be slavery. As to what was to be done with the remaining part south of the line, nothing was said; but perhaps the fair implication was, that it should come in with slavery if it should so choose. The southern part, except a portion heretofore mentioned, afterwards did come in with slavery, as the State of Arkansas. All these many years since 1820, the northern part had remained a wilderness. At length settlements began in it also. In due course, Iowa came in as a free state, and Minnesota was given a territorial government, without removing the slavery restriction. Finally the sole remaining part, north of the line, Kansas and Nebraska, was to be organized; and it is proposed, and carried, to blot out the old dividing line of thirty-four years standing, and to open the whole of that country to the introduction of slavery.

Now, this, to my mind, is manifestly unjust. After an angry and dangerous controversy, the parties made friends by dividing the bone of contention. The one party first appropriates her own share, beyond all power to be disturbed in the possession of it; and then seizes the share of the other party. It is as if two starving men had divided their only loaf; the one had hastily swallowed his half, and then grabbed the other half just as he was putting it to his mouth!

. . . Equal justice to the South, it is said, requires us to consent to the extending of slavery to new countries. That is to say, inasmuch as you do not object to my taking my hog to Nebraska, therefore I must not object to you taking your slave. Now, I admit this is perfectly logical, if there is no difference between hogs and Negroes. But while you thus require me to deny the humanity of the Negro, I wish to ask whether you of the South yourselves, have ever been willing to do as much? It is kindly provided that of all those who come into the world, only a small percentage are natural tyrants. That percentage is no larger in the slave states than in the free. The great majority, south as well as north, have human sympathies, of which they can no more divest themselves than they can of their sensibility to physical pain. These sympathies in the bosoms of the Southern people, manifest in many ways, their sense of the wrong of slavery, and their consciousness that, after all, there is humanity in the Negro. If they deny this, let me address them a few plain questions. In 1820 you joined the North, almost unanimously, in declaring the African slave trade piracy, and in annexing to it the punishment of death. Why did you do this? If you did not feel that it was wrong, why did you join in providing that men should be hung for it? The practice was no more than bringing wild Negroes from Africa, to sell to such as would buy them. But you never thought of hanging men for catching and selling wild horses, wild buffaloes or wild bears.

Again, you have amongst you, a sneaking individual, of the class of native tyrants, known as the "slave-dealer." He watches your necessities, and crawls up to buy your slave, at a speculating price. If you cannot help it, you sell to him; but if you can help it, you drive him from your door. You despise him utterly. You do not recognize him as a friend, or even as an honest man. Your children must not play with his; they may rollick freely with the little Negroes, but not with the "slave-dealers' " children. If you are obliged to deal with him, you try to get through the job without so much as touching him. It is common with you to join hands with the men you meet; but with the slave-dealer you avoid the ceremony—instinctively shrinking from the snaky contact. If he grows rich and retires from business, you still remember him, and still keep up the ban of non-intercourse upon him and his family. Now why is this? You do not so treat the man who deals in corn, cattle or tobacco. . . .

Douglas had proposed that the inhabitants of a territory be allowed to decide the question of slavery for themselves—an alluring solution to a nation fervently attached to the principle of self-government. Lincoln dissented.

But one great argument in the support of the repeal of the Missouri Compromise, is still to come. That argument is "the sacred right of self-government." It seems our distinguished Senator has found great difficulty in getting his antagonists, even in the Senate to meet him fairly on this argument—some poet has said

"Fools rush in where angels fear to tread."

At the hazard of being thought one of the fools of this quotation, I meet that argument—I rush in, I take that bull by the horns.

I trust I understand, and truly estimate the right of self-government. My faith in the proposition that each man should do precisely as he pleases with all which is exclusively his own, lies at the foundation of the sense of justice there is in me. I extend the principle to communities of men, as well as to individuals. I so extend it, because it is politically wise, as well as naturally just: politically wise, in saving us from broils about matters which do not concern us. Here, or at Washington, I would not trouble myself with the oyster laws of Virginia, or the cranberry laws of Indiana.

The doctrine of self-government is right—absolutely and eternally right—but it has no just application, as here attempted. Or perhaps I should rather say that whether it has such just application depends upon whether a Negro is *not* or *is* a man. If he is *not* a man, why in that case, he who *is* a man may, as a matter of self-government, do just as he pleases with him. But if the Negro *is* a man, is it not to that extent, a total destruction of self-government, to say that he too shall not govern *himself?* When the white man governs himself that is self-government; but when he governs himself, and also governs *another* man, that is *more* than self-government—that is despotism. If the Negro is a *man,* why then my an-

169

cient faith teaches me that "all men are created equal;" and that there can be no moral right in connection with one man's making a slave of another.

Judge Douglas frequently, with bitter irony and sarcasm, paraphrases our argument by saying "The white people of Nebraska are good enough to govern themselves, *but they are not good enough to govern a few miserable Negroes!!*"

Well I doubt not that the people of Nebraska are, and will continue to be as good as the average of people elsewhere. I do not say the contrary. What I do say is, that no man is good enough to govern another man, *without that other's consent.* I say this is the leading principle—the sheet anchor of American republicanism. Our Declaration of Independence says:

"We hold these truths to be self-evident: that all men are created equal; that they are endowed by their Creator with certain inalienable rights; that among these are life, liberty and the pursuit of happiness. That to secure these rights, governments are instituted among men, deriving their just powers from the consent of the governed."

I have quoted so much at this time merely to show that according to our ancient faith, the just powers of governments are derived from the consent of the governed. Now the relation of masters and slaves is, *pro tanto,* a total violation of this principle. The master not only governs the slave without his consent; but he governs him by a set of rules altogether different from those which he prescribes for himself. Allow *all* the governed an equal voice in the government, and that, and that only is self-government.

Let it not be said I am contending for the establishment of political and social equality between the whites and blacks. I have already said the contrary. I am not now combating the argument of *necessity,* arising from the fact that the blacks are already amongst us; but I am combating what is set up as *moral* argument for allowing them to be taken where they have never yet been— arguing against the *extension* of a bad thing, which where it already exists, we must of necessity, manage as we best can.

In support of his application of the doctrine of self-government, Senator Douglas has sought to bring to his aid the opinions and examples of our revolutionary fathers. I am glad he has done this. I love the sentiments of those old-time men; and shall be most happy to abide by their opinions. He shows us that when it was in contemplation for the colonies to break off from Great Britain, and set up a new government for themselves, several of the states instructed their delegates to go for the measure *provided each state should be allowed to regulate its domestic concerns in its own way.* I do not quote; but this in substance. This was right. I see nothing objectionable in it. I also think it probable that it had some reference to the existence of slavery amongst them. I will not deny that it had. But had it, in any reference to the carrying of slavery into *new countries?* That is the question; and we will let the fathers themselves answer it.

This same generation of men, and mostly the same individuals of the generation, who declared this principle—who declared independence—who fought the War of the Revolution through—who afterwards made the Constitution under which we still live—these same men passed the Ordinance of '87, declaring that slavery should never go to the Northwest Territory. I have no doubt Judge Douglas thinks they were very inconsistent in this. It is a question of discrimination between them and him. But there is not an inch of ground left for his claiming that their opinions—their example—their authority—are on his side in this controversy.

Again, is not Nebraska, while a territory, a part of us? Do we not own the country? And if we surrender the control of it, do we not surrender the right of self-government? It is part of ourselves. If you say we shall not control it because it is *only* part, the same is true of every other part; and when all the parts arc gone, what has become of the whole? What is then left of us? What use for the general government, when there is nothing left for it to govern?

Lincoln saw that slavery was a national rather than a regional problem: the plain citizen in New England or Ohio had a stake in what happened in Nebraska.

But you say this question should be left to the people of Nebraska, because they are more particularly interested. If this be the rule, you must leave it to each individual to say for himself whether he will have slaves. What better moral right have thirty-one citizens of Nebraska to say, that the thirty-second shall not hold slaves, than the people of the thirty-one states have to say that slavery shall not go into the thirty-second state at all?

But if it is a sacred right for the people of Nebraska to take and hold slaves there, it is equally their sacred right to buy them where they can buy them cheapest; and that undoubtedly will be on the coast of Africa; provided you will consent to not hang them for going there to buy them. You must remove this restriction too, from the sacred right of self-government. I am aware you say that taking slaves from the states to Nebraska, does not make slaves of freemen; but the African slave-trader can say just as much. He does not catch free Negroes and bring them here. He finds them already slaves in the hands of their black captors, and he honestly buys them at the rate of about a red cotton handkerchief a head. This is very cheap, and it is a great abridgement of the sacred right of self-government to hang men for engaging in this profitable trade!

. . . Whether slavery shall go into Nebraska, or other new territories, is not a matter of exclusive concern to the people who may go there. The whole nation is interested that the best use shall be made of these territories. We want them for the homes of free white people. This they cannot be, to any considerable extent, if slavery shall be planted within them. Slave states are places for poor white people to remove *from;* not to remove *to.* New free states are the places for poor people to go to and better their condition. For this use, the nation needs these territories.

Still further; there are constitutional relations between the slave and free states, which are degrading to the latter. We are under legal obligations to catch and return their runaway slaves to them—a sort of dirty, disagreeable job, which I believe, as a general rule the slave-holders will not perform for one another. Then again, in the control of the government—the management of the partnership affairs—they have greatly the advantage of us. By the Constitution, each state has two Senators—each has a number of Representatives; in proportion to the number of its people—and each has a number of presidential electors, equal to the whole number of its Senators and Representatives together. But in ascertaining the number of the people, for this purpose, five slaves are counted as being equal to three whites. The slaves do not vote; they are only counted and so used, as to swell the influence of the white people's votes. . . .

Now all this is manifestly unfair; yet I do not mention it to complain of it, in so far as it is already settled. It is in the Constitution; and I do not, for that cause, or any other cause, propose to

172

destroy, or alter, or disregard the Constitution. I stand to it, fairly, fully, and firmly.

But when I am told I must leave it altogether to *other people* to say whether new partners are to be bred up and brought into the firm, on the same degrading terms against me, I respectfully demur. I insist, that whether I shall be a whole man, or only the half of one, in comparison with others, is a question in which I am somewhat concerned; and one which no other man can have a sacred right of deciding for me. If I am wrong in this—if it really be a sacred right of self-government, in the man who shall go to Nebraska, to decide whether he will be the *equal* of me or the *double* of me, then after he shall have exercised that right, and thereby shall have reduced me to a still smaller fraction of a man than I already am, I should like for some gentleman deeply skilled in the mysteries of sacred rights, to provide himself with a microscope, and peep about, and find out, if he can, what has become of my sacred rights! They will surely be too small for detection with the naked eye.

Finally, I insist, that if there is *anything* which it is the duty of the *whole people* to never entrust to any hands but their own, that thing is the preservation and perpetuity, of their own liberties, and institutions. And if they shall think, as I do, that the extension of slavery endangers them, more than any, or all other causes, how recreant to themselves, if they submit the question, and with it, the fate of their country, to a mere handful of men, bent only on temporary self-interest. If this question of slavery extension were an insignificant one—one having no power to do harm—it might be shuffled aside in this way. But being, as it is, the great Behemoth of danger, shall the strong grip of the nation be loosened upon him, to entrust him to the hands of such feeble keepers?

I have done with this mighty argument of self-government. Go, sacred thing! Go in peace.

Who, Lincoln asked, was risking the peace: the "incendiary" abolitionist or the slaveholder who insisted on invading free territory?

But Nebraska is urged as a great Union-saving measure. Well I too, go for saving the Union. Much as I hate slavery, I would consent to the extension of it rather than see the Union dissolved, just as I would consent to any *great* evil, to avoid a *greater* one.

But when I go to Union-saving, I must believe, at least, that the means I employ has some adaptation to the end. To my mind, Nebraska has no such adaptation.

"It hath no relish of salvation in it."

It is an aggravation, rather, of the only one thing which ever endangers the Union. When it came upon us, all was peace and quiet. The nation was looking to the forming of new bonds of union; and a long course of peace and prosperity seemed to lie before us. In the whole range of possibility, there scarcely appears to me to have been anything, out of which the slavery agitation could have been revived, except the very project of repealing the Missouri Compromise. Every inch of territory we owned, already had a definite settlement of the slavery question, and by which, all parties were pledged to abide. Indeed, there was no uninhabited country on the continent, which we could acquire; if we except some extreme northern regions, which are wholly out of the question. In this state of case, the genius of discord himself, could scarcely have invented a way of again setting us by the ears, but by turning back and destroying the peace measures of the past. The councils of that genius seem to have prevailed, the Missouri Compromise was repealed; and here we are, in the midst of a new slavery agitation, such, I think, as we have never seen before.

Who is responsible for this? Is it those who resist the measure; or those who, causelessly, brought it forward, and pressed it through, having reason to know, and, in fact, knowing it must and would be so resisted? It could not but be expected by its author, that it would be looked upon as a measure for the extension of slavery, aggravated by a gross breach of faith. Argue as you will, and long as you will, this is the naked *front* and *aspect,* of the measure. And in this aspect, it could not but produce agitation. Slavery is founded in the selfishness of man's nature—opposition to it, is in his love of justice. These principles are an eternal antagonism; and when brought into collision so fiercely, as slavery extension brings them, shocks, and throes, and convulsions must ceaselessly follow. Repeal the Missouri Compromise—repeal all compromises—repeal the Declaration of Independence—repeal all past history, you still cannot repeal human nature. It still will be the abundance of man's heart, that slavery extension is wrong;

and out of the abundance of his heart, his mouth will continue to speak. . . .

The Missouri Compromise ought to be restored. For the sake of the Union, it ought to be restored. We ought to elect a House of Representatives which will vote its restoration. If by any means, we omit to do this, what follows? Slavery may or may not be established in Nebraska. But whether it be or not, we shall have repudiated—discarded from the councils of the nation—the *spirit* of *compromise;* for who after this will ever trust in a national compromise? The spirit of mutual concession—that spirit which first gave us the Constitution, and which has thrice saved the Union— we shall have strangled and cast from us forever. And what shall we have in lieu of it? The South flushed with triumph and tempted to excesses; the North, betrayed, as they believe, brooding on wrong and burning for revenge. One side will provoke; the other resent. The one will taunt, the other defy; one aggresses, the other retaliates. Already a few in the North, defy all constitutional restraints, resist the execution of the fugitive slave law, and even menace the institution of slavery in the states where it exists.

Already a few in the South, claim the constitutional right to take to and hold slaves in the free states—demand the revival of the slave trade; and demand a treaty with Great Britain by which fugitive slaves may be reclaimed from Canada. As yet they are but few on either side. It is a grave question for the lovers of the Union, whether the final destruction of the Missouri Compromise, and with it the spirit of all compromise will or will not embolden and embitter each of these, and fatally increase the numbers of both.

But restore the Compromise, and what then? We thereby restore the national faith, the national confidence, the national feeling of brotherhood. We thereby reinstate the spirit of concession and compromise—that spirit which has never failed us in past perils, and which may be safely trusted for all the future. The South ought to join in doing this. The peace of the nation is as dear to them as to us. In memories of the past and hopes of the future, they share as largely as we. It would be on their part, a great act—great in its spirit, and great in its effect. It would be worth to the nation a hundred years' purchase of peace and prosperity. And what of sacrifice would they make? They only surrender to us, what they gave us for a consideration long, long ago; what they have not now, asked for, struggled or cared for; what has been thrust upon them, not less to their own astonishment than to ours.

But it is said we cannot restore it; that though we elect every member of the lower house, the Senate is still against us. It is quite true, that of the Senators who passed the Nebraska bill, a majority of the whole Senate will retain their seats in spite of the elections of this and the next year. But if at these elections, their several constituencies shall clearly express their will against Nebraska, will these Senators disregard their will? Will they neither obey, nor make room for those who will?

But even if we fail to technically restore the Compromise, it is still a great point to carry a popular vote in favor of the restoration. The moral weight of such a vote cannot be estimated too highly. The authors of Nebraska are not at all satisfied with the destruction of the Compromise—an endorsement of this *principle,* they proclaim to be the great object. With them, Nebraska alone is a small matter—to establish a principle, for *future use,* is what they particularly desire.

That future use is to be the planting of slavery wherever in the wide world, local and unorganized opposition cannot prevent it. Now if you wish to give them this endorsement—if you wish to establish this principle—do so. I shall regret it; but it is your right. On the contrary if you are opposed to the principle—intend to give it no such endorsement—let no wheedling, no sophistry, divert you from throwing a direct vote against it.

Some men, mostly Whigs, who condemn the repeal of the Missouri Compromise, nevertheless hesitate to go for its restoration, lest they be thrown in company with the abolitionist. Will they allow me as an old Whig to tell them good humoredly, that I think this is very silly? Stand with anybody that stands *right*. Stand with him while he is right and *part* with him when he goes wrong. Stand *with* the abolitionist in restoring the Missouri Compromise; and stand *against* him when he attempts to repeal the fugitive slave law. In the latter case you stand with the southern disunionist. What of that? you are still right. In both cases you are right. In both cases you oppose the dangerous extremes. In both you stand on middle ground and hold the ship level and steady. In both you are national and nothing less than national. This is good old Whig ground. To desert such ground, because of any company, is to be less than a Whig—less than a man—less than an American.

In concluding, Lincoln returned to the moral theme, speaking with an eloquence which he never surpassed.

I particularly object to the *new* position which the avowed principle of this Nebraska law gives to slavery in the body politic. I object to it because it assumes that there *can be moral right* in the enslaving of one man by another. I object to it as a dangerous dalliance for a free people—a sad evidence that, feeling prosperity we forget right—that liberty, as a principle, we have ceased to revere. I object to it because the fathers of the republic eschewed, and rejected it. The argument of "Necessity" was the only argument they ever admitted in favor of slavery; and so far, and so far only as it carried them, did they ever go. They found the institution existing among us, which they could not help; and they cast blame upon the British king for having permitted its introduction. *Before* the Constitution, they prohibited its introduction into the Northwestern Territory—the only country we owned, then free from it. At the framing and adoption of the Constitution, they forbore to so much as mention the word "slave" or "slavery" in the whole instrument. In the provision for the recovery of fugitives, the slave is spoken of as a *"person held to service or labor."* In that prohibiting the abolition of the African slave trade for twenty years, that trade is spoken of as "The migration or importation of such persons as any of the states *now existing,* shall think proper to admit," &c. These are the only provisions alluding to slavery. Thus, the thing is hid away, in the Constitution, just as an afflicted man hides away a wen or a cancer, which he dares not cut out at once, lest he bleed to death; with the promise, nevertheless, that the cutting may begin at the end of a given time. Less than this our fathers *could* not do; and *more* they *would* not do. Necessity drove them so far, and farther, they would not go. But this is not all. The earliest Congress, under the Constitution, took the same view of slavery. They hedged and hemmed it into the narrowest limits of necessity. . . .

But *now* it is to be transformed into a "sacred right." Nebraska brings it forth, places it on the high road to extension and perpetuity; and, with a pat on its back, says to it, "Go, and God speed you." Henceforth it is to be the chief jewel of the nation—the very

The Living Lincoln

figure-head of the ship of state. Little by little, but steadily as man's march to the grave, we have been giving up the *old* for the *new* faith. Near eighty years ago we began by declaring that all men are created equal; but now from that beginning we have run down to the other declaration, that for *some* men to enslave *others* is a "sacred right of self-government." These principles cannot stand together. They are as opposite as God and Mammon; and whoever holds to the one, must despise the other. When Pettit, in connection with his support of the Nebraska bill, called the Declaration of Independence "a self-evident lie" he only did what consistency and candor require all other Nebraska men to do. Of the forty-odd Nebraska Senators who sat present and heard him, no one rebuked him. Nor am I apprized that any Nebraska newspaper, or any Nebraska orator, in the whole nation, has ever yet rebuked him. If this had been said among Marion's men, Southerners though they were, what would have become of the man who said it? If this had been said to the men who captured André, the man who said it, would probably have been hung sooner than André was. If it had been said in old Independence Hall, seventy-eight years ago, the very doorkeeper would have throttled the man, and thrust him into the street.

Let no one be deceived. The spirit of Seventy-six and the spirit of Nebraska, are utter antagonisms; and the former is being rapidly displaced by the latter.

Fellow-countrymen: Americans south, as well as north, shall we make no effort to arrest this? Already the liberal party throughout the world, express the apprehension "that the one retrograde institution in America, is undermining the principles of progress, and fatally violating the noblest political system the world ever saw." This is not the taunt of enemies, but the warning of friends. Is it quite safe to disregard it—to despise it? Is there no danger to liberty itself, in discarding the earliest practice, and first precept of our ancient faith? In our greedy chase to make profit of the Negro, let us beware, lest we "cancel and tear to pieces" even the white man's charter of freedom.

Our republican robe is soiled, and trailed in the dust. Let us re-purify it. Let us turn and wash it white, in the spirit, if not the blood, of the Revolution. Let us turn slavery from its claims of "moral right," back upon its existing legal rights, and its arguments of "necessity." Let us return it to the position our fathers gave it; and there let it rest in peace. Let us re-adopt the Declara-

178

tion of Independence, and with it, the practices, and policy, which harmonize with it. Let North and South—let all Americans—let all lovers of liberty everywhere—join in the great and good work. If we do this, we shall not only have saved the Union; but we shall have so saved it, as to make, and to keep it, forever worthy of the saving. We shall have so saved it, that the succeeding millions of free happy people, the world over, shall rise up, and call us blessed, to the latest generations.

In the election, held on November 7, the Anti-Nebraska forces won a majority in the Illinois legislature. Lincoln saw an opportunity to displace his old antagonist, James Shields, in the United States Senate. With characteristic directness, he began to build his fences.

Clinton, DeWitt Co.
Nov. 10. 1854

Mr. Charles Hoyt
Dear Sir:
　　You used to express a good deal of partiality for me; and if you are still so, now is the time. Some friends here are really for me, for the U. S. Senate; and I should be very grateful if you could make a mark for me among your members. Please write me at all events, giving me the names, post offices, and *"political position"* of members round about you. Direct to Springfield.
　　Let this be confidential. Yours truly

A. Lincoln—

To give strength to the local Anti-Nebraska ticket, Lincoln had stood for the Illinois House of Representatives and had been elected. Now, in the belief that the office would hurt his chances for election to the United States Senate, he took a decisive step.

Springfield,
Novr. 25— 1854

N. W. Matheny:
Clerk of the county court
　　of Sangamon County, Illinois
　　Sir: I hereby decline to accept the office of Representative in the General Assembly, for the said county of Sangamon, to which office I am reported to have been elected on the 7th. of Novr. inst. I therefore desire that you notify the Governor of this

vacancy, in order that legal steps be taken to fill the same. Your Obt. Servt.

A. Lincoln—

The Republican Party, with youthful zeal, leaned farther toward abolitionism than Lincoln was willing to go. Partly from political caution, partly because he had not yet thought out his own course, he evaded a commitment.

Springfield,
Novr. 27. 1854

I. Codding, Esq
Dear Sir
   Your note of the 13th. requesting my attendance of the Republican State Central Committee, on the 17th. inst. at Chicago, was, owing to my absence from home, received on the evening of that day (17th) only. While I have pen in hand allow me to say I have been perplexed some to understand why my name was placed on that committee. I was not consulted on the subject; nor was I apprized of the appointment, until I discovered it by accident two or three weeks afterwards. I suppose my opposition to the principle of slavery is as strong as that of any member of the Republican party; but I had also supposed that the *extent* to which I feel authorized to carry that opposition, practically, was not at all satisfactory to that party. The leading men who organized that party, were present, on the 4th. of Oct. at the discussion between Douglas and myself at Springfield, and had full opportunity to not misunderstand my position. Do I misunderstand theirs? Please write, and inform me. Yours truly

A. Lincoln—

Joseph Gillespie, of Edwardsville, had served in the Whig ranks as long as Lincoln, and could be a formidable competitor for the Senate seat. He could be an equally strong ally.

Springfield,
Dec: 1– 1854

J. Gillespie, Esq
My dear Sir
   I have really got it into my head to try to be United States Senator; and if I could have your support my chances would be

reasonably good. But I know, and acknowledge, that you have as just claims to the place as I have; and therefore I do not ask you to yield to me, if you are thinking of becoming a candidate yourself. If, however, you are not, then I should like to be remembered affectionately by you; and also, to have you make a mark for me with the Anti-Nebraska members, down your way. If you know, and have no objection to tell, let me know whether Trumbull intends to make a push. If he does, I suppose the two men in St. Clair, and one or both in Madison will be for him.

We have the legislature clearly enough on joint ballot; but the Senate is very close; and Calhoun told me today that the Nebraska men will stave off the election if they can. Even if we get into joint vote, we shall have difficulty to unite our forces.

Please write me, and let this be confidential.   Your friend as ever

A. Lincoln—

Lincoln took time enough from his political proselyting to write a legal opinion tinged with compassion.

December 18, 1854

John Fitzgerald, eighteen years of age, able-bodied, but without pecuniary means, came directly from Ireland to Springfield, Illinois, and there stopped, and sought employment, with no present intention of returning to Ireland, or going elsewhere. After remaining in the city some three weeks, part of the time employed, and part not, he fell sick, and became a public charge. It has been submitted to me, whether the city of Springfield, or the county of Sangamon is, by law, to bear the charge.

It is my opinion, and decision, that the city is to bear it. I base this upon the construction I give the 4th. Section of the 13th. Article of the new city charter (Approved March 2, 1854). I think the legislature intended that all public charges, arising from the indigence of persons, *resident* within the city, were to be borne by the city—and not by the county. I think it was not the intention that this class of charges was to be parcelled out between the city and county, by critical discussions on the words "citizen," "pauper," and the like.

Dec: 18– 1854.

A. Lincoln—

The Living Lincoln

One of Lincoln's strongest supporters was Elihu B. Washburne of Galena, recently re-elected to Congress. Lincoln kept him informed of what went on in the Illinois legislature. The Springfield lawyer did not allow his hopes to cloud his vision.

(CONFIDENTIAL)

Springfield,
January 6– 1855

Hon: E. B. Washburne.
My dear Sir:

I telegraphed you as to the organization of the two houses. . . .

As to the senatorial election I think very little more is known than was before the meeting of the legislature. Besides the ten or a dozen, on our side, who are willing to be known as candidates, I think there are fifty secretly watching for a chance. I do not know that it is much advantage to have the largest number of votes at the start. If I did know this to be an advantage I should feel better; for I cannot doubt but I have more committals than any other one man. Your district comes up tolerably well for me; but not unanimously by any means – George Gage is for me, as you know. J. H. Adams is not committed to me but I think will be for me. Mr. Talcott will not be for me as a first choice. Dr. Little and Mr. Sargent are openly for me. Prof. Pinckney is for me, but wishes to be quiet. Dr. Whitney writes me that Rev. Mr. Lawrence will be for me; and his manner to me so indicates; but he has not spoken it out. Mr. Swan, I have some slight hopes of. Turner says he is not committed; and I shall get him whenever I can make it appear to be his interest to go for me. Dr. Lyman and old Mr. Diggins will never go for me as a first choice. M. P. Sweet is here as a candidate; and I understand he claims that he has 22 members committed to him. I think some part of his estimate must be based on insufficient evidence; as I cannot well see where they are to be found; and as I can learn the name of one only – Day of La Salle. Still, it may be so. There are more than 22 Anti-Nebraska members who are not committed to me. Tell Norton that Mr. Strunk and Mr. Wheeler come out plump for me; and for which I thank him. Judge Parks I have decided hopes for; but he says he is not committed. I understand myself as having 26 committals; and I

182

do not think any other one man has ten—may be mistaken though. The whole legislature stands,

Senate — A.N. 13 N. 12—
H.R. " 44 " 31—
       $\overline{57}$ " $\overline{43}$

$\overline{43}$

14 maj. All here, but Kinney, of St. Clair.

Our special election here is plain enough when understood. Our adversaries pretended to be running no candidate, secretly notified all their men to be on hand; and, favored by a very rainy day got a complete snap judgment on us. In Novr. Sangamon gave Yates 2166 votes. On the rainy day she gave our man only 984—leaving him 82 votes behind. After all, the result is not of the least consequence. The Locos kept up a great chattering over it till the organization of the HR. since which they all seem to have forgotten it. . . .

Yours as ever
A. Lincoln—

Delayed by a snow storm that crippled transportation, and held back by the inability of factions to unite, the legislature made its tardy choice. An unembittered Lincoln gave Washburne a full report.

Springfield,
Feby. 9–1855

Hon: E. B. Washburne—
My dear Sir:

The agony is over at last; and the result you doubtless know. I write this only to give you some particulars to explain what might appear difficult of understanding. I began with 44 votes, Shields 41, and Trumbull 5—yet Trumbull was elected. In fact 47 different members voted for me—getting three new ones on the second ballot, and losing four old ones. How came my 47 to yield to T's 5? It was Govr. Matteson's work. He has been secretly a candidate every since (before even) the fall election. All the members round about the canal were Anti-Nebraska; but were, nevertheless nearly all Democrats, and old personal friends of his. His plan was to privately impress them with the belief that he was as good Anti-Nebraska as anyone else—at least could be secured to be so by instructions, which could be easily passed. In this way he got from four to six of that sort of men to really prefer his election to that of any other man—all "sub rosa" of course. One notable instance of this sort was with Mr. Strunk of Kankakee. At the beginning of the session he came a volunteer to tell me he was for me & would walk a hundred miles to elect me; but lo, it was not long before he leaked it out that he was going for me the first few ballots & then for Govr. Matteson.

The Nebraska men, of course, were not for Matteson; but when they found they could elect no avowed Nebraska man they tardily determined, to let him get whomever of our men he could by whatever means he could and ask him no questions. In the meantime Osgood, Don. Morrison & Trapp of St. Clair had openly gone over from us. With the united Nebraska force, and their re-cruits, open & covert, it gave Matteson more than enough to elect him. We saw into it plainly ten days ago; but with every possible effort, could not head it off. All that remained of the Anti-Nebraska force, excepting Judd, Cook, Palmer, Baker & Allen of Madison, & two or three of the secret Matteson men, would go into caucus, & I could get the nomination of that caucus. But the three Senators & one of the two representatives above named "could never vote for a Whig" and this incensed some twenty Whigs to "think" they would never vote for the man of the five. So we stood, and so we went into the fight yesterday; the Nebraska men very confident of the election of Matteson, though denying that he was a candidate; and we very much believing also, that they would elect him. But they wanted first to make a show of good faith to Shields by voting for him a few times, and our secret Matteson men also wanted to make a show of good faith by voting with us a few times. So we led off. On the seventh ballot, I think, the signal was given to the Neb. men, to turn on to Matteson, which they acted on to a man, with one exception; my old friend Strunk going with them giving him 44 votes. Next ballot the re-maining Neb. man, & one pretended Anti- went on to him, giving him 46. The next still another giving him 47, wanting only three of an election. In the meantime, our friends with a view of detain-ing our expected bolters had been turning from me to Trumbull till he had risen to 35 & I had been reduced to 15. These would never desert me except by my direction; but I became satisfied that if we could prevent Matteson's election one or two ballots more, we could not possibly do so a single ballot after my friends should begin to return to me from Trumbull. So I determined to strike at once; and accordingly advised my remaining friends to go for him, which they did & elected him on that the 10th. ballot.

Such is the way the thing was done. I think you would have done the same under the circumstances; though Judge Davis, who came down this morning, declares he never would have consented to the 47 men being controlled by the 5. I regret my defeat moderately, but I am not nervous about it. I could have headed off every combination and been elected, had it not been for Matteson's double game—and his defeat now gives me more pleasure than my own gives me pain. On the whole, it is perhaps as well for our general cause that Trumbull is elected. The Neb. men confess that they hate it worse than anything that could have happened. It is a great consolation to see them worse whipped than I am. I tell them it is their own fault—that they had abundant opportunity to choose between him & me, which they declined, and instead forced it on me to decide between him & Matteson.

With my grateful acknowledgments for the kind, active, and continued interest you have taken for me in this matter, allow me to subscribe myself   Yours forever

A. Lincoln—

Although the passage of twenty-three years had dimmed Lincoln's memory, he succeeded in recalling details of his service in the Black Hawk War.

Springfield, Ills,
May 14— 1855

W. F. Boggs, Esq.
Kingston, Mo.

Although my Christian name is *Abraham*, and not *Edward*, the within letter is evidently intended for me. Whether I ever gave Mr. Barnett a discharge I cannot remember; nor do I know whether it would now be proper for me to give him one, not having, or knowing where to find, any of the old rolls or papers of my company. I do very well remember, however, that Clardy Barnett, a small man, with a scar on his face, and not far from my own age, which is now 46, did serve more than fourteen days (near forty I think) in the company of which I had the command as

185

The Living Lincoln

Captain, in Col. —— Thompson's Regiment of Mounted Volunteers, in the Black Hawk War of 1832 — and that he was entitled to an honorable discharge. We went from Sangamon County, Illinois; and Samuel Whiteside of Madison Co, Ills, was our Brigadier General. Yours &c.

A. Lincoln —

The Whig Party, never held together by strong convictions, was falling apart, yet Lincoln was not ready to affiliate with the Republicans. To Owen Lovejoy, ardent abolitionist, brother of the martyred Elijah P. Lovejoy, and Republican leader, Lincoln explained his attitude with quiet candor.

Springfield,
August 11 – 1855

Hon: Owen Lovejoy:
My dear Sir:

Yours of the 7th. was received the day before yesterday. Not even *you* are more anxious to prevent the extension of slavery than I; and yet the political atmosphere is such, just now, that I fear to do anything, lest I do wrong. Know-nothingism has not yet entirely tumbled to pieces — nay, it is even a little encouraged by the late elections in Tennessee, Kentucky & Alabama. Until we can get the elements of this organization, there is not sufficient materials to successfully combat the Nebraska democracy with. We cannot get them so long as they cling to a hope of success under their own organization; and I fear an open push by us now, may offend them, and tend to prevent our ever getting them. About us here, they are mostly my old political and personal friends; and I have hoped their organization would die out without the painful necessity of my taking an open stand against them. Of their principles I think little better than I do of those of the slavery extensionists. Indeed I do not perceive how any one professing to be sensitive to the wrongs of the Negroes, can join in a league to degrade a class of white men.

I have no objection to "fuse" with anybody provided I can fuse on ground which I think is right; and I believe the opponents of slavery extension could now do this, if it were not for this K.N.ism. In many speeches last summer I advised those who did me the honor of a hearing to "stand with anybody who stands right"—and I am still quite willing to follow my own advice. I lately saw, in the Quincy Whig, the report of a preamble and resolutions, made by Mr. Williams, as chairman of a committee, to a public meeting and adopted by the meeting. I saw them but once, and have them not now at command; but so far as I can remember them, they occupy about the ground I should be willing to "fuse" upon.

As to my personal movements this summer, and fall, I am quite busy trying to pick up my lost crumbs of last year. I shall be here till September; then to the circuit till the 20th. then to Cincinnati, awhile, after a patent right case; and back to the circuit to the end of November. I can be seen here any time this month; and at Bloomington at any time from the 10th. to the 17th. of September. As to an extra session of the legislature, I should know no better how to bring that about, than to lift myself over a fence by the straps of my boots. Yours truly

A. Lincoln—

More emotionally, Lincoln defined his principles to a professor of law in Transylvania College, at Lexington, Kentucky. Robertson, visiting Springfield in Lincoln's absence, had left a copy of his *Scrap Book on Law and Politics, Men and Times.* Lincoln's acknowledgment foreshadowed by almost three years the theme of one of his greatest speeches.

Springfield, Ills.
Aug. 15. 1855

Hon: Geo. Robertson
Lexington, Ky.
My dear Sir:
The volume you left for me has been received. I am really grateful for the honor of your kind remembrance, as well as for the book. The partial reading I have already given it, has afforded me much of both pleasure and instruction. It was new to me that the exact question which led to the Missouri Compromise, had arisen before it arose in regard to Missouri; and that you had taken so prominent a part in it. Your short, but able and patriotic speech upon that occasion, has not been improved upon since, by those holding the same views; and, with all the lights you then had, the views you took appear to me as very reasonable.

The Living Lincoln

You are not a friend of slavery in the abstract. In that speech you spoke of *"the peaceful extinction* of *slavery"* and used other expressions indicating your belief that the thing was, at some time, to have an end. Since then we have had thirty-six years of experience; and this experience has demonstrated, I think, that there is no peaceful extinction of slavery in prospect for us. The signal failure of Henry Clay, and other good and great men, in 1849, to effect anything in favor of gradual emancipation in Kentucky, together with a thousand other signs, extinguishes that hope utterly. On the question of liberty, as a principle, we are not what we have been. When we were the political slaves of King George, and wanted to be free, we called the maxim that "all men are created equal" a self-evident truth; but now when we have grown fat, and have lost all dread of being slaves ourselves, we have become so greedy to be *masters* that we call the same maxim "a self-evident lie." The Fourth of July has not quite dwindled away; it is still a great day—*for burning fire-crackers!!!*

The spirit which desired the peaceful extinction of slavery, has itself become extinct, with the *occasion,* and the *men* of the Revolution. Under the impulse of that occasion, nearly half the states adopted systems of emancipation at once; and it is a significant fact, that not a single state has done the like since. So far as peaceful, voluntary emancipation is concerned, the condition of the Negro slave in America, scarcely less terrible to the contemplation of a free mind, is now as fixed, and hopeless of change for the better, as that of the lost souls of the finally impenitent. The Autocrat of all the Russias will resign his crown, and proclaim his subjects free republicans sooner than will our American masters voluntarily give up their slaves.

Our political problem now is "Can we, as a nation, continue together *permanently—forever—*half-slave, and half-free?" The problem is too mighty for me. May God, in his mercy, superintend the solution. Your much obliged friend, and humble servant

A. Lincoln—

To Joshua Speed, Lincoln unburdened himself with frankness. Over the years, the sight of manacled slaves that he had once described to Speed's sister in mere wonderment had taken on a grim aspect. Yet he saw no reason why differing opinions should disrupt an old friendship.

National Emergence

Springfield, Aug: 24, 1855

Dear Speed:

You know what a poor correspondent I am. Ever since I received your very agreeable letter of the 22nd. of May I have been intending to write you in answer to it. You suggest that in political action now, you and I would differ. I suppose we would; not quite as much, however, as you may think. You know I dislike slavery; and you fully admit the abstract wrong of it. So far there is no cause of difference. But you say that sooner than yield your legal right to the slave—especially at the bidding of those who are not themselves interested, you would see the Union dissolved. I am not aware that *any one* is bidding you to yield that right; very certainly *I* am not. I leave that matter entirely to yourself. I also acknowledge *your* rights and *my* obligations, under the Constitution, in regard to your slaves. I confess I hate to see the poor creatures hunted down, and caught, and carried back to their stripes, and unrewarded toils; but I bite my lip and keep quiet. In 1841 you and I had together a tedious low-water trip, on a steamboat from Louisville to St. Louis. You may remember, as I well do, that from Louisville to the mouth of the Ohio there were, on board, ten or a dozen slaves, shackled together with irons. That sight was a continual torment to me; and I see something like it every time I touch the Ohio, or any other slave-border. It is hardly fair for you to assume, that I have no interest in a thing which has, and continually exercises, the power of making me miserable. You ought rather to appreciate how much the great body of the Northern people do crucify their feelings, in order to maintain their loyalty to the Constitution and the Union.

I do oppose the extension of slavery, because my judgment and feelings so prompt me; and I am under no obligation to the contrary. If for this you and I must differ, differ we must. You say if you were President, you would send an army and hang the leaders of the Missouri outrages upon the Kansas elections; still, if Kansas fairly votes herself a slave state, she must be admitted, or the Union must be dissolved. But how if she votes herself a slave state *unfairly*—that is, by the very means for which you say you would hang men? Must she still be admitted, or the Union be dissolved? That will be the phase of the question when it first becomes a practical one. In your assumption that there may be a *fair* decision of the slavery question in Kansas, I plainly see you and I would differ about the Nebraska law. I look upon that enactment not as a *law,* but as *violence* from the beginning. It was conceived in violence, passed in violence, is maintained in violence, and is being executed in violence. I say it was *conceived* in violence, because the destruction of the Missouri Compromise, under the circumstances, was nothing less than violence. It was *passed* in violence, because it could not have passed at all but for the votes of many members, in violent disregard of the known will of their constituents. It is *maintained* in violence because the elections since, clearly demand its repeal, and this demand is openly disregarded. *You* say men ought to be hung for the way they are executing that law; and *I* say the way it is being executed is quite as good as any of its antecedents. It is being executed in the precise way which was intended from the first; else why does no Nebraska man express astonishment or condemnation? Poor Reeder is the only public man who has been silly enough to believe that any thing like fairness was ever intended; and he has been bravely undeceived.

That Kansas will form a slave constitution, and, with it, will ask to be admitted into the Union, I take to be an already settled question; and so settled by the very means you so pointedly condemn. By every principle of law, ever held by any court, north or south, every Negro taken to Kansas is free; yet in utter disregard of this—in the spirit of violence merely—that beautiful legislature gravely passes a law to hang men who shall venture to inform a Negro of his legal rights. This is the substance, and real object of the law. If, like Haman, they should hang upon the gallows of their own building, I shall not be among the mourners for their fate.

In my humble sphere, I shall advocate the restoration of the Missouri Compromise, so long as Kansas remains a territory; and when, by all these foul means, it seeks to come into the Union as a slave state, I shall oppose it. I am very loth, in any case, to withhold my assent to the enjoyment of property *acquired,* or *located,* in good faith; but I do not admit that *good faith,* in taking a Negro to Kansas, to be held in slavery, is a *possibility* with any man. Any man who has sense enough to be the controller of his own property, has too much sense to misunderstand the outrageous character of this whole Nebraska business. But I digress. In my opposition to the admission of Kansas I shall have some company; but we may be beaten. If we are, I shall not, on that account, attempt to dissolve the Union. On the contrary, if we succeed, there will be enough of us to take care of the Union. I think it probable, however, we shall be beaten. Standing as a unit among yourselves, you can, directly, and indirectly, bribe enough of our men to carry the day—as you could on an open proposition to establish monarchy. Get hold of some man in the North, whose position and ability is such, that he can make the support of your measure—whatever it may be—a *Democratic party necessity,* and the thing is done. *Apropos* of this, let me tell you an anecdote. Douglas introduced the Nebraska bill in January. In February afterwards, there was a call session of the Illinois legislature. Of the one hundred members composing the two branches of that body, about seventy were Democrats. These latter held a caucus, in which the Nebraska bill was talked of, if not formally discussed. It was thereby discovered that just three, and no more, were in favor of the measure. In a day or two Douglas' orders came on to have resolutions passed approving the bill; and they were passed by large majorities!!! The truth of this is vouched for by a bolting Democratic member. The masses too, Democratic as well as Whig, were even nearer unanimous against it; but as soon as the party necessity of supporting it, became apparent, the way the Democracy began to see the *wisdom* and *justice* of it, was perfectly astonishing.

You say if Kansas fairly votes herself a free state, as a Christian you will rather rejoice at it. All decent slave-holders *talk* that way; and I do not doubt their candor. But they never *vote* that way. Although in a private letter, or conversation, you will express your preference that Kansas shall be free, you would vote for no man for Congress who would say the same thing publicly. No such man could be elected from any district in any slave state. You think Stringfellow & Co. ought to be hung; and yet, at the next presidential election you will vote for the exact type and representative of Stringfellow. The slave-breeders and slave-traders, are a small, odious and detested class, among you; and yet in politics, they dictate the course of all of you, and are as completely your masters, as you are the masters of your own Negroes.

You enquire where I now stand. That is a disputed point. I think I am a Whig; but others say there are no Whigs, and that I am an abolitionist. When I was at Washington I voted for the Wilmot Proviso as good as forty times, and I never heard of any one attempting to unwhig me for that. I now do no more than oppose the *extension* of slavery.

I am not a Know-Nothing. That is certain. How could I be? How can any one who abhors the oppression of Negroes, be in favor of degrading classes of white people? Our progress in degeneracy appears to me to be pretty rapid. As a nation, we began by declaring that *"all men are created equal."* We now practically read it "all men are created equal, *except Negroes.*" When the Know-Nothings get control, it will read "all men are created equal, except Negroes, *and foreigners, and Catholics.*" When it comes to this I should prefer emigrating to some country where they make no pretence of loving liberty—to Russia, for instance, where despotism can be taken pure, and without the base alloy of hypocrisy.

Mary will probably pass a day or two in Louisville in October. My kindest regards to Mrs. Speed. On the leading subject of this letter, I have more of her sympathy than I have of yours.

And yet let me say I am　　Your friend forever

A. Lincoln—

After almost thirty years, Lincoln could still recommend the course he had followed to a young man aspiring to the law.

Springfield,
Novr. 5– 1855

Isham Reavis, Esq.
My dear Sir:

I have just reached home, and found your letter of the 23rd. ult. I am from home too much of my time, for a young man to read law with me advantageously. If you are resolutely determined to make a lawyer of yourself, the thing is more than half-done already. It is but a small matter whether you read *with* anybody or not. I did not read with anyone. Get the books, and read and study them till you understand them in their principal features; and that is the main thing. It is of no consequence to be in a large town while you are reading. I read at New Salem, which never had three hundred people living in it. The *books,* and your *capacity* for understanding them, are just the same in all places. Mr. Dummer *

---

* In 1837 Henry E. Dummer had made an opening for Lincoln in John T. Stuart's law office by removing from Springfield to Beardstown. There Dummer still practiced.

is a very clever man and an excellent lawyer (much better than I, in law-learning); and I have no doubt he will cheerfully tell you what books to read, and also loan you the books.

Always bear in mind that your own resolution to succeed, is more important than any other one thing. Very truly Your friend
A. Lincoln

Lincoln cherished the right of the professional man to set his own fees.

Springfield, Illinois,
February 21, 1856.

Mr. George P. Floyd,
Quincy, Illinois.
Dear Sir:
I have just received yours of 16th, with check on Flagg & Savage for twenty-five dollars. You must think I am a high-priced man. You are too liberal with your money.

Fifteen dollars is enough for the job. I send you a receipt for fifteen dollars, and return to you a ten dollar bill. Yours truly,
A. Lincoln.

The practical politician, aware that idealism counts for nothing until it is registered in votes, spoke in a letter to Lyman Trumbull, who occupied the seat in the United States Senate to which Lincoln had aspired eighteen months earlier. In John McLean, a seventy-one-year-old associate justice of the United States Supreme Court, Lincoln saw more political strength than posterity has discerned. William H. Bissell was the Republican nominee for Governor.

Springfield, June 7, 1856

Hon: Lyman Trumbull
My dear Sir:
The news of Buchanan's nomination came yesterday; and a good many Whigs, of conservative feelings, and slight pro-slavery proclivities, withal, are inclining to go for him, and will do it, unless the Anti-Nebraska nomination shall be such as to divert them. The man to effect that object is Judge McLean; and his nomination would save every Whig, except such as have already gone over hook and line, as Singleton, Morrison, Constable, & others. J. T. Stuart, Anthony Thornton, James M. Davis (the old settler) and

others like them, will heartily go for McLean, but will everyone go for Buchanan, as against Chase, Banks, Seward, Blair or Fremont? I think they would stand Blair or Fremont for Vice-President—but not more.

Now there is a grave question to be considered. Nine-tenths of the Anti-Nebraska votes have to come from old Whigs. In setting stakes, is it safe to totally disregard them? Can we possibly win, if we do so? So far they have been disregarded. I need not point out the instances.

I think I may trust you to believe I do not say this on my own personal account. I am *in,* and shall go for any one nominated unless he be *"platformed"* expressly, or impliedly, on some ground which I may think wrong.

Since the nomination of Bissell we are in good trim in Illinois, save at the point I have indicated. If we can save pretty nearly all the Whigs, we shall elect him, I think, by a very large majority.

I address this to you, because your influence in the Anti-Nebraska nomination will be greater than that of any other Illinoisan.

Let this be confidential. Yours very truly

A. Lincoln

In the spring of 1856 Lincoln joined the Republican Party. In mid-June the Republican National Convention nominated John C. Fremont for the presidency—and gave an indication of Lincoln's growing reputation when 110 delegates voted for him as the vice-presidential nominee.

In the ensuing campaign, Lincoln made more than fifty speeches. None was printed in its entirety, but the tenor of all may be inferred from the few passages which a reporter for the *Weekly North-Western Gazette* of Galena recorded verbatim when Lincoln spoke there on July 23.

Mr. LINCOLN was addressing himself to the opponents of Fremont and the Republican party, and had referred to the charge of "sectionalism," and then spoke something as follows in relation to another charge, and said:

"You further charge us with being Disunionists. If you mean that it is our aim to dissolve the Union, for myself I answer, that is untrue; for those who act with me I answer, that it is untrue. Have you heard us assert that as our aim? Do you really believe that such is our aim? Do you find it in our platform, our speeches, our conversation, or anywhere? If not, withdraw the charge.

"But, you may say, that though it is not your *aim*, it will be the result, if we succeed, and that we are therefore Disunionists in fact. This is a grave charge you make against us, and we certainly have a right to demand that you specify in what way we are to dissolve the Union. How are we to effect this?

"The only specification offered is volunteered by Mr. Fillmore, in his Albany speech. His charge is, that if we elect a President and Vice President both from the free states, it will dissolve the Union. This is open folly. The Constitution provides, that the President and Vice President of the United States shall be of different states; but says nothing as to the latitude and longitude of those states. In 1828, Andrew Jackson of Tennessee, and John C. Calhoun of South Carolina, were elected President and Vice President, both from slave states; but no one thought of dissolving the Union then, on that account. In 1840, Harrison of Ohio, and Tyler of Virginia, were elected. In 1841, Harrison died, and John Tyler succeeded to the Presidency, and William R. King, of Alabama, was elected acting Vice-President by the Senate; but no one supposed that the Union was in danger. In fact, at the very time Mr. Fillmore uttered this idle charge, the state of things in the United States disproved it. Mr. Pierce of New Hampshire, and Mr. Bright of Indiana,—both from free states,—are President and Vice President; and the Union stands, and *will* stand. You do not contend that it ought to dissolve the Union, and the facts show that it *won't;* therefore, the charge may be dismissed without further consideration.

"No other specification is made, and the only one that could be made is, that the restoration of the restriction of '87, making the United States territory free territory, would dissolve the Union. Gentlemen, it will require a decided majority to pass such an act. We, the majority, being able constitutionally to do all that we purpose, would have no desire to dissolve the Union. Do you say that such restriction of slavery would be unconstitutional and that some of the states would not submit to its enforcement? I grant you that an unconstitutional act is not a law; but I do not ask, and will not take your construction of the Constitution. The Supreme Court of the United States is the tribunal to decide such questions, and we will submit to its decisions; and if you do also, there will be an end of the matter. Will you? If not, who are the Disunionists, you or we? We, the majority, would not strive to dissolve the Union; and if any attempt is made it must be by you, who so loudly stigmatize us as Disunionists. But the Union, in any event, won't be dissolved. We don't want to dissolve it, and if you attempt it, *we won't let you.* With the purse and sword, the army and navy and treasury in our hands and at our command, you *couldn't do it.* This government would be very weak, indeed, if a majority, with a disciplined army and navy, and a well-filled treasury, could not preserve itself, when attacked by an unarmed, undisciplined, unorganized minority.

"All this talk about the dissolution of the Union is humbug— nothing but folly. *We won't* dissolve the Union, and *you shan't.*"

To the President of Illinois College at nearby Jacksonville, Lincoln read a little lesson on the motives that move men of principle.

Springfield,
Sept. 27. 1856

Rev. J. M. Sturtevant
Jacksonville, Ills
My dear Sir:
Owing to absence yours of the 16th. was not received till the day-before-yesterday. I thank you for your good opinion of me personally, and still more for the deep interest you take in the cause of our common country. It pains me a little that you have deemed it necessary to point out to me how I may be compensated for throwing myself in the breach now. This assumes that I am merely calculating the chances of personal advancement. Let me assure you that I decline to be a candidate for Congress, on my clear conviction, that my running would *hurt,* & not *help* the cause. I am willing to make any personal sacrifice, but I am not willing to do, what in my own judgment, is, a sacrifice of the cause itself. Very truly Yours

A. Lincoln

"The truth about Mr. Lincoln," said William H. Herndon, "is that he read less and thought more than any man in his sphere in America." Herndon exaggerated, but only by magnifying a truth. Lincoln thought incessantly; and often, to give his thoughts precision, he committed them to paper. Here is a reflection on his own career as contrasted with that of Stephen A. Douglas.

[*December, 1856*]

Twenty-two years ago Judge Douglas and I first became acquainted. We were both young then; he a trifle younger than I. Even then, we were both ambitious; I, perhaps, quite as much so as he. With *me,* the race of ambition has been a failure—a flat failure; with *him* it has been one of splendid success. His name fills the nation; and is not unknown, even, in foreign lands. I affect no contempt for the high eminence he has reached. So reached, that the oppressed of my species, might have shared with me in the elevation, I would rather stand on that eminence, than wear the richest crown that ever pressed a monarch's brow.

In the presidential election of 1856 James Buchanan, Democrat, defeated Fremont and Millard Fillmore, the candidate of the American, or Know-Nothing, party. But in Illinois, the Republican state ticket swept the field. Chicago Republicans celebrated the result with a banquet, on December 10, at which Lincoln was an honored guest. By pre-arrangement he responded to the first of the regular toasts: "The Union—The North will maintain it—the South will not depart therefrom."

December 10, 1856

We have another annual presidential message. Like a rejected lover, making merry at the wedding of his rival, the President felicitates hugely over the late presidential election. He considers the result a signal triumph of good principles and good men, and a very pointed rebuke of bad ones. He says the people did it. He forgets that the "people," as he complacently calls only those who voted for Buchanan, are in a minority of the whole people, by about four hundred thousand voters—one full tenth of all the voters. Remembering this, he might perceive that the "rebuke" may not be quite as durable as he seems to think—that the majority may not choose to remain permanently rebuked by that minority.

The President thinks the great body of us Fremonters, being ardently attached to liberty, in the abstract, were duped by a few wicked and designing men. There is a slight difference of opinion

197

on this. We think *he,* being ardently attached to the hope of a second term, *in the concrete,* was duped by men who had liberty every way. He is in the cat's paw. By much dragging of chestnuts from the fire for others to eat, his claws are burnt off to the gristle, and he is thrown aside as unfit for further use. As the fool said to King Lear, when his daughters had turned him out of doors, "He's a shelled pea's cod."

So far as the President charges us "with a desire to change the domestic institutions of existing states"; and of "doing everything in our power to deprive the Constitution and the laws of moral authority," for the whole party, on *belief,* and for myself, on *knowledge* I pronounce the charge an unmixed, and unmitigated falsehood.

Our government rests in public opinion. Whoever can change public opinion, can change the government, practically just so much. Public opinion, on any subject, always has a *"central idea,"* from which all its minor thoughts radiate. That "central idea" in our political public opinion, at the beginning was, and until recently has continued to be, "the equality of men." And although it was always submitted patiently to whatever of inequality there seemed to be as matter of actual necessity, its constant working has been a steady progress towards the practical equality of all men. The late presidential election was a struggle, by one party, to discard that central idea, and to substitute for it the opposite idea that slavery is right, in the abstract, the workings of which, as a central idea, may be the perpetuity of human slavery, and its extension to all countries and colors. Less than a year ago, the Richmond *Enquirer,* an avowed advocate of slavery, regardless of color, in order to favor his views, invented the phrase, "state equality," and now the President, in his message, adopts the *Enquirer's* catch-phrase, telling us the people "have asserted the constitutional equality of each and all of the states of the Union as states." The President flatters himself that the new central idea is completely inaugurated; and so, indeed, it is, so far as the mere fact of a presidential election can inaugurate it. To us it is left to know that the majority of the people have not yet declared for it, and to hope that they never will.

All of us who did not vote for Mr. Buchanan, taken together, are a majority of four hundred thousand. But, in the late contest we were divided between Fremont and Fillmore. Can we not come together, for the future? Let everyone who really believes, and is resolved, that free society is not, *and shall not be,* a failure, and who can conscientiously declare that in the past contest he has done only what he thought best—let every one have charity to believe that every other one can say as much. Thus let bygones be bygones. Let past differences, as nothing be; and with steady eye on the real issue, let us reinaugurate the good old "central ideas" of the Republic. We *can* do it. The human heart *is* with us—God is with us. We shall again be able not to declare, that "all states as states, are equal," nor yet that "all citizens as citizens are equal," but to renew the broader, better declaration, including both these and much more, that "all *men* are created equal."

An outburst of temper on Mrs. Lincoln's part put her husband in a humiliating position. He could not make the necessary apology without revealing some of the tensions of his home life.

Springfield, Ill., February 20, 1857.

(PRIVATE.)
John E. Rosette, Esq.
Dear Sir:
Your note about the little paragraph in the Republican was received yesterday, since which time I have been too unwell to notice it. I had not supposed you wrote or approved it. The whole originated in mistake. You know by the conversation with me that I thought the establishment of the paper unfortunate, but I always expected to throw no obstacle in its way, and to patronize it to the extent of taking and paying for one copy. When the paper was brought to my house, my wife said to me, "Now are you going to take another worthless little paper?" I said to her *evasively,* "I have not directed the paper to be left." From this, in my absence, she sent the message to the carrier. This is the whole story. Yours truly,

A. Lincoln.

As a Republican, Lincoln evaluated the party and its prospects.

[c. February 28, 1857]
Upon those men who are, in sentiment, opposed to the spread, and nationalization of slavery, rests the task of preventing it. The

Republican organization is the embodiment of that sentiment; though, as yet, it by no means embraces all the individuals holding that sentiment. The party is newly formed; and in forming, old party ties had to be broken, and the attractions of party pride, and influential leaders were wholly wanting. In spite of old differences, prejudices, and animosities, its members were drawn together by a paramount common danger. They formed and manouvered in the face of the disciplined enemy, and in the teeth of all his persistent misrepresentations. Of course, they fell far short of gathering in all of their own. And yet, a year ago, they stood up, an army over thirteen hundred thousand strong. That army is, today, the best hope of the nation, and of the world. Their work is before them; and from which they may not guiltlessly turn away.

On March 6, 1857, the Supreme Court of the United States handed down a decision in the case of a Negro whose status as slave or freeman had come to dramatize the slavery issue. Dred Scott, a slave, had been taken by his master to Illinois and later to Wisconsin Territory. After four years his master took him back to Missouri. Years later, Dred Scott sued for his freedom in the Missouri courts, contending that residence on free soil had effected his emancipation. In time the case reached the Supreme Court.

Each of the nine justices wrote a separate opinion, but that of Chief Justice Taney represented the majority. Taney held that Scott was not a citizen of the United States or the state of Missouri, and therefore could not sue in the Federal courts. Not content with deciding the issue, the Chief Justice went further: the Missouri Compromise was unconstitutional. Thus in effect he upheld one of the basic provisions of Douglas's Nebraska Bill. Had Taney set out purposely to infuriate the anti-slavery forces of the country he could have chosen no surer means.

While bitter recriminations over the court's decision rocked the country, the grand jury of the United States Court met in Springfield. Learning that Douglas was in the city, the jurors invited him to speak on the issues of the day, and particularly the Dred Scott decision. When he responded on June 12 Representatives' Hall in the State House was crowded to capacity. Lincoln sat in the audience.

Two weeks later Lincoln stood in the same room to reply in behalf of the Republicans of Illinois. Instead of limiting himself to the technical weaknesses of the Dred Scott decision he sought, and found, a broader base.

June 26, 1857

Fellow Citizens:

I am here tonight, partly by the invitation of some of you, and partly by my own inclination. Two weeks ago Judge Douglas spoke here on the several subjects of Kansas, the Dred Scott decision, and Utah. I listened to the speech at the time, and have read the report of it since. It was intended to controvert opinions which I think just, and to assail (politically, not personally,) those men who, in common with me, entertain those opinions. For this reason I wished then, and still wish, to make some answer to it, which I now take the opportunity of doing. . . .

Judicial decisions are of greater or less authority as precedents, according to circumstances. That this should be so, accords both with common sense, and the customary understanding of the legal profession.

If this important decision had been made by the unanimous concurrence of the judges, and without any apparent partisan bias, and in accordance with legal public expectation, and with the steady practice of the departments throughout our history, and had been, in no part, based on assumed historical facts which are not really true; or, if wanting in some of these, it had been before the court more than once, and had there been affirmed and re-affirmed through a course of years, it then might be, perhaps would be, factious, nay, even revolutionary, to not acquiesce in it as a precedent.

But when, as it is true we find it wanting in all these claims to the public confidence, it is not resistance, it is not factious, it is not even disrespectful, to treat it as not having yet quite established a settled doctrine for the country. . . .

I have said, in substance, that the Dred Scott decision was, in part, based on assumed historical facts which were not really true; and I ought not to leave the subject without giving some reasons for saying this; I therefore give an instance or two, which I think fully sustain me. Chief Justice Taney, in delivering the opinion of the majority of the court, insists at great length that Negroes were no part of the people who made, or for whom was made, the Declaration of Independence, or the Constitution of the United States. . . . This assumption is a mistake. In some trifling particulars, the condition of that race has been ameliorated; but, as a whole, in this country, the change between then and now is decidedly the other way; and their ultimate destiny has never appeared so hopeless as in the last three or four years. In two of the five states—New Jersey and North Carolina—that then gave the free Negro the right of voting, the right has since been taken away; and in a third—New York—it has been greatly abridged; while it has not been extended, so far as I know, to a single additional state, though the number of the states has more than doubled. In those days, as I understand, masters could, at their own pleasure, emancipate their slaves; but since then, such legal restraints have been made upon emancipation, as to amount almost to prohibition. In those days, legislatures held the unquestioned power to abolish slavery in their respective states; but now it is becoming quite fashionable for state constitutions to withhold that power from the legislatures. In those days, by common consent, the spread of the black man's bondage to new countries was prohibited; but now, Congress decides that it *will* not continue the prohibition, and the Supreme Court decides that it *could* not if it would. In those days, our Declaration of Independence was held sacred by all, and thought to include all; but now, to aid in making the bondage of the Negro universal and eternal, it is assailed, and sneered at, and construed, and hawked at, and torn, till, if its framers could rise from their graves, they could not at all recognize it. All the powers of earth seem rapidly combining against him. Mammon is after him; ambition follows, and philosophy follows, and the theology of the day is fast joining the cry. They have him in his prison house; they have searched his person, and left no prying instrument with him. One after another they have closed the heavy iron doors upon him, and now they have him, as it were, bolted in with a lock of a hundred keys, which can never be unlocked without the concurrence of every key; the keys in the hands of a hundred different men, and they scattered to a hundred different and distant places; and they stand musing as to what invention, in all the dominions of mind and matter, can be produced to make the impossibility of his escape more complete than it is.

It is grossly incorrect to say or assume, that the public estimate of the Negro is more favorable now than it was at the origin of the government.

Three years and a half ago, Judge Douglas brought forward

his famous Nebraska bill. The country was at once in a blaze. He scorned all opposition, and carried it through Congress. Since then he has seen himself superseded in a presidential nomination, by one indorsing the general doctrine of his measure, but at the same time standing clear of the odium of its untimely agitation, and its gross breach of national faith; and he has seen that successful rival constitutionally elected, not by the strength of friends, but by the division of adversaries, being in a popular minority of nearly four hundred thousand votes. He has seen his chief aids in his own state, Shields and Richardson, politically speaking, successively tried, convicted, and executed, for an offense not their own, but his. And now he sees his own case, standing next on the docket for trial.

There is a natural disgust in the minds of nearly all white people, to the idea of an indiscriminate amalgamation of the white and black races; and Judge Douglas evidently is basing his chief hope, upon the chances of being able to appropriate the benefit of this disgust to himself. If he can, by much drumming and repeating, fasten the odium of that idea upon his adversaries, he thinks he can struggle through the storm. He therefore clings to this hope, as a drowning man to the last plank. He makes an occasion for lugging it in from the opposition to the Dred Scott decision. He finds the Republicans insisting that the Declaration of Independence includes *all* men, black as well as white; and forthwith he boldly denies that it includes Negroes at all, and proceeds to argue gravely that all who contend it does, do so only because they want to vote, and eat, and sleep, and marry with Negroes! He will have it that they cannot be consistent else. Now I protest against that counterfeit logic which concludes that, because I do not want a black woman for a *slave* I must necessarily want her for a *wife*. I need not have her for either, I can just leave her alone. In some respects she certainly is not my equal; but in her natural right to eat the bread she earns with her own hands without asking leave of any one else, she is my equal, and the equal of all others.

Chief Justice Taney, in his opinion in the Dred Scott case, admits that the language of the Declaration is broad enough to include the whole human family, but he and Judge Douglas argue that the authors of that instrument did not intend to include Negroes, by the fact that they did not at once, actually place them on an equality with the whites. Now this grave argument comes to just nothing at all, by the other fact, that they did not at once, *or*

ever afterwards, actually place all white people on an equality with
one or another. And this is the staple argument of both the Chief
Justice and the Senator, for doing this obvious violence to the
plain unmistakable language of the Declaration. I think the authors
of that notable instrument intended to include *all* men, but they
did not intend to declare all men equal *in all respects.* They did
not mean to say all were equal in color, size, intellect, moral de-
velopments, or social capacity. They defined with tolerable dis-
tinctness, in what respects they did consider all men created equal
—equal in "certain inalienable rights, among which are life, liberty,
and the pursuit of happiness." This they said, and this meant. They
did not mean to assert the obvious untruth, that all were then actually enjoying that equality, nor yet, that they were about to confer it immediately upon them. In fact they had no power to confer
such a boon. They meant simply to declare the *right,* so that the
enforcement of it might follow as fast as circumstances should
permit. They meant to set up a standard maxim for free society,
which should be familiar to all, and revered by all; constantly
looked to, constantly labored for, and even though never perfectly
attained, constantly approximated, and thereby constantly spreading and deepening its influence, and augmenting the happiness and
value of life to all people of all colors everywhere. The assertion
that "all men are created equal" was of no practical use in effecting
our separation from Great Britain; and it was placed in the Declaration, not for that, but for future use. Its authors meant it to be,
thank God, it is now proving itself, a stumbling block to those who
in after times might seek to turn a free people back into the hateful
paths of despotism. They knew the proneness of prosperity to
breed tyrants, and they meant when such should re-appear in this
fair land and commence their vocation they should find left for
them at least one hard nut to crack.

I have now briefly expressed my view of the *meaning* and *objects* of that part of the Declaration of Independence which declares that "all men are created equal.". . .

Then Lincoln quoted Douglas on the same subject.

"No man can vindicate the character, motives and conduct of
the signers of the Declaration of Independence, except upon the
hypothesis that they referred to the white race alone, and not to
the African, when they declared all men to have been created

equal—that they were speaking of British subjects on this continent being equal to British subjects born and residing in Great Britain—that they were entitled to the same inalienable rights, and among them were enumerated life, liberty and the pursuit of happiness. The Declaration was adopted for the purpose of justifying the colonists in the eyes of the civilized world in withdrawing their allegiance from the British crown, and dissolving their connection with the mother country."

My good friends, read that carefully over some leisure hour, and ponder well upon it—see what a mere wreck—mangled ruin—it makes of our once glorious Declaration.

"They were speaking of British subjects on this continent being equal to British subjects born and residing in Great Britain!" Why, according to this, not only Negroes but white people outside of Great Britain and America are not spoken of in that instrument. The English, Irish and Scotch, along with white Americans, were included to be sure, but the French, Germans and other white people of the world are all gone to pot along with the Judge's inferior races.

I had thought the Declaration promised something better than the condition of British subjects; but no, it only meant that we should be *equal* to them in their own oppressed and *unequal* condition. According to that, it gave no promise that having kicked off the King and Lords of Great Britain, we should not at once be saddled with a King and Lords of our own.

I had thought the Declaration contemplated the progressive improvement in the condition of all men everywhere; but no, it merely "was adopted for the purpose of justifying the colonists in the eyes of the civilized world in withdrawing their allegiance from the British crown, and dissolving their connection with the mother country." Why, that object having been effected some eighty years ago, the Declaration is of no practical use now—mere rubbish—old wadding left to rot on the battlefield after the victory is won.

I understand you are preparing to celebrate the Fourth, tomorrow week. What for? The doings of that day had no reference to the present; and quite half of you are not even descendants of those who were referred to at that day. But I suppose you will celebrate; and will even go so far as to read the Declaration. Suppose after you read it once in the old-fashioned way, you read it once more with Judge Douglas' version. It will then run thus: "We hold these truths to be self-evident that all British subjects who were on this continent eighty-one years ago, were created equal to all British subjects born and *then* residing in Great Britain."

And now I appeal to all—to Democrats as well as others,—are you really willing that the Declaration shall be thus frittered away? —thus left no more at most, than an interesting memorial of the dead past? thus shorn of its vitality, and practical value; and left without the *germ* or even the *suggestion* of the individual rights of man in it?

But Judge Douglas is especially horrified at the thought of the mixing blood by the white and black races: agreed for once—a thousand times agreed. There are white men enough to marry all the white women, and black men enough to marry all the black women; and so let them be married. On this point we fully agree with the Judge; and when he shall show that his policy is better adapted to prevent amalgamation than ours we shall drop ours, and adopt his. . . .

I have said that the separation of the races is the only perfect preventive of amalgamation. I have no right to say all the members of the Republican party are in favor of this, nor to say that as a party they are in favor of it. There is nothing in their platform directly on the subject. But I can say a very large proportion of its members are for it, and that the chief plank in their platform— opposition to the spread of slavery—is most favorable to that separation.

Such separation, if ever effected at all, must be effected by colonization; and no political party, as such, is now doing anything directly for colonization. Party operations at present only favor or retard colonization incidentally. The enterprise is a difficult one; but "when there is a will there is a way;" and what colonization needs most is a hearty will. Will springs from the two elements of moral sense and self-interest. Let us be brought to believe it is morally right, and, at the same time, favorable to, or, at least, not against, our interest, to transfer the African to his native clime, and we shall find a way to do it, however great the task may be. The children of Israel, to such numbers as to include four hundred thousand fighting men, went out of Egyptian bondage in a body.

How differently the respective courses of the Democratic and Republican parties incidentally bear on the question of forming a will—a public sentiment—for colonization, is easy to see. The Republicans inculcate, with whatever of ability they can, that the Negro is a man; that his bondage is cruelly wrong, and that the field of his oppression ought not to be enlarged. The Democrats deny his manhood; deny, or dwarf to insignificance, the wrong of his bondage; so far as possible, crush all sympathy for him, and cultivate and excite hatred and disgust against him; compliment themselves as Union-savers for doing so; and call the indefinite outspreading of his bondage "a sacred right of self-government."

The plainest print cannot be read through a gold eagle; and it will be ever hard to find many men who will send a slave to Liberia, and pay his passage while they can send him to a new country, Kansas for instance, and sell him for fifteen hundred dollars, and the rise.

As the last months of the year 1857 slipped past Lincoln contemplated, at first with satisfaction, a quarrel among his Democratic adversaries. Rebelling against the party dictatorship of President Buchanan, Douglas had broken with the administration over a constitution for Kansas—the Lecompton constitution—which he considered a violation of the principle of popular sovereignty.

On this ground, Douglas's stand coincided with that of the Republicans. "Perhaps," some eastern members of the party seemed to be saying, "this man deserves our support when he comes up for reelection in 1858." When Horace Greeley, editor of the New York *Tribune,* took this tack Lincoln became apprehensive. He intended to give Douglas the race of his life, and wanted no interference from distant doctrinaires who knew nothing of the Little Giant's real principles and did not understand the political situation in Illinois.

Bloomington, Dec. 28, 1857–

Hon. Lyman Trumbull.
Dear Sir:

What does the New-York Tribune mean by its constant eulogizing, and admiring, and magnifying of Douglas? Does it, in this, speak the sentiments of the Republicans at Washington? Have they concluded that the Republican cause, generally, can be best promoted by sacrificing us here in Illinois? If so we would like to know it soon; it will save us a great deal of labor to surrender at once.

As yet I have heard of no Republican here going over to

Douglas; but if the Tribune continues to din his praises into the ears of its five or ten thousand Republican readers in Illinois, it is more than can be hoped that all will stand firm.

I am not complaining. I only wish a fair understanding. Please write me at Springfield. Your Obt. Servt.

A. Lincoln—

In writing to the editor of the Greenville, Illinois, *Advocate,* Lincoln assumed that he would be the Republican candidate to oppose Douglas. But Lincoln still worried over the possibility that his opponent would receive some Republican support.

Springfield,
May 15. 1858

J. F. Alexander, Esq
Greenville, Ills.
My dear Sir:

I reached home a week ago and found yours of the 1st. inviting me to name a time to meet and address a political meeting in Bond County. It is too early, considering that when I once begin making political speeches I shall have no respite till November. The *labor* of that I might endure, but I really cannot spare the time from my business.

Nearer the time I will try to meet the people of Bond, if they desire.

I will only say now that, as I understand, there remains all the difference there ever was between Judge Douglas & the Republicans—*they* insisting that Congress *shall,* and *he* insisting that Congress *shall not,* keep slavery out of the territories *before & up to the time* they form state constitutions. No Republican has ever contended that, *when* a constitution is to be formed, any but the *people* of the territory shall form it. Republicans have never contended that Congress should *dictate* a constitution to any state or territory; but they have contended that the people should be *perfectly* free to form their constitution in their own way—as *perfectly* free from the *presence* of *slavery* amongst them, as from every other improper influence.

In voting together in opposition to a constitution being forced upon the people of Kansas, neither Judge Douglas nor the Republicans, has conceded anything which was ever in dispute between them. Yours very truly

A. Lincoln

To another editor, Charles L. Wilson of the Chicago *Journal,* Lincoln again made clear his apprehension. But he refused to see treachery in Greeley's preference for Douglas.

Springfield,
June 1. 1858.

Charles L. Wilson, Esq.
My Dear Sir
    Yours of yesterday, with the inclosed newspaper slip, is received. I have never said, or thought more, as to the inclination of some of our Eastern Republican friends to favor Douglas, than I expressed in your hearing on the evening of the 21st. April, at the state library in this place. I have believed—do believe now—that Greeley, for instance, would be rather pleased to see Douglas re-elected over me or any other Republican; and yet I do not believe it is so, because of any secret arrangement with Douglas. It is because he thinks Douglas' superior position, reputation, experience, and *ability,* if you please, would more than compensate for his lack of a pure Republican position, and therefore, his re-election do the general cause of Republicanism, more good, than would the election of any one of our better undistinguished pure Republicans. I do not know how *you* estimate Greeley, but *I* consider him incapable of corruption, or falsehood. He denies that he directly is taking part in favor of Douglas, and I believe him. Still his *feeling* constantly manifests itself in his paper, which, being so extensively read in Illinois, is, and will continue to be, a drag upon us. I have also thought that Govr. Seward too, feels about as Greeley does; but not being a newspaper editor, his feeling, in this respect, is not much manifested. I have no idea that he is, by conversations or by letters, urging Illinois Republicans to vote for Douglas.
    As to myself, let me pledge you my word that neither I, nor any friend of mine so far as I know, has been setting stake against Gov. Seward. No combination has been made *with* me, or *proposed* to me, in relation to the next presidential candidate. The same thing is true in regard to the next Governor of our state. I am not di-

rectly or indirectly committed to anyone; nor has anyone made any advance to me upon the subject. I have had many free conversations with John Wentworth; but he never dropped a remark that led me to suspect that he wishes to be Governor. Indeed, it is due to truth to say that while he has uniformly expressed himself for me, he has never hinted at any condition.

The signs are that we shall have a good convention on the 16th. and I think our prospects generally, are improving some every day. I believe we need nothing so much as to get rid of unjust suspicions of one another. Yours very truly

A. Lincoln.

Lincoln, asked to supply a sketch of his life for the *Dictionary of Congress,* chose to put on record the barest essentials of his life, seemingly unaware that he had become a man of more than local reputation.

June [15?] 1858

Born, February 12, 1809, in Hardin County, Kentucky.
Education defective.
Profession, a lawyer.
Have been a captain of volunteers in Black Hawk War.
Postmaster at a very small office.
Four times a member of the Illinois legislature, and was a
member of the lower house of Congress. Yours, etc.,

A. Lincoln.

VII. A House Divided

1858 By the early summer of 1858, Lincoln had clearly won the right to contest the re-election of Douglas, whose term in the United States Senate would expire that year. Lincoln's near-victory in 1855 gave him an advantage over all other aspirants, and the high ground of his speeches in the three years that had followed made his position as leader of the party unassailable. The only dissidents were the eastern Republicans who continued to hint that the party in Illinois might be wise not to oppose Douglas. To put these meddlers in their place the Republican State Convention, meeting in Springfield on June 16, 1858, unanimously passed a resolution declaring that "Abraham Lincoln is the first and only choice of the Republicans of Illinois for the United States Senate."

Lincoln had been preparing his speech of acceptance for several weeks. As ideas occurred to him he wrote them on stray scraps of paper and stored them in his hat. Shortly before the convention he arranged the scraps in sequence and copied them on sheets. Thus, on the evening of June 16, when he spoke in the Hall of the House of Representatives, he had a manuscript before him, but he knew its content so thoroughly that he needed to give it only a passing glance.

On the evening before the convention Lincoln had read his speech to a group of leaders of the party. Almost without exception they protested the figure of the house divided. One said that it was ahead of its time; another contended that it would drive away many new recruits from the Democratic ranks; to a third it was simply "a damned fool utterance." Lincoln replied that the time had come for bringing the plain facts before the people. If he should be defeated for telling the truth, he was willing to pay the price. The next day he delivered his speech as he had prepared it.

The Living Lincoln

Mr. President and Gentlemen of the Convention.

If we could first know *where* we are, and *whither* we are tending, we could then better judge *what* to do, and *how* to do it.

We are now far into the *fifth* year, since a policy was initiated, with the *avowed* object, and *confident* promise, of putting an end to slavery agitation.

Under the operation of that policy, that agitation has not only, *not ceased,* but has *constantly augmented.*

In *my* opinion, it *will* not cease, until a *crisis* shall have been reached, and passed.

"A house divided against itself cannot stand."

I believe this government cannot endure, permanently half-*slave* and half-*free.*

I do not expect the Union to be *dissolved*—I do not expect the house to *fall*—but I *do* expect it will cease to be divided.

It will become *all* one thing, or *all* the other.

Either the *opponents* of slavery, will arrest the further spread of it, and place it where the public mind shall rest in the belief that it is in course of ultimate extinction; or its *advocates* will push it forward, till it shall become alike lawful in *all* the states, *old* as well as *new*—*North* as well as *South.*

Have we no *tendency* to the latter condition?

Let any one who doubts, carefully contemplate that now almost complete legal combination—piece of *machinery* so to speak —compounded of the Nebraska doctrine, and the Dred Scott decision. Let him consider not only *what work* the machinery is adapted to do, and *how well* adapted; but also, let him study the *history* of its construction, and trace, if he can, or rather *fail,* if he can, to trace the evidences of design, and concert of action, among its chief bosses, from the beginning.

But, so far, *Congress* only, had acted; and an *indorsement* by the people, *real* or apparent, was indispensable, to *save* the point already gained, and give chance for more.

The new year of 1854 found slavery excluded from more than half the states by state constitutions, and from most of the national territory by congressional prohibition.

Four days later, commenced the struggle, which ended in repealing that congressional prohibition.

This opened all the national territory to slavery; and was the first point gained.

This necessity had not been overlooked; but had been provided

212

for, as well as might be, in the notable argument of *"squatter sovereignty,"* otherwise called *"sacred right of self-government,"* which latter phrase, though expressive of the only rightful basis of any government, was so perverted in this attempted use of it as to amount to just this: That if any *one* man, choose to enslave *another,* no *third* man shall be allowed to object.

That argument was incorporated into the Nebraska bill itself, in the language which follows: *"It being the true intent and meaning of this act not to legislate slavery into any territory or state, nor exclude it therefrom; but to leave the people thereof perfectly free to form and regulate their domestic institutions in their own way, subject only to the Constitution of the United States."*

Then opened the roar of loose declamation in favor of "Squatter Sovereignty," and "sacred right of self-government."

"But," said opposition members, "let us be more *specific* — let us *amend* the bill so as to expressly declare that the people of the territory *may* exclude slavery." "Not we," said the friends of the measure; and down they voted the amendment.

While the Nebraska bill was passing through Congress, a *law case,* involving the question of a Negro's freedom, by reason of his owner having voluntarily taken him first into a free state and then a territory covered by the congressional prohibition, and held him as a slave, for a long time in each, was passing through the U. S. Circuit Court for the District of Missouri; and both Nebraska bill and law suit were brought to a decision in the same month of May, 1854. The Negro's name was "Dred Scott," which name now designates the decision finally made in the case.

Before the *then* next presidential election, the law case came *to,* and was argued *in* the Supreme Court of the United States; but the *decision* of it was deferred until *after* the election. Still, *before* the election, Senator Trumbull, on the floor of the Senate, requests the leading advocate of the Nebraska bill to state *his opinion* whether the people of a territory can constitutionally exclude slavery from their limits; and the latter answers, "That is a question for the Supreme Court."

The election came. Mr. Buchanan was elected, and the *indorsement,* such as it was, secured. That was the *second* point gained. The indorsement, however, fell short of a clear popular majority by nearly four hundred thousand votes, and so, perhaps, was not overwhelmingly reliable and satisfactory.

The *outgoing* President, in his last annual message, as impressively as possible *echoed back* upon the people the *weight* and *authority* of the indorsement.

The Supreme Court met again; *did not* announce their decision, but ordered a re-argument.

The presidential inauguration came, and still no decision of the court; but the *incoming* President, in his inaugural address, fervently exhorted the people to abide by the forthcoming decision, *whatever it might be.*

Then, in a few days, came the decision.

The reputed author of the Nebraska bill finds an early occasion to make a speech at this capitol indorsing the Dred Scott decision, and vehemently denouncing all opposition to it.

The new President, too, seizes the early occasion of the Silliman letter to *indorse* and strongly *construe* that decision, and to express his *astonishment* that any different view had ever been entertained.

At length a squabble springs up between the President and the author of the Nebraska bill, on the *mere* question of *fact,* whether the Lecompton constitution was or was not, in any just sense, made by the people of Kansas; and in that squabble the latter declares that all he wants is a fair vote for the people, and that he *cares* not whether slavery be voted *down* or voted *up*. I do not understand his declaration that he cares not whether slavery be voted down or voted up, to be intended by him other than as an *apt definition* of the *policy* he would impress upon the public mind—the *principle* for which he declares he has suffered much, and is ready to suffer to the end.

And well may he cling to that principle. If he has any parental feeling, well may he cling to it. That principle, is the only *shred* left of his original Nebraska doctrine. Under the Dred Scott decision, "squatter sovereignty" squatted out of existence, tumbled down like temporary scaffolding—like the mould at the foundry served through one blast and fell back into loose sand—helped to carry an election, and then was kicked to the winds. His late *joint* struggle with the Republicans, against the Lecompton constitution, involves nothing of the original Nebraska doctrine. That struggle was made on a point, the right of a people to make their own constitution, upon which he and the Republicans have never differed.

The several points of the Dred Scott decision, in connection with Senator Douglas' "care not" policy, constitute the piece of machinery, in its *present* state of advancement. This was the third point gained.

The *working* points of that machinery are:

First, that no Negro slave, imported as such from Africa, and no descendant of such slave can ever be a *citizen* of any state, in the sense of that term as used in the Constitution of the United States.

This point is made in order to deprive the Negro, in every possible event, of the benefit of this provision of the United States Constitution, which declares that—

"The citizens of each state shall be entitled to all privileges and immunities of citizens in the several states."

Secondly, that "subject to the Constitution of the United States," neither *Congress* nor a *Territorial Legislature* can exclude slavery from any United States territory.

This point is made in order that individual men may *fill up* the territories with slaves, without danger of losing them as property, and thus to enhance the chances of *permanency* to the institution through all the future.

Thirdly, that whether the holding a Negro in actual slavery in a free state, makes him free, as against the holder, the United States courts will not decide, but will leave to be decided by the courts of any slave state the Negro may be forced into by the master.

This point is made, not to be pressed *immediately;* but, if acquiesced in for a while, and apparently *indorsed* by the people at an election, *then* to sustain the logical conclusion that what Dred Scott's master might lawfully do with Dred Scott, in the free state of Illinois, every other master may lawfully do with any other *one,* or one *thousand* slaves, in Illinois, or in any other free state.

Auxiliary to all this, and working hand in hand with it, the Nebraska doctrine, or what is left of it, is to *educate* and *mould* public opinion, at least *Northern* public opinion, to not *care* whether slavery is voted *down* or voted *up.*

This shows exactly where we now *are;* and *partially* also whither we are tending.

It will throw additional light on the latter, to go back, and run the mind over the string of historical facts already stated. Several things will *now* appear less *dark* and *mysterious* than they did *when* they were transpiring. The people were to be left "perfectly free" "subject only to the Constitution." What the *Constitution* had to do with it, outsiders could not *then* see. Plainly enough *now,* it was an exactly fitted *niche,* for the Dred Scott decision to afterwards come in, and declare the *perfect freedom* of the people, to be just no freedom at all.

Why was the amendment, expressly declaring the right of the people to exclude slavery, voted down? Plainly enough *now,* the adoption of it, would have spoiled the niche for the Dred Scott decision.

Why was the court decision held up? Why, even a Senator's individual opinion withheld, till *after* the presidential election? Plainly enough *now,* the speaking out *then* would have damaged the *"perfectly free"* argument upon which the election was to be carried.

Why the *outgoing* President's felicitation on the indorsement? Why the delay of a reargument? Why the incoming President's *advance* exhortation in favor of the decision?

These things *look* like the cautious *patting* and *petting* a spirited horse, preparatory to mounting him, when it is dreaded that he may give the rider a fall.

And why the hasty after indorsements of the decision by the President and others?

We can not absolutely *know* that all these exact adaptations are the result of preconcert. But when we see a lot of framed timbers, different portions of which we know have been gotten out at different times and places and by different workmen—Stephen, Franklin, Roger and James,* for instance—and when we see these timbers joined together, and see they exactly make the frame of a house or a mill, all the tenons and mortices exactly fitting, and all the lengths and proportions of the different pieces exactly adapted to their respective places, and not a piece too many or too few—not omitting even scaffolding—or, if a single piece be lacking, we can see the place in the frame exactly fitted and prepared to yet bring such piece in—in *such* a case, we find it impossible to not *believe* that Stephen and Franklin and Roger and James all understood one another from the beginning, and all worked upon a common *plan* or *draft* drawn up before the first lick was struck.

It should not be overlooked that, by the Nebraska bill, the people of a *state* as well as *territory,* were to be left *"perfectly free"* *"subject only to the Constitution."*

* Douglas, Pierce, Taney, and Buchanan.

A House Divided

Why mention a *state?* They were legislating for *territories,* and not *for* or *about* states. Certainly the people of a state *are* and *ought to be* subject to the Constitution of the United States; but why is mention of this *lugged* into this merely *territorial* law? Why are the people of a *territory* and the people of a *state* therein *lumped* together, and their relation to the Constitution therein treated as being *precisely* the same?

While the opinion of *the court,* by Chief Justice Taney, in the Dred Scott case, and the separate opinions of all the concurring judges, expressly declare that the Constitution of the United States neither permits Congress nor a territorial legislature to exclude slavery from any United States territory, they all *omit* to declare whether or not the same Constitution permits a *state,* or the people of a state, to exclude it.

Possibly, this was a mere *omission;* but who can be *quite* sure, if McLean or Curtis * had sought to get into the opinion a declaration of unlimited power in the people of a *state* to exclude slavery from their limits, just as Chase and Macy † sought to get such declaration, in behalf of the people of a territory, into the Nebraska bill—I ask, who can be quite *sure* that it would not have been voted down, in the one case, as it had been in the other.

The nearest approach to the point of declaring the power of a state over slavery, is made by Judge Nelson. He approaches it more than once, using the precise idea, and *almost* the language too, of the Nebraska act. On one occasion his exact language is, "except in cases where the power is restrained by the Constitution of the United States, the law of the state is supreme over the subject of slavery within its jurisdiction."

In what *cases* the power of the *states* is so restrained by the U. S. Constitution, is left an *open* question, precisely as the same question, as to the restraint on the power of the *territories* was left open in the Nebraska act. Put *that* and *that* together, and we have another nice little niche, which we may, ere long, see filled with another Supreme Court decision, declaring that the Constitution of the United States does not permit a *state* to exclude slavery from its limits.

And this may especially be expected if the doctrine of "care not whether slavery be voted *down* or voted *up,*" shall gain upon the

* Justices of the Supreme Court.

† Senator Salmon P. Chase of Ohio and Representative Daniel Macy of Indiana.

public mind sufficiently to give promise that such a decision can be maintained when made.

Such a decision is all that slavery now lacks of being alike lawful in all the states.

Welcome or unwelcome, such decision *is* probably coming, and will soon be upon us, unless the power of the present political dynasty shall be met and overthrown.

We shall *lie down* pleasantly dreaming that the people of *Missouri* are on the verge of making their state *free;* and we shall *awake* to the *reality,* instead, that the *Supreme* Court has made *Illinois* a *slave* state.

To meet and overthrow the power of that dynasty, is the work now before all those who would prevent that consummation.

That is *what* we have to do.

But *how* can we best do it?

There are those who denounce us *openly* to their *own* friends, and yet whisper *us softly,* that *Senator Douglas* is the *aptest* instrument there is, with which to effect that object. *They* do *not* tell us, nor has *he* told us, that he *wishes* any such object to be effected. They wish us to *infer* all, from the facts, that he now has a little quarrel with the present head of the dynasty; and that he has regularly voted with us, on a single point, upon which, he and we, have never differed.

They remind us that *he* is a very *great man,* and that the largest of *us* are very small ones. Let this be granted. But "a *living dog* is better than a *dead lion.*" Judge Douglas, if not a *dead* lion *for this work,* [is] at least a *caged* and *toothless* one. How can he oppose the advances of slavery? He don't *care* anything about it. His avowed *mission is impressing* the "public heart" to *care* nothing about it.

A leading Douglas Democratic newspaper thinks Douglas' superior talent will be needed to resist the revival of the African slave trade.

Does Douglas believe an effort to revive that trade is approaching? He has not said so. Does he *really* think so? But if it is, how can he resist it? For years he has labored to prove it a *sacred right* of white men to take Negro slaves into the new territories. Can he possibly show that it is *less* a sacred right to *buy* them where they can be bought cheapest? And, unquestionably they can be bought *cheaper in Africa* than in *Virginia.*

He has done all in his power to reduce the whole question of slavery to one of a mere *right of property;* and as such, how can *he* oppose the foreign slave trade—how can he refuse that trade in that "property" shall be "perfectly free"—unless he does it as a *protection* to the home production? And as the home *producers* will probably not *ask* the protection, he will be wholly without a ground of opposition.

Senator Douglas holds, we know, that a man may rightfully be *wiser today* than he was *yesterday*—that he may rightfully *change* when he finds himself wrong.

But, can we for that reason, run ahead, and *infer* that he *will* make any particular change, of which he, himself, has given no intimation? Can we *safely* base *our* action upon any such *vague* inference?

Now, as ever, I wish to not *misrepresent* Judge Douglas' *position*, question his *motives*, or do ought that can be personally offensive to him.

Whenever, *if ever*, he and we can come together on *principle* so that *our great cause* may have assistance from *his great ability*, I hope to have interposed no adventitious obstacle.

But clearly, he is not *now* with us—he does not *pretend* to be—he does not *promise* to *ever* be.

Our cause, then, must be intrusted to, and conducted by its own undoubted friends—those whose hands are free, whose hearts are in the work—who *do care* for the result.

Two years ago the Republicans of the nation mustered over thirteen hundred thousand strong.

We did this under the single impulse of resistance to a common danger, with every external circumstance against us.

Of *strange, discordant,* and even, *hostile* elements, we gathered from the four winds, and *formed* and fought the battle through, under the constant hot fire of a disciplined, proud, and pampered enemy.

Did we brave all *then,* to *falter* now?—*now*—when that same enemy is *wavering,* dissevered and belligerent?

The result is not doubtful. We shall not fail—if we stand firm, we shall not fail.

Wise counsels may *accelerate* or *mistakes delay* it, but, sooner or later, the victory is *sure* to come.

Lincoln soon learned that the party managers who had objected to his "House Divided" opening had been sound prophets. Many readers were disturbed by what they took to be a prediction of impending disunion. To the editor of the Chicago *Daily Democratic Press,* then on the verge of consolidating with the Chicago *Tribune,* Lincoln tried to convey his true meaning.

Springfield,
June 23, 1858

Jno. L. Scripps, Esq
My dear Sir

Your kind note of yesterday is duly received. I am much flattered by the estimate you place on my late speech; and yet I am much mortified that any part of it should be construed so differently from anything intended by me. The language, "place it where the public mind shall rest in the belief that it is in course of ultimate extinction," I used deliberately, not dreaming then, nor believing now, that it asserts, or intimates, any power or purpose, to interfere with slavery in the states where it exists. But, to not cavil about language, I declare that whether the clause used by me, will bear such construction or not, I never so intended it. I have declared a thousand times, and now repeat that, in my opinion, neither the general government, nor any other power outside of the slave states, can constitutionally or rightfully interfere with slaves or slavery where it already exists. I believe that whenever the effort to spread slavery into the new territories, by whatever means, and into the free states themselves, by Supreme Court decisions, shall be fairly headed off, the institution will then be in course of ultimate extinction; and by the language used I meant only this.

I do not intend this for publication; but still you may show it to anyone you think fit. I think I shall, as you suggest, take some early occasion to publicly repeat the declaration I have already so often made as before stated. Yours very truly

A. Lincoln

In preparation for an active campaign, Lincoln began to marshal his financial resources.

Springfield,
June 25– 1858

A. Campbell, Esq
My dear Sir

In 1856 you gave me authority to draw on you for any sum not exceeding five hundred dollars. I see clearly that such a privilege would be more available now than it was then. I am aware that times are tighter now than they were then. Please write me at all events; and whether you can now do anything or not, I shall continue grateful for the past. Yours very truly

A Lincoln

The senatorial campaign had barely started when Lincoln's stand on the Mexican War came out of the past to trouble him. Joseph Medill was one of the publishers of the sturdily Republican Chicago *Tribune*.

Springfield,
June 25 1858

J Medill, Esq
My dear Sir

Your note of the 23rd. did not reach me till last evening. The Times article I saw yesterday morning. I will give you a brief history of facts, upon which you may rely with entire confidence, and from which you can frame such articles or paragraphs as you see fit.

I was in Congress but a single term. I was a candidate when the Mexican War broke out—and I then took the ground, which I never varied from, that the administration had done wrong in getting us into the war, but that the officers and soldiers who went to the field must be supplied and sustained at all events. I was elected the first Monday of August 1846, but, in regular course, only took my seat December 6, 1847. In the interval all the battles had been fought, and the war was substantially ended, though our army was still in Mexico, and the treaty of peace was not finally concluded till May 30, 1848. Col. E. D. Baker had been elected to Congress from the same district, for the regular term next preceding mine; but having gone to Mexico himself, and having resigned his seat in Congress, a man by the name of John Henry, was elected to fill Baker's vacancy, and so came into Congress before I did. On the 23rd. day of February 1847 (the very day I believe, Col. John Hardin was killed at Buena Vista, and certainly more than nine months before I took a seat in Congress) a bill corresponding with great accuracy to that mentioned by the Times, passed the House of Representatives, and *John Henry* voted against it, as may be seen in the Journal of that session at pages 406–7. The bill became a law; and is found in the U. S. Statutes at Large—Vol. 9. page 149.

This I suppose is the real origin of the Times' attack upon me. In its blind rage to assail me, it has seized on a vague recollection of Henry's vote, and appropriated it to me. I scarcely think anyone is quite vile enough to make such a charge in such terms, without some slight belief in the truth of it.

Henry was my personal and political friend; and, as I thought, a very good man; and when I first learned of that vote, I well remember how astounded and mortified I was. This very bill, voted against by Henry, passed into a law, and made the appropriations for the year ending June 30, 1848—extending a full month beyond the actual and formal ending of the war. When I came into Congress, money was needed to meet the appropriations made, and to be made; and accordingly on the 17th. day of Feb. 1848, a bill to borrow 18,500,000. passed the House of Representatives, for which I voted, as will appear by the Journal of that session page 426, 427. The act itself, reduced to 16,000,000 (I suppose in the Senate) is found in U. S. Statutes at Large Vol. 9– 217.

Again, on the 8th. of March 1848, a bill passed the House of Representatives, for which I voted, as may be seen by the Journal 520–521. It passed into a law, and is found in U. S. Statutes at Large page 215 and forward. The last section of the act, on page 217—contains an appropriation of 800,000. for clothing the volunteers.

It is impossible to refer to all the votes I gave but the above I think are sufficient as specimens; and you may safely deny that I ever gave any vote for withholding any supplies whatever, from officers or soldiers of the Mexican War. I have examined the Journals a good deal; and besides I cannot be mistaken; for I had my eye always upon it. I must close to get this into the mail. Yours very truly

A. Lincoln

Douglas opened his campaign for reelection with a speech at Chicago on the evening of July 9. Lincoln sat on the balcony of the Tremont House, from which Douglas spoke. The following evening Lincoln spoke from the same place.

In opening his address Lincoln made a point of acknowledging his opponent's courtesy. "I was furnished with a seat very convenient for hearing him," Lincoln said, "and was otherwise very courteously treated by him and his friends, for which I thank him and them." Lincoln spent several minutes in denying that the Republicans had formed an alliance with Douglas's Democratic enemies, and in denouncing

A House Divided

the "popular sovereignty" policy of his rival. He then turned to a defense of his "House Divided" speech.

July 10, 1858

Judge Douglas made two points upon my recent speech at Springfield. He says they are to be the issues of this campaign. The first one of these points he bases upon the language in a speech which I delivered at Springfield, which I believe I can quote correctly from memory. I said there that "we are now far into the fifth year since a policy was instituted for the avowed object and with the confident promise of putting an end to slavery agitation; under the operation of that policy, that agitation had [not] only not ceased, but has constantly augmented."—[A voice—"That's the very language."] "I believe it will not cease until a crisis shall have been reached and passed. A house divided against itself cannot stand. I believe this government cannot endure permanently half-slave and half-free." [Applause.] "I do not expect the Union to be dissolved,"—I am quoting from my speech—"I do not expect the house to fall, but I do expect it will cease to be divided. It will become all one thing or the other. Either the opponents of slavery will arrest the spread of it, and place it where the public mind shall rest in the belief that it is in the course of ultimate extinction, or its advocates will push it forward until it shall become alike lawful in all the states, North as well as South." ["Good, good."]

That is the paragraph. In this paragraph which I have quoted in your hearing, and to which I ask the attention of all, Judge Douglas thinks he discovers great political heresy. I want your attention particularly to what he has inferred from it. He says I am in favor of making all the states of this Union uniform in all their internal regulations; that in all their domestic concerns I am in favor of making them entirely uniform. He draws this inference from the language I have quoted to you. He says that I am in favor of making war by the North upon the South for the extinction of slavery; that I am also in favor of inviting (as he expresses it) the South to a war upon the North, for the purpose of nationalizing slavery. Now, it is singular enough, if you will carefully read that passage over, that I did not say that I was in favor of anything in it. I only said what I expected would take place. I made a prediction only—it may have been a foolish one perhaps. I did not even say that I desired that slavery should be put in course of ultimate extinction.

I do say so now, however, [great applause] so there need be no longer any difficulty about that. It may be written down in the great speech. [Applause and laughter.]

Gentlemen, Judge Douglas informed you that this speech of mine was probably carefully prepared. I admit that it was. I am not master of language; I have not a fine education; I am not capable of entering into a disquisition upon dialectics, as I believe you call it; but I do not believe the language I employed bears any such construction as Judge Douglas put upon it. But I don't care about a quibble in regard to words. I know what I meant, and I will not leave this crowd in doubt, if I can explain it to them, what I really meant in the use of that paragraph.

I am not, in the first place, unaware that this government has endured eighty-two years, half-slave and half-free. I know that. I am tolerably well acquainted with the history of the country, and I know that it has endured eighty-two years, half-slave and half-free. I *believe*—and that is what I meant to allude to there—I *believe* it has endured because, during all that time, until the introduction of the Nebraska bill, the public mind did rest, all the time, in the belief that slavery was in course of ultimate extinction. ["Good!" "Good!" and applause.] That was what gave us the rest that we had through that period of eighty-two years; at least, so I believe. I have always hated slavery, I think as much as any abolitionist. [Applause.] I have been an Old Line Whig. I have always hated it, but I have always been quiet about it until this new era of the introduction of the Nebraska bill began. I always believed that everybody was against it, and that it was in course of ultimate extinction. [Pointing to Mr. Browning, who stood near by.] Browning thought so; the great mass of the nation have rested in the belief that slavery was in course of ultimate extinction. They had reason so to believe.

The adoption of the Constitution and its attendant history led the people to believe so; and that such was the belief of the framers of the Constitution itself. Why did those old men, about the time of the adoption of the Constitution, decree that slavery should not go into the new territory, where it had not already gone? Why declare that within twenty years the African slave trade, by which slaves are supplied, might be cut off by Congress? Why were all these acts? I might enumerate more of these acts—but enough. What were they but a clear indication that the framers of the Constitution intended and expected the ultimate extinction of that institution. [Cheers.] And now, when I say, as I said in my speech that Judge Douglas has quoted from, when I say that I think the opponents of slavery will resist the farther spread of it, and place it where the public mind shall rest with the belief that it is in course of ultimate extinction, I only mean to say, that they will place it where the founders of this government originally placed it.

I have said a hundred times, and I have now no inclination to take it back, that I believe there is no right, and ought to be no inclination in the people of the free states to enter into the slave states, and interfere with the question of slavery at all. I have said that always. Judge Douglas has heard me say it—if not quite a hundred times, at least as good as a hundred times; and when it is said that I am in favor of interfering with slavery where it exists, I know it is unwarranted by anything I have ever *intended,* and, as I believe, by anything I have ever *said.* If, by any means, I have ever used language which could fairly be so construed, (as, however, I believe I never have,) I now correct it. . . .

The audience broke into cheers as a delegation from the Seventh Ward marched in. Lincoln waited, then struck again at Douglas.

Now in relation to his inference that I am in favor of a general consolidation of all the local institutions of the various states. I will attend to that for a little while, and try to inquire, if I can, how on earth it could be that any man could draw such an inference from anything I said. I have said, very many times, in Judge Douglas' hearing, that no man believed more than I in the principle of self-government; that it lies at the bottom of all my ideas of just government, from beginning to end. I have denied that his use of that term applies properly. But for the thing itself, I deny that any man has ever gone ahead of me in his devotion to the principle, whatever he may have done in efficiency in advocating it. I think that I have said it in your hearing—that I believe each individual is naturally entitled to do as he pleases with himself and the fruit of his labor, so far as it in no wise interferes with any other man's rights—[applause]—that each community, as a state, has a right to do exactly as it pleases with all the concerns within that state that interfere with the rights of no other state, and that the general government, upon principle, has no right to interfere with anything other than that general class of things that does concern the whole. I have said that at all times. I have said, as illustrations, that I do not believe in the right of Illinois to interfere with the cranberry laws of Indiana, the oyster laws of Virginia, or the liquor laws of Maine. I have said these things over and over again, and I repeat them here as my sentiments.

How is it, then, that Judge Douglas infers, because I hope to see slavery put where the public mind shall rest in the belief that it is in the course of ultimate extinction, that I am in favor of Illinois going over and interfering with the cranberry laws of Indiana? What can authorize him to draw any such inference? I suppose there might be one thing that at least enabled *him* to draw such an inference that would not be true with me or with many others, that is, because he looks upon all this matter of slavery as an exceedingly little thing—this matter of keeping one-sixth of the population of the whole nation in a state of oppression and tyranny unequalled in the world. He looks upon it as being an exceedingly little thing—only equal to the question of the cranberry laws of Indiana—as something having no moral question in it—as something on a par with the question of whether a man shall pasture his land with cattle, or plant it with tobacco—so little and so small a thing, that he concludes, if I could desire that anything should be done to bring about the ultimate extinction of that little thing, I must be in favor of bringing about an amalgamation of all the other little things in the Union. Now, it so happens—and there, I presume, is the foundation of this mistake—that the Judge thinks thus; and it so happens that there is a vast portion of the American people that do *not* look upon that matter as being this very little thing. They look upon it as a vast moral evil; they can prove it is such by the writings of those who gave us the blessings of liberty which we enjoy, and that they so looked upon it, and not as an evil merely confining itself to the states where it is situated; and while we agree that, by the Constitution we assented to, in the states where it exists we have no right to interfere with it because it is in the Constitution and we are by both duty and inclination to stick by that Constitution in all its letter and spirit from beginning to end. [Great applause.]

So much then as to my disposition—my wish—to have all the state legislatures blotted out, and to have one general consolidated government, and a uniformity of domestic regulations in all the states, by which I suppose it is meant if we raise corn here, we

must make sugar cane grow here too, and we must make those
which grow North, grow in the South. All this I suppose he understands I am in favor of doing. Now, so much for all this nonsense
—for I must call it so. The Judge can have no issue with me on a
question of establishing uniformity in the domestic regulations of
the states. . . .

In a passage on the Dred Scott decision Lincoln went over ground
that he had already covered in his Dred Scott speech of June 26, 1857.
His argument led him to a stirring affirmation of faith in the promise
of the Declaration of Independence. On that note he closed.

Now, it happens that we meet together once every year, some-
time about the 4th of July, for some reason or other. These 4th of
July gatherings I suppose have their uses. If you will indulge me,
I will state what I suppose to be some of them.

We are now a mighty nation, we are thirty—or about thirty
millions of people, and we own and inhabit about one-fifteenth
part of the dry land of the whole earth. We run our memory back
over the pages of history for about eighty-two years and we discover that we were then a very small people in point of numbers,
vastly inferior to what we are now, with a vastly less extent of
country,—with vastly less of everything we deem desirable among
men,—we look upon the change as exceedingly advantageous to us
and to our posterity, and we fix upon something that happened
away back, as in some way or other being connected with this rise
of prosperity. We find a race of men living in that day whom we
claim as our fathers and grandfathers; they were iron men, they
fought for the principle that they were contending for; and we understood that by what they then did it has followed that the degree
of prosperity that we now enjoy has come to us. We hold this annual celebration to remind ourselves of all the good done in this
process of time of how it was done and who did it, and how we are
historically connected with it; and we go from these meetings in
better humor with ourselves—we feel more attached the one to the
other, and more firmly bound to the country we inhabit. In every
way we are better men in the age, and race, and country in which
we live for these celebrations.

But after we have done all this we have not yet reached the
whole. There is something else connected with it. We have besides
these men—descended by blood from our ancestors—among us

The Living Lincoln

perhaps half our people who are not descendants at all of these men, they are men who have come from Europe—German, Irish, French and Scandinavian—men that have come from Europe themselves, or whose ancestors have come hither and settled here, finding themselves our equals in all things. If they look back through this history to trace their connection with those days by blood, they find they have none, they cannot carry themselves back into that glorious epoch and make themselves feel that they are part of us, but when they look through that old Declaration of Independence they find that those old men say that "We hold these truths to be self-evident, that all men are created equal," and then they feel that that moral sentiment taught in that day evidences their relation to those men, that it is the father of all moral principle in them, and that they have a right to claim it as though they were blood of the blood, and flesh of the flesh of the men who wrote that Declaration, [loud and long-continued applause] and so they are. That is the electric cord in that Declaration that links the hearts of patriotic and liberty-loving men together, that will link those patriotic hearts as long as the love of freedom exists in the minds of men throughout the world. [Applause.]

Now, sirs, for the purpose of squaring things with this idea of "don't care if slavery is voted up or voted down," for sustaining the Dred Scott decision [A voice—"Hit him again"], for holding that the Declaration of Independence did not mean anything at all, we have Judge Douglas giving his exposition of what the Declaration of Independence means, and we have him saying that the people of America are equal to the people of England. According to his construction, you Germans are not connected with it. Now I ask you in all soberness, if all these things, if indulged in, if ratified, if confirmed and endorsed, if taught to our children, and repeated to them, do not tend to rub out the sentiment of liberty in the country, and to transform this government into a government of some other form. Those arguments that are made, that the inferior race are to be treated with as much allowance as they are capable of enjoying; that as much is to be done for them as their condition will allow. What are these arguments? They are the arguments that kings have made for enslaving the people in all ages of the world. You will find that all the arguments in favor of kingcraft were of this class; they always bestrode the necks of the people, not that they wanted to do it, but because the people were better off for being ridden. That is their argument, and this argument of the Judge is the same old serpent that says you work and I eat, you toil and I will enjoy the fruits of it. Turn it whatever way you will—whether it come from the mouth of a king, an excuse for enslaving the people of his country, or from the mouth of men of one race as a reason for enslaving the men of another race, it is all the same old serpent, and I hold if that course of argumentation that is made for the purpose of convincing the public mind that we should not care about this, should be granted, it does not stop with the Negro. I should like to know if taking this old Declaration of Independence, which declares that all men are equal upon principle and making exceptions to it where will it stop. If one man says it does not mean a Negro, why not another say it does not mean some other man? If that Declaration is not the truth, let us get the statute book, in which we find it and tear it out! Who is so bold as to do it! [Voices—"me" "no one," &c.] If it is not true let us tear it out! [cries of "no, no,"] let us stick to it then, [cheers] let us stand firmly by it then. [Applause.] . . .

Back in Springfield, Lincoln appraised his encounter with the Little Giant. Gustave Koerner, former Lieutenant Governor of Illinois, was a strong force in the German wing of the Republican Party.

Springfield,
July 15. 1858

Hon. G. Koerner:
My dear Sir
I have just been called on by one of our German Republicans here, to ascertain if Mr. Hecker could not be prevailed on to visit this region, and address the Germans, at this place, and a few others at least. Please ascertain & write me. He would, of course, have to be paid something. Find out from him about how much.

I have just returned from Chicago. Douglas took nothing by his motion there. In fact, by his rampant indorsement of the Dred Scott decision he drove back a few Republicans who were favorably inclined towards him. His tactics just now, in part, is to make it appear that he is having a triumphal entry into, and march through the country; but it is all as bombastic and hollow as Napoleon's bulletins sent back from his campaign in Russia. I was present at his reception in Chicago, and it certainly was very large and imposing; but judging from the opinions of others better acquainted with faces there, and by the strong call for me to speak, when he closed, I really believe we could have voted him down in that very crowd. Our meeting, twenty-four hours after, called only twelve hours before it came together and got up without trumpery, was nearly as large, and five times as enthusiastic.

I write this, for your private eye, to assure you that there is no solid shot, in these bombastic parades of his. Yours very truly

A. Lincoln

Again Lincoln spoke in reply to Douglas. The place was Springfield, the date July 17. Douglas took the stand in the afternoon in a grove on the north side of the city; Lincoln in the evening at the State House.

Lincoln opened by admitting that he entered the senatorial contest under a disadvantage. The northern part of the state, where Republican strength was centered, had fewer seats in the legislature than its fast-growing population warranted. Douglas, therefore, could win by a minority of the popular vote.

Another drawback was Lincoln's own lack of prominence. For political effect, he exaggerated his insignificance.

. . . Senator Douglas is of world wide renown. All the anxious politicians of his party, or who have been of his party for years past, have been looking upon him as certainly, at no distant day, to be the President of the United States. They have seen in his round, jolly, fruitful face, postoffices, landoffices, marshalships, and cabinet appointments, chargeships and foreign missions, bursting and sprouting out in wonderful exuberance ready to be laid hold of by their greedy hands. [Great laughter.] And as they have been gazing upon this attractive picture so long, they cannot, in the little distraction that has taken place in the party, bring themselves to give up the charming hope; but with greedier anxiety they rush about him, sustain him, and give him marches, triumphal entries, and receptions beyond what even in the days of his highest prosperity they could have brought about in his favor. On the contrary nobody has ever expected me to be President. In my poor, lean, lank, face, nobody has ever seen that any cabbages were sprouting out. [Tremendous cheering and laughter.] These are disadvantages all, taken together, that the Republicans labor under. *We* have to

A House Divided

fight this battle upon principle, and upon principle alone. I am, in a certain sense, made the standard-bearer in behalf of the Republicans. I was made so merely because there had to be some one so placed—I being in no wise, preferable to any other one of the twenty-five—perhaps a hundred we have in the Republican ranks. Then I say I wish it to be distinctly understood and borne in mind, that we have to fight this battle without many—perhaps without any—of the external aids which are brought to bear against us. So I hope those with whom I am surrounded have principle enough to nerve themselves for the task and leave nothing undone, that can be fairly done, to bring about the right result.

With arguments now familiar, Lincoln attacked "popular sovereignty" and Douglas's effort to win votes from the stand he had taken on the Lecompton constitution. Lincoln then went on the defensive. Douglas, too, was making political capital out of the "House Divided" doctrine.

. . . When he was preparing his plan of campaign, Napoleon-like, in New York, as appears by two speeches I have heard him deliver since his arrival in Illinois, he gave special attention to a speech of mine, delivered here on the 16th of June last. He says that he carefully read that speech. He told us that at Chicago a week ago last night, and he repeated it at Bloomington last night. Doubtless, he repeated it again today, though I did not hear him. In the two first places—Chicago and Bloomington—I heard him; today I did not. [A voice—Yes; he said the same thing.] He said he had carefully examined that speech; *when,* he did not say; but there is no reasonable doubt it was when he was in New York preparing his plan of campaign. I am glad he did read it carefully. He says it was evidently prepared with great care. I freely admit it was prepared with care. I claim not to be more free from errors than others—perhaps scarcely so much; but I was very careful not to put anything in that speech as a matter of fact, or make any inferences which did not appear to me to be true, and fully warrantable. If I had made any mistake I was willing to be corrected; if I had drawn any inference in regard to Judge Douglas, or anyone else, which was not warranted, I was fully prepared to modify it as soon as discovered. I planted myself upon the truth, and the truth only, so far as I knew it, or could be brought to know it.

Having made that speech with the most kindly feeling towards

231

The Living Lincoln

Judge Douglas, as manifested therein, I was gratified when I found that he had carefully examined it, and had detected no error of fact, nor any inference against him, nor any misrepresentations, of which he thought fit to complain. In neither of the two speeches I have mentioned, did he make any such complaint. I will thank anyone who will inform me that he, in his speech today, pointed out anything I had stated, respecting him, as being erroneous. I presume there is no such thing. I have reason to be gratified that the care and caution used in that speech, left it so that he, most of all others interested in discovering error, has not been able to point out one thing against him which he could say was wrong. He seizes upon the doctrines he supposes to be included in that speech, and declares that upon them will turn the issues of this campaign. He then quotes, or attempts to quote, from my speech. I will not say that he willfully misquotes, but he does fail to quote accurately. His attempt at quoting is from a passage which I believe I can quote accurately from memory. I shall make the quotation now, with some comments upon it, as I have already said, in order that the Judge shall be left entirely without excuse for misrepresenting me. I do so now, as I hope, for the last time. I do this in great caution, in order that if he repeats his misrepresentation, it shall be plain to all that he does so willfully. If, after all, he still persists, I shall be compelled to reconstruct the course I have marked out for myself, and draw upon such humble resources as I have, for a new course, better suited to the real exigencies of the case. I set out in this campaign, with the intention of conducting it strictly as a gentleman, in substance at least, if not in the outside polish. The latter I shall never be, but that which constitutes the inside of a gentleman I hope I understand, and am not less inclined to practice than others. [Cheers.] It was my purpose and expectation that this canvass would be conducted upon principle, and with fairness on both sides; and it shall not be my fault, if this purpose and expectation shall be given up.

He charges, in substance, that I invite a war of sections; that I propose all the local institutions of the different states shall become consolidated and uniform. What is there in the language of that speech which expresses such purpose, or bears such construction? I have again and again said that I would not enter into any of the states to disturb the institution of slavery. Judge Douglas said, at Bloomington, that I used language most able and ingenious

232

A House Divided

for concealing what I really meant; and that while I had protested against entering into the slave states, I nevertheless did mean to go on the banks of Ohio and throw missiles into Kentucky to disturb them in their domestic institutions.

I said, in that speech, and I meant no more, that the institution of slavery ought to be placed in the very attitude where the framers of this government placed it, and left it. I do not understand that the framers of our Constitution left the people of the free states in the attitude of firing bombs or shells into the slave states. I was not using that passage for the purpose for which he infers I did use it. I said: "We are now far advanced into the fifth year since a policy was created for the avowed object and with the confident promise of putting an end to slavery agitation. Under the operation of that policy that agitation has not only not ceased, but has constantly augmented. In my opinion it will not cease till a crisis shall have been reached and passed. 'A house divided against itself can not stand.' I believe that this government cannot endure permanently half-slave and half-free. It will become all one thing or all the other. Either the opponents of slavery will arrest the further spread of it, and place it where the public mind shall rest in the belief that it is in the course of ultimate extinction, or its advocates will push it forward till it shall become alike lawful in all the states, old as well as new, North as well as South."

Now you all see, from that quotation, I did not express my *wish* on anything. In that passage I indicated no wish or purpose of my own; I simply expressed my *expectation*. Cannot the Judge perceive the distinction between a *purpose* and an *expectation*. I have often expressed an expectation to die, but I have never expressed a *wish* to die. I said at Chicago, and now repeat, that I am quite aware this government has endured, half-slave and half-free, for eighty-two years. I understand that little bit of history. I expressed the opinion I did, because I perceived—or thought I perceived—a new set of causes introduced. I did say, at Chicago, in my speech there, that I do wish to see the spread of slavery arrested and to see it placed where the public mind shall rest in the belief that it is in course of ultimate extinction. I said that because I supposed, when the public mind shall rest in that belief, we shall have peace on the slavery question. I have believed—and now believe—the public mind did rest on that belief up to the introduction of the Nebraska bill.

The Living Lincoln

Although I have ever been opposed to slavery, so far I rested in the hope and belief that it was in course of ultimate extinction. For that reason, it had been a minor question with me. I might have been mistaken; but I had believed, and now believe, that the whole public mind, that is the mind of the great majority, had rested in that belief up to the repeal of the Missouri Compromise. But upon that event, I became convinced that either I had been resting in a delusion, or the institution was being placed on a new basis—a basis for making it perpetual, national and universal. Subsequent events have greatly confirmed me in that belief. I believe that bill to be the beginning of a conspiracy for that purpose. So believing, I have since then considered that question a paramount one. So believing, I have thought the public mind will never rest till the power of Congress to restrict the spread of it, shall again be acknowledged and exercised on the one hand, or on the other, all resistance be entirely crushed out. I have expressed that opinion, and I entertain it to-night. It is denied that there is any tendency to the nationalization of slavery in these states.

Mr. Brooks, of South Carolina, in one of his speeches, when they were presenting him with canes, silver plate, gold pitchers and the like, for assaulting Senator Sumner, distinctly affirmed his opinion that when this Constitution was formed, it was the belief of no man that slavery would last to the present day.

He said, what I think, that the framers of our Constitution placed the institution of slavery where the public mind rested in the hope that it was in course of ultimate extinction. But he went on to say that the men of the present age, by their experience, have become wiser than the framers of the Constitution; and the invention of the cotton gin had made the perpetuity of slavery a necessity in this country.

As another piece of evidence tending to the same point:—Quite recently in Virginia, a man—the owner of slaves—made a will providing that after his death certain of his slaves should have their freedom if they should so choose, and go to Liberia, rather than remain in slavery. They chose to be liberated. But the persons to whom they would descend as property, claimed them as slaves. A suit was instituted, which finally came to the supreme court of Virginia, and was therein decided against the slaves, upon the ground that a Negro cannot make a choice—that they had no legal power to choose—could not perform the condition upon which their freedom depended.

I do not mention this with any purpose of criticizing, but to connect it with the arguments as affording additional evidence of the change of sentiment upon this question of slavery in the direction of making it perpetual and national. I argue now as I did before, that there is such a tendency, and I am backed not merely by the facts, but by the open confession in the slave states.

For more than a year Douglas had been contending that the Dred Scott decision had settled the question of slavery in the territories. Lincoln had refused to accept the decision as a political rule. Pivoting on this point, he took the offensive.

The plain truth is simply this: Judge Douglas is *for* Supreme Court decisions when he likes and against them when he does not like them. He is for the Dred Scott decision because it tends to nationalize slavery—because it is part of the original combination for that object. It so happens, singularly enough, that I never stood opposed to a decision of the Supreme Court till this. On the contrary, I have no recollection that he was ever particularly in favor of one till this. He never was in favor of any, nor opposed to any, till the present one, which helps to nationalize slavery.

Free men of Sangamon—free men of Illinois—free men everywhere—judge ye between him and me, upon this issue.

He says this Dred Scott case is a very small matter at most—that it has no practical effect; that at best, or rather, I suppose, at worst, it is but an abstraction. I submit that the proposition that the thing which determines whether a man is free or a slave, is rather *concrete* than *abstract*. I think you would conclude that it was, if your liberty depended upon it, and so would Judge Douglas if his liberty depended upon it. But suppose it was on the question of spreading slavery over the new territories that he considers it as being merely an abstract matter, and one of no practical importance. How has the planting of slavery in new countries always been effected? It has now been decided that slavery cannot be kept out of our new territories by any legal means. In what does our new territories now differ in this respect, from the old colonies when slavery was first planted within them? It was planted as Mr. Clay once declared, and as history proves true, by individual men in spite of the wishes of the people; the mother government refusing to prohibit it, and withholding from the people of the colonies the authority to prohibit it for themselves. Mr. Clay says this was one of the great and just causes of complaint against Great Britain by the colonies, and the best apology we can now make for having the institution amongst us. In that precise condition our Nebraska politicians have at last succeeded in placing our own new territories; the government will not prohibit slavery within them, nor allow the people to prohibit it.

I defy any man to find any difference between the policy which originally planted slavery in these colonies and that policy which now prevails in our own new territories. If it does not go into them, it is only because no individual wishes it to go. The Judge indulged himself, doubtless, today, with the question as to what I am going to do with or about the Dred Scott decision. Well, Judge, will you please tell me what you did about the Bank decision? Will you not graciously allow us to do with the Dred Scott decision precisely as you did with the Bank decision? You succeeded in breaking down the moral effect of that decision; did you find it necessary to amend the Constitution? or to set up a court of Negroes in order to do it?

There is one other point. Judge Douglas has a very affectionate leaning towards the Americans and Old Whigs. Last evening, in a sort of weeping tone, he described to us a death-bed scene. He had been called to the side of Mr. Clay, in his last moments, in order that the genius of "popular sovereignty" might duly descend from the dying man and settle upon him, the living and most worthy successor. He could do no less than promise that he would devote the remainder of his life to "popular sovereignty;" and then the great statesman departs in peace. By this part of the "plan of the campaign," the Judge has evidently promised himself that tears shall be drawn down the cheeks of all Old Whigs, as large as half-grown apples.

Mr. Webster, too, was mentioned; but it did not quite come to a death-bed scene, as to him. It would be amusing, if it were not disgusting, to see how quick these Compromise-breakers administer on the political effects of their dead adversaries, trumping up claims never before heard of, and dividing the assets among themselves. If I should be found dead tomorrow morning, nothing but my insignificance could prevent a speech being made on my authority, before the end of next week. It so happens that in that "popular sovereignty" with which Mr. Clay was identified, the Missouri Compromise was expressly reserved; and it was a little singular if Mr. Clay cast his mantle upon Judge Douglas on purpose to have that Compromise repealed.

Again, the Judge did not keep faith with Mr. Clay when he first brought in his Nebraska bill. He left the Missouri Compromise unrepealed, and in his report accompanying the bill, he told the world he did it on purpose. The manes of Mr. Clay must have been in great agony, till thirty days later, when "popular sovereignty" stood forth in all its glory.

One more thing. Last night Judge Douglas tormented himself with horrors about my disposition to make Negroes perfectly equal with white men in social and political relations. He did not stop to show that I have said any such thing, or that it legitimately follows from anything I have said, but he rushes on with his assertions. I adhere to the Declaration of Independence. If Judge Douglas and his friends are not willing to stand by it, let them come up and amend it. Let them make it read that all men are created equal except Negroes. Let us have it decided, whether the Declaration of Independence, in this blessed year of 1858, shall be thus amended. In his construction of the Declaration last year he said it only meant that Americans in America were equal to Englishmen in England. Then, when I pointed out to him that by that rule he excludes the Germans, the Irish, the Portuguese, and all the other people who have come amongst us since the Revolution, he reconstructs his construction. In his last speech he tells us it meant Europeans.

I press him a little further, and ask if it meant to include the Russians in Asia? or does he mean to exclude that vast population from the principles of our Declaration of Independence? I expect ere long he will introduce another amendment to his definition. He is not at all particular. He is satisfied with anything which does not endanger the nationalizing of Negro slavery. It may draw white men down, but it must not lift Negroes up. Who shall say, "I am the superior, and you are the inferior?"

My declarations upon this subject of Negro slavery may be misrepresented, but cannot be misunderstood. I have said that I do not understand the Declaration to mean that all men were created equal in all respects. They are not our equal in color; but I suppose that it does mean to declare that all men are equal in some respects; they are equal in their right to "life, liberty, and the pursuit of happiness." Certainly the Negro is not our equal in color—perhaps not in many other respects; still, in the right to put into his mouth the bread that his own hands have earned, he is the equal of every other man, white or black. In pointing out that more has been given you, you cannot be justified in taking away the little which has been given him. All I ask for the Negro is that if you do not like him, let him alone. If God gave him but little, that little let him enjoy.

When our government was established, we had the institution of slavery among us. We were in a certain sense compelled to tolerate its existence. It was a sort of necessity. We had gone through our struggle and secured our own independence. The framers of the Constitution found the institution of slavery amongst their other institutions at the time. They found that by an effort to eradicate it, they might lose much of what they had already gained. They were obliged to bow to the necessity. They gave power to Congress to abolish the slave trade at the end of twenty years. They also prohibited it in the territories where it did not exist. They did what they could and yielded to the necessity for the rest. I also yield to all which follows from that necessity. What I would most desire would be the separation of the white and black races.

One more point on this Springfield speech which Judge Douglas says he has read so carefully. I expressed my belief in the existence of a conspiracy to perpetuate and nationalize slavery. I did not profess to know it, nor do I now. I showed the part Judge Douglas had played in the string of facts, constituting to my mind, the proof of that conspiracy. I showed the parts played by others.

I charged that the people had been deceived into carrying the last presidential election, by the impression that the people of the territories might exclude slavery if they chose, when it was known in advance by the conspirators, that the court was to decide that neither Congress nor the people could so exclude slavery. These charges are more distinctly made than anything else in the speech.

Judge Douglas has carefully read and re-read that speech. He has not, so far as I know, contradicted those charges. In the two speeches which I heard he certainly did not. On his own tacit admission I renew that charge. I charge him with having been a party to that conspiracy and to that deception for the sole purpose of nationalizing slavery.

Partly by accident, partly by Lincoln's planning, the campaigning of the two contestants had assumed the pattern of a debate. At Chicago, Douglas had spoken on July 9; Lincoln had replied the next day. At Springfield, on the 17th, Douglas had spoken in the afternoon, Lincoln in the evening. The challenger now moved to make the pattern formal and to extend it to the entire state. Norman B. Judd, a Chicago lawyer, was chairman of the Republican State Central Committee.

Chicago, Ills.
July 24, 1858.

Hon. S. A. Douglas
My Dear Sir
Will it be agreeable to you to make an arrangement for you and myself to divide time, and address the same audiences during the present canvass? Mr. Judd, who will hand you this, is authorized to receive your answer; and, if agreeable to you, to enter into the terms of such arrangement. Your Obt. Servt

A. Lincoln

Douglas answered querulously, but agreed to formal debates in the seven congressional districts in which the two men had not already made major speeches. Lincoln did not allow his opponent's insinuations to stand unchallenged.

Springfield,
July 29. 1858

Hon. S. A. Douglas
Dear Sir
Yours of the 24th. in relation to an arrangement to divide time and address the same audiences, is received; and, in apology for not sooner replying, allow me to say that when I sat by you at dinner yesterday I was not aware that you had answered my note, nor certainly, that my own note had been presented to you. An hour after I saw a copy of your answer in the Chicago Times; and, reaching home, I found the original awaiting me. Protesting that your insinuations of attempted unfairness on my part are unjust;

and with the hope that you did not very considerately make them, I proceed to reply. To your statement that "It has been suggested recently that an arrangement had been made to bring out a third candidate for the U. S. Senate who, with yourself, should canvass the state in opposition to me &c." I can only say that such suggestion must have been made by yourself; for certainly none such has been made by, or to me; or otherwise, to my knowledge. Surely you did not *deliberately* conclude, as you insinuate, that I was expecting to draw you into an arrangement, of terms to be agreed on by yourself, by which a third candidate, and myself, "in concert, might be able to take the opening and closing speech in every case."

As to your surprise that I did not sooner make the proposal to divide time with you, I can only say I made it as soon as I resolved to make it. I did not know but that such proposal would come from you; I waited respectfully to see. It may have been well known to you that you went to Springfield for the purpose of agreeing on the plan of campaign; but it was not so known to me. When your appointments were announced in the papers, extending only to the 21st. of August, I, for the first time, considered it certain that you would make no proposal to me; and then resolved, that if my friends concurred, I would make one to you. As soon thereafter as I could see and consult with friends satisfactorily, I did make the proposal. It did not occur to me that the proposed arrangement could derange your plan, after the latest of your appointments already made. After that, there was, before the election, largely over two months of clear time.

For you to say that we have already spoken at Chicago and Springfield, and that on both occasions I had the concluding speech, is hardly a fair statement. The truth rather is this. At Chicago, July 9th, you made a carefully prepared conclusion on my speech of June 16th.; twenty-four hours after I made a hasty conclusion on yours of the 9th.; you had six days to prepare, and concluded on me again at Bloomington on the 16th.; twenty-four hours after I concluded on you again at Springfield. In the meantime you had made another conclusion on me at Springfield, which I did not hear, and of the contents of which I knew nothing when I spoke; so that your speech made in daylight, and mine at night of the 17th. at Springfield were both made in perfect independence of each other. The dates of making all these speeches, will show, I think, that in the matter of time for preparation, the advantage has all been on your side; and that none of the external circumstances have stood to my advantage.

I agree to an arrangement for us to speak at the seven places you have named, and at your own times, provided you name the times at once, so that I, as well as you, can have to myself the time not covered by the arrangement. As to other details, I wish perfect reciprocity, and no more. I wish as much time as you, and that conclusions shall alternate. That is all. Your obedient Servant

A. Lincoln—

P.S. As matters now stand, I shall be at no more of your exclusive meetings; and for about a week from today a letter from you will reach me at Springfield.   *A.L.*

To a Quincy, Illinois, lawyer who had offered a tactical suggestion, Lincoln made a shrewd forecast of the way in which Douglas would escape from a logical trap.

Springfield,
July 31. 1858.

Henry Asbury, Esq
My dear Sir

Yours of the 28th. is received. The points you propose to press upon Douglas, he will be very hard to get up to. But I think you labor under a mistake when you say no one cares how he answers. This implies that it is equal with him whether he is injured here or at the South. That is a mistake. He cares nothing for the South —he knows he is already dead there. He only leans southward now to keep the Buchanan party from growing in Illinois. You shall have hard work to get him directly to the point whether a teritorial legislature has or has not the power to exclude slavery. But if you succeed in bringing him to it, though he will be compelled to say it possesses no such power; he will instantly take ground that slavery cannot actually exist in the teritories, unless the people desire it, and so give it protective teritorial legislation. If this offends the South he will let it offend them; as at all events he means to hold on to his chances in Illinois. You will soon learn by the papers that both the Judge and myself, are to be in Quincy on the 13th. of October, when & where I expect the pleasure of seeing you. Yours very truly

A. Lincoln.

Lincoln, willing to concede a point, though unwilling to let it pass without notice, closed the arrangements for the debates.

Springfield,
July 31. 1858.

Hon. S. A. Douglas:
Dear Sir
Yours of yesterday, naming places, times, and terms, for joint discussions between us, was received this morning. Although, by the terms, as you propose, you take *four* openings and closes to my *three,* I accede, and thus close the arrangement. I direct this to you at Hillsboro; and shall try to have both your letter and this, appear in the Journal and Register of Monday morning. Your Obt. Servt.

A. Lincoln—

VIII. "These Poor Tongues"

1858   T H E attention of the entire nation focussed on the seven formal debates, each with opening, reply, and rejoiner, each stenographically reported. Illinoisans, however, were much more likely to appraise the contestants from the speeches they made in the intervals between the debates. When Lincoln began his campaign with a speech at Beardstown on August 12, Douglas was already in the field. From that time until the end of October, both men pressed themselves to the limit in campaigning of the most arduous kind. Each man traveled from town to town by whatever conveyance was available—river steamer, primitive railroad, horse and buggy—put up in the miserable inns of small towns, rode in parades, met with local leaders, and spoke for an hour or two from an open platform or the stage of a hall. Broiling sun or chill rain, deep dust or deeper mud, meant nothing to the candidates or to the crowds that came to hear them.

Voters saw two men as different as men could be. Although Douglas was little more than five feet in height, his broad shoulders, massive chest, and deep musical voice conveyed an impression of strength and sturdiness. Lincoln—thin, bony, awkward—stood a foot above his rival. His voice, as he began to speak, would be high-pitched and nasal, but as he warmed to his work the pitch would drop and his words would carry to the outer limits of a crowd of thousands. Both were canny, experienced debaters, quick to exploit any weakness in the other's argument. At forty-five and forty-nine—Lincoln was the older—they had reached the full maturity of their powers.

On August 21, the day of the first joint debate, the town of Ottawa, located on the Illinois River in the north-central part of the state, found itself bursting with 10,000 visitors. Early in the afternoon two rival processions escorted the speakers to the public square. Eager partisans pressed so closely around the stand that time was lost in clearing the way for the debaters and reporters,

243

but after some skirmishing they were in their places. The crowd quieted.

Douglas opened with characteristic aggressiveness. Lincoln and Lyman Trumbull, Douglas charged, had conspired to dissolve the old Whig and Democratic parties, and to form from members of both an Abolition party misnamed Republican. For their labors, both were to go to the United States Senate. Trumbull collected his reward in 1855; Lincoln was now trying to collect his. Douglas also pounced on Lincoln's "House Divided" speech and its divisive tendencies, and censured his opponent for his stand on the Dred Scott decision.

Early in his speech Douglas posed a series of questions:

"I desire to know whether Mr. Lincoln today stands as he did in 1854, in favor of the unconditional repeal of the fugitive slave law. I desire him to answer whether he stands pledged today, as he did in 1854, against the admission of any more slave states into the Union, even if the people want them. I want to know whether he stands pledged against the admission of a new state into the Union with such a constitution as the people of that state may see fit to make. I want to know whether he stands today pledged to the abolition of slavery in the District of Columbia. I desire him to answer whether he stands pledged to the prohibition of the slave trade between the different states. I desire to know whether he stands pledged to prohibit slavery in all the territories of the United States, north as well as south of the Missouri Compromise line. I desire him to answer whether he is opposed to the acquisition of any more territory unless slavery is first prohibited therein."

Tauntingly, Douglas explained. "I ask Abraham Lincoln to answer these questions, in order that when I trot him down to lower Egypt I may put the same questions to him. My principles are the same everywhere. I can proclaim them alike in the North, the South, the East, and the West. My principles will apply wherever the Constitution prevails and the American flag waves. I desire to know whether Mr. Lincoln's principles will bear transplanting from Ottawa to Jonesboro? I put these questions to him today distinctly, and ask an answer."

Douglas also interjected a personal reference, seemingly friendly but filled with veiled slights:

"In the remarks I have made on this platform, and the position of Mr. Lincoln upon it, I mean nothing personally disrespectful or unkind to that gentleman. I have known him for nearly twenty-five years. There were many points of sympathy between us when we first got acquainted. We were both comparatively boys, and both struggling with poverty in a strange land. I was a school teacher in the town of Winchester, and he a flourishing grocery-keeper in the town of Salem. He was more successful in his occupation than I was in mine, and hence more fortunate in this world's goods. Lincoln is one of those peculiar men who perform with admirable skill everything which they undertake. I made as good a school teacher as I could and when a cabinet-maker I made a good bedstead and tables, although my old boss said I succeeded better with bureaus and secretaries than anything else; but I believe that Lincoln was always more successful in business than I, for his business enabled him to get into the legislature. I met him there, however, and had a sympathy with him, because of the uphill struggle we both had in life. He was then just as good at telling an anecdote as now. He could beat any of the boys wrestling, or running a foot race, in pitching quoits or tossing a copper, could ruin more liquor than all the boys of the town together, and the dignity and impartiality with which he presided at a horse race or fist fight, excited the admiration and won the praise of everybody that was present and participated. I sympathised with him, because he was struggling with difficulties and so was I.

"Mr. Lincoln served with me in the legislature in 1836, when we both retired, and he subsided, or became submerged, and he was lost sight of as a public man for some years. In 1846, when Wilmot introduced his celebrated proviso, and the abolition tornado swept over the country, Lincoln again turned up as a member of Congress from the Sangamon district. I was then in the Senate of the United States, and was glad to welcome my old friend and companion. Whilst in Congress, he distinguished himself by his opposition to the Mexican War, taking the side of the common enemy against his own country; and when he returned home he found that the indignation of the people followed him everywhere, and he was again submerged or obliged to retire into private life, forgotten by his former friends."

Lincoln, placed on the defensive by Douglas's opening, denied that he and Douglas were parties to a conspiracy. After taking notice of Douglas's personal aspersions, the Republican candidate argued that

245

he had not advocated national discord when he used the "House Divided" figure.

The Judge is wofully at fault about his early friend Lincoln being a "grocery keeper." [Laughter.] I don't know as it would be a great sin, if I had been, but he is mistaken. Lincoln never kept a grocery anywhere in the world. [Laughter.] It is true that Lincoln did work the latter part of one winter in a small still house, up at the head of a hollow. [Roars of laughter.] And so I think my friend, the Judge, is equally at fault when he charges me at the time when I was in Congress of having opposed our soldiers who were fighting in the Mexican War. The Judge did not make his charge very distinctly but I can tell you what he can prove by referring to the record. You remember I was an Old Whig, and whenever the Democratic party tried to get me to vote that the war had been righteously begun by the President, I would not do it. But whenever they asked for any money, or land warrants, or anything to pay the soldiers there, during all that time, I gave the same votes that Judge Douglas did. [Loud applause.] You can think as you please as to whether that was consistent. Such is the truth; and the Judge has the right to make all he can out of it. But when he, by a general charge, conveys the idea that I withheld supplies from the soldiers who were fighting in the Mexican War, or did anything else to hinder the soldiers, he is, to say the least, grossly and altogether mistaken, as a consultation of the records will prove to him.

As I have not used up so much of my time as I had supposed, I will dwell a little longer upon one or two of these minor topics upon with the Judge has spoken. He has read from my speech in Springfield, in which I say that "a house divided against itself cannot stand." Does the Judge say it *can* stand? [Laughter.] I don't know whether he does or not. The Judge does not seem to be attending to me just now, but I would like to know if it is his opinion that a house divided against itself *can stand*. If he does, then there is a question of veracity, not between him and me, but between the Judge and an authority of a somewhat higher character. [Laughter and applause.]

Now, my friends, I ask your attention to this matter for the purpose of saying something seriously. I know that the Judge may readily enough agree with me that the maxim which was put forth by the Saviour is true, but he may allege that I misapply it; and the Judge has a right to urge that, in my application, I do misapply it, and then I have a right to show that I do *not* misapply it. When he undertakes to say that because I think this nation, so far as the question of slavery is concerned, will all become one thing or all the other, I am in favor of bringing about a dead uniformity in the various states, in all their institutions, he argues erroneously. The great variety of the local institutions in the states, springing from differences in the soil, differences in the face of the country, and in the climate, are bonds of Union. They do not make "a house divided against itself," but they make a house united. If they produce in one section of the country what is called for by the wants of another section, and this other section can supply the wants of the first, they are not matters of discord but bonds of union, true bonds of union. But can this question of slavery be considered as among *these* varieties in the institutions of the country? I leave it to you to say whether, in the history of our government, this institution of slavery has not always failed to be a bond of union, and, on the contrary, been an apple of discord and an element of division in the house. [Cries of "Yes, yes," and applause.] I ask you to consider whether, so long as the moral constitution of men's minds shall continue to be the same, after this generation and assemblage shall sink into the grave, and another race shall arise, with the same moral and intellectual development we have—whether, if that institution is standing in the same irritating position in which it now is, it will not continue an element of division? [Cries of "Yes, yes."] If so, then I have a right to say that in regard to this question, the Union is a house divided against itself, and when the Judge reminds me that I have often said to him that the institution of slavery has existed for eighty years in some states, and yet it does not exist in some others, I agree to the fact, and I account for it by looking at the position in which our fathers originally placed it—restricting it from the new territories where it had not gone, and legislating to cut off its source by the abrogation of the slave trade, thus putting the seal of legislation *against its spread*. The public mind *did* rest in the belief that it was in the course of ultimate extinction. [Cries of "Yes, yes."]

But lately, I think—and in this I charge nothing on the Judge's motives—lately, I think, that he, and those acting with him, have placed that institution on a new basis, which looks to the *perpetu-*

ity and nationalization of slavery. [Loud cheers.] And while it is placed upon this new basis, I say, and I have said, that I believe we shall not have peace upon the question until the opponents of slavery arrest the further spread of it, and place it where the public mind shall rest in the belief that it is in the course of ultimate extinction; or, on the other hand, that its advocates will push it forward until it shall become alike lawful in all the states, old as well as new, North as well as South. Now, I believe if we could arrest the spread, and place it where Washington, and Jefferson, and Madison placed it, it *would be* in the course of ultimate extinction, and the public mind *would,* as for eighty years past, believe that it was in the course of ultimate extinction. The crisis would be past and the institution might be let alone for a hundred years, if it should live so long, in the states where it exists, yet it would be going out of existence in the way best for both the black and the white races.

Progressing in his argument, Lincoln repeated the conspiracy charge that he had first levelled at the Democrats in his "House Divided" address. To support it, he drew on the Dred Scott decision and its consequences as he saw them.

Now my friends I wish you to attend for a little while to one or two other things in that Springfield speech. My main object was to show, so far as my humble ability was capable of showing to the people of this country, what I believed was the truth—that there was a *tendency,* if not a conspiracy among those who have engineered this slavery question for the last four or five years, to make slavery perpetual and universal in this nation. . . . I do not say that I *know* such a conspiracy to exist. To that, I reply *I believe it.* If the Judge says that I do *not* believe it, then *he* says what *he* does not know, and falls within his own rule, that he who asserts a thing which he does not know to be true, falsifies as much as he who knowingly tells a falsehood. I want to call your attention to a little discussion on that branch of the case, and the evidence which brought my mind to the conclusion which I expressed as my *belief.* If, in arraying that evidence, I had stated anything which was false or erroneous, it needed but that Judge Douglas should point it out, and I would have taken it back with all the kindness in the world. I do not deal in that way. If I have brought forward anything not a fact, if he will point it out, it will not even ruffle me to take it back. But if he will not point out anything erroneous in the evidence, is it not rather for him to show, by a comparison of the evidence that I have *reasoned* falsely, than to call the "kind, amiable, intelligent gentleman," a liar? [Cheers and laughter.] If I have reasoned to a false conclusion, it is the vocation of an able debater to show by argument that I have wandered to an erroneous conclusion. . . .

I ask the attention of the people here assembled and elsewhere, to the course that Judge Douglas is pursuing every day as bearing upon this question of making slavery national. Not going back to the records but taking the speeches he makes, the speeches he made yesterday and day before and makes constantly all over the country—I ask your attention to them. In the first place what is necessary to make the institution national? Not war. There is no danger that the people of Kentucky will shoulder their muskets and with a young nigger stuck on every bayonet march into Illinois and force them upon us. There is no danger of our going over there and making war upon them. Then what is necessary for the nationalization of slavery? It is simply the next Dred Scott decision. It is merely for the Supreme Court to decide that no *state* under the Constitution can exclude it, just as they have already decided that under the Constitution neither Congress nor the territorial legislature can do it. When that is decided and acquiesced in, the whole thing is done.

This being true, and this being the way as I think that slavery is to be made national, let us consider what Judge Douglas is doing every day to that end. In the first place, let us see what influence he is exerting on public sentiment. In this and like communities, public sentiment is everything. With public sentiment, nothing can fail; without it nothing can succeed. Consequently he who moulds public sentiment, goes deeper than he who enacts statutes or pronounces decisions. He makes statutes and decisions possible or impossible to be executed. This must be borne in mind, as also the additional fact that Judge Douglas is a man of vast influence, so great that it is enough for many men to profess to believe anything, when they once find out that Judge Douglas professes to believe it. Consider also the attitude he occupies at the head of a large party—a party which he claims has a majority of all the voters in the country. This man sticks to a decision which forbids the people of a territory from excluding slavery, and he does so not because he says it is right in itself—he does not give any opinion on that—but because it has been *decided by the court,* and being decided by the court, he is, and you are bound to take it in your political action as *law*—not that he judges at all of its merits, but because a decision of the court is to him a *"Thus saith the Lord."* [Applause.] He places it on that ground alone, and you will bear in mind that thus committing himself unreservedly to this decision, *commits him to the next one* just as firmly as to this. He did not commit himself on account of the merit or demerit of the decision, but it is a *Thus saith the Lord.* The next decision, as much as this, will be a *thus saith the Lord.* There is nothing that can divert or turn him away from this decision. It is nothing that I point out to him that his great prototype, Gen. Jackson, did not believe in the binding force of decisions. It is nothing to him that Jefferson did not so believe. I have said that I have often heard him approve of Jackson's course in disregarding the decision of the Supreme Court pronouncing a National Bank constitutional. He says, I did not hear him say so. He denies the accuracy of my recollection. I say he ought to know better than I, but I will make no question about this thing, though it still seems to me that I heard him say it twenty times. [Applause and laughter.] I will tell him though, that he now claims to stand on the Cincinnati platform, which affirms that Congress *cannot* charter a National Bank, in the teeth of that old standing decision that Congress *can* charter a bank. [Loud applause.]

And I remind him of another piece of history on the question of respect for judicial decisions, and it is a piece of Illinois history, belonging to a time when the large party to which Judge Douglas belonged, were displeased with a decision of the Supreme Court of Illinois, because they had decided that a Governor could not remove a Secretary of State. You will find the whole story in Ford's History of Illinois, and I know that Judge Douglas will not deny that he was then in favor of overslaughing that decision by the mode of adding five new Judges, so as to vote down the four old ones. Not only so, but it ended in *the Judge's sitting down on that very bench as one of the five new Judges to break down the four old ones.* [Cheers and laughter.] It was in this way precisely that he got his title of Judge. Now, when the Judge tells me that men appointed conditionally to sit as members of a court, will have to be catechised beforehand upon some subject, I say "You know

Judge; you have tried it." [Laughter.] When he says a court of this kind will lose the confidence of all men, will be prostituted and disgraced by such a proceeding, I say, "You know best, Judge; you have been through the mill." [Great laughter.]

But I cannot shake Judge Douglas' teeth loose from the Dred Scott decision. Like some obstinate animal (I mean no disrespect,) that will hang on when he has once got his teeth fixed, you may cut off a leg, or you may tear away an arm, still he will not relax his hold. And so I may point out to the Judge, and say that he is bespattered all over, from the beginning of his political life to the present time, with attacks upon judicial decisions—I may cut off limb after limb of his public record, and strive to wrench him from a single dictum of the Court—yet I cannot divert him from it. He hangs to the last, to the Dred Scott decision. [Loud cheers.] These things show there is a purpose *strong as death and eternity* for which he adheres to this decision, and for which he will adhere to *all other decisions* of the same Court. [Vociferous applause.]

An Irishman—and therefore a Democrat—in the audience called out: "Give us something besides Dred Scott!"

Yes; no doubt you want to hear something that don't hurt. [Laughter and applause.] Now, having spoken of the Dred Scott decision, one more word and I am done. Henry Clay, my beau ideal of a statesman, the man for whom I fought all my humble life —Henry Clay once said of a class of men who would repress all tendencies to liberty and ultimate emancipation, that they must, if they would do this, go back to the era of our independence, and muzzle the cannon which thunders its annual joyous return; they must blow out the moral lights around us; they must penetrate the human soul, and eradicate there the love of liberty; and then and not till then, could they perpetuate slavery in this country! [Loud cheers.] To my thinking, Judge Douglas is, by his example and vast influence, doing that very thing in this community, [cheers,] when he says that the Negro has nothing in the Declaration of Independence. Henry Clay plainly understood the contrary. Judge Douglas is going back to the era of our Revolution, and to the extent of his ability, muzzling the cannon which thunders its annual joyous return. When he invites any people willing to have slavery, to establish it, he is blowing out the moral lights around

251

us. [Cheers.] When he says he "cares not whether slavery is voted down or voted up,"—that it is a sacred right of self-government— he is in my judgment penetrating the human soul and eradicating the light of reason and the love of liberty in this American people. [Enthusiastic and continued applause.] And now I will only say that when, by all these means and appliances, Judge Douglas shall succeed in bringing public sentiment to an exact accordance with his own views—when these vast assemblages shall echo back all these sentiments—when they shall come to repeat his views and to avow his principles, and to say all that he says on these mighty questions—then it needs only the formality of the second Dred Scott decision, which he endorses in advance, to make slavery alike lawful in all the states—old as well as new, North as well as South.

On August 27, at Freeport in strongly Republican northern Illinois, Lincoln and Douglas met again. In opening, Lincoln took up the questions which Douglas had asked at Ottawa, and then propounded four of his own.

Ladies and Gentlemen—
On Saturday last, Judge Douglas and myself first met in public discussion. He spoke one hour, I an hour-and-a-half, and he replied for half-an-hour. The order is now reversed. I am to speak an hour, he an hour-and-a-half, and then I am to reply for half-an-hour. I propose to devote myself during the first hour to the scope of what was brought within the range of his half-hour speech at Ottawa. Of course there was brought within the scope in that half-hour's speech something of his own opening speech. In the course of that opening argument Judge Douglas proposed to me seven distinct interrogatories. In my speech of an hour-and-a-half, I attended to some other parts of his speech, and incidentally, as I thought, answered one of the interrogatories then. I then distinctly intimated to him that I would answer the rest of his interrogatories on condition only that he should agree to answer as many for me. He made no intimation at the time of the proposition, nor did he in his reply allude at all to that suggestion of mine. I do him no injustice in saying that he occupied at least half of his reply in dealing with me as though I had *refused* to answer his interrogatories. I now propose that I will answer any of the interrogatories, upon condition that he will answer questions from me not exceeding the

same number. I give him an opportunity to respond. The Judge remains silent. I now say to you that I will answer his interrogatories, whether he answers mine or not; [applause] and that after I have done so, I shall propound mine to him. [Applause.]

I have supposed myself, since the organization of the Republican party at Bloomington, in May, 1856, bound as a party man by the platforms of the party, then and since. If in any interrogatories which I shall answer I go beyond the scope of what is within these platforms it will be perceived that no one is responsible but myself.

Having said thus much, I will take up the Judge's interrogatories as I find them printed in the Chicago *Times,* and answer them *seriatim.* In order that there may be no mistake about it, I have copied the interrogatories in writing, and also my answers to them. The first one of these interrogatories is in these words:

Question 1. "I desire to know whether Lincoln today stands, as he did in 1854, in favor of the unconditional repeal of the fugitive slave law?"

Answer. I do not now, nor ever did, stand in favor of the unconditional repeal of the fugitive slave law. [Cries of "good," "good."]

Q. 2. "I desire him to answer whether he stands pledged today, as he did in 1854, against the admission of any more slave states into the Union, even if the people want them?"

A. I do not now, nor ever did, stand pledged against the admission of any more slave states into the Union.

Q. 3. "I want to know whether he stands pledged against the admission of a new state into the Union with such a constitution as the people of that state may see fit to make."

A. I do not stand pledged against the admission of a new state into the Union, with such a constitution as the people of that state may see fit to make. [Cries of "good," "good."]

Q. 4. "I want to know whether he stands today pledged to the abolition of slavery in the District of Columbia?"

A. I do not stand today pledged to the abolition of slavery in the District of Columbia.

Q. 5. "I desire him to answer whether he stands pledged to the prohibition of the slave trade between the different states?"

A. I do not stand pledged to the prohibition of the slave trade between the different states.

Q. 6. "I desire to know whether he stands pledged to prohibit

253

slavery in all the territories of the United States, North as well as South of the Missouri Compromise line."

A. I am impliedly, if not expressly, pledged to a belief in the *right* and *duty* of Congress to prohibit slavery in all the United States territories. [Great applause.]

Q. 7. "I desire him to answer whether he is opposed to the acquisition of any new territory unless slavery is first prohibited therein."

A. I am not generally opposed to honest acquisition of territory; and, in any given case, I would or would not oppose such acquisition, accordingly as I might think such acquisition would or would not aggravate the slavery question among ourselves. [Cries of "good," "good."]

Now, my friends, it will be perceived upon an examination of these questions and answers, that so far I have only answered that I was not *pledged* to this, that or the other. The Judge has not framed his interrogatories to ask me anything more than this, and I have answered in strict accordance with the interrogatories, and have answered truly that I am not *pledged* at all upon any of the points to which I have answered. But I am not disposed to hang upon the exact form of his interrogatory. I am rather disposed to take up at least some of these questions, and state what I really think upon them.

As to the first one, in regard to the Fugitive Slave law, I have never hesitated to say, and I do not now hesitate to say, that I think, under the Constitution of the United States, the people of the Southern states are entitled to a congressional Fugitive Slave law. Having said that, I have had nothing to say in regard to the existing Fugitive Slave law further than that I think it should have been framed so as to be free from some of the objections that pertain to it, without lessening its efficiency. And inasmuch as we are not now in an agitation in regard to an alteration or modification of that law, I would not be the man to introduce it as a new subject of agitation upon the general question of slavery.

In regard to the other question of whether I am pledged to the admission of any more slave states into the Union, I state to you very frankly that I would be exceedingly sorry ever to be put in a position of having to pass upon that question. I should be exceedingly glad to know that there would never be another slave state admitted into the Union [applause]; but I must add, that if slavery shall be kept out of the territories during the territorial existence of any one given territory, and then the people shall, having a fair chance and a clear field, when they come to adopt the constitution, do such an extraordinary thing as to adopt a slave constitution, uninfluenced by the actual presence of the institution among them, I see no alternative, if we own the country, but to admit them into the Union. [Applause.]

The third interrogatory is answered by the answer to the second, it being, as I conceive, the same as the second.

The fourth one is in regard to the abolition of slavery in the District of Columbia. In relation to that, I have my mind very distinctly made up. I should be exceedingly glad to see slavery abolished in the District of Columbia. [Cries of "good, good."] I believe that Congress possesses the constitutional power to abolish it. Yet as a member of Congress, I should not with my present views, be in favor of *endeavoring* to abolish slavery in the District of Columbia, unless it would be upon these conditions. *First,* that the abolition should be gradual. *Second,* that it should be on a vote of the majority of qualified voters in the District, and *third,* that compensation should be made to unwilling owners. With these three conditions, I confess I would be exceedingly glad to see Congress abolish slavery in the District of Columbia, and, in the language of Henry Clay, "sweep from our Capital that foul blot upon our nation." [Loud applause.]

In regard to the fifth interrogatory, I must say here, that as to the question of the abolition of the slave trade between the different states, I can truly answer, as I have, that I am *pledged* to nothing about it. It is a subject to which I have not given that mature consideration that would make me feel authorized to state a position so as to hold myself entirely bound by it. In other words, that question has never been prominently enough before me to induce me to investigate whether we really have the constitutional power to do it. I could investigate it if I had sufficient time, to bring myself to a conclusion upon that subject, but I have not done so, and I say so frankly to you here, and to Judge Douglas. I must say, however, that if I should be of opinion that Congress does possess the constitutional power to abolish the slave trade among the different states, I should still not be in favor of the exercise of that power unless upon some conservative principle as I conceive it, akin to what I have said in relation to the abolition of slavery in the District of Columbia.

My answer as to whether I desire that slavery should be prohibited in all the territories of the United States is full and explicit within itself, and cannot be made clearer by any comments of mine. So I suppose in regard to the question whether I am opposed to the acquisition of any more territory unless slavery is first prohibited therein, my answer is such that I could add nothing by way of illustration, or making myself better understood, than the answer which I have placed in writing.

Now in all this, the Judge has me and he has me on the record. I suppose he had flattered himself that I was really entertaining one set of opinions for one place and another set for another place— that I was afraid to say at one place what I uttered at another. What I am saying here I suppose I say to a vast audience as strongly tending to abolitionism as any audience in the state of Illinois, and I believe I am saying that which, if it would be offensive to any persons and render them enemies to myself, would be offensive to persons in this audience.

I now proceed to propound to the Judge the interrogatories, so far as I have framed them. I will bring forward a new installment when I get them ready. [Laughter.] I will bring them forward now, only reaching to number four.

The first one is—

Question 1. If the people of Kansas shall, by means entirely unobjectionable in all other respects, adopt a state constitution, and ask admission into the Union under it, *before* they have the requisite number of inhabitants according to the English bill— some ninety-three thousand—will you vote to admit them? [Applause.]

Q. 2. Can the people of a United States territory, in any lawful way, against the wish of any citizen of the United States, exclude slavery from its limits prior to the formation of a state constitution? [Renewed applause.]

Q. 3. If the Supreme Court of the United States shall decide that states can not exclude slavery from their limits, are you in favor of acquiescing in, adopting and following such decision as a rule of political action? [Loud applause.]

Q. 4. Are you in favor of acquiring additional territory, in disregard of how such acquisition may affect the nation on the slavery question? [Cries of "good," "good."]

Douglas answered forthrightly. "First," he said, "he [Lincoln] desires to know if the people of Kansas shall form a constitution by means entirely proper and unobjectionable and ask admission into the Union as a state, before they have the requisite population for a member of Congress, whether I will vote for that admission. . . . In reference to Kansas, it is my opinion, that as she has population enough to constitute a slave state, she has people enough for a free state."

Douglas's reply to Lincoln's second question would be known as the "Freeport Doctrine," and would be the subject of endless argument. By his answer, Douglas would hold the voters of Illinois but lose, beyond hope of recovery, the pro-slavery South. He chose his words carefully:

"The next question propounded to me by Mr. Lincoln is, can the people of a territory in any lawful way against the wishes of any citizen of the United States; exclude slavery from their limits prior to the formation of a state constitution? I answer emphatically, as Mr. Lincoln has heard me answer a hundred times from every stump in Illinois, that in my opinion the people of a territory can, by lawful means, exclude slavery from their limits prior to the formation of a state constitution. Mr. Lincoln knew that I had argued that question over and over again. He heard me argue the Nebraska bill on that principle all over the state in 1854, in 1855 and in 1856, and he has no excuse for pretending to be in doubt as to my position on that question. It matters not what way the Supreme Court may hereafter decide as to the abstract question whether slavery may or may not go into a territory under the Constitution, the people have the lawful means to introduce it or exclude it as they please, for the reason that slavery cannot exist a day or an hour anywhere, unless it is supported by local police regulations. Those police regulations can only be established by the local legislature, and if the people are opposed to slavery they will elect representatives to that body who will by unfriendly legislation effectually prevent the introduction of it into their midst. If, on the contrary, they are for it, their legislation will favor its extension. Hence, no matter what the decision of the Supreme Court may be on that abstract question, still the right of the people to make a slave territory or a free territory is perfect and complete under the Nebraska bill. I hope Mr. Lincoln deems my answer satisfactory on that point."

The Living Lincoln

In replying to Lincoln's third question Douglas resorted to ridicule:
"The third question which Mr. Lincoln presented is, if the Supreme Court of the United States shall decide that a state of this Union cannot exclude slavery from its own limits will I submit to it? I am amazed that Lincoln should ask such a question. . . . He might as well ask me, suppose Mr. Lincoln should steal a horse would I sanction it; and it would be as genteel in me to ask him, in the event he stole a horse, what ought to be done with him. He casts an imputation upon the Supreme Court of the United States by supposing that they would violate the Constitution of the United States. I tell him that such a thing is not possible."

Subsequently Lincoln had added a question to his original three. Douglas answered that with candor.

"The fourth question of Mr. Lincoln is, are you in favor of acquiring additional territory in disregard as to how such acquisition may affect the Union on the slavery question? . . . I answer that whenever it becomes necessary, in our growth and progress to acquire more territory, that I am in favor of it, without reference to the question of slavery, and when we have acquired it, I will leave the people free to do as they please, either to make it slave or free territory, as they prefer."

Mid-September found the candidates in the somnolent little town of Jonesboro in the southernmost part of Illinois. The region, settled by Southerners, was pro-slavery in its sympathies and heavily Democratic. Douglas made the debate the occasion for stressing his position on the Negro.

"I hold," he asserted, "that a Negro is not and never ought to be a citizen of the United States. I hold that this government was made on the white basis, by white men, for the benefit of white men and none others. I do not believe that the Almighty made the Negro capable of self-government. . . . I say to you, my fellow-citizens, that in my opinion the signers of the Declaration had no reference to the Negro whatever when they declared all men to be created equal. They desired to express by that phrase, white men, men of European birth and European descent, and had no reference either to the Negro, the savage Indians, the Fejee, the Malay, or any other inferior and degraded race, when they spoke of the equality of men. . . .

"My friends, I am in favor of preserving this government as our

fathers made it. It does not follow by any means that because a Negro
is not your equal or mine that hence he must necessarily be a slave. On
the contrary, it does follow that we ought to extend to the Negro every
right, privilege, every immunity which he is capable of enjoying consistent with the good of society. When you ask me what these rights are,
what their nature and extent is, I tell you that that is a question which
each state of this Union must decide for itself. Illinois has already decided the question. We have decided that the Negro must not be a slave
within our limits, but we have also decided that the Negro shall not be
a citizen within our limits; that he shall not vote, hold office, or exercise
any political rights. I maintain that Illinois, as a sovereign state, has a
right thus to fix her policy with reference to the relation between the
white man and the Negro; but while we had the right to decide the
question for ourselves we must recognize the same right in Kentucky
and in every other state to make the same decision, or a different
one. . . .

"The Dred Scott decision covers the whole question, and declares
that each state has the right to settle this question of suffrage for itself, and all questions as to the relations between the white man and the
Negro. . . . I receive it as law, and I say that while those states are
adopting regulations on that subject disgusting and abhorrent, according to my views, I will not make war on them if they will mind their
own business and let us alone."

Obviously, Douglas hoped to prod his Republican opponent into
defining his own attitude on the place of the Negro, but Lincoln chose
to ignore the challenge, and instead, exploited Douglas's Freeport doctrine.

The second interrogatory that I propounded to him [Douglas
at Freeport] was this:

Q. 2. Can the people of a United States territory, in any lawful way, against the wish of any citizen of the United States, exclude slavery from its limits prior to the formation of a state constitution?

To this Judge Douglas answered that they can lawfully exclude slavery from the Territory prior to the formation of a constitution. He goes on to tell us how it can be done. As I understand
him, he holds that it can be done by the territorial legislature refusing to make any enactments for the protection of slavery in the

territory, and especially by adopting unfriendly legislation to it. For the sake of clearness I state it again; that they can exclude slavery from the territory, 1st, by withholding what he assumes to be an indispensable assistance to it in the way of legislation; and 2d, by unfriendly legislation. If I rightly understand him, I wish to ask your attention for a while to his position.

In the first place, the Supreme Court of the United States has decided that any congressional prohibition of slavery in the territories is unconstitutional—that they have reached this proposition as a conclusion from their former proposition that the Constitution of the United States expressly recognizes property in slaves, and from that other constitutional provision that no person shall be deprived of property without due process of law. Hence they reach the conclusion that as the Constitution of the United States expressly recognizes property in slaves, and prohibits any person from being deprived of property without due process of law, to pass an act of Congress by which a man who owned a slave on one side of a line would be deprived of him if he took him on the other side, is depriving him of that property without due process of law. That I understand to be the decision of the Supreme Court. I understand also that Judge Douglas adheres most firmly to that decision; and the difficulty is, how is it possible for any power to exclude slavery from the territory unless in violation of that decision? That is the difficulty. . . .

I hold that the proposition that slavery cannot enter a new country without police regulations is historically false. It is not true at all. I hold that the history of this country shows that the institution of slavery was originally planted upon this continent *without* these "police regulations" which the Judge now thinks necessary for the actual establishment of it. Not only so, but is there not another fact—how came this Dred Scott decision to be made? It was made upon the case of a Negro being taken and actually held in slavery in Minnesota Territory, claiming his freedom because the act of Congress prohibited his being so held there. *Will the Judge pretend that Dred Scott was not held there without police regulations?* There is at least one matter of record as to his having been held in slavery in the territory, not only without police regulations, but in the teeth of congressional legislation supposed to be valid at the time. This shows that there is vigor enough in slavery to plant itself in a new country even against unfriendly legislation. It takes not only law but the *enforcement* of law to keep it out. That is the history of this country upon the subject.

I wish to ask one other question. It being understood that the Constitution of the United States guarantees property in slaves in the territories, if there is any infringement of the right of that property, would not the United States Courts, organized for the government of the territory, apply such remedy as might be necessary in that case? It is a maxim held by the courts, that there is no wrong without its remedy; and the courts have a remedy for whatever is acknowledged and treated as a wrong.

Again: I will ask you my friends, if you were elected members of the legislature, what would be the first thing you would have to do before entering upon your duties? *Swear to support the Constitution of the United States.* Suppose you believe, as Judge Douglas does, that the Constitution of the United States guarantees to your neighbor the right to hold slaves in that territory—that they are his property—how can you clear your oaths unless you give him such legislation as is necessary to enable him to enjoy that property? What do you understand by supporting the constitution of a state or of the United States? Is it not to give such constitutional helps to the rights established by that constitution as may be practically needed? Can you, if you swear to support the Constitution, and believe that the Constitution establishes a right, clear your oath, without giving it support? Do you support the Constitution if, knowing or believing there is a right established under it which needs specific legislation, you withhold that legislation? Do you not violate and disregard your oath? I can conceive of nothing plainer in the world. There can be nothing in the words "support the Constitution," if you may run counter to it by refusing support to any right established under the Constitution. And what I say here will hold with still more force against the Judge's doctrine of "unfriendly legislation." How could you, having sworn to support the Constitution, and believing it guaranteed the right to hold slaves in the territories, assist in legislation *intended to defeat that right?* That would be violating your own view of the Constitution. Not only so, but if you were to do so, how long would it take the courts to hold your votes unconstitutional and void? Not a moment.

Lastly I would ask—is not Congress, itself, under obligation to give legislative support to any right that is established under the United States Constitution? I repeat the question—is not Congress, itself, bound to give legislative support to any right that is established in the United States Constitution? A member of Congress swears to support the Constitution of the United States, and if he sees a right established by that Constitution which needs specific legislative protection, can he clear his oath without giving that protection? Let me ask you why many of us who are opposed to slavery upon principle give our acquiescence to a fugitive slave law? Why do we hold ourselves under obligations to pass such a law, and abide by it when it is passed? Because the Constitution makes provision that the owners of slaves shall have the right to reclaim them. It gives the right to reclaim slaves, and that right is, as Judge Douglas says, a barren right, unless there is legislation that will enforce it.

The mere declaration, "No person held to service or labor in one state under the laws thereof, escaping into another, shall in consequence of any law or regulation therein be discharged from such service or labor, but shall be delivered up on claim of the party to whom such service or labor may be due," is powerless without specific legislation to enforce it. Now on what ground would a member of Congress who is opposed to slavery in the abstract vote for a fugitive law, as I would deem it my duty to do? Because there is a constitutional right which needs legislation to enforce it. And although it is distasteful to me, I have sworn to support the Constitution, and having so sworn I cannot conceive that I do support it if I withheld from that right any necessary legislation to make it practical. And if that is true in regard to a fugitive slave law, is the right to have fugitive slaves reclaimed any better fixed in the Constitution than the right to hold slaves in the territories? For this decision is a just exposition of the Constitution as Judge Douglas thinks. Is the one right any better than the other? Is there any man who while a member of Congress would give support to the one any more than the other? If I wished to refuse to give legislative support to slave property in the territories, if a member of Congress, I could not do it holding the view that the Constitution establishes that right. If I did it at all, it would be because I deny that this decision properly construes the Constitution. But if I acknowledge with Judge Douglas that this decision properly construes the Constitution, I cannot conceive that I would be less than a perjured man if I should refuse in Congress to give such protection to that property as in its nature it needed.

Lincoln closed with a personal reference to Douglas. Name-calling and innuendoes as to Douglas's fondness for liquor revealed the extent to which the stresses of a strenuous campaign had distorted Lincoln's usual good judgment.

Now, my fellow citizens, I will detain you only a little while longer. My time is very nearly out. I find a report of a speech made by Judge Douglas at Joliet, since we last met at Freeport—published I believe in the *Missouri Republican*—on the 9th of this month, in which Judge Douglas says:

"You know at Ottawa, I read this platform, and asked him if he concurred in each and all of the principles set forth in it. He would not answer these questions. At last I said frankly, 'I wish you to answer them, because when I get them up here where the color of your principles is a little darker than in Egypt, I intend to trot you down to Jonesboro.' The very notice that I was going to take him down to Egypt made him tremble in the knees so that he had to be carried from the platform. He laid up seven days, and in the meantime held a consultation with his political physicians, they had Lovejoy and Farnsworth and all the leaders of the Abolition party, they consulted it all over, and at last Lincoln came to the conclusion that he would answer, so he came up to Freeport last Friday."

Now that statement altogether furnishes a subject for philosophical contemplation. [Laughter.] I have been treating it in that way, and I have really come to the conclusion that I can explain it in no other way than by believing the Judge is crazy. [Renewed laughter.] If he was in his right mind, I cannot conceive how he would have risked disgusting the four or five thousand of his own friends who stood there, and knew, as to my having been carried from the platform, that there was not a word of truth in it.

JUDGE DOUGLAS—Didn't they carry you off?

Mr. LINCOLN—There; that question illustrates the character of this man Douglas, exactly. He smiles now and says, "Didn't they carry you off?" But he says then, *"He had to be carried off;"* and he said it to convince the country that he had so completely broken me down by his speech that I had to be carried away. Now he seeks to dodge it, and asks, "Didn't they carry you off?" Yes, they did. *But, Judge Douglas, why didn't you tell the truth?* [Great laughter and cheers.] I would like to know why you didn't tell the truth about it. [Continued laughter.] And then again, "He laid up seven days." He puts this in print for the people of the country to read as a serious document. I think if he had been in his sober senses he would not have risked that barefacedness in the presence of thousands of his own friends, who knew that I made speeches within six of the seven days at Henry, Marshall County; Augusta, Hancock County, and Macomb, McDonough County, including all the necessary travel to meet him again at Freeport at the end of the six days. Now I say, there is no charitable way to look at that statement, except to conclude that he is actually crazy. [Laughter.]

There is another thing in that statement that alarmed me very greatly as he states it, that he was going to "trot me down to Egypt." Thereby he would have you to infer that I would not come to Egypt unless he forced me—that I could not be got here, unless he, giant-like, had hauled me down here. [Laughter.] That statement he makes, too, in the teeth of the knowledge that I had made the stipulation to come down here, *and that he himself had been very reluctant to enter into the stipulation.* [Cheers and laughter.] More than all this, Judge Douglas, when he made that statement must have been crazy, and wholly out of his sober senses, or else he would have known that when he got me down here—that promise—that windy promise—of his powers to annihilate me, wouldn't amount to anything. Now, how little do I look like being carried away trembling? Let the Judge go on, and after he is done with his half-hour, I want you all, if I can't go home myself, to let me stay and rot here; and if anything happens to the Judge, if I cannot carry him to the hotel and put him to bed, let me stay here and rot. [Great laughter.] I say, then, there is something *extraordinary* in this statement? I ask you if you know any other living man who would make such a statement? [Cries of "No," "no." "Yes," "yes."] I will ask my friend Casey, over there, if he would do such a thing? [Casey dropped his head and said nothing.] Would he send that out and have his men take it as the truth? Did the Judge talk of trotting me down to Egypt to scare me to death? Why, I know this people better than he does. I was raised just a little east of here. I am a part of this people. But the Judge was raised further north, and perhaps he has some horrid idea of what this people might be induced to do. [Roars of laughter and cheers.] But really I have talked about this matter perhaps longer than I ought, for it is no great thing, and yet the smallest are often the most difficult things to deal with. The Judge has set about seriously trying to make the impression that when we meet at different places I am literally in his clutches—that I am a poor, helpless, decrepit mouse, and that I can do nothing at all. This is one of the ways he has taken to create that impression. I don't know any other way to meet it, except this. I don't want to quarrel with him—to call him a liar—but when I come square up to him I don't know what else to call him, if I must tell the truth out. [Cheers and laughter.] I want to be at peace, and reserve all my fighting powers for necessary occasions. My time, now, is very nearly out, and I give up the trifle that is left to the Judge to let him set my knees trembling again, if he can.

Three days later, at Charleston in the eastern part of the state, the debaters devoted most of their time to an extraneous subject—the course of Lyman Trumbull in the United States Senate. But Lincoln did define his own position on the Negro.

September 18, 1858

While I was at the hotel today an elderly gentleman called upon me to know whether I was really in favor of producing a perfect equality between the Negroes and white people. [Great laughter.] While I had not proposed to myself on this occasion to say much on that subject, yet as the question was asked me I thought I would occupy perhaps five minutes in saying something in regard to it. I will say then that I am not, nor ever have been in favor of bringing about in any way the social and political equality of the white and black races, [applause]—that I am not nor ever have been in favor of making voters or jurors of Negroes, nor of qualifying them to hold office, nor to intermarry with white people; and I will say in addition to this that there is a physical difference between the white and black races which I believe will forever forbid the two races living together on terms of social and political equality. And inasmuch as they cannot so live, while they do remain together there must be the position of superior and inferior, and I as much as any other man am in favor of having the superior position assigned to the white race.

I say upon this occasion I do not perceive that because the

265

white man is to have the superior position the Negro should be denied everything. I do not understand that because I do not want a Negro woman for a slave I must necessarily want her for a wife. [Cheers and laughter.] My understanding is that I can just let her alone. I am now in my fiftieth year, and I certainly never have had a black woman for either a slave or a wife. So it seems to me quite possible for us to get along without making either slaves or wives of Negroes. I will add to this that I have never seen to my knowledge a man, woman or child who was in favor of producing a perfect equality, social and political, between Negroes and white men. I recollect of but one distinguished instance that I ever heard of so frequently as to be entirely satisfied of its correctness—and that is the case of Judge Douglas' old friend Col. Richard M. Johnson. [Laughter.] I will also add to the remarks I have made, (for I am not going to enter at large upon this subject,) that I have never had the least apprehension that I or my friends would marry Negroes if there was no law to keep them from it, [laughter] but as Judge Douglas and his friends seem to be in great apprehension that they might, if there were no law to keep them from it, [roars of laughter] I give him the most solemn pledge that I will to the very last stand by the law of this state, which forbids the marrying of white people with Negroes. [Continued laughter and applause.] I will add one further word, which is this, that I do not understand there is any place where an alteration of the social and political relations of the Negro and the white man can be made except in the state legislature—not in the Congress of the United States—and as I do not really apprehend the approach of any such thing myself, and as Judge Douglas seems to be in constant horror that some such danger is rapidly approaching, I propose as the best means to prevent it that the Judge be kept at home and placed in the state legislature to fight the measure. [Uproarious laughter and applause.] I do not propose dwelling longer at this time on this subject. . . .

I mentioned in a certain speech of mine which has been printed, that the Supreme Court had decided that a Negro could not possibly be made a citizen, and without saying what was my ground of complaint in regard to that, or whether I had any ground of complaint, Judge Douglas has from that thing manufactured nearly everything that he ever says about my disposition to produce an equality between the Negroes and the white people.

"These Poor Tongues"

[Laughter and applause.] If any one will read my speech, he will find I mentioned that as one of the points decided in the course of the Supreme Court opinions, but I did not state what objection I had to it. But Judge Douglas tells the people what my objection was when I did not tell them myself. [Loud applause and laughter.] Now my opinion is that the different states have the power to make a Negro a citizen under the Constitution of the United States if they choose. The Dred Scott decision decides that they have not that power. If the state of Illinois had that power I should be opposed to the exercise of it. [Cries of "good," "good," and applause.] That is all I have to say about it.

At home for a week-end in late September, Lincoln helped an impecunious friend.

September 25, 1858

My old friend, Henry Chew, the bearer of this, is in a straight for some furniture to commence housekeeping. If any person will furnish him, twenty-five dollars' worth, and he does not pay for it by the first of January next, I will.*

A. Lincoln

Again in the thick of the campaign, Lincoln put politics out of mind long enough to compose verses for the daughters of the innkeeper at Winchester, Illinois.

September 28, 1858

To Rosa—

You are young, and I am older;
   You are hopeful, I am not—
Enjoy life, ere it grow colder—
   Pluck the roses ere they rot.

Teach your beau to heed the lay—
   That sunshine soon is lost in shade—
That *now's* as good as any day—
   To take thee, Rosa, ere she fade.

Winchester, Sep. 28. 1858.

A. Lincoln—

* He did.

The Living Lincoln

September 30, 1858

To Linnie—

    A sweet plaintive song did I hear,
      And I fancied that she was the singer—
    May emotions as pure, as that song set astir
      Be the worst that the future shall bring her.

Winchester Sep. 30– 1858–

                   A. Lincoln–

By the time of the fifth debate, held on the campus of Knox College at Galesburg on October 7, both candidates had already discussed all the issues that could be injected into the campaign. Each, therefore, began to work out a summation of his position. Lincoln's came in his reply to Douglas's opening speech.

My Fellow-Citizens—

A very large portion of the speech which Judge Douglas has addressed to you has previously been delivered and put in print. [Laughter.] I do not mean that for a hit upon the Judge at all. [Renewed laughter.] If I had not been interrupted, I was going to say that such an answer as I was able to make to a very large portion of it, had already been more than once made and published. There has been an opportunity afforded to the public to see our respective views upon the topics discussed in a large portion of the speech which he has just delivered. I make these remarks for the purpose of excusing myself for not passing over the entire ground that the Judge has traversed. I however desire to take up some of the points that he has attended to, and ask your attention to them, and I shall follow him backwards upon some notes which I have taken, reversing the order by beginning where he concluded.

The Judge has alluded to the Declaration of Independence, and insisted that Negroes are not included in that Declaration; and that it is a slander upon the framers of that instrument, to suppose that Negroes were meant therein; and he asks you: Is it possible to believe that Mr. Jefferson, who penned the immortal paper, could have supposed himself applying the language of that instrument to the Negro race, and yet held a portion of that race in slavery? Would he not at once have freed them? I only have to remark upon this part of the Judge's speech, (and that, too, very briefly, for I shall not detain myself, or you, upon that point for any great

268

length of time,) that I believe the entire records of the world, from the date of the Declaration of Independence up to within three years ago, may be searched in vain for one single affirmation, from one single man, that the Negro was not included in the Declaration of Independence. I think I may defy Judge Douglas to show that he ever said so, that Washington ever said so, that any President ever said so, that any member of Congress ever said so, or that any living man upon the whole earth ever said so, until the necessities of the present policy of the Democratic party, in regard to slavery, had to invent that affirmation. [Tremendous applause.] And I will remind Judge Douglas and this audience, that while Mr. Jefferson was the owner of slaves, as undoubtedly he was, in speaking upon this very subject, he used the strong language that "he trembled for his country when he remembered that God was just"; and I will offer the highest premium in my power to Judge Douglas if he will show that he, in all his life, ever uttered a sentiment at all akin to that of Jefferson. [Great applause and cries of "Hit him again," "good," "good."] . . .

Now a few words in regard to these extracts from speeches of mine, which Judge Douglas has read to you, and which he supposes are in very great contrast to each other. Those speeches have been before the public for a considerable time, and if they have any inconsistency in them, if there is any conflict in them the public have been able to detect it. When the Judge says, in speaking on this subject, that I make speeches of one sort for the people of the northern end of the state, and of a different sort for the southern people, he assumes that I do not understand that my speeches will be put in print and read north and south. I knew all the while that the speech that I made at Chicago and the one I made at Jonesboro and the one at Charleston, would all be put in print and all the reading and intelligent men in the community would see them and know all about my opinions. And I have not supposed, and do not now suppose, that there is any conflict whatever between them. ["They are all good speeches!" "Hurrah for Lincoln!"] But the Judge will have it that if we do not confess that there is a sort of inequality between the white and black races, which justifies us in making them slaves, we must, then, insist that there is a degree of equality that requires us to make them our wives. [Loud applause, and cries, "Give it to him;" "Hit him again."] Now, I have all the while taken a broad distinction in regard to that matter; and that is all there is in these different speeches which he arrays here, and the entire reading of either of the speeches will show that that distinction was made.

Perhaps by taking two parts of the same speech, he could have got up as much of a conflict as the one he has found. I have all the while maintained, that in so far as it should be insisted that there was an equality between the white and black races that should produce a perfect social and political equality, it was an impossibility. This you have seen in my printed speeches, and with it I have said, that in their right to "life, liberty and the pursuit of happiness," as proclaimed in that old Declaration, the inferior races are our equals. [Long-continued cheering.] And these declarations I have constantly made in reference to the abstract moral question, to contemplate and consider when we are legislating about any new country which is not already cursed with the actual presence of the evil—slavery. I have never manifested any impatience with the necessities that spring from the actual presence of black people amongst us, and the actual existence of slavery amongst us where it does already exist; but I have insisted that, in legislating for new countries, where it does not exist, there is no just rule other than that of moral and abstract right! With reference to those new countries, those maxims as to the right of a people to "life, liberty and the pursuit of happiness," were the just rules to be constantly referred to. There is no misunderstanding this, except by men interested to misunderstand it. [Applause.] I take it that I have to address an intelligent and reading community, who will peruse what I say, weigh it, and then judge whether I advance improper or unsound views, or whether I advance hypocritical, and deceptive, and contrary views in different portions of the country. I believe myself to be guilty of no such thing as the latter, though, of course, I cannot claim that I am entirely free from all error in the opinions I advance.

The Judge has also detained us a while in regard to the distinction between his party and our party. His he assumes to be a national party—ours, a sectional one. He does this in asking the question whether this country has any interest in the maintenance of the Republican party? He assumes that our party is altogether sectional—that the party to which he adheres is national; and the argument is, that no party can be a rightful party—can be based upon rightful principles—unless it can announce its principles everywhere. I presume that Judge Douglas could not go into Russia and announce the doctrine of our national democracy; he could not denounce the doctrine of kings, and emperors, and monarchies, in Russia; and it may be true of this country, that in some places we may not be able to proclaim a doctrine as clearly true as the truth of democracy, because there is a section so directly opposed to it that they will not tolerate us in doing so. Is it the true test of the soundness of a doctrine, that in some places people won't let you proclaim it? [No, no, no.] Is that the way to test the truth of any doctrine? [No, no, no.] Why, I understood that at one time the people of Chicago would not let Judge Douglas preach a certain favorite doctrine of his. [Laughter and cheers.] I commend to his consideration the question, whether he takes that as a test of the unsoundness of what he wanted to preach. [Loud cheers.]

There is another thing to which I wish to ask attention for a little while on this occasion. What has always been the evidence brought forward to prove that the Republican party is a sectional party? The main one was that in the southern portion of the Union the people did not let the Republicans proclaim their doctrine amongst them. That has been the main evidence brought forward—that they had no supporters, or substantially none, in the slave states. The South have not taken hold of our principles as we announce them; nor does Judge Douglas now grapple with those principles. We have a Republican state platform, laid down in Springfield in June last, stating our position all the way through the questions before the country. We are now far advanced in this canvass. Judge Douglas and I have made perhaps forty speeches apiece, and we have now for the fifth time met face to face in debate, and up to this day I have not found either Judge Douglas or any friend of his taking hold of the Republican platform or laying his finger upon anything in it that is wrong. [Cheers.] I ask you all to recollect that. Judge Douglas turns away from the platform of principles to the fact that he can find people somewhere who will not allow us to announce those principles. [Applause.] If he had great confidence that our principles were wrong, he would take hold of them and demonstrate them to be wrong. But he does not do so. The only evidence he has of their being wrong is in the fact that there are people who won't allow us to preach them. I ask again, is that the way to test the soundness of a doctrine? [Cries of "No," "No."] . . .

The Living Lincoln

The Judge tells, in proceeding, that he is opposed to making any odious distinctions between free and slave states. I am altogether unaware that the Republicans are in favor of making any odious distinctions between the free and slave states. But there still is a difference, I think, between Judge Douglas and the Republicans in this. I suppose that the real difference between Judge Douglas and his friends, and the Republicans on the contrary, is that the Judge is not in favor of making any difference between slavery and liberty—that he is in favor of eradicating, of pressing out of view, the questions of preference in this country for free over slave institutions; and consequently every sentiment he utters discards the idea that there is any wrong in slavery. Everything that emanates from him or his coadjutors in their course of policy, carefully excludes the thought that there is anything wrong in slavery. All their arguments, if you will consider them, will be seen to exclude the thought that there is anything whatever wrong in slavery. If you will take the Judge's speeches, and select the short and pointed sentences expressed by him—as his declaration that he "don't care whether slavery is voted up or down"—you will see at once that this is perfectly logical, if you do not admit that slavery is wrong. If you do admit that it is wrong, Judge Douglas cannot logically say that he don't care whether a wrong is voted up or voted down. Judge Douglas declares that if any community want slavery they have a right to have it. He can say that logically, if he says that there is no wrong in slavery; but if you admit that there is a wrong in it, he cannot logically say that anybody has a right to do wrong. He insists that, upon the score of equality, the owners of slaves and owners of property—of horses and every other sort of property—should be alike and hold them alike in a new territory. That is perfectly logical, if the two species of property are alike and are equally founded in right. But if you admit that one of them is wrong, you cannot institute any equality between right and wrong.

And from this difference of sentiment—the belief on the part of one that the institution is wrong, and a policy springing from that belief which looks to the arrest of the enlargement of that wrong; and this other sentiment, that it is no wrong, and a policy sprung from that sentiment which will tolerate no idea of preventing that wrong from growing larger, and looks to there never being an end of it through all the existence of things,—arises the real difference between Judge Douglas and his friends, on the one hand,

and the Republicans on the other. Now, I confess myself as belonging to that class in the country who contemplate slavery as a moral, social and political evil, having due regard for its actual existence amongst us and the difficulties of getting rid of it in any satisfactory way, and to all the constitutional obligations which have been thrown about it; but, nevertheless, desire a policy that looks to the prevention of it as a wrong, and looks hopefully to the time when as a wrong it may come to an end. [Great applause.]

At Quincy, on the Mississippi River, Lincoln refined his summation. Here Carl Schurz, German university graduate and liberal Republican, saw Lincoln for the first time. Later Schurz put on record this impression:

"Mr. Lincoln was to open with an allowance of one hour. . . . His voice was not musical, rather high-keyed, and apt to turn into a shrill treble in moments of excitement; but it was not positively disagreeable. It had an exceedingly penetrating, far-reaching quality. . . . His gesture was awkward. He swung his long arms sometimes in a very ungraceful manner. Now and then he would, to give particular emphasis to a point, bend his knees and body with a sudden downward jerk, and then shoot up again with a vehemence that raised him to his tiptoes and made him look much taller than he really was. . . .

"There was, however, in all he said, a tone of earnest truthfulness, of elevated, noble sentiment, and of kindly sympathy, which added greatly to the strength of his argument, and became, as in the course of his speech he touched upon the moral side of the question in debate, powerfully impressive. Even when attacking his opponent with keen satire or invective, which, coming from any other speaker, would have sounded bitter and cruel, there was still a certain something in his utterance making his hearers feel that those thrusts came from a reluctant heart, and that he would much rather have treated his foe as a friend."

October 13, 1858

The Judge, in his concluding speech at Galesburg, says that I was pushing this matter to a personal difficulty, to avoid the responsibility for the enormity of my principles. I say to the Judge and to this audience now, that I will again state our principles as well as I hastily can in all their enormity, and if the Judge hereafter chooses to confine himself to a war upon these principles, he will probably not find me departing from the same course.

The Living Lincoln

We have in this nation this element of domestic slavery. It is a matter of absolute certainty that it is a disturbing element. It is the opinion of all the great men who have expressed an opinion upon it, that it is a dangerous element. We keep up a controversy in regard to it. That controversy necessarily springs from difference of opinion, and if we can learn exactly—can reduce to the lowest elements—what that difference of opinion is, we perhaps shall be better prepared for discussing the different systems of policy that we would propose in regard to that disturbing element. I suggest that the difference of opinion, reduced to its lowest terms, is no other than the difference between the men who think slavery a wrong and those who do not think it wrong. The Republican party think it wrong—we think it is a moral, a social and a political wrong. We think it is a wrong not confining itself merely to the persons or the states where it exists, but that it is a wrong in its tendency, to say the least, that extends itself to the existence of the whole nation. Because we think it wrong, we propose a course of policy that shall deal with it as a wrong. We deal with it as with any other wrong, in so far as we can prevent its growing any larger, and so deal with it that in the run of time there may be some promise of an end to it. We have a due regard to the actual presence of it amongst us and the difficulties of getting rid of it in any satisfactory way, and all the constitutional obligations thrown about it. I suppose that in reference both to its actual existence in the nation, and to our constitutional obligations, we have no right at all to disturb it in the states where it exists, and we profess that we have no more inclination to disturb it than we have the right to do it. We go further than that; we don't propose to disturb it where, in one instance, we think the Constitution would permit us. We think the Constitution would permit us to disturb it in the District of Columbia. Still we do not propose to do that, unless it should be in terms which I don't suppose the nation is very likely soon to agree to—the terms of making the emancipation gradual and compensating the unwilling owners. Where we suppose we have the constitutional right, we restrain ourselves in reference to the actual existence of the institution and the difficulties thrown about it. We also oppose it as an evil so far as it seeks to spread itself. We insist on the policy that shall restrict it to its present limits. We don't suppose that in doing this we violate anything due to the actual

274

presence of the institution, or anything due to the constitutional guarantees thrown around it.

We oppose the Dred Scott decision in a certain way, upon which I ought perhaps to address you a few words. We do not propose that when Dred Scott has been decided to be a slave by the court, we, as a mob, will decide him to be free. We do not propose that, when any other one, or one thousand, shall be decided by that court to be slaves, we will in any violent way disturb the rights of property thus settled; but we nevertheless do oppose that decision as a political rule which shall be binding on the voter, to vote for nobody who thinks it wrong, which shall be binding on the members of Congress or the President to favor no measure that does not actually concur with the principles of that decision. We do not propose to be bound by it as a political rule in that way, because we think it lays the foundation not merely of enlarging and spreading out what we consider an evil, but it lays the foundation for spreading that evil into the states themselves. We propose so resisting it as to have it reversed if we can, and a new judicial rule established upon this subject.

I will add this, that if there be any man who does not believe that slavery is wrong in the three aspects which I have mentioned, or in any one of them, that man is misplaced, and ought to leave us. While, on the other hand, if there be any man in the Republican party who is impatient over the necessity springing from its actual presence, and is impatient of the constitutional guarantees thrown around it, and would act in disregard of these, he too is misplaced standing with us. He will find his place somewhere else; for we have a due regard, so far as we are capable of understanding them, for all these things. This, gentlemen, as well as I can give it, is a plain statement of our principles in all their enormity.

I will say now that there is a sentiment in the country contrary to me—a sentiment which holds that slavery is not wrong, and therefore it goes for policy that does not propose dealing with it as a wrong. That policy is the Democratic policy, and that sentiment is the Democratic sentiment. If there be a doubt in the mind of anyone of this vast audience that this is really the central idea of the Democratic party, in relation to this subject, I ask him to bear with me while I state a few things tending, as I think, to prove that proposition. In the first place, the leading man—I think I may do my friend Judge Douglas the honor of calling him such—advocating the present Democratic policy, never himself says it is wrong. He has the high distinction, so far as I know, of never having said slavery is either right or wrong. [Laughter.] Almost everybody else says one or the other, but the Judge never does. If there be a man in the Democratic party who thinks it is wrong, and yet clings to that party, I suggest to him in the first place that his leader don't talk as he does, for he never says that it is wrong. In the second place, I suggest to him that if he will examine the policy proposed to be carried forward, he will find that he carefully excludes the idea that there is anything wrong in it. If you will examine the arguments that are made on it, you will find that everyone carefully excludes the idea that there is anything wrong in slavery.

Perhaps that Democrat who says he is as much opposed to slavery as I am, will tell me that I am wrong about this. I wish him to examine his own course in regard to this matter a moment, and then see if his opinion will not be changed a little. You say it is wrong; but don't you constantly object to anybody else saying so? Do you not constantly argue that this is not the right place to oppose it? You say it must not be opposed in the free states, because slavery is not here; it must not be opposed in the slave states, because it is there; it must not be opposed in politics, because that will make a fuss; it must not be opposed in the pulpit, because it is not religion. [Loud cheers.] Then where is the place to oppose it? There is no suitable place to oppose it. There is no place in the country to oppose this evil overspreading the continent, which you say yourself is coming. Frank Blair and Gratz Brown tried to get up a system of gradual emancipation in Missouri, had an election in August and got beat, and you, Mr. Democrat, threw up your hat, and halloed "hurrah for Democracy." [Enthusiastic cheers.]

So I say again that in regard to the arguments that are made, when Judge Douglas says he "don't care whether slavery is voted up or voted down," whether he means that as an individual expression of sentiment, or only as a sort of statement of his views on national policy, it is alike true to say that he can thus argue logically if he don't see anything wrong in it; but he cannot say so logically if he admits that slavery is wrong. He cannot say that he would as soon see a wrong voted up as voted down. When Judge Douglas says that whoever, or whatever community, wants slaves, they have a right to have them, he is perfectly logical if there is nothing wrong in the institution; but if you admit that it is wrong, he cannot logically say that anybody has a right to do wrong. When he says that slave property and horse and hog property are alike to be allowed to go into the territories, upon the principles of equality, he is reasoning truly, if there is no difference between them as property; but if the one is property, held rightfully, and the other is wrong, then there is no equality between the right and wrong; so that, turn it in any way you can, in all the arguments sustaining the Democratic policy, and in that policy itself, there is a careful, studied exclusion of the idea that there is anything wrong in slavery. Let us understand this. I am not, just here, trying to prove that we are right and they are wrong. I have been stating where we and they stand, and trying to show what is the real difference between us; and I now say that whenever we can get the question distinctly stated—can get all these men who believe that slavery is in some of these respects wrong, to stand and act with us in treating it as a wrong—then, and not till then, I think we will in some way come to an end of this slavery agitation. [Prolonged cheers.]

On October 15, the candidates met for the last time at Alton, where twenty-one years earlier a pro-slavery mob had murdered Elijah P. Lovejoy for persisting in publishing an anti-slavery newspaper. Gustave Koerner pictured the effect of two months of hard campaigning on the two men:

"Here I met, for the first time since 1856, Judge Douglas, who in his genial manner shook hands with me, apparently quite cordially. But I was really shocked at the condition he was in. His face was bronzed, which was natural enough, but it was also bloated, and his looks were haggard, and his voice almost extinct. In conversation he merely whispered. In addressing his audience he made himself understood only by an immense strain, and then only to a very small circle immediately near him. He had the opening and conclusion. His speech, however, was as good as any he had delivered. Lincoln, although sunburned, was as fresh as if he had just entered the campaign, and as cool and collected as ever. Without any apparent effort he stated his propositions clearly and tersely, and his whole speech was weighted with noble and deep thoughts."

The Judge alludes very often in the course of his remarks to the exclusive right which the states have to decide the whole thing for themselves. I agree with him very readily that the different states have that right. He is but fighting a man of straw when he assumes that I am contending against the right of the states to do as they please about it. Our controversy with him is in regard to the new territories. We agree that when the states come in as states they have the right and the power to do as they please. We have no power as citizens of the free states or in our federal capacity as members of the federal Union through the general government, to disturb slavery in the states where it exists. We profess constantly that we have no more inclination than belief in the power of the government to disturb it; yet we are driven constantly to defend ourselves from the assumption that we are warring upon the rights of the *states*. What I insist upon is, that the new territories shall be kept free from it while in the territorial condition. Judge Douglas assumes that we have no interest in them—that we have no right whatever to interfere. I think we have some interest. I think that as white men we have. Do we not wish for an outlet for our surplus population, if I may so express myself? Do we not feel an interest in getting to that outlet with such institutions as we would like to have prevail there? If *you* go to the territory opposed to slavery and another man comes upon the same ground with his slave, upon the assumption that the things are equal, it turns out that he has the equal right all his way and you have no part of it your way. If he goes in and makes it a slave territory, and by consequence a slave state, is it not time that those who desire to have it a free state were on equal ground? Let me suggest it in a different way. How many Democrats are there about here ["a thousand"] who have left slave states and come into the free state of Illinois to get rid of the institution of slavery? [Another voice—"a thousand and one."] I reckon there are a thousand and one. [Laughter.] I will ask you, if the policy you are now advocating had prevailed when this country was in a territorial condition, where would you have gone to get rid of it? [Applause.] Where would you have found your free state or territory to go to? And when hereafter, for any cause, the people in this place shall desire to find new homes, if they wish to be rid of the institution, where will they find the place to go to? [Loud cheers.]

Now irrespective of the moral aspect of this question as to whether there is a right or wrong in enslaving a Negro, I am still in favor of our new territories being in such a condition that white men may find a home—may find some spot where they can better their condition—where they can settle upon new soil and better their condition in life. [Great and continued cheering.] I am in favor of this not merely (I must say it here as I have elsewhere) for our own people who are born amongst us, but as an outlet for *free white people everywhere,* the world over—in which Hans and Baptiste and Patrick, and all other men from all the world, may find new homes and better their conditions in life. [Loud and long continued applause.]

I have stated upon former occasions, and I may as well state again, what I understand to be the real issue in this controversy between Judge Douglas and myself. On the point of my wanting to make war between the free and the slave states, there has been no issue between us. So, too, when he assumes that I am in favor of introducing a perfect social and political equality between the white and black races. These are false issues, upon which Judge Douglas has tried to force the controversy. There is no foundation in truth for the charge that I maintain either of these propositions. The real issue in this controversy—the one pressing upon every mind—is the sentiment on the part of one class that looks upon the institution of slavery *as a wrong,* and of another class that *does not* look upon it as a wrong. The sentiment that contemplates the institution of slavery in this country as a wrong is the sentiment of the Republican party. It is the sentiment around which all their actions —all their arguments circle—from which all their propositions radiate. They look upon it as being a moral, social and political wrong; and while they contemplate it as such, they nevertheless have due regard for its actual existence among us, and the difficulties of getting rid of it in any satisfactory way and to all the constitutional obligations thrown about it. Yet having a due regard for these, they desire a policy in regard to it that looks to its not creating any more danger. They insist that it should as far as may be, *be treated* as a wrong, and one of the methods of treating it as a wrong is to *make provision that it shall grow no larger.* [Loud applause.] They also desire a policy that looks to a peaceful end of slavery at sometime, as being wrong. These are the views they entertain in regard to it as I understand them; and all their sentiments—all their arguments and propositions are brought within this range. I have said and I repeat it here, that if there be a man amongst us who does not think that the institution of slavery is wrong in any one of the aspects of which I have spoken, he is misplaced and ought not to be with us. And if there be a man amongst us who is so impatient of it as a wrong as to disregard its actual presence among us and the difficulty of getting rid of it suddenly in a satisfactory way, and to disregard the constitutional obligations thrown about it, that man is misplaced if he is on our platform. We disclaim sympathy with him in practical action. He is not placed properly with us. . . .

The Democratic policy in regard to that institution will not tolerate the merest breath, the slightest hint, of the least degree of wrong about it. Try it by some of Judge Douglas' arguments. He says he "don't care whether it is voted up or voted down" in the territories. I do not care myself in dealing with that expression, whether it is intended to be expressive of his individual sentiments on the subject, or only of the national policy he desires to have established. It is alike valuable for my purpose. Any man can say that who does not see anything wrong in slavery, but no man can logically say it who does see a wrong in it; because no man can logically say he don't care whether a wrong is voted up or voted down. He may say he don't care whether an indifferent thing is voted up or down, but he must logically have a choice between a right thing and a wrong thing. He contends that whatever community wants slaves has a right to have them. So they have if it is not a wrong. But if it is a wrong, he cannot say people have a right to do wrong. He says that upon the score of equality, slaves should be allowed to go in a new territory, like other property. This is strictly logical if there is no difference between it and other property. If it and other property are equal, his argument is entirely logical. But if you insist that one is wrong and the other right, there is no use to institute a comparison between right and wrong. You may turn over everything in the Democratic policy from beginning to end, whether in the shape it takes on the statute book, in the shape it takes in the Dred Scott decision, in the shape it takes in conversation or the shape it takes in short maxim-like arguments—it everywhere carefully excludes the idea that there is anything wrong in it.

The end of the long debate was moments away. Lincoln brought months of argument to a simple issue, so clear that no one could misunderstand it, so freighted with moral significance that none could regard it with an easy conscience.

"These Poor Tongues"

That is the real issue. That is the issue that will continue in this country when these poor tongues of Judge Douglas and myself shall be silent. It is the eternal struggle between these two principles—right and wrong—throughout the world. They are the two principles that have stood face to face from the beginning of time; and will ever continue to struggle. The one is the common right of humanity and the other the divine right of kings. It is the same principle in whatever shape it develops itself. It is the same spirit that says, "You work and toil and earn bread, and I'll eat it." [Loud applause.] No matter in what shape it comes, whether from the mouth of a king who seeks to bestride the people of his own nation and live by the fruit of their labor, or from one race of men as an apology for enslaving another race, it is the same tyrannical principle. I was glad to express my gratitude at Quincy, and I re-express it here to Judge Douglas—*that he looks to no end of the institution of slavery.* That will help the people to see where the struggle really is. It will hereafter place with us all men who really do wish the wrong may have an end. And whenever we can get rid of the fog which obscures the real question—when we can get Judge Douglas and his friends to avow a policy looking to its perpetuation—we can get out from among them that class of men and bring them to the side of those who treat it as a wrong. Then there will soon be an end of it, and that end will be its "ultimate extinction." Whenever the issue can be distinctly made, and all extraneous matter thrown out so that men can fairly see the real difference between the parties, this controversy will soon be settled, and it will be done peaceably too. There will be no war, no violence. It will be placed again where the wisest and best men of the world, placed it. Brooks of South Carolina once declared that when this Constitution was framed, its framers did not look to the institution existing until this day. When he said this, I think he stated a fact that is fully borne out by the history of the times. But he also said they were better and wiser men than the men of these days; yet the men of these days had experience which they had not, and by the invention of the cotton gin it became a necessity in this country that slavery should be perpetual. I now say that willingly or unwillingly, purposely or without purpose, Judge Douglas has been the most prominent instrument in changing the position of the institution of slavery which the fathers of the government

281

expected to come to an end ere this—*and putting it upon Brooks'
cotton gin basis,* [great applause,]—placing it where he openly
confesses he has no desire there shall ever be an end of it. [Re-
newed applause.]

Lincoln brought his campaign to an end with an address in Springfield on October 30. In his conclusion—the only part of his speech that
has been preserved—he spoke movingly of his own motives.

My friends, today closes the discussions of this canvass. The
planting and the culture are over; and there remains but the preparation, and the harvest.

I stand here surrounded by friends—some *political, all personal*
friends, I trust. May I be indulged, in this closing scene, to say a
few words of myself. I have borne a laborious, and, in some respects
to myself, a painful part in the contest. Through all, I have neither
assailed, nor wrestled with any part of the Constitution. The legal
right of the Southern people to reclaim their fugitives I have constantly admitted. The legal right of Congress to interfere with their
institution in the states, I have constantly denied. In resisting the
spread of slavery to new territory, and with that, what appears
to me to be a tendency to subvert the first principle of free government itself my whole effort has consisted. To the best of my judgment I have labored *for,* and not *against* the Union. As I have not
felt, so I have not expressed any harsh sentiment towards our
Southern brethren. I have constantly declared, as I really believed,
the only difference between them and us, is the difference of circumstances.

I have meant to assail the motives of no party, or individual;
and if I have, in any instance (of which I am not conscious) departed from my purpose, I regret it.

I have said that in some respects the contest has been painful to
me. Myself, and those with whom I act have been constantly accused of a purpose to destroy the union; and bespattered with every
imaginable odious epithet; and some who were friends, as it were
but yesterday have made themselves most active in this. I have
cultivated patience, and made no attempt at a retort.

Ambition has been ascribed to me. God knows how sincerely I
prayed from the first that this field of ambition might not be opened.
I claim no insensibility to political honors; but today could the Mis-

souri restriction be restored, and the whole slavery question replaced on the old ground of "toleration" by *necessity* where it exists, with unyielding hostility to the spread of it, on principle, I would, in consideration, gladly agree, that Judge Douglas should never be *out,* and I never *in,* an office, so long as we both or either, live.

On the same day Lincoln tried to combat an untruth that accused him of bigotry.

Springfield,
Oct. 30, 1858

Edward Lusk, Esq
Dear Sir
I understand the story is still being told, and insisted upon, that I have been a Know Nothing. I repeat, what I stated in a public speech at Meredosia, that I am not, nor ever have been, connected with the party called the Know Nothing party, or party calling themselves the American party. *Certainly* no man of truth, and I *believe,* no man of good character for truth can be found to say on his own knowledge that I ever was connected with that party. Yours very truly

A. Lincoln

On November 2 the voters gave their decision. The popular vote for Republican representatives and senators exceeded the vote for Democrats by more than 4,000, but because of the apportionment and holdover senators (elected in Illinois for four-year terms) Douglas won a clear majority of members of the legislature.

Lincoln, intent as he had been on victory, did not allow defeat to embitter him. Instead, he took an early opportunity to urge State Central Chairman Judd to remove, for Lyman Trumbull's benefit, the cause of his own defeat.

Springfield Nov 15 1858

Hon N B Judd
My dear Sir
I have the pleasure to inform you that I am convalescent and hoping these lines may find you in the same improving state of health. Doubtless you have suspected for some time that I entertain a personal wish for a term in the US Senate; and had the suspicion

taken the shape of a direct charge, I think I could not have truthfully denied it. But let the past as nothing be.

For the future my view is that the fight must go on. The returns here are not yet completed, but it is believed that Dougherty's vote will be slightly greater than Miller's majority over Fondey. We have some hundred and twenty thousand clear Republican votes. That pile is worth keeping together. It will elect a state treasurer two years hence.

In that day I shall fight in the ranks, but I shall be in no one's way for any of the places. I am especially for Trumbull's reelection; and by the way this brings me to the principal object of this letter. Can you not take your draft of an apportionment law, and carefully revise it till it shall be strictly & obviously just in all particulars, & then by an early & persistent effort get enough of the enemy's men to enable you to pass it. I believe if you & Peck make a job of it begin early & work earnestly & quietly, you can succeed in it. Unless something be done Trumbull is eventually beaten two years hence. Take this into serious consideration. Yours as ever

A Lincoln

Even in defeat Lincoln was willing to bear his full share of the costs of the campaign.

Springfield, Nov. 16. 1858

Hon: N. B. Judd
My dear Sir

Yours of the 15th. is just received. I wrote *you* the same day. As to the pecuniary matter, I am willing to pay according to my ability; but I am the poorest hand living to get others to pay. I have been on expenses so long without earning anything that I am absolutely without money now for even household purposes. Still, if you can put in two hundred and fifty dollars for me towards discharging the debt of the committee, I will allow it when you and I settle the private matter between us. This, with what I have already paid, and with an outstanding note of mine, will exceed my subscription of five hundred dollars. This too, is exclusive of my ordinary expenses during the campaign, all which being added to my loss of time and business, bears pretty heavily upon one no better off in world's goods than I; but as I had the post of honor, it is not for me to be over-nice.

"These Poor Tongues"

You are feeling badly. *"And this too shall pass away."* Never fear. Yours as ever

A. Lincoln

Lincoln was a patient man, but his forebearance had limits. This he demonstrated when a firm of wholesalers, in St. Louis, pressed immoderately for results in a series of collection cases which he and Herndon had undertaken to handle.

Springfield,
Novr. 17. 1858

Messrs S. C. Davis & Co
Gentlemen

You perhaps need not to be reminded how I have been personally engaged the last three or four months. Your letter to Lincoln & Herndon, of Oct. 1st. complaining that the lands of those against whom we obtained judgments last winter for you, have not been sold on execution has just been handed to me today. I will try to "explain how our" (your) "interests have been so much neglected" as you choose to express it. After these judgments were obtained we wrote you that under our law, the selling of land on execution is a delicate and dangerous, matter; that it could not be done safely, without a careful examination of titles; and also of the *value* of the property. Our letters to you will show this. To do this would require a canvass of half the state. We were puzzled, & you sent no definite instructions. At length we employed a young man to visit all the localities, and make as accurate a report on titles and values as he could. He did this, expending three or four weeks' time, and as he said, over a hundred dollars of his own money in doing so. When this was done we wrote you, asking if we should sell and bid in for you in accordance with this information. This letter you never answered.

My mind is made up. I will have no more to do with this class of business. I can do business in court, but I cannot, and will not follow executions all over the world. The young man who collected the information for us is an active young lawyer living at Carrollton, Greene County I think. We promised him a share of the compensation we should ultimately receive. He must be somehow paid; and I believe you would do well to turn the whole business over to him. I believe we have had, of legal fees, which you are to recover back from the defendants, one hundred dollars. I would not go through the same labor and vexation again for five hundred; still, if you will clear us of Mr. William Fishback (such is his name) we will be most happy to surrender to him, or to any other person you may name. Yours &c

A. Lincoln

To Henry Asbury, who had suggested the second question which Lincoln had put to Douglas at Freeport, Lincoln voiced resolution and faith in ultimate victory.

Springfield,
Novr. 19, 1858

Henry Asbury, Esq
My dear Sir

Yours of the 13th. was received some days ago. The fight must go on. The cause of civil liberty must not be surrendered at the end of *one,* or even, one *hundred* defeats. Douglas had the ingenuity to be supported in the late contest both as the best means to *break down,* and to *uphold* the slave interest. No ingenuity can keep those antagonistic elements in harmony long. Another explosion will soon come. Yours truly

A. Lincoln—

Lincoln took steps to preserve the full record of the debates. He appealed first to one of the publishers of the Chicago *Tribune.*

Springfield,
Novr. 20, 1858

Dr. C. H. Ray
My dear Sir

I wish to preserve a set of the late debates (if they may be called so) between Douglas and myself. To enable me to do so, please get two copies of each number of your paper containing the whole, and send them to me by express; and I will pay you for the papers & for your trouble. I wish the two sets, in order to lay one away in the raw, and to put the other in a scrapbook. Remember, if part of any debate is on *both* sides of one sheet, it will take two sets to make one scrapbook.

I believe, according to a letter of yours to Hatch you are "feeling like h—ll yet." Quit that. You will soon feel better. Another "blow-up" is coming; and we shall have fun again. Douglas managed to be supported both as the best instrument to *put down* and to *uphold* the slave power; but no ingenuity can long keep these antagonisms in harmony. Yours as ever

A. Lincoln

When Lincoln did not hear from Ray, he turned to a young lawyer whom he had come to know in circuit practice.

Springfield
Nov. 30. 1858

H. C. Whitney, Esq
My dear Sir:
Being desirous of preserving in some permanent form, the late joint discussions between Douglas and myself, ten days ago I wrote to Dr. Ray, requesting him to forward to me, by express, two sets of the nos. of the Tribune, which contain the reports of those discussions. Up to date I have no word from him on the subject. Will you, if in your power procure them and forward them to me by express? If you will, I will pay all charges, and be greatly obliged to boot.

Hoping to meet you before long I remain   As ever your friend
A. Lincoln

Whitney, after considerable trouble, collected the newspapers and Lincoln expressed his thanks. In less than two years, as the result of his foresight and tenacity, the debates would be permanently preserved in book form.

Springfield,
Dec. 25. 1858

H. C. Whitney Esq
My dear Sir:
I have received yours of the 23, inquiring whether I received the newspapers you sent me by express. I did receive them, and am very much obliged. There is some probability that my scrapbook will be reprinted; and if it shall, I will save you a copy. Your friend as ever

A. Lincoln—

IX. The Making of a Candidate

1859-1860 ON January 5, 1859, the General Assembly of Illinois confirmed the result of the fall election by returning Stephen A. Douglas to the United States Senate. By this time Lincoln had put defeat behind him and had plunged again into his law practice—partly to make up for the time he had lost and the money he had spent in the preceding six months, and partly to push the memory of failure from his mind. In January and February the United States courts and the state Supreme Court absorbed him. When they adjourned he started on the old familiar round of circuit courts.

But Lincoln could no longer devote himself wholly to the law. His debates with Douglas had been reported all over the country. A short six months earlier the name of Abraham Lincoln had hardly been mentioned outside the state of Illinois; now millions knew it. Letters came from strangers asking for Lincoln's views on political questions; others begged for speeches. Despite defeat, he had become a man of national prominence.

A group of Boston Republicans organized a celebration in honor of the birthday of Thomas Jefferson. Lincoln answered his invitation with a careful letter.

Springfield, Ills.
April 6. 1859

Messrs. Henry L. Pierce, & others.
Gentlemen
Your kind note inviting me to attend a festival in Boston, on the 13th. inst. in honor of the birthday of Thomas Jefferson, was duly received. My engagements are such that I cannot attend.

The Making of a Candidate

Bearing in mind that about seventy years ago, two great political parties were first formed in this country, that Thomas Jefferson was the head of one of them, and Boston the headquarters of the other, it is both curious and interesting that those supposed to descend politically from the party opposed to Jefferson, should now be celebrating his birthday in their own original seat of empire, while those claiming political descent from him have nearly ceased to breathe his name everywhere.

Remembering too, that the Jefferson party were formed upon their supposed superior devotion to the *personal* rights of men, holding the rights of *property* to be secondary only, and greatly inferior, and then assuming that the so-called Democracy of today, are the Jefferson, and their opponents, the anti-Jefferson parties, it will be equally interesting to note how completely the two have changed hands as to the principle upon which they were originally supposed to be divided.

The Democracy of today hold the *liberty* of one man to be absolutely nothing, when in conflict with another man's right of *property*. Republicans, on the contrary, are for both the *man* and the *dollar;* but in cases of conflict, the man *before* the dollar.

I remember once being much amused at seeing two partially intoxicated men engage in a fight with their greatcoats on, which fight, after a long, and rather harmless contest, ended in each having fought himself *out* of his own coat, and *into* that of the other. If the two leading parties of this day are really identical with the two in the days of Jefferson and Adams, they have performed about the same feat as the two drunken men.

But soberly, it is now no child's play to save the principles of Jefferson from total overthrow in this nation.

One would start with great confidence that he could convince any sane child that the simpler propositions of Euclid are true; but, nevertheless, he would fail, utterly, with one who should deny the definitions and axioms. The principles of Jefferson are the definitions and axioms of free society. And yet they are denied, and evaded, with no small show of success. One dashingly calls them "glittering generalities"; another bluntly calls them "self-evident lies"; and still others insidiously argue that they apply only to "superior races."

These expressions, differing in form, are identical in object and effect—the supplanting the principles of free government, and restoring those of classification, caste, and legitimacy. They would delight a convocation of crowned heads, plotting against the people. They are the vanguard — the miners, and sappers — of returning despotism. We must repulse them, or they will subjugate us.

This is a world of compensations; and he who would *be* no slave, must consent to *have* no slave. Those who deny freedom to others, deserve it not for themselves; and, under a just God, cannot long retain it.

All honor to Jefferson — to the man who, in the concrete pressure of a struggle for national independence by a single people, had the coolness, forecast, and capacity to introduce into a merely revolutionary document, an abstract truth, applicable to all men and all times, and so to embalm it there, that today, and in all coming days, it shall be a rebuke and a stumbling-block to the very harbingers of re-appearing tyranny and oppression. Your obedient Servant

A. Lincoln —

Some saw in Lincoln the next Republican candidate for the Presidency. Partly from modesty, partly because he knew the movement to be premature, Lincoln refused to be enticed by the editor of the Rock Island *Register*.

Springfield,
April 16. 1859.

T. J. Pickett, Esq
My dear Sir.

Yours of the 13th. is just received. My engagements are such that I cannot, at any very early day, visit Rock Island, to deliver a lecture, or for any other object.

As to the other matter you kindly mention, I must, in candor, say I do not think myself fit for the Presidency. I certainly am flattered, and gratified, that some partial friends think of me in that connection; but I really think it best for our cause that no concerted effort, such as you suggest, should be made.

Let this be considered confidential. Yours very truly
A. Lincoln —

To Salmon P. Chase, Governor of Ohio and aspirant for the Republican nomination, Lincoln wrote a generous note.

The Making of a Candidate

Hon: S. P. Chase
Dear Sir

Reaching home yesterday I found your kind note of the 14th. informing me that you have given Mr. Whitney the appointment he desired; and also mentioning the present encouraging aspects of the Republican cause—and our Illinois canvass of last year. I thank you for the appointment. Allow me also to thank you as being one of the very few distinguished men, whose sympathy we in Illinois did receive last year, of all those whose sympathy we thought we had reason to expect.

Of course I would have preferred success; but failing in that, I have no regrets for having rejected all advice to the contrary, and resolutely made the struggle. Had we thrown ourselves into the arms of Douglas, as re-electing him by our votes would have done, the Republican cause would have been annihilated in Illinois, and, as I think, demoralized, and prostrated everywhere for years, if not forever. As it is, in the language of Benton "we are clean" and the Republican star gradually rises higher everywhere. Yours truly.

A. Lincoln

As editor of the *Illinois Staats-Anzeiger* of Springfield, Theodore Canisius undoubtedly knew how Lincoln would reply to a question concerning the action of Massachusetts in raising the voting qualifications for naturalized citizens.

Springfield, May 17, 1859

Dr. Theodore Canisius
Dear Sir:

Your note asking, in behalf of yourself and other German citizens, whether I am for or against the constitutional provision in regard to naturalized citizens, lately adopted by Massachusetts; and whether I am for or against a fusion of the Republicans, and other opposition elements, for the canvass of 1860, is received.

Massachusetts is a sovereign and independent state; and it is no privilege of mine to scold her for what she does. Still, if from what she *has done*, an inference is sought to be drawn as to what I *would do*, I may, without impropriety, speak out. I say then, that, as I understand the Massachusetts provision, I am against its adoption in Illinois, or in any other place, where I have a right to oppose it. Understanding the spirit of our institutions to aim at

The Living Lincoln

the *elevation* of men, I am opposed to whatever tends to *degrade* them. I have some little notoriety for commiserating the oppressed condition of the Negro; and I should be strangely inconsistent if I could favor any project for curtailing the existing rights of *white men,* even though born in different lands, and speaking different languages from myself.

As to the matter of fusion, I am for it, if it can be had on Republican grounds; and I am not for it on any other terms. A fusion on any other terms, would be as foolish as unprincipled. It would lose the whole North, while the common enemy would still carry the whole South. The question of *men* is a different one. There are good patriotic men, and able statesmen, in the South whom I would cheerfully support, if they would now place themselves on Republican ground. But I am against letting down the Republican standard a hair's breadth.

I have written this hastily, but I believe it answers your questions substantially.* Yours truly

A. Lincoln

Anxious to hold together the radical and conservative wings of the party, especially in Illinois, Lincoln appealed to Chase for aid.

Springfield, Ills.
June 9. 1859

Hon: S. P. Chase:
Dear Sir

Please pardon the liberty I take in addressing you, as I now do. It appears by the papers that the late Republican state convention of Ohio adopted a platform, of which the following is one plank, "A repeal of the atrocious Fugitive Slave law."

This is already damaging us here. I have no doubt that if that plank be even *introduced* into the next Republican National convention, it will explode it. Once introduced, its supporters and its opponents will quarrel irreconcilably. The latter believe the U. S. Constitution declares that a fugitive slave *"shall be delivered up"*; and they look upon the above plank as dictated by the spirit which declares a fugitive slave *"shall not be delivered up."*

I enter upon no argument one way or the other; but I assure

* Two weeks after this letter was written, Lincoln secretly bought Canisius' paper, thus assuring its support of the Republican cause.

you the cause of Republicanism is hopeless in Illinois, if it be in any way made responsible for that plank. I hope you can, and will, contribute something to relieve us from it. Your Obt. Servt.

A. Lincoln

Mindful of newspaper support, Lincoln acknowledged a debt and made a pledge.

Springfield
June 15. 1859

Press & Tribune Co
Gentlemen
Herewith is a little draft to pay for your daily another year from today. I suppose I shall take the Press & Tribune so long as it, and I both live, unless I become unable to pay for it. In its devotion to our cause always, and to me personally last year I owe it a debt of gratitude, which I fear I shall never be able to pay. Yours very truly

A. Lincoln—

Still determined to prevent costly splits in the party, Lincoln turned to a Republican Congressman from Indiana.

Springfield, Ills, July 6, 1859.

Hon: Schuyler Colfax:
My dear Sir:
I much regret not seeing you while you were here among us. Before learning that you were to be at Jacksonville on the 4th. I had given my word to be at another place. Besides a strong desire to make your personal acquaintance, I was anxious to speak with you on politics, a little more fully than I can well do in a letter. My main object in such conversation would be to hedge against divisions in the Republican ranks generally, and particularly for the contest of 1860. The point of danger is the temptation in different localities to *"platform"* for something which will be popular just there, but which, nevertheless, will be a firebrand elsewhere, and especially in a national convention. As instances, the movement against foreigners in Massachusetts; in New Hampshire, to make obedience to the Fugitive Slave law, punishable as a crime; in Ohio, to repeal the Fugitive Slave law; and squatter sovereignty in Kansas. In these things there is explosive matter enough to blow up

293

half a dozen national conventions, if it gets into them; and what gets very rife outside of conventions is very likely to find its way into them. What is desirable, if possible, is that in every local convocation of Republicans, a point should be made to avoid everything which will distract Republicans elsewhere. Massachusetts Republicans should have looked beyond their noses; and then they could not have failed to see that tilting against foreigners would ruin us in the whole Northwest. New Hampshire and Ohio should forbear tilting against the Fugitive Slave law in such way as to utterly overwhelm us in Illinois with the charge of enmity to the Constitution itself. Kansas, in her confidence that she can be saved to freedom on "squatter sovereignty"—ought not to forget that to prevent the spread and nationalization of slavery is a national concern, and must be attended to by the nation. In a word, in every locality we should look beyond our noses; and at least say *nothing* on points where it is probable we shall disagree.

I write this for your eye only; hoping however that if you see danger as I think I do, you will do what you can to avert it. Could not suggestions be made to the leading men in the state and congressional conventions; and so avoid, to some extent at least, these apples of discord? Yours very truly

A. Lincoln

On the same theme Lincoln wrote to a lawyer of Columbus, Ohio, who was active in the Republican organization of that state. Again Lincoln disavowed interest in the Presidency.

Springfield, Ills.
July 28. 1859

Hon. Samuel Galloway
My dear Sir:
Your very complimentary, not to say flattering letter of the 23rd. inst. is received. Dr. Reynolds had induced me to expect you here; and I was disappointed, not a little, by your failure to come. And yet I fear you have formed an estimate of me which can scarcely be sustained on a personal acquaintance.

Two things done by the Ohio Republican convention—the repudiation of Judge Swan, and the "plank" for a repeal of the Fugitive Slave law—I very much regretted. These two things are of a piece; and they are viewed by many good men, sincerely opposed to slavery, as a struggle against, and in disregard of, the Constitution itself. And it is the very thing that will greatly endanger our cause, if it be not kept out of our national convention. There is another thing our friends are doing which gives me some uneasiness. It is their leaning towards *"popular sovereignty."* There are three substantial objections to this. First, no party can command respect which sustains this year, what it opposed last. Secondly, Douglas, (who is the most dangerous enemy of liberty, because the most insidious one) would have little support in the North, and by consequence, no capital to trade on in the South, if it were not for our friends thus magnifying him and his humbug. But lastly, and chiefly, Douglas' popular sovereignty, accepted by the public mind, as a just principle, nationalizes slavery, and revives the African slave trade, inevitably. Taking slaves into new territories, and buying slaves in Africa, are identical things—identical *rights* or identical *wrongs*—and the argument which establishes one will establish the other. Try a thousand years for a sound reason why Congress shall not hinder the people of Kansas from having slaves, and when you have found it, it will be an equally good one why Congress should not hinder the people of Georgia from importing slaves from Africa.

As to Gov. Chase, I have a kind side for him. He was one of the few distinguished men of the nation who gave us, in Illinois, their sympathy last year. I never saw him, suppose him to be able, and right-minded; but still he may not be the most suitable as a candidate for the Presidency.

I must say I do not think myself fit for the Presidency. As you propose a correspondence with me, I shall look for your letters anxiously.

I have not met Dr. Reynolds since receiving your letter; but when I shall, I will present your respects, as requested. Yours very truly

A. Lincoln

Lincoln still worried over the possibility that the Republican party might adopt Douglas.

[*c. September, 1859?*]

[1]

What will Douglas do now? He does not quite know himself. Like a skillful gambler he will play for all the chances. His first wish is to be the nominee of the Charleston convention, without any new test. The Democratic party proper do not wish to let it go just that way. They are thinking of getting up a slave code test for him. They better not. Their true policy is to let him into the convention, beat him then, and give him no plausible excuse to bolt the nomination. But if they press the slave code test upon him, he will not take it; but, as in the case of Lecompton, will appeal to the North on his bravery in opposing it. True the logic of his position, as an indorser of the Dred Scott decision imperatively requires him to go the slave code. Honestly believing in that decision, he cannot, without perjury, refuse to go the slave code. But he will refuse. He never lets the logic of principle, displace the logic of success. And then, when he thus turns again to the North, we shall have the Lecompton phase of politics reproduced on a larger scale. It will then be a question whether the Republican party of the nation shall make him President, in magnanimous gratitude for having opposed a slave code, just as it was, last year, a question whether the Illinois Republicans should re-elect him Senator, in magnanimous gratitude for having opposed Lecompton. Some larger gentlemen will then have a chance of swallowing the same pill which they somewhat persistently prescribed for us little fellows last year. I hope they will not swallow it. For the sake of the *cause*, rather than the *men*, I hope they will not swallow it. The Republican cause cannot live by Douglas' position. His position, whether for or against a slave code, for or against Lecompton, leads inevitably to the nationalizing and perpetuity of slavery, and the Republican cause cannot live by it. Dallying with Douglas is, at best, for Republicans, only loss of labor, and loss of time. Wander with him however long, at last they must turn back and strike for a policy, which shall deal with slavery as a wrong, restrain its enlargement, and look to its termination.

[11]

The effort to prove that our fathers who framed the government under which we live, understood that a proper division of local from federal authority, and some provision of the Constitution, both forbid the federal government to control slavery in the federal territories, is as if, when a man stands before you, so that you see him, and lay your hand upon him, you should go about examining his tracks, and insisting therefrom, that he is not present, but somewhere else. They *did,* through the federal government, control slavery in the federal territories. They did the identical thing, which D. insists they understood they ought not to do.

[III]

Negro equality! Fudge!! How long, in the government of a God great enough to make and maintain this Universe, shall there continue knaves to vend, and fools to gulp, so low a piece of demagogism as this.

The demand for speeches became irresistible. In August, Lincoln spoke at Council Bluffs, Iowa, where he had gone on personal business. In September, at the insistence of Ohio Republicans, he spoke at Columbus and Cincinnati, taking as his target an article by Douglas in that month's issue of *Harper's.* Republicans of Indianapolis heard him when he stopped there en route to Springfield. On the last day of the month he made the principal address at the Wisconsin State Fair, held at Madison.

The occasion called for a non-political speech and Lincoln complied, yet there were political overtones to much of what he said.

September 30, 1859
Members of the Agricultural Society and Citizens of Wisconsin:

Agricultural fairs are becoming an institution of the country; they are useful in more ways than one; they bring us together, and thereby make us better acquainted, and better friends than we otherwise would be. From the first appearance of man upon the earth, down to very recent times, the words *"stranger"* and *"enemy"* were *quite* or *almost,* synonymous. Long after civilized nations had defined robbery and murder as high crimes, and had affixed severe punishments to them, when practiced among and upon their own people respectively, it was deemed no offence, but even meritorious, to rob, and murder, and enslave *strangers,* whether as nations or as individuals. Even yet, this has not totally disappeared. The man of the highest moral cultivation, in spite of all which abstract principle can do, likes him whom he *does* know, much better than him whom he does *not* know. To correct the evils, great and small, which spring from want of sympathy, and from positive enmity, among *strangers,* as nations, or as individuals, is one of the highest functions of civilization. To this end our agricultural fairs contrib-

297

The Living Lincoln

ute in no small degree. They make more pleasant, and more strong, and more durable, the bond of social and political union among us. Again, if, as Pope declares, "happiness is our being's end and aim," our fairs contribute much to that end and aim, as occasions of recreation—as holidays. Constituted as man is, he has positive need of occasional recreation; and whatever can give him this, associated with virtue and advantage, and free from vice and disadvantage, is a positive good. Such recreation our fairs afford. They are a present pleasure, to be followed by no pain, as a consequence; they are a present pleasure, making the future more pleasant. . . .

One feature, I believe, of every fair, is a regular *address*. The Agricultural Society of the young, prosperous, and soon to be, great state of Wisconsin, has done me the high honor of selecting me to make that address upon this occasion—an honor for which I make my profound, and grateful acknowledgement.

I presume I am not expected to employ the time assigned me, in the mere flattery of the farmers, as a class. My opinion of them is that, in proportion to numbers, they are neither better nor worse than other people. In the nature of things they are more numerous than any other class; and I believe there really are more attempts at flattering them than any other; the reason of which I cannot perceive, unless it be that they can cast more votes than any other. On reflection, I am not quite sure that there is not cause of suspicion against you, in selecting me, in some sort a politician, and in no sort a farmer, to address you.

But farmers, being the most numerous class, it follows that their interest is the largest interest. It also follows that that interest is most worthy of all to be cherished and cultivated—that if there be inevitable conflict between that interest and any other, that other should yield.

Again, I suppose it is not expected of me to impart to you much specific information on agriculture. You have no reason to believe, and do not believe, that I possess it—if that were what you seek in this address, any one of your own number, or class, would be more able to furnish it.

You, perhaps, do expect me to give some general interest to the occasion; and to make some general suggestions, on practical matters. I shall attempt nothing more. And in such suggestions by me, quite likely very little will be new to you, and a large part of the rest possibly already known to be erroneous. . . .

The Making of a Candidate

The world is agreed that *labor* is the source from which human wants are mainly supplied. There is no dispute upon this point. From this point, however, men immediately diverge. Much disputation is maintained as to the best way of applying and controlling the labor element. By some it is assumed that labor is available only in connection with capital—that nobody labors, unless somebody else, owning capital, somehow, by the use of that capital, induces him to do it. Having assumed this, they proceed to consider whether it is best that capital shall *hire* laborers, and thus induce them to work by their own consent; or *buy* them, and drive them to it without their consent. Having proceeded so far they naturally conclude that all laborers are necessarily either *hired* laborers, or *slaves*. They further assume that whoever is once a *hired* laborer, is fatally fixed in that condition for life; and thence again that his condition is as bad as, or worse than that of a slave. This is the *"mud-sill"* theory.

Lincoln did not forget that he once had been a hired hand. He knew that free labor could prosper only on free soil.

But another class of reasoners hold the opinion that there is no *such* relation between capital and labor, as assumed; and that there is no such thing as a freeman being fatally fixed for life, in the condition of a hired laborer, that both these assumptions are false, and all inferences from them groundless. They hold that labor is prior to, and independent of, capital; that, in fact, capital is the fruit of labor, and could never have existed if labor had not *first* existed—that labor can exist without capital, but that capital could never have existed without labor. Hence they hold that labor is the superior—greatly the superior—of capital.

They do not deny that there is, and probably always will be, *a* relation between labor and capital. The error, as they hold, is in assuming that the *whole* labor of the world exists within that relation. A few men own capital; and that few avoid labor themselves, and with their capital, hire, or buy, another few to labor for them. A large majority belong to neither class—neither work for others, nor have others working for them. Even in all our slave states, except South Carolina, a majority of the whole people of all colors, are neither slaves nor masters. In these free states, a large majority are neither *hirers* nor *hired*. Men, with their families—wives, sons and daughters—work for themselves, on their farms, in their houses

299

and in their shops, taking the whole product to themselves, and asking no favors of capital on the one hand, nor of hirelings or slaves on the other. It is not forgotten that a considerable number of persons mingle their own labor with capital; that is, labor with their own hands, and also buy slaves or hire freemen to labor for them; but this is only a *mixed,* and not a *distinct* class. No principle stated is disturbed by the existence of this mixed class. Again, as has already been said, the opponents of the *"mud-sill"* theory insist that there is not, of necessity, any such thing as the free hired laborer being fixed to that condition for life. There is demonstration for saying this. Many independent men, in this assembly, doubtless a few years ago were hired laborers. And their case is almost if not quite the general rule.

The prudent, penniless beginner in the world, labors for wages awhile, saves a surplus with which to buy tools or land, for himself; then labors on his own account another while, and at length hires another new beginner to help him. This, say its advocates, is *free* labor—the just and generous, and prosperous system, which opens the way for all—gives hope to all, and energy, and progress, and improvement of condition to all. If any continue through life in the condition of the hired laborer, it is not the fault of the system, but because of either a dependent nature which prefers it, or improvidence, folly, or singular misfortune. I have said this much about the elements of labor generally, as introductory to the consideration of a new phase which that element is in process of assuming. The old general rule was that *educated* people did not perform manual labor. They managed to eat their bread, leaving the toil of producing it to the uneducated. This was not an insupportable evil to the working bees, so long as the class of drones remained very small. But *now,* especially in these free states, nearly all are educated—quite too nearly all, to leave the labor of the uneducated, in any wise adequate to the support of the whole. It follows from this that henceforth educated people must labor. Otherwise, education itself would become a positive and intolerable evil. No country can sustain, in idleness, more than a small percentage of its numbers. The great majority must labor at something productive. From these premises the problem springs, "How can *labor* and *education* be the most satisfactorily combined?"

By the *"mud-sill"* theory it is assumed that labor and education are incompatible; and any practical combination of them impossible. According to that theory, a blind horse upon a treadmill, is a perfect illustration of what a laborer should be—all the better for being blind, that he could not tread out of place, or kick understandingly. According to that theory, the education of laborers, is not only useless, but pernicious, and dangerous. In fact, it is, in some sort, deemed a misfortune that laborers should have heads at all. Those same heads are regarded as explosive materials, only to be safely kept in damp places, as far as possible from that peculiar sort of fire which ignites them. A Yankee who could invent a strong *handed* man without a head would receive the everlasting gratitude of the "mud-sill" advocates.

But free labor says "no!" Free labor argues that, as the Author of man makes every individual with one head and one pair of hands, it was probably intended that heads and hands should co-operate as friends; and that that particular head, should direct and control that particular pair of hands. As each man has one mouth to be fed, and one pair of hands to furnish food, it was probably intended that that particular pair of hands should feed that particular mouth—that each head is the natural guardian, director, and protector of the hands and mouth inseparably connected with it; and that being so, every head should be cultivated, and improved, by whatever will add to its capacity for performing its charge. In one word free labor insists on universal education. . . .

To Lincoln, there was more than dirt in farming. He was an early spokesman for that wedding of science and plow which would make American agriculture pre-eminent.

This leads to the further reflection, that no other human occupation opens so wide a field for the profitable and agreeable combination of labor with cultivated thought, as agriculture. I know of nothing so pleasant to the mind, as the discovery of anything which is at once *new* and *valuable*—nothing which so lightens and sweetens toil, as the hopeful pursuit of such discovery. And how vast, and how varied a field is agriculture, for such discovery. The mind, already trained to thought, in the country school, or higher school, cannot fail to find there an exhaustless source of profitable enjoyment. Every blade of grass is a study; and to produce two, where there was but one, is both a profit and a pleasure. And not grass alone; but soils, seeds, and seasons—hedges, ditches, and fences, draining, droughts, and irrigation—plowing, hoeing, and harrowing—reaping, mowing, and threshing—saving crops, pests of crops, diseases of crops, and what will prevent or cure them—implements, utensils, and machines, their relative merits, and how to improve them—hogs, horses, and cattle—sheep, goats, and poultry—trees, shrubs, fruits, plants, and flowers—the thousand things of which these are specimens—each a world of study within itself.

In all this, book-learning is available. A capacity, and taste, for reading, gives access to whatever has already been discovered by others. It is the key, or one of the keys, to the already solved problems. And not only so. It gives a relish, and facility, for successfully pursuing the yet unsolved ones. The rudiments of science, are available, and highly valuable. Some knowledge of botany assists in dealing with the vegetable world—with all growing crops. Chemistry assists in the analysis of soils, selection, and application of manures, and in numerous other ways. The mechanical branches of natural philosophy, are ready help in almost everything; but especially in reference to implements and machinery.

The thought recurs that education—cultivated thought—can best be combined with agricultural labor, or any labor, on the principle of *thorough* work—that careless, half-performed, slovenly work, makes no place for such combination. And thorough work, again, renders sufficient, the smallest quantity of ground to each man. And this again, conforms to what must occur in a world less inclined to wars, and more devoted to the arts of peace, than heretofore. Population must increase rapidly—more rapidly than in former times—and ere long the most valuable of all arts, will be the art of deriving a comfortable subsistence from the smallest area of soil. No community whose every member possesses this art, can ever be the victim of oppression in any of its forms. Such community will be alike independent of crowned-kings, money-kings, and land-kings. . . .

I will detain you but a moment longer. Some of you will be successful, and such will need but little philosophy to take them home in cheerful spirits; others will be disappointed, and will be in a less happy mood. To such, let it be said, "Lay it not too much to heart." Let them adopt the maxim, "Better luck next time"; and then, by renewed exertion, make that better luck for themselves.

And by the successful, and the unsuccessful, let it be remembered, that while occasions like the present, bring their sober and durable benefits, the exultations and mortifications of them, are but temporary; that the victor shall soon be the vanquished, if he relax in his exertion; and that the vanquished this year, may be victor the next, in spite of all competition.

It is said an eastern monarch once charged his wise men to invent him a sentence, to be ever in view, and which should be true and appropriate in all times and situations. They presented him the words: *"And this, too, shall pass away."* How much it expresses! How chastening in the hour of pride!—how consoling in the depths of affliction! "And this, too, shall pass away." And yet let us hope it is not *quite* true. Let us hope, rather, that by the best cultivation of the physical world, beneath and around us; and the intellectual and moral world within us, we shall secure an individual, social, and political prosperity and happiness, whose course shall be onward and upward, and which, while the earth endures, shall not pass away.

Lincoln's willingness to express his views on political questions hinted that his ambition was stirring. His correspondent was a physician at Reading, Pennsylvania—and Pennsylvania Republicans were ardent proponents of a protective tariff.

Clinton,
Oct. 11th. 1859

Dr. Edward Wallace:
My dear Sir:
I am here, just now, attending court. Yesterday, before I left Springfield, your brother, Dr. William S. Wallace, showed me a letter of yours, in which you kindly mention my name, inquire for my tariff views; and suggest the propriety of my writing a letter upon the subject. I was an old Henry Clay tariff Whig. In old times I made more speeches on that subject, than on any other. I have not since changed my views. I believe yet, if we could have a moderate, carefully adjusted, protective tariff, so far acquiesced in, as to not be a perpetual subject of political strife, squabbles, charges, and uncertainties, it would be better for us. Still, it is my opinion that, just now, the revival of that question, will not advance the cause itself, or the man who revives it. I have not thought much upon the subject recently; but my general impression is, that the necessity for a protective tariff will, ere long, force its old opponents to take it up; and then its old friends can join in, and estab-

lish it on a more firm and durable basis. We, the Old Whigs, have been entirely beaten out on the tariff question; and we shall not be able to re-establish the policy, until the absence of it, shall have demonstrated the necessity for it, in the minds of men heretofore opposed to it.

With this view, I should prefer, to not now, write a public letter upon the subject. I therefore wish this to be considered confidential.

I shall be very glad to receive a letter from you. Yours truly
A. Lincoln—

To a supporter of Simon Cameron, U. S. Senator, Republican boss of Pennsylvania, and presidential aspirant, Lincoln admitted for the first time that his name might be on the national ticket. Still, he cautiously turned down an invitation to join forces with the Pennsylvanian.

Springfield, Ills.
Nov. 1. 1859

W. E. Frazer, Esq
Dear Sir:
Yours of the 24th. ult. was forwarded to me from Chicago. It certainly is important to secure Pennsylvania for the Republicans, in the next presidential contest; and not unimportant to, also, secure Illinois. As to the ticket you name, I shall be heartily for it, *after* it shall have been fairly nominated by a Republican national convention; and I cannot be committed to it *before*. For my single self, I have enlisted for the permanent success of the Republican cause; and, for this object, I shall labor faithfully in the ranks, unless, as I think not probable, the judgment of the party shall assign me a different position. If the Republicans of the great state of Pennsylvania, shall present Mr. Cameron as their candidate for the Presidency, such an indorsement of his fitness for the place, could scarcely be deemed insufficient. Still, as I would not like the *public* to know, so I would not like *myself* to know I had entered a combination with any man, to the prejudice of all others whose friends respectively may consider them preferable. Yours truly
A. Lincoln

Early in December, Lincoln visited Kansas. While in Leavenworth, where he made two speeches, he stopped at the home of an old friend,

304

The Making of a Candidate

Mark W. Delahay. In Mary Delahay's autograph album Lincoln left a record of his visit.

December 7, 1859

Dear Mary

With pleasure I write my name in your album. Ere long some younger man will be more happy to confer *his* name upon *you*.

Don't allow it, Mary, until fully assured that he is worthy of the happiness. Dec. 7 – 1859   Your friend

A. Lincoln

Jesse W. Fell, of Normal, Illinois, believed that Lincoln had a good chance to win the Republican nomination. He needed, however, to be better known, particularly in the East. Fell induced Lincoln to write an account of his life, and sent the manuscript to Joseph J. Lewis, of West Chester, Pennsylvania, who made it the basis of a biographical article which he published in the *Chester County Times* on February 11, 1860. The article, widely copied by Republican papers, gave thousands of readers their first personal glimpse of the Western candidate.

Springfield,
Dec. 20. 1859

J. W. Fell, Esq
My dear Sir:

Herewith is a little sketch, as you requested. There is not much of it, for the reason, I suppose, that there is not much of me.

If anything be made out of it, I wish it to be modest, and not to go beyond the material. If it were thought necessary to incorporate anything from any of my speeches, I suppose there would be no objection. Of course it must not appear to have been written by myself. Yours very truly .

A. Lincoln

I was born Feb. 12, 1809, in Hardin County, Kentucky. My parents were both born in Virginia, of undistinguished families – second families, perhaps I should say. My mother, who died in my tenth year, was of a family of the name of Hanks, some of whom now reside in Adams, and others in Macon counties, Illinois. My paternal grandfather, Abraham Lincoln, emigrated from Rocking-ham County, Virginia, to Kentucky, about 1781 or 2, where, a year or two later, he was killed by Indians, not in battle, but by stealth, when he was laboring to open a farm in the forest. His ancestors, who were Quakers, went to Virginia from Berks County, Pennsylvania. An effort to identify them with the New England family of the same name ended in nothing more definite, than a similarity of Christian names in both families, such as Enoch, Levi, Mordecai, Solomon, Abraham, and the like.

My father, at the death of his father, was but six years of age; and he grew up, literally without education. He removed from Kentucky to what is now Spencer County, Indiana, in my eighth year. We reached our new home about the time the state came into the Union. It was a wild region, with many bears and other wild animals still in the woods. There I grew up. There were some schools, so called; but no qualification was ever required of a teacher, beyond *"readin, writin, and cipherin,"* to the rule of three. If a straggler supposed to understand Latin, happened to sojourn in the neighborhood, he was looked upon as a wizard. There was absolutely nothing to excite ambition for education. Of course when I came of age I did not know much. Still somehow, I could read, write, and cipher to the rule of three; but that was all. I have not been to school since. The little advance I now have upon this store of education, I have picked up from time to time under the pressure of necessity.

I was raised to farm work, which I continued till I was twenty-two. At twenty-one I came to Illinois, and passed the first year in Illinois—Macon County. Then I got to New Salem, (at that time in Sangamon, now in Menard County), where I remained a year as a sort of clerk in a store. Then came the Black Hawk War; and I was elected a Captain of Volunteers—a success which gave me more pleasure than any I have had since. I went the campaign, was elated, ran for the legislature the same year (1832) and was beaten —the only time I have been beaten by the people. The next, and three succeeding biennial elections, I was elected to the legislature. I was not a candidate afterwards. During this legislative period I had studied law, and removed to Springfield to practice it. In 1846 I was once elected to the lower House of Congress. Was not a candidate for re-election. From 1849 to 1854, both inclusive, practiced law more assiduously than ever before. Always a Whig in politics, and generally on the Whig electoral tickets, making active canvasses. I was losing interest in politics, when the repeal of the

The Making of a Candidate

Missouri Compromise aroused me again. What I have done since then is pretty well known.

If any personal description of me is thought desirable, it may be said, I am, in height, six feet, four inches, nearly; lean in flesh, weighing, on an average, one hundred and eighty pounds; dark complexion, with coarse black hair, and grey eyes—no other marks or brands recollected. Yours very truly

A. Lincoln

Hon. J. W. Fell.

Lincoln's debates with Douglas were on the press. The editor of the Chicago *Times,* spokesman for the Douglas Democrats, had heard that the Republican contestant had revised his speeches. Lincoln entered a denial.

Springfield, Jan. 24. 1860

Jas. W. Sheahan, Esq
Dear Sir

Yours of the 21st., requesting copies of my speeches now in progress of publication in Ohio, is received. I have no such copies now at my control; having sent the only set I ever had, to Ohio. Mr. Geo. M. Parsons has taken an active part among those who have the matter in charge, in Ohio; and I understand Messrs. Follett, Foster & Co are to be the publishers. I make no objection to any satisfactory arrangement you may make with Mr. Parsons and the publishers; and, if it will facilitate you, you are at liberty to show them this note.

You labor under a mistake, somewhat injurious to me, if you suppose I have *revised* the speeches, in any just sense of the word. I only made some small verbal corrections, mostly such as an intelligent reader would make for himself; not feeling justified to do more, when republishing the speeches along with those of Senator Douglas—his and mine being mutually answers and replies to one another. Yours truly

A. Lincoln.

Norman B. Judd, chairman of the republican State Central Committee, smarted under the charge that he had given Lincoln only lukewarm support in 1858. In December, 1859, Lincoln had written an open letter in which he avowed his faith in Judd's loyalty. Lincoln appealed for a return favor.

Springfield Feb. 9, 1860

Hon. N. B. Judd,
Dear Sir:

I am not in a position where it would hurt much for me to not be nominated on the national ticket; but I am where it would hurt some for me to not get the Illinois delegates. What I expected when I wrote the letter to Messrs Dole and others is now happening. Your discomfited assailants are most bitter against me; and they will, for revenge upon me, lay to the Bates egg in the South, and to the Seward egg in the North, and go far towards squeezing me out in the middle with nothing. Can you not help me a little in this matter, in your end of the vineyard?

I mean this to be private. Yours as ever

A. Lincoln

The ghost of the "House Divided" speech would not be laid.

Springfield,
Feb. 14. 1860

Messrs. O. P. Hall
J. R. Fullinwider & W. F. Correll.
Gentlemen.

Your letter, in which among other things, you ask "what I meant when I said this Union could not stand half-slave and half-free—and also what I meant when I said a house divided against itself could not stand" is received, and I very cheerfully answer it as plainly as I may be able. You misquote, to some material extent, what I did say; which induces me to think you have not very carefully read the speech in which the expressions occur which puzzle you to understand. For this reason and because the language I used is as plain as I can make it, I now quote at length the whole paragraph in which the expressions which puzzle you occur. It is as follows: "We are now far into the fifth year since a policy was initiated with the avowed object, and confident promise of putting an end to slavery agitation. Under the operation of that policy that agitation has not only not ceased but constantly augmented. I believe it will not cease until a crisis shall have been reached, and

The Making of a Candidate

passed. A house divided against itself cannot stand. I believe this government can not endure *permanently*, half-slave, and half-free. I do not expect the Union to be dissolved; I do not expect the house to fall; but I do expect it will cease to be divided. It will become all one thing, or all the other. Either the opponents of slavery will arrest the further spread of it, and place it where the public mind shall rest in the belief that it is in course of ultimate extinction; or its advocates will push it forward till it will become alike lawful in all the states, old as well as new, North as well as South."

That is the whole paragraph; and it puzzles me to make my meaning plainer. Look over it carefully, and conclude I meant all I said and did not mean anything I did not say, and you will have my meaning. Douglas attacked me upon this, saying it was a declaration of war between the slave and the free states. You will perceive I said no such thing, and I assure you I thought of no such thing.

If I had said "I believe this government can not *last always*, half-slave and half-free" would you understand it any better than you do? "Endure permanently" and "last always" have exactly the same meaning.

If you, or any of you, will state to me some meaning which you suppose I had, I can, and will instantly tell you whether that was my meaning. Yours very truly

A. Lincoln

In February, 1860, an invitation of the Young Men's Republican Union took Lincoln to New York. He had spent weeks in preparing his speech, carefully documenting his thesis that the framers of the Constitution had tolerated slavery of necessity, and had looked forward to a day when it would not be a blot upon the nation's name. On the evening of February 27, at Cooper Institute, he spoke to an audience liberally sprinkled with distinguished men. In the first half of his address he arrayed the historical evidence. Then he turned to argument, addressing the people of the South as if they sat before him.

But enough! *Let all who believe that "our fathers, who framed the government under which we live, understood this question just as well, and even better, than we do now," speak as they spoke, and act as they acted upon it. This is all Republicans ask—all Republicans desire—in relation to slavery. As those fathers marked it, so let it be again marked, as an evil not to be extended, but to be tolerated and protected only because of and so far as its actual presence among us makes that toleration and protection a necessity. Let all the guaranties those fathers gave it, be, not grudgingly, but fully and fairly maintained.* For this Republicans contend, and with this, so far as I know or believe, they will be content.

And now, if they would listen—as I suppose they will not—I would address a few words to the Southern people.

I would say to them:—You consider yourselves a reasonable and a just people; and I consider that in the general qualities of reason and justice you are not inferior to any other people. Still, when you speak of us Republicans, you do so only to denounce us as reptiles, or, at the best, as no better than outlaws. You will grant a hearing to pirates or murderers, but nothing like it to "Black Republicans." In all your contentions with one another, each of you deems an unconditional condemnation of "Black Republicanism" as the first thing to be attended to. Indeed, such condemnation of us seems to be an indispensable prerequisite—license, so to speak—among you to be admitted or permitted to speak at all. Now, can you, or not, be prevailed upon to pause and to consider whether this is quite just to us, or even to yourselves? Bring forward your charges and specifications, and then be patient long enough to hear us deny or justify.

You say we are sectional. We deny it. That makes an issue; and the burden of proof is upon you. You produce your proof; and what is it? Why, that our party has no existence in your section—gets no votes in your section. The fact is substantially true; but does it prove the issue? If it does, then in case we should, without change of principle, begin to get votes in your section, we should thereby cease to be sectional. You cannot escape this conclusion; and yet, are you willing to abide by it? If you are, you will probably soon find that we have ceased to be sectional, for we shall get votes in your section this very year. You will then begin to discover, as the truth plainly is, that your proof does not touch the issue. The fact that we get no votes in your section, is a fact of your making, and not of ours. And if there be fault in that fact, that fault is primarily yours, and remains so until you show that we repel you by some wrong principle or practice. If we do repel you by any wrong principle or practice, the fault is ours; but this brings you to where you ought to have started—to a discussion of the right or wrong of our principle. If our principle, put in practice, would wrong your section for the benefit of ours, or for any other object, then our principle, and we with it, are sectional, and are justly opposed and denounced as such. Meet us, then, on the question of whether our principle, put in practice, would wrong your section; and so meet us as if it were possible that something may be said on our side. Do you accept the challenge? No! Then you really believe that the principle which "our fathers who framed the government under which we live" thought so clearly right as to adopt it, and indorse it again and again, upon their official oaths, is in fact so clearly wrong as to demand your condemnation without a moment's consideration.

Some of you delight to flaunt in our faces the warning against sectional parties given by Washington in his Farewell Address. Less than eight years before Washington gave that warning, he had, as President of the United States, approved and signed an act of Congress, enforcing the prohibition of slavery in the Northwestern Territory, which act embodied the policy of the government upon that subject up to and at the very moment he penned that warning; and about one year after he penned it, he wrote La Fayette that he considered that prohibition a wise measure, expressing in the same connection his hope that we should at some time have a confederacy of free states.

Bearing this in mind, and seeing that sectionalism has since arisen upon this same subject, is that warning a weapon in your hands against us, or in our hands against you? Could Washington himself speak, would he cast the blame of that sectionalism upon us, who sustain his policy, or upon you who repudiate it? We respect that warning of Washington, and we commend it to you, together with his example pointing to the right application of it.

But you say you are conservative—eminently conservative—while we are revolutionary, destructive, or something of the sort. What is conservatism? Is it not adherence to the old and tried, against the new and untried? We stick to, contend for, the identical old policy on the point in controversy which was adopted by "our fathers who framed the government under which we live"; while you with one accord reject, and scout, and spit upon that old policy, and insist upon substituting something new. True, you disagree among yourselves as to what that substitute shall be. You are divided on new propositions and plans, but you are unanimous in

311

rejecting and denouncing the old policy of the fathers. Some of you are for reviving the foreign slave trade; some for a congressional slave code for the territories; some for Congress forbidding the territories to prohibit slavery within their limits; some for maintaining slavery in the territories through the judiciary; some for the "gur-reat pur-rinciple" that "if one man would enslave another, no third man should object," fantastically called "popular sovereignty"; but never a man among you in favor of federal prohibition of slavery in federal territories, according to the practice of "our fathers who framed the government under which we live." Not one of all your various plans can show a precedent or an advocate in the century within which our government originated. Consider, then, whether your claim of conservatism for yourselves, and your charge of destructiveness against us, are based on the most clear and stable foundations.

Again, you say we have made the slavery question more prominent than it formerly was. We deny it. We admit that it is more prominent, but we deny that we made it so. It was not we, but you, who discarded the old policy of the fathers. We resisted, and still resist, your innovation; and thence comes the greater prominence of the question. Would you have that question reduced to its former proportions? Go back to that old policy. What has been will be again, under the same conditions. If you would have the peace of the old times, readopt the precepts and policy of the old times.

You charge that we stir up insurrections among your slaves. We deny it; and what is your proof? Harper's Ferry! John Brown!! John Brown was no Republican; and you have failed to implicate a single Republican in his Harper's Ferry enterprise. If any member of our party is guilty in that matter, you know it or you do not know it. If you do know it, you are inexcusable for not designating the man and proving the fact. If you do not know it, you are inexcusable for asserting it, and especially for persisting in the assertion after you have tried and failed to make the proof. You need not be told that persisting in a charge which one does not know to be true, is simply malicious slander.

Some of you admit that no Republican designedly aided or encouraged the Harper's Ferry affair; but still insist that our doctrines and declarations necessarily lead to such results. We do not believe it. We know we hold to no doctrine, and make no declaration, which were not held to and made by "our fathers who framed the government under which we live." You never dealt fairly by us in relation to this affair. When it occurred, some important state elections were near at hand, and you were in evident glee with the belief that, by charging the blame upon us, you could get an advantage of us in those elections. The elections came, and your expectations were not quite fulfilled. Every Republican man knew that, as to himself at least, your charge was a slander, and he was not much inclined by it to cast his vote in your favor. Republican doctrines and declarations are accompanied with a continual protest against any interference whatever with your slaves, or with you about your slaves. Surely, this does not encourage them to revolt. True, we do, in common with "our fathers, who framed the government under which we live," declare our belief that slavery is wrong; but the slaves do not hear us declare even this. For anything we say or do, the slaves would scarcely know there is a Republican party. I believe they would not, in fact, generally know it but for your misrepresentations of us, in their hearing. In your political contests among yourselves, each faction charges the other with sympathy with Black Republicanism; and then, to give point to the charge, defines Black Republicanism to simply be insurrection, blood and thunder among the slaves.

Slave insurrections are no more common now than they were before the Republican party was organized. What induced the Southampton insurrection, twenty-eight years ago, in which, at least, three times as many lives were lost as at Harper's Ferry? You can scarcely stretch your very elastic fancy to the conclusion that Southampton was "got up by Black Republicanism." In the present state of things in the United States, I do not think a general, or even a very extensive slave insurrection, is possible. The indispensable concert of action cannot be attained. The slaves have no means of rapid communication; nor can incendiary freemen, black or white, supply it. The explosive materials are everywhere in parcels; but there neither are, nor can be supplied, the indispensable connecting trains.

Much is said by Southern people about the affection of slaves for their masters and mistresses; and a part of it, at least, is true. A plot for an uprising could scarcely be devised and communicated to twenty individuals before some one of them, to save the life of a favorite master or mistress, would divulge it. This is the rule; and the slave revolution in Hayti was not an exception to it, but a case

313

occurring under peculiar circumstances. The gunpowder plot of British history, though not connected with slaves, was more in point. In that case, only about twenty were admitted to the secret; and yet one of them, in his anxiety to save a friend, betrayed the plot to that friend, and, by consequence, averted the calamity. Occasional poisonings from the kitchen, and open or stealthy assassinations in the field, and local revolts extending to a score or so, will continue to occur as the natural results of slavery; but no general insurrection of slaves, as I think, can happen in this country for a long time. Whoever much fears, or much hopes for such an event, will be alike disappointed.

In the language of Mr. Jefferson, uttered many years ago, "It is still in our power to direct the process of emancipation, and deportation, peaceably, and in such slow degrees, as that the evil will wear off insensibly; and their places be, *pari passu,* filled up by free white laborers. If, on the contrary, it is left to force itself on, human nature must shudder at the prospect held up."

Mr. Jefferson did not mean to say, nor do I, that the power of emancipation is in the federal government. He spoke of Virginia; and, as to the power of emancipation, I speak of the slaveholding states only. The federal government, however, as we insist, has the power of restraining the extension of the institution—the power to insure that a slave insurrection shall never occur on any American soil which is now free from slavery.

John Brown's effort was peculiar. It was not a slave insurrection. It was an attempt by white men to get up a revolt among slaves, in which the slaves refused to participate. In fact, it was so absurd that the slaves, with all their ignorance, saw plainly enough it could not succeed. That affair, in its philosophy, corresponds with the many attempts, related in history, at the assassination of kings and emperors. An enthusiast broods over the oppression of a people till he fancies himself commissioned by Heaven to liberate them. He ventures the attempt, which ends in little else than his own execution. Orsini's attempt on Louis Napoleon, and John Brown's attempt at Harper's Ferry were, in their philosophy, precisely the same. The eagerness to cast blame on old England in the one case, and on New England in the other, does not disprove the sameness of the two things.

And how much would it avail you, if you could, by the use of John Brown, Helper's book, and the like, break up the Republican organization? Human action can be modified to some extent, but human nature cannot be changed. There is a judgment and a feeling against slavery in this nation, which cast at least a million and a half of votes. You cannot destroy that judgment and feeling—that sentiment—by breaking up the political organization which rallies around it. You can scarcely scatter and disperse an army which has been formed into order in the face of your heaviest fire; but if you could, how much would you gain by forcing the sentiment which created it out of the peaceful channel of the ballot-box, into some other channel? What would that other channel probably be? Would the number of John Browns be lessened or enlarged by the operation?

But you will break up the Union rather than submit to a denial of your constitutional rights.

That has a somewhat reckless sound; but it would be palliated, if not fully justified, were we proposing, by the mere force of numbers, to deprive you of some right, plainly written down in the Constitution. But we are proposing no such thing.

When you make these declarations, you have a specific and well-understood allusion to an assumed constitutional right of yours, to take slaves into the federal territories, and to hold them there as property. But no such right is specifically written in the Constitution. That instrument is literally silent about any such right. We, on the contrary, deny that such a right has any existence in the Constitution, even by implication.

Your purpose, then, plainly stated, is, that you will destroy the government, unless you be allowed to construe and enforce the Constitution as you please, on all points in dispute between you and us. You will rule or ruin in all events.

This, plainly stated, is your language. Perhaps you will say the Supreme Court has decided the disputed constitutional question in your favor. Not quite so. But waiving the lawyer's distinction between dictum and decision, the court have decided the question for you in a sort of way. The court have substantially said, it is your constitutional right to take slaves into the federal territories, and to hold them there as property. When I say the decision was made in a sort of way, I mean it was made in a divided court, by a bare majority of the Judges, and they not quite agreeing with one another in the reasons for making it; that it is so made as that its avowed supporters disagree with one another about its meaning, and that it was mainly based upon a mistaken statement of fact—the statement in the opinion that "the right of property in a slave is distinctly and expressly affirmed in the Constitution."

An inspection of the Constitution will show that the right of property in a slave is not "*distinctly* and *expressly* affirmed" in it. Bear in mind, the Judges do not pledge their judicial opinion that such right is *impliedly* affirmed in the Constitution; but they pledge their veracity that it is "*distinctly* and *expressly*" affirmed there—"distinctly," that is, not mingled with anything else—"expressly," that is, in words meaning just that, without the aid of any inference, and susceptible of no other meaning.

If they had only pledged their judicial opinion that such right is affirmed in the instrument by implication, it would be open to others to show that neither the word "slave" nor "slavery" is to be found in the Constitution, nor the word "property" even, in any connection with language alluding to the things slave, or slavery, and that wherever in that instrument the slave is alluded to, he is called a "person;"—and wherever his master's legal right in relation to him is alluded to, it is spoken of as "service or labor which may be due,"—as a debt payable in service or labor. Also, it would be open to show, by contemporaneous history, that this mode of alluding to slaves and slavery, instead of speaking of them, was employed on purpose to exclude from the Constitution the idea that there could be property in man.

To show all this, is easy and certain.

When this obvious mistake of the Judges shall be brought to their notice, is it not reasonable to expect that they will withdraw the mistaken statement, and reconsider the conclusion based upon it?

And then it is to be remembered that "our fathers, who framed the government under which we live"—the men who made the Constitution—decided this same constitutional question in our favor, long ago—decided it without division among themselves, when making the decision; without division among themselves about the meaning of it after it was made, and, so far as any evidence is left, without basing it upon any mistaken statement of facts.

Under all these circumstances, do you really feel yourselves justified to break up this government, unless such a court decision as yours is, shall be at once submitted to as a conclusive and final rule of political action? But you will not abide the election of a Repub-

The Making of a Candidate

lican President! In that supposed event, you say, you will destroy the Union; and then, you say, the great crime of having destroyed it will be upon us! That is cool. A highwayman holds a pistol to my ear, and mutters through his teeth, "Stand and deliver, or I shall kill you, and then you will be a murderer!"

To be sure, what the robber demanded of me—my money—was my own; and I had a clear right to keep it; but it was no more my own than my vote is my own; and the threat of death to me, to extort my money, and the threat of destruction to the Union, to extort my vote, can scarcely be distinguished in principle.

A few words now to Republicans. *It is exceedingly desirable that all parts of this great confederacy shall be at peace, and in harmony, one with another. Let us Republicans do our part to have it so. Even though much provoked, let us do nothing through passion and ill temper. Even though the Southern people will not so much as listen to us, let us calmly consider their demands, and yield to them if, in our deliberate view of our duty, we possibly can.* Judging by all they say and do, and by the subject and nature of their controversy with us, let us determine, if we can, what will satisfy them.

Will they be satisfied if the territories be unconditionally surrendered to them? We know they will not. In all their present complaints against us, the territories are scarcely mentioned. Invasions and insurrections are the rage now. Will it satisfy them, if, in the future, we have nothing to do with invasions and insurrections? We know it will not. We so know, because we know we never had anything to do with invasions and insurrections; and yet this total abstaining does not exempt us from the charge and the denunciation.

The question recurs, what will satisfy them? Simply this: We must not only let them alone, but we must, somehow, convince them that we do let them alone. This, we know by experience, is no easy task. We have been so trying to convince them from the very beginning of our organization, but with no success. In all our platforms and speeches we have constantly protested our purpose to let them alone; but this has had no tendency to convince them. Alike unavailing to convince them, is the fact that they have never detected a man of us in any attempt to disturb them.

These natural, and apparently adequate means all failing, what will convince them? This, and this only: cease to call slavery *wrong,* and join them in calling *it right.* And this must be done thoroughly—done in *acts* as well as in *words.* Silence will not be tolerated—we must place ourselves avowedly with them. Senator Douglas's new sedition law must be enacted and enforced, suppressing all declarations that slavery is wrong, whether made in politics, in presses, in pulpits, or in private. We must arrest and return their fugitive slaves with greedy pleasure. We must pull down our free state constitutions. The whole atmosphere must be disinfected from all taint of opposition to slavery, before they will cease to believe that all their troubles proceed from us.

I am quite aware they do not state their case precisely in this way. Most of them would probably say to us, "Let us alone, *do* nothing to us, and *say* what you please about slavery." But we do let them alone—have never disturbed them—so that, after all, it is what we say, which dissatisfies them. They will continue to accuse us of doing, until we cease saying.

I am also aware they have not, as yet, in terms, demanded the overthrow of our free state constitutions. Yet those constitutions declare the wrong of slavery, with more solemn emphasis, than do all other sayings against it; and when all these other sayings shall have been silenced, the overthrow of these constitutions will be demanded, and nothing be left to resist the demand. It is nothing to the contrary, that they do not demand the whole of this just now. Demanding what they do, and for the reason they do, they can voluntarily stop nowhere short of this consummation. Holding, as they do, that slavery is morally right, and socially elevating, they cannot cease to demand a full national recognition of it, as a legal right, and a social blessing.

Nor can we justifiably withhold this, on any ground save our conviction that slavery is wrong. If slavery is right, all words, acts, laws, and constitutions against it, are themselves wrong, and should be silenced, and swept away. If it is right, we cannot justly object to its nationality—its universality; if it is wrong, they cannot justly insist upon its extension—its enlargement. All they ask, we could readily grant, if we thought slavery right; all we ask, they could as readily grant, if they thought it wrong. Their thinking it right, and our thinking it wrong, is the precise fact upon which depends the whole controversy. Thinking it right, as they do, they are not to blame for desiring its full recognition, as being right; but, thinking it wrong, as we do, can we yield to them? Can we cast our votes with their view, and against our own? In view of our moral, social and political responsibilties, can we do this?

Wrong as we think slavery is, we can yet afford to let it alone where it is, because that much is due to the necessity arising from its actual presence in the nation; but can we, while our votes will prevent it, allow it to spread into the national territories, and to overrun us here in these free states? If our sense of duty forbids this, then let us stand by our duty, fearlessly and effectively. Let us be diverted by none of those sophistical contrivances wherewith we are so industriously plied and belabored—contrivances such as groping for some middle ground between the right and the wrong, vain as the search for a man who should be neither a living man nor a dead man—such as a policy of "don't care" on a question about which all true men do care—such as Union appeals beseeching true Union men to yield to Disunionists, reversing the divine rule, and calling, not the sinners, but the righteous to repentance— such as invocations to Washington, imploring men to unsay what Washington said, and undo what Washington did.

Neither let us be slandered from our duty by false accusations against us, nor frightened from it by menaces of destruction to the government nor of dungeons to ourselves. *Let us have faith that right makes might, and in that faith, let us, to the end, dare to do our duty as we understand it.*

Lincoln left New York to visit his son Robert at Phillips Exeter Academy, and to speak at several cities in New England. From Exeter he wrote to Mrs. Lincoln. Only a part of his letter has survived.

[*Exeter, N. H. March 4, 1860*]
. . . I have been unable to escape this toil. If I had foreseen it, I think I would not have come East at all. The speech at New York, being within my calculation before I started, went off passably well and gave me no trouble whatever. The difficulty was to make nine others, before reading audiences who had already seen all my ideas in print. . . .

In a speech at New Haven, Lincoln covered familiar ground, but he also touched on a new subject—William H. Seward's "irrepressible conflict" doctrine, so close to his own "house divided" prediction.

The Living Lincoln

I see the signs of the approaching triumph of the Republicans in the bearing of their political adversaries. A great deal of their war with us nowadays is mere bushwhacking. [*Laughter.*] At the Battle of Waterloo, when Napoleon's cavalry had charged again and again upon the unbroken squares of British infantry, at last they were giving up the attempt, and going off in disorder, when some of the officers in mere vexation and complete despair fired their pistols at those solid squares. The Democrats are in that sort of extreme desperation; it is nothing else. [Laughter.] I will take up a few of these *arguments*.

There is "THE IRREPRESSIBLE CONFLICT." [Applause.] How they rail at Seward for that saying! They repeat it constantly; and although the proof has been thrust under their noses again and again, that almost every good man since the formation of our government has uttered that same sentiment, from Gen. Washington, who "trusted that we should yet have a confederacy of free states," with Jefferson, Jay, Monroe, down to the latest days, yet they refuse to notice that at all, and persist in railing at Seward for saying it. Even Roger A. Pryor, editor of the Richmond Enquirer, uttered the same sentiment in almost the same language, and yet so little offence did it give the Democrats that he was sent for to Washington to edit the States—the Douglas organ there, while Douglas goes into hydrophobia and spasms of rage because Seward dared to repeat it. [Great applause.] This is what I call bushwhacking, a sort of argument that they must know any child can see through.

Lincoln faced an audience aroused over a local strike. His remarks on labor and capital were based on his own experience.

Another specimen of this bushwhacking, that "shoe strike." [Laughter.] Now be it understood that I do not pretend to know all about the matter. I am merely going to speculate a little about some of its phases. And at the outset, *I am glad to see that a system of labor prevails in New England under which laborers* CAN *strike* when they want to [Cheers], where they are not obliged to work under all circumstances, and are not tied down and obliged to labor whether you pay them or not! [Cheers.] I *like* the system which lets a man quit when he wants to, and wish it might prevail everywhere. [Tremendous applause.] One of the reasons why I am opposed to slavery is just here. What is the true condition of the laborer? I take it that it is best for all to leave each man free to acquire property as fast as he can. Some will get wealthy. I don't believe in a law to prevent a man from getting rich; it would do more harm than good. So while we do not propose any war upon capital, we do wish to allow the humblest man an equal chance to get rich with everybody else. [Applause.] When one starts poor, as most do in the race of life, free society is such that he knows he can better his condition; he knows that there is no fixed condition of labor, for his whole life. I am not ashamed to confess that twenty-five years ago I was a hired laborer, mauling rails, at work on a flat-boat—just what might happen to any poor man's son! [Applause.] I want every man to have the chance—and I believe a black man is entitled to it—in which he *can* better his condition—when he may look forward and hope to be a hired laborer this year and the next, work for himself afterward, and finally to hire men to work for him! That is the true system. Up here in New England, you have a soil that scarcely sprouts black-eyed beans, and yet where will you find wealthy men so wealthy, and poverty so rarely in extremity? There is not another such place on earth! [Cheers.] I desire that if you get too thick here, and find it hard to better your condition on this soil, you may have a chance to strike and go somewhere else, where you may not be degraded, nor have your family corrupted by forced rivalry with Negro slaves. I want you to have a clean bed, and no snakes in it! [Cheers.] Then you can better your condition, and so it may go on and on in one ceaseless round so long as man exists on the face of the earth!

Lincoln was willing to promise help to Mark W. Delahay, and just as unwilling to countenance Delahay's suggestion that the Kansas delegation to the Republican National Convention might be bought.

Springfield, Ills— Mar— 16, 1860

Dear Delahay—

I have just returned from the East. Before leaving, I received your letter of Feb. 6; and on my return I find those of the 17th. & 19th. with Genl. Lane's note inclosed in one of them.

I sincerely wish you could be elected one of the first Senators for Kansas; but how to help you I do not know. If it were permissible for me to interfere, I am not personally acquainted with a single member of your legislature. If my known friendship for you could be of any advantage, that friendship was abundantly manifested by me last December while in Kansas. If any member had written me, as you say some have Trumbull, I would very readily answer him. I shall write Trumbull on the subject at this sitting.

I understood, while in Kansas, that the state legislature will not meet until the state is admitted. Was that the right understanding?

As to your kind wishes for myself, allow me to say I cannot enter the ring on the money basis—first, because, in the main, it is wrong; and secondly, I have not, and cannot get, the money. I say, in the main, the use of money is wrong; but for certain objects, in a political contest, the use of some, is both right, and indispensable. With me, as with yourself, this long struggle has been one of great pecuniary loss. I now distinctly say this. If you shall be appointed a delegate to Chicago, I will furnish one hundred dollars to bear the expenses of the trip.

Present my respects to Genl. Lane; and say to him, I shall be pleased to hear from him at any time. Your friend, as ever

A. Lincoln—

P.S. I have not yet taken the newspaper slip to the Journal. I shall do that tomorrow; and then send you the paper as requested.

A. L.

Lincoln had judged his own prospects with uncanny accuracy. He would welcome the support of the Ohio delegation if he could have it without hurting the chances of Ohio's favorite son, Salmon P. Chase.

Chicago, March 24, 1860

Hon. Samuel Galloway
My dear Sir:

I am here attending a trial in court. Before leaving home I received your kind letter of the 15th. Of course I am gratified to know I have friends in Ohio who are disposed to give me the highest evidence of their friendship and confidence. Mr Parrott of the legislature, had written me to the same effect. If I have any chance, it consists mainly in the fact that the *whole* opposition would vote for me if nominated. (I don't mean to include the proslavery opposition of the South, of course.) My name is new in the field; and I suppose I am not the *first* choice of a very great many. Our policy, then, is to give no offence to others—leave them in a mood to come to us, if they shall be compelled to give up their first love. This, too, is dealing justly with all, and leaving us in a mood to support heartily whoever shall be nominated. I believe I have once before told you that I especially wish to do no ungenerous thing towards Governor Chase, because he gave us his sympathy in 1858, when scarcely any other distinguished man did. Whatever you may do for me, consistently with these suggestions, will be appreciated, and gratefully remembered.

Please write me again. Yours very truly

A. Lincoln

Another Ohioan, R. M. Corwine of Cincinnati, informed Lincoln that the Ohio delegation was divided, and asked him how the leading candidates stood in Illinois. Lincoln's analysis omitted himself.

Springfield, Ill., April 6th. 1860.

Hon. R. M. Corwine.
My Dear Sir

Reaching home yesterday after an absence of more than two weeks, I found your letter of the 24th of March. Remembering that when not a very great man begins to be mentioned for a very great position, his head is very likely to be a little turned, I concluded I am not the fittest person to answer the questions you ask. Making due allowance for this, I think Mr. Seward is the very best candidate we could have for the north of Illinois, and the very *worst* for the south of it. The estimate of Gov. Chase here is neither better nor worse than that of Seward, except that he is a newer man. They are regarded as being almost the same, seniority giving Seward the inside track. Mr. Bates, I think, would be the best man for the south of our state, and the worst for the north of it. If Judge McLean was fifteen, or even ten years younger, I think he would be stronger than either, in our state, taken as a whole; but his great age, and the recollection of the deaths of Harrison and Taylor have, so far, prevented his being much spoken of here.

I really believe we can carry the state for either of them, or for anyone who may be nominated; but doubtless it would be easier to do it with some than with others.

I feel myself disqualified to speak of myself in this matter. I feel this letter will be of little value to you; but I can make it no better, under the circumstances. Let it be strictly confidential, not that there is anything really objectionable in it, but because it might be misconstrued. Yours very truly,

A. Lincoln.

The Living Lincoln

To remove doubts in the mind of a friend—the editor of a newspaper in Iroquois County, Illinois—Lincoln explained how he came to make his Cooper Union address, and to be paid for it.

Springfield, April 6, 1860.

C. F. McNeill, Esq.—
Dear Sir:

Reaching home yesterday, I found yours of the 23d. March, inclosing a slip from *The Middleport Press*. It is not true that I ever *charged* anything for a political speech in my life—but this much is true: Last October I was requested, by letter, to deliver some sort of speech in Mr. Beecher's church, in Brooklyn, $200 being offered in the first letter. I wrote that I could do it in February, provided they would take a political speech, if I could find time to get up no other. They agreed, and subsequently I informed them the speech would have to be a political one. When I reached New York, I, for the first time, learned that the place was changed to "Cooper Institute." I made the speech, and left for New Hampshire, where I have a son at school, neither asking for pay nor having any offered me. Three days after, a check for $200— was sent to me, at N. H., and I took it, *and did not know it was wrong*. My understanding now is, though I knew nothing of it at the time, that they did charge for admittance, at the Cooper Institute, and that they took in more than twice $200.

I have made this explanation to you as a friend; but I wish no explanation made to our enemies. What they want is a squabble and a fuss; and that they can have if we explain; and they cannot have if we don't.

When I returned through New York from New England I was told by the gentlemen who sent me the check, that a drunken vagabond in the Club, having learned something about the $200, made the exhibition out of which *The Herald* manufactured the article quoted by *The Press* of your town.

My judgment is, and therefore my request is, that you give no denial, and no explanations.

Thanking you for your kind interest in the matter, I remain,
Yours truly,

A. Lincoln.

If Harvey G. Eastman, the proprietor of a business college at Poughkeepsie, made the inquiry that Lincoln suggested, Eastman

The Making of a Candidate

learned that the photograph in question was taken by Mathew Brady, who would someday become almost as well known as his subject.

Springfield, Ills.
April 7. 1860

H. G. Eastman, Esq
Dear Sir

Yours of March 18th. addressed to me at Chicago, and requesting my photograph is received. I have not a single one now at my control; but I think you can easily get one at New York. While I was there I was taken to one of the places where they get up such things, and I suppose they got my shadow, and can multiply copies indefinitely. Any of the Republican Club men there can show you the place. Yours truly

A. Lincoln

Lincoln would not be disappointed if he should fail to win the nomination, but he had reached the point where he was doing all he could to win. Babcock was the editor of the New Haven *Palladium.*

Springfield, Ills.
April 14. 1860

Jas. F. Babcock, Esq
My dear Sir:

Reaching home, after a short absence, I find your obliging letter of the 8th. I was very anxious for the result in Connecticut, and am much gratified that it is all safe.

As to the presidential nomination, claiming no greater exemption from selfishness than is common, I still feel that my whole aspiration should be, and therefore must be, to be placed anywhere, or nowhere, as may appear most likely to advance our cause.

As to the names of confidential friends here, with whom you might correspond, I give you David Davis, Bloomington, Ills.

Julius White, Chicago, ″
Dr. I. A. W. Buck, Aurora, ″
A. Sympson, Carthage ″

I will add that Hon J. W. Grimes & Hon. S. R. Curtis, Senator & Representative from Iowa, are very friendly to me, though I do not know that they favor my nomination. The following named gentlemen are probably for me—and would like to correspond with you.

The Living Lincoln

Hon: Saml. Galloway, Columbus, O.
   "   Robt. C. Schenck, Dayton, O.
   "   J. W. Gorden, Indianapolis, Ia.
   W. T. Page, Esq. Evansville, Ia.
   Hawkins Taylor, Esq. Keokuk, Iowa

Please do not understand that I wish to task you with the opening of a correspondence with all these gentlemen; I mean no more than to furnish you the names, and leave the rest to your own pleasure.

Please make my respects to your family, and believe me Yours very truly

A. Lincoln—

For Lyman Trumbull, in the United States Senate, Lincoln repeated his analysis of the political situation in Illinois. When he wrote, the Democratic National Convention, in session at Charleston, South Carolina, was deadlocked by the sectional differences that would soon fracture the party.

Springfield,
April 29. 1860

Hon: L. Trumbull:
My dear Sir:
    Yours of the 24th. was duly received; and I have postponed answering it, hoping by the result at Charleston, to know who is to lead our adversaries, before writing. But Charleston hangs fire, and I wait no longer.

As you request, I will be entirely frank. The taste *is* in my mouth a little; and this, no doubt, disqualifies me, to some extent, to form correct opinions. You may confidently rely, however, that by no advice or consent of mine, shall my pretensions be pressed to the point of endangering our common cause.

Now, as to my opinions about the chances of others in Illinois. I think neither Seward nor Bates can carry Illinois if Douglas shall be on the track; and that either of them can, if he shall not be. I rather think McLean could carry it with D. on or off—in other words, I think McLean is stronger in Illinois, taking all sections of it, than either S. or B; and I think S. the weakest of the three. I hear no objection to McLean, except his age; but that objection seems to occur to everyone; and it is possible it might leave him no

326

stronger than the others. By the way, if we should nominate him, how would we save to ourselves the chance of filling his vacancy in the court? Have him hold on up to the moment of his inauguration? Would that course be no drawback upon us in the canvass?

Recurring to Illinois, we want something here quite as much as, and which is harder to get than, the electoral vote—the legislature. And it is exactly in this point that Seward's nomination would be hard upon us. Suppose he should gain us a thousand votes in Winnebago, it would not compensate for the loss of fifty in Edgar.

A word now for your own special benefit. You better write no letters which can possibly be distorted into opposition, or quasi-opposition to me. There are men on the constant watch for such things out of which to prejudice my peculiar friends against you. While I have no more suspicion of you than I have of my best friend living, I am kept in a constant struggle against suggestions of this sort. I have hesitated some to write this paragraph, lest you should suspect I do it for my own benefit, and not for yours; but on reflection I conclude you will not suspect me.

Let no eye but your own see this—not that there is anything wrong, or even ungenerous, in it; but it would be misconstrued. Your friend as ever

A. Lincoln

As the Republican convention approached, Lincoln now included his own prospects in his forecasting. He also revealed the names of those in whose hands he had placed his political fortunes.

PRIVATE

Springfield, Ills. May 2. 1860.

Hon: R. M. Corwine
Dear Sir:
Yours of the 30th. ult. is just received. After what you have said, it is perhaps proper I should post you, so far as I am able, as to the "lay of the land." First then, I think the Illinois delegation will be unanimous for me at the start; and no other delegation will. A few individuals in other delegations would like to go for me at the start, but may be restrained by their colleagues. It is represented to me, by men who ought to know, that the whole of Indiana might not be difficult to get. You know how it is in Ohio. I am certainly not the first choice there; and yet I have not heard

that anyone makes any positive objection to me. It is just so everywhere so far as I can perceive. Everywhere, except in Illinois, and possibly Indiana, one or another is preferred to me, but there is no positive objection. This is the ground as it now appears. I believe you personally know C. M. Allen, of Vincennes, Ia. He is a delegate, and has notified me that the entire Ia. delegation will be in Chicago the same day you name—Saturday the 12th. My friends Jesse K. Dubois, our Auditor, & Judge David Davis, will probably be there ready to confer with friends from other states. Let me hear from you again when anything occurs. Yours very truly

A. Lincoln

Lincoln knew and admired the works of only a few authors. One was Robert Burns.

Springfield, May 2, 1860.

Mr. James G. Wilson.
My Dear Friend:
I am greatly obliged for the volume of your friend Fitz Greene Halleck's poems. Many a month has passed since I have met with anything more admirable than his beautiful lines on Burns. With Alnwick Castle, Marco Bozzaris, and Red Jacket, I am also much pleased.

It is wonderful that you should have seen and known a sister of Robert Burns. You must tell me something about her when we meet again. Yours very truly,

A. Lincoln.

Dr. Edward Wallace, to whom Lincoln had written before, drew another letter on the tariff.

Springfield, Ills. May 12. 1860

Dr. Edward Wallace:
My dear Sir
Your brother, Dr. W. S. Wallace, shows me a letter of yours, in which you request him to inquire if you may use a letter of mine to you, in which something is said upon the tariff question. I do not precisely remember what I did say in that letter; but I presume I said nothing substantially different from what I shall say now.

In the days of Henry Clay I was a Henry Clay-tariff-man; and

The Making of a Candidate

my views have undergone no material change upon that subject. I now think the tariff question ought not to be agitated in the Chicago convention; but that all should be satisfied on that point, with a presidential candidate, whose antecedents give assurance that he would neither seek to force a tariff law by executive influence; nor yet to arrest a reasonable one, by a veto, or otherwise. Just such a candidate I desire shall be put in nomination. I really have no objection to these views being publicly known; but I do wish to thrust no letter before the public now, upon any subject. Save me from the appearance of obtrusion; and I do not care who sees this, or my former letter. Yours very truly

A. Lincoln.

To his managers in the Republican National Convention, now in session in Chicago, Lincoln pencilled a message on the margin of a copy of the St. Louis *Missouri Democrat.*

[*May 17, 1860*]

I agree with Seward in his "Irrepressible Conflict," but I do not endorse his "Higher Law" doctrine. *Make no contracts that will bind me.*

On the third ballot, taken on the morning of May 18, the convention nominated Abraham Lincoln as the Republican candidate for President. The following evening an official committee, headed by George Ashmun of Massachusetts, chairman of the convention, called on the candidate at his home to convey formal notice of his selection. To Ashmun's notification speech Lincoln made a brief reply.

May 19, 1860

Mr. Chairman and gentlemen of the committee, I tender you, and through you to the Republican National Convention, and all the people represented in it, my profoundest thanks for the high honor done me, which you now formally announce.

Deeply, and even painfully sensible of the great responsibility which is inseparable from that honor—a responsibility which I could almost wish had fallen upon some one of the far more eminent men and experienced statesmen whose distinguished names were before the Convention, I shall, by your leave, consider more fully the resolutions of the Convention, denominated the platform, and without unseasonable delay, respond to you, Mr. Chairman, in writing—not doubting now, that the platform will be found satisfactory, and the nomination accepted.

And now, I will not longer defer the pleasure of taking you, and each of you, by the hand.

Four days later Lincoln sent Ashmun a formal letter of acceptance.

Springfield, Ills. May 23. 1860

Hon: George Ashmun:
President of the Republican National Convention.
Sir:

I accept the nomination tendered me by the Convention over which you presided, and of which I am formally apprized in the letter of yourself and others, acting as a committee of the convention, for that purpose.

The declaration of principles and sentiments, which accompanies your letter, meets my approval; and it shall be my care not to violate, or disregard it, in any part.

Imploring the assistance of Divine Providence, and with due regard to the views and feelings of all who were represented in the convention; to the rights of all the states, and territories, and people of the nation; to the inviolability of the Constitution, and the perpetual union, harmony, and prosperity of all, I am most happy to co-operate for the practical success of the principles declared by the Convention. Your obliged friend, and fellow citizen

A. Lincoln

X. The Republican Nominee

1860   As a presidential candidate, Lincoln proposed to remain in Springfield and let the party stalwarts carry the campaign to the people. By this course he would follow the time-honored convention which held that an aspirant for the Presidency should have nothing to do with getting himself elected. At the same time, by making no public statements, he would give his opponents no handholds.

But if Lincoln would not go to the people, the people would come to him. He would have thousands of visitors—party leaders, plain Republicans, the merely curious. Since he could not receive these sovereign Americans properly in the small and dingy quarters of Lincoln & Herndon, the Governor's office in the State House was placed at his disposal. There, a few days after the nomination, Lincoln established himself, with John G. Nicolay, a young man who had been employed by the Secretary of State, as his secretary.

The nomination deluged Lincoln with congratulations. To distinguished well-wishers, and to personal acquaintances, he wrote in his own neat script. One of his first letters went to the Ohio Republican who had hoped that he, rather than Lincoln, would be the choice of the convention.

Springfield, Ills. May 26, 1860.

Hon. S. P. Chase.
My Dear Sir:
It gave me great pleasure to receive yours, mistakenly dated, May 17. Holding myself the humblest of all whose names were before the convention, I feel in especial need of the assistance of all; and I am glad—very glad—of the indication that you stand ready. It is a great consolation that so nearly all—all except Mr.

331

Bates & Mr. Clay, I believe, — of those distinguished and able men, are already in high position to do service in the common cause. Your Obt Servt

A. Lincoln

The Kentucky abolitionist who had aspired, unsuccessfully, to the vice-presidential nomination, received a letter calculated to ease his disappointment.

Springfield, Ills.
May 26. 1860

Hon. C. M. Clay.
My dear Sir:
Yours of the 21st. is received, and for which I sincerely thank you. The humblest of all whose names were before the convention, I shall, in the canvass, and especially afterwards, if the result shall devolve the administration upon me, need the support of all the talent, popularity, and courage, North and South, which is in the party; and it is with sincere gratification that I receive this early indication of your unwavering purpose to stand for the right. Your Obt. Servt.

A. Lincoln

In Colfax's words of congratulation — "I need not say how heartily I join with your *original* friends in their greetings to you" — Lincoln found a cue for a deft reply.

Springfield, Ills.
May 26. 1860

PRIVATE
Hon. Schuyler Colfax
My dear Sir:
Your very kind, and acceptable letter of the 18th was received two or three days since.
You distinguish between yourself and my *original* friends — a distinction which, by your leave, I propose to forget.
I have acted upon your suggeston, and also upon my own impulse, in relation to our old friend R. W. T.* Yours very truly

A. Lincoln

* Richard W. Thompson, of Indiana, who, Colfax had suggested, would like to hear from Lincoln.

The Republican Nominee

Caleb B. Smith, who, at Chicago, had worked mightily in Lincoln's behalf with the Indiana delegation, received thanks and an expression of cautious optimism.

Springfield, Ills. May 26. 1860

Hon: C. B. Smith —
My dear Sir:
Yours of the 21st. was duly received; but I have found no time till now, to say a word in the way of answer. I am, indeed, much indebted to Indiana; and, as my home friends tell me, much to you personally. Your saying you no longer consider Ia.* a doubtful state, is very gratifying. The thing starts well everywhere — too well, I almost fear, to last. But we are in, and stick or go through, must be the word.

Let me hear from Indiana occasionally. Your friend, as ever
A. Lincoln.

The clerk of the circuit court at Elizabethtown, Kentucky, gave Lincoln an opportunity to lay aside politics momentarily and to indulge his interest in family history.

Springfield, Ills.
May 28. 1860

Hon. Saml. Haycraft
Dear Sir:
Your recent letter, without date, is received. Also the copy of your speech on the contemplated Daniel Boone monument, which I have not yet had time to read. In the main you are right about my history. My father was Thomas Lincoln, and Mrs. Sally Johnston, was his second wife. You are mistaken about my mother — her maiden name was Nancy Hanks. I was not born at Elizabethtown; but my mother's first child, a daughter, two years older than myself, and now long since deceased, was. I was born Feb. 12. 1809, near where Hodgenville now is, then in Hardin County. I do not think I ever saw you, though I very well know who you are — so well that I recognized your handwriting, on opening your letter, before I saw the signature. My recollection is that Ben. Helm was first clerk, that you succeeded him, that Jack Thomas and William Farleigh graduated in the same office, and that your handwritings were all very similar. Am I right?

* In 1860, a common abbreviation for Indiana.

The Living Lincoln

My father has been dead near ten years; but my stepmother, (Mrs. Johnston) is still living.

I am really very glad of your letter, and shall be pleased to receive another at any time. Yours very truly

A. Lincoln

Ambitious biographers invaded Springfield. One of the first was John Locke Scripps of the Chicago *Press & Tribune.* Grateful for the paper's support, Lincoln took time to write, in the third person, a long autobiographical sketch. Scripps made it the basis of his *Life of Abraham Lincoln,* the best of the campaign biographies.

[*c. June, 1860*]

Abraham Lincoln was born Feb. 12, 1809, then in Hardin, now in the more recently formed county of Larue, Kentucky. His father, Thomas, & grandfather, Abraham, were born in Rockingham County, Virginia, whither their ancestors had come from Berks County, Pennsylvania. His lineage has been traced no farther back than this. The family were originally Quakers, though in later times they have fallen away from the peculiar habits of that people. The grandfather Abraham, had four brothers—Isaac, Jacob, John & Thomas. So far as known, the descendants of Jacob and John are still in Virginia. Isaac went to a place near where Virginia, North Carolina, and Tennessee, join; and his descendants are in that region. Thomas came to Kentucky, and after many years, died there, whence his descendants went to Missouri. Abraham, grandfather of the subject of this sketch, came to Kentucky, and was killed by Indians about the year 1784. He left a widow, three sons and two daughters. The eldest son, Mordecai, remained in Kentucky till late in life, when he removed to Hancock County, Illinois, where soon after he died, and where several of his descendants still reside. The second son, Josiah, removed at an early day to a place on Blue River, now within Harrison [Hancock] County, Indiana; but no recent information of him, or his family, has been obtained. The eldest sister, Mary, married Ralph Crume and some of her descendants are now known to be in Breckenridge County, Kentucky. The second sister, Nancy, married William Brumfield, and her family are not known to have left Kentucky, but there is no recent information from them. Thomas, the youngest son, and father of the present subject, by the early death of his father, and very narrow circumstances of his mother, even in childhood was a wandering laboring boy, and grew up literally without education. He never did more in the way of writing than to bunglingly sign his own name. Before he was grown, he passed one year as a hired hand with his uncle Isaac on Watauga, a branch of the Holston River. Getting back into Kentucky, and having reached his 28th. year, he married Nancy Hanks—mother of the present subject—in the year 1806. She also was born in Virginia; and relatives of hers of the name of Hanks, and of other names, now reside in Coles, in Macon, and in Adams counties, Illinois, and also in Iowa. The present subject has no brother or sister of the whole or half blood. He had a sister, older than himself, who was grown and married, but died many years ago, leaving no child. Also a brother, younger than himself, who died in infancy. Before leaving Kentucky he and his sister were sent for short periods, to A.B.C. schools, the first kept by Zachariah Riney, and the second by Caleb Hazel.

At this time his father resided on Knob Creek, on the road from Bardstown Ky. to Nashville Tenn. at a point three, or three and a half miles south or southwest of Atherton's ferry on the Rolling Fork. From this place he removed to what is now Spencer County, Indiana, in the autumn of 1816, A. then being in his eighth year. This removal was partly on account of slavery; but chiefly on account of the difficulty in land titles in Ky. He settled in an unbroken forest; and the clearing away of surplus wood was the great task ahead. A. though very young, was large of his age, and had an axe put into his hands at once; and from that till within his twenty-third year, he was almost constantly handling that most useful instrument—less, of course, in plowing and harvesting seasons. At this place A. took an early start as a hunter, which was never much improved afterwards. (A few days before the completion of his eighth year, in the absence of his father, a flock of wild turkeys approached the new log cabin, and A. with a rifle gun, standing inside, shot through a crack, and killed one of them. He has never since pulled a trigger on any larger game.) In the autumn of 1818 his mother died; and a year afterwards his father married Mrs. Sally Johnston, at Elizabethtown, Ky—a widow, with three children of her first marriage. She proved a good and kind mother to A. and is still living in Coles Co. Illinois. There were no children of this second marriage. His father's residence continued at the same place in Indiana, till 1830. While here A. went to

A.B.C. schools by littles, kept successively by Andrew Crawford, ——Sweeney, and Azel W. Dorsey. He does not remember any other. The family of Mr. Dorsey now reside in Schuyler Co. Illinois. A. now thinks that the aggregate of all his schooling did not amount to one year. He was never in a college or academy as a student; and never inside of a college or academy building till since he had a law license. What he has in the way of education, he has picked up. After he was twenty-three, and had separated from his father, he studied English grammar, imperfectly of course, but so as to speak and write as well as he now does. He studied and nearly mastered the six books of Euclid, since he was a member of Congress. He regrets his want of education, and does what he can to supply the want. In his tenth year he was kicked by a horse, and apparently killed for a time. When he was nineteen, still residing in Indiana, he made his first trip upon a flatboat to New Orleans. He was a hired hand merely; and he and a son of the owner, without other assistance, made the trip. The nature of part of the cargo load, as it was called—made it necessary for them to linger and trade along the sugar coast—and one night they were attacked by seven Negroes with intent to kill and rob them. They were hurt some in the melee, but succeeded in driving the Negroes from the boat, and then "cut cable," "weighed anchor" and left.

March 1st. 1830—A. having just completed his 21st. year, his father and family, with the families of the two daughters and sons-in-law, of his stepmother, left the old homestead in Indiana, and came to Illinois. Their mode of conveyance was wagons drawn by ox teams, and A. drove one of the teams. They reached the county of Macon, and stopped there some time within the same month of March. His father and family settled a new place on the north side of the Sangamon River, at the junction of the timberland and prairie, about ten miles westerly from Decatur. Here they built a log cabin, into which they removed, and made sufficient of rails to fence ten acres of ground, fenced and broke the ground, and raised a crop of sown corn upon it the same year. These are, or are supposed to be, the rails about which so much is being said just now, though they are far from being the first, or only rails ever made by A.

The sons-in-law, were temporarily settled at other places in the county. In the autumn all hands were greatly afflicted with ague and fever, to which they had not been used, and by which they

336

were greatly discouraged—so much so that they determined on leaving the county. They remained however, through the succeeding winter, which was the winter of the very celebrated "deep snow" of Illinois. During that winter, A. together with his stepmother's son, John D. Johnston, and John Hanks, yet residing in Macon County, hired themselves to one Denton Offutt, to take a flatboat from Beardstown, Illinois to New Orleans; and for that purpose, were to join him—Offutt—at Springfield, Ills. so soon as the snow should go off. When it did go off which was about the 1st of March 1831—the county was so flooded, as to make traveling by land impracticable; to obviate which difficulty they purchased a large canoe and came down the Sangamon River in it. This is the time and the manner of A's first entrance into Sangamon County. They found Offutt at Springfield, but learned from him that he had failed in getting a boat at Beardstown. This led to their hiring themselves to him at $12 per month, each; and getting the timber out of the trees and building a boat at old Sangamon Town on the Sangamon River, seven miles N.W. of Springfield, which boat they took to New Orleans, substantially upon the old contract. It was in connection with this boat that occurred the ludicrous incident of sewing up the hogs' eyes. Offutt bought thirty-odd large fat live hogs, but found difficulty in driving them from where he purchased them to the boat, and thereupon conceived the whim that he could sew up their eyes and drive them where he pleased. No sooner thought of than decided, he put his hands, including A. at the job, which they completed—all but the driving. In their blind condition they could not be driven out of the lot or field they were in. This expedient failing, they were tied and hauled on carts to the boat. It was near the Sangamon River, within what is now Menard County.

During this boat enterprise acquaintance with Offutt, who was previously an entire stranger, he conceived a liking for A. and believing he could turn him to account, he contracted with him to act as clerk for him, on his return from New Orleans, in charge of a store and mill at New Salem, then in Sangamon, now in Menard County. Hanks had not gone to New Orleans, but having a family, and being likely to be detained from home longer than at first expected, had turned back from St. Louis. He is the same John Hanks who now engineers the "rail enterprise" at Decatur; and is a first cousin to A's mother. A's father, with his own family & others mentioned, had, in pursuance of their intention, removed from Macon to Coles County. John D. Johnston, the stepmother's son, went to them; and A. stopped indefinitely, and, for the first time, as it were, by himself at New Salem, before mentioned. This was in July 1831. Here he rapidly made acquaintances and friends. In less than a year Offutt's business was failing—had almost failed,—when the Black Hawk War of 1832—broke out. A. joined a volunteer company, and to his own surprise, was elected captain of it. He says he has not since had any success in life which gave him so much satisfaction. He went the campaign, served near three months, met the ordinary hardships of such an expedition, but was in no battle. He now owns in Iowa, the land upon which his own warrants for this service, were located. Returning from the campaign, and encouraged by his great popularity among his immediate neighbors, he, the same year, ran for the legislature and was beaten—his own precinct, however, casting its votes 277 for and 7, against him. And this too while he was an avowed Clay man, and the precinct the autumn afterwards, giving a majority of 115 to Genl. Jackson over Mr. Clay. This was the only time A. was ever beaten on a direct vote of the people. He was now without means and out of business, but was anxious to remain with his friends who had treated him with so much generosity, especially as he had nothing elsewhere to go to. He studied what he should do—thought of learning the blacksmith trade—thought of trying to study law—rather thought he could not succeed at that without a better education. Before long, strangely enough, a man offered to sell and did sell, to A. and another as poor as himself, an old stock of goods, upon credit. They opened as merchants; and he says that was *the* store. Of course they did nothing but get deeper and deeper in debt. He was appointed postmaster at New Salem—the office being too insignificant, to make his politics an objection. The store winked out. The surveyor of Sangamon, offered to depute to A. that portion of his work which was within his part of the county. He accepted, procured a compass and chain, studied Flint and Gibson a little, and went at it. This procured bread, and kept soul and body together. The election of 1834 came, and he was then elected to the legislature by the highest vote cast for any candidate. Major John T. Stuart, then in full practice of the law, was also elected. During the canvass, in a private conversation he encouraged A. to study law. After the election he borrowed books of Stuart, took them home with him, and went at it in good earnest.

The Republican Nominee

He studied with nobody. He still mixed in the surveying to pay board and clothing bills. When the legislature met, the law books were dropped, but were taken up again at the end of the session. He was re-elected in 1836, 1838, and 1840. In the autumn of 1836 he obtained a law license, and on April 15, 1837 removed to Springfield, and commenced the practice, his old friend, Stuart taking him into partnership. March 3rd. 1837, by a protest entered upon the Ills. House Journal of that date, at pages 817, 818, A. with Dan Stone, another representative of Sangamon, briefly defined his position on the slavery question; and so far as it goes, it was then the same that it is now. The protest is as follows—(Here insert it) * In 1838, & 1840 Mr. L's party in the legislature voted for him as speaker; but being in the minority, he was not elected. After 1840 he declined a re-election to the legislature. He was on the Harrison electoral ticket in 1840, and on that of Clay in 1844, and spent much time and labor in both those canvasses. In Nov. 1842 he was married to Mary, daughter of Robert S. Todd, of Lexington, Kentucky. They have three living children, all sons— one born in 1843, one in 1850, and one in 1853. They lost one, who was born in 1846. In 1846, he was elected to the lower House of Congress, and served one term only, commencing in Dec. 1847 and ending with the inauguration of Gen. Taylor, in March 1849. All the battles of the Mexican War had been fought before Mr. L. took his seat in Congress, but the American army was still in Mexico, and the treaty of peace was not fully and formally ratified till the June afterwards. Much has been said of his course in Congress in regard to this war. A careful examination of the Journals and Congressional Globe shows, that he voted for all the supply measures which came up, and for all the measures in any way favorable to the officers, soldiers, and their families, who conducted the war through; with this exception that some of these measures passed without yeas and nays, leaving no record as to how particular men voted. The Journals and Globe also show him voting that the war was unnecessarily and unconstitutionally begun by the President of the United States. This is the language of Mr. Ashmun's amendment, for which Mr. L. and nearly or quite all, other Whigs of the H.R. voted.

Mr. L's reasons for the opinion expressed by this vote were briefly that the President had sent Genl. Taylor into an inhabited part of the country belonging to Mexico, and not to the U. S. and

* See p. 15.

339

thereby had provoked the first act of hostility—in fact the commencement of the war; that the place, being the country bordering on the east bank of the Rio Grande, was inhabited by native Mexicans, born there under the Mexican government; and had never submitted to, nor been conquered by Texas, or the U. S. nor transferred to either by treaty—that although Texas claimed the Rio Grande as her boundary, Mexico had never recognized it, the people on the ground had never recognized it, and neither Texas nor the U. S. had ever enforced it—that there was a broad desert between that, and the country over which Texas had actual control—that the country where hostilities commenced, having once belonged to Mexico, must remain so, until it was somehow legally transferred, which had never been done.

Mr. L. thought the act of sending an armed force among the Mexicans, was *unnecessary,* inasmuch as Mexico was in no way molesting, or menacing the U. S. or the people thereof; and that it was *unconstitutional,* because the power of levying war is vested in Congress, and not in the President. He thought the principal motive for the act, was to divert public attention from the surrender of "Fifty-four, forty, or fight" to Great Britain, on the Oregon boundary question.

Mr. L. was not a candidate for re-election. This was determined upon, and declared before he went to Washington, in accordance with an understanding among Whig friends, by which Col. Hardin, and Col. Baker had each previously served a single term in the same district.

In 1848, during his term in Congress, he advocated Gen. Taylor's nomination for the Presidency, in opposition to all others, and also took an active part for his election, after his nomination—speaking a few times in Maryland, near Washington, several times in Massachusetts, and canvassing quite fully his own district in Illinois, which was followed by a majority in the district of over 1500 for Gen. Taylor.

Upon his return from Congress he went to the practice of the law with greater earnestness than ever before. In 1852 he was upon the Scott electoral ticket, and did something in the way of canvassing, but owing to the hopelessness of the cause in Illinois, he did less than in previous presidential canvasses.

In 1854, his profession had almost superseded the thought of politics in his mind, when the repeal of the Missouri compromise aroused him as he had never been before.

The Republican Nominee

In the autumn of that year he took the stump with no broader practical aim or object than to secure, if possible, the re-election of Hon. Richard Yates to Congress. His speeches at once attracted a more marked attention than they had ever before done. As the canvass proceeded, he was drawn to different parts of the state, outside of Mr. Yates' district. He did not abandon the law, but gave his attention, by turns, to that and politics. The state agricultural fair was at Springfield that year, and Douglas was announced to speak there.

In the canvass of 1856, Mr. L. made over fifty speeches, no one of which, so far as he remembers, was put in print. One of them was made at Galena, but Mr. L. has no recollection of any part of it being printed; nor does he remember whether in that speech he said anything about a Supreme Court decision. He may have spoken upon that subject; and some of the newspapers may have reported him as saying what is now ascribed to him; but he thinks he could not have expressed himself as represented.

With worn patience, Lincoln tried to establish, for all time, the proper spelling of his given name.

Springfield, Ills. June 4 1860

Hon: George Ashmun
My dear Sir

It seems as if the question whether my first name is "Abraham" or "Abram" will never be settled. It is *"Abraham"* and if the letter of acceptance is not yet in print, you may, if you think fit, have my signature thereto printed *"Abraham Lincoln."* Exercise your own judgment about this. Yours as ever,

A. Lincoln.

In a second letter to Haycraft, Lincoln indulged in an attempt at humor that he would regret.

Springfield, Ills. June 4, 1860

PRIVATE
Hon. Saml. Haycraft.
Dear Sir:

Your second letter, dated May 31st. is received. You suggest that a visit to the place of my nativity might be pleasant to me. Indeed it would. But would it be safe? Would not the people Lynch me?

The Living Lincoln

The place on Knob Creek, mentioned by Mr. Read, I remember very well; but I was not born there. As my parents have told me, I was born on Nolin, very much nearer Hodgin's-Mill than the Knob Creek place is. My earliest recollection, however, is of the Knob Creek place.

Like yourself I belonged to the Whig party from its origin to its close. I never belonged to the American party organization; nor ever to a party called a Union party; though I hope I neither am, or ever have been, less devoted to the Union than yourself, or any other patriotic man.

It may not be altogether without interest to let you know that my wife is a daughter of the late Robert S. Todd, of Lexington Ky —and that a half-sister of hers is the wife of Ben. Hardin Helm, born and raised at your town, but residing at Louisville now, as I believe. Yours very truly

A. Lincoln.

Lincoln's nomination gave the proprietors of the Burnet House, in Cincinnati, the opportunity to collect an overdue bill. William M. Dickson, to whom Lincoln turned for help, had married a cousin of Mrs. Lincoln.

Springfield, Ills.
June 7. 1860

Hon: W. M. Dickson.
My dear Sir:

Your telegraphic despatch, the day of the nomination, was received; as also was, in due course, your kind letter of May 21st. with Cousin Annie's note at the end of it.

I have just now received a letter from Cincinnati, of which the following is a copy.

"Cincinnati, June 5. 1860

"Hon A. Lincoln
Dr. Sir:

We are extremely sorry to be under the necessity of calling your attention to the inclosed bill during your sojourn at the 'Burnet' in Sept. last; but it appears there is no remedy left us other than to advise you of its never having been paid. We relied upon the Republican committee, but as yet have not been able to find any-

The Republican Nominee

one willing to take the responsibility of paying same—consequently advise you in the premises. Very Respy. Yours,

Johnson, Saunders & Co"

The inclosed bill is as follows:

"Burnet House
Cincinnati, Sept. 19– 1859

"Hon: A. Lincoln
To Johnson, Saunders & Co. Dr.

Board & Parlor self & family	37.50
Extra Suppers. 3.50. Wines, Liquors & cigars 7.50.	11.00
Occupancy of room No. 15. committee.	5.00
	$53.50"

Now this may be right, but I have a slight suspicion of it, for two or three reasons. First, when I left, I called at the office of the hotel, and was there distinctly told the bill "was settled" "was all right" or words to that effect. Secondly, it seems a little steep that "Board & parlor" from Saturday 7½ P.M. to Monday 10½ A.M. for a man, woman, and one small child, should be $37.50. Thirdly, we had no extra suppers, unless having tea at our room the first evening, was such. We were in the house over the time of five meals, three only of which we took in the house. We did not once dine in the house. As to wines, liquors & cigars, we had none— absolutely none. These last may have been in room 15, by order of committee, but I do not recollect them at all.

Please look into this, and write me. I can and will pay it if it is right; but I do not wish to be "diddled!" Please do what you do quietly, having no fuss about it. Yours very truly

A. Lincoln

A letter questioning Lincoln's honesty brought a testy reply.

Springfield,
June 9, 1860

Mrs. Deziah Vance
Madam

Your letter of June 5th. is received. I have no money collected by me for Mr. Vance, and I had ceased trying to collect any for him long before his death. You speak of my letters to Mr. Vance;

and if I remember, they will show that the charge of Mr. Vance's claim here was transferred to Mr. W. H. Herndon. I think his claim was against a man, or men, by the name of Vanmeter. I never keep anybody's money, which I collect, an hour longer than I can find a chance to turn it over to him. If you doubt this, get some of the busy-bodies who are imposing on you in this matter, to find somebody who will swear he paid me money for Mr. Vance. If there is any such man he can be found.

If, as you say, Mr. Trimble spoke to me, and I gave him no satisfaction, it was because the truth was not satisfactory. Let Mr. Trimble or anyone else come here and see the man or men, of whom they or you, think I received money for Mr. Vance, and learn of them how the truth is. I have no papers in my hands, belonging to Mr. Vance. I do not certainly know, but my opinion is that nothing can be got on those old claims, or that old claim of Mr. Vance. Yours &c

A. Lincoln

Lincoln denied a rumor that he had served wine to the members of the committee that had notified him of his nomination. The beverage was ice water.

Springfield, Ills.
June 11. 1860

PRIVATE & CONFIDENTIAL
J. Mason Haight, Esq
My dear Sir—

I think it would be improper for me to write, or say anything to, or for, the public, upon the subject of which you inquire. I therefore wish the letter I do write to be held as strictly confidential. Having kept house sixteen years, and having never held the "cup" to the lips of my friends then, my judgment was that I should not, in my new position, change my habit in this respect. What actually occurred upon the occasion of the committee visiting me, I think it would be better for others to say. Yours Respectfully

A. Lincoln

Lincoln, somewhat embarrassed, learns that Dickson has paid the Burnet House bill.

The Republican Nominee

Springfield, Ills.
June 15. 1860

Hon: W. M. Dickson
My dear Sir

Yours inclosing receipt of "Burnet House" is received; and I sincerely thank you for your attention to this business. Let it stand as it is for the present, with the distinct understanding that you are not to ultimately lose the money.

Give my love to Cousin Annie. Yours very truly

A. Lincoln

When Follett, Foster & Co., Columbus, Ohio, publishers, announced an "authorized" campaign biography they came close to losing the friend they had made by publishing the Lincoln-Douglas Debates.

ESPECIALLY CONFIDENTIAL

Springfield, Ills. June 19, 1860

Hon: Saml. Galloway:
My dear Sir

Your very kind letter of the 15th. is received. Messrs. Follett, Foster & Co's Life of me is *not* by my authority; and I have scarcely been so much astounded by anything, as by their public announcement that it is authorized by me. They have fallen into some strange misunderstanding. I certainly knew they contemplated publishing a biography, and I certainly did not object to their doing so, *upon their own responsibility*. I even took pains to facilitate them. But, at the same time, I made myself tiresome, if not hoarse, with repeating to Mr. Howard, their only agent seen by me, my protest that I *authorized nothing*—would be *responsible for nothing*. How, they could so misunderstand me, passes comprehension. As a matter, *wholly my own*, I would authorize no biography, without *time*, and *opportunity* to carefully examine and consider ever word of it; and, in this case, in the nature of things, I can have no such time and opportunity. But, in my present position, when, by the lessons of the past, and the united voice of all discreet friends, I am neither to write or speak a word for the public, how dare I to send forth, by my authority, a volume of hundreds of pages, for adversaries to make points upon without end. Were I to do so, the convention would have a right to reassemble, and substitute another name for mine.

The Living Lincoln

For these reasons, I would not look at the proof sheets. I am determined to maintain the position of truly saying I never saw the proof sheets, or any part of their work, before its publication.

Now, do not mistake me. I feel great kindness for Messrs. F. F. & Co—do not think they have intentionally done wrong. There may be nothing wrong in their proposed book. I sincerely hope there will not. I barely suggest that you, or any of the friends there, on the party account, look it over, & exclude what you may think would embarrass the party—bearing in mind, at all times, that I *authorize nothing*—will be *responsible* for *nothing*. Your friend, as ever

A. Lincoln

Because of his long friendship with A. G. Henry, now living in Oregon Territory, Lincoln could indulge in the optimism that he was reluctant to reveal to the rank and file of party workers.

Springfield, Ills. July 4, 1860

My dear Doctor:

Your very agreeable letter of May 15th. was received three days ago. We are just now receiving the first sprinkling of your Oregon election returns—not enough, I think, to indicate the result. We should be too happy if both Logan and Baker should triumph.

Long before this you have learned who was nominated at Chicago. We know not what a day may bring forth; but, today, it looks as if the Chicago ticket will be elected. I think the chances were more than equal that we could have beaten the Democracy *united*. Divided, as it is, its chance appears indeed very slim. But great is Democracy in resources; and it may yet give its fortunes a turn. It is under great temptation to do something; but what can it do which was not thought of, and found impracticable, at Charleston and Baltimore? The signs now are that Douglas and Breckenridge will each have a ticket in every state. They are driven to this to keep up their bombastic claims of *nationality*, and to avoid the charge of *sectionalism* which they have so much lavished upon us.

It is an amusing fact, after all Douglas has said about *nationality*, and *sectionalism*, that I had more votes from the Southern section at Chicago, than he had at Baltimore! In fact, there was more of the Southern section represented at Chicago, than in the Douglas rump concern at Baltimore!!

The Republican Nominee

Our boy, in his tenth year, (the baby when you left) has just had a hard and tedious spell of scarlet fever; and he is not yet beyond all danger. I have a headache, and a sore throat upon me now, inducing me to suspect that I have an inferior type of the same thing.

Our eldest boy, Bob, has been away from us nearly a year at school, and will enter Harvard University this month. He promises very well, considering we never controlled him much.

Write again when you receive this. Mary joins in sending our kindest regards to Mrs. H., yourself, and all the family. Your friend, as ever

A. Lincoln—

Lincoln decided that it was time to establish a closer relationship with Hannibal Hamlin, his running mate.

Springfield, Illinois, July 18, 1860.

My dear Sir:

It appears to me that you and I ought to be acquainted, and accordingly I write this as a sort of introduction of myself to you. You first entered the Senate during the single term I was a member of the House of Representatives, but I have no recollection that we were introduced. I shall be pleased to receive a line from you.

The prospect of Republican success now appears very flattering, so far as I can perceive. Do you see anything to the contrary? Yours truly,

A. Lincoln.

Through a trusted friend, a lawyer of Quincy, Illinois, Lincoln tried to kill a canard.

CONFIDENTIAL

Springfield, Ills.
July 21, 1860

Hon. A. Jonas:
My dear Sir

Yours of the 20th. is received. I suppose as good, or even better, men than I may have been in American, or Know Nothing lodges; but in point of fact, I never was in one, at Quincy, or elsewhere. I was never in Quincy but one day and two nights, while

The Living Lincoln

Know Nothing lodges were in existence, and you were with me that day and both those nights. I had never been there before in my life; and never afterwards, till the joint debate with Douglas in 1858. It was in 1854, when I spoke in some hall there, and after the speaking, you, with others, took me to an oyster saloon, passed an hour there, and you walked with me to, and parted with me at, the Quincy House, quite late at night. I left by stage for Naples before daylight in the morning, having come in by the same route, after dark, the evening previous to the speaking, when I found you waiting at the Quincy House to meet me. A few days after I was there, Richardson, as I understood, started this same story about my having been in a Know Nothing lodge. When I heard of the charge, as I did soon after, I taxed my recollection for some incident which could have suggested it; and I remembered that on parting with you the last night, I went to the office of the hotel to take my stage passage for the morning, was told that no stage office for that line was kept there, and that I must see the driver, before retiring, to insure his calling for me in the morning; and a servant was sent with me to find the driver, who after taking me a square or two, stopped me, and stepped perhaps a dozen steps farther, and in my hearing called to someone, who answered him apparently from the upper part of a building, and promised to call with the stage for me at the Quincy House. I returned and went to bed; and before day the stage called and took me. This is all.

That I never was in a Know Nothing lodge in Quincy, I should expect, could be easily proved, by respectable men, who were always in the lodges and never saw me there. An affidavit of one or two such would put the matter at rest.

And now, a word of caution. Our adversaries think they can gain a point, if they could force me to openly deny this charge, by which some degree of offence would be given to the Americans. For this reason, it must not publicly appear that I am paying any attention to the charge. Yours truly

A. Lincoln

In a letter to George C. Latham, a Springfield boy who had attended Phillips Exeter Academy with Robert Lincoln, Lincoln reflected the concern he had felt when his own son, a year earlier, had failed to pass the Harvard entrance examinations.

The Republican Nominee

My dear George

I have scarcely felt greater pain in my life than on learning yesterday from Bob's letter, that you had failed to enter Harvard University. And yet there is very little in it, if you will allow no feeling of *discouragement* to seize, and prey upon you. It is a *certain* truth, that you *can* enter, and graduate in, Harvard University; and having made the attempt, you *must* succeed in it. *"Must"* is the word.

I know not how to aid you, save in the assurance of one of mature age, and much severe experience, that you *can* not fail, if you resolutely determine, that you *will* not.

The president of the institution, can scarcely be other than a kind man; and doubtless he would grant you an interview, and point out the readiest way to remove, or overcome, the obstacles which have thwarted you.

In your temporary failure there is no evidence that you may not yet be a better scholar, and a more successful man in the great struggle of life, than many others, who have entered college more easily.

Again I say let no feeling of discouragement prey upon you, and in the end you are sure to succeed.

With more than a common interest I subscribe myself Very truly your friend,

A. Lincoln.

Simeon Francis now published *The Oregon Farmer* at Portland. Lincoln sent him local news and a prediction based on the break-up of the Democratic Party. In successive conventions at Baltimore the Democrats had nominated two tickets—one headed by Stephen A. Douglas and Herschel V. Johnson, the other, proslavery in sympathy, by John C. Breckenridge and Joseph Lane. Even before the Republican convention remnants of the Whig and American parties had formed the Constitutional Union Party with John Bell and Edward Everett as candidates for President and Vice-President. Small wonder that Lincoln should be sure of victory.

Springfield, Ills. Aug. 4. 1860

Friend Francis—

I have had three letters from you—one, a long one, received in

February; one, telling me of the deputation of Mr. Greeley to cast the vote of Oregon, in the Chicago convention, received a few days before that convention; and one written since you knew the result of your Oregon election, received a few days ago. I have not, till now, attempted an answer to any of them, because I disliked to write you a mere note, and because I could not find time to write at length.

Your brother Allen has returned from California, and, I understand, intends remaining here. Josiah is running his J. P. court, about as when you left. We had a storm here last night which did considerable damage, the largest single instance of which, was to the Withies. A wall of their brick shop building was thrown in, and, it is said destroyed ten thousand dollars' worth of carriages. I have heard of no personal injury done.

When you wrote, you had not learned of the doings of the Democratic convention at Baltimore; but you will be in possession of it all long before this reaches you. I hesitate to say it, but it really appears now, as if the success of the Republican ticket is inevitable. We have no reason to doubt any of the states which voted for Fremont. Add to these, Minnesota, Pennsylvania, and New Jersey, and the thing is done. Minnesota is as sure as such a thing can be; while the Democracy are so divided between Douglas and Breckenridge in Penn. & N. J. that they are scarcely less sure. Our friends are also confident in Indiana and Illinois. I should expect the same division would give us a fair chance in Oregon. Write me what you think on that point.

We were very anxious here for David Logan's election. I think I will write him before long. If you see Col. Baker, give him my respects. I do hope he may not be tricked out of what he has fairly earned.

Make my kindest regards to Mrs. Francis; and tell her I both hope and believe she is not so unhappy as when I saw her last. Your friend, as ever

A. Lincoln

Lincoln learned how easily a partisan newspaper correspondent could twist an innocent remark into something sinister. The candidate appealed to a member of the Republican National Committee to help undo the damage.

The Republican Nominee

Springfield, Ills.
Aug. 16, 1860

Hon. George G. Fogg—
My dear Sir:

I am annoyed some by the printed paragraph below, in relation to myself, taken from the N. Y. Herald's correspondence from this place of August 8th.

"He had, he said, on one occasion been invited to go into Kentucky and revisit some of the scenes with whose history his father in his lifetime had been identified. On asking by letter whether Judge Lynch would be present, he received no response; and he therefore came to the conclusion that the invitation was a trap laid by some designing person to inveigle him into a slave state for the purpose of doing violence to his person."

This is decidedly wrong. I did not say it. I do not impugn the correspondent. I suppose he misconceived the statement from the following incident. Soon after the Chicago nomination I was written to by a highly respectable gentleman of Hardin County, Ky, inquiring if I was a son of Thomas Lincoln, whom he had known long ago, in that county. I answered that I was, and that I was myself born there. He wrote again, and, among other things, (did not *invite* me but) simply *inquired* if it would not be agreeable to me to revisit the scenes of my childhood. I replied, among other things, "It would indeed; but would you not Lynch me?" He did not write again.

I have, *playfully,* (and never otherwise) related this incident several times; and I suppose I did so to the Herald correspondent, though I do not remember it. If I did, it is all that I did say, from which the correspondent could have inferred his statement.

Now, I dislike, exceedingly, for Kentuckians to understand that I am charging them with a purpose to inveigle me, and do violence to me. Yet I cannot go into the newspapers. Would not the editor of the Herald, upon being shown this letter, insert the short correction, which you find upon the inclosed scrap?

Please try him, unless you perceive some sufficient reason to the contrary. In no event, let my name be publicly used. Yours very truly

A. Lincoln

The Living Lincoln

CORRECTION

We have such assurance as satisfies us that our correspondent writing from Springfield, Ills, under date of Aug. 8– was mistaken in representing Mr. Lincoln as expressing a suspicion of a design to inveigle him into Kentucky for the purpose of doing him violence. Mr. Lincoln neither entertains, nor has intended to express any such suspicion.

Lincoln hurried an explanation to Samuel Haycraft.

Springfield, Ills. Aug. 16. 1860

Hon. Saml. Haycraft
My dear Sir:
 A correspondent of the New York Herald, who was here a week ago, writing to that paper, represents me as saying I had been invited to visit Kentucky, but that I suspected it was a trap to inveigle me into Kentucky, in order to do violence to me.
 This is wholly a mistake. I said no such thing. I do not remember, but possibly I did mention my correspondence with you. But very certainly I was not guilty of stating, or insinuating, a suspicion of any intended violence, deception, or other wrong, against me, by you, or any other Kentuckian. Thinking this Herald correspondence might fall under your eye, I think it due to myself to enter my protest against the correctness of this part of it. I scarcely think the correspondent was malicious; but rather that he misunderstood what was said. Yours very truly

A. Lincoln.

Haycraft replied that he had recognized at once that Lincoln had written in jest, and offered to make a statement to that effect to the New York *Herald.*

Springfield, Ill
Aug 23 1860

Hon. Sam Haycraft
My dear Sir:
 Yours of the 19th. is just received. I now fear I may have given you some uneasiness by my last letter. I did not mean to intimate

that I had, to any extent, been involved, or embarrassed, by you; nor yet, to draw from you anything to relieve myself from difficulty. My only object was to assure you that I had not, as represented by the Herald correspondent, charged you with an attempt to inveigle me into Kentucky to do me violence. I believe no such thing of you, or of Kentuckians generally; and I dislike to be represented to them as slandering them in that way. Yours truly

A. Lincoln

Charles Hanks, posing as a relative who had known the Republican nominee intimately, published a letter scoffing at Lincoln's prowess in rail-splitting. John Hanks, Charles' brother, asked Lincoln how well he had known Charles. In replying, Lincoln drew on memories of his life thirty years earlier. The Hanks brothers were first cousins of Lincoln's mother.

Springfield, Ills.
Aug. 24. 1860

John Hanks, Esq
My dear Sir:
Yours of the 23rd. is received. My recollection is that I never lived in the same neighborhood with Charles Hanks till I came to Macon County, Illinois, after I was twenty-one years of age. As I understand, he and I were born in different counties of Kentucky, and never saw each other in that state; that while I was a very small boy my father removed to Indiana, and your father with his family remained in Kentucky for many years. At length you, a young man grown, came to our neighborhood, and were at our house, off and on, a great deal for three, four, or five years; and during the time, your father, with his whole family, except William, Charles, and William Miller, who had married one of your sisters, came to the same neighborhood in Indiana, and remained a year or two, and then went to Illinois. William, Charles, and William Miller, had removed directly from Kentucky to Illinois, not even passing through our neighborhood in Indiana.

Once, a year or two before I came to Illinois, Charles, with some others, had been back to Kentucky, and returning to Illinois, passed through our neighborhood in Indiana. He stopped, I think, but one day, (certainly not as much as three); and this was the first time I ever saw him in my life, and the *only* time, till I came to

The Living Lincoln

Illinois, as before stated. The year I passed in Macon County I was with him a good deal—mostly on his own place, where I helped him at breaking prairie, with a joint team of his and ours, which in turn, broke some on the new place we were improving.

This is, as I remember it. Don't let this letter be made public by any means. Yours very truly

A. Lincoln

To Joseph Medill of the Chicago *Press & Tribune,* Lincoln showed how closely, in spite of his apparent aloofness, he was following the campaign.

PRIVATE

Springfield,
Sept. 4. 1860

J. Medill, Esq
My dear Sir

Yours of Aug. 30th. for some cause, only reached me last night. As to Pennsylvania, I have a letter from Gen. Cameron, dated Aug. 29th. in which, among other things, he says:

"You may as well be getting your inaugural address ready, so as to have plenty of time to make it short. If possible we are daily becoming stronger in Pennsylvania, and in New Jersey all is right."

Last night, just as I had read your letter, Mr. David Taggart called upon me. He is a very intelligent gentleman, lately was Speaker of the Penn. Senate, and is now upon our electoral ticket, and residing at Northumberland. He left home Thursday the 30th.; and he is very confident that Penn. is abundantly safe, both for Curtin in Oct— & the national ticket in Novr. This from Cameron & Taggart, constitutes my latest news from Penn.

I am more annoyed by what you write me of Maine. Long ago I had heard about danger of two members of Congress there; but at least six weeks since Mr. Hamlin wrote me "all *is* safe in New England"; and very recently Mr. Fogg of N. H. wrote from N. York saying: "We are having a desperate fight in Maine; but it will end in a splendid triumph for us." He had just come from Maine.

What you say about the northern 30 counties of Illinois pleases me. Keep good your promise that they will give as much majority as they did for Fremont, and we will let you off. We cannot be

354

beaten, nor even hard run, in the state, if that holds true. Yours as ever

A Lincoln.

When a man attains sudden prominence he hears from friends and acquaintances whom he has not seen for many years. Nathaniel Grigsby had known Lincoln in Spencer County, Indiana.

Springfield, Ills. Sep. 20, 1860

Nathaniel Grigsby, Esq
My dear Sir:
Your letter of July 19th. was received only a few days ago, having been mailed by your brother at Gentryville, Ia. on the 12th. of this month. A few days ago, Gov. Wood, of Quincy told me he saw you, and that you said you had written me. I had not then received your letter.

Of our three families who removed from Indiana together, my father, Squire Hall, and John D. Johnston, are dead—and all the rest of us are yet living. Of course the younger ones are grown up, marriages contracted, and new ones born. I have three boys now, the oldest of which is seventeen years of age.

There is now a Republican electoral ticket in Missouri, so that you can vote for me if your neighbors will let you. I would advise you not to get into any trouble about it. Give my kindest regards to your brother Charles.

Within the present year I have had two letters from John Gorden, who is living somewhere in Missouri,—I forget exactly where—and he says his father and mother are both still living near him. Yours very truly

A. Lincoln

Distant relatives also make themselves known.

Springfield, Ills. Sept. 21 1860

John Chrisman, Esq
My dear Sir
Yours of the 13th. was duly received. I have no doubt that you and I are related. My grandfather's Christian name was "Abra-

ham." He had four brothers—Isaac, Jacob, John & Thomas. They were born in Pennsylvania, and my grandfather, and some, if not all the others, in early life removed to Rockingham Co. Virginia. There my father—named Thomas—was born. From there my grandfather removed to Kentucky, and was killed by Indians, about the year 1784. His brother Thomas, who was my father's uncle— also removed to Kentucky—to Fayette Co. I think—where, as I understand he lived, and died. I close, by repeating, I have no doubt you and I are related. Yours very truly

A. Lincoln

A member of the Hanks clan turned up in Oregon.

Springfield, Ills. Sep. 24, 1860

Dear John

Your letter of July 22— was received a few days ago. If your father and mother desire you to come home, it is a delicate matter for me to advise you not to do it. Still, as you ask my advice, it is that if you are doing well, you better stick to it. If you have a good start there, and should give it up, you might not get it again, here, or elsewhere. It cannot be other than their first wish that you shall do well.

And now, as to politics, I am very much obliged to you for what you offer to do for me in Oregon. This side of the Rocky Mountains things appear reasonably well for the general result. In opposing David Logan, at the late congressional election in Oregon, I suppose you did what you thought was right; and when a man does what he thinks is right, he does the best he can. Still, I am sorry you did not think differently, as I knew David from his childhood, and he studied law in our office when his father and I were partners.

I heard from our relations over at Charleston, about three weeks ago, and they were well then.

Write me again when you receive this. Your Uncle

A. Lincoln

Pennsylvania, Indiana, and Ohio held elections for state officers on October 9. Lincoln sent the results to Herndon, who was making a

The Republican Nominee

Republican speech at nearby Petersburg when Lincoln's letter was handed to him.

Springfield Ills Oct. 10th 1860

Dear William:

I cannot give you details, but it is entirely certain that Pennsylvania and Indiana have gone Republican very largely, Penn 25,-000 & Indiana 5 to 10. Ohio of course is safe. Yours as ever

A. Lincoln.

An eleven-year-old girl who lived in Westfield, New York, wrote Lincoln an artless letter in which she told him he would look better with a beard. Soon afterward, he grew one.

PRIVATE

Springfield, Ills.
Oct 19. 1860

Miss. Grace Bedell
My dear little Miss.

Your very agreeable letter of the 15th. is received.

I regret the necessity of saying I have no daughters. I have three sons—one seventeen, one nine, and one seven, years of age. They, with their mother, constitute my whole family.

As to the whiskers, having never worn any, do you not think people would call it a piece of silly affection if I were to begin it now? Your very sincere well-wisher

A. Lincoln.

More than ordinary warmth marks a letter to an old friend and former neighbor of Spencer County.

Springfield, Ills.
Oct. 23. 1860

David Turnham, Esq
My dear old friend:

Your kind letter of the 17th. is received. I am indeed very glad to learn you are still living and well. I well remember when you and I last met, after a separation of fourteen years, at the cross-road voting place, in the fall of 1844. It is now sixteen years more and we are both no longer young men. I suppose you are a grandfather; and I, though married much later in life, have a son nearly grown.

I would much like to visit the old home, and old friends of my boyhood, but I fear the chance for doing so soon, is not very good. Your friend & and sincere well-wisher

A. Lincoln

Fame had not stifled Lincoln's generous impulses.

Springfield, Oct. 24 1860

The lady bearer of this, says she has freight at the depot, which she cannot get without four dollars. If this be correct, let her have the freight, and I will pay you any amount not exceeding four dollars on presentation of this note.*

A. Lincoln.

From Fort Leavenworth, Kansas, Major David Hunter sent word of a rumored assassination plot. Lincoln decided that Hunter might be a useful source of information about the loyalty of the army.

PRIVATE & CONFIDENTIAL

Springfield, Ills. Oct. 26. 1860

Maj. David Hunter:
My dear Sir:

Your very kind letter of the 20th. was duly received, and for which, please accept my thanks.

I have another letter from a writer unknown to me, saying the officers of the army at Fort Kearney, have determined, in case of Republican success, at the approaching presidential election, to take themselves, and the arms at that point, south, for the purpose of resistance to the government. While I think there are many chances to one that this is a humbug, it occurs to me that any real movement of this sort in the army would leak out and become known to you. In such case, if it would not be unprofessional, or dishonorable (of which you are to be judge) I shall be much obliged if you will apprize me of it. Yours very truly

A. Lincoln

George D. Prentice, editor of the Louisville *Journal,* was one of many persons who urged Lincoln to make a public statement to allay

* Five days later Lincoln paid.

The Republican Nominee

the rising disaffection in the South. To all, Lincoln replied substantially as he did to Prentice.

Lincoln's "Confidential" endorsement, though undated, suggests that he refrained from sending the letter until after the election.

PRIVATE & CONFIDENTIAL

Springfield, Ills. Oct. 29. 1860

(Copy)

Geo. D. Prentice, Esq
My dear Sir:

Yours of the 26th. is just received. Your suggestion that I, in a certain event, shall write a letter, setting forth my conservative views and intentions, is certainly a very worthy one. But would it do any good? If I were to labor a month, I could not express my conservative views and intentions more clearly and strongly, than they are expressed in our platform, and in my many speeches already in print, and before the public. And yet even you, who do occasionally speak of me in terms of personal kindness, give no prominence to these oft-repeated expressions of conservative views and intentions; but busy yourself with appeals to all conservative men, to vote for Douglas—to vote any way which can possibly defeat me—thus impressing your readers that you think I am the very worst man living. If what I have already said has failed to convince you, no repetition of it would convince you. The writing of your letter, now before me, gives assurance that you would publish such a letter from me as you suggest; but, till now, what reason had I to suppose the Louisville Journal, even, would publish a *repetition* of that which is already at its command, and which it does not press upon the public attention?

And, now my friend—for such I esteem you personally—do not misunderstand me. I have not decided that I will not do substantially what you suggest. I will not forbear doing so, merely on *punctilio* and pluck. If I do finally abstain, it will be because of apprehension that it would do harm. For the good men of the South—and I regard the majority of them as such—I have no objection to repeat seventy and seven times. But I have *bad* men also to deal with, both North and South—men who are eager for something new upon which to base new misrepresentations—men who would like to frighten me, or, at least, to fix upon me the character of timidity and cowardice. They would seize upon almost any letter I could write, as being an *"awful coming down."* I intend keeping my eye upon these gentlemen, and to not unnecessarily put any weapons in their hands. Yours very truly

A. Lincoln

[The following endorsement appears on the back:]

CONFIDENTIAL

The within letter was written on the day of its date, and, on reflection, withheld till now. It expresses the views I still entertain.

A. Lincoln

XI. A Period of Waiting

1860-1861 ON November 8, 1860, Abraham Lincoln was elected President of the United States. He received 1,866,452 votes against 2,815,617 cast for his three opponents, but in the Electoral College he had a clear majority.

Before the results were known, Lincoln asked his Vice-President to come to Chicago for a meeting.

CONFIDENTIAL

Springfield, Ills. Nov. 8, 1860

Hon. H. Hamlin.
My dear Sir.
    I am anxious for a personal interview with you at as early a day as possible. Can you, without much inconvenience, meet me at Chicago? If you can, please name as early a day as you conveniently can, and telegraph me; unless there be sufficient time, before the day named, to communicate by mail. Yours very truly
A. Lincoln.

Five days after the election Lincoln made his final contribution to his correspondence with Samuel Haycraft, who had expressed the hope that Robert L. Wintersmith, a Lincoln elector, would not be over-looked when the victors came to divide the spoils.

PRIVATE, AND CONFIDENTIAL

Springfield, Ills. Nov. 13. 1860

Hon. Samuel Haycraft
My dear Sir.
    Yours of the 9th. just received. I can only answer briefly. Rest fully assured that the good people of the South who will put themselves in the same temper and mood towards me which you do, will find no cause to complain of me.

361

The Living Lincoln

While I cannot, as yet, make any committal as to offices, I sincerely hope I may find it in my power to oblige the friends of Mr. Wintersmith. Yours very truly,

A. Lincoln.

Lincoln took advantage of a letter of congratulation from Joshua F. Speed to invite his old friend to a reunion in Chicago.

Springfield. Ills. Nov. 19. 1860

Dear Speed—

Yours of the 14th. is received. I shall be at Chicago Thursday the 22nd. inst. and one or two succeeding days. Could you not meet me there?

Mary thinks of going with me; and therefore I suggest that Mrs. S. accompany you.

Please let this be private, as I prefer a very great crowd should not gather at Chicago.

Respects to Mrs. S. Your friend, as ever

A. Lincoln

Although determined to issue no reassuring statement, Lincoln made a concession to persistent pressure: he gave Lyman Trumbull a conciliatory passage for inclusion in the speech which Trumbull made at a Republican jubilation meeting held at Springfield on November 20. Trumbull did not use the second paragraph.

November 20, 1860

I have labored in, and for, the Republican organization with entire confidence that whenever it shall be in power, each and all of the states will be left in as complete control of their own affairs respectively, and at as perfect liberty to choose, and employ, their own means of protecting property, and preserving peace and order within their respective limits, as they have ever been under any administration. Those who have voted for Mr. Lincoln, have expected, and still expect this; and they would not have voted for him had they expected otherwise. I regard it as extremely fortunate for the peace of the whole country, that this point, upon which the Republicans have been so long, and so persistently misrepresented, is now to be brought to a practical test, and placed beyond the possibility of doubt. Disunionists *per se,* are now in hot haste to get out of the Union, precisely because they perceive they can not, much longer, maintain apprehension among the Southern people that their homes, and firesides, and lives, are to endangered by the action of the federal government. With such *"Now, or never"* is the maxim.

I am rather glad of this military preparation in the South. It will enable the people the more easily to suppress any uprisings there, which their misrepresentations of purposes may have encouraged.

Lincoln had contended, in letters to George D. Prentice and others, that the secessionists would ignore any peaceful gesture he might make. In a letter to the editor of the New York *Times* he cited Trumbull's speech, without confessing his own part in it, to prove his point.

PRIVATE & CONFIDENTIAL

Springfield, Ills.
Nov. 28. 1860

Hon. H. J. Raymond
My dear Sir

Yours of the 14th. was received in due course. I have delayed so long to answer it, because my reasons for not coming before the public in any form just now, had substantially appeared in your paper (The Times), and hence I feared they were not deemed sufficient by you, else you would not have written me as you did.

I now think we have a demonstration in favor of my view. On the 20th. inst. Senator Trumbull made a short speech which I suppose you have both seen and approved. Has a single newspaper, heretofore against us, urged that speech upon its readers with a purpose to quiet public anxiety? Not one, so far as I know. On the contrary the Boston Courier, and its class, hold me responsible for the speech, and endeavor to inflame the North with the belief that it foreshadows an abandonment of Republican ground by the incoming administration; while the Washington Constitution, and its class hold the same speech up to the South as an open declaration of war against them.

This is just as I expected, and just what would happen with any declaration I could make. These political fiends are not half sick enough yet. "Party malice" and not "public good" possesses them

363

entirely. "They seek a sign, and no sign shall be given them." At least such is my present feeling and purpose. Yours very truly

A. Lincoln

In two simultaneous letters Lincoln notified his chief rival for the nomination, William H. Seward, that he would be appointed Secretary of State.

Springfield, Ills. Dec. 8 1860

My dear Sir:

With your permission, I shall, at the proper time, nominate you to the Senate, for confirmation, as Secretary of State, for the United States.

Please let me hear from you at your own earliest convenience. Your friend and obedient servant

A. Lincoln.

Hon. William H. Seward,
Washington   D. C.

PRIVATE & CONFIDENTIAL

Springfield Ills. Dec. 8. 1860

My dear Sir:

In addition to the accompanying, and more formal note, inviting you to take charge of the State Department, I deem it proper to address you this. Rumors have got into the newspapers to the effect that the department, named above, would be tendered you, as a compliment, and with the expectation that you would decline it. I beg you to be assured that I have said nothing to justify these rumors. On the contrary, it has been my purpose, from the day of the nomination at Chicago, to assign you, by your leave, this place in the administration. I have delayed so long to communicate that purpose, in deference to what appeared to me to be a proper caution in the case. Nothing has been developed to change my view in the premises; and I now offer you the place, in the hope that you will accept it, and with the belief that your position in the public eye, your integrity, ability, learning, and great experience, all combine to render it an appointment pre-eminently fit to be made.

One word more. In regard to the patronage, sought with so much eagerness and jealousy, I have prescribed for myself the maxim, "Justice to all"; and I earnestly beseech your co-operation in keeping the maxim good. Your friend, and obedient servant

A. Lincoln—

Hon. William H. Seward
Washington   D. C.

From Washington, Trumbull had written Lincoln to inform him that some Republicans were inclined to consider compromises on the question of slavery extension. Lincoln quickly proclaimed his own inflexible opposition.

PRIVATE, & CONFIDENTIAL
Springfield, Ills. Dec. 10. 1860

Hon. L. Trumbull.
My dear Sir:
Let there be no compromise on the question of *extending* slavery. If there be, all our labor is lost, and, ere long, must be done again. The dangerous ground—that into which some of our friends have a hankering to run—is Pop. Sov. Have none of it. Stand firm. The tug has to come, & better now, than any time hereafter. Yours as ever

A. Lincoln.

An inquiring letter from John A. Gilmer of North Carolina, a Southern Congressman with strong pro-Union sympathies, could not be ignored. But Lincoln would not permit his reply to be published.

STRICTLY CONFIDENTIAL
Springfield, Ill. Dec 15, 1860.

Hon. John A. Gilmer:
My dear Sir—
Yours of the 10th is received. I am greatly disinclined to write a letter on the subject embraced in yours; and I would not do so, even privately as I do, were it not that I fear you might misconstrue my silence. Is it desired that I shall shift the ground upon which I have been elected? I cannot do it. You need only to acquaint yourself with that ground, and press it on the attention of the South. It is all in print and easy of access. May I be pardoned if I ask whether even you have ever attempted to procure the reading of the Republican platform, or my speeches, by the Southern people? If not, what reason have I to expect that any additional production

365

of mine would meet a better fate? It would make me appear as if I repented for the crime of having been elected, and was anxious to apologize and beg forgiveness. To so represent me, would be the principal use made of any letter I might now thrust upon the public. My old record cannot be so used; and that is precisely the reason that some new declaration is so much sought.

Now, my dear sir, be assured, that I am not questioning *your* candor; I am only pointing out, that, while a new letter would hurt the cause which I think a just one, you can quite as well effect every patriotic object with the old record. Carefully read pages 18, 19, 74, 75, 88, 89, & 267 of the volume of Joint Debates between Senator Douglas and myself, with the Republican platform adopted at Chicago, and all your questions will be substantially answered. I have no thought of recommending the abolition of slavery in the District of Columbia, nor the slave trade among the slave states, even on the conditions indicated; and if I were to make such recommendation, it is quite clear Congress would not follow it.

As to employing slaves in arsenals and dockyards, it is a thing I never thought of in my life, to my recollection, till I saw your letter; and I may say of it, precisely as I have said of the two points above.

As to the use of patronage in the slave states, where there are few or no Republicans, I do not expect to inquire for the politics of the appointee, or whether he does or not own slaves. I intend in that matter to accommodate the people in the several localities, if they themselves will allow me to accommodate them. In one word, I never have been, am not now, and probably never shall be, in a mood of harassing the people, either North or South.

On the territorial question, I am inflexible, as you see my position in the book. On that, there is a difference between you and us; and it is the only substantial difference. You think slavery is right and ought to be extended; we think it is wrong and ought to be restricted. For this, neither has any just occasion to be angry with the other.

As to the state laws, mentioned in your sixth question, I really know very little of them. I never have read one. If any of them are in conflict with the fugitive slave clause, or any other part of the Constitution, I certainly should be glad of their repeal; but I could hardly be justified, as a citizen of Illinois, or as President of the United States, to recommend the repeal of a statute of Vermont, or South Carolina.

A Period of Waiting

With the assurance of my highest regards I subscribe myself Your obt. Servt.,

A. Lincoln

P.S. The documents referred to, I suppose you will readily find in Washington.   *A. L.*

When the chairman of the Indiana State Republican Committee wrote from Washington implying that certain Republicans were not averse to some form of popular sovereignty, and that many thought the South should be represented in the Cabinet, Lincoln again stated his position.

CONFIDENTIAL

Springfield Ills.
Dec. 18. 1860

Hon. Jno. D. Defrees.
My dear Sir

Yours of the 15th. is received. I am sorry any Republican inclines to dally with Pop. Sov. of any sort. It acknowledges that slavery has equal rights with liberty, and surrenders all we have contended for. Once fastened on us as a settled policy, filibustering for all south of us, and making slave states of it, follows in spite of us, with an early Supreme Court decision, holding our free state constitutions to be unconstitutional.

Would Scott or Stephens go into the cabinet? And if yea, on what terms? Do they come to me? or I go to them? or are we to lead off in open hostility to each other? Yours truly

A. Lincoln

The editor of the New York *Times* presumed to send Lincoln a letter from a rabidly secessionist member of the Mississippi legislature. The President-Elect came close to losing his temper.

CONFIDENTIAL

Springfield, Ills.
Dec. 18, 1860

Hon. H. J. Raymond
My dear Sir

Yours of the 14th. is received. What a very mad man your correspondent, Smedes is. Mr. Lincoln is not pledged to the ultimate extinction of slavery; does not hold the black man to be the equal of the white, unqualifiedly as Mr. S. states it; and never did stigmatize their white people as immoral & unchristian; and Mr. S. cannot prove one of his assertions true.

Mr. S. seems sensitive on the questions of morals and Christianity. What does he think of a man who makes charges against another which he does not know to be true, and could easily learn to be false?

As to the pitcher story, it is a forgery out and out. I never made but one speech in Cincinnati—the last speech in the volume containing the Joint Debates between Senator Douglas and myself. I have never yet seen Gov. Chase. I was never in a meeting of Negroes in my life; and never saw a pitcher presented by anybody to anybody.

I am much obliged by your letter, and shall be glad to hear from you again when you have anything of interest. Yours truly

A. Lincoln

Lincoln stiffened in preparation for the crisis. The day before he wrote to Congressman Washburne, South Carolina had passed her Ordinance of Secession.

CONFIDENTIAL

Springfield, Ills.
Dec. 21. 1860

Hon. E. B. Washburne
My dear Sir:

Last night I received your letter giving an account of your interview with Gen. Scott, and for which I thank you. Please present my respects to the General, and tell him, confidentially, I shall be obliged to him to be as well prepared as he can to either *hold,* or *retake,* the forts, as the case may require, at, and after the inauguration. Yours as ever

A. Lincoln

Lincoln reasoned with Alexander H. Stephens of Georgia, whom he had known and admired when both men were Whig members of the same Congress.

A Period of Waiting

Springfield, Ills.
Dec. 22, 1860

Hon. A. H. Stephens—
My dear Sir

Your obliging answer to my short note is just received, and for which please accept my thanks. I fully appreciate the present peril the country is in, and the weight of responsibility on me.

Do the people of the South really entertain fears that a Republican administration would, *directly,* or *indirectly,* interfere with their slaves, or with them, about their slaves? If they do, I wish to assure you, as once a friend, and still, I hope, not an enemy, that there is no cause for such fears.

The South would be in no more danger in this respect, than it was in the days of Washington. I suppose, however, this does not meet the case. You think slavery is *right* and ought to be extended; while we think it is *wrong* and ought to be restricted. That I suppose is the rub. It certainly is the only substantial difference between us. Yours very truly

A. Lincoln

Greatly disturbed by a rumor of what he considered a treasonable intention on the part of the Buchanan administration, Lincoln prepared for the worst.

Springfield, Ills. Dec. 24, 1860

Hon. Lyman Trumbull
My dear Sir

I expect to be able to offer Mr. Blair a place in the cabinet; but I cannot, as yet, be committed on the matter, to any extent whatever.

Dispatches have come here two days in succession, that the forts in South Carolina, will be surrendered by the order, or consent at least, of the President.

I can scarcely believe this; but if it prove true, I will, if our friends at Washington concur, announce publicly at once that they are to be retaken after the inauguration. This will give the Union men a rallying cry, and preparation will proceed somewhat on their side, as well as on the other. Yours as ever

A. Lincoln.

The Living Lincoln

Lincoln moved to redeem a pledge, more implied than expressed, that his managers had made at the Chicago convention.

Springfield, Ills.
Dec. 31, 1860

Hon. Simon Cameron
My dear Sir:

I think fit to notify you now, that by your permission, I shall, at the proper time, nominate you to the U. S. Senate, for confirmation as Secretary of the Treasury, or as Secretary of War—which of the two, I have not yet definitely decided. Please answer at your own earliest convenience. Your Obt. Servt.

A. Lincoln—

At the proposed appointment of Cameron, opposition erupted. In his long and devious political career were unsavory episodes which his many enemies lost no time in exploiting. Lincoln, impressed by their representations, asked the Pennsylvanian to decline the proffered position.

PRIVATE
Springfield, Ills. Jan. 3, 1861

Hon. Simon Cameron
My dear Sir

Since seeing you things have developed which make it impossible for me to take you into the cabinet. You will say this comes of an interview with McClure; and this is partly, but not wholly true. The more potent matter is wholly outside of Pennsylvania; and yet I am not at liberty to specify it. Enough that it appears to me to be sufficient. And now I suggest that you write me declining the appointment, in which case I do not object to its being known that it was tendered you. Better do this at once, before things so change, that you cannot honorably decline, and I be compelled to openly recall the tender. No person living knows, or has an intimation that I write this letter. Yours truly

A. Lincoln

P.S. Telegraph me instantly, on receipt of this, saying "All right." *A. L.*

Cameron made no response, yet Lincoln was wise enough in the ways of politics to be sure that a United States Senator who was also the Republican czar of the second largest state would be heard from.

A Period of Waiting

But there might be a way out. If Cameron could be induced to remain in the Senate by the promise of the Pennsylvania patronage, Lincoln's problem would be solved.

The harassed President-Elect explained the situation to Senator Trumbull, who had reported that many Republicans in the Senate were opposed to Cameron's appointment as Secretary of the Treasury.

VERY CONFIDENTIAL

Springfield, Ills.
Jan. 7. 1861

Hon. Lyman Trumbull
My dear Sir

Yours of the 3rd. is just received. The democrats of our H.R. refused to make a quorum today, trying, as I understand, to prevent your re-election. I trust that before this reaches you, the telegraph will have informed you that they have failed, and you have triumphed.

Gen. C. has not been offered the Treasury, and, I think, will not be. It seems to me not only highly proper, but a *necessity,* that Gov. Chase shall take that place. His ability, firmness, and purity of character, produce the propriety; and that he alone can reconcile Mr. Bryant, and his class, to the appointment of Gov. S. to the State Department produces the necessity. But then comes the danger that the protectionists of Pennsylvania will be dissatisfied; and, to clear this difficulty, Gen. C. must be brought to co-operate. He would readily do this for the War Department. But then comes the fierce opposition to his having any department, threatening even to send charges into the Senate to procure his rejection by that body. Now, what I would most like, and what I think he should prefer too, under the circumstances, would be to retain his place in the Senate; and if that place has been promised to another, let that other take a respectable, and reasonably lucrative place abroad. Also let Gen. C's friends be, with entire fairness, cared for in Pennsylvania, and elsewhere.

I may mention before closing that besides the very fierce opposition to Gen. C. he is more amply recommended for a place in the cabinet, than any other man.

I have a great notion to post Judd fully in this matter, and get him to visit Washington, and in his quiet way, try to adjust it satisfactorily. Yours as ever

A. Lincoln.

The Living Lincoln

Instead of writing, Cameron sent an emissary. Lincoln, wrestling with his prickliest problem, tried to undo the damage caused by his original letter of January 3.

Springfield, Ills.
Jan. 13. 1861

Hon. Simon Cameron
My dear Sir:

At the suggestion of Mr. Sanderson, and with hearty good will besides, I herewith send you a letter dated Jan. 3rd. — the same in date, as the last you received from me. I thought best to give it that date, as it is, in some sort, to take the place of that letter. I learn, both by a letter of Mr. Swett, and from Mr. Sanderson, that your feelings were wounded by the *terms* of my letter really of the 3rd. I wrote that letter under great anxiety, and perhaps I was not as guarded in its terms as I should have been; but I beg you to be assured, I intended no offence. My great object was to have you act quickly — if possible, before the matter should be complicated with the Penn. senatorial election. Destroy the offensive letter, or return it to me.

I say to you now I have not doubted that you would perform the duties of a department ably and faithfully. Nor have I for a moment intended to ostracize your friends. If I should make a cabinet appointment for Penn. before I reach Washington, I will not do so without consulting you, and giving all the weight to your views and wishes which I consistently can. This I have always intended. Yours truly

A. Lincoln.

[ENCLOSURE]

Springfield, Ills.
Jan. 3. 1861

Hon. Simon Cameron
My dear Sir:

When you were here about the last of December, I handed you a letter saying I should at the proper time, nominate you to the Senate for a place in the cabinet. It is due to you, and to truth, for me to say you were here by my invitation, and not upon any suggestion of your own. You have not, as yet, signified to me, whether you would accept the appointment; and, with much pain, I now say to you, that you will relieve me from great embarrassment by allowing me to recall the offer. This springs from an unexpected complication; and not from any change of my view as to the ability or faithfulness with which you would discharge the duties of the place.

I now think I will not definitely fix upon any appointment for Pennsylvania until I reach Washington. Your Obt. Servt.

A. Lincoln.

In planning to visit his stepmother in Coles County, Lincoln did not forget his homespun friend and relative, John Hanks.

Springfield, Jan. 28. 1861

Dear John

I now think I will pass Decatur, going to Coles, on the day after tomorrow—Wednesday, the 30th. of the month. Be ready, and go along. Yours as ever

A. Lincoln

Lincoln reiterated his determination that there should be no modification of the Republican party's stand on the "now vexed question" of the extension of slavery to the territories.

PRIVATE & CONFIDENTIAL

Springfield, Ills. Feb. 1. 1861

Hon. W. H. Seward
My dear Sir

On the 21st. ult. Hon. W. Kellogg, a Republican M.C of this state whom you probably know, was here, in a good deal of anxiety, seeking to ascertain to what extent I would be consenting for our friends to go in the way of compromise on the now vexed question. While he was with me I received a dispatch from Senator Trumbull, at Washington, alluding to the same question, and telling me to await letters. I thereupon told Mr. Kellogg that when I should receive these letters, posting me as to the state of affairs at Washington, I would write you, requesting you to let him see my letter. To my surprise when the letters mentioned by Judge Trumbull came, they made no allusion to the "vexed question." This baffled me so much that I was near not writing you at all, in compliance with what I had said to Judge Kellogg.

373

The Living Lincoln

I say now, however, as I have all the while said, that on the territorial question—that is, the question of extending slavery under the national auspices,—I am inflexible. I am for no compromise which *assists* or *permits* the extension of the institution on soil owned by the nation. And any trick by which the nation is to acquire territory, and then allow some local authority to spread slavery over it, is as obnoxious as any other.

I take it that to effect some such result as this, and to put us again on the high-road to a slave empire is the object of all these proposed compromises. I am against it.

As to fugitive slaves, District of Columbia, slave trade among the slave states, and whatever springs of necessity from the fact that the institution is amongst us, I care but little, so that what is done be comely, and not altogether outrageous. Nor do I care much about New Mexico, if further extension were hedged against. Yours very truly

A. Lincoln—

Preparatory to leaving for Washington, Lincoln turned over valuable papers, representing the bulk of his estate, to the Secretary of the Springfield Marine and Fire Insurance Company, his bank.

[February 9? 1861]

Abraham Lincoln leaves with the undersigned for safe-keeping, and to receive interest, the following papers—

One note of A. J. Van Deren, J. M. Vanderen, Cyrus W. Van Deren, security, and Lewis Johnson, for one thousand dollars, balance due, interest at ten per cent, paid up to March 18— 1861.

Two notes of N. W. Edwards, together amounting to fifteen hundred and eighty-seven dollars and ninety cents, interest at ten per cent due from Jan. 16. 1860.

Two notes of Smith, Edwards & Co, for aggregate balance of one thousand dollars, and interest at ten per cent from Jan. 16. 1861.

One note of J. K. Lewis and Thomas Lewis, for one hundred and fifty dollars, interest at ten per cent due from April 22, 1860.

One note, and mortgage of Isaac Lindsay, for six hundred dollars, interest at ten per cent, due from August 28. 1860.

A Period of Waiting

One note & mortgage, of William Cline, for seven hundred and fifty dollars, interest at ten per cent from Nov. 22. 1859.

One note & mortgage of J. Ruckel, for five hundred dollars, interest at ten per cent, due from Sep 28 – 1860.

One note of John Cook, for seven hundred and fifty dollars, interest due, from April 17, 1860.

One Springfield City bond, for one thousand dollars reduced by two payments to $666.67.

One certificate of six shares of Alton & Sangamon Railroad stock

One certificate of scholarship in Illionis State University.

One note of N. B. Judd, for three thousand dollars, with interest at ten per cent from Sep 1. 1859.

> Policy of insurance
> Lease of house
> Notes on Haines,

Rob. Irwin.

On the morning of February 11, Lincoln proceeded alone to the depot of the Great Western Railway. In the waiting room he greeted friends. Then he stepped to the rear platform of the last car of the special train that was to carry him to Washington. While a light rain fell on those who had gathered to wish him well, he spoke his last words to his neighbors.

February 11, 1861

My friends—

No one, not in my situation, can appreciate my feeling of sadness at this parting. To this place, and the kindness of these people, I owe everything. Here I have lived a quarter of a century, and have passed from a young to an old man. Here my children have been born, and one is buried. I now leave, not knowing when, or whether ever, I may return, with a task before me greater than that which rested upon Washington. Without the assistance of that Divine Being, who ever attended him, I cannot succeed. With that assistance I cannot fail. Trusting in Him, who can go with me, and remain with you and be everywhere for good, let us confidently hope that all will yet be well. To His care commending you, as I hope in your prayers you will commend me, I bid you an affectionate farewell.

The next two weeks, lacking one day, Lincoln would spend en route to Washington, giving many thousands an opportunity to see the lanky Westerner who was to be the next President. He would attend receptions, ride in processions, and make dozens of speeches. Whether by design or through fatigue, what he said was usually innocuous, sometimes vapid. But he made a few exceptions. When he spoke on the evening of February 11 from the balcony of the Bates House in Indianapolis, he probed fundamental questions and indicated, without committing himself, that he would not permit the seceding South to leave the Union unhindered.

February 11, 1861

It is not possible, in my journey to the national capital, to address assemblies like this which may do me the great honor to meet me as you have done, but very briefly. I should be entirely worn out if I were to attempt it. I appear before you now to thank you for this very magnificent welcome which you have given me, and still more for the very generous support which your state recently gave to the political cause of the whole country, and the whole world. [Applause.]. . . .

The words "coercion" and "invasion" are in great use about these days. Suppose we were simply to try if we can, and ascertain what is the meaning of these words. Let us get, if we can, the exact definitions of these words—not from dictionaries, but from the men who constantly repeat them—what things they mean to express by the words. What, then, is "coercion"? What is "invasion"? Would the marching of an army into South Carolina, for instance, without the consent of her people, and in hostility against them, be coercion or invasion? I very frankly say, I think it would be invasion, and it would be coercion too, if the people of that country were forced to submit. But if the government, for instance, but simply insists upon holding its own forts, or retaking those forts which belong to it,— [cheers,]—or the enforcement of the laws of the United States in the collection of duties upon foreign importations,—[renewed cheers,] —or even the withdrawal of the mails from those portions of the country where the mails themselves are habitually violated; would any or all of these things be coercion? Do the lovers of the Union

A Period of Waiting

contend that they will resist coercion or invasion of any state, understanding that any or all of these would be coercing or invading a state? If they do, then it occurs to me that the means for the preservation of the Union they so greatly love, in their own estimation, is of a very thin and airy character. [Applause.] If sick, they would consider the little pills of the homeopathist as already too large for them to swallow. In their view, the Union, as a family relation, would not be anything like a regular marriage at all, but only as a sort of free-love arrangement,—[laughter,]—to be maintained on what that sect calls passionate attraction. [Continued laughter.] But, my friends, enough of this.

What is the particular sacredness of a state? I speak not of that position which is given to a state in and by the Constitution of the United States, for that all of us agree to—we abide by; but that position assumed, that a state can carry with it out of the Union that which it holds in sacredness by virtue of its connection with the Union. I am speaking of that assumed right of a state, as a primary principle, that the Constitution should rule all that is less than itself, and ruin all that is bigger than itself. [Laughter.] But, I ask, wherein does consist that right? If a state, in one instance, and a county in another, should be equal in extent of territory, and equal in the number of people, wherein is that state any better than the county? Can a change of name change the right? By what principle of original right is it that one-fiftieth or one-ninetieth of a great nation, by calling themselves a state, have the right to break up and ruin that nation as a matter of original principle? Now, I ask the question—I am not deciding anything—[laughter,]—and with the request that you will think somewhat upon that subject and decide for yourselves, if you choose, when you get ready,—where is the mysterious, original right, from principle, for a certain district of country with inhabitants, by merely being called a state, to play tyrant over all its own citizens, and deny the authority of everything greater than itself. [Laughter.] I say I am deciding nothing, but simply giving something for you to reflect upon; and, with having said this much, and having declared, in the start, that I will make no long speeches, I thank you again for this magnificent welcome, and bid you an affectionate farewell. [Cheers.]

Ten days later, at Trenton, New Jersey, Lincoln recalled the emotions aroused by his first knowledge of the Revolutionary struggle.

The Living Lincoln

February 21, 1861

Mr. President and Gentlemen of the Senate of the State of New Jersey:

I am very grateful to you for the honorable reception of which I have been the object. I cannot but remember the place that New Jersey holds in our early history. In the early revolutionary struggle, few of the states among the old thirteen had more of the battlefields of the country within their limits than old New Jersey.

May I be pardoned if, upon this occasion, I mention that away back in my childhood, the earliest days of my being able to read, I got hold of a small book, such a one as few of the younger members have ever seen, Weems' "Life of Washington." I remember all the accounts there given of the battlefields and struggles for the liberties of the country, and none fixed themselves upon my imagination so deeply as the struggle here at Trenton, New Jersey. The crossing of the river; the contest with the Hessians; the great hardships endured at that time, all fixed themselves on my memory more than any single revolutionary event; and you all know, for you have all been boys, how these early impressions last longer than any others. I recollect thinking then, boy even though I was, that there must have been something more than common that those men struggled for. I am exceedingly anxious that that thing which they struggled for; that something even more than national independence; that something that held out a great promise to all the people of the world to all time to come; I am exceedingly anxious that this Union, the Constitution, and the liberties of the people shall be perpetuated in accordance with the original idea for which that struggle was made, and I shall be most happy indeed if I shall be an humble instrument in the hands of the Almighty, and of this, his almost chosen people, for perpetuating the object of that great struggle.

You give me this reception, as I understand, without distinction of party. I learn that this body is composed of a majority of gentlemen who, in the exercise of their best judgment in the choice of a chief magisrate, did not think I was the man. I understand, nevertheless, that they came forward here to greet me as the constitutional President of the United States—as citizens of the United States, to meet the man who, for the time being, is the representative man of the nation, united by a purpose to perpetuate the Union and liberties of the people. As such, I accept this reception more gratefully than I could do did I believe it was tendered to me as an individual.

At Independence Hall, on the anniversary of Washington's birth, Lincoln put the most fundamental of his political convictions into words. He would speak several other times that day—the last of his prolonged trip—but he would not approach either the confessional depth or the resolute strength of this short address.

February 22, 1861

Mr. Cuyler:

I am filled with deep emotion at finding myself standing here in the place where were collected together the wisdom, the patriotism, the devotion to principle, from which sprang the institutions under which we live. You have kindly suggested to me that in my hands is the task of restoring peace to our distracted country. I can say in return, sir, that all the political sentiments I entertain have been drawn, so far as I have been able to draw them, from the sentiments which originated, and were given to the world from this hall in which we stand. I have never had a feeling politically that did not spring from the sentiments embodied in the Declaration of Independence. [Great cheering.] I have often pondered over the dangers which were incurred by the men who assembled here and adopted that Declaration of Independence—I have pondered over the toils that were endured by the officers and soldiers of the army, who achieved that independence. [Applause.] I have often inquired of myself, what great principle or idea it was that kept this confederacy so long together. It was not the mere matter of the separation of the colonies from the mother land; but something in that Declaration giving liberty, not alone to the people of this country, but hope to the world for all future time. [Great applause.] It was that which gave promise that in due time the weights should be lifted from the shoulders of all men, and that *all* should have an equal chance. [Cheers.] This is the sentiment embodied in that Declaration of Independence.

Now, my friends, can this country be saved upon that basis? If it can, I will consider myself one of the happiest men in the world if I can help to save it. If it can't be saved upon that principle, it will be truly awful. But, if this country cannot be saved without giving up that principle—I was about to say I would rather be assassinated on this spot than to surrender it. [Applause.]

Now, in my view of the present aspect of affairs, there is no need of bloodshed and war. There is no necessity for it. I am not in favor of such a course, and I may say in advance, there will be no bloodshed unless it be forced upon the government. The government will not use force unless force is used against it. [Prolonged applause and cries of "That's the proper sentiment."]

My friends, this is a wholly unprepared speech. I did not expect to be called upon to say a word when I came here—I supposed I was merely to do something towards raising a flag. I may, therefore, have said something indiscreet, [cries of "no, no"], but I have said nothing but what I am willing to live by, and, in the pleasure of Almighty God, die by.

On the evening of February 22 Lincoln was told that detectives had discovered a plot to assassinate him when he passed through Baltimore. Though skeptical, he yielded to the insistence of his friends, abandoned his published schedule, and set out at once, in secret, for the capital. He arrived safely the following morning and went at once to Willard's Hotel, where he would remain until the inauguration.

For the next ten days the President-Elect received visitors, attended a few functions, and conferred with Republican leaders. Whenever he could he polished his inaugural address. Before leaving Springfield he had completed a draft, and had had a few copies printed in the office of the *Illinois State Journal* for friends and advisers to read. At the suggestion of Orville H. Browning, Lincoln softened a declaration of purpose, "All the power at my disposal will be used to reclaim the public property and places which have fallen; to hold, occupy and possess these, and all other property and places belonging to the government . . . ," by deleting the words, "to reclaim the public property and places which have fallen." Seward proposed the addition of a closing paragraph which would give the address an emotional appeal. Lincoln accepted the idea and rewrote Seward's uninspired language into a passage of rare beauty. Other changes were those small substitutions which a sensitive craftsman is constantly making in the interest of clarity and cadence.

No President ever approached his inauguration in the brittle atmosphere which pervaded the country on March 4, 1861. Seven states had declared themselves out of the Union. Lincoln made clear his conviction that secession was revolution, but at the same time he assured the people of the South that the new administration would give them no cause for leaving the Union. Beyond that, he counseled patience, hoping, apparently, that if the resort to arms could be forestalled both sections would see the folly of disunion and take up again their former peaceful partnership.

March 4, 1861

Fellow citizens of the United States:

In compliance with a custom as old as the government itself, I appear before you to address you briefly, and to take, in your presence, the oath prescribed by the Constitution of the United States, to be taken by the President "before he enters on the execution of his office."

I do not consider it necessary, at present, for me to discuss those matters of administration about which there is no special anxiety, or excitement.

Apprehension seems to exist among the people of the Southern states, that by the accession of a Republican administration, their property, and their peace, and personal security, are to be endangered. There has never been any reasonable cause for such apprehension. Indeed, the most ample evidence to the contrary has all the while existed, and been open to their inspection. It is found in nearly all the published speeches of him who now addresses you. I do but quote from one of those speeches when I declare that "I have no purpose, directly or indirectly, to interfere with the institution of slavery in the states where it exists. I believe I have no lawful right to do so, and I have no inclination to do so." Those who nominated and elected me did so with full knowledge that I had made this, and many similar declarations, and had never recanted them. And more than this, they placed in the platform, for my acceptance, and as a law to themselves, and to me, the clear and emphatic resolution which I now read:

"*Resolved,* That the maintenance inviolate of the rights of the states, and especially the right of each state to order and control its own domestic institutions according to its own judgment exclusively, is essential to that balance of power on which the perfection and endurance of our political fabric depend; and we denounce the lawless invasion by armed force of the soil of any state or territory, no matter under what pretext, as among the gravest of crimes."

I now reiterate these sentiments: and in doing so, I only press upon the public attention the most conclusive evidence of which the case is susceptible, that the property, peace and security of no section are to be in anywise endangered by the now incoming administration. I add too, that all the protection which, consistently with the Constitution and the laws, can be given, will be cheerfully given to all the states when lawfully demanded, for whatever cause —as cheerfully to one section, as to another.

There is much controversy about the delivering up of fugitives from service or labor. The clause I now read is as plainly written in the Constitution as any other of its provisions:

"No person held to service or labor in one state, under the laws thereof, escaping into another, shall, in consequence of any law or regulation therein, be discharged from such service or labor, but shall be delivered up on claim of the party to whom such service or labor may be due."

It is scarcely questioned that this provision was intended by those who made it, for the reclaiming of what we call fugitive slaves; and the intention of the law-giver is the law. All members of Congress swear their support to the whole Constitution—to this provision as much as to any other. To the proposition, then, that slaves whose cases come within the terms of this clause, "shall be delivered up," their oaths are unanimous. Now, if they would make the effort in good temper, could they not, with nearly equal unanimity, frame and pass a law, by means of which to keep good that unanimous oath?

There is some difference of opinion whether this clause should be enforced by national or by state authority; but surely that difference is not a very material one. If the slave is to be surrendered, it can be of but little consequence to him, or to others, by which authority it is done. And should anyone, in any case, be content that his oath shall go unkept, on a merely unsubstantial controversy as to *how* it shall be kept?

Again, in any law upon this subject, ought not all the safeguards of liberty known in civilized and humane jurisprudence to be introduced, so that a free man be not, in any case, surrendered as a slave? And might it not be well, at the same time, to provide by law for the enforcement of that clause in the Constitution which guarantees that "The citizens of each state shall be entitled to all privileges and immunities of citizens in the several states?"

I take the official oath today, with no mental reservations, and with no purpose to construe the Constitution or laws, by any hypercritical rules. And while I do not choose now to specify particular acts of Congress as proper to be enforced, I do suggest, that it will be much safer for all, both in official and private stations, to conform to, and abide by, all those acts which stand unrepealed, than to violate any of them, trusting to find impunity in having them held to be unconstitutional.

It is seventy-two years since the first inauguration of a President under our national Constitution. During that period fifteen different and greatly distinguished citizens, have, in succession, administered the executive branch of the government. They have conducted it through many perils; and, generally, with great success. Yet, with all this scope for precedent, I now enter upon the same task for the brief constitutional term of four years, under great and peculiar difficulty. A disruption of the Federal Union heretofore only menaced, is now formidably attempted.

I hold, that in contemplation of universal law, and of the Constitution, the Union of these states is perpetual. Perpetuity is implied, if not expressed, in the fundamental law of all national governments. It is safe to assert that no government proper, ever had a provision in its organic law for its own termination. Continue to execute all the express provisions of our national Constitution, and the Union will endure forever—it being impossible to destroy it, except by some action not provided for in the instrument itself.

Again, if the United States be not a government proper, but an association of states in the nature of contract merely, can it, as a contract, be peaceably unmade, by less than all the parties who made it? One party to a contract may violate it—break it, so to speak; but does it not require all to lawfully rescind it?

Descending from these general principles, we find the proposition that, in legal contemplation, the Union is perpetual, confirmed by the history of the Union itself. The Union is much older than the Constitution. It was formed in fact, by the Articles of Association in 1774. It was matured and continued by the Declaration of Independence in 1776. It was further matured and the faith of all the then thirteen states expressly plighted and engaged that it should be perpetual, by the Articles of Confederation in 1778.

And finally, in 1787, one of the declared objects for ordaining and establishing the Constitution, was *"to form a more perfect union."*

But if destruction of the Union, by one, or by a part only, of the states, be lawfully possible, the Union is *less* perfect than before the Constitution, having lost the vital element of perpetuity.

It follows from these views that no state, upon its own mere motion, can lawfully get out of the Union,—that *resolves* and *ordinances* to that effect are legally void; and that acts of violence, within any state or states, against the authority of the United States, are insurrectionary or revolutionary, according to circumstances.

I therefore consider that, in view of the Constitution and the laws, the Union is unbroken; and, to the extent of my ability, I shall take care, as the Constitution itself expressly enjoins upon me, that the laws of the Union be faithfully executed in all the states. Doing this I deem to be only a simple duty on my part; and I shall perform it, so far as practicable, unless my rightful masters, the American people, shall withhold the requisite means, or, in some authoritative manner, direct the contrary. I trust this will not be regarded as a menace, but only as the declared purpose of the Union that it *will* constitutionally defend, and maintain itself.

In doing this there needs to be no bloodshed or violence; and there shall be none, unless it be forced upon the national authority. The power confided to me, will be used to hold, occupy, and possess the property, and places belonging to the government, and to collect the duties and imposts; but beyond what may be necessary for these objects, there will be no invasion—no using of force against, or among the people anywhere. Where hostility to the United States, in any interior locality, shall be so great and so universal, as to prevent competent resident citizens from holding the federal offices, there will be no attempt to force obnoxious strangers among the people for that object. While the strict legal right may exist in the government to enforce the exercise of these offices, the attempt to do so would be so irritating, and so nearly impracticable with all, that I deem it better to forego, for the time, the uses of such offices.

The mails, unless repelled, will continue to be furnished in all parts of the Union. So far as possible, the people everywhere shall have that sense of perfect security which is most favorable to calm thought and reflection. The course here indicated will be followed,

A Period of Waiting

unless current events, and experience, shall show a modification, or change, to be proper; and in every case and exigency, my best discretion will be exercised, according to circumstances actually existing, and with a view and a hope of a peaceful solution of the national troubles, and the restoration of fraternal sympathies and affections.

That there are persons in one section, or another who seek to destroy the Union at all events, and are glad of any pretext to do it, I will neither affirm or deny; but if there be such, I need address no word to them. To those, however, who really love the Union, may I not speak?

Before entering upon so grave a matter as the destruction of our national fabric, with all its benefits, its memories, and its hopes, would it not be wise to ascertain precisely why we do it? Will you hazard so desperate a step, while there is any possibility that any portion of the ills you fly from, have no real existence? Will you, while the certain ills you fly to, are greater than all the real ones you fly from? Will you risk the commission of so fearful a mistake?

All profess to be content in the Union, if all constitutional rights can be maintained. Is it true, then, that any right, plainly written in the Constitution, has been denied? I think not. Happily the human mind is so constituted, that no party can reach to the audacity of doing this. Think, if you can, of a single instance in which a plainly written provision of the Constitution has ever been denied. If, by the mere force of numbers, a majority should deprive a minority of any clearly written constitutional right, it might, in a moral point of view, justify revolution—certainly would, if such right were a vital one. But such is not our case. All the vital rights of minorities, and of individuals, are so plainly assured to them, by affirmations and negations, guarantees and prohibitions, in the Constitution, that controversies never arise concerning them. But no organic law can ever be framed with a provision specifically applicable to every question which may occur in practical administration. No foresight can anticipate, nor any document of reasonable length contain express provisions for all possible questions. Shall fugitives from labor be surrendered by national or by state authority? The Constitution does not expressly say. *May* Congress prohibit slavery in the territories? The Constitution does not expressly say. *Must* Congress protect slavery in the territories? The Constitution does not expressly say.

From questions of this class spring all our constitutional controversies, and we divide upon them into majorities and minorities. If the minority will not acquiesce, the majority must, or the government must cease. There is no other alternative; for continuing the government, is acquiescence on one side or the other. If a minority, in such case, will secede rather than acquiesce, they make a precedent which, in turn, will divide and ruin them; for a minority of their own will secede from them, whenever a majority refuses to be controlled by such minority. For instance, why may not any portion of a new confederacy, a year or two hence, arbitrarily secede again, precisely as portions of the present Union now claim to secede from it. All who cherish disunion sentiments, are now being educated to the exact temper of doing this. Is there such perfect identity of interests among the states to compose a new Union, as to produce harmony only, and prevent renewed secession?

Plainly, the central idea of secession, is the essence of anarchy. A majority, held in restraint by constitutional checks, and limitations, and always changing easily, with deliberate changes of popular opinions and sentiments, is the only true sovereign of a free people. Whoever rejects it, does, of necessity, fly to anarchy or to despotism. Unanimity is impossible; the rule of a minority, as a permanent arrangement, is wholly inadmissible; so that, rejecting the majority principle, anarchy, or despotism in some form, is all that is left.

I do not forget the position assumed by some, that constitutional questions are to be decided by the Supreme Court; nor do I deny that such decisions must be binding in any case, upon the parties to a suit, as to the object of that suit, while they are also entitled to very high respect and consideration, in all parallel cases, by all other departments of the government. And while it is obviously possible that such decision may be erroneous in any given case, still the evil effect following it, being limited to that particular case, with the chance that it may be overruled, and never become a precedent for other cases, can better be borne than could the evils of a different practice. At the same time the candid citizen must confess that if the policy of the government, upon vital questions, affecting the whole people, is to be irrevocably fixed by decisions of the Supreme Court, the instant they are made, in ordinary litigation between parties, in personal actions, the people will have ceased to be their own rulers, having, to that extent, practically resigned their government, into the hands of that eminent tribunal. Nor is there, in this view, any assault upon the court, or the judges. It is a duty, from which they may not shrink, to decide cases properly brought before them; and it is no fault of theirs, if others seek to turn their decisions to political purposes.

One section of our country believes slavery is *right,* and ought to be extended, while the other believes it is *wrong,* and ought not to be extended. This is the only substantial dispute. The fugitive slave clause of the Constitution, and the law for the suppression of the foreign slave trade, are each as well enforced, perhaps, as any law can ever be in a community where the moral sense of the people imperfectly supports the law itself. The great body of the people abide by the dry legal obligation in both cases, and a few break over in each. This, I think, cannot be perfectly cured; and it would be worse in both cases *after* the separation of the sections, than before. The foreign slave trade, now imperfectly suppressed, would be ultimately revived without restriction, in one section; while fugitive slaves, now only partially surrendered, would not be surrendered at all, by the other.

Physically speaking we cannot separate. We cannot remove our respective sections from each other, nor build an impassable wall between them. A husband and wife may be divorced, and go out of the presence, and beyond the reach of each other; but the different parts of our country cannot do this. They cannot but remain face to face; and intercourse, either amicable or hostile, must continue between them. Is it possible then to make that intercourse more advantageous, or more satisfactory, *after* separation than *before?* Can aliens make treaties easier than friends can make laws? Can treaties be more faithfully enforced between aliens, than laws can among friends? Suppose you go to war, you cannot fight always; and when, after much loss on both sides, and no gain on either, you cease fighting, the identical old questions, as to terms of intercourse, are again upon you.

This country, with its institutions, belongs to the people who inhabit it. Whenever they shall grow weary of the existing government, they can exercise their *constitutional* right of amending it, or their *revolutionary* right to dismember, or overthrow it. I cannot be ignorant of the fact that many worthy, and patriotic citizens are desirous of having the national Constitution amended. While I make no recommendation of amendments, I fully recognize the rightful authority of the people over the whole subject, to be exercised in either of the modes prescribed in the instrument itself; and I should, under existing circumstances, favor, rather than oppose, a fair opportunity being afforded the people to act upon it.

I will venture to add that, to me, the convention mode seems preferable, in that it allows amendments to originate with the people themselves, instead of only permitting them to take, or reject, propositions, originated by others, not especially chosen for the purpose, and which might not be precisely such, as they would wish to either accept or refuse. I understand a proposed amendment to the Constitution—which amendment, however, I have not seen, has passed Congress, to the effect that the federal government, shall never interfere with the domestic institutions of the states, including that of persons held to service. To avoid misconstruction of what I have said, I depart from my purpose not to speak of particular amendments, so far as to say that, holding such a provision to now be implied constitutional law, I have no objection to its being made express, and irrevocable.

The chief magistrate derives all his authority from the people, and they have conferred none upon him to fix terms for the separation of the states. The people themselves can do this also if they choose; but the executive, as such, has nothing to do with it. His duty is to administer the present government, as it came to his hands, and to transmit it, unimpaired by him, to his successor.

Why should there not be a patient confidence in the ultimate justice of the people? Is there any better, or equal hope, in the world? In our present differences, is either party without faith of being in the right? If the Almighty Ruler of nations, with his eternal truth and justice, be on your side of the North, or on yours of the South, that truth, and that justice, will surely prevail, by the judgment of this great tribunal, the American people.

By the frame of the government under which we live, this same people have wisely given their public servants but little power for mischief; and have, with equal wisdom, provided for the return of that little to their own hands at very short intervals.

While the people retain their virtue, and vigilance, no administration, by any extreme of wickedness or folly, can very seriously injure the government, in the short space of four years.

My countrymen, one and all, think calmly and *well,* upon this whole subject. Nothing valuable can be lost by taking time. If there be an object to *hurry* any of you, in hot haste, to a step which you would never take *deliberately,* that object will be frustrated by taking time; but no good object can be frustrated by it. Such of you as are now dissatisfied, still have the old Constitution unimpaired, and, on the sensitive point, the laws of your own framing under it; while the new administration will have no immediate power, if it would, to change either. If it were admitted that you who are dissatisfied, hold the right side in the dispute, there still is no single good reason for precipitate action. Intelligence, patriotism, Christianity, and a firm reliance on Him, who has never yet forsaken this favored land, are still competent to adjust, in the best way, all our present difficulty.

In *your* hands, my dissatisfied fellow-countrymen, and not in *mine,* is the momentous issue of civil war. The government will not assail *you.* You can have no conflict, without being yourselves the aggressors. *You* have no oath registered in Heaven to destroy the government, while *I* shall have the most solemn one to "preserve, protect and defend" it.

I am loath to close. We are not enemies, but friends. We must not be enemies. Though passion may have strained, it must not break our bonds of affection. The mystic chords of memory, stretching from every battlefield, and patriot grave, to every living heart and hearthstone, all over this broad land, will yet swell the chorus of the Union, when again touched, as surely they will be, by the better angels of our nature.

XII. The Irrepressible
Conflict

1861 THE American Civil War was an extremely complicated phenomenon. Factors of politics, of economics, of mass psychology, of constitutional law, of manners and customs and morals each played its part in shaping the bloodiest civil war in history. Logic and emotion frequently were in conflict. The classic symbol of this contradiction was the horseman who late one April afternoon rode alone across the bridge that led from Washington to Arlington Heights. That day the chief command of the Union armies had been offered him. The mind of Robert E. Lee admitted that secession was revolution and that slavery was a political and moral evil, but the heart of Robert E. Lee would not permit him to take up arms against his native Virginia.

Sitting lost in thought before the fireplace in the White House, Lincoln reduced the complex issues of those first weeks in the Presidency to the two points that forbade compromise. First was the constitutional problem: Lincoln saw secession simply and clearly as illegal, and therefore as a course of action that must be resisted. Second was the belief, voiced by the Vice President of the Confederacy, that his government recognized "the truth that the Negro is not equal to the white man, that slavery—subordination to the superior race—is his natural and normal condition." To Lincoln this proposition was morally abhorrent, and therefore must be resisted.

There exists no written record to establish the precise moment when Lincoln decided that war was inevitable. Was it before or after Sumter was fired upon? A President of Lincoln's temperament must at least accept the necessity of war before he can prepare for it. It is true that until the last fatal moment Lincoln hoped the innate reasonableness of people would prevail and prevent the calamity of war. It is true that he preferred to shift testing the great point at issue—the defense of the established military installations of the United States—from Sumter to Fort Pickens, where the atmosphere was less filled with the emotional sparks of Southern firebrands.

In either case, the stakes were fundamentally of legal rather than military importance. After only a few days in office, Lincoln knew that twenty thousand troops would be required to defend Sumter for whatever slight strategic value the fort might provide; and the army and navy differed heatedly over whether there was even a remote chance of transporting these troops to the point of danger. But there existed no need to re-enforce the small garrison inside Sumter to establish the morality of the situation. Attack meant aggression and pin-pointed the constitutional responsibility for what, at some point or other, Lincoln had to accept as the irresistible conflict.

Lincoln's position, previous to Sumter, was perilous. No clearcut mandate could be drawn from the election that sent him to the White House. Winfield Scott, his commanding general, was now so infirm that he could no longer mount a horse. Within the cabinet were three personalities—William H. Seward from New York, Secretary of State; Salmon P. Chase from Ohio, Secretary of the Treasury; and Simon Cameron from Pennsylvania, Secretary of War—who had coveted the presidential nomination at Chicago and who held no illusions concerning Lincoln's limited experience in administrative or military matters.

Yet one day Seward would describe Lincoln as "the best man of us all" and history would concur in that opinion. Lincoln's greatness rests in this triumph, and the triumph itself rests in the character of Lincoln. Steadfastness of will, fairness of judgment, humility of self, growth of mind and bigness of heart were the invincible attributes that Lincoln brought to Washington in those dark, bitter years when democracy as a workable form of government stood on trial before the world.

Early in March, Lincoln received ominous news. The government of South Carolina had decreed that Major Anderson, commanding Fort Sumter in Charleston Harbor, no longer would be permitted to purchase supplies in the city. Before the President decided on his next move, he asked General Scott for information.

Executive Mansion, March 9, 1861.

Lieutenant General Scott:
My dear Sir:
On the 5th inst. I received from the Hon. Joseph Holt, the then faithful and vigilant Secretary of War, a letter of that date, inclosing a letter and accompanying documents received by him on the 4th inst. from Major Robert Anderson commanding at Fort Sumter, South Carolina; and copies of all which I now transmit. Immediately on the receipt of them by me, I transmitted the whole to you for your consideration; and the same day you returned the package to me with your opinion endorsed upon it, a copy of which opinion I now also transmit to you. Learning from you verbally that since then you have given the subject a more full and thorough consideration, you will much oblige me by giving answers, in writing, to the following interrogatories:

1st To what point of time can Major Anderson maintain his position at Fort Sumter, without fresh supplies or reinforcement?

2d. Can you, with all the means now in your control, supply or reinforce Fort Sumter within that time?

3d If not, what amount of means and of what description, in addition to that already at your control, would enable you to supply and reinforce that fortress within the time?

Please answer these, adding such statements, information, and counsel as your great skill and experience may suggest. Your obedient Servant

A. Lincoln.

With each day the tension mounted, yet a week later in a note to the Secretary of the Navy Lincoln showed that he had not lost his interest in the personal problems of others.

Executive Mansion
March 16/61

Hon. Gideon Welles
Dear Sir
The bearer (William) is a servant who has been with me for some time & in whom I have confidence as to his integrity and faithfulness. He wishes to enter your service. The difference of

color between him & the other servants is the cause of our separation. If you can give him employment you will confer a favour on Yours truly

A. Lincoln.

In a letter to John T. Stuart, Lincoln tried with the utmost tact to help Elizabeth Todd Grimsley, his "Cousin Lizzie" in Springfield.

PRIVATE

Washington, March 30, 1861

Dear Stuart:

Cousin Lizzie shows me your letter of the 27th. The question of giving her the Springfield post office troubles me. You see I have already appointed William Jayne a territorial governor, and Judge Trumbull's brother to a land office. Will it do for me to go on and justify the declaration that Trumbull and I have divided out all the offices among our relatives? Dr. Wallace, you know, is needy, and looks to me; and I personally owe him much.

I see by the papers, a vote is to be taken as to the post office. Could you not set up Lizzie and beat them all? She, being here, need know nothing of it, & therefore there would be no indelicacy on her part. Yours as ever

A. Lincoln

Secretary of State Seward occupied an ambiguous position in the Sumter crisis. At heart an appeaser—Henry Adams called him "the wily old scarecrow"—Seward assured Alabama's John A. Campbell, who still remained a member of the United States Supreme Court, that Sumter would be evacuated. But Seward did not speak for Lincoln, as the South assumed. April approached, Sumter remained garrisoned, and Seward, feeling increasingly awkward, sent the White House "Some Thoughts for the President's Consideration." There is strong doubt as to whether Lincoln ever sent the following reply. After reading what he had written, he may have put the pages aside and handled the matter orally.

Executive Mansion April 1, 1861

Hon: W. H. Seward:

My dear Sir:

Since parting with you I have been considering your paper dated this day, and entitled "Some thoughts for the President's consideration." The first proposition in it is, "1st. We are at the end of a month's administration, and yet without a policy, either domestic or foreign."

At the *beginning* of that month, in the inaugural, I said "The power confided to me will be used to hold, occupy and possess the property and places belonging to the government, and to collect the duties, and imposts." This had your distinct approval at the time; and, taken in connection with the order I immediately gave General Scott, directing him to employ every means in his power to strengthen and hold the forts, comprises the exact domestic policy you now urge, with the single exception, that it does not propose to abandon Fort Sumter.

Again, I do not perceive how the reinforcement of Fort Sumter would be done on a slavery, or party issue, while that of Fort Pickens would be on a more national, and patriotic one.

The news received yesterday in regard to St. Domingo, certainly brings a new item within the range of our foreign policy; but up to that time we have been preparing circulars, and instructions to ministers, and the like, all in perfect harmony, without even a suggestion that we had no foreign policy.

Upon your closing propositions, that "whatever policy we adopt, there must be an energetic prosecution of it"

"For this purpose it must be somebody's business to pursue and direct it incessantly"

"Either the President must do it himself, and be all the while active in it, or"

"Devolve it on some member of his cabinet"

"Once adopted, debates on it must end, and all agree and abide" I remark that if this must be done, *I* must do it. When a general line of policy is adopted, I apprehend there is no danger of its being changed without good reason, or continuing to be a subject of unnecessary debate; still, upon points arising in its progress, I wish, and suppose I am entitled to have the advice of all the cabinet. Your Obt. Servt.

A. Lincoln

Before dawn on April 12 the Confederate batteries opened on Fort Sumter. Anderson and his garrison withstood for more than thirty hours the uneven duelling by cannon, then surrendered when fire spread toward the powder magazine. On Sunday, April 14, Stephen A. Douglas conferred for two hours with Lincoln. The mind and heart of the Little Giant stanchly supported the fateful proclamation that the President issued next day.

April 15, 1861

BY THE PRESIDENT OF THE UNITED STATES
A PROCLAMATION

Whereas the laws of the United States have been for some time past, and now are opposed, and the execution thereof obstructed, in the States of South Carolina, Georgia, Alabama, Florida, Mississippi, Louisiana and Texas, by combinations too powerful to be suppressed by the ordinary course of judicial proceedings, or by the powers vested in the Marshals by law,

Now therefore, I, Abraham Lincoln, President of the United States, in virtue of the power in me vested by the Constitution, and the laws, have thought fit to call forth, and hereby do call forth, the militia of the several states of the Union, to the aggregate number of seventy-five thousand, in order to suppress said combinations, and to cause the laws to be duly executed. The details, for this object, will be immediately communicated to the state authorities through the War Department.

I appeal to all loyal citizens to favor, facilitate and aid this effort to maintain the honor, the integrity, and the existence of our national union, and the perpetuity of popular government; and to redress wrongs already long enough endured.

I deem it proper to say that the first service assigned to the forces hereby called forth will probably be to re-possess the forts, places, and property which have been seized from the Union; and in every event, the utmost care will be observed, consistently with the objects aforesaid, to avoid any devastation, any destruction of, or interference with, property, or any disturbance of peaceful citizens in any part of the country.

And I hereby command the persons composing the combinations aforesaid to disperse, and retire peaceably to their respective abodes within twenty days from this date.

Deeming that the present condition of public affairs presents an extraordinary occasion, I do hereby, in virtue of the power in me vested by the Constitution, convene both Houses of Congress. Senators and Representatives are therefore summoned to assemble at their respective chambers, at 12 o'clock, noon, on Thursday, the fourth day of July, next, then and there to consider and determine, such measures, as, in their wisdom, the public safety, and interest may seem to demand.

In Witness Whereof I have hereunto set my hand, and caused the Seal of the United States to be affixed.

[L.S.]   Done at the city of Washington this fifteenth day of April in the year of our Lord One thousand, Eight hundred and Sixty-one, and of the Independence of the United States the Eighty-fifth.

Abraham Lincoln

By the President
WILLIAM H. SEWARD, Secretary of State.

What were the thoughts and duties of the President in those first days when the nation split in two? Here are glimpses into the types of urgencies that confronted Lincoln—the never-ending streams of office-seekers, the newer streams of requests for appointments in army and navy, an autograph hunter to satisfy.

[c. April 15, 1861]

If there is any secessionist in your department, I wish you would remove him, and give the place to Mr. S. C. Atkinson; or, if, in any way you can give him a place, I shall be obliged.

Mr. Huffman, Collector.

A. Lincoln

Executive Mansion
April 15. 1861

Lieut. General Scott:
My dear Sir:

Col. Peter G. Washington tells me it is my duty to call an officer to the command of the District of Columbia militia now in the U. S. service, and that he, by rank in the District militia, is entitled to the place.

Is it my duty to call, or designate, such officer? and if yea, is Col. Washington, by military law, usage, or courtesy, entitled to the place?

Please investigate & inform me   Your Obt. Servt.

A. Lincoln

The Irrepressible Conflict

Executive Mansion.
April 15, 1861.

Hon. Sec. of Navy,
My dear Sir:—
I must relieve myself of the remaining California appointments. The charge against Samuel Bell is unsustained, and, in fact, in a good degree, disproved. I therefore request that you send me a commission for him as Navy Agent   Very truly,

A. Lincoln.

Executive Mansion
April 17, 1861

Hon. Atty. Gen.
My dear Sir:
Two of the judges for Nebraska have been appointed. Please send me your briefs as to the remaining judge and the attorney & marshal.   Yours truly,

A. Lincoln

Executive Mansion
April 17— 1861

Hon. Sec. of State—
Dear Sir
The Gov. of Nebraska has been appointed. Will you please send me your brief for *Secretary* of that territory?   Yours truly

A. Lincoln

Executive Mansion
April 17. 1861

Hon. Gideon Welles.
My dear Sir:
I have no reason to doubt that Mr. James S. Chalker, the bearer of this, is, as he says, the author of the "Wide Awake" order. As he is your townsman, you will know; and if it is all straight, please add your recommendation to mine, that he have some suitable appointment in the army, which he desires. When you shall have added your word, send the whole to the War Department. Yours truly

A. Lincoln

The Living Lincoln

Executive Mansion
April 18. 1861

Hon. W. H. Seward.
My dear Sir

You astonish me by saying Mr. Weed understands there is some alienation, or enmity of feeling, on my part towards him. Nothing like it. I shall be glad to see him any time, & have wondered at not having seen him here already. Yours very truly

A. Lincoln

Executive Mansion
April 18. 1861

Dr. Edward Wallace
Dear Sir

Having today concluded to appoint you Naval Officer at Philadelphia, I now, at the request of Dr. Luther, a strong and honorable competitor of yours, and at the urgent request of Gen. Cameron also, earnestly solicit you to appoint Col. John C. Meyers, of your own city, the deputy Naval Officer. You will personally oblige me by doing this, besides smoothing things which otherwise might be a little rough.   Yours very truly

A. Lincoln

Executive Mansion
April 18. 1861

Hon. Sec. of Navy
Dear Sir

Be here on Philadelphia appointments, at 12. o'clock today. Yours truly

A. Lincoln

White House, April 19, 1861.

Whoever in later times shall see this, and look at the date, will readily excuse the writer for not having indulged in sentiment, or poetry. With all kind regards for Miss Smith.

A. Lincoln.

The North responded with patriotic zeal; bands blared; volunteers rushed to enlist. In Maryland, however, Southern sympathizers growled

398

The Irrepressible Conflict

militantly; and on April 19 a Baltimore mob attacked the Sixth Massachusetts Infantry as it traveled to Washington. Four soldiers were killed, several wounded. A committee of fifty, representing the Young Men's Christian Associations of Baltimore, appealed to the President to avoid future disturbances. An aroused Lincoln faced the issue squarely.

April 22, 1861

You, gentlemen, come here to me to ask for peace on any terms, and yet have no word of condemnation for those who are making war on us. You express great horror of bloodshed, and yet would not lay a straw in the way of those who are organizing in Virginia and elsewhere to capture this city. The rebels attack Fort Sumter, and your citizens attack troops sent to the defense of the government, and the lives and property in Washington, and yet you would have me break my oath and surrender the government without a blow. There is no Washington in that—no Jackson in that—no manhood nor honor in that. I have no desire to invade the South; but I must have troops to defend this Capital. Geographically it lies surrounded by the soil of Maryland; and mathematically the necessity exists that they should come over her territory. Our men are not moles, and can't dig under the earth; they are not birds, and can't fly through the air. There is no way but to march across, and that they must do. But in doing this there is no need of collision. Keep your rowdies in Baltimore, and there will be no bloodshed. Go home and tell your people that if they will not attack us, we will not attack them; but if they do attack us, we will return it, and that severely.

Maryland's ex-senator, Reverdy Johnson, asked Lincoln to assure him that the forces gathering in Washington would not be used to invade Maryland or Virginia. There was no lack of stiffness in the spine of the man in the White House.

CONFIDENTIAL
Executive Mansion, April 24th 1861.
Hon. Reverdy Johnson
My dear Sir:
Your note of this morning is just received. I forebore to answer yours of the 22d because of my aversion (which I thought you

understood,) to getting on paper, and furnishing new grounds for misunderstanding.

I *do* say the sole purpose of bringing troops *here* is to defend this capital.

I *do* say I have no purpose to *invade* Virginia, with them or any other troops, as I understand the word *invasion*. But suppose Virginia sends her troops, or admits others through her borders, to assail this capital, am I not to repel them, even to the crossing of the Potomac if I can?

Suppose Virginia erects, or permits to be erected, batteries on the opposite shore, to bombard the city, are we to stand still and see it done? In a word, if Virginia strikes us, are we not to strike back, and as effectively as we can?

Again, are we not to hold Fort Monroe (for instance) if we can? I have no objection to declare a thousand times that I have no purpose to *invade* Virginia or any other state, but I do not mean to let them invade us without striking back. Yours truly

A. Lincoln

Even the high emotionalism of war could not persuade Lincoln to forsake hastily one of the most precious principles enunciated in the Bill of Rights.

Washington, April 25– 1861.

Lieutenant General Scott
My dear Sir:

The Maryland legislature assembles tomorrow at Annapolis; and, not improbably, will take action to arm the people of that state against the United States. The question has been submitted to, and considered by me, whether it would not be justifiable, upon the ground of necessary defence, for you, as commander in chief of the United States army, to arrest, or disperse the members of that body. I think it would *not* be justifiable; nor, efficient for the desired object.

First, they have a clearly legal right to assemble; and, we cannot know in advance, that their action will not be lawful, and peaceful. And if we wait until they shall *have* acted, their arrest, or dispersion, will not lessen the effect of their action.

Secondly, we *can* not permanently prevent their action. If we arrest them, we cannot long hold them as prisoners; and when liberated, they will immediately re-assemble, and take their action. And, precisely the same if we simply disperse them. They will immediately re-assemble in some other place.

I therefore conclude that it is only left to the commanding general to watch, and await their action, which, if it shall be to arm their people against the United States, he is to adopt the most prompt, and efficient means to counteract, even, if necessary, to the bombardment of their cities—and in the extremest necessity, the suspension of the writ of habeas corpus. Your Obedient Servant

A. Lincoln.

The defender of Sumter received a gracious note from his commander-in-chief.

Washington, D. C.
May 1. 1861

Major Robert Anderson
My dear Sir

A few days ago I caused an official letter to be written you through the War Department, expressive of the approbation and gratitude I considered due you and your command from this government.

I now write this, as a purely private and social letter, to say I shall be much gratified to see you here at your earliest convenience, when and where I can personally testify my appreciation of your services and fidelity; and, perhaps, explain some things on my part, which you may not have understood.

I shall also be very glad to see any of the officers who served with you at Fort Sumter, and whom it might be convenient and agreeable for you to invite to accompany you here. Your Obt. Servt.

A. Lincoln

Captain Gustavus V. Fox commanded the expedition that the President had sent to provision Sumter. It was characteristic of Lincoln to take the responsibility when a mission seemed to fail and to leave to others a sense of high duty well performed.

The Living Lincoln

Washington, D. C.
May 1, 1861

Capt. G. V. Fox
My dear Sir

I sincerely regret that the failure of the late attempt to provision Fort Sumter, should be the source of any annoyance to you. The practicability of your plan was not, in fact, brought to a test. By reason of a gale, well known in advance to be possible, and not improbable, the tugs, an essential part of the plan, never reached the ground; while, by an accident, for which you were in no wise responsible, and possibly I, to some extent was, you were deprived of a war vessel with her men, which you deemed of great importance to the enterprise.

I most cheerfully and truly declare that the failure of the undertaking has not lowered you a particle, while the qualities you developed in the effort, have greatly heightened you, in my estimation. For a daring and dangerous enterprise, of a similar character, you would, today, be the man, of all my acquaintances, whom I would select.

You and I both anticipated that the cause of the country would be advanced by making the attempt to provision Fort Sumter, even if it should fail; and it is no small consolation now to feel that our anticipation is justified by the result. Very truly your friend

A. Lincoln

Almost a month of war found Lincoln still bedeviled by problems of patronage. A note of irritability crept into his correspondence.

Executive Department
May 6, 1861

Hon. Sec. of Treasury
Dear Sir

The Secretary of State this moment introduces to me Mr. James Gordon Bennett, Jr. who tenders to the U. S. service, a fine yacht of 160 tons burthen. If you allow him an interview, which I ask for him, he will talk with you about putting some other vessels of the same class, into the service. We send this subject to you because we believe these vessels may be made most available in the revenue service. Yours truly

A. Lincoln

The Irrepressible Conflict

Washington D. C.
May 6, 1861

Hon. F. S. Corkran
My dear Sir

I am quite sure you are not aware how much I am disobliged by the refusal to give Mr. F. S. Evans a place in the custom house. I had no thought that the men to whom I had given the higher offices would be so ready to disoblige me. I still wish you would give Mr. Evans the place of deputy Naval Officer. Yours &c.

A. Lincoln

Executive Mansion
May 8. 1861

Hon. Comr. of Pensions,
My dear Sir

Once more I ask you to find a clerkship for a man of your own name—O. D. Barret, of Oswego Co. New York. Yours truly

A. Lincoln

Executive Mansion, May 8, 1861.

My dear Sir:

I am told there is an office in your department called "The Superintending Architect of the Treasury Department, connected with the Bureau of Construction," which is now held by a man of the name of Young, and wanted by a gentleman of the name of Christopher Adams.

Ought Mr. Young to be removed, and if yea, ought Mr. Adams to be appointed? Mr. Adams is magnificently recommended; but the great point in his favor is that Thurlow Weed and Horace Greeley join in recommending him. I suppose the like never happened before, and never will again; so that it is now or never. What say you? Yours truly,

A. Lincoln.

Washington, D. C.
May 8. 1861

Hon. W. B. Thomas.
Collector
My dear Sir

I do not *demand,* or *insist,* even, that you shall make any appointment in your office; but I would be much obliged if you could

The Living Lincoln

give a place to [blank] Ridgeway, or to such person as a widow sister of his—a Mrs. Corneau—would name. It is for her sake I make this request, she being an acquaintance and very highly valued friend of mine. Yours very truly

A. Lincoln

Executive Mansion, May 10, 1861.

My dear Sir:

I have felt myself obliged to refuse the post office at this place to my old friend Nathan Sargent, which wounds him, and consequently me, very deeply. He now says there is an office in your department, called the "Commissioner of Customs," which the incumbent, a Mr. Ingham, wishes to vacate. I will be much obliged if you agree for me to appoint Mr. Sargent to this place. Yours very truly,

A. Lincoln.

To Anderson, now commanding in Kentucky, Lincoln recommended an old friend who could be trusted with a military mission.

Washington, D. C.
May 14. 1861

Col. Robert Anderson
My dear Sir

Some time ago, and before it was arranged for you to go west, as now, the question was upon us how arms sent to Cincinnati for Kentuckians, could surely be put in the hands of friends, and not of enemies; and, for this purpose, and without their knowledge, Messrs Crittenden, Guthrie, and Joshua F. Speed, bearer of this, or any one of them, were designated to distribute the arms, in their discretion. After you left here last week it occurred to us that you could perform this service as safely, and perhaps more expeditiously, by reason that you will be on the spot, and will not have to wait for the co-operation of any one; and a direction was accordingly sent to the parties forwarding the arms to Cincinnati. It now occurs further that the kind assistance of these gentlemen may still be valuable to you in this, and perhaps other matters; and when it shall so appear to you it is hoped you will avail yourself of it. Mr. Speed, though less known to the world than the other gentlemen, is far better known to me than either of them; and I have the utmost confidence in his loyalty and integrity, and also in his judgment on any subject which he professes to understand. I think you will find him a most agreeable companion, and at the same time a most valuable assistant in our common cause. Yours very truly

A. Lincoln

In Missouri the same train often carried one car for Confederate recruits, another car for Union soldiers. Brigadier General William S. Harney was not Scott's choice as the man for this trouble spot. Harney was relieved April 21, restored to command May 8, and then placed on indefinite leave May 16. Lincoln appealed to a shrewd political mind for guidance.

PRIVATE
Washington D. C. May 18. 1861

Hon. F. P. Blair
My Dear Sir.

We have a good deal of anxiety here about St. Louis. I understand an order has gone from the War Department to you, to be delivered or withheld in your discretion, relieving Gen. Harney from his command. I was not quite satisfied with the order when it was made, though on the whole I thought it best to make it; but since then I have become more doubtful of its propriety. I do not write now to countermand it; but to say I wish you would withhold it, unless in your judgment the necessity to the contrary is very urgent.

There are several reasons for this. We better have him a *friend* than an *enemy*. It will dissatisfy a good many who otherwise would be quiet. More than all, we first relieved him, then restored him, & now if we relieve him again, the public will ask, "why all this vacillation."

Still if, in your judgment, it is *indispensable* let it be so. Yours very truly

A. Lincoln

At the suggestion of Robert Irwin, old Springfield friend, Lincoln supported the appointment of George Dennison for the coveted post of

The Living Lincoln

Naval Officer of New York. Parke Godwin (Lincoln deleted the name) charged Dennison with dishonesty. But Lincoln had been a lawyer and could see how circumstances might have trapped Dennison. The President's sense of fair play emerged in a letter to Salmon P. Chase.

Executive Mansion, May 18, 1861.

My dear Sir:

The suggestions of your note accompanying the commission for Mr. Dennison as Naval Officer at New York have been considered in the same spirit of kindness in which I know they were offered. They present the very difficulty which has embarrassed me from the first in the case: that Mr. Dennison has not the position in the public eye which would lead to the expectation of his receiving so high an office. I believe I have told you fully what it was, and is, that pressed me to appoint him: the urgent solicitation of an old friend who has served me all my life, and who has never before received or asked anything in return. His (Mr. Dennison's) good character was vouched for from the start by many at New York, including Mr. Opdyke.

At length, when I was, as it were, in the very act of appointing him, Mr.——— made a general charge of dishonesty against him. I pressed him for particulars, and it turned out that Mr. Dennison in his business as a lawyer had got some printing done for his clients, becoming personally responsible for the work, and had not paid for it when dunned. While this, if true, is certainly not to be commended, I believe the like might, in some cases, be proven upon me. They are a class of debts which our clients ought to pay, and when we are personally dunned for them we sometimes hang fire. Besides, Mr. Dennison went far toward a satisfactory explanation of one case; and while Mr.——— intimated that there were other cases, he did not specify them.

I consider that the charge of dishonesty has failed; and it now seems to me more difficult to change my purpose than if the charge had never been made. Yours as ever,

A. Lincoln.

Often the prosecution of the war became involved in local pressures, prejudices, and interests. In such moments Lincoln's quiet reasoning and honest humility helped to resolve tensions and conflicts. In the spirit of a national leader the President wrote to Governor Edwin D. Morgan of New York.

Washington, D. C.
May 20. 1861

His Excellency
Gov. E. D. Morgan
My dear Sir:

Yours of the 19th. is received. Your letter to the Secretary of War I have not seen.

To not shirk just responsibility, I suppose I ought to admit that I had much to do with the matter of which you complain.

The committee came here some time last week, saying there were fourteen regiments in N. Y. city, not within the 38 you were organizing; that *something must* be done with them,—that they could not safely keep them longer, nor safely disband them. I could not see—cannot yet—how it could wrong you, or the regiments you were raising, for these 14 to move forward at once, provided yours, too, should be received when ready. But aware of my own ignorance in military matters, I sent to Genl. Scott to get his opinion whether the thing could be safely done, both as to the question of confusion, and also whether the govt. could advantageously keep and use the *whole*. His answer was that the *whole* should come—of the 14, 5 to come here, & 9 to Fortress Monroe. I thought the whole difficulty was solved, and directed an order to be made accordingly. I was even pleased with it; because I had been trying for two weeks to begin the collecting of a force at Fortress Monroe, and it now appeared as if this would begin.

Next day & after the committee had gone, I was brought to fear that a squabble was to arise between you and the committee, by which neither your regiments nor theirs, would move in any reasonable time; to avoid which, I wrote one of the committee—Mr. Russell—to send them at once.

I am very loath to do any wrong; but I do not see yet wherein this was a wrong.

I certainly did not know that any regiments especially under your control were to be sent forward by the committee; but I do not perceive the *substantial* wrong, even in such a case. That it may be a *technical* wrong, I can readily understand—but we are in no condition to waste time on technicalities.

The Living Lincoln

The enthusiastic uprising of the people in our cause, is our great reliance; and we can not safely give it any check, even though it overflows, and runs in channels not laid down in any chart.

In ordering the 14 regiments forward, no intimation was intended, that you were failing in activity, or in any duty. On the contrary, I acknowledge you have done, & are doing nobly; and for which I tender you my sincere thanks. Yours very truly

A. Lincoln

The personal tragedy of war struck directly at Lincoln when his young friend, Colonel Elmer E. Ellsworth, was killed by Rebel sympathizers at Alexandria, Virginia on May 24. Lincoln turned to the sad task of writing to Ephraim D. and Phoebe Ellsworth, the colonel's parents. With beautiful tenderness the President sought to comfort the stricken couple.

Washington D. C.
May 25. 1861

To the Father and Mother of Col.
Elmer E. Ellsworth:
My dear Sir and Madam,
In the untimely loss of your noble son, our affliction here, is scarcely less than your own. So much of promised usefulness to one's country, and of bright hopes for one's self and friends, have rarely been so suddenly dashed, as in his fall. In size, in years, and in youthful appearance, a boy only, his power to command men, was surpassingly great. This power, combined with a fine intellect, an indomitable energy, and a taste altogether military, constituted in him, as seemed to me, the best natural talent, in that department, I ever knew. And yet he was singularly modest and deferential in social intercourse. My acquaintance with him began less than two years ago; yet through the latter half of the intervening period, it was as intimate as the disparity of our ages, and my engrossing engagements, would permit. To me, he appeared to have no indulgences or pastimes; and I never heard him utter a profane, or an intemperate word. What was conclusive of his good heart, he never forgot his parents. The honors he labored for so laudably, and, in the sad end, so gallantly gave his life, he meant for them, no less than for himself.

In the hope that it may be no intrusion upon the sacredness of your sorrow, I have ventured to address you this tribute to the memory of my young friend, and your brave and early fallen child.

May God give you that consolation which is beyond all earthly power. Sincerely your friend in a common affliction—

A. Lincoln

The extreme patience and tact with which Lincoln dealt with military protocol was reflected in a letter to General Scott. "Nothing can be more kind than your courtesy to me in a matter so exclusively within your own competency as the appointment of a quarter Master general," Scott replied. Meigs received the post.

PRIVATE

Executive Mansion. June 5. 1861

Lieut. Genl. Scott
My dear Sir

Doubtless you begin to understand how disagreeable it is to me to do a thing arbitrarily, when it is unsatisfactory to others associated with me.

I very much wish to appoint Col. Meigs Quarter-Master General, and yet Gen. Cameron does not quite consent. I have come to know Col. Meigs quite well for a short acquaintance, and, so far as I am capable of judging I do not know one who combines the qualities of masculine intellect, learning and experience of the right sort, and physical power of labor and endurance so well as he.

I know he has great confidence in you, always sustaining so far as I have observed, your opinions, against any differing ones.

You will lay me under one more obligation, if you can and will use your influence to remove Gen. Cameron's objection. I scarcely need tell you I have nothing personal in this, having never seen or heard of Col. Meigs, until about the end of last March. Your obt. Servt,

A. Lincoln

Doubtless no President ever entered the White House possessing less technical military knowledge, yet none surpassed Lincoln in an earnest effort to learn the profession of war. A small lot of Enfield pattern rifles was probably the subject of this letter to Captain John A. Dahlgren.

The Living Lincoln

Executive Mansion
June 10. 1861

Capt. Dahlgren,
My dear Sir
    You have seen Mr. Blunt's new gun. What think you of it? Would the government do well to purchase some of them? Should they be of the size of the one exhibited? or of different sizes? Yours truly

A. Lincoln

    I saw this gun myself, and witnessed some experiments with it; and I really think it worthy the attention of the government.
    June 10, 1861

A. Lincoln

    William P. Dole received from the President a list of shocking reasons why Anson Dart was not the man to supervise Indian affairs in the Washington Territory.

Executive Mansion
June [c. 11], 1861

Hon. W. P. Dole
Comr. of Ind. Affrs.
My dear Sir
    Some time ago I directed you to designate a suitable person to be Superintendent of Indian Affairs in Washington Territory, saying I would appoint the person you would so designate. You designated Anson Dart; and I now have the following reasons for not appointing him, all coming to my knowledge since I gave you the direction mentioned.
    1st.   A member of the present Cabinet tells me that during Genl. Taylor's administration Dart distinctly tendered money to him for his influence to get an office from Gen. Taylor.
    2nd.   A member of the present H.R. from Wisconsin writes me over his own name that Dart is an immoral and dishonest man; and that if nominated, he will go before the Senate and procure his rejection if possible.
    3rd.   One of the Senators from Oregon tells me that Dart's character is very bad in that county; that he is universally understood out there to have left his family at home, and kept a prosti-

tute while there; and that, if nominated, he will, in the Senate, procure his rejection if possible.

4th. The other Senator from Oregon tells me Dart's character is very odious and bad in that county; and that Dart, last winter, distinctly proposed to him that if he would procure his appointment to the Oregon Indian Superintendency, he would give him a thousand dollars the day the appointment should be made, and five hundred a year, as long as he should hold the office.

I presume you knew nothing of these things; and that neither you or I could knowingly be for such a man. Yours truly

A. Lincoln

Lincoln deleted the first two sentences before sending this letter to his brother-in-law, who, on August 8, was appointed captain and commissary of subsistence.

Washington D. C.   June 19, 1861

Hon. N. W. Edwards
My dear Sir:

It pains me to hear you speak of being ruined in your pecuniary affairs. I still hope you are injured only, and not ruined. When you wrote me some time ago in reference to looking up something in the Departments here, I thought I would inquire into the thing and write you, but the extraordinary pressure upon me diverted me from it, and soon it passed out of my mind. The thing you proposed, it seemed to me, I ought to understand myself before it was set on foot by my direction or permission; and I really had no *time* to make myself acquainted with it. Nor have I yet. And yet I am unwilling, of course, that you should be deprived of a chance to make something, if it can be done without injustice to the government, or to any individual. If you choose to come here and point out to me how this can be done, I shall not only not object, but shall be gratified to be able to oblige you. Your friend as ever

A. Lincoln

Lincoln affixed his name to a document first circulated in 1833. Reputedly President Harrison died before he could sign the certificate.

411

The Living Lincoln

[c. July 4, 1861]

TEMPERANCE DECLARATION OF ELEVEN PRESIDENTS
OF THE UNITED STATES

Being satisfied from observation and experience, as well as from medical testimony, that ardent spirits, as a drink, is not only needless, but hurtful and that the entire disuse of it would tend to promote the health, the virtue and happiness of the community: we hereby express our conviction, that should the citizens of the United States, and especially all young men, discountenance entirely the use of it, they would not only promote their own personal benefit, but the good of the country and of the world.

James Madison,	James K. Polk,
John Quincy Adams,	Zachary Taylor,
Andrew Jackson,	Millard Fillmore,
Martin Van Buren,	Franklin Pierce,
John Tyler,	James Buchanan,

Abraham Lincoln.

Four months after taking office, Lincoln convened a special session of Congress. The Springfield lawyer who had become the chief executive of a divided nation seized this opportunity to plead before the bar of history the rectitude of the course he had pursued. Clearly, deliberately, brilliantly, Lincoln argued the case against the South as the agressor, against Virginia as virtually an armed fortress of the Confederacy, and against attitudes in the border states that furthered disunion. Lincoln's special message spoke both to the North of 1861 and to American descendants, North and South, throughout the ages.

July 4, 1861

Fellow-citizens of the Senate and House of Representatives:

Having been convened on an extraordinary occasion, as authorized by the Constitution, your attention is not called to any ordinary subject of legislation.

At the beginning of the present presidential term, four months ago, the functions of the federal government were found to be generally suspended within the several states of South Carolina, Georgia, Alabama, Mississippi, Louisiana, and Florida, excepting only those of the Post Office Department.

Within these states, all the forts, arsenals, dockyards, custom-houses, and the like, including the movable and stationary property in, and about them, had been seized, and were held in open hostility to this government, excepting only Forts Pickens, Taylor, and Jefferson, on, and near the Florida coast, and Fort Sumter, in Charleston harbor, South Carolina. The forts thus seized had been put in improved condition; new ones had been built; and armed forces had been organized, and were organizing, all avowedly with the same hostile purpose.

The forts remaining in the possession of the federal government, in, and near, these states, were either besieged or menaced by warlike preparations; and especially Fort Sumter was nearly surrounded by well protected hostile batteries, with guns equal in quality to the best of its own, and outnumbering the latter as perhaps ten to one. A disproportionate share, of the federal muskets and rifles, had somehow found their way into these states, and had been seized, to be used against the government. Accumulations of the public revenue, lying within them, had been seized for the same object. The navy was scattered in distant seas; leaving but a very small part of it within the immediate reach of the government. Officers of the federal army and navy, had resigned in great numbers; and, of those resigning, a large proportion had taken up arms against the government. Simultaneously, and in connection with all this, the purpose to sever the federal Union, was openly avowed. In accordance with this purpose, an ordinance had been adopted in each of these states, declaring the states, respectively, to be separated from the national Union. A formula for instituting a combined government of these states had been promulgated; and this illegal organization, in the character of Confederate States, was already invoking recognition, aid, and intervention, from foreign powers.

Finding this condition of things, and believing it to be an imperative duty upon the incoming executive, to prevent, if possible, the consummation of such attempt to destroy the federal Union, a choice of means to that end became indispensable. This choice was made; and was declared in the inaugural address. The policy chosen looked to the exhaustion of all peaceful measures, before a resort to any stronger ones. It sought only to hold the public places and property, not already wrested from the government, and to collect the revenue; relying for the rest, on time, discussion, and the ballot-box. It promised a continuance of the mails, at government expense, to the very people who were resisting the government; and it gave repeated pledges against any disturbance to any of the people, or any of their rights. Of all that which a president might constitutionally, and justifiably, do in such a case, everything was foreborne, without which, it was believed possible to keep the government on foot.

On the 5th of March, (the present incumbent's first full day in office) a letter of Major Anderson, commanding at Fort Sumter, written on the 28th of February, and received at the War Department on the 4th of March, was, by that Department, placed in his hands. This letter expressed the professional opinion of the writer, that reinforcements could not be thrown into that fort within the time for his relief, rendered necessary by the limited supply of provisions, and with a view of holding possession of the same, with a force of less than twenty thousand good, and well-disciplined men. This opinion was concurred in by all the officers of his command; and their *memoranda* on the subject, were made enclosures of Major Anderson's letter. The whole was immediately laid before Lieutenant General Scott, who at once concurred with Major Anderson in opinion. On reflection, however, he took full time, consulting with other officers, both of the army and the navy; and, at the end of four days, came reluctantly, but decidedly, to the same conclusion as before. He also stated at the same time that no such sufficient force was then at the control of the government, or could be raised, and brought to the ground, within the time when the provisions in the fort would be exhausted. In a purely military point of view, this reduced the duty of the administration, in the case, to the mere matter of getting the garrison safely out of the fort.

It was believed, however, that to so abandon that position, under the circumstances, would be utterly ruinous; that the *necessity* under which it was to be done, would not be fully understood —that, by man, it would be construed as a part of a *voluntary* policy—that, at home, it would discourage the friends of the Union, embolden its adversaries, and go far to insure to the latter, a recognition abroad—that, in fact, it would be our national destruction consummated. This could not be allowed. Starvation was not yet upon the garrison; and ere it would be reached, *Fort Pickens* might be reinforced. This last, would be a clear indication of *policy,* and would better enable the country to accept the evacuation of Fort

Sumter, as a military *necessity*. An order was at once directed to be sent for the landing of the troops from the Steamship Brooklyn, into Fort Pickens. This order could not go by land, but must take the longer, and slower route by sea. The first return news from the order was received just one week before the fall of Fort Sumter. The news itself was, that the officer commanding the Sabine, to which vessel the troops had been transferred from the Brooklyn, acting upon some *quasi* armistice of the late administration, (and of the existence of which, the present administration, up to the time the order was dispatched, had only too vague and uncertain rumors, to fix attention) had refused to land the troops. To now reinforce Fort Pickens, before a crisis would be reached at Fort Sumter was impossible—rendered so by the near exhaustion of provisions in the latter-named fort. In precaution against such a conjuncture, the government had, a few days before, commenced preparing an expedition, as well adapted as might be, to relieve Fort Sumter, which expedition was intended to be ultimately used, or not, according to circumstances. The strongest anticipated case, for using it, was now presented; and it was resolved to send it forward. As had been intended, in this contingency, it was also resolved to notify the Governor of South Carolina, that he might expect an attempt would be made to provision the fort; and that, if the attempt should not be resisted, there would be no effort to throw in men, arms, or ammunition, without further notice, or in case of an attack upon the fort. This notice was accordingly given; whereupon the fort was attacked, and bombarded to its fall, without even awaiting the arrival of the provisioning expedition.

It is thus seen that the assault upon, and reduction of, Fort Sumter, was, in no sense, a matter of self-defense on the part of the assailants. They well knew that the garrison in the fort could, by no possibility, commit aggression upon them. They knew—they were expressly notified—that the giving of bread to the few brave and hungry men of the garrison, was all which would on that occasion be attempted, unless themselves, by resisting so much, should provoke more. They knew that this government desired to keep the garrison in the fort, not to assail them, but merely to maintain visible possession, and thus to preserve the Union from actual, and immediate dissolution—trusting, as herein-before stated, to time, discussion, and the ballot-box, for final adjustment; and they assailed, and reduced the fort, for precisely the reverse object—to drive out the visible authority of the federal Union, and thus force it to immediate dissolution.

That this was their object, the executive well understood; and having said to them in the inaugural address, "You can have no conflict without being yourselves the aggressors," he took pains, not only to keep this declaration good, but also to keep the case so free from the power of ingenious sophistry, as that the world should not be able to misunderstand it. By the affair at Fort Sumter, with its surrounding circumstances, that point was reached. Then, and thereby, the assailants of the government, began the conflict of arms, without a gun in sight, or in expectancy, to return their fire, save only the few in the fort, sent to that harbor, years before, for their own protection, and still ready to give that protection, in whatever was lawful. In this act, discarding all else, they have forced upon the country, the distinct issue: "Immediate dissolution, or blood."

Clearly Lincoln understood the fundamental issue of the war. Later, at Gettysburg, he would restate this conviction in words of lasting power and beauty.

And this issue embraces more than the fate of these United States. It presents to the whole family of man, the question, whether a constitutional republic, or a democracy—a government of the people, by the same people—can, or cannot, maintain its territorial integrity, against its own domestic foes. It presents the question, whether discontented individuals, too few in numbers to control administration, according to organic law, in any case, can always, upon the pretences made in this case, or on any other pretences, or arbitrarily, without any pretence, break up their government, and thus practically put an end to free government upon the earth. It forces us to ask: "Is there, in all republics, this inherent, and fatal weakness?" "Must a government, of necessity, be too *strong* for the liberties of its own people, or too *weak* to maintain its own existence?"

So viewing the issue, no choice was left but to call out the war power of the government; and so to resist force, employed for its destruction, by force, for its preservation. . . .

Soon after the first call for militia, it was considered a duty to authorize the commanding general, in proper cases, according to his discretion, to suspend the privilege of the writ of habeas corpus; or, in other words, to arrest, and detain, without resort to the ordinary processes and forms of law, such individuals as he might deem dangerous to the public safety. This authority has purposely been exercised but very sparingly. Nevertheless, the legality and propriety of what has been done under it, are questioned; and the attention of the country has been called to the proposition that one who is sworn to "take care that the laws be faithfully executed," should not himself violate them. Of course some consideration was given to the questions of power, and propriety, before this matter was acted upon. The whole of the laws which were required to be faithfully executed, were being resisted, and failing of execution, in nearly one-third of the states. Must they be allowed to finally fail of execution, even had it been perfectly clear, that by the use of the means necessary to their execution, some single law, made in such extreme tenderness of the citizen's liberty, that practically, it relieves more of the guilty, than of the innocent, should, to a very limited extent, be violated? To state the question more directly, are all the laws, *but one*, to go unexecuted, and the government itself go to pieces, lest that one be violated? Even in such a case, would not the official oath be broken, if the government should be overthrown, when it was believed that disregarding the single law, would tend to preserve it? But it was not believed that this question was presented. It was not believed that any law was violated. The provision of the Constitution that "The privilege of the writ of habeas corpus, shall not be suspended unless when, in cases of rebellion or invasion, the public safety may require it," is equivalent to a provision—is a provision—that such privilege may be suspended when, in cases of rebellion, or invasion, the public safety *does* require it. It was decided that we have a case of rebellion, and that the public safety does require the qualified suspension of the privilege of the writ which was authorized to be made. Now it is insisted that Congress, and not the executive, is vested with this power. But the Constitution itself, is silent as to which, or who, is to exercise the power; and as the provision was plainly made for a dangerous emergency, it cannot be believed the framers of the instrument intended, that in every case, the danger should run its course, until Congress could be called together; the very assembling of which might be prevented, as was intended in this case, by the rebellion. . . .

The Living Lincoln

Earlier in this message Lincoln had referred to "the power of ingenious sophistry" that had underscored the conspiracy of the Confederacy. Now with sledge-hammer blows he returned to this attack upon the makers of disunion.

It might seem, at first thought, to be of little difference whether the present movement at the South be called "secession" or "rebellion." The movers, however, well understand the difference. At the beginning, they knew they could never raise their treason to any respectable magnitude, by any name which implies *violation* of law. They knew their people possessed as much of moral sense, as much of devotion to law and order, and as much pride in, and reverence for, the history, and government, of their common country, as any other civilized, and patriotic people. They knew they could make no advancement directly in the teeth of these strong and noble sentiments. Accordingly they commenced by an insidious debauching of the public mind. They invented an ingenious sophism, which, if conceded, was followed by perfectly logical steps, through all the incidents, to the complete destruction of the Union. The sophism itself is, that any state of the Union may, *consistently* with the national Constitution, and therefore *lawfully,* and *peacefully,* withdraw from the Union, without the consent of the Union, or of any other state. The little disguise that the supposed right is to be exercised only for just cause, themselves to be the sole judge of its justice, is too thin to merit any notice.

With rebellion thus sugar-coated, they have been drugging the public mind of their section for more than thirty years; and, until at length, they have brought many good men to a willingness to take up arms against the government the day *after* some assemblage of men have enacted the farcical pretence of taking their state out of the Union, who could have been brought to no such thing the day *before*.

This sophism derives much—perhaps the whole—of its currency, from the assumption, that there is some omnipotent, and sacred supremacy, pertaining to a *state*—to each state of our federal Union. Our states have neither more, nor less power, than that reserved to them, in the Union, by the Constitution—no one of them ever having been a state *out* of the Union. The original ones passed into the Union even *before* they cast off their British colonial dependence; and the new ones each came into the Union

418

directly from a condition of dependence, excepting Texas. And even Texas, in its temporary independence, was never designated a state. The new ones only took the designation of states, on coming into the Union, while that name was first adopted for the old ones, in, and by, the Declaration of Independence. Therein the "United Colonies" were declared to be "Free and Independent States"; but, even then, the object plainly was not to declare their independence of *one another,* or of the *Union;* but directly the contrary, as their mutual pledge, and their mutual action, before, at the time, and afterwards, abundantly show. The express plighting of faith, by each and all of the original thirteen, in the Articles of Confederation, two years later, that the Union shall be perpetual, is most conclusive. Having never been states, either in substance, or in name, *outside* of the Union, whence this magical omnipotence of "state rights," asserting a claim of power to lawfully destroy the Union itself? Much is said about the "sovereignty" of the states; but the word, even, is not in the national Constitution; nor, as is believed, in any of the state constitutions. What is a "sovereignty," in the political sense of the term? Would it be far wrong to define it "A political community, without a political superior"? Tested by this, no one of our states, except Texas, ever was a sovereignty. And even Texas gave up the character on coming into the Union; by which act, she acknowledged the Constitution of the United States, and the laws and treaties of the United States made in pursuance of the Constitution, to be, for her, the supreme law of the land. The states have their *status* IN the Union, and they have no other *legal status*. If they break from this, they can only do so against law, and by revolution. The Union, and not themselves separately, procured their independence, and their liberty. By conquest, or purchase, the Union gave each of them, whatever of independence, and liberty, it has. The Union is older than any of the states; and, in fact it created them as states. Originally, some dependent colonies made the Union; and, in turn, the Union threw off their old dependence, for them, and made them states, such as they are. Not one of them ever had a state constitution, independent of the Union. Of course, it is not forgotten that all the new states framed their constitutions, before they entered the Union; nevertheless, dependent upon, and preparatory to, coming into the Union.

Unquestionably the states have the powers, and rights, reserved to them in, and by the national Constitution; but among these, surely, are not included all conceivable powers, however mischievous, or destructive; but, at most, such only, as were known in the world, at the time, as governmental powers; and certainly, a power to destroy the government itself, had never been known as a governmental—as a merely administrative power. This relative matter of national power, and state rights, as a principle, is no other than the principle of *generality,* and *locality.* Whatever concerns the whole, should be confided to the whole—to the general government; while, whatever concerns *only* the state, should be left exclusively, to the state. This is all there is of original principle about it. Whether the national Constitution, in defining boundaries between the two, has applied the principle with exact accuracy, is not to be questioned. We are all bound by that defining, without question.

What is now combatted, is the position that secession is *consistent* with the Constitution—is *lawful,* and *peaceful.* It is not contended that there is any express law for it; and nothing should ever be implied as law, which leads to unjust, or absurd consequences. . . .

The seceders insist that our Constitution admits of secession. They have assumed to make a national constitution of their own, in which, of necessity, they have either *discarded,* or *retained,* the right of secession, as they insist, it exists in ours. If they have discarded it, they thereby admit that, on principle, it ought not to be in ours. If they have retained it, by their own construction of ours they show that to be consistent they must secede from one another, whenever they shall find it the easiest way of settling their debts, or effecting any other selfish, or unjust object. The principle itself is one of disintegration, and upon which no government can possibly endure. . . .

It may be affirmed, without extravagance, that the free institutions we enjoy, have developed the powers, and improved the condition, of our whole people, beyond any example in the world. Of this we now have a striking, and an impressive illustration. So large an army as the government has now on foot, was never before known, without a soldier in it, but who had taken his place there, of his own free choice. But more than this: there are many single regiments whose members, one and another, possess full practical knowledge of all the arts, sciences, professions, and whatever else, whether useful or elegant, is known in the world; and there is scarcely one, from which there could not be selected, a president, a cabinet, a congress, and perhaps a court, abundantly competent to administer the government itself. Nor do I say this is not true, also, in the army of our late friends, now adversaries, in this contest; but if it is, so much better the reason why the government, which has conferred such benefits on both them and us, should not be broken up. Whoever, in any section, proposes to abandon such a government, would do well to consider, in deference to what principle it is, that he does it—what better he is likely to get in its stead—whether the substitute will give, or be intended to give, so much of good to the people. There are some foreshadowings on this subject. Our adversaries have adopted some Declarations of Independence; in which, unlike the good old one, penned by Jefferson, they omit the words "all men are created equal." Why? They have adopted a temporary national constitution, in the preamble of which, unlike our good old one, signed by Washington, they omit "We, the people," and substitute "We, the deputies of the sovereign and independent states." Why? Why this deliberate pressing out of view, the rights of men, and the authority of the people?

Lincoln's message now approached its conclusion. To every man, woman and child who must sacrifice to sustain the Union he gave a special dignity.

This is essentially a people's contest. On the side of the Union, it is a struggle for maintaining in the world, that form, and substance of government, whose leading object is, to elevate the condition of men—to lift artificial weights from all shoulders—to clear the paths of laudable pursuit for all—to afford all, an unfettered start, and a fair chance, in the race of life. Yielding to partial, and temporary departures, from necessity, this is the leading object of the government for whose existence we contend.

I am most happy to believe that the plain people understand, and appreciate this. It is worthy of note, that while in this, the government's hour of trial, large numbers of those in the army and navy, who have been favored with the offices, have resigned, and proved false to the hand which had pampered them, not one common soldier, or common sailor is known to have deserted his flag.

Great honor is due to those officers who remain true, despite the example of their treacherous associates; but the greatest honor, and most important fact of all, is the unanimous firmness of the common soldiers, and common sailors. To the last man, so far as known, they have successfully resisted the traitorous efforts of those, whose commands, but an hour before, they obeyed as absolute law. This is the patriotic instinct of the plain people. They understand, without an argument, that destroying the government, which was made by Washington, means no good to them.

Our popular government has often been called an experiment. Two points in it, our people have already settled—the successful *establishing*, and the successful *administering* of it. One still remains—its successful *maintenance* against a formidable attempt to overthrow it. It is now for them to demonstrate to the world, that those who can fairly carry an election, can also suppress a rebellion —that ballots are the rightful, and peaceful, successors of bullets; and that when ballots have fairly, and constitutionally, decided, there can be no successful appeal, back to bullets; that there can can be no successful appeal, except to ballots themselves, at succeeding elections. Such will be a great lesson of peace; teaching men that what they cannot take by an election, neither can they take it by a war—teaching all, the folly of being the beginners of a war.

Lest there be some uneasiness in the minds of candid men, as to what is to be the course of the government, towards the Southern states, *after* the rebellion shall have been suppressed, the executive deems it proper to say, it will be his purpose then, as ever, to be guided by the Constitution, and the laws; and that he probably will have no different understanding of the powers, and duties of the federal government, relatively to the rights of the states, and the people, under the Constitution, than that expressed in the inaugural address.

He desires to preserve the government, that it may be administered for all, as it was administered by the men who made it. Loyal citizens everywhere, have the right to claim this of their government; and the government has no right to withhold, or neglect it. It is not perceived that, in giving it, there is any coercion, any conquest, or any subjugation, in any just sense of those terms.

The Constitution provides, and all the states have accepted the provision, that "The United States shall guarantee to every state in this Union a republican form of government." But, if a state may lawfully go out of the Union, having done so, it may also discard the republican form of government; so that to prevent its going out, is an indispensable *means,* to the *end,* of maintaining the guaranty mentioned; and when an end is lawful and obligatory, the indispensable means to it, are also lawful, and obligatory.

It was with the deepest regret that the executive found the duty of employing the war power, in defence of the government, forced upon him. He could but perform this duty, or surrender the existence of the government. No compromise, by public servants, could, in this case, be a cure; not that compromises are not often proper, but that no popular government can long survive a marked precedent, that those who carry an election, can only save the government from immediate destruction, by giving up the main point, upon which the people gave the election. The people themselves, and not their servants, can safely reverse their own deliberate decisions. As a private citizen, the executive could not have consented that these institutions shall perish; much less could he, in betrayal of so vast, and so sacred a trust, as these free people had confided to him. He felt that he had no moral right to shrink; nor even to count the chances of his own life, in what might follow. In full view of his great responsibility, he has, so far, done what he has deemed his duty. You will now, according to your own judgment, perform yours. He sincerely hopes that your views, and your action, may so accord with his, as to assure all faithful citizens, who have been disturbed in their rights, of a certain, and speedy restoration to them, under the Constitution, and the laws.

And having thus chosen our course, without guile, and with pure purpose, let us renew our trust in God, and go forward without fear, and with manly hearts.

Abraham Lincoln

July 4, 1861.

"Father Abraham" writes an indulgent note.

[*July 4, 1861*]

Horatio N. Taft, the boy-bearer of this, wishes to be a page. By the within, his father seems to be willing; and, as he is a playmate of my little boys, I am quite willing.

A. Lincoln

The Living Lincoln

Within ninety days, sang Northern patriots as they joined the army, Jeff Davis would be dangled from a sour apple tree. Lincoln was eager to strike a blow, though Scott argued that the army was not ready. Then at Manassas Junction the Union suffered the humiliating defeat of First Bull Run. It was not easy afterward for Lincoln to forget how Scott had called himself the "greatest coward in America." An anguished and gallant old soldier poured out his heart to the President: "I deserve removal because I did not stand up, when my army was not in condition to fight, and resist it to the last." Alone in the White House, what might Lincoln think? Four days after Bull Run, he completed these memoranda of military policy suggested by the North's first defeat.

July 23. 1861.

1 Let the plan for making the blockade effective be pushed forward with all possible dispatch.

2 Let the volunteer forces at Fort Monroe & vicinity—under Genl. Butler—be constantly drilled, disciplined, and instructed without more for the present.

3. Let Baltimore be held, as now, with a gentle, but firm, and certain hand.

4 Let the force now under Patterson, or Banks, be strengthened, and made secure in its possition.

5. Let the forces in Western Virginia act, till further orders, according to instructions, or orders from Gen. McClellan.

6. Let Gen. Fremont push forward his organization, and operations in the West as rapidly as possible, giving rather special attention to Missouri.

7 Let the forces late before Manassas, except the three-months men, be reorganized as rapidly as possible, in their camps here and about Arlington.

8. Let the three-months forces, who decline to enter the longer service, be discharged as rapidly as circumstances will permit.

9 Let the new volunteer forces be brought forward as fast as possible; and especially into the camps on the two sides of the river here.

July 27, 1861

When the foregoing shall have been substantially attended to—
1. Let Manassas Junction, (or some point on one or other of

the railroads near it;); and Strasburg, be seized, and permanently held, with an open line from Washington to Manassas; and an open line from Harper's Ferry to Strasburg—the military men to find the way of doing these.

    2.   This done, a joint movement from Cairo on Memphis; and from Cincinnati on East Tennessee.

Tired lines lengthened around the President's eyes. The urgency of the war seemed to quicken and to pile up details large and small. To each Lincoln turned, weighing the consequences carefully.

July 25, 1861

Let the four artillery companies which have been in actual service at Cairo for some time, be mustered in regularly for the three years service, and so done that they be paid from the beginning of their actual service.

A. Lincoln

July 25 1861

Will Lieut. Genl. Scott please see Professor Lowe, once more about his balloon?

A Lincoln

July 25, 1861.

July 25, 1861

Hon: Sec. of State
Dear Sir
    The bearer of this wishes to have a son appointed consul to Spezia; and if you have no objection, I have none.

A. Lincoln

July 25. 1861

July 25, 1861

If the Adjutant General can get the regiment together on the terms proposed, I think it will be a good corps, and ought to be accepted.

A. Lincoln

July 25, 1861.

The Living Lincoln

c. July 25, 1861

Col. Wallace, bearer of this, commands one of the Illinois regiments, just ordered to be received, wishes a copy of the order to take to Illinois. Please let him have it.

A. Lincoln

Executive Mansion
July 26, 1861.

Hon. Secretary of War
Dear Sir

Please let Reuben B. Hatch of Illinois, be appointed an Assistant Quartermaster, and assigned to the brigade of General Prentiss, in Illinois.

Also let Speed Butler of Illinois be appointed Commissary of Subsistence, and assigned to the brigade of General Pope, in Illinois.

Your obedient Servant

Abraham Lincoln.

July 26, 1861

Lewis E. Johnson, desires to be a Paymaster of Volunteers. He is the son of Hon. Reverdy Johnson who much desires the appointment.

A. Lincoln.

July 26, 1861.

I wish this to be done when the time comes.   *A. L.*

The inadequacies of the Union army were found in all branches, among them the Medical Corps. One of the grimmest battles that had to be won, one observer said, was to save Union soldiers from "death from the frying pan." To touchy General John C. Fremont, commanding the Department of Missouri, Lincoln artfully broached the subject of medical supervision.

Washington, August 2d 1861.

To Major Genl. Fremont,

Godfrey Aigner, M.D. has been selected by the Sanitary Commission to visit the camps of a portion of your department, to report upon circumstances affecting their health, and to advise the officers in regard to means for sustaining and improving the sanitary condition of their men. As Doctor Aigner will only act consistently with the strictest rules of military discipline, and as it will be his duty to sustain your authority and meet your wishes in all respects, your countenance, aid and support is confidently requested to be extended to him, in facilitating his movements and strengthening his influence. Yours truly

A. Lincoln

The rising exigencies of war did not lessen for the President the haggling for appointments, both civil and military. This sampling covers a period of twelve days.

Executive Mansion
August 10. 1861

Hon. Sec. of War.
My dear Sir
　　If Ohio is not already overstocked with paymasterships of Volunteers, let Richard P. L. Baber have one. I personally wish this done. Yours truly

A. Lincoln

Executive Mansion
August 10. 1861

Hon. Sec. of War
My dear Sir
　　It is said Capt. McKnabb, or, McNabb, in Utah, has been dismissed from the army on the charge of being a disunionist; and that he wishes a hearing to enable him to show that the charge is false. Fair play is a jewel. Give him a chance if you can. Yours truly

A. Lincoln

Executive Mansion
August 13. 1861

Hon. Sec. of War
My dear Sir
　　Let *now* Brigadier Genl. David Hunter be a Major General of Volunteers to be assigned to a Division of Illinois Volunteers. Also

let George H. Stoneman, and William F. Smith, both now in the service, each be a Brigadier General of Volunteers. Also Henry W. Benham, a Brigadier General of Volunteers. I mean Capt. Benham, so often spoken of, and am not sure I have his Christian name correct; but you will know. Yours truly

A. Lincoln

Why may not this young man have Venice, which is only $750– or Nice, which has fees only? Senator Pomeroy is very anxious for it.

A. Lincoln

Aug. 13. 1861.

August 14, 1861

It is said Capt. Dallas was rejected by the Senate through mistake. If Gen. Thomas can be satisfied, to a reasonable degree of certainty, that this is true, let Capt. Dallas be reappointed at once.

A. Lincoln

Aug. 14. 1861

Washington, August 15, 1861

Hon. James Pollock
My dear Sir:

You must make a job of it, and provide a place for the bearer of this, Elias Wampole. Make a job of it with the Collector, and have it done. You *can* do it for me, and you *must*. Yours as ever.

A. Lincoln

Executive Mansion
August 17, 1861

Hon. Sec. of War
My dear Sir

These gentlemen—Samuel Gamage, and Charles R. Saunders— are Californians, who were well recommended for offices which have been given to others. I am now willing that they should be appointed Paymasters of Volunteers, as Californians. Yours truly

A. Lincoln

The Irrepressible Conflict

Executive Mansion, August 17, 1861.

Hon. Secretary of War:

My dear Sir:

Unless there be reason to the contrary, not known to me, make out a commission for Simon B. Buckner, of Kentucky, as a Brigadier General of Volunteers. It is to be put into the hands of General Anderson, and delivered to General Buckner or not, at the discretion of General Anderson. Of course it is to remain a secret unless and until the commission is delivered. Yours, truly,

A. Lincoln.

Executive Mansion
August 17– 1861

Hon. Sec. of War

My dear Sir–

Let Henry Wager Halleck, of California, be appointed a Major General in the *Regular Army*. I make this appointment on Gen. Scott's recommendation; and I am sure he said to me verbally that the appointment is to be in the Regular Army, though a memorandum on the subject handed me by one of his aids, says "of volunteers." Perhaps the Adjt. Genl. should communicate with Genl. Scott, on the question. Yours truly

A. Lincoln

August 17, 1861

I repeat that if Adjutant Genl. Thomas is reasonably well satisfied that Capt. Dallas was rejected by the Senate through misapprehension of facts, he is to be re-appointed. It is the opinion of the Adjutant General, and of Genl. Franklin, as shown by what they have written within, that he is a good officer. Aug. 17. 1861.

A. Lincoln

Executive Mansion
August 19, 1861

Hon. Sec. of War

My dear Sir

At the request of Brigadier General Anderson, I have con-

429

cluded to appoint George H. Thomas, of the 2nd. Cavalry, a Brigadier General of Volunteers.

Also, let the Hon. James Shields, now of California, be appointed a Brigadier General of Volunteers.

Also, Col. Michael Corcoran, now a prisoner at Richmond. Yours truly

A. Lincoln

Executive Mansion
August 20. 1861

Hon. Sec. of State
My dear Sir.

Mr. Zebina Eastman, of Chicago, Ills. is one of the earliest, and most efficient of our free-soil laborers. If a position, with even moderate pay, could be found for him in England, he is just the man to reach the sympathies of the English people, to the extent that he can come in contact with them. He is more than a common man, in his sphere; and I shall be very glad if you can find out, or fix out for him, some such place as I have indicated. Yours truly

A. Lincoln

Executive Mansion, August 22, 1861.

Hon. Secretary of War.
Sir:

Victor B. Bell, now of Colorado, is one of my most valued friends; and one of the best, if not the very best clerk I ever knew. I would like for him to be an Asst. Quarter Master or Commissary of Subsistence of Volunteers.

Can you not fix it for me? Yours truly,

A. Lincoln.

August 22, 1861.

The primary necessity of the war in the West was to keep Kentucky and Missouri neutral until the Union sentiment in these states could prevail. The situation in Kentucky was peculiar: although the state legislature remained loyal to the Union, the Governor, Beriah Magoffin, openly sympathized with the Confederacy. Magoffin protested Union recruitment and the establishment of camps in Kentucky, but Lincoln stood firm.

Washington, D. C.
August 24. 1861

To His Excellency
B. Magoffin
Governor of the State of Kentucky.
Sir:

Your letter of the 19th. inst. in which you *"urge the removal from the limits of Kentucky of the military force now organized, and in camp within said state"* is received.

I may not possess full and precisely accurate knowledge upon this subject; but I believe it is true that there is a military force in camp within Kentucky, acting by authority of the United States, which force is not very large, and is not now being augmented.

I also believe that some arms have been furnished to this force by the United States.

I also believe this force consists exclusively of Kentuckians, having their camp in the immediate vicinity of their own homes, and not assailing, or menacing, any of the good people of Kentucky.

In all I have done in the premises, I have acted upon the urgent solicitation of many Kentuckians, and in accordance with what I believed, and still believe, to be the wish of a majority of all the Union-loving people of Kentucky.

While I have conversed on this subject with many eminent men of Kentucky, including a large majority of her members of Congress, I do not remember that any one of them, or any other person, except your Excellency and the bearers of your Excellency's letter, has urged me to remove the military force from Kentucky, or to disband it. One other very worthy citizen of Kentucky did solicit me to have the augmenting of the force suspended for a time.

Taking all the means within my reach to form a judgment, I do not believe it is the popular wish of Kentucky that this force shall be removed beyond her limits; and, with this impression, I must respectfully decline to so remove it.

The Living Lincoln

I most cordially sympathize with your Excellency, in the wish to preserve the peace of my own native state, Kentucky; but it is with regret I search, and cannot find, in your not-very-short letter, any declaration, or intimation, that you entertain any desire for the preservation of the federal Union.* Your Obedient Servant,

A. Lincoln

In command in Missouri was John C. Fremont, famed as an explorer and the presidential standard bearer for the Republican party in 1856. Fremont spoke extravagantly of the expedition he planned to capture New Orleans, but his ability to deal with the Confederate forces that he immediately opposed was thoroughly ineffective. Then, without authority, Fremont issued a proclamation that gave him the power under martial law to seize the property of all persons in Missouri who had enlisted with the Confederate cause and to free their slaves. To anti-slavery radicals Fremont was overnight a hero; to Lincoln, who knew that Democrats in the North would support the war on no basis except preservation of the Union, and who well could fear for what Fremont's action might do to crush Unionist sentiment in Kentucky, the proclamation threatened disastrous repercussions. The President had no intention of permitting a general in the field to usurp his authority.

PRIVATE AND CONFIDENTIAL

Washington D. C. Sept. 2, 1861.

Major General Fremont:
My dear Sir:

Two points in your proclamation of August 30th give me some anxiety. First, should you shoot a man, according to the proclama· tion, the Confederates would very certainly shoot our best man in their hands in retaliation; and so, man for man, indefinitely. It is therefore my order that you allow no man to be shot, under the proclamation, without first having my approbation or consent.

Secondly, I think there is great danger that the closing paragraph, in relation to the confiscation of property, and the liberating slaves of traitorous owners, will alarm our Southern Union friends, and turn them against us—perhaps ruin our rather fair prospect for Kentucky. Allow me therefore to ask, that you will as of your own motion, modify that paragraph so as to conform to the *first* and

---

* Magoffin resigned the following August.

fourth sections of the act of Congress, entitled, "An act to confiscate property used for insurrectionary purposes," approved August, 6th, 1861, and a copy of which act I herewith send you. This letter is written in a spirit of caution and not of censure.

I send it by a special messenger, in order that it may certainly and speedily reach you. Yours very truly

A. Lincoln

[ENDORSEMENT]

Copy of letter sent to Gen. Fremont, by special messenger leaving Washington Sep. 3. 1861.

Fremont's behavior in St. Louis became scandalous. His headquarters resembled a showy court over which he presided like a disdainful potentate. Scott thought that if General David Hunter, then commanding at Rolla, Missouri, could be transferred to Fremont's staff "some rash measures might be staved off." Probably with tongue in cheek, Lincoln acquiesced.

Washington D. C. Sep. 9. 1861

Major Genl. David Hunter
My dear Sir:

Gen. Fremont needs assistance which it is difficult to give him. He is losing the confidence of men near him, whose support any man in his position must have to be successful. His cardinal mistake is that he isolates himself, & allows nobody to see him; and by which he does not know what is going on in the very matter he is dealing with. He needs to have, by his side, a man of large experience. Will you not, for me, take that place? Your rank is one grade too high to be ordered to it; but will you not serve the country, and oblige me, by taking it voluntarily?

[No Signature]

Section 4 of the Act of Congress, August 6, 1861, to which Lincoln referred in this letter to Fremont, read as follows: "Provided that any person held to service or labor, by laws of any state, to another, the owner to such claim to labor loses his claim if person held to labor is employed in hostile service against the government."

The Living Lincoln

Washington, D. C.
Sep. 11. 1861.

Major General John C. Fremont.
Sir:

Yours of the 8th. in answer to mine of 2nd. inst. is just received. Assuming that you, upon the ground, could better judge of the necessities of your position than I could at this distance, on seeing your proclamation of August 30th. I perceived no general objection to it. The particular clause, however, in relation to the confiscation of property and the liberation of slaves, appeared to me to be objectionable, in its nonconformity to the Act of Congress passed the 6th. of last August upon the same subjects; and hence I wrote you expressing my wish that that clause should be modified accordingly. Your answer, just received, expresses the preference on your part, that I should make an open order for the modification, which I very cheerfully do. It is therefore ordered that the said clause of said proclamation be so modified, held, and construed, as to conform to, and not to transcend, the provisions on the same subject contained in the act of Congress entitled "An Act to confiscate property used for insurrectionary purposes" Approved, August 6. 1861; and that said act be published at length with this order. Your Obt. Servt

A. Lincoln.

Lincoln matched the anger of the Fremonts with a temperate statement of fact.

Washington, D. C. Sep. 12. 1861

Mrs. Genl. Fremont
My dear Madam—

Your two notes of today are before me. I answered the letter you bore me from Gen. Fremont, on yesterday; and not hearing from you during the day, I sent the answer to him by mail.

It is not exactly correct, as you say you were told by the elder Mr. Blair, to say that I sent Postmaster General Blair to St. Louis to examine into that Department, and report. Postmaster General Blair did go, with my approbation, to see and converse with Gen. Fremont as a friend.

I do not feel authorized to furnish you with copies of letters in my possession without the consent of the writers.

The Irrepressible Conflict

No impression has been made on my mind against the honor or integrity of Gen. Fremont; and I now enter my protest against being understood as acting in any hostility towards him. Your Obt. Servt

A. Lincoln

Orville H. Browning had been appointed to fill in the Senate the unexpired term of Stephen A. Douglas. For attacking the revocation of Fremont's proclamation, Browning drew a reprimand as sharp as a slap in the face.

Executive Mansion
Washington Sept 22d 1861.

Hon. O. H. Browning
My dear Sir

Yours of the 17th is just received; and coming from you, I confess it astonishes me. That you should object to my adhering to a law, which you had assisted in making, and presenting to me, less than a month before, is odd enough. But this is a very small part. Genl. Fremont's proclamation, as to confiscation of property, and the liberation of slaves, is *purely political,* and not within the range of *military* law, or necessity. If a commanding general finds a necessity to seize the farm of a private owner, for a pasture, an encampment, or a fortification, he has the right to do so, and to so hold it, as long as the necessity lasts; and this is within military law, because within military necessity. But to say the farm shall no longer belong to the owner, or his heirs forever; and this as well when the farm is not needed for military purposes as when it is, is purely political, without the savor of military law about it. And the same is true of slaves. If the general needs them, he can seize them, and use them; but when the need is past, it is not for him to fix their permanent future condition. That must be settled according to laws made by lawmakers, and not by military proclamations. The proclamation in the point in question, is simply "dictatorship." It assumes that the general may do *anything* he pleases—confiscate the lands and free the slaves of *loyal* people, as well as of disloyal ones. And going the whole figure I have no doubt would be more popular with some thoughtless people, than that which has been done! But I cannot assume this reckless position; nor allow others to assume it on my responsibility. You speak of it as being the only means of *saving* the government. On the contrary it is itself the surrender of the government. Can it be pretended that it is any longer the government of the U. S.—any government of Constitution and laws,—wherein a general, or a President, may make permanent rules of property by proclamation?

I do not say Congress might not with propriety pass a law, on the point, just such as General Fremont proclaimed. I do not say I might not, as a member of Congress, vote for it. What I object to, is, that I as President, shall expressly or impliedly seize and exercise the permanent legislative functions of the government.

So much as to principle. Now as to policy. No doubt the thing was popular in some quarters, and would have been more so if it had been a general declaration of emancipation. The Kentucky legislature would not budge till that proclamation was modified; and Gen. Anderson telegraphed me that on the news of Gen. Fremont having actually issued deeds of manumission, a whole company of our volunteers threw down their arms and disbanded. I was so assured, as to think it probable, that the very arms we had furnished Kentucky would be turned against us. I think to lose Kentucky is nearly the same as to lose the whole game. Kentucky gone, we cannot hold Missouri, nor, as I think, Maryland. These all against us, and the job on our hands is too large for us. We would as well consent to separation at once, including the surrender of this capital. On the contrary, if you will give up your restlessness for new positions, and back me manfully on the grounds upon which you and other kind friends gave me the election, and have approved in my public documents, we shall go through triumphantly.

You must not understand I took my course on the proclamation *because* of Kentucky. I took the same ground in a private letter to General Fremont before I heard from Kentucky.

You think I am inconsistent because I did not also forbid Gen. Fremont to shoot men under the proclamation. I understand that part to be within military law; but I also think, and so privately wrote Gen. Fremont, that it is impolitic in this, that our adversaries have the power, and will certainly exercise it, to shoot as many of our men as we shoot of theirs. I did not say this in the public letter, because it is a subject I prefer not to discuss in the hearing of our enemies.

The Irrepressible Conflict

There has been no thought of removing Gen. Fremont on any ground connected with his proclamation; and if there has been any wish for his removal on any ground, our mutual friend Sam. Glover can probably tell you what it was. I hope no real necessity for it exists on any ground.

Suppose you write to Hurlbut and get him to resign. Your friend as ever

A. Lincoln

The hot, muggy summer passed. After Bull Run confidence mounted steadily in the South. Confederate enlistments almost kept pace with enlistments in the North. By the autumn of 1861 Rebel forces under arms numbered about 150,000 and Union forces about 180,000. Lincoln lived now with one problem uppermost in his mind—how could the North strike a telling blow in battle? By October he had worked out a memorandum for a campaign that wisely co-ordinated the employment of forces east and west.

c. October 1, 1861

On, or about the 5th. of October, (the exact day to be determined hereafter) I wish a movement made to seize and hold a point on the railroad connecting Virginia and Tennessee, near the Mountain pass called Cumberland Gap.

That point is now guarded against us by Zollicoffer, with 6000 or 8000, rebels at Barboursville, Kentucky, say twenty-five miles from the Gap towards Lexington.

We have a force of 5000 or 6000, under General Thomas, at Camp Dick Robinson, about twenty-five miles from Lexington, and seventy-five from Zollicoffer's camp on the road between the two, which is not a railroad, anywhere between Lexington and the point to be seized—and along the whole length of which the Union sentiment among the people largely predominates.

We have military possession of the railroads from Cincinnati to Lexington, and from Louisville to Lexington, and some Home Guards under General Crittenden are on the latter line.

We have possession of the railroad from Louisville to Nashville, Tenn, so far as Muldrough's Hill, about forty miles, and the rebels have possession of that road all south of there. At the Hill we have a force of 8000 under Gen. Sherman; and about an equal

437

force of rebels is a very short distance south, under Gen. Buckner.

We have a large force at Paducah, and a smaller at Fort Holt, both on the Kentucky side, with some at Bird's Point, Cairo, Mound City, Evansville, & New Albany, all on the other side; and all which, with the gun-boats on the river, are, perhaps, sufficient to guard the Ohio from Louisville to its mouth.

About supplies of troops, my general idea is that all from Wisconsin, Minnesota, Iowa, Illinois, Missouri, and Kansas, not now elsewhere, be left to *Fremont*.

All from Indiana and Michigan, not now elsewhere, be sent to Anderson at Louisville.

All from Ohio, needed in Western Virginia be sent there; and any remainder, be sent to Mitchell at Cincinnati, for Anderson.

All east of the mountains be appropriated to McClellan, and to the coast.

As to movements, my idea is that the one for the coast, and that on Cumberland Gap be simultaneous; and that, in the meantime, preparation, vigilant watching, and the defensive only be acted upon— (this however, not to apply to Fremont's operations in northern and middle Missouri) —that before these movements, Thomas and Sherman shall respectively watch, but not attack Zollicoffer, and Buckner.

That when the coast and Gap movements shall be ready, Sherman is merely to stand fast; while all at Cincinnati, and all at Louisville with all on the lines, concentrate rapidly at Lexington, and thence to Thomas' camp joining him, and the whole thence upon the Gap.

It is for the military men to decide whether they can find a pass through the mountains at or near the Gap, which cannot be defended by the enemy, with a greatly inferior force, and what is to be done in regard to this.

The coast and Gap movements made, Generals McClellan and Fremont, in their respective departments, will avail themselves of any advantages the diversions may present.

As the concept grew that the war was not simply a swift little action to be decided somewhere in Virginia, but was a conflict that must in time affect all parts of the nation, a letter to Samuel R. Curtis, stationed at St. Louis, reflected a concern that Lincoln experienced frequently. Were his commanding generals qualified?

The Irrepressible Conflict

Washington, D. C.
Oct. 7. 1861.

Brig: Genl. S. R. Curtis
My dear Sir:

Without prejudice, and looking to nothing but justice, and the public interest, I am greatly perplexed about Gen: Fremont: In your position, you cannot but have a correct judgment in the case; and I beseech you to answer Gen. Cameron, when he hands you this, "Ought Gen: Fremont to be relieved from, or retained in his present command?" It shall be entirely confidential; but you can perceive how indispensable it is to justice & the public service, that I should have, an intelligent, unprejudiced, and judicious opinion from some professional military man on the spot, to assist me in the case. Yours very truly

A. Lincoln

Lincoln welcomed rare chances to indulge his sense of humor. The fortunate mother was Mrs. Mary Buckley, a widow with six children.

Executive Mansion
Oct. 17, 1861

Majr. Ramsay
My dear Sir

The lady—bearer of this—says she has two sons who want to work. Set them at it, if possible. Wanting to work is so rare a merit, that it should be encouraged. Yours truly

A. Lincoln

Again General Curtis heard from Lincoln regarding Fremont, and the one factor above all others that would decide the President's attitude toward his generals is clearly suggested.

Executive Mansion,
Washington, Oct. 24, 1861.

Brig: Genl. S. R. Curtis
Dear Sir:

On receipt of this, with the accompanying inclosures, you will take safe, certain, and suitable measures to have the inclosure addressed to Major General Fremont, delivered to him, with all reasonable dispatch—subject to these conditions only, that if, when

Gen. Fremont shall be reached by the messenger (yourself, or anyone sent by you) he shall then have, in personal command, fought
and won a battle, or shall then be actually in a battle, or shall then
be in the immediate presence of the enemy, in expectation of a battle, it is not to be delivered, but held for further orders. After, and
not till after, the delivery to Gen. Fremont, let the inclosure addressed to Gen. Hunter be delivered to him. Your Obt. Servt.

A. Lincoln

General George B. McClellan, who had been hammering raw recruits into disciplined soldiers for the Army of the Potomac, is called by
Lincoln to a higher duty.

PRIVATE

Executive Mansion
Nov. 1. 1861

Major General Geo. B. McClellan
My dear Sir

Lieut. Genl. Scott having been, upon his own application,
placed on the list of retired officers, with his advice, and the concurrence of the entire cabinet, I have designated you to command
the whole army. You will, therefore, assume this enlarged duty at
once, conferring with me so far as necessary. Yours truly

A. Lincoln

P.S. For the present, let Gen. Wool's command be excepted.

A L

Lincoln graciously announced the retirement of an eminent military
figure—Winfield Scott, hero of the War with Mexico, whose efforts in
bolstering army morale during the last weeks of the Buchanan administration had been a service of equal magnitude.

Executive Mansion, Washington, November 1, 1861.

On the 1st day of November, A.D. 1861, upon his own application to the President of the United States, Brevet Lieutenant General Winfield Scott is ordered to be placed, and hereby is placed,
upon the list of retired officers of the Army of the United States,
without reduction in his current pay, subsistence, or allowances.

The American people will hear with sadness and deep emotion

that General Scott has withdrawn from the active control of the army, while the President and a unanimous cabinet express their own and the nation's sympathy in his personal affliction and their profound sense of the important public services rendered by him to his country during his long and brilliant career, among which will ever be gratefully distinguished his faithful devotion to the Constitution, the Union, and the Flag, when assailed by parricidal rebellion.

Abraham Lincoln.

XIII. From Belmont to Second Manassas

1861-1862   ACROSS the Mississippi River from Columbus, Kentucky, in 1861 three shanties, stuck in Missouri mud, comprised the town of Belmont. Along the river bluffs Confederate guns contested any approach by land or water to this desolate community. Nearby some three thousand Rebel troops camped without the least fear of attack.

Unexpectedly, on the seventh of November, a Union general scarcely known outside his home state of Illinois sailed down the river on a routine reconnaisance mission. Instead of turning and running, as good military sense seemed to dictate, the general decided to pick a fight. After four hours of mean, vicious struggle, neither side could claim a clear victory. Yet, for two results, the action at Belmont was memorable. The Confederate forces there had been intended as reinforcements elsewhere in Missouri at a time when the Union's hold on that border state was critically jeopardized—a plan that now had to be abandoned. Equally important, perhaps, was the cool-headed way the Union general led his soldiers out of a trap that could have produced disaster. For the first time men in the ranks sang the praises of Ulysses S. Grant.

To Lincoln the name of Grant meant almost nothing, yet before another year had passed this would be a name that the President pondered with increasing interest. Ultimately the President would believe that in Grant he had found a general he could trust. Upon that decision the war turned.

Necessarily this discovery came slowly. The summer and autumn of 1861 were months of personal torment for Lincoln, when, in bitter self-appraisal, he lived with a growing sense of inadequacy. What preparation had he to serve as the civilian leader of great armies operating on widely separated battlefields? Again, had he been impulsive and reckless in pressing for the action that had led to the costly defeat at First Bull Run? McClellan followed Scott in command, and Lincoln, almost as though he felt chastised, exhibited extraordinary talents of patience and personal humility in holding his emotions in check. Quickly, McClellan revealed ability as an efficient organizer, as a diligent builder of defenses, as a zealous drill master. In letters to his wife, however, he became a fantastic egotist: "I almost think that were I to win some small success now I could become Dictator." He denied any such ambition and thought that he displayed "admirable self-denial."

Unfortunately Lincoln did not read McClellan's mail to his wife. In good faith the President accepted McClellan's boasts of how, with one crushing blow, he intended to smash the Confederate army across the Potomac. Lincoln well could believe in McClellan, for his military accomplishments were impressive. A graduate of West Point, the general had served with distinction in the War with Mexico, had written a manual on the art of war, and had translated from the French a treatise on bayonet exercises.

Washington sweltered through the summer of 1861, and hands flicking any sort of fan that would create a breeze disclosed an edginess that the heat alone could not explain. On the south side of the Potomac rose Confederate batteries that threatened the capital's outlet to the sea. Above Harper's Ferry the Confederates cut the tracks of the Baltimore and Ohio, thereby severing the city's main link to the West. McClellan grew snappish when asked at what point he proposed to stop these tactics. The Confederates outnumbered him, McClellan said in bad humor; he would move when he was ready. The general who believed that he might have become dictator had been wise in not pushing his luck. McClellan possessed no flair for risking his kingdom.

A dry Indian summer passed into a crisp autumn. Out of Ohio stomped "Bluff Ben" Wade, growing more profane with each mile in his demands to know when that old hen McClellan was going to hatch a little military action. The horse face and whiskey tenor of Zacariah Chandler of Michigan added Republican assent to the chorus of senatorial dissatisfaction. Lincoln must have recognized some echo of the hornet's buzz that had swirled around his head after the removal of Fremont. The President pleaded for faith in

McClellan; the Senators, having minds of their own, established an investigating committee.

In effect, Lincoln's leadership was being questioned, yet from the beginning of the war he did much better than he realized. Every waking hour, he was trying to win. He grasped quickly the essential strategy that would defeat the South. Among his earliest acts was the creation of four blockading squadrons, and whereas the ports of the Confederacy never were sealed off completely, all Southern shipping was reduced by more than seven-eighths. Moreover he soon recognized that there must be a co-ordinated plan of action whereby the armies of the East drove steadily on Richmond while the armies in the West protected the neutrality of the border states, opened the Mississippi, and then moved northward into Virginia.

Lincoln never underestimated the psychological advantage the South gained from fighting for a way of life upon soil that it considered its homeland. The longer the war was protracted the stronger grew the South's hope that the North would lose interest in a conflict which it could stop without immediately losing or altering its manners and customs. Also with time European support could throw the balance in favor of the Confederacy. Obviously, when all factors were weighed, more than rash impulse had spurred Lincoln to precipitate the battle at Manassas Junction.

Yet in November of 1861 the President still must live with the fact that the North remained unprepared for war. Among the callers at the White House was Congressman Elihu B. Washburne, who had visited Illinois troops after Belmont, and, in the phrase of the day, had promised "to drop a flea" in Lincoln's ear upon returning to Washington. General John A. McClernand was a prominent Illinois Democrat from Springfield. Lincoln wrote in the tone of a fellow-townsman.

Washington. Nov. 10. 1861

Brigadier General McClernand
My Dear Sir
This is not an official but a social letter. You have had a battle, and without being able to judge as to the precise measure of its value, I think it is safe to say that you, and all with you have done honor to yourselves and the flag and service to the country. Most gratefully do I thank you and them. In my present position, I must care for the whole nation; but I hope it will be no injustice to any

other state, for me to indulge a little home pride, that Illinois does not disappoint us.

I have just closed a long interview with Mr. Washburne in which he has detailed the many difficulties you, and those with you labor under. Be assured, we do not forget or neglect you. Much, very much, goes undone: but it is because we have not the power to do it faster than we do. Some of your forces are without arms, but the same is true here, and at every other place where we have considerable bodies of troops. The plain matter-of-fact is, our good people have rushed to the rescue of the government, faster than the government can find arms to put into their hands.

It would be agreeable to each division of the army to know its own precise destination: but the government cannot immediately, nor inflexibly at any time, determine as to all; nor if determined, can it tell its *friends* without at the same time telling its *enemies*.

We know you do all as wisely and well as you can; and you will not be deceived if you conclude the same is true of us. Please give my respects and thanks to all. Yours very truly

A. Lincoln.

The North found no more devoted supporter of the Union or of Lincoln than Stephen A. Douglas, who, overtaxing his strength, died suddenly in Chicago. A perplexing afternoon in the White House for Lincoln was reflected in a memorandum of an interview with the widow of the Illinois senator.

Robert Douglas was then twelve years old, Stephen Douglas, Jr., a year younger.

Executive Mansion, Nov. 27 – 1861

Yesterday Mrs. Douglas called, saying she is guardian of the minor children of her late husband; that she is being urged, against her inclination, to send them South, on the plea of avoiding the confiscation of their property there, and asking my counsel in the case.

I expect the United States will overcome the attempt to confiscate property, because of loyalty to the government; but if not, I still do not expect the property of absent minor children will be confiscated. I therefore think Mrs. Douglas may safely act her pleasure in the premises.

But it is especially dangerous for my name to be connected with

the matter; for nothing would more certainly excite the secessionists to do the worst they can against the children.

One evening, when McClellan ignored a call from the President by
going to bed, Lincoln said: "I will hold McClellan's horse, if he will
only bring us success." After this incident, however, the general was
summoned to the White House whenever Lincoln wished to see him,
and soon he received a memorandum that jabbed at his essential weaknesses. To the President's first question, McClellan pencilled in the margin: "If bridge trains ready—By Dec. 15.—probably 25th." McClellan
answered the second question by writing the figure "71,000," the third
with the figure "33,000."

c. December 1, 1861

If it were determined to make a forward movement of the
Army of the Potomac, without awaiting further increase of numbers, or better drill & discipline, how *long* would it require to actually get in motion?

After leaving all that would be necessary, how many troops
could join the movement from southwest of the river?

How many from northeast of it?

Suppose, then, that of those southwest of the river 50,000
move forward and menace the enemy at Centerville.

The remainder of the movable force on that side move rapidly
to the crossing of the Ocoquan by the road from Alexandria towards Richmond; there to be joined by the whole movable force
from northeast of the river, having landed from the Potomac just
below the mouth of the Ocoquan, moved by land up the south side
of that stream to the crossing point named; then the whole move
together, by the road thence to Brentsville, and beyond, to the railroad just south of its crossing of Broad Run, a strong detachment
of cavalry having gone rapidly ahead to destroy the railroad
bridges south and north of the point.

If the crossing of the Ocoquan by those from above be resisted,
those landing from the Potomac below to take the resisting force of
the enemy in rear; or, if the landing from the Potomac be resisted,
those crossing the Ocoquan from above to take that resisting force
in rear. Both points will probably not be successfully resisted at the
same time.

From Belmont to Second Manassas

The force in front of Centreville, if pressed too hardly, should fight back slowly into the intrenchments behind them.

Armed vessels and transportation should remain at the Potomac landing to cover a possible retreat.

A tired President prepared his annual message to Congress. His references to the conduct of the war were brief, and seemed addressed principally to foreign powers, who always had found their chief resources of commerce centered in the North. Turning to domestic problems, Lincoln gave attention first to the need for judicial reforms.

December 3, 1861

. . . There are three vacancies on the bench of the Supreme Court—two by the decease of Justices Daniel and McLean, and one by the resignation of Justice Campbell. I have so far forborne making nominations to fill these vacancies for reasons which I will now state. Two of the outgoing judges resided within the states now overrun by revolt; so that if successors were appointed in the same localities, they could not now serve upon their circuits; and many of the most competent men there, probably would not take the personal hazard of accepting to serve, even here, upon the supreme bench. I have been unwilling to throw all the appointments northward, thus disabling myself from doing justice to the South on the return of peace; although I may remark that to transfer to the North one which has heretofore been in the South, would not, with reference to territory and population, be unjust.

During the long and brilliant judicial career of Judge McLean his circuit grew into an empire—altogether too large for any one judge to give the courts therein more than a nominal attendance—rising in population from one million four hundred and seventy-thousand eighteen, in 1830, to six million one hundred and fifty-one thousand four hundred and five, in 1860.

Besides this, the country generally has outgrown our present judicial system. If uniformity was at all intended, the system requires that all the states shall be accommodated with circuit courts, attended by supreme judges, while, in fact, Wisconsin, Minnesota, Iowa, Kansas, Florida, Texas, California, and Oregon, have never had any such courts. Nor can this well be remedied without a change of the system; because the adding of judges to the Supreme

447

Court, enough for the accommodation of all parts of the country, with circuit courts, would create a court altogether too numerous for a judicial body of any sort. And the evil, if it be one, will increase as new states come into the Union. Circuit courts are useful, or they are not useful. If useful, no state should be denied them; if not useful, no state should have them. Let them be provided for all, or abolished as to all.

Three modifications occur to me, either of which, I think, would be an improvement upon our present system. Let the Supreme Court be of convenient number in every event. Then, first, let the whole country be divided into circuits of convenient size, the supreme judges to serve in a number of them corresponding to their own number, and independent circuit judges be provided for all the rest. Or, secondly, let the supreme judges be relieved from circuit duties, and circuit judges provided for all the circuits. Or, thirdly, dispense with circuit courts altogether, leaving the judicial functions wholly to the district courts and an independent Supreme Court.

I respectfully recommend to the consideration of Congress the present condition of the statute laws, with the hope that Congress will be able to find an easy remedy for many of the inconveniences and evils which constantly embarrass those engaged in the practical administration of them. Since the organization of the government, Congress has enacted some five thousand acts and joint resolutions, which fill more than six thousand closely printed pages, and are scattered through many volumes. Many of these acts have been drawn in haste and without sufficient caution, so that their provisions are often obscure in themselves, or in conflict with each other, or at least so doubtful as to render it very difficult for even the best informed persons to ascertain precisely what the statute law really is.

It seems to me very important that the statute laws should be made as plain and intelligible as possible, and be reduced to as small a compass as may consist with the fullness and precision of the will of the legislature and the perspicuity of its language. This, well done, would, I think, greatly facilitate the labors of those whose duty it is to assist in the administration of the laws, and would be a lasting benefit to the people, by placing before them, in a more accessible and intelligible form, the laws which so deeply concern their interests and their duties.

From Belmont to Second Manassas

I am informed by some whose opinions I respect, that all the acts of Congress now in force, and of a permanent and general nature, might be revised and re-written, so as to be embraced in one volume (or at most, two volumes) of ordinary and convenient size. And I respectfully recommend to Congress to consider of the subject, and, if my suggestion be approved, to devise such plan as to their wisdom shall seem most proper for the attainment of the end proposed. . . .

The judicial reforms urged by Lincoln brought passage of an act, approved July 15, 1862, that created nine circuits and repealed all acts giving district courts the power of circuit courts, while additional legislation the following year created a tenth circuit for California and Oregon and fixed the number of justices of the Supreme Court at nine plus the chief justice. A law authorizing the simplification of public statutes was not passed until 1866.

Lincoln gave careful attention to other domestic problems of the day, suggesting legislation that resulted the next May in the establishment of the Department of Agriculture, then turned to relations with the border states and a significant victory that had been won there.

The relations of the government with the Indian tribes have been greatly disturbed by the insurrection, especially in the southern superintendency and in that of New Mexico. The Indian country south of Kansas is in the possession of insurgents from Texas and Arkansas. The agents of the United States appointed since the 4th. of March for this superintendency have been unable to reach their posts, while the most of those who were in office before that time have espoused the insurrectionary cause, and assume to exercise the powers of agents by virtue of commissions from the insurrectionists. It has been stated in the public press that a portion of those Indians have been organized as a military force, and are attached to the army of the insurgents. Although the government has no official information upon this subject, letters have been written to the Commissioner of Indian Affairs by several prominent chiefs, giving assurance of their loyalty to the United States, and expressing a wish for the presence of federal troops to protect them. It is believed that upon the repossession of the country by the federal forces the Indians will readily cease all hostile demonstrations, and resume their former relations to the government.

449

Agriculture, confessedly the largest interest of the nation, has not a department, nor a bureau, but a clerkship only, assigned to it in the government. While it is fortunate that this great interest is so independent in its nature as to not have demanded and extorted more from the government, I respectfully ask Congress to consider whether something more cannot be given voluntarily with general advantage.

Annual reports exhibiting the condition of our agriculture, commerce, and manufactures would present a fund of information of great practical value to the country. While I make no suggestion as to details, I venture the opinion that an agricultural and statistical bureau might profitably be organized.

The execution of the laws for the suppression of the African slave trade, has been confided to the Department of the Interior. It is a subject of gratulation that the efforts which have been made for the suppression of this inhuman traffic, have been recently attended with unusual success. Five vessels being fitted out for the slave trade have been seized and condemned. Two mates of vessels engaged in the trade, and one person in equipping a vessel as a slaver, have been convicted and subjected to the penalty of fine and imprisonment, and one captain, taken with a cargo of Africans on board his vessel, has been convicted of the highest grade of offence under our laws, the punishment of which is death.

The territories of Colorado, Dakota and Nevada, created by the last Congress, have been organized, and civil administration has been inaugurated therein under auspices especially gratifying, when it is considered that the leaven of treason was found existing in some of these new countries when the federal officers arrived there.

The abundant natural resources of these territories, with the security and protection afforded by organized government, will doubtless invite to them a large immigration when peace shall restore the business of the country to its accustomed channels. I submit the resolutions of the legislature of Colorado, which evidence the patriotic spirit of the people of the territory. So far the authority of the United States has been upheld in all the territories, as it is hoped it will be in the future. I commend their interests and defence to the enlightened and generous care of Congress. . . .

The last ray of hope for preserving the Union peaceably, expired at the assault upon Fort Sumter; and a general review of

what has occurred since may not be unprofitable. What was pain,
fully uncertain then, is much better defined and more distinct now;
and the progress of events is plainly in the right direction. The insurgents confidently claimed a strong support from north of Mason
and Dixon's line; and the friends of the Union were not free from
apprehension on the point. This, however, was soon settled definitely and on the right side. South of the line, noble little Delaware
led off right from the first. Maryland was made to *seem* against the
Union. Our soldiers were assaulted, bridges were burned, and railroads torn up, within her limits; and we were many days, at one
time, without the ability to bring a single regiment over her soil to
the capital. Now, her bridges and railroads are repaired and open
to the government; she already gives seven regiments to the cause
of the Union and none to the enemy; and her people, at a regular
election, have sustained the Union, by a larger majority, and a
larger aggregate vote than they ever before gave to any candidate,
or any question. Kentucky, too, for some time in doubt, is now decidedly, and, I think, unchangeably, ranged on the side of the Union. Missouri is comparatively quiet; and I believe cannot again be
overrun by the insurrectionists. These three states of Maryland,
Kentucky, and Missouri, neither of which would promise a single
soldier at first, have now an aggregate of not less than forty thousand in the field, for the Union; while, of their citizens, certainly
not more than a third of that number, and they of doubtful where-
abouts, and doubtful existence, are in arms against it. After a somewhat bloody struggle of months, winter closes on the Union people
of western Virginia, leaving them masters of their own country.

An insurgent force of about fifteen hundred, for months domi-
nating the narrow peninsular region, constituting the counties of
Accomac and Northampton, and known as eastern shore of Virginia, together with some contiguous parts of Maryland, have laid
down their arms; and the people there have renewed their allegiance to, and accepted the protection of, the old flag. This leaves
no armed insurrectionist north of the Potomac, or east of the
Chesapeake.

Also we have obtained a footing at each of the isolated points,
on the southern coast, of Hatteras, Port Royal, Tybee Island, near
Savannah, and Ship Island; and we likewise have some general accounts of popular movements, in behalf of the Union, in North
Carolina and Tennessee.

The Living Lincoln

These things demonstrate that the cause of the Union is advancing steadily and certainly southward. . . .

The issue of war, as Lincoln saw it, rested fundamentally in what was a proper—and healthful—relationship between labor and capital.

It continues to develop that the insurrection is largely, if not exclusively, a war upon the first principle of popular government —the rights of the people. Conclusive evidence of this is found in the most grave and maturely considered public documents, as well as in the general tone of the insurgents. In those documents we find the abridgement of the existing right of suffrage and the denial to the people of all right to participate in the selection of public officers, except the legislative, boldly advocated, with labored arguments to prove that large control of the people in government, is the source of all political evil. Monarchy itself is sometimes hinted at as a possible refuge from the power of the people.

In my present position, I could scarcely be justified were I to omit raising a warning voice against this approach of returning despotism.

It is not needed, nor fitting here, that a general argument should be made in favor of popular institutions; but there is one point, with its connections, not so hackneyed as most others, to which I ask a brief attention. It is the effort to place *capital* on an equal footing with, if not above *labor*, in the structure of government. It is assumed that labor is available only in connection with capital; that nobody labors unless somebody else, owning capital, somehow by the use of it, induces him to labor. This assumed, it is next considered whether it is best that capital shall *hire* laborers, and thus induce them to work by their own consent, or *buy* them, and drive them to it without their consent. Having proceeded so far, it is naturally concluded that all laborers are either *hired* laborers, or what we call slaves. And further it is assumed that whoever is once a hired laborer, is fixed in that condition for life.

Now, there is no such relation between capital and labor as assumed; nor is there any such thing as a free man being fixed for life in the condition of a hired laborer. Both these assumptions are false, and all inferences from them are groundless.

Labor is prior to, and independent of, capital. Capital is only the fruit of labor, and could never have existed if labor had not first existed. Labor is the superior of capital, and deserves much the higher consideration. Capital has its rights, which are as worthy of protection as any other rights. Nor is it denied that there is, and probably always will be, a relation between labor and capital, producing mutual benefits. The error is in assuming that the whole labor of community exists within that relation. A few men own capital, and that few avoid labor themselves, and, with their capital, hire or buy another few to labor for them. A large majority belong to neither class—neither work for others, nor have others working for them. In most of the southern states, a majority of the whole people of all colors are neither slaves nor masters; while in the northern a large majority are neither hirers nor hired. Men with their families—wives, sons, and daughters—work for themselves, on their farms, in their houses, and in their shops, taking the whole product to themselves, and asking no favors of capital on the one hand, nor of hired laborers or slaves on the other. It is not forgotten that a considerable number of persons mingle their own labor with capital—that is, they labor with their own hands, and also buy or hire others to labor for them; but this is only a mixed, and not a distinct class. No principle stated is disturbed by the existence of this mixed class.

Again: as has already been said, there is not, of necessity, any such thing as the free hired laborer being fixed to that condition for life. Many independent men everywhere in these states, a few years back in their lives, were hired laborers. The prudent, penniless beginner in the world, labors for wages awhile, saves a surplus with which to buy tools or land for himself; then labors on his own account another while, and at length hires another new beginner to help him. This is the just, and generous, and prosperous system, which opens the way to all—gives hope to all, and consequent energy, and progress, and improvement of condition to all. No men living are more worthy to be trusted than those who toil up from poverty—none less inclined to take, or touch, aught which they have not honestly earned. Let them beware of surrendering a political power which they already possess, and which, if surrendered, will surely be used to close the door of advancement against such as they, and to fix new disabilities and burdens upon them, till all of liberty shall be lost.

From the first taking of our national census to the last are seventy years; and we find our population at the end of the period eight times as great as it was at the beginning. The increase of those

453

other things which men deem desirable has been even greater. We thus have at one view, what the popular principle applied to government, through the machinery of the states and the Union, has produced in a given time; and also what, if firmly maintained, it promises for the future. There are already among us those, who, if the Union be preserved, will live to see it contain two hundred and fifty millions. The struggle of today, is not altogether for today— it is for a vast future also. With a reliance on Providence, all the more firm and earnest, let us proceed in the great task which events have devolved upon us.

December 3, 1861

Abraham Lincoln

From the country of Lincoln's boyhood came a gift that the President valued. Lincoln's Aunt Mary, a year older than his father, had been born in 1775.

Executive Mansion,
Washington, Dec. 4, 1861.

My dear Madam

I take great pleasure in acknowledging the receipt of your letter of Nov. 26; and in thanking you for the present by which it was accompanied. A pair of socks so fine, and soft, and warm, could hardly have been manufactured in any other way than the old Kentucky fashion. Your letter informs me that your maiden name was Crume, and that you were raised in Washington County, Kentucky, by which I infer that an uncle of mine by marriage was a relative of yours. Nearly, or quite sixty years ago, Ralph Crume married Mary Lincoln, a sister of my father, in Washington County, Kentucky.

Accept my thanks, and believe me   Very truly   Your friend
A. Lincoln.

Mrs. Susannah Weathers
Rossville, Clinton Co, Ind.

Wherever Lincoln turned, tensions of war awaited him. The published report of General Lorenzo Thomas, covering conditions in Missouri leading to Fremont's removal, disturbed General Curtis, who felt that "conversations drawn out" of him upon Lincoln's "confidential assurance" had alienated him with Fremont's friends. Curtis hoped that he had not lost "the respect of those who best know all the circumstances." Lincoln did not deny that Curtis had been used badly.

Washington, D. C.
Dec. 12. 1861

PRIVATE
Brig. Genl. S. R. Curtis.
My dear Sir.

I snatch a moment to both thank you, and apologize to you. In all sincerity I thank you for the complete and entirely satisfactory manner in which you executed the trusts I confided to you by letter.

You, and others, particularly, and the public service generally, were wronged, and injured by the publication of Gen. Thomas' report, on his return from the West. I have no apology only to say it never would have been done, if I had had the least suspicion it was to be done. Being done, I thought the maxim "least said, soonest mended" applied to the case. Yours very truly

A. Lincoln

Lincoln, facing his own limitations, borrowed from the Library of Congress books on military history and theory, but when he tried to discuss this reading with McClellan he was brushed aside. What the President must discover about generals probably had not been included in the textbooks. When Major General David Hunter learned that the command in Kentucky had gone to a mere brigadier, he wailed to Lincoln: "I am very deeply mortified, humiliated, insulted and disgraced." By return mail Hunter received a scorching reproof.

Executive Mansion, Washington,
Dec. 31, 1861.

Major General Hunter.
Dear Sir:

Yours of the 23rd. is received; and I am constrained to say it is difficult to answer so ugly a letter in good temper. I am, as you intimate, losing much of the great confidence I placed in you, not from any act or omission of yours touching the public service, up to the time you were sent to Leavenworth, but from the flood of grumbling dispatches and letters I have seen from you since. I knew you were being ordered to Leavenworth at the time it was done; and I aver that with as tender a regard for your honor and your sensibilities as I had for my own, it never occurred to me that you were being "humiliated, insulted and disgraced"; nor have I, up to this day, heard an intimation that you have been wronged, coming from anyone but yourself. No one has blamed you for the retrograde movement from Springfield, nor for the information you gave Gen. Cameron; and this you could readily understand, if it were not for your unwarranted assumption that the ordering you to Leavenworth must necessarily have been done as a *punishment* for some *fault*. I thought then, and think yet, the position assigned to you is as responsible, and as honorable, as that assigned to Buell. I know that Gen. McClellan expected more important results from it. My impression is that at the time you were assigned to the new western department, it had not been determined to replace Gen. Sherman in Kentucky; but of this I am not certain, because the idea that a command in Kentucky was very desirable, and one in the farther West, very undesirable, had never occurred to me. You constantly speak of being placed in command of only 3000. Now tell me, is not this mere impatience? Have you not known all the while that you are to command four or five times that many?

I have been, and am sincerely your friend; and if, as such, I dare to make a suggestion, I would say you are adopting the best possible way to ruin yourself. "Act well your part, there all the honor lies." He who does *something* at the head of one regiment, will eclipse him who does *nothing* at the head of a hundred. Your friend as ever.

A. Lincoln

McClellan fell ill. Whether Little Mac wheezed with a cold or burned with typhoid fever no one would say, but obviously his interest in military affairs had been suspended. By telegram and letter Lincoln turned hopefully to the West, where Major General Henry W. Halleck now commanded the Department of Missouri.

Washington, D. C.
Jany. 1. 1861 [1862]

Majr. Genl. Halleck
St. Louis, Mo.

Gen. McClellan should not yet be disturbed with business. I think Gen. Buell and yourself should be in communication and concert at once. I write you tonight, and also telegraph and write him.

A. Lincoln.

Executive Mansion, Washington, January 1, 1862.
My dear General Halleck:

General McClellan is not dangerously ill, as I hope, but would better not to be disturbed with business. I am very anxious that, in case of General Buell's moving toward Nashville, the enemy shall not be greatly reinforced, and I think there is danger he will be from Columbus. It seems to me that a real or feigned attack upon Columbus from up-river at the same time would either prevent this or compensate for it by throwing Columbus into our hands. I wrote General Buell a letter similar to this, meaning that he and you shall communicate and act in concert, unless it be your judgment and his that there is no necessity for it. You and he will understand much better than I how to do it. Please do not lose time in this matter. Yours, very truly,

A. Lincoln.

Doubtless this note cheered McClellan, but the meeting with the senators had been far stormier than Lincoln suggested.

Executive Mansion
Jany. 1. 1862

My dear General

I hear that the doings of an investigating committee, give you some uneasiness. You may be entirely relieved on this point. The gentlemen of the committee were with me an hour and a half last night; and I found them in a perfectly good mood.

As their investigation brings them acquainted with facts, they are rapidly coming to think of the whole case as all sensible men would. Yours as ever

A. Lincoln

Gen. McClellan.

From hour to hour the President's dejection grew. The impatience for action mounted; Chase spoke as though the North was bankrupt. "The bottom is out of the tub," Lincoln told one White House caller and another heard him suggest taking the field in person. From the West, where he wanted Halleck and Buell to act in concert, all he received was objections. With diffidence, Lincoln tried once more to nudge Don Carlos Buell.

Executive Mansion,
Washington, January 6th, 1862.

Brig. Gen. Buell
My dear Sir:

Your dispatch of yesterday has been received, and it disappoints and distresses me. I have shown it to Gen. McClellan, who says he will write you today. I am not competent to criticize your views; and therefore what I offer is merely in justification of myself. Of the two, I would rather have a point on the railroad south of Cumberland Gap, than Nashville, first, because it cuts a great artery of the enemy's communication, which Nashville does not, and secondly because it is in the midst of loyal people, who would rally around it, while Nashville is not. Again, I cannot see why the movement on East Tennessee would not be a diversion in your favor, rather than a disadvantage, assuming that a movement towards Nashville is the main object.

But my distress is that our friends in East Tennessee are being hanged and driven to despair, and even now I fear, are thinking of taking rebel arms for the sake of personal protection. In this we lose the most valuable stake we have in the South. My dispatch, to which yours is an answer, was sent with the knowledge of Senator Johnson and Representative Maynard of East Tennessee, and they will be upon me to know the answer, which I cannot safely show them. They would despair—possibly resign to go and save their families somehow, or die with them.

I do not intend this to be an order in any sense, but merely, as intimated before, to show you the grounds of my anxiety. Yours very Truly

A. Lincoln

Antislavery radicals openly mocked Lincoln's moderate approach to emancipation. The political fire-eaters, who wanted to deal a stunning blow to the "rebellious traitors" in the South, found a wily ally in Simon Cameron. Without the President's knowledge, the annual report of the Secretary of War called for emancipation and the arming of slaves. The report already had gone to postmasters for distribution when Lincoln learned of the passage; he ordered the document recalled, the proposals deleted. But the press knew there had been two versions, and the political ferment quickened. Quietly, Lincoln seized the right opportunity to separate Cameron from his official family.

Executive Mansion,
Washington, Jan. 11, 1862.

PRIVATE

Dear Sir

Though I have said nothing hitherto in response to your wish, expressed long since, to resign your seat in the cabinet, I have not been unmindful of it. I have been only unwilling to consent to a change at a time, and under circumstances which might give occasion to misconstruction, and unable, till now to see how such misconstruction could be avoided.

But the desire of Mr. Clay to return home and to offer his services to his country in the field enables me now to gratify your wish, and at the same time evince my personal regard for you, and my confidence in your ability, patriotism, and fidelity to public trust.

I therefore tender to your acceptance, if you still desire to resign your present position, the post of Minister to Russia. Should you accept it, you will bear with you the assurance of my undiminished confidence, of my affectionate esteem, and of my sure expectation that, near the great sovereign whose personal and hereditary friendship for the United States, so much endears him to Americans, you will be able to render services to your country, not less important than those you could render at home. Very sincerely Your friend

A. Lincoln

The first military requirement of the North had been to strengthen Union sympathies in Missouri, Kentucky, western Virginia and eastern Tennessee. Yet Lincoln's study of military fundamentals made him understand that the scattered deployment of troops into such areas could not produce ultimate victory. Again he tried to make Buell see how the war must be fought.

COPY—one also sent to Gen. Halleck.
Executive Mansion,
Washington, Jan. 13, 1862.

Brig. Genl. Buell.

My dear Sir:

Your dispatch of yesterday is received, in which you say "I

have received your letter and Gen. McClellan's; and will, at once devote all my efforts to your views, and his." In the midst of my many cares, I have not seen, or asked to see, Gen. McClellan's letter to you. For my own views, I have not offered, and do not now offer them as orders; and while I am glad to have them respectfully considered, I would blame you to follow them contrary to your own clear judgment—unless I should put them in the form of orders. As to Gen. McClellan's views, you understand your duty in regard to them better than I do. With this preliminary, I state my general idea of this war to be that we have the *greater* numbers, and the enemy has the *greater* facility of concentrating forces upon points of collision; that we must fail, unless we can find some way of making *our* advantage an overmatch for *his;* and that this can only be done by menacing him with superior forces at *different* points, at the *same* time; so that we can safely attack, one, or both, if he makes no change; and if he *weakens* one to *strengthen* the other, forbear to attack the strengthened one, but seize, and hold the weakened one, gaining so much. To illustrate, suppose last summer, when Winchester ran away to reinforce Manassas, we had forborne to attack Manassas, but had seized and held Winchester. I mention this to illustrate, and not to criticize. I did not lose confidence in McDowell, and I think less harshly of Patterson than some others seem to. In application of the general rule I am suggesting, every particular case will have its modifying circumstances, among which the most constantly present, and most difficult to meet, will be the want of perfect knowledge of the enemy's movements. This had its part in the Bull Run case; but worse, in that case, was the expiration of the terms of the three-months men. Applying the principle to your case, my idea is that Halleck shall menace Columbus, and "down river" generally; while you menace Bowling Green, and East Tennessee. If the enemy shall concentrate at Bowling Green, do not retire from his front; yet do not fight him there, either, but seize Columbus and East Tennessee, one or both, left exposed by the concentration at Bowling Green. It is matter of no small anxiety to me and one which I am sure you will not overlook, that the East Tennessee line, is so long, and over so bad a road. Yours very truly

A. Lincoln.

The secretive, suspicious, sharp-tongued Edwin McMasters Stanton, who succeeded Cameron as Secretary of War, posed new problems for

From Belmont to Second Manassas

Lincoln. Differences of opinion became inevitable. Here was one of the earliest.

Executive Mansion
January 22. 1862

Hon Sec of War
My Dear Sir

On reflection I think it will not do as a rule for the Adjutant General to attend me wherever I go; not that I have any objection to his presence, but that it would be an uncompensating incumbrance both to him and me. When it shall occur to me to go anywhere, I wish to be free to go at once, and not to have to notify the Adjutant General, and wait till he can get ready. It is better too, for the public service, that he shall give his time to the business of his office, and not to personal attendance on me. While I thank you for the kindness of the suggestion, my view of the matter is as I have stated. Yours truly

A. Lincoln

Lincoln at last lost patience with McClellan's continuing delays and issued a special order for the Army of the Potomac to advance on Richmond by way of Manassas Junction. McClellan objected and proposed an alternate plan. In reply the President again disclosed a mind that could do its own military thinking.

Executive Mansion,
Washington, Feb. 3, 1862.

Major General McClellan
My dear Sir:

You and I have distinct, and different plans for a movement of the Army of the Potomac—yours to be down the Chesapeake, up the Rappahannock to Urbana, and across land to the terminus of the railroad on the York River—, mine to move directly to a point on the railroad southwest of Manassas.

If you will give me satisfactory answers to the following questions, I shall gladly yield my plan to yours.

1st. Does not your plan involve a greatly larger expenditure of *time*, and *money* than mine?

2nd. Wherein is a victory *more certain* by your plan than mine?

3rd. Wherein is a victory *more valuable* by your plan than mine?

4th. In fact, would it not be *less* valuable, in this, that it would break no great line of the enemy's communications, while mine would?

5th. In case of disaster, would not a safe retreat be more difficult by your plan than by mine? Yours truly

A. Lincoln

[MEMORANDUM ACCOMPANYING LETTER OF PRESIDENT TO GENERAL MCCLELLAN, DATED FEBRUARY 3, 1862]

1. Suppose the enemy should attack us in force *before* we reach the Ocoquan, what? In view of the possibility of this, might it not be safest to have our entire force to move together from above the Ocoquan?

2. Suppose the enemy, in force, shall dispute the crossing of the Ocoquan, what? In view of this, might it not be safest for us to cross the Ocoquan at Colchester rather than at the village of Ocoquan? This would cost the enemy two miles more of travel to meet us, but would, on the contrary, leave us two miles further from our ultimate destination.

3. Suppose we reach Maple valley without an attack, will we not be attacked there, in force, by the enemy marching by the several roads from Manassas? and if so, what?

That same day Lincoln turned from the uncertainties of war to a problem on which he could speak with complete authority.

February 3, 1862

Abraham Lincoln,
President of the United States of America.
To His Majesty Somdetch Phra Paramendr Maha Mongut,
King of Siam,
&c., &c.

Great and Good Friend:

I have received Your Majesty's two letters of the date of February 14th., 1861.

I have also received in good condition the royal gifts which accompanied those letters,—namely, a sword of costly materials and exquisite workmanship; a photographic likeness of Your Majesty and of Your Majesty's beloved daughter; and also two elephants' tusks of length and magnitude such as indicate that they could have belonged only to an animal which was a native of Siam.

Your Majesty's letters show an understanding that our laws forbid the President from receiving these rich presents as personal treasures. They are therefore accepted in accordance with Your Majesty's desire as tokens of your good will and friendship for the American people. Congress being now in session at this capital, I have had great pleasure in making known to them this manifestation of Your Majesty's munificence and kind consideration.

Under their directions the gifts will be placed among the archives of the government, where they will remain perpetually as tokens of mutual esteem and pacific dispositions more honorable to both nations than any trophies of conquest could be.

I appreciate most highly Your Majesty's tender of good offices in forwarding to this government a stock from which a supply of elephants might be raised on our own soil. This government would not hesitate to avail itself of so generous an offer if the object were one which could be made practically useful in the present condition of the United States.

Our political jurisdiction, however, does not reach a latitude so low as to favor the multiplication of the elephant, and steam on land, as well as on water, has been our best and most efficient agent of transportation in internal commerce.

I shall have occasion at no distant day to transmit to Your Majesty some token of indication of the high sense which this government entertains of Your Majesty's friendship.

Meantime, wishing for Your Majesty a long and happy life, and for the generous and emulous people of Siam the highest possible prosperity, I commend both to the blessing of Almighty God. Your Good Friend,

Abraham Lincoln.

Washington, February 3, 1862.
By the President:
   WILLIAM H. SEWARD, Secretary of State.

On the morning of February 16 Fort Donelson, key to the Cumberland River, surrendered unconditionally to the general who had shown so much flair at Belmont. Growing in confidence as commander-in-chief, Lincoln spoke instantly of safeguards necessary to insure Grant's victory. Three days later a naval force under Captain Andrew H. Foote occupied Clarksville, Tennessee.

Executive Mansion,
Washington, Feb. 16, 1862

Major General Halleck
St. Louis, Mo.

You have Fort Donelson safe, unless Grant shall be overwhelmed from outside, to prevent which latter will, I think, require all the vigilance, energy, and skill of yourself & Buell, acting in full co-operation. Columbus will not get at Grant, but the force from Bowling Green will. They hold the railroad from Bowling Green to within a few miles of Donelson, with the bridge at Clarksville undisturbed. It is unsafe to rely that they will not dare to expose Nashville to Buell. A small part of their force can retire slowly towards Nashville, breaking up the railroad as they go, and keep Buell out of that city twenty days. Meantime Nashville will be abundantly defended by forces from all South & perhaps from here at Manassas. Could not a cavalry force from Gen. Thomas on the upper Cumberland, dash across, almost unresisted, and cut the railroad at or near Knoxville, Tenn.? In the midst of a bombardment at Donelson, why could not a gunboat run up and destroy the bridge at Clarksville? Our success or failure at Donelson is vastly important; and I beg you to put your soul in the effort. I send a copy to Buell.

A. Lincoln

Union army camps were besieged by runaway Negroes. Radical Republicans still pressed for action, and even Lincoln could not deny that emancipation would win the support of liberal opinion in Europe. But Lincoln had promised the border states that he would not attack slavery within their territories, a pledge he had no wish to break. The President offered a possible solution in a special message to Congress.

March 6, 1862

Fellow-citizens of the Senate, and House of Representatives,

I recommend the adoption of a Joint Resolution by your honorable bodies which shall be substantially as follows:

From Belmont to Second Manassas

"Resolved that the United States ought to co-operate with any state which may adopt gradual abolishment of slavery, giving to such state pecuniary aid, to be used by such state in its discretion, to compensate for the inconveniences public and private, produced by such change of system."

If the proposition contained in the resolution does not meet the approval of Congress and the country, there is the end; but if it does command such approval, I deem it of importance that the states and people immediately interested, should be at once distinctly notified of the fact, so that they may begin to consider whether to accept or reject it. The federal government would find its highest interest in such a measure, as one of the most efficient means of self-preservation. The leaders of the existing insurrection entertain the hope that this government will ultimately be forced to acknowledge the independence of some part of the disaffected region, and that all the slave states north of such part will then say "the Union, for which we have struggled, being already gone, we now choose to go with the southern section." To deprive them of this hope, substantially ends the rebellion; and the initiation of emancipation completely deprives them of it, as to all the states initiating it. The point is not that *all* the states tolerating slavery would very soon, if at all, initiate emancipation; but that, while the offer is equally made to all, the more northern shall, by such initiation, make it certain to the more southern, that in no event, will the former ever join the latter, in their proposed confederacy. I say "initiation" because, in my judgment, gradual, and not sudden emancipation, is better for all. In the mere financial, or pecuniary view, any Member of Congress, with the census tables and Treasury reports before him, can readily see for himself how very soon the current expenditures of this war would purchase, at fair valuation, all the slaves in any named state. Such a proposition, on the part of the general government, sets up no claim of a right, by federal authority, to interfere with slavery within state limits, referring, as it does, the absolute control of the subject, in each case, to the state and its people, immediately interested. It is proposed as a matter of perfectly free choice with them.

In the annual message last December, I thought fit to say "The Union must be preserved; and hence all indispensable means must be employed." I said this, not hastily, but deliberately. War has been made, and continues to be, an indispensable means to this end. A practical re-acknowledgment of the national authority would render the war unnecessary, and it would at once cease. If, however, resistance continues, the war must also continue; and it is impossible to foresee all the incidents, which may attend and all the ruin which may follow it. Such as may seem indispensable, or may obviously promise great efficiency towards ending the struggle, must and will come.

The proposition now made, though an offer only, I hope it may be esteemed no offence to ask whether the pecuniary consideration tendered would not be of more value to the states and private persons concerned, than are the institution, and property in it, in the present aspect of affairs.

While it is true that the adoption of the proposed resolution would be merely initiatory, and not within itself a practical measure, it is recommended in the hope that it would soon lead to important practical results. In full view of my great responsibility to my God, and to my country, I earnestly beg the attention of Congress and the people to the subject.

Abraham Lincoln

March 6. 1862.

Neither war nor slavery could relieve the pressure of patronage, which in this case reached halfway round the world.

Executive Mansion,
Washington, March 7, 1862.

Hon. Sec. of State
My dear Sir:

Mr. James F. B. Marshall, of Mass. is now with me on the question of the Honolulu Commissioner. It pains me some that this tilt for the place of Col. Baker's friend grows so fierce, now the Col. is no longer alive to defend him. I presume, however, we shall have no rest from it. Mr. Marshall appears to be a very intelligent gentleman, and well acquainted with the affairs of the Sandwich Islands. The California delegation also expect the place for some one of their citizens. In self-defence I am disposed to say "Make a selection and send it to me." Yours truly

A. Lincoln.

From Belmont to Second Manassas

Lincoln lost no chance to press for compensated emancipation.

Executive Mansion,
Washington, March 9, 1862.

PRIVATE
Hon. Henry J. Raymond:
My dear Sir:

I am grateful to the New York journals, and not less so to the Times than to others, for their kind notices of the late special message to Congress. Your paper, however, intimates that the proposition, though well-intentioned, must fail on the score of expense. I do hope you will reconsider this. Have you noticed the facts that less than one half-day's cost of this war would pay for all the slaves in Delaware, at four hundred dollars per head?—that eighty-seven days' cost of this war would pay for all in Delaware, Maryland, District of Columbia, Kentucky, and Missouri at the same price? Were those states to take the step, do you doubt that it would shorten the war more than eighty-seven days, and thus be an actual saving of expense? Please look at these things, and consider whether there should not be another article in the Times? Yours very truly,

A. Lincoln

Lincoln writes an unconventional prescription for an ailing son.

Washington, D. C. March 10, 1862

No. 79

RIGGS & Co.
Pay to "Tad" (when he is well enough to present) *or bearer*

Five ———————————————— *Dollars*

$5/00

A. Lincoln

The day after the *Monitor* checkmated the *Merrimac,* the President saw a need for great caution.

Executive Mansion
March 10, 1862

Hon. Sec. of Navy
My dear Sir

I have just seen Lieut. Worden, who says the "Monitor" could be boarded and captured very easily—first, after boarding, by

467

wedging the turret, so that it would not turn, and then by pouring water in her & drowning her machinery. He is decidedly of opinion she should not go sky-larking up to Norfolk. Yours truly

A. Lincoln

Evidence indicates that Lincoln composed this communication which Stanton transmitted to McClellan.

War Department, March 13, 1862.

The President having considered the plan of operations agreed upon by yourself and the commanders of army corps, makes no objection to the same, but gives the following directions as to its execution:

1st. Leave such force at Manassas Junction as shall make it entirely certain that the enemy shall not repossess himself of that position and line of communication.

2d. Leave Washington secure.

3d. Move the remainder of the force down the Potomac, choosing a new base at Fortress Monroe, or anywhere between here and there; or, at all events, move such remainder of the army at once in pursuit of the enemy by some route.

Edwin M. Stanton,
Secretary of War.

Seven o'clock, forty minutes.
Major General George B. McClellan.

Nathaniel Hawthorne was a member of the Massachusetts delegation that presented the President with "an elegant whip." Lincoln addressed his brief reply to Representative Charles R. Train.

March 13, 1862.

I thank you, Mr. Train, for your kindness in presenting me with this truly elegant and highly creditable specimen of the handiwork of the mechanics of your state of Massachusetts, and I beg of you to express my hearty thanks to the donors. It displays a perfection of workmanship which I really wish I had time to acknowledge in more fitting words, and I might then follow your idea that it is suggestive, for it is evidently expected that a good deal of whipping is to be done. But, as we meet here socially, let us not think only of whipping rebels, or of those who seem to think only of whipping Negroes, but of those pleasant days which it is to be hoped are in store for us, when, seated behind a good pair of horses, we can crack our whips and drive through a peaceful, happy and prosperous land. With this idea, gentlemen, I must leave you for my business duties.

The "domestic affliction" was the death of eleven-year-old William Wallace Lincoln. "It is hard, hard to have him die!" the President said.

Executive Mansion,
Washington, March 19, 1862.

Dr. Samuel Boyd Tobey:
My dear Sir:
A domestic affliction, of which doubtless you are informed, has delayed me so long in making acknowledgment for the very kind and appropriate letter, signed, on behalf, and by direction of a meeting of the representatives of the Society of Friends for New England, held at Providence, Rhode Island the 8th. of second month 1862, by Samuel Boyce, clerk, and presented to me by yourself and associates.

Engaged, as I am, in a great war, I fear it will be difficult for the world to understand how fully I appreciate the principles of peace, inculcated in this letter, and everywhere, by the Society of Friends. Grateful to the good people you represent for their prayers in behalf of our common country, I look forward hopefully to an early end of war, and return of peace. Your obliged friend

A. Lincoln

To the editor of the New York *Tribune* Lincoln restated the basic principles that he believed must govern any action on emancipation.

PRIVATE

Executive Mansion,
Washington, March 24, 1862.

Hon. Horace Greeley—
My dear Sir:
Your very kind letter of the 16th. to Mr. Colfax, has been shown me by him. I am grateful for the generous sentiments and purposes expressed towards the administration. Of course I am anxious to see the policy proposed in the late special message, go

forward; but you have advocated it from the first, so that I need to say little to you on the subject. If I were to suggest anything it would be that as the North are already for the measure, we should urge it *persuasively,* and not *menacingly,* upon the South. I am a little uneasy about the abolishment of slavery in this District, not but I would be glad to see it abolished, but as to the time and manner of doing it. If some one or more of the border states would move fast, I should greatly prefer it; but if this cannot be in a reasonable time, I would like the bill to have the three main features—gradual—compensation—and vote of the people—I do not talk to Members of Congress on the subject, except when they ask me. I am not prepared to make any suggestion about confiscation. I may drop you a line hereafter. Yours truly

A. Lincoln

McClellan prepared to attack Richmond by moving up the Peninsula between the York and James rivers. Lincoln distrusted the plan and insisted that forces under Fremont and McDowell be left behind for the adequate protection of Washington. Stonewall Jackson threatened the capital and Lincoln reacted as the Confederates hoped he would.

PRIVATE

Executive Mansion,
Washington, March 31, 1862.

Major General McClellan
My dear Sir
This morning I felt constrained to order Blenker's Division to Fremont; and I write this to assure you that I did so with great pain, understanding that you would wish it otherwise. If you could know the full pressure of the case, I am confident you would justify it—even beyond a mere acknowledgment that the commander-in-chief, may order what he pleases. Yours very truly

A. Lincoln

McClellan dallied on the Peninsula, laying siege to Yorktown instead of assaulting its unimpressive works. The novelty of going aloft in a balloon to reconnoiter the enemy had not provided much information—certainly nowhere near enough to overcome the general's innate fears. Lincoln chafed at the delay, the constant barrage of complaints and excuses, and wrote bluntly to his general.

Washington,
April 9. 1862

Major General McClellan.
My dear Sir.

Your despatches complaining that you are not properly sustained, while they do not offend me, do pain me very much.

Blencker's Division was withdrawn from you before you left here; and you knew the pressure under which I did it, and, as I thought, acquiesced in it—certainly not without reluctance.

After you left, I ascertained that less than twenty thousand unorganized men, without a single field battery, were all you designed to be left for the defence of Washington, and Manassas Junction; and part of this even, was to go to Gen. Hooker's old position. Gen. Banks' corps, once designed for Manassas Junction, was diverted, and tied up on the line of Winchester and Strausburg, and could not leave it without again exposing the upper Potomac, and the Baltimore and Ohio Railroad. This presented, (or would present, when McDowell and Sumner should be gone) a great temptation to the enemy to turn back from the Rappahanock, and sack Washington. My explicit order that Washington should, by the judgment of *all* the commanders of army corps, be left entirely secure, had been neglected. It was precisely this that drove me to detain McDowell.

I do not forget that I was satisfied with your arrangement to leave Banks at Manassas Junction; but when that arrangement was broken up, and *nothing* was substituted for it, of course I was not satisfied. I was constrained to substitute something for it myself. And now allow me to ask "Do you really think I should permit the line from Richmond, *via* Manassas Junction, to this city to be entirely open, except what resistance could be presented by less than twenty thousand unorganized troops?" This is a question which the country will not allow me to evade.

There is a curious mystery about the *number* of the troops now with you. When I telegraphed you on the 6th. saying you had over a hundred thousand with you, I had just obtained from the Secretary of War, a statement, taken as he said, from your own returns, making 108,000 then with you, and *en route* to you. You now say you will have but 85,000, when all *en route* to you shall have reached you. How can the discrepancy of 23,000 be accounted for?

As to Gen. Wool's command, I understand it is doing for you precisely what a like number of your own would have to do, if that command was away.

I suppose the whole force which has gone forward for you, is with you by this time; and if so, I think it is the precise time for you to strike a blow. By delay the enemy will relatively gain upon you—that is, he will gain faster, by *fortifications* and *re-inforcements,* than you can by re-inforcements alone.

And, once more let me tell you, it is indispensable to *you* that you strike a blow. *I* am powerless to help this. You will do me the justice to remember I always insisted, that going down the Bay in search of a field, instead of fighting at or near Manassas, was only shifting, and not surmounting, a difficulty—that we would find the same enemy, and the same, or equal, intrenchments, at either place. The country will not fail to note—is now noting—that the present hesitation to move upon an intrenched enemy, is but the story of Manassas repeated.

I beg to assure you that I have never written you, or spoken to you, in greater kindness of feeling than now, nor with a fuller purpose to sustain you, so far as in my most anxious judgment, I consistently can. *But you must act.* Yours very truly

A. Lincoln

May arrived. Lincoln's uneasiness mounted.

(CYPHER)

Executive Mansion,
Washington, May 1, 1862.

Major Gen. McClellan
Near York-Town, Va.

Your call for Parrott guns from Washington alarms me—chiefly because it argues indefinite procrastination. Is anything to be done?

A. Lincoln

By May 4, McClellan was ready to bombard Yorktown, then discovered the place evacuated. A wire told Washington: "I shall push the

enemy to the wall." With Stanton and Chase, Lincoln visited Fortress
Monroe, McClellan's headquarters, the camps of the army. Across the
bay at Norfolk lurked the *Merrimac,* a threat that McClellan ignored.
Lincoln slammed his hat on the floor. Later, at his orders, gunboats
attacked Confederate batteries at Sewall's Point and Union troops
forced the surrender of Norfolk. Chase said: "So has ended a brilliant
week's campaign of the President." The moment was hardly propitious
for McClellan to request authority to remove subordinates "who prove
themselves incompetent." Lincoln responded tartly.

Fort Monroe, Va.
May 9, 1862.

Major General McClellan.
My dear Sir:

I have just assisted the Secretary of War in framing the part of
a despatch to you, relating to army corps, which despatch of course
will have reached you long before this will. I wish to say a few
words to you privately on this subject. I ordered the army corps
organization not only on the unanimous opinion of the twelve generals whom you had selected and assigned as generals of division.
but also on the unanimous opinion of every *military man* I could
get an opinion from, and every modern military book, yourself only
excepted. Of course, I did not, on my own judgment, pretend to
understand the subject. I now think it indispensable for you to
know how your struggle against it is received in quarters which we
cannot entirely disregard. It is looked upon as merely an effort to
pamper one or two pets, and to persecute and degrade their supposed rivals. I have had no word from Sumner, Heintzelman, or
Keyes. The commanders of these corps are of course the three
highest officers with you, but I am constantly told that you have no
consultation or communication with them; that you consult and
communicate with nobody but General Fitz John Porter, and perhaps General Franklin. I do not say these complaints are true or
just; but at all events it is proper you should know of their existence. Do the commanders of corps disobey your orders in anything?

When you relieved General Hamilton of his command the
other day, you thereby lost the confidence of at least one of your
best friends in the Senate. And here let me say, not as applicable
to you personally, that Senators and Representatives speak of me

in their places as they please, without question; and that officers of the army must cease addressing insulting letters to them for taking no greater liberty with them.

But, to return, are you strong enough—are you strong enough, even with my help—to set your foot upon the necks of Sumner, Heintzelman, and Keyes all at once? This is a practical and very serious question for you.

The success of your army and the cause of the country are the same; and of course I only desire the good of the cause. Yours truly

A. Lincoln.

To a committee from the General Synod of the Evangelical Lutheran Church, the President expressed gratitude for resolutions supporting the suppression of the rebellion and the maintenance of the Constitution.

May 13, 1862

Gentlemen:

I welcome here the representatives of the Evangelical Lutherans of the United States. I accept with gratitude their assurances of the sympathy and support of that enlightened, influential, and loyal class of my fellow-citizens in an important crisis which involves, in my judgment, not only the civil and religious liberties of our own dear land, but in a large degree the civil and religious liberties of mankind in many countries and through many ages. You well know, gentlemen, and the world knows, how reluctantly I accepted this issue of battle forced upon me, on my advent to this place, by the internal enemies of our country. You all know, the world knows the forces and the resources the public agents have brought into employment to sustain a government against which there has been brought not one complaint of real injury committed against society, at home or abroad. You all may recollect that in taking up the sword thus forced into our hands this government appealed to the prayers of the pious and the good, and declared that it placed its whole dependence upon the favor of God. I now humbly and reverently, in your presence, reiterate the acknowledgment of that dependence, not doubting that, if it shall please the Divine Being who determines the destinies of nations that this shall remain a united people, they will, humbly seeking the Divine guidance, make their prolonged national existence a source of new benefits to themselves and their successors, and to all classes and conditions of mankind.

Historian John Lothrop Motley, whom Lincoln appointed minister to Austria, was Mary's father.

Executive Mansion,
Washington, May 17, 1862.

Miss Mary Motley—
A friend of yours (a young gentleman of course) tells me you do me the honor of requesting my autograph. I could scarcely refuse any young lady—certainly not the daughter of your distinguished father. Yours truly

A. Lincoln

Lincoln vouches for the integrity of Stanton.

PRIVATE

Executive Mansion
May 21, 1862.

James G. Bennett, Esq
Dear Sir:
Thanking you again for the able support given by you, through the Herald, to what I think the true cause of the country, and also for your kind expressions towards me personally, I wish to correct an erroneous impression of yours in regard to the Secretary of War. He mixes no politics whatever with his duties; knew nothing of Gen. Hunter's proclamation; and he and I alone got up the counter-proclamation. I wish this to go no further than to you, while I do wish to assure you it is true. Yours truly

A. Lincoln

With the Union army committed to a major campaign on the Peninsula, Stonewall Jackson struck suddenly at Front Royal, raced Banks to Winchester, almost trapping the Northern forces there, and now pursued Banks in his retreat to Harper's Ferry. In this critical situation Lincoln appealed to Halleck, commanding the Department of the Mississippi.

The Living Lincoln

Major Genl. Halleck
Near Corinth, Tenn. [*Mississippi*]

Several despatches from Assistant Secretary Scott, and one from Gov. Morton, asking re-inforcements for you have been received. I beg you to be assured we do the best we can. I mean to cast no blame when I tell you each of our commanders along our line from Richmond to Corinth supposes himself to be confronted by numbers superior to his own. Under this pressure we thinned the line on the upper Potomac until yesterday it was broken, at heavy loss to us, and Gen. Banks put in great peril, out of which he is not yet extricated, and may be actually captured. We need men to repair this breach, and have them not at hand.

My dear general, I feel justified to rely very much on you. I believe you and the brave officers and men with you, can and will get the victory at Corinth.

A. Lincoln

Jackson's bold campaign in the Shenandoah Valley imperilled Washington. On the Peninsula, McClellan cried for more troops. But Lincoln saw the greater need. If possible, Jackson must be cut off.

(SEND IN CYPHER)

War Department
Washington City, D. C.
May 25. 1862 8½ P.M.

Major Gen. McClellan

Your despatch received. Banks was at Strasburg with about six thousand men, Shields having been taken from him to swell a column for McDowell to aid you at Richmond, and the rest of his force scattered at various places. On the 23rd. a rebel force of seven to ten thousand fell upon one regiment and two companies guarding the bridge at Front Royal, destroying it entirely, crossed the Shenandoah, and on the 24th. (yesterday) pushed to get north of Banks on the road to Winchester. Banks ran a race with them, beating them into Winchester yesterday evening. This morning a battle ensued between the two forces in which Banks was beaten back into full retreat towards Martinsburg, and probably is broken up into a total rout. Geary, on the Manassas Gap R.R. just now reports that Jackson is now near Front Royal with ten thousand following up & supporting as I understand, the force now pursuing Banks. Also that another force of ten thousand is near Orleans following on in the same direction. Stripped bare, as we are here, it will be all we can do to prevent them crossing the Potomac at Harper's Ferry, or above. We have about twenty thousand of McDowell's force moving back to the vicinity of Front Royal; and Gen. Fremont, who was at Franklin, is moving to Harrisonburg, both these movements intended to get in the enemy's rear. One more of McDowell's brigades is ordered through here to Harper's Ferry. The rest of his force remains, for the present, at Fredericksburg. We are sending such regiments and dribs from here and Baltimore, as we can spare, to Harper's Ferry, supplying their places, in some sort, by calling in militia from the adjacent states. We also have eighteen cannon on the road to Harper's Ferry of which arm, there is not a single one yet at that point. This is now our situation. If McDowell's force was now beyond our reach, we should be utterly helpless. Apprehension of something like this, and no unwillingness to sustain you, has always been my reason for withholding McDowell's force from you. Please understand this, and do the best you can with the force you have.

A Lincoln

Lincoln kept his head. The wily Jackson ducked back up the Valley. The victory that McClellan claimed for Porter, which McClellan called "one of the handsomest things in the war," revealed to the Confederates that he was opening the way for McDowell to join him, the precise movement Jackson was ordered to prevent. Lincoln did not suspect that he was being outguessed—that the Valley campaign was intended to keep McDowell off the Peninsula. In this reply to McClellan, Lincoln deleted these words in conclusion: "and last I must be the Judge as to the *duty,* of the government in this respect."

Washington City, D. C.
May 28, 1862. 8.40 P.M.

Maj. Gen. McClellan
I am very glad of Gen. F. J. Porter's victory. Still, if it was a total rout of the enemy, I am puzzled to know why the Richmond and Fredericksburg Railroad was not seized. Again, as you say you have *all* the railroads but the Richmond and Fredericksburg,

The Living Lincoln

I am puzzled to see how, lacking that, you can have any, except the scrap from Richmond to West Point. The scrap of the Virginia Central from Richmond to Hanover Junction, without more, is simply nothing.

That the whole force of the enemy is concentrating in Richmond, I think cannot be certainly known to you or me. Saxton, at Harper's Ferry, informs us that a large force (supposed to be Jackson's and Ewell's) forced his advance from Charlestown today. Gen. King telegraphs us from Fredericksburg that contrabands give certain information that fifteen thousand left Hanover Junction Monday morning to re-inforce Jackson. I am painfully impressed with the importance of the struggle before you; and I shall aid you all I can consistently with my view of due regard to all points.

A. Lincoln

Lincoln sensed the imminence of battle on the Peninsula.

Washington City, D. C.
June 1. 1862. 9½ [A.M.]

Major Gen. McClellan
You are probably engaged with the enemy. I suppose he made the attack. Stand well on your guard—hold all your ground, or yield any only inch by inch and in good order. This morning we merge Gen. Wool's department into yours, giving you command of the whole, and sending Gen. Dix to Fortress Monroe, and Gen. Wool to Fort McHenry. We also send Gen. Sigel to report to you for duty.

A. Lincoln

On May 31, at Fair Oaks or Seven Pines, the Rebels had struck south of the Chickahominy. McClellan could only report that a bloody battle continued.

Washington City, D. C.
June 1, 1862. 5. P.M.

Major Gen. McClellan.
Thanks for what you *could*, and *did* say, in your despatch of noon today to the Sec. of War. If the enemy shall not have renewed the attack this afternoon, I think the hardest of your work is done.

Shields' advance came in collision with part of the enemy yesterday evening six miles from Front Royal in a direction between

From Belmont to Second Manassas

Winchester & Strasburg, driving them back, capturing a few prisoners and one rifled cannon. Firing in that direction today, heard both from Harper's Ferry and Front Royal, indicate a probability that Fremont has met the enemy.

We have concluded to send Gen. Sigel to Harper's Ferry, so that what I telegraphed you about him this morning, is revoked. Dix goes to Fort Monroe tonight.

A. Lincoln

Despite the mounting cares of war, the fatherly heart of Lincoln dictated a private letter to Stanton. The boy was reappointed to West Point, but did not graduate.

PRIVATE

War Department
Washington City, D. C.
June 5. 1862

Hon. Sec. of War.
My dear Sir

Herewith I return you the papers in relation to the proposed reappointment of William Kellogg, Jr. to a cadetship. Upon Gen. Totten's statement of the case I think it is natural that he should feel as he expresses himself. And yet the case comes upon me in the very strongest way to be painful to me. Hon. William Kellogg, the father, is not only a Member of Congress from my state, but he is my personal friend of more than twenty years' standing, and of whom I had many personal kindnesses. This matter touches him very deeply—the feelings of a father for a child—as he thinks, all the future of his child. I cannot be the instrument to crush his heart. According to strict rule he has the right to make the renomination. Let the appointment be made. It needs not to become a precedent. Hereafter let no resignation be accepted under demerit amounting to cause for dismissal, unless upon express stipulation in writing that the cadet resigning shall not be re-nominated. In this I mean no censure upon Gen. Totten; and although I have marked this note *"private"* I am quite willing for him to see it. Yours truly

A. Lincoln.

At Cross Keys on June 8 and at Port Republic next day, Jackson defeated Fremont and Shields. Perhaps if, as ordered, Fremont had gone to Harrisonburg, he might have blocked Jackson. But Jackson had no intention of being caught; his mission was to immobilize Mc-Dowell by threatening Washington, then turn up on the Peninsula. Lincoln chafed to realize how easily Jackson played cat-and-mouse with the Union generals.

Washington City, D. C.
June 13 1862

Major Gen. Fremont

We cannot afford to keep your force, and Banks', and Mc-Dowell's, engaged in keeping Jackson south of Strasburg and Front Royal. You fought Jackson alone, and worsted him. He can have no substantial reinforcement, so long as a battle is pending at Richmond. Surely you and Banks in supporting distance are capable of keeping him from returning to Winchester. But if Sigel be sent forward to you, and McDowell (as he must) be put to other work, Jackson will break through at Front Royal again. He is already on the right side of the Shenandoah to do it, and on the wrong side of it to attack you. The orders already sent you and Banks place you and him in the proper positions for the work assigned you. Jackson cannot move his whole force on either of you, before the other can learn of it, and go to his assistance. He cannot divide his force, sending part against each of you because he will be too weak for either. Please do as I directed in the order of the 8th. and my despatch of yesterday, the 12th. and neither you nor Banks will be overwhelmed by Jackson. By proper scouts-lookouts, and beacons of smoke by day, and fires by night, you can always have timely notice of the enemy's approach. I know not as to you, but by some, this has been too much neglected.

A. Lincoln

Three days later Lincoln again faced the shortcomings of a general who seemed to be doing his best fighting behind a telegraph key.

"CYPHER"

Washington City, D. C.
June 16, 1862

Major General Fremont
Mount Jackson, Va.

Your despatch of yesterday reminding me of a supposed understanding that I would furnish you a corps of thirty-five thousand men, and asking of me "the fulfillment of this understanding" is received. I am ready to come to a fair settlement of accounts with you on the fulfillment of understandings.

Early in March last, when I assigned you to the command of the Mountain Department, I did tell you I would give you all the force I could, and that I hoped to make it reach thirty five thousand. You, at the same time told me that, within a reasonable time, you would seize the railroad at, or east of, Knoxville, Tenn. if you could. There was then in the department a force supposed to be twenty-five thousand—the exact number as well known to you as to me. After looking about two or three days you called and distinctly told me that if I would add the Blenker division to the force already in the department, you would undertake the job. The Blenker division contained ten thousand; and at the expense of great dissatisfaction to Gen. McClellan, I took it from his army, and gave it to you. My promise was literally fulfilled. I had given you all I could, and I had given you very nearly if not quite thirty-five thousand.

Now for yours. On the 23rd. of May, largely over two months afterwards, you were at Franklin, Va, not within three hundred miles of Knoxville, nor within eighty miles of any part of the railroad east of it—and not moving forward, but telegraphing here that you could not move for lack of everything. Now, do not misunderstand me. I do not say you have not done all you could. I presume you met unexpected difficulties; and I beg you to believe that as surely as you have done your best, so have I. I have not the power now to fill up your corps to thirty-five thousand. I am not demanding of you to do the work of thirty-five thousand. I am only asking of you to stand cautiously on the defensive, get your force in order, and give such protection as you can to the valley of the Shenandoah, and to Western Virginia. Have you received the orders? and will you act upon them?

A. Lincoln.

If possible, Lincoln's irritation with McClellan increased.

Washington, June 26, 1862.

Major General McClellan:
    Your three despatches of yesterday in relation to the affair, ending with the statement that you completely succeeded in making

your point, are very gratifying. The later one of 6:15 P.M., suggesting the probability of your being overwhelmed by 200,000, and talking of where the responsibility will belong, pains me very much. I give you all I can, and act on the presumption that you will do the best you can with what you have, while you continue, ungenerously I think, to assume that I could give you more if I would. I have omitted and shall omit no opportunity to send you reenforcements whenever I possibly can.

A. Lincoln

Young Quintin was the son of Mrs. Lincoln's cousin, Ann Todd Campbell. He graduated from West Point in 1866.

Washington D. C.
June 28. 1862

Cadet Quintin Campbell
My dear Sir
Your good mother tells me you are feeling very badly in your new situation. Allow me to assure you it is a perfect certainty that you will, very soon, feel better—quite happy—if you only stick to the resolution you have taken to procure a military education. I am older than you, have felt badly myself, and *know,* what I tell you is true. Adhere to your purpose and you will soon feel as well as you ever did. On the contrary, if you falter, and give up, you will lose the power of keeping any resolution, and will regret it all your life. Take the advice of a friend, who, though he never saw you, deeply sympathizes with you, and stick to your purpose. Sincerely your friend

A. Lincoln

After Joseph E. Johnston was wounded in early June, Lee assumed the Confederate command on the Peninsula. With the purpose of Jackson's movements clear, Lincoln rushed ten regiments of McDowell's corps to McClellan. Before McClellan attacked, however, Lee punched at the Union forces north of the Chickahominy—the start of the Seven Days' Battle. From McClellan, admitting that he knew not "the full history of the day," came the first word of that fighting. The losses on both sides he reported as "terrible." Lincoln braced himself for a possible disaster.

Washington City, D. C.
June 28– 1862

Major Gen. McClellan

Save your army at all events. Will send re-inforcements as fast as we can. Of course they cannot reach you today, tomorrow, or next day. I have not said you were ungenerous for saying you needed re-inforcement. I thought you were ungenerous in assuming that I did not send them as fast as I could. I feel any misfortune to you and your army quite as keenly as you feel it yourself. If you have had a drawn battle, or a repulse, it is the price we pay for the enemy not being in Washington. We protected Washington, and the enemy concentrated on you; had we stripped Washington, he would have been upon us before the troops sent could have got to you. Less than a week ago you notified us that re-inforcements were leaving Richmond to come in front of us. It is the nature of the case, and neither you or the government that is to blame. Please tell at once the present condition and aspect of things.

A. Lincoln

P.S. Gen. Pope thinks if you fall back, it would be much better towards York River, than towards the James. As Pope now has charge of the Capital, please confer with him through the telegraph. *A. L.*

On the first day at Mechanicsville, McClellan stopped Lee's attack; but the following day at Gaines' Mill victory belonged to the Rebels. The general who had fancied he could have become dictator lost his nerve—and apparently his head as well, for 60,000 troops that might have been employed against the weak side of Lee's line were not used. Typically, McClellan wired Stanton: "If I save this army now, I tell you plainly that I owe no thanks to you or to any other person in Washington." The supervisor of military telegrams ordered the sentence deleted before the message was shown to the Secretary of War.

Lincoln grew haggard. "I must die sometime," he told an old friend. Criticism mounted against both McClellan and the President. Seward heard from Lincoln in these moments of bitter despair.

The Living Lincoln

Executive Mansion
June 28. 1862.

Hon. W. H. Seward
My dear Sir

My view of the present condition of the war is about as follows:
The evacuation of Corinth, and our delay by the flood in the Chicahominy, has enabled the enemy to concentrate too much force in Richmond for McClellan to successfully attack. In fact there soon will be no substantial rebel force anywhere else. But if we send all the force from here to McClellan, the enemy will, before we can know of it, send a force from Richmond and take Washington. Or, if a large part of the western army be brought here to McClellan, they will let us have Richmond, and retake Tennessee, Kentucky, Missouri &c. What should be done is to hold what we have in the West, open the Mississippi, and take Chatanooga & East Tennessee, without more—a reasonable force should, in every event, be kept about Washington for its protection. Then let the country give us a hundred thousand new troops in the shortest possible time, which added to McClellan, directly or indirectly, will take Richmond, without endangering any other place which we now hold—and will substantially end the war. I expect to maintain this contest until successful, or till I die, or am conquered, or my term expires, or Congress or the country forsakes me; and I would publicly appeal to the country for this new force, were it not that I fear a general panic and stampede would follow—so hard is it to have a thing understood as it really is. I think the new force should be all, or nearly all infantry, principally because such can be raised most cheaply and quickly. Yours very truly
A. Lincoln

July first brought news from McClellan of "another day of desperate fighting . . . you must send me reenforcements . . . very promptly." Lincoln tried to make McClellan face reality.

Executive Mansion,
Washington, July 1 1862.

Major Genl. McClellan—

It is impossible to re-inforce you for your present emergency. If we had a million of men we could not get them to you in time. We have not the men to send. If you are not strong enough to face the enemy you must find a place of security, and wait, rest, and repair. Maintain your ground if you can; but save the army at all events, even if you fall back to Fortress Monroe. We still have strength enough in the country, and will bring it out.

A. Lincoln

Later that day Washington again heard from McClellan. He had repulsed Lee and was regrouping his forces along a ridge that paralleled the James River. He needed 50,000 reserves instantly. A passage of the dispatch read: "I must apologize for the probable incoherency of this letter. I am exhausted by want of sleep and constant anxiety." The gentleness in Lincoln responded at once.

Washington, D. C.,
July 2 1862.

Major Gen. McClellan

Your despatch of Tuesday morning induces me to hope your army is having some rest. In this hope, allow me to reason with you a moment. When you ask for fifty thousand men to be promptly sent you, you surely labor under some gross mistake of fact. Recently you sent papers showing your disposal of forces, made last spring, for the defence of Washington, and advising a return to that plan. I find it included in, and about Washington seventy-five thousand men. Now please be assured, I have not men enough to fill that very plan by fifteen thousand. All of Fremont in the Valley, all of Banks, all of McDowell, not with you, and all in Washington, taken together do not exceed, if they reach sixty thousand. With Wool and Dix added to those mentioned, I have not, outside of your army, seventy-five thousand men east of the mountains. Thus, the idea of sending you fifty thousand, or any other considerable force promptly, is simply absurd. If in your frequent mention of responsibility, you have the impression that I blame you for not doing more than you can, please be relieved of such impression. I only beg that in like manner, you will not ask impossibilities of me. If you think you are not strong enough to take Richmond just now, I do not ask you to try just now. Save the army, material and personal; and I will strengthen it for the offensive again, as fast as I can. The governors of eighteen states offer me a new levy of three hundred thousand, which I accept.

A. Lincoln

The Living Lincoln

Lincoln had delegated Seward to ask the Governors of the North for more troops. While recognizing difficulties, the responses generally were encouraging. The Governor of New York heard from Lincoln by letter; to other Union Governors this message was telegraphed.

Washington,
July 3. 1862. [10:30 A.M.*]*

Gov. E. D. Morgan
My dear Sir—

I should not want the half of three hundred thousand new troops, if I could have them *now*. If I had fifty thousand additional troops here *now,* I believe I could substantially close the war in two weeks. But *time* is *everything;* and if I get fifty thousand new men in a month, I shall have lost twenty thousand old ones during the same month, having gained only thirty thousand, with the difference between old and new troops still against me. The quicker you send, the fewer you will have to send. *Time* is everything. Please act in view of this. The enemy having given up Corinth, it is not wonderful that he is thereby enabled to check us for a time at Richmond.

A. Lincoln.

The campaign on the Peninsula proved that the Army of the Potomac could fight magnificently, yet it had been thrown back. Another aspect of that campaign was the emergence of Lee—a general to respect, perhaps to fear. McClellan, believing he might still win with fresh troops, sent his chief-of-staff to Washington to plead his case. Lincoln, however, was a military realist.

War Department Washington City, D. C.
July 4. 1862

Major Gen. McClellan:

I understand your position as stated in your letter, and by Gen. Marcy. To reinforce you so as to enable you to resume the offensive within a month, or even six weeks, is impossible. In addition to that arrived, and now arriving from the Potomac, (about ten thousand, I suppose) and about ten thousand I hope you will have from Burnside very soon, and about five thousand from Hunter a little later, I do not see how I can send you another man within a month. Under these circumstances the defensive, for the present, must be your only care. Save the army—first, where you are, if you *can;* and secondly, by removal, if you must. You, on the ground, must be the judge as to which you will attempt, and of the means for effecting it. I but give it as opinion, that with the aid of the gunboats, and the re-inforcements mentioned above, you can hold your present position, provided, and so long as, you can keep the James River open below you. If you are not tolerably confident you can keep the James River open, you had better remove as soon as possible. I do not remember that you have expressed any apprehension as to the danger of having your communication cut on the river below you; yet I do not suppose it can have escaped your attention. Yours very truly

 A. Lincoln

P.S. If, at any time, you feel able to take the offensive, you are not restrained from doing so.   *A. L.*

McClellan wired on July 4: "Our whole army is drawn up for review in its positions, bands playing, salutes being fired, and all things looking bright."

 Washington City, D. C.
July 5, 1862.

Major Genl. McClellan

A thousand thanks for the relief your two despatches of 12 & 1 P.M. yesterday—give me. Be assured the heroism and skill of yourself, officers, and men, are, and forever will be appreciated. If you can hold your present position, we shall *"hive"* the enemy yet.

 A. Lincoln

Enormous pressure was exerted on Lincoln to relieve McClellan and the President paid his second surprise visit to the headquarters of his general, now at Harrison Landing. When, mounted on a horse, Lincoln reviewed the troops at least one soldier feared that at any moment his legs might become entangled with those of the animal. But other soldiers, believing in the President's ability to understand what they suffered, said: "When he finds out, it will be stopped."

From the field Lincoln went to West Point to confer with Winfield Scott, then on July 11 gave the command of all land forces to General Henry W. Halleck. Next day the President invited to the White House the representatives from the border states, urging them to end the war with ballots rather than bullets. Twenty members of this group responded on July 14, denying the practicability of Lincoln's arguments; and the following day eight others signed a minority report of approval.

July 12, 1862

Gentlemen.

After the adjournment of Congress, now very near, I shall have no opportunity of seeing you for several months. Believing that you of the border states hold more power for good than any other equal number of Members, I feel it a duty which I cannot justifiably waive, to make this appeal to you. I intend no reproach or complaint when I assure you that in my opinion, if you all had voted for the resolution in the gradual emancipation message of last March, the war would now be substantially ended. And the plan therein proposed is yet one of the most potent, and swift means of ending it. Let the states which are in rebellion see, definitely and certainly, that, in no event, will the states you represent ever join their proposed confederacy, and they cannot, much longer maintain the contest. But you cannot divest them of their hope to ultimately have you with them so long as you show a determination to perpetuate the institution within your own states. Beat them at elections, as you have overwhelmingly done, and, nothing daunted, they still claim you as their own. You and I know what the lever of their power is. Break that lever before their faces, and they can shake you no more forever.

Most of you have treated me with kindness and consideration; and I trust you will not now think I improperly touch what is exclusively your own, when, for the sake of the whole country I ask "Can you, for your states, do better than to take the course I urge?" Discarding *punctillio,* and maxims adapted to more manageable times, and looking only to the unprecedentedly stern facts of our case, can you do better in any possible event? You prefer that the constitutional relation of the states to the nation shall be practically restored, without disturbance of the institution; and if this were done, my whole duty, in this respect, under the constitution, and my oath of office, would be performed. But it is not done, and we are trying to accomplish it by war. The incidents of the war cannot be avoided. If the war continue long, as it must, if the object be not sooner attained, the institution in your states will be extinguished by mere friction and abrasion—by the mere incidents of the war. It will be gone, and you will have nothing valuable in lieu of it. Much of its value is gone already. How much better for you, and for your people, to take the step which, at once, shortens the war, and secures substantial compensation for that which is sure to be wholly lost in any other event. How much better to thus save the money which else we sink forever in the war. How much better to do it while we can, lest the war ere long render us pecuniarily unable to do it. How much better for you, as seller, and the nation as buyer, to sell out, and buy out, that without which the war could never have been, than to sink both the thing to be sold, and the price of it, in cutting one another's throats.

I do not speak of emancipation *at once,* but of a *decision* at once to emancipate *gradually.* Room in South America for colonization, can be obtained cheaply, and in abundance; and when numbers shall be large enough to be company and encouragement for one another, the freed people will not be so reluctant to go.

I am pressed with a difficulty not yet mentioned—one which threatens division among those who, united are none too strong. An instance of it is known to you. Gen. Hunter is an honest man. He was, and I hope, still is, my friend. I valued him none the less for his agreeing with me in the general wish that all men everywhere, could be free. He proclaimed all men free within certain states, and I repudiated the proclamation. He expected more good, and less harm from the measure, than I could believe would follow. Yet in repudiating it, I gave dissatisfaction, if not offence, to many whose support the country cannot afford to lose. And this is not the end of it. The pressure, in this direction, is still upon me, and is increasing. By conceding what I now ask, you can relieve me, and much more, can relieve the country, in this important point. Upon these considerations I have again begged your attention to the message of March last. Before leaving the Capital, consider and discuss it among yourselves. You are patriots and statesmen; and, as such, I pray you, consider this proposition; and, at the least, commend it to the consideration of your states and people. As you would perpetuate popular government for the best people in the world, I beseech you that you do in no wise omit this. Our common country is in great peril, demanding the loftiest views, and boldest action to bring it speedy relief. Once relieved, its form of government is saved to the world; its beloved history, and cherished memories, are vindicated; and its happy future fully assured, and rendered inconceivably grand. To you, more than to any others, the privilege is given, to assure that happiness, and swell that grandeur, and to link your own names therewith forever.

George Pomroy's mother, a Civil War nurse from Chelsea, Massachusetts, had nursed Mrs. Lincoln and Tad a few months earlier.

> *Executive Mansion,*
> *Washington, July 15. 1862.*

Hon. Sec. of War
My dear Sir:

This young man—George K. Pomroy—is the son of one of the best women I ever knew—a widow who has lost all her other children, and has cheerfully given this one to the war, and devotes herself exclusively to nursing our sick and wounded soldiers. I wish to do something for him, and, even, to strain a point for that object. I wish you would see him, and give him a second Lieutenancy in the regular army, in the first vacancy not already promised. He has already served nearly a year in the volunteers. This shall be your voucher. Yours truly

> *A. Lincoln*

In April a combined naval and army force seized New Orleans. Brigadier General John S. Phelps served as military governor of Arkansas and Louisiana until June, when Colonel George P. Shepley became military governor of Louisiana. From the beginning of occupation of the port the Union's commanding general, Bejamin F. Butler, displayed a rare talent for antagonizing everyone, and among the nicknames attached to him was "Beast" Butler. Many foreign consuls protested Butler's arrogant actions, and it was as a special agent for the State Department to investigate these complaints that Reverdy Johnson had gone to Louisiana. Whatever Union feeling had existed there, Johnson wrote Lincoln, had nearly subsided "from the impression that it is the *purpose* of the Govt. to force the Emancipation of the slaves." Unless this impression was altered at once, Johnson warned the President, "this State cannot be, for years, if ever, reinstated in the Union." Only four days had passed since Lincoln had revealed to his cabinet the somewhat astonishing news that he was considering a proclamation that would free the slaves in rebellious states. Both political pressure at home and moral persuasion abroad were in Lincoln's mind as, step by step, he moved toward a historic decision.

PRIVATE

Executive Mansion,
Washington, July 26, 1862.

Hon Reverdy Johnson
My Dear Sir.

Yours of the 16th. by the hand of Governor Shepley is received. It seems the Union feeling in Louisiana is being crushed out by the course of General Phelps. Please pardon me for believing that is a false pretense. The people of Louisiana—all intelligent people everywhere—know full well, that I never had a wish to touch the foundations of their society, or any right of theirs. With perfect knowledge of this, they forced a necessity upon me to send armies among them, and it is their own fault, not mine, that they are annoyed by the presence of General Phelps. They also know the remedy—know how to be cured of General Phelps. Remove the necessity of his presence. And might it not be well for them to consider whether they have not already had *time* enough to do this? If they can conceive of anything worse than General Phelps, within my power, would they not better be looking out for it? They very well know the way to avert all this is simply to take their place in the Union upon the old terms. If they will not do this, should they not receive harder blows rather than lighter ones?

You are ready to say I apply to *friends* what is due only to *enemies.* I distrust the *wisdom* if not the *sincerity* of friends, who would hold my hands while my enemies stab me. This appeal of professed friends has paralyzed me more in this struggle than any other one thing. You remember telling me the day after the Baltimore mob in April 1861, that it would crush all Union feeling in Maryland for me to attempt bringing troops over Maryland soil to Washington. I brought the troops notwithstanding, and yet there was Union feeling enough left to elect a legislature the next autumn which in turn elected a very excellent Union U. S. Senator!

I am a patient man—always willing to forgive on the Christian terms of repentance; and also to give ample *time* for repentance. Still I must save this government if possible. What I *cannot* do, of course I *will* not do; but it may as well be understood, once for all, that I shall not surrender this game leaving any available card unplayed. Yours truly

A. Lincoln

Principal loyalists in New Orleans were Cuthbert Bullitt (who later would serve as acting collector of customs and U. S. marshal for Louisiana) and Thomas J. Durant. General Nathaniel P. Banks thought that Lincoln's letter to Bullitt "is one of the best" and should be published. There is no indication, however, that it was ever printed.

PRIVATE

Washington D. C.
July 28. 1862

Cuthbert Bullitt Esq
New Orleans La.
Sir:

The copy of a letter addressed to yourself by Mr. Thomas J. Durant, has been shown to me. The writer appears to be an able, a dispassionate, and an entirely sincere man. The first part of the letter is devoted to an effort to show that the secession ordinance of Louisiana was adopted against the will of a majority of the people. This is probably true; and in that fact may be found some instruction. Why did they allow the ordinance to go into effect? Why did they not assert themselves? Why stand passive and allow themselves to be trodden down by a minority? Why did they not hold popular meetings, and have a convention of their own, to express and enforce the true sentiment of the state? If preorganization was against them *then,* why not do this *now,* that the United States army is present to protect them? The paralysis—the dead palsy—of the government in this whole struggle is, that this class of men will do nothing for the government, nothing for themselves, except demanding that the government shall not strike its open enemies, lest they be struck by accident!

Mr. Durant complains that in various ways the relation of master and slave is disturbed by the presence of our army; and he considers it particularly vexatious that this, in part, is done under cover of an act of Congress, while constitutional guaranties are suspended on the plea of military necessity. The truth is, that what is done, and omitted, about slaves, is done and omitted on the same military necessity. It is a military necessity to have men and money; and we can get neither, in sufficient numbers, or amounts, if we keep from, or drive from, our lines, slaves coming to them. Mr. Durant cannot be ignorant of the pressure in this direction; nor of my efforts to hold it within bounds till he, and such as he shall have time to help themselves.

I am not posted to speak understandingly on all the police regulations of which Mr. Durant complains. If experience shows any one of them to be wrong, let them be set right. I think I can perceive, in the freedom of trade, which Mr. Durant urges, that he would relieve both friends and enemies from the pressure of the blockade. By this he would serve the enemy more effectively than the enemy is able to serve himself. I do not say or believe that to serve the enemy is the purpose of Mr. Durant; or that he is conscious of any purpose, other than national and patriotic ones. Still, if there were a class of men who, having no choice of sides in the contest, were anxious only to have quiet and comfort for themselves while it rages, and to fall in with the victorious side at the end of it, without loss to themselves, their advice as to the mode of conducting the contest would be precisely such as his is. He speaks of no duty—apparently thinks of none—resting upon Union men. He even thinks it injurious to the Union cause that they should be restrained in trade and passage without taking sides. They are to touch neither a sail nor a pump, but to be merely passengers,— deadheads at that—to be carried snug and dry, throughout the storm, and safely landed right side up. Nay, more; even a mutineer is to go untouched lest these sacred passengers receive an accidental wound.

Of course the rebellion will never be suppressed in Louisiana, if the professed Union men there will neither help to do it, nor permit the government to do it without their help.

Now, I think the true remedy is very different from what is suggested by Mr. Durant. It does not lie in rounding the rough angles of the war, but in removing the necessity for the war. The people of Louisiana who wish protection to person and property, have but to reach forth their hands and take it. Let them, in good faith, re-inaugurate the national authority, and set up a state government conforming thereto under the Constitution. They know how to do it, and can have the protection of the army while doing it. The army will be withdrawn so soon as such state government can dispense with its presence; and the people of the state can then upon the old constitutional terms, govern themselves to their own liking. This is very simple and easy.

If they will not do this, if they prefer to hazard all for the sake of destroying the government, it is for them to consider whether it is probable I will surrender the government to save them from losing all. If they decline what I suggest, you scarcely need to ask what I will do. What would you do in my position? Would you drop the war where it is? Or, would you prosecute it in future, with elder-stalk squirts, charged with rose water? Would you deal lighter blows rather than heavier ones? Would you give up the contest, leaving any available means unapplied?

I am in no boastful mood. I shall not do *more* than I can, and I shall do *all* I can to save the government, which is my sworn duty as well as my personal inclination. I shall do nothing in malice. What I deal with is too vast for malicious dealing. Yours truly

A. Lincoln

The prominent New York financier and Democrat, August Belmont, was the recipient of this letter.

July 31, 1862.

Dear Sir:

You send to Mr. Weed an extract from a letter written at New Orleans the 9th instant, which is shown to me. You do not give the writer's name; but plainly he is a man of ability, and probably of some note. He says: "The time has arrived when Mr. Lincoln must take a decisive course. Trying to please everybody, he will satisfy nobody. A vacillating policy in matters of importance is the very worst. Now is the time, if ever, for honest men who love their country to rally to its support. Why will not the North say officially that it wishes for the restoration of the Union as it was?"

And so, it seems, this is the point on which the writer thinks I have no policy. Why will he not read and understand what I have said?

The substance of the very declaration he desires is in the inaugural, in each of the two regular messages to Congress, and in many, if not all, the minor documents issued by the executive since the inauguration.

From Belmont to Second Manassas

Broken eggs cannot be mended; but Louisiana has nothing to do now but to take her place in the Union as it was, barring the already broken eggs. The sooner she does so, the smaller will be the amount of that which will be past mending. This government cannot much longer play a game in which it stakes all, and its enemies stake nothing. Those enemies must understand that they cannot experiment for ten years trying to destroy the government, and if they fail still come back into the Union unhurt. If they expect in any contingency to ever have the Union as it was, I join with the writer in saying, "Now is the time."

How much better it would have been for the writer to have gone at this, under the protection of the army at New Orleans, than to have sat down in a closet writing complaining letters northward! Yours truly,

A. Lincoln.

Greeley unleashed a bitter editorial attack upon the policy Lincoln pursued with regard to the slaves of Rebels. Among the nine specific charges were accusations that the President was "strangely and disastrously remiss . . . with regard to the emancipating provisions of the new Confiscation Act," that he was "unduly influenced" by "certain fossil politicians hailing from the Border Slaves States," and that what the country required of Lincoln was "a frank, declared, unqualified, ungrudging execution of the laws of the land . . ." The President's reply was moderate in tone, but no one could mistake his position.

Executive Mansion,
Washington, August 22, 1862.

Hon. Horace Greely:
Dear Sir

I have just read yours of the 19th. addressed to myself through the New York Tribune. If there be in it any statements, or assumptions of fact, which I may know to be erroneous, I do not, now and here, controvert them. If there be in it any inferences which I may believe to be falsely drawn, I do not now and here, argue against them. If there be perceptible in it an impatient and dictatorial tone, I waive it in deference to an old friend, whose heart I have always supposed to be right.

As to the policy I "seem to be pursuing" as you say, I have not meant to leave any one in doubt.

The Living Lincoln

I would save the Union. I would save it the shortest way under the Constitution. The sooner the national authority can be restored; the nearer the Union will be "the Union as it was." If there be those who would not save the Union, unless they could at the same time *save* slavery, I do not agree with them. If there be those who would not save the Union unless they could at the same time *destroy* slavery, I do not agree with them. My paramount object in this struggle *is* to save the Union, and is *not* either to save or to destroy slavery. If I could save the Union without freeing *any* slave I would do it, and if I could save it by freeing *all* the slaves I would do it; and if I could save it by freeing some and leaving others alone I would also do that. What I do about slavery, and the colored race, I do because I believe it helps to save the Union; and what I forbear, I forbear because I do *not* believe it would help to save the Union. I shall do *less* whenever I shall believe what I am doing hurts the cause, and I shall do *more* whenever I shall believe doing more will help the cause. I shall try to correct errors when shown to be errors; and I shall adopt new views so fast as they shall appear to be true views.

I have here stated my purpose according to my view of *official* duty; and I intend no modification of my oft-expressed *personal* wish that all men everywhere could be free. Yours,

A. Lincoln

The failure of McClellan's Peninsular campaign taught Lincoln a number of military lessons. The North could not fight the gentlemanly defensive war that McClellan preferred, but must strike aggressively to crush the armies of the South. Also, Lincoln must acknowledge that the professional soldier was not necessarily a master of the art of war; indeed, his judgment could prove the worst of any. Despite the fact that John Pope had been successful in opening the Mississippi south of Memphis, it was with tongue-in-cheek that Lincoln brought him east to command. Pope quickly justified this reservation, for his vainglorious braggadocio everywhere aroused rensentment and ridicule. Meanwhile Lee, who relied on boldness, sent Jackson racing around Pope's right flank, and a second Union debacle was in the making at Manassas. A distraught, sleepless Lincoln tried to piece together the truth as Jackson maneuvered to rejoin Lee and Longstreet, coming through undefended Thoroughfare Gap, massed on Pope's left flank.

From Belmont to Second Manassas

Aug. 27. 4./30 P.M. *1862*

Major Gen. Burnside
Falmouth, Va.
    Do you hear anything from Pope?

A. Lincoln

War Department, August 27, 1862.

Is the railroad bridge over Bull Run destroyed?
Colonel Haupt.

A. Lincoln.

War Department, August 27, 1862.

    What became of our forces which held the bridge till twenty minutes ago, as you say?
Colonel Haupt.

A. Lincoln.

Aug. 27. 4 P.M. *1862.*

Major General McClellan
Alexandria, Va
    What news from the front?

A Lincoln

Aug. 28. 2/40 P.M. *1862*

Major Genl. Burnside
Falmouth, Va
    Any news from Gen. Pope?

A. Lincoln

Aug. 28. 2/40 P.M. *1862*

Col. Haupt.
Alexandria, Va.
    Yours received. *How* do you learn that the rebel forces at Manassas are large and commanded by several of their best generals?

A. Lincoln

The Living Lincoln

Washington, D. C.,
Aug. 29. 2/30 P.M. 1862.

Major Genl. Burnside
Falmouth, Va.

Any further news? Does Col. Devin mean that sound of firing was heard in direction of Warrenton, as stated, or in direction of Warrenton Junction?

A. Lincoln

War Department, August 29, 1862.

What news from direction of Manassas? What generally?
Colonel Haupt.

A. Lincoln

War Department,
Washington, D. C.,
Aug. 29. 2/30. 1862.

Major Genl. McClellan
Alexandria, Va.

What news from direction of Manassas Junction? What generally?

A. Lincoln

Washington, D. C.,
Aug. 29. 1862.

Major Genl. McClellan
Alexandria, Va

Yours of today just received. I think your first alternative, towit, "to concentrate all our available forces to open communication with Pope," is the right one. But I wish not to control. That I now leave to Gen. Halleck, aided by your counsels.

A. Lincoln

August 30. 8/35 PM. 1862

Major Genl. Banks.
Manassas Junction, Va

Please tell me what news.

A Lincoln

From Belmont to Second Manassas

Washington, D. C.,
Aug. 30, 10/20 AM *1862.*

Col. Haupt.
Alexandria, Va.
> What news?

A. Lincoln

Aug. 30. 1862, 3/50. P.M

Col. Haupt,
Alexandria, Va
> Please send me the latest news.

A. Lincoln

United States Military Telegraph.
Aug. 31. 7/10 A.M. *1862*

Col. Haupt,
Alexandria, Va
> What news? Do you hear firing this morning?

A. Lincoln

Again beaten Union troops straggled into Washington from Manassas. Understandably, Lincoln meditated upon the role played by Divine Will in the war that rent the nation.

[September 2, 1862?]

The will of God prevails. In great contests each party claims to act in accordance with the will of God. Both *may* be, and one *must* be wrong. God cannot be *for,* and *against* the same thing at the same time. In the present civil war it is quite possible that God's purpose is something different from the purpose of either party—and yet the human instrumentalities, working just as they do, are of the best adaptation to effect His purpose. I am almost ready to say this is probably true—that God wills this contest, and wills that it shall not end yet. By His mere quiet power, on the minds of the now contestants, He could have either *saved* or *destroyed* the Union without a human contest. Yet the contest began. And having begun He could give the final victory to either side any day. Yet the contest proceeds.

XIV. From Antietam to Vicksburg

1862-1863 C ONGRESSIONAL elections approached. The tempo of war increased, both on its military and political fronts.

Confederate strategy, either by design or luck, seemed aimed to deal the North a crushing blow in both arenas. Lee, flushed with the victory at Second Manassas, invaded Maryland. Buell, on his way to Louisville, found the Rebel Bragg stalking him along the Ohio River. Richmond well could feel satisfied if it could close the second year of war with the line of battle in the East pushed north of Maryland, which had not seceded; and the line of battle in the West pushed beyond Kentucky, which also had remained loyal to the Union.

Lee's advance threatened immediate disaster. He must be stopped by the Army of the Potomac, and the army trusted only McClellan. Reluctantly, Lincoln restored to command a general in whom he had little confidence.

And a constant whip at Lincoln's back now was the slavery question. At a public meeting on September 7 in Bryan Hall, Chicago, Christians of all denominations adopted a memorial in favor of national emancipation. Lincoln had decided weeks earlier to issue a proclamation, yet here he argued the matter as if it were an open question.

September 13, 1862
The subject presented in the memorial is one upon which I have thought much for weeks past, and I may even say for months. I am approached with the most opposite opinions and advice, and that by religious men, who are equally certain that they represent

500

the Divine will. I am sure that either the one or the other class is mistaken in that belief, and perhaps in some respects both. I hope it will not be irreverent for me to say that if it is probable that God would reveal his will to others, on a point so connected with my duty, it might be supposed he would reveal it directly to me; for, unless I am more deceived in myself than I often am, it is my earnest desire to know the will of Providence in this matter. *And if I can learn what it is I will do it!* These are not, however, the days of miracles, and I suppose it will be granted that I am not to expect a direct revelation. I must study the plain physical facts of the case, ascertain what is possible and learn what appears to be wise and right. The subject is difficult, and good men do not agree. For instance, the other day four gentlemen of standing and intelligence from New York called, as a delegation, on business connected with the war; but, before leaving, two of them earnestly beset me to proclaim general emancipation, upon which the other two at once attacked them! You know, also, that the last session of Congress had a decided majority of anti-slavery men, yet they could not unite on this policy. And the same is true of the religious people. Why, the rebel soldiers are praying with a great deal more earnestness, I fear, than our own troops, and expecting God to favor their side; for one of our soldiers, who had been taken prisoner, told Senator Wilson, a few days since, that he met with nothing so discouraging as the evident sincerity of those he was among in their prayers. But we will talk over the merits of the case.

What *good* would a proclamation of emancipation from me do, especially as we are now situated? I do not want to issue a document that the whole world will see must necessarily be inoperative, like the Pope's bull against the comet! Would *my word* free the slaves, when I cannot even enforce the Constitution in the rebel states? Is there a single court, or magistrate, or individual that would be influenced by it there? And what reason is there to think it would have any greater effect upon the slaves than the late law of Congress, which I approved, and which offers protection and freedom to the slaves of rebel masters who come within our lines? Yet I cannot learn that that law has caused a single slave to come over to us. And suppose they could be induced by a proclamation of freedom from me to throw themselves upon us, *what should we do with them?* How can we feed and care for such a multitude? Gen. Butler wrote me a few days since that he was

501

issuing more rations to the slaves who have rushed to him than to all the white troops under his command. They *eat*, and that is all, though it is true Gen. Butler is feeding the whites also by the thousand; for it nearly amounts to a famine there. If, now, the pressure of the war should call off our forces from New Orleans to defend some other point, what is to prevent the masters from reducing the blacks to slavery again; for I am told that whenever the rebels take any black prisoners, free or slave, they immediately auction them off! They did so with those they took from a boat that was aground in the Tennessee river a few days ago. And then *I am very ungenerously attacked for it!* For instance, when, after the late battles at and near Bull Run, an expedition went out from Washington under a flag of truce to bury the dead and bring in the wounded, and the rebels seized the blacks who went along to help and sent them into slavery, Horace Greeley said in his paper that the government would probably do nothing about it. What *could* I do?

But, asked the delegates, what would he have done if white men had been seized? Lincoln ignored the question and continued.

Now, then, tell me, if you please, what possible result of good would follow the issuing of such a proclamation as you desire? Understand, I raise no objection against it on legal or constitutional grounds; for, as commander-in-chief of the army and navy, in time of war, I suppose I have a right to take any measure which may best subdue the enemy. Nor do I urge objections of a moral nature, in view of possible consequences of insurrection and massacre at the South. I view the matter as a practical war measure, to be decided upon according to the advantages or disadvantages it may offer to the suppression of the rebellion.

Members of the delegation advanced arguments that Lincoln countered one by one.

I admit that slavery is the root of the rebellion, or at least its *sine qua non*. The ambition of politicians may have instigated them to act, but they would have been impotent without slavery as their instrument. I will also concede that emancipation would help us in Europe, and convince them that we are incited by something more than ambition. I grant further that it would help *somewhat* at the North, though not so much, I fear, as you and those you represent imagine. Still, some additional strength would be added in that way to the war. And then unquestionably it would weaken the rebels by drawing off their laborers, which is of great importance. But I am not so sure we could do much with the blacks. If we were to arm them, I fear that in a few weeks the arms would be in the hands of the rebels; and indeed thus far we have not had arms enough to equip our white troops. I will mention another thing, though it meet only your scorn and contempt: There are fifty thousand bayonets in the Union armies from the border slave states. It would be a serious matter if, in consequence of a proclamation such as you desire, they should go over to the rebels. I do not think they all would—not so many indeed as a year ago, or as six months ago—not so many to-day as yesterday. Every day increases their Union feeling. They are also getting their pride enlisted, and want to beat the rebels. Let me say one thing more: I think you should admit that we already have an important principle to rally and unite the people in the fact that constitutional government is at stake. This is a fundamental idea, going down about as deep as anything.

Lincoln would not dismiss the delegates, however, without giving them some hope.

Do not misunderstand me, because I have mentioned these objections. They indicate the difficulties that have thus far prevented my action in some such way as you desire. I have not decided against a proclamation of liberty to the slaves, but hold the matter under advisement. And I can assure you that the subject is on my mind, by day and night, more than any other. Whatever shall appear to be God's will I will do. I trust that, in the freedom with which I have canvassed your views, I have not in any respect injured your feelings.

Lee's invasion of Maryland ended at Antietam Creek, where the lucky capture of his plan of action finally produced a victory for McClellan. Lincoln had been waiting for some such change in military fortune to support his next political offensive. On September 22, five days after Antietam, he issued a warning that after January 1, 1863 all slaves in states still in rebellion would be declared free. "God bless you for this noble act," wrote Hannibal Hamlin, reflecting the general sentiment in the North. A note of pessimism ran through Lincoln's response.

503

The Living Lincoln

Executive Mansion,
Washington, September 28, 1862.

My Dear Sir:

Your kind letter of the 25th is just received. It is known to some that while I hope something from the proclamation, my expectations are not as sanguine as are those of some friends. The time for its effect southward has not come; but northward the effect should be instantaneous.

It is six days old, and while commendation in newspapers and by distinguished individuals is all that a vain man could wish, the stocks have declined, and troops come forward more slowly than ever. This, looked soberly in the face, is not very satisfactory. We have fewer troops in the field at the end of six days than we had at the beginning—the attrition among the old outnumbering the addition by the new. The North responds to the proclamation sufficiently in breath; but breath alone kills no rebels.

I wish I could write more cheerfully; nor do I thank you the less for the kindness of your letter. Yours very truly,

A. Lincoln.

The President went to Maryland to visit the Army of the Potomac. At Frederick he spoke informally: the strain of war had changed his life.

October 4, 1862

In my present position it is hardly proper for me to make speeches. Every word is so closely noted that it will not do to make trivial ones, and I cannot be expected to be prepared to make a matured one just now. If I were as I have been most of my life, I might perhaps, talk amusing to you for half-an-hour, and it wouldn't hurt anybody; but as it is, I can only return my sincere thanks for the compliment paid our cause and our common country.

Antietam forced Lee back into Virginia, but McClellan missed the opportunity to inflict a fatal blow. Too much hesitancy, attacks that were not co-ordinated, reserves that were never employed let Lee escape into the Shenandoah Valley. Still the Confederates were not well based to protect Richmond—why did McClellan continue to dissipate

504

his advantage? After Lincoln visited headquarters, Halleck ordered McClellan to "cross the Potomac and give battle or drive the enemy south." The cautious general refused to budge. Patiently Lincoln tried again to make McClellan move.

Executive Mansion,
Washington, Oct. 13, 1862.

Major General McClellan
My dear Sir

You remember my speaking to you of what I called your over-cautiousness. Are you not over-cautious when you assume that you cannot do what the enemy is constantly doing? Should you not claim to be at least his equal in prowess, and act upon the claim?

As I understand, you telegraph Gen. Halleck that you cannot subsist your army at Winchester unless the railroad from Harper's Ferry to that point be put in working order. But the enemy does now subsist his army at Winchester at a distance nearly twice as great from railroad transportation as you would have to do without the railroad last named. He now wagons from Culpeper C.H. which is just about twice as far as you would have to do from Harper's Ferry. He is certainly not more than half as well provided with wagons as you are. I certainly should be pleased for you to have the advantage of the railroad from Harper's Ferry to Winchester, but it wastes all the remainder of autumn to give it to you; and, in fact ignores the question of *time,* which cannot, and must not be ignored.

Again, one of the standard maxims of war, as you know, is "to operate upon the enemy's communications as much as possible without exposing your own." You seem to act as if this applies *against* you, but cannot apply in your *favor.* Change positions with the enemy, and think you not he would break your communication with Richmond within the next twenty-four hours? You dread his going into Pennsylvania. But if he does so in full force, he gives up his communications to you absolutely, and you have nothing to do but to follow, and ruin him; if he does so with less than full force, fall upon, and beat what is left behind all the easier.

Exclusive of the water line, you are now nearer Richmond than the enemy is by the route that you *can,* and he *must* take. Why can you not reach there before him, unless you admit that he is more than your equal on a march. His route is the arc of a circle, while yours is the chord. The roads are as good on yours as on his.

You know I desired, but did not order, you to cross the Potomac below, instead of above the Shenandoah and Blue Ridge. My idea was that this would at once menace the enemy's communications, which I would seize if he would permit. If he should move northward I would follow him closely, holding his communications. If he should prevent our seizing his communications, and move towards Richmond, I would press closely to him, fight him if a favorable opportunity should present, and, at least, try to beat him to Richmond on the inside track. I say "try"; if we never try, we shall never succeed. If he make a stand at Winchester, moving neither north or south, I would fight him there, on the idea that if we cannot beat him when he bears the wastage of coming to us, we never can when we bear the wastage of going to him. This proposition is a simple truth, and is too important to be lost sight of for a moment. In coming to us, he tenders us an advantage which we should not waive. We should not so operate as to merely drive him away. As we must beat him somewhere, or fail finally, we can do it, if at all, easier near to us, than far away. If we cannot beat the enemy where he now is, we never can, he again being within the entrenchments of Richmond.

Recurring to the idea of going to Richmond on the inside track, the facility of supplying from the side away from the enemy is remarkable—as it were, by the different spokes of a wheel extending from the hub towards the rim—and this whether you move directly by the chord, or on the inside arc, hugging the Blue Ridge more closely. The chord-line, as you see, carries you by Aldie, Hay-Market, and Fredericksburg; and you see how turnpikes, railroads, and finally, the Potomac by Acquia Creek, meet you at all points from Washington. The same, only the lines lengthened a little, if you press closer to the Blue Ridge part of the way. The gaps through the Blue Ridge I understand to be about the following distances from Harper's Ferry, to wit: Vestal's five miles; Gregorie's, thirteen, Snicker's eighteen, Ashby's, twenty-eight, Manassas, thirty-eight, Chester forty-five, and Thornton's fifty-three. I should think it preferable to take the route nearest the enemy, disabling him to make an important move without your knowledge, and compelling him to keep his forces together, for dread of you. The gaps would enable you to attack if you should wish. For a great part of the way, you would be practically between the enemy and both Washington and Richmond, enabling us to spare you the greatest number of troops from here. When at length, running for Richmond ahead of him enables him to move this way; if he does so, turn and attack him in rear. But I think he should be engaged long before such point is reached. It is all easy if our troops march as well as the enemy; and it is unmanly to say they cannot do it.

This letter is in no sense an order. Yours truly

A. Lincoln.

In the Illinois State Historical Library at Springfield a miniature brass cannon is preserved with this note.

Capt. Dahlgren may let "Tad" have a little gun that he cannot hurt himself with.

A. Lincoln

Oct. 14, 1862.

Lincoln authorized a political general to raise his own troops for a campaign against Vicksburg. Grant, about to fight for the same objective, knew nothing of these negotiations.

October 20, 1862

This order, though marked confidential, may be shown by Gen. McClernand, to Governors, and even others, when, in his discretion, he believes so doing to be indispensable to the progress of the expedition. I add that I feel deep interest in the success of the expedition, and desire it to be pushed forward with all possible despatch, consistently with the other parts of the military service.

A. Lincoln

Oct. 20. 1862.

Lincoln's sarcasm hurtled at McClellan with the force of a howitzer shell.

Washington City, D. C.
Oct. 24 [25]. 1862

Majr. Genl. McClellan

I have just read your despatch about sore-tongued and fatigued horses. Will you pardon me for asking what the horses of your army have done since the Battle of Antietam that fatigues anything?

A. Lincoln

Lincoln, deeply mystical, constantly brooded over the conflict between war's bloodshed and suffering and the beneficent purpose of an all-powerful God. Occasionally, as in this interview with Eliza P. Gurney, he brought his reflections to the surface. His visitor was the widow of Joseph J. Gurney, English Quaker, philosopher, and author of religious works.

October 26, 1862

I am glad of this interview, and glad to know that I have your sympathy and prayers. We are indeed going through a great trial —a fiery trial. In the very responsible position in which I happen to be placed, being a humble instrument in the hands of our Heavenly Father, as I am, and as we all are, to work out His great purposes, I have desired that all my works and acts may be according to His will, and that it might be so, I have sought His aid—but if after endeavoring to do my best in the light which He affords me, I find my efforts fail, I must believe that for some purpose unknown to me, He wills it otherwise. If I had had my way, this war would never have been commenced; if I had been allowed my way this war would have been ended before this, but we find it still continues; and we must believe that He permits it for some wise purpose of his own, mysterious and unknown to us; and though with our limited understandings we may not be able to comprehend it, yet we cannot but believe, that He who made the world still governs it.

Lincoln endeavored to approach McClellan in a more conciliatory mood.

Executive Mansion, Washington,
Oct. 27. 1862

Majr. Gen. McClellan.

Yours of yesterday received. Most certainly I intend no injustice to any; and if I have done any, I deeply regret it. To be told after more than five weeks total inaction of the army, and during which period we had sent to that army every fresh horse we pos-

From Antietam to Vicksburg

sibly could, amounting in the whole to 7918, that the cavalry horses were too much fatigued to move, presented a very cheerless, almost hopeless, prospect for the future; and it may have forced something of impatience into my despatches. If not recruited, and rested then, when could they ever be? I suppose the river is rising, and I am glad to believe you are crossing.

A. Lincoln

Before the day was over, however, the President lost patience.

Executive Mansion, Washington,
October 27, 1862. [3:25 P.M.*]*

Major-General McClellan:
Your dispatch of 3 P.M. today, in regard to filling up old regiments with drafted men, is received, and the request therein shall be complied with as far as practicable.

And now I ask a distinct answer to the question, Is it your purpose not to go into action again until the men now being drafted in the states are incorporated into the old regiments?

A. Lincoln.

The congressional elections went against the administration. Carl Schurz had one explanation for the causes of this reversal, Lincoln another.

"PRIVATE & CONFIDENTIAL"

Executive Mansion,
Washington, Nov. 10. 1862.

Gen. Schurz.
My dear Sir
Yours of the 8th. was, today, read to me by Mrs. S. We have lost the elections; and it is natural that each of us will believe, and say, it has been because his peculiar view was not made sufficiently prominent. I think I know what it was, but I may be mistaken. Three main causes told the whole story. 1. The Democrats were left in a majority by our friends going to the war. 2. The Democrats observed this & determined to reinstate themselves in power, and 3. Our newspapers, by vilifying and disparaging the administration, furnished them all the weapons to do it with. Certainly, the ill-success of the war had much to do with this.

509

You give a different set of reasons. If you had not made the following statements, I should not have suspected them to be true. "The defeat of the administration is the administration's own fault." (Opinion.) "It admitted its professed opponents to its counsels." (Asserted as a fact.) "It placed the army, now a great power in this Republic, into the hands of its enemies." (Asserted as a fact.) "In all personal questions, to be hostile to the party of the government, seemed to be a title to consideration." (Asserted as a fact.) "If to forget the great rule, that if you are true to your friends, your friends will be true to you, and that you make your enemies stronger by placing them upon an equality with your friends." "Is it surprising that the opponents of the administration should have got into their hands the government of the principal states, after they have had for a long time the principal management of the war, the great business of the national government."

I cannot dispute about the matter of opinion. On the three matters (stated as facts) I shall be glad to have your evidence upon them when I shall meet you. The plain facts, as they appear to me, are these. The administration came into power, very largely in a minority of the popular vote. Notwithstanding this, it distributed to its party friends as nearly all the civil patronage as any administration ever did. The war came. The administration could not even start in this, without assistance outside of its party. It was mere nonsense to suppose a minority could put down a majority in rebellion. Mr. Schurz (now Gen. Schurz) was about here then & I do not recollect that he then considered all who were not Republicans, were enemies of the government, and that none of them must be appointed to military positions. He will correct me if I am mistaken. It so happened that very few of our friends had a military education or were of the profession of arms. It would have been a question whether the war should be conducted on military knowledge, or on political affinity, only that our own friends (I think Mr. Schurz included) seemed to think that such a question was inadmissible. Accordingly I have scarcely appointed a Democrat to a command, who was not urged by many Republicans and opposed by none. It was so as to McClellan. He was first brought forward by the Republican Governor of Ohio, & claimed, and contended for at the same time by the Republican Governor of Pennsylvania. I received recommendations from the Republican delegations in Congress, and I believe every one of them recommended a majority of Democrats. But, after all many Republicans were appointed; and I mean no disparagement to them when I say I do not see that their superiority of success has been so marked as to throw great suspicion on the good faith of those who are not Republicans. Yours truly,

A. Lincoln

Lincoln explained to a distinguished jurist the politics of war.

PRIVATE

Executive Mansion,
Washington, Nov. 19, 1862.

Judge S. Treat
St. Louis, Mo.
My dear Sir
Your very patriotic and judicious letter, addressed to Judge Davis, in relation to the Mississippi, has been left with me by him for perusal. You do not estimate the value of the object you press, more highly than it is estimated here. It is now the object of particular attention. It has not been neglected, as you seem to think, because the West was divided into different military departments. The cause is much deeper. The country will not allow us to send our whole western force down the Mississippi, while the enemy sacks Louisville and Cincinnati. Possibly it would be better if the country would allow this, but it will not. I confidently believed, last September that we could end the war by allowing the enemy to go to Harrisburg and Philadelphia, only that we could not keep down mutiny, and utter demoralization among the Pennsylvanians. And this, though very unhandy sometimes, is not at all strange. I presume if an army was starting today for New Orleans, and you confidently believed that St. Louis would be sacked in consequence, you would be in favor of stopping such army.

We are compelled to watch all these things. With great respect Your Obt. Servt

A. Lincoln

Lincoln's footnote to history was based on an incident of the Revolution when John Hook, a suspected Tory, sued for two steers commandeered by the hungry patriots. Describing the surrender at York-

The Living Lincoln

town, Henry concluded: "But hark! what notes of discord are these which disturb the general joy, and silence the acclamations of victory — they are the notes of *John Hook,* hoarsely bawling through the American camp, *beef! beef! beef!*"

PRIVATE

Executive Mansion,
Washington, Nov. 20. 1862.

Hon. George Robertson
My dear Sir.

Your despatch of yesterday is just received. I believe you are acquainted with the American classics, (if there be such) and probably remember a speech of Patrick Henry, in which he represented a certain character in the revolutionary times, as totally disregarding all questions of country, and "hoarsely bawling, beef! beef!! beef!!!"

Do you not know that I may as well surrender this contest, directly, as to make any order, the obvious purpose of which would be to return fugitive slaves? Yours very truly

A. Lincoln

Nathaniel P. Banks, given Butler's command in New Orleans, had promised swift, aggressive action. Instead, he seemed to out-delay McClellan — no mean feat, from Lincoln's experience — and demanded supplies that he could never use. Soon the army had nicknamed N. P. Banks "Nothing Positive."

Executive Mansion,
Washington, Nov. 22, 1862.

My dear General Banks

Early last week you left me in high hope with your assurance that you would be off with your expedition at the end of that week, or early in this. It is now the end of this, and I have just been overwhelmed and confounded with the sight of a requisition made by you, which, I am assured, cannot be filled, and got off within an hour short of two months! I inclose you a copy of the requisition, in some hope that it is not genuine — that you have never seen it.

My dear General, this expanding, and piling up of *impedimenta,* has been, so far, almost our ruin, and will be our final ruin if it is not abandoned. If you had the articles of this requisition

512

upon the wharf, with the necessary animals to make them of any use, and forage for the animals, you could not get vessels together in two weeks to carry the whole, to say nothing of your twenty thousand men; and, having the vessels, you could not put the cargoes aboard in two weeks more. And, after all, where you are going, you have no use for them. When you parted with me, you had no such idea in your mind. I know you had not, or you could not have expected to be off so soon as you said. You must get back to something like the plan you had then, or your expedition is a failure before you start. You must be off before Congress meets. You would be better off anywhere, and especially where you are going, for not having a thousand wagons, doing nothing but hauling forage to feed the animals that draw them, and taking at least two thousand men to care for the wagons and animals, who otherwise might be two thousand good soldiers.

Now dear General, do not think this is an ill-natured letter— it is the very reverse. The simple publication of this requisition would ruin you. Very truly your friend

A. Lincoln

Schurz continued his post mortems on the elections. He did not blame Lincoln for placing Democrats like McClellan, Buell and Halleck in high military positions, "but it was unfortunate that you sustained them . . . after they had been found failing;—failing not only in a political but also in a military sense." Schurz reiterated: "It is best that you . . . should see the fact in its true light and appreciate its significance: *the result of the elections was a most serious and severe reproof administered to the administration.*" In replying, Lincoln drew heavily on his resources of patience and reason.

Executive Mansion,
Washington, Nov. 24. 1862.

Gen. Carl Schurz
My dear Sir

I have just received, and read, your letter of the 20th. The purport of it is that we lost the late elections, and the administration is failing, because the war is unsuccessful; and that I must not flatter myself that I am not justly to blame for it. I certainly know that if the war fails, the administration fails, and that I *will* be blamed for it, whether I deserve it or not. And I ought to be blamed, if I could do better. You think I could do better; therefore you blame me already. I think I could not do better; therefore I blame you for blaming me. I understand you *now* to be willing to accept the help of men, who are not Republicans, provided they have "heart in it." Agreed. I want no others. But who is to be the judge of hearts, or of "heart in it"? If I must discard my own judgment, and take yours, I must also take that of others; and by the time I should reject all I should be advised to reject, I should have none left, Republicans, or others—not even yourself. For, be assured, my dear sir, there are men who have "heart in it" that think you are performing your part as poorly as you think I am performing mine. I certainly have been dissatisfied with the slowness of Buell and McClellan; but before I relieved them I had great fears I should not find successors to them, who would do better; and I am sorry to add, that I have seen little since to relieve those fears. I do not clearly see the prospect of any more rapid movements. I fear we shall at last find out that the difficulty is in our case, rather than in particular generals. I wish to disparage no one—certainly not those who sympathize with me; but I must say I need success more than I need sympathy, and that I have not seen the so much greater evidence of getting success from my sympathizers, than from those who are denounced as the contrary. It does seem to me that in the field the two classes have been very much alike, in what they have done, and what they have failed to do. In sealing their faith with their blood, Baker, and Lyon, and Bohlen, and Richardson, Republicans, did all that men could do; but did they any more than Kearney, and Stevens, and Reno, and Mansfield, none of whom were Republicans, and some, at least of whom, have been bitterly, and repeatedly, denounced to me as secession sympathizers? I will not perform the ungrateful task of comparing cases of failure.

In answer to your question "Has it not been publicly stated in the newspapers, and apparently proved as a fact, that from the commencement of the war, the enemy was continually supplied with information by some of the confidential subordinates of as important an officer as Adjutant General Thomas?" I must say "no" so far as my knowledge extends. And I add that if you can give any tangible evidence upon that subject, I will thank you to come to the city and do so. Very truly Your friend

A. Lincoln

From Antietam to Vicksburg

Ambrose E. Burnside, one of McClellan's corps commanders, now led the Army of the Potomac. The President's uneasiness continued.

Executive Mansion, Washington,
Nov. 25. 1862. [11:30 A.M.]

Major General Burnside.
Falmouth, Va.

If I should be in a boat off Aquia Creek, at dark tomorrow (Wednesday) evening, could you, without inconvenience, meet me & pass an hour or two with me?

A. Lincoln

The President went to Acquia Creek with his own notions of how to beat Lee. His generals did not agree with him.

Steamer Baltimore
Off Acquia Creek, Va.
Nov. 27. 1862

Major General Halleck
Sir:

I have just had a long conference with Gen. Burnside. He believes that Gen. Lee's whole army, or nearly the whole of it is in front of him, at and near Fredericksburg. Gen. B. says he could take into battle now any day, about, one hundred and ten thousand men, that his army is in good spirit, good condition, good moral, and that in all respects he is satisfied with officers and men; that he does not want more men with him, because he could not handle them to advantage; that he thinks he can cross the river in face of the enemy and drive him away, but that, to use his own expression, it is somewhat risky. I wish the case to stand more favorable than this in two respects. First, I wish his crossing of the river to be nearly free from risk; and secondly, I wish the enemy to be prevented from falling back, accumulating strength as he goes, into his intrenchments at Richmond. I therefore propose that Gen. B. shall not move immediately; that we accumulate a force on the south bank of the Rappahannock – at, say, Port Royal, under protection of one or two gun-boats, as nearly up to twenty-five thousand strong as we can. At the same time another force of about the same strength as high up the Pamunkey, as can be protected by gunboats. These being ready, let all three forces move simultane-

515

The Living Lincoln

ously, Gen. B.'s force in its attempt to cross the river, the Rappahannock force moving directly up the south side of the river to his assistance, and ready, if found admissible, to deflect off to the turnpike bridge over the Mattapony in the direction of Richmond. The Pamunkey force to move as rapidly as possible up the north side of the Pamunkey, holding all the bridges and especially the turnpike bridge immediately north of Hanover C.H.; hurry north, and seize and hold the Mattapony bridge before mentioned, and also, if possible, press higher up the streams and destroy the railroad bridges. Then, if Gen. B. succeeds in driving the enemy from Fredericksburg, he the enemy no longer has the road to Richmond, but we have it and can march into the city. Or, possibly, having forced the enemy from his line, we could move upon, and destroy his army. Gen. B.'s main army would have the same line of supply and retreat as he has now provided; the Rappahannock force would have that river for supply, and gun-boats to fall back upon; and the Pamunkey force would have that river for supply, and a line between the two rivers—Pamunkey & Mattapony—along which to fall back upon its gun-boats. I think the plan promises the best results, with the least hazard, of any now conceivable.

Note—The above plan, proposed by me, was rejected by Gen. Halleck & Gen. Burnside, on the ground that we could not raise and put in position, the Pamunkey force without too much waste of time.

A. L.

Lincoln's annual message to Congress reviewed the country's relations with other nations, and, considering the dangers involved in maintaining a blockade of 3,000 miles of sea-coast, struck a satisfactory balance. One solution to the slavery problem, however, had met stubborn foreign resistence.

December 1, 1862

. . . Applications have been made to me by many free Americans of African descent to favor their emigration, with a view to such colonization as was contemplated in recent acts of Congress. Other parties, at home and abroad—some from interested motives, others upon patriotic considerations, and still others influenced by philanthropic sentiments—have suggested similar measures; while, on the other hand, several of the Spanish-American republics have protested against the sending of such colonies to their respective territories. Under these circumstances, I have declined to move any such colony to any state, without first obtaining the consent of its government, with an agreement on its part to receive and protect such emigrants in all the rights of freemen; and I have, at the same time, offered to the several states situated within the tropics, or having colonies there, to negotiate with them, subject to the advice and consent of the Senate, to favor the voluntary emigration of persons of that class to their respective territories, upon conditions which shall be equal, just, and humane. Liberia and Hayti are, as yet, the only countries to which colonists of African descent from here, could go with certainty of being received and adopted as citizens; and I regret to say such persons, contemplating colonization, do not seem so willing to migrate to those countries, as to some others, nor so willing as I think their interest demands. I believe, however, opinion among them, in this respect, is improving; and that, ere long, there will be an augmented, and considerable migration to both these countries, from the United States. . . .

In the territories the war had produced a different kind of hostility.

The Indian tribes upon our frontiers have, during the past year, manifested a spirit of insubordination, and, at several points, have engaged in open hostilities against the white settlements in their vicinity. The tribes occupying the Indian country south of Kansas, renounced their allegiance to the United States, and entered into treaties with the insurgents. Those who remained loyal to the United States were driven from the country. The chief of the Cherokees has visited this city for the purpose of restoring the former relations of the tribe with the United States. He alleges that they were constrained, by superior force, to enter into treaties with the insurgents, and that the United States neglected to furnish the protection which their treaty stipulations required.

In the month of August last the Sioux Indians, in Minnesota, attacked the settlements in their vicinity with extreme ferocity, killing, indiscriminately, men, women, and children. This attack was wholly unexpected, and, therefore, no means of defence had been provided. It is estimated that not less than eight hundred persons were killed by the Indians, and a large amount of property was destroyed. How this outbreak was induced is not definitely known, and suspicions, which may be unjust, need not to be stated. Information was received by the Indian bureau, from different sources, about the time hostilities were commenced, that a simultaneous attack was to be made upon the white settlements by all the tribes between the Mississippi River and the Rocky Mountains. The state of Minnesota has suffered great injury from this Indian war. A large portion of her territory has been depopulated, and a severe loss has been sustained by the destruction of property. The people of that state manifest much anxiety for the removal of the tribes beyond the limits of the state as a guarantee against future hostilities. The Commissioner of Indian Affairs will furnish full details. I submit for your especial consideration whether our Indian system shall not be remodelled. Many wise and good men have impressed me with the belief that this can be profitably done. . . .

Other portions of the message encouraged the laying of a transatlantic cable and the construction of a transcontinental railroad. Then Lincoln proposed three amendments to the Constitution: 1. to provide compensation to every state which would abolish slavery before the year 1900; 2. to compensate loyal masters whose slaves had been freed by the chances of war; and 3. to authorize Congress to appropriate money for colonizing free Negroes with their own consent. The President proceeded to justify what would amount to a social revolution.

I beg indulgence to discuss these proposed articles at some length. Without slavery the rebellion could never have existed; without slavery it could not continue.

Among the friends of the Union there is great diversity, of sentiment, and of policy, in regard to slavery, and the African race amongst us. Some would perpetuate slavery; some would abolish it suddenly, and without compensation; some would abolish it gradually, and with compensation; some would remove the freed people from us, and some would retain them with us; and there are yet other minor diversities. Because of these diversities, we waste much strength in struggles among ourselves. By mutual concession we should harmonize, and act together. This would be compromise; but it would be compromise among the friends, and not with the enemies of the Union. These articles are intended to embody a plan of such mutual concessions. If the plan shall be adopted, it is assumed that emancipation will follow, at least, in several of the states. . . .

The emancipation will be unsatisfactory to the advocates of perpetual slavery; but the length of time should greatly mitigate their dissatisfaction. The time spares both races from the evils of sudden derangement—in fact, from the necessity of any derangement—while most of those whose habitual course of thought will be disturbed by the measure will have passed away before its consummation. They will never see it. Another class will hail the prospect of emancipation, but will deprecate the length of time. They will feel that it gives too little to the now living slaves. But it really gives them much. It saves them from the vagrant destitution which must largely attend immediate emancipation in localities where their numbers are very great; and it gives the inspiring assurance that their posterity shall be free forever. The plan leaves to each state, choosing to act under it, to abolish slavery now, or at the end of the century, or at any intermediate time, or by degrees, extending over the whole or any part of the period; and it obliges no two states to proceed alike. It also provides for compensation, and generally the mode of making it. This, it would seem, must further mitigate the dissatisfaction of those who favor perpetual slavery, and especially of those who are to receive the compensation. Doubtless some of those who are to pay, and not to receive will object. Yet the measure is both just and economical. In a certain sense the liberation of slaves is the destruction of property—property acquired by descent, or by purchase, the same as any other property. It is no less true for having been often said, that the people of the South are not more responsible for the original introduction of this property, than are the people of the North; and when it is remembered how unhesitatingly we all use cotton and sugar, and share the profits of dealing in them, it may not be quite safe to say, that the South has been more responsible than the North for its continuance. If then, for a common object, this property is to be sacrificed is it not just that it be done at a common charge?

And if, with less money, or money more easily paid, we can preserve the benefits of the Union by this means, than we can by the war alone, is it not also economical to do it? Let us consider it then. Let us ascertain the sum we have expended in the war since compensated emancipation was proposed last March, and consider whether, if that measure had been promptly accepted, by even some of the slave states, the same sum would not have done more to close the war, than has been otherwise done. If so the measure would save money, and, in that view, would be a prudent and economical measure. Certainly it is not so easy to pay *something* as it is to pay *nothing;* but it is easier to pay a *large* sum than it is to pay a larger one. And it is easier to pay any sum *when* we are able, than it is to pay it *before* we are able. The war requires large sums, and requires them at once. The aggregate sum necessary for compensated emancipation, of course, would be large. But it would require no ready cash; nor the bonds even, any faster than the emancipation progresses. This might not, and probably would not, close before the end of the thirty-seven years. At that time we shall probably have a hundred millions of people to share the burden, instead of thirty-one millions, as now. And not only so, but the increase of our population may be expected to continue for a long time after that period, as rapidly as before; because our territory will not have become full. I do not state this inconsiderately. At the same ratio of increase which we have maintained, on an average, from our first national census, in 1790, until that of 1860, we should, in 1900, have a population of 103,208,415. . . .

The proposed emancipation would shorten the war, perpetuate peace, insure this increase of population, and proportionately the wealth of the country. With these, we should pay all the emancipation would cost, together with our other debt, easier than we should pay our other debt, without it. If we had allowed our old national debt to run at six per cent. per annum, simple interest, from the end of our revolutionary struggle until today, without paying anything on either principal or interest, each man of us would owe less upon that debt now, than each man owed upon it then; and this because our increase of men, through the whole period, has been greater than six per cent.; has run faster than the interest upon the debt. Thus, time alone relieves a debtor nation, so long as its population increases faster than unpaid interest accumulates on its debt.

This fact would be no excuse for delaying payment of what is justly due; but it shows the great importance of time in this connexion—the great advantage of a policy by which we shall not have to pay until we number a hundred millions, what, by a different policy, we would have to pay now, when we number but thirty-one millions. In a word, it shows that a dollar will be much harder to pay for the war, than will be a dollar for emancipation on the proposed plan. And then the latter will cost no blood, no precious life. It will be a saving of both. . . .

I cannot make it better known than it already is, that I strongly favor colonization. And yet I wish to say there is an objection urged against free colored persons remaining in the country, which is largely imaginary, if not sometimes malicious.

It is insisted that their presence would injure, and displace white labor and white laborers. If there ever could be a proper time for mere catch arguments, that time surely is not now. In times like the present, men should utter nothing for which they would not willingly be responsible through time and in eternity. Is it true, then, that colored people can displace any more white labor, by being free, than by remaining slaves? If they stay in their old places, they jostle no white laborers; if they leave their old places, they leave them open to white laborers. Logically, there is neither more nor less of it. Emancipation, even without deportation, would probably enhance the wages of white labor, and, very surely, would not reduce them. Thus, the customary amount of labor would still have to be performed; the freed people would surely not do more than their old proportion of it, and very probably, for a time, would do less, leaving an increased part to white laborers, bringing their labor into greater demand, and, consequently, enhancing the wages of it. With deportation, even to a limited extent, enhanced wages to white labor is mathematically certain. Labor is like any other commodity in the market—increase the demand for it, and you increase the price of it. Reduce the supply of black labor, by colonizing the black laborer out of the country, and, by precisely so much, you increase the demand for, and wages of, white labor. . . .

I do not forget the gravity which should characterize a paper addressed to the Congress of the nation by the Chief Magistrate of the nation. Nor do I forget that some of you are my seniors, nor that many of you have more experience than I, in the conduct of public affairs. Yet I trust that in view of the great responsibility resting upon me, you will perceive no want of respect to yourselves, in any undue earnestness I may seem to display.

Is it doubted, then, that the plan I propose, if adopted, would shorten the war, and thus lessen its expenditure of money and of

The Living Lincoln

blood? Is it doubted that it would restore the national authority and national prosperity, and perpetuate both indefinitely? Is it doubted that we here—Congress and executive—can secure its adoption? Will not the good people respond to a united, and earnest appeal from us? Can we, can they, by any other means, so certainly, or so speedily, assure these vital objects? We can succeed only by concert. It is not "can *any* of us *imagine* better?" but "can we *all* do better?" Object whatsoever is possible, still the question recurs "can we do better?" The dogmas of the quiet past, are inadequate to the stormy present. The occasion is piled high with difficulty, and we must rise with the occasion. As our case is new, so we must think anew, and act anew. We must disenthrall ourselves, and then we shall save our country.

With rarely equalled eloquence, Lincoln concluded his message.

Fellow-citizens, *we* cannot escape history. We of this Congress and this administration, will be remembered in spite of ourselves. No personal significance, or insignificance, can spare one or another of us. The fiery trial through which we pass, will light us down, in honor or dishonor, to the latest generation. We *say* we are for the Union. The world will not forget that we say this. We know how to save the Union. The world knows we do know how to save it. We—even *we here*—hold the power, and bear the responsibility. In *giving* freedom to the *slave,* we *assure* freedom to the *free*—honorable alike in what we give, and what we preserve. We shall nobly save, or meanly lose, the last best, hope of earth. Other means may succeed; this could not fail. The way is plain, peaceful, generous, just—a way which, if followed, the world will forever applaud, and God must forever bless.

Abraham Lincoln

December 1, 1862.

In mid-December Burnside suffered a dreadful defeat at Fredericksburg. Dissident Republicans suggested many courses that Lincoln could pursue—place a Republican at the head of the army, resign as President, reshuffle his cabinet. "Seward is Lincoln's evil genius," wrote Joseph Medill of the Chicago *Tribune*. Behind the scenes the ambitious Chase, resenting the friendship that had developed between Seward and Lincoln, played a sly hand. But two brief messages and a letter would tell the story of how Lincoln handled an unhappy political crisis.

522

From Antietam to Vicksburg

He assented to a meeting of a senatorial committee, and, to everyone's surprise, also invited the members of his cabinet. Chase was caught flat-footed; his back-stage whisperings could not be reiterated face-to-face. Both Seward and Chase resigned. "I've got a pumpkin in each end of my bag," Lincoln said—and wrote his letter.

> *Executive Mansion,*
> *Washington, Dec. 18. 1862.*
>
> *Hon. Jacob Collamer.*
> *My dear Sir:*
> I will see the committee named, at 7 P.M. today.
> *A. Lincoln*

> Secretary of the Treasury, please do not go out of town.
> *A. Lincoln.*
> *December 20, 1862.*

> (C O P Y)
>
> *Executive Mansion,*
> *Washington, December 20. 1862.*
>
> *Hon. William H. Seward, &*
> *Hon. Salmon P. Chase.*
> *Gentlemen:*
> You have respectively tendered me your resignations, as Secretary of State, and Secretary of the Treasury of the United States. I am apprised of the circumstances which may render this course personally desirable to each of you; but, after most anxious consideration, my deliberate judgment is, that the public interest does not admit of it. I therefore have to request that you will resume the duties of your departments respectively. Your Obt. Servt.
> *A. Lincoln.*
> P.S. Same as above sent to Gov. Chase   *A L.*
> P.S. Same as above sent to Gov. Seward.   *A L.*
> Note—Postscripts, like the above are to respective letters.

Lincoln's tender wisdom—and memories of a happier past—were reflected in a letter to Fanny McCullough, whose father was killed in battle near Coffeeville, Mississippi. The President had known William McCullough as clerk of the McLean County Circuit Court at Bloomington, Illinois.

The Living Lincoln

Executive Mansion,
Washington, December 23, 1862.

Dear Fanny

It is with deep grief that I learn of the death of your kind and brave father; and, especially, that it is affecting your young heart beyond what is common in such cases. In this sad world of ours, sorrow comes to all; and, to the young, it comes with bitterest agony, because it takes them unawares. The older have learned to ever expect it. I am anxious to afford some alleviation of your present distress. Perfect relief is not possible, except with time. You cannot now realize that you will ever feel better. Is not this so? And yet it is a mistake. You are sure to be happy again. To know this, which is certainly true, will make you some less miserable now. I have had experience enough to know what I say; and you need only to believe it, to feel better at once. The memory of your dear father, instead of an agony, will yet be a sad sweet feeling in your heart, of a purer, and holier sort than you have known before.

Please present my kind regards to your afflicted mother.

Your sincere friend

A. Lincoln.

Miss Fanny McCullough.

With the approach of a new year, one question overshadowed all others. Would Lincoln issue the Emancipation Proclamation, as he had promised? The President kept his word. The document, great in historical significance, was prosaic in language except for the next to closing paragraph, which Chase suggested. Tired from a day of handshaking, Lincoln worried that his signature might not appear firm.

January 1, 1863

BY THE PRESIDENT OF THE UNITED STATES OF AMERICA:

A PROCLAMATION.

Whereas, on the twenty-second day of September, in the year of our Lord one thousand eight hundred and sixty-two, a proclamation was issued by the President of the United States, containing, among other things, the following, to wit:

"That on the first day of January, in the year of our Lord one thousand eight hundred and sixty-three, all persons held as slaves within any State or designated part of a State, the people whereof shall then be in rebellion against the United States, shall be then,

524

thenceforward, and forever free; and the Executive Government of the United States, including the military and naval authority thereof, will recognize and maintain the freedom of such persons, and will do no act or acts to repress such persons, or any of them, in any efforts they may make for their actual freedom.

"That the Executive will, on the first day of January aforesaid, by proclamation, designate the States and parts of States, if any, in which the people thereof, respectively, shall then be in rebellion against the United States; and the fact that any State, or the people thereof, shall on that day be, in good faith, represented in the Congress of the United States by members chosen thereto at elections wherein a majority of the qualified voters of such State shall have participated, shall, in the absence of strong countervailing testimony, be deemed conclusive evidence that such State, and the people thereof, are not then in rebellion against the United States."

Now, therefore I, Abraham Lincoln, President of the United States, by virtue of the power in me vested as Commander-in-Chief, of the Army and Navy of the United States in time of actual armed rebellion against authority and government of the United States, and as a fit and necessary war measure for suppressing said rebellion, do, on this first day of January, in the year of our Lord one thousand eight hundred and sixty-three, and in accordance with my purpose so to do publicly proclaimed for the full period of one hundred days, from the day first above mentioned, order and designate as the States and parts of States wherein the people thereof respectively, are this day in rebellion against the United States, the following, to wit:

Arkansas, Texas, Louisiana, (except the Parishes of St. Bernard, Plaquemines, Jefferson, St. Johns, St. Charles, St. James, Ascension, Assumption, Terrebonne, Lafourche, St. Mary, St. Martin, and Orleans, including the City of New Orleans) Mississippi, Alabama, Florida, Georgia, South Carolina, North Carolina, and Virginia, (except the forty-eight counties designated as West Virginia, and also the counties of Berkley, Accomac, Northampton, Elizabeth City, York, Princess Ann, and Norfolk, including the cities of Norfolk & Portsmouth); and which excepted parts are, for the present, left precisely as if this proclamation were not issued.

And by virtue of the power, and for the purpose aforesaid, I do order and declare that all persons held as slaves within said designated States, and parts of States, are, and henceforward shall be free; and that the executive government of the United States, including the military and naval authorities thereof, will recognize and maintain the freedom of said persons.

And I hereby enjoin upon the people so declared to be free to abstain from all violence, unless in necessary self-defence; and I recommend to them that, in all cases when allowed, they labor faithfully for reasonable wages.

And I further declare and make known, that such persons of suitable condition, will be received into the armed service of the United States to garrison forts, positions, stations, and other places, and to man vessels of all sorts in said service.

And upon this act, sincerely believed to be an act of justice, warranted by the Constitution, upon military necessity, I invoke the considerate judgment of mankind, and the gracious favor of Almighty God.

In witness whereof, I have hereunto set my hand and caused the seal of the United States to be affixed.

[L.S.] Done at the City of Washington, this first day of January, in the year of our Lord one thousand eight hundred and sixty-three, and of the Independence of the United States of America the eighty-seventh.

By the President:

Abraham Lincoln

WILLIAM H. SEWARD, Secretary of State.

Among the New York's callers at the White House was Burnside, importuning Lincoln to make a decision which he felt to be beyond his competence. Distraught, the President turned to a military adviser, who had become adept at temporizing.

Executive Mansion,
Washington, January 1. 1863.

Major Gen. Halleck
My dear Sir:

Gen. Burnside wishes to cross the Rappahannock with his army, but his Grand Division commanders all oppose the movement. If in such a difficulty as this you do not help, you fail me precisely in the point for which I sought your assistance. You know what Gen. Burnside's plan is; and it is my wish that you go with him to the ground, examine it as far as practicable, confer with the officers, getting their judgment, and ascertaining their temper, in a word, gather all the elements for forming a judgment of your own; and then tell Gen. Burnside that you *do* approve, or that you do *not* approve his plan. Your military skill is useless to me, if you will not do this. Yours very truly

A Lincoln

[*Endorsement*]
Withdrawn, because considered harsh by Gen. Halleck.   *A.L.*
Jan. 1. 1862 [*1863*]

For another caller, harassed by the insatiable demands of war, Lincoln did the little that he could.

Executive Mansion,
Washington, Jany. 1, 1863.

Hon. Sec. of War:
Dear Sir:
Yesterday a piteous appeal was made to me by an old lady of genteel appearance, saying she had, with what she thought sufficient assurance that she would not be disturbed by the government, fitted up the two south divisions of the old "Duff Green" building in order to take boarders, and has boarders already in it, & others, including M.C.s. engaged, and that now she is ordered to be out of it by Saturday the 3rd. inst.; and that, independently of the ruin it brings on her, by her lost outlay, she neither has, nor can find another shelter for her own head. I know nothing about it myself, but promised to bring it to your notice. Yours truly

A. Lincoln

In St. Louis the vexing problem of loyalty had become entangled with freedom of conscience and religion. To the commander of the Department of Missouri, Lincoln stated a basic principle.

Executive Mansion,
Washington, January 2, 1863.

Major General Curtis
My dear Sir:
Yours of Dec. 29th. by the hand of Mr. Strong is just received. The day I telegraphed you suspending the order in relation to Dr. McPheeters, he, with Mr. Bates, the Attorney General, appeared before me, and left with me a copy of the order mentioned. The Dr. also showed me the copy of an oath which he said he had taken, which is, indeed, very strong, and specific. He also verbally

assured me that he had constantly prayed in church for the President and government, as he had always done before the present war. In looking over the recitals in your order, I do not see that this matter of the prayer, as he states it, is negatived; nor that any violation of his oath is charged; nor, in fact, that any thing specific is alleged against him. The charges are all general—that he has a rebel wife & rebel relations, that he sympathizes with rebels, and that he exercises rebel influence. Now, after talking with him, I tell you frankly, I believe he does sympathize with the rebels; but the question remains whether such a man, of unquestioned good moral character, who has taken such an oath as he has, and cannot even be charged of violating it, and who can be charged with no other specific act or omission, can, with safety to the government be exiled, upon the suspicion of his secret sympathies. But I agree that this must be left to you who are on the spot; and if, after all, you think the public good requires his removal, my suspension of the order is withdrawn, only with this qualification that the time during the suspension, is not to be counted against him. I have promised him this.

But I must add that the U. S. government must not, as by this order, undertake to run the churches. When an individual, in a church or out of it, becomes dangerous to the public interest, he must be checked; but let the churches, as such take care of themselves. It will not do for the U. S. to appoint trustees, supervisors, or other agents for the churches. Yours very truly

A. Lincoln

Affairs in Missouri continued to plague the President. This time the question involved the peculiar practice of levying assessments on Southern sympathizers—a source of discord compounded by bad feeling between the Governor and department commander. Lincoln, devoid of false pride, incapable of holding grudges, tried to infuse Samuel R. Curtis with some of the same spirit.

Executive Mansion,
Washington, January 5, 1863.

Major General Curtis
My dear Sir:
I am having a good deal of trouble with Missouri matters, and I now sit down to write you particularly about it. One class of

friends believe in greater severity, and another in greater leniency, in regard to arrests, banishments, and assessments. As usual in such cases, each questions the other's motives. On the one hand it is insisted that Gov. Gamble's Unionism, at most, is not better than a secondary spring of action—that hunkerism, and a wish for political influence, stand before Unionism, with him. On the other hand, it is urged that arrests, banishments, and assessments are made more for private malice, revenge, and pecuniary interest, than for the public good. This morning I was told by a gentleman who, I have no doubt believes what he says, that in one case of assessments for *ten* thousand dollars, the different persons who paid, compared receipts, and found they had paid thirty thousand dollars. If this be true, the inference is that the collecting agents pocketed the odd twenty thousand. And true or not, in the instance, nothing but the sternest necessity can justify the making and maintaining of a system so liable to such abuses. Doubtless the necessity for the making of the system in Missouri *did* exist, and whether it continues for the maintenance of it, is now a practical, and very important question. Some days ago Governor Gamble telegraphed me asking that the assessments, outside of St. Louis County, might be suspended, as they already have been within it; and this morning all the Members of Congress here from Missouri, but one, lay a paper before me asking the same thing. Now, my belief is that Gov. Gamble is an honest and true man, not less so than yourself; that you and he could confer together on this, and other Missouri questions with great advantage to the public; that each knows something which the other does not, and that, acting together, you could about double your stock of pertinent information. May I not hope that you and he will attempt this? I could at once safely do, (or you could safely do without me) whatever you and he agree upon. There is absolutely no reason why you should not agree. Yours as ever

A. Lincoln

P.S. I forgot to say that Hon. James S. Rollins, M.C. from one of the Missouri districts wishes that, upon his personal responsibility, Rev. John M. Robinson, of Columbia, Mo. James L. Matthews of Boone County, Mo, and James L. Stephens, also of Boone County, Mo. may be allowed to return to their respective homes. Major Rollins leaves with me very strong papers from the neighbors of these men, whom he says he knows to be true men.

He also says he has many constituents who he thinks are rightfully exiled; but that he thinks these three should be allowed to return. Please look into the case, and oblige Major Rollins if you consistently can. Yours truly

A. Lincoln

From Tennessee, Rosecrans claimed victory in a battle at Stone River that resembled bloody Shiloh.

Executive Mansion,
Washington, Jan. 5. 1863

Major General W. S. Rosecrans
Murfreesboro, Tenn.

Your despatch announcing retreat of enemy has just reached here. God bless you, and all with you! Please tender to all, and accept for yourself, the nation's gratitude for yours, and their, skill, endurance, and dauntless courage.

A Lincoln

The Religious Society of Friends in Iowa believed that the Emancipation Proclamation was "intrinsically right" and wrote Lincoln "in Christian love." The President also believed that he followed the will of God.

Executive Mansion,
Washington, January 5, 1863

My Good Friends

The Honorable Senator Harlan has just placed in my hands your letter of the 27th of December which I have read with pleasure and gratitude.

It is most cheering and encouraging for me to know that in the efforts which I have made and am making for the restoration of a righteous peace to our country, I am upheld and sustained by the good wishes and prayers of God's people. No one is more deeply than myself aware that without His favor our highest wisdom is but as foolishness and that our most strenuous efforts would avail nothing in the shadow of His displeasure. I am conscious of no desire for my country's welfare, that is not in consonance with His will, and of no plan upon which we may not ask His blessing. It seems to me that if there be one subject upon which all good men may unitedly agree, it is imploring the gracious favor of the God of Nations upon the struggles our people are making for the preservation of their precious birthright of civil and religious liberty. Very truly Your friend

A. Lincoln.

To   Caleb Russell } Secretaries
      Sallie A. Fenton

John A. McClernand allowed a mirage to divert him from his proper concern—the campaign against Vicksburg. High officers in the Confederate army, he informed Lincoln, desired peace, by which they meant the restoration of the Union as it had been before the issuance of the Emancipation Proclamation. In reply, Lincoln laid down terms from which he would never deviate.

Executive Mansion,
Washington, January 8. 1863.

Major General McClernand
My dear Sir

Your interesting communication by the hand of Major Scates is received. I never did ask more, nor ever was willing to accept less, than for all the states, and the people thereof, to take and hold their places, and their rights, in the Union, under the Constitution of the United States. For this alone have I felt authorized to struggle; and I seek neither more nor less now. Still, to use a coarse, but an expressive figure, broken eggs cannot be mended. I have issued the Emancipation Proclamation, and I cannot retract it.

After the commencement of hostilities I struggled nearly a year and a half to get along without touching the "institution"; and when finally I conditionally determined to touch it, I gave a hundred days' fair notice of my purpose, to all the states and people, within which time they could have turned it wholly aside, by simply again becoming good citizens of the United States. They chose to disregard it, and I made the peremptory proclamation on what appeared to me to be a military necessity. And being made, it must stand. As to the states not included in it, of course they can have their rights in the Union as of old. Even the people of the states included, if they choose, need not to be hurt by it. Let them adopt systems of apprenticeship for the colored people, conforming sub-

531

stantially to the most approved plans of gradual emancipation; and, with the aid they can have from the general government, they may be nearly as well off, in this respect, as if the present trouble had not occurred, and much better off than they can possibly be if the contest continues persistently.

As to any dread of my having a "purpose to enslave, or exterminate, the whites of the South," I can scarcely believe that such dread exists. It is too absurd. I believe you can be my personal witness that no man is less to be dreaded for undue severity, in any case.

If the friends you mention really wish to have peace upon the old terms, they should act at once. Every day makes the case more difficult. They can so act, with entire safety, so far as I am concerned.

I think you would better not make this letter public; but you may rely confidently on my standing by whatever I have said in it. Please write me if anything more comes to light. Yours very truly

A. Lincoln.

With emancipation proclaimed, the North turned to the recruitment of Negroes. Gently, Lincoln urged the use of colored troops on reluctant commanders.

PRIVATE & CONFIDENTIAL

Executive Mansion,
Washington, January 14, 1863.

Major General Dix
My dear Sir:
The proclamation has been issued. We were not succeeding — at best, were progressing too slowly — without it. Now, that we have it, and bear all the disadvantage of it, (as we do bear some in certain quarters) we must also take some benefit from it, if practicable. I therefore will thank you for your well considered opinion whether Fortress Monroe, and Yorktown, one or both, could not, in whole or in part, be garrisoned by colored troops, leaving the white forces now necessary at those places, to be employed elsewhere. Yours very truly

A. Lincoln

From the workingmen of Manchester, England, hard hit by the shutting off of Southern cotton, came warm approval of the Emancipation Proclamation. They wrote in part: "One thing alone has, in the past, lessened our sympathy with your country and our confidence in it; we mean the ascendancy of politicians who not merely maintained Negro slavery, but desired to extend and root it more firmly." Lincoln understood the great weapon of psychological warfare that had come to him, and used it with skill.

> *Executive Mansion, Washington,*
> *January 19, 1863.*

To the workingmen of Manchester:

I have the honor to acknowledge the receipt of the address and resolutions which you sent to me on the eve of the new year.

When I came, on the fourth day of March, 1861, through a free and constitutional election, to preside in the government of the United States, the country was found at the verge of civil war. Whatever might have been the cause, or whosesoever the fault, one duty paramount to all others was before me, namely, to maintain and preserve at once the Constitution and the integrity of the federal republic. A conscientious purpose to perform this duty is a key to all the measures of administration which have been, and to all which will hereafter be pursued. Under our form of government, and my official oath, I could not depart from this purpose if I would. It is not always in the power of governments to enlarge or restrict the scope of moral results which follow the policies that they may deem it necessary for the public safety, from time to time, to adopt.

I have understood well that the duty of self-preservation rests solely with the American people. But I have at the same time been aware that favor or disfavor of foreign nations might have a material influence in enlarging and prolonging the struggle with disloyal men in which the country is engaged. A fair examination of history has seemed to authorize a belief that the past action and influences of the United States were generally regarded as having been beneficent towards mankind. I have therefore reckoned upon the forbearance of nations. Circumstances, to some of which you kindly allude, induced me especially to expect that if justice and good faith should be practiced by the United States, they would encounter no hostile influence on the part of Great Britain. It is now a pleasant duty to acknowledge the demonstration you have given of your desire that a spirit of peace and amity towards this country may prevail in the councils of your Queen, who is respected and esteemed in your own country only more than she is by the kindred nation which has its home on this side of the Atlantic.

I know and deeply deplore the sufferings which the workingmen at Manchester and in all Europe are called to endure in this crisis. It has been often and studiously represented that the attempt to overthrow this government, which was built upon the foundation of human rights, and to substitute for it one which should rest exclusively on the basis of human slavery, was likely to obtain the favor of Europe. Through the actions of our disloyal citizens the workingmen of Europe have been subjected to a severe trial, for the purpose of forcing their sanction to that attempt. Under these circumstances, I cannot but regard your decisive utterance upon the question as an instance of sublime Christian heroism which has not been surpassed in any age or in any country. It is, indeed, an energetic and reinspiring assurance of the inherent power of truth and of the ultimate and universal triumph of justice, humanity, and freedom. I do not doubt that the sentiments you have expressed will be sustained by your great nation, and, on the other hand, I have no hesitation in assuring you that they will excite admiration, esteem, and the most reciprocal feelings of friendship among the American people. I hail this interchange of sentiment, therefore, as an augury that, whatever else may happen, whatever misfortune may befall your country or my own, the peace and friendship which now exist between the two nations will be, as it shall be my desire to make them, perpetual.

Abraham Lincoln.

John A. McClernand had been reduced by Grant to a corps commander in the Vicksburg campaign. The bitter general believed that Halleck had conspired to take from him the army he had recruited on the orders of Lincoln and Stanton. To Lincoln, McClernand charged Halleck with every mistake since Corinth. The President replied with calm advice.

Executive Mansion,
Washington, January 22. 1863.

Major Gen. McClernand
My dear Sir:

Yours of the 7th. was received yesterday. I need not recite, because you remember the contents. The charges, in their nature, are such that I must know as much about the facts involved, as you can. I have too many *family* controversies, (so to speak) already on my hands, to voluntarily, or so long as I can avoid it, take up another. You are now doing well—well for the country, and well for yourself—much better than you could possibly be, if engaged in open war with Gen. Halleck. Allow me to beg, that for your sake, for my sake, & for the country's sake, you give your whole attention to the better work.

Your success upon the Arkansas, was both brilliant and valuable, and is fully appreciated by the country and government. Yours truly

A. Lincoln

In late January Lincoln reluctantly concluded that Burnside was incapable of commanding the Army of the Potomac. With misgivings, the President turned to another corps commander who had been one of Burnside's harshest critics. Lincoln knew that Hooker boasted too much and drank more than was good for him. "He can fight," Nicolay and Hay heard the President remark, ". . . but whether he can 'keep tavern' for a large army is another matter." The situation called for a forthright letter. Lincoln wrote a masterpiece.

Executive Mansion,
Washington, January 26, 1863.

Major General Hooker:
General.

I have placed you at the head of the Army of the Potomac. Of course I have done this upon what appear to me to be sufficient reasons. And yet I think it best for you to know that there are some things in regard to which, I am not quite satisfied with you. I believe you to be a brave and a skilful soldier, which, of course, I like. I also believe you do not mix politics with your profession, in which you are right. You have confidence in yourself, which is a valuable, if not an indispensable quality. You are ambitious, which, within reasonable bounds, does good rather than harm. But I think that during Gen. Burnside's command of the army, you have taken counsel of your ambition, and thwarted him as much as you could, in which you did a great wrong to the country, and to a most meritorious and honorable brother officer. I have heard, in such way as to believe it, of your recently saying that both the army and the government needed a dictator. Of course it was not *for* this, but in spite of it, that I have given you the command. Only those generals who gain successes, can set up dictators. What I now ask of you is military success, and I will risk the dictatorship. The government will support you to the utmost of its ability, which is neither more nor less than it has done and will do for all commanders. I much fear that the spirit which you have aided to infuse into the army, of criticizing their commander, and withholding confidence from him, will now turn upon you. I shall assist you as far as I can, to put it down. Neither you, nor Napoleon, if he were alive again, could get any good out of an army, while such a spirit prevails in it.

And now, beware of rashness. Beware of rashness, but with energy, and sleepless vigilance, go forward, and give us victories. Yours very truly

A. Lincoln

Beset with cares of every variety, Lincoln rode out a peeve with gusto.

Executive Mansion,
Washington, March 9, 1863.

Mrs. L. H. Phipps

Yours of the 8th. is received. It is difficult for you to understand, what is, nevertheless true, that the bare reading of a letter of that length requires more than any one person's share of my time. And when read, what is it but an evidence that you intend to importune me for one thing, and another, and another, until, in self-defence, I must drop all and devote myself to find a place, even though I remove somebody else to do it, and thereby turn him & his friends upon me for indefinite future importunity, and hindrance from the legitimate duties for which I am supposed to be placed here? Yours &c.

A. Lincoln

The ebbing of enthusiasm for the war put a Democrat in the Governor's Mansion at Albany. Lincoln moved to establish an understanding.

From Antietam to Vicksburg

Executive Mansion,
Washington, March 23, 1863.

His Excellency
Gov. Seymour
Dear Sir:

You and I are substantially strangers; and I write this chiefly that we may become better acquainted. I, for the time being, am at the head of a nation which is in great peril; and you are at the head of the greatest state of that nation. As to maintaining the nation's life, and integrity, I assume, and believe, there cannot be a difference of *purpose* between you and me. If we should differ as to the *means,* it is important that such difference should be as small as possible—that it should not be enhanced by unjust suspicions on one side or the other. In the performance of my duty, the co-operation of your state, as that of others, is needed—in fact, is indispensable. This alone is a sufficient reason why I should wish to be at a good understanding with you. Please write me at least as long a letter as this—of course, saying in it, just what you think fit. Yours very truly

A. Lincoln

Lincoln pressed his desire to use Negro troops on the military governor of Tennessee.

Executive Mansion,
Washington, March 26. 1863.

Hon. Andrew Johnson
My dear Sir:

I am told you have at least *thought* of raising a Negro military force. In my opinion the country now needs no specific thing so much as some man of your ability, and position, to go to this work. When I speak of your position, I mean that of an eminent citizen of a slave state, and himself a slaveholder. The colored population is the great *available* and yet *unavailed* of, force for restoring the Union. The bare sight of fifty thousand armed, and drilled black soldiers on the banks of the Mississippi, would end the rebellion at once. And who doubts that we can present that

537

sight, if we but take hold in earnest? If you *have* been thinking of it please do not dismiss the thought. Yours truly

A. Lincoln

With Tad, Lincoln spent a week with the Army of the Potomac. Through field glasses he could see Fredericksburg. He surprised a blasphemous ambulance driver with the comment: "You swear just like Governor Seward." Doubtless during this visit Lincoln wrote the following memorandum of Hooker's plan of campaign against Richmond. Later changes in strategy led to the Battle of Chancellorsville.

[*c. April 6–10, 1863*]

My opinion is, that just now, with the enemy directly ahead of us, there is *no* eligible route for us into Richmond; and consequently a question of preference between the Rappahannock route, and the James River route is a contest about nothing. Hence our prime object is the enemy's army in front of us, and is not with, or about, Richmond—at all, unless it be incidental to the main object.

What then? The two armies are face to face with a narrow river between them. Our communications are shorter and safer than are those of the enemy. For this reason, we can, with equal powers fret him more than he can us. I do not think that by raids towards Washington he can derange the Army of the Potomac at all. He has no distant operations which can call any of the Army of the Potomac away; we have such operations which may call him away, at least in part. While he remains intact, I do not think we should take the disadvantage of attacking him in his entrenchments; but we should continually harass and menace him, so that he shall have no leisure, nor safety in sending away detachments. If he weakens himself, then pitch into him.

The "Gen. S." of this letter was Stoneman, whose cavalry must disrupt Confederate communications and threaten Richmond if the next move against Lee was to be properly screened.

Executive Mansion,
Washington, April 15. 1863

Major General Hooker

It is now 10-15 P.M. An hour ago I received your letter of this morning, and a few minutes later your despatch of this evening. The latter gives me considerable uneasiness. The rain and mud, of course, were to be calculated upon. Gen. S. is not moving rapidly enough to make the expedition come to anything. He has now been out three days, two of which were unusually fine weather, and all three without hindrance from the enemy, and yet he is not twenty-five miles from where he started. To reach his point, he still has sixty to go; another river, the Rapidan, to cross, and will be hindered by the enemy. By arithmetic, how many days will it take him to do it? I do not know that any better can be done, but I greatly fear it is another failure already. Write me often. I am very anxious. Yours truly

A. Lincoln

Lincoln makes a gracious social secretary for Mrs. Lincoln.

Executive Mansion,
Washington, April 22, 1863.

Hon. Charles Sumner
My dear Sir

Mrs. L. is embarrassed a little. She would be pleased to have your company again this evening, at the opera, but she fears she may be taxing you. I have undertaken to clear up the little difficulty. If, for any reason, it will tax you, decline, without any hesitation; but if it will not, consider yourself already invited, and drop me a note. Yours very truly

A. Lincoln.

Among Lincoln's many burdens was one Francis L. Capen, Certified Practical Meteorologist & Expert in Computing Changes in Weather.

April 28, 1863

It seems to me Mr. Capen knows nothing about the weather, in advance. He told me three days ago that it would not rain again till the 30th. of April or 1st. of May. It is raining now & has been for ten hours. I cannot spare any more time to Mr. Capen.

April. 28. 1863.

A Lincoln

On May 6 Hooker was badly battered at Chancellorsville and his army forced to withdraw across the Rappahannock. Noah Brooks, at the White House, reported that Lincoln moaned: "My God! My God!

What will the country say? What *will* the country say?" Yet it was a thoroughly composed President who, the next day, put defeat behind him and looked to the future.

> *Head-Quarters, Army of the Potomac,*
> *May. 7 1863.*

Major General Hooker.
My dear Sir

The recent movement of your army is ended without effecting its object, except perhaps some important breakings of the enemy's communications. What next? If possible I would be very glad of another movement early enough to give us some benefit from the fact of the enemy's communications being broken, but neither for this reason or any other, do I wish anything done in desperation or rashness. An early movement would also help to supersede the bad moral effect of the recent one, which is sure to be considerably injurious. Have you already in your mind a plan wholly, or partially formed? If you have, prosecute it without interference from me. If you have not, please inform me, so that I, incompetent as I may be, can try to assist in the formation of some plan for the army. Yours as ever

> *A Lincoln*

Across the Rappahannock the two armies watched each other like hostile dogs. Though anxious for victory, Lincoln counseled caution.

> *Executive Mansion, Washington,*
> *May 14. 1863.*

Major General Hooker
My dear Sir:

When I wrote you on the 7th. I had an impression that possibly, by an early movement, you could get some advantage from the supposed facts that the enemy's communications were disturbed and that he was somewhat deranged in position. That idea has now passed away, the enemy having re-established his communications, regained his positions and actually received reinforcements. It does not now appear probable to me that you can gain anything by an early renewal of the attempt to cross the Rappahannock. I therefore shall not complain, if you do no more, for a time, than to keep the enemy at bay, and out of other mischief, by menaces and occasional cavalry raids, if practicable; and to put your own army in good condition again. Still, if in your own clear judgment, you can renew the attack successfully, I do not mean to restrain you. Bearing upon this last point, I must tell you I have some painful intimations that some of your corps and division commanders are not giving you their entire confidence. This would be ruinous, if true; and you should therefore, first of all, ascertain the real facts beyond all possibility of doubt. Yours truly

A. Lincoln

When St. Louisans objected to the appointment of General John M. Schofield as commander of the Department of Missouri, Lincoln issued an ultimatum.

Executive Mansion,
Washington,
May 15, 1863. [9 P.M.]

Hon. H. T. Blow
C. D. Drake & others
St. Louis, Mo

Your despatch of today is just received. It is very painful to me that you in Missouri cannot, or will not, settle your factional quarrel among yourselves. I have been tormented with it beyond endurance for months, by both sides. Neither side pays the least respect to my appeals to your reason. I am now compelled to take hold of the case.

A. Lincoln

From elsewhere in the West came heartening news. Grant suddenly transported his army south of Vicksburg, crossed into Mississippi, abandoned his base of supplies, and in a series of bold, brilliant maneuvers separated the Confederate armies of Pemberton and Joseph E. Johnston, then laid seige to the city. The moment was scarcely a happy one for even an old friend and stanch supporter to suggest a reshuffling of Lincoln's military organization.

PRIVATE & CONFIDENTIAL

Executive Mansion,
Washington, May 26. 1863.

Hon. I. N. Arnold.
My dear Sir:

Your letter advising me to dismiss Gen. Halleck is received. If the public believe, as you say, that he has driven Fremont, Butler, and Sigel from the service, they believe what I know to be false;

so that if I were to yield to it, it would only be to be instantly beset by some other demand based on another falsehood equally gross. You know yourself that Fremont was relieved at his own request, before Halleck could have had anything to do with it—went out near the end of June, while Halleck only came in near the end of July. I know equally well that no wish of Halleck's had anything to do with the removal of Butler or Sigel. Sigel, like Fremont, was relieved at his own request, pressed upon me almost constantly for six months, and upon complaints that could have been made as justly by almost any corps commander in the army, and more justly by some. So much for the way they got out. Now a word as to their not getting back. In the early spring, Gen. Fremont sought active service again; and, as it seemed to me, sought it in a very good, and reasonable spirit. But he holds the highest rank in the army, except McClellan, so that I could not well offer him a subordinate command. Was I to displace Hooker, or Hunter, or Rosecrans, or Grant, or Banks? If not, what was I to do? And similar to this, is the case of both the others. One month after Gen. Butler's return, I offered him a position in which I thought and still think, he could have done himself the highest credit, and the country the greatest service, but he declined it. When Gen. Sigel was relieved, at his own request as I have said, of course I had to put another in command of his corps. Can I instantly thrust that other out to put him in again?

And now my good friend, let me turn your eyes upon another point. Whether Gen. Grant shall or shall not consummate the capture of Vicksburg, his campagn from the beginning of this month up to the twenty-second day of it, is one of the most brilliant in the world. His corps commanders, & Division commanders, in part, are McClernand, McPherson, Sherman, Steele, Hovey, Blair, & Logan. And yet taking Gen. Grant & these seven of his generals, and you can scarcely name one of them that has not been constantly denounced and opposed by the same men who are now so anxious to get Halleck out, and Fremont & Butler & Sigel in. I believe no one of them went through the Senate easily, and certainly one failed to get through at all. I am compelled to take a more impartial and unprejudiced view of things. Without claiming to be your superior, which I do not, my position enables me to understand my duty in all these matters better than you possibly can, and I hope you do not yet doubt my integrity. Your friend, as ever

A. Lincoln

From Antietam to Vicksburg

Wise to the dangerous cross-currents of politics, Lincoln counselled Schofield on the course to pursue in Missouri.

Executive Mansion,
Washington, May 27. 1863.

Gen. J. M. Schofield
My dear Sir:

Having relieved Gen. Curtis and assigned you to the command of the Department of the Missouri—I think it may be of some advantage for me to state to you why I did it. I did not relieve Gen. Curtis because of any full conviction that he had done wrong by commission or omission. I did it because of a conviction in my mind that the Union men of Missouri, constituting, when united, a vast majority of the whole people, have entered into a pestilent factional quarrel among themselves, Gen. Curtis, perhaps not of choice, being the head of one faction, and Gov. Gamble that of the other. After months of labor to reconcile the difficulty, it seemed to grow worse and worse until I felt it my duty to break it up somehow; and as I could not remove Gov. Gamble, I had to remove Gen. Curtis. Now that you are in the position, I wish you to undo nothing merely because Gen. Curtis or Gov. Gamble did it; but to exercise your own judgment, and do *right* for the public interest. Let your military measures be strong enough to repel the invader and keep the peace, and not so strong as to unnecessarily harass and persecute the people. It is a difficult *role,* and so much greater will be the honor if you perform it well. If both factions, or neither, shall abuse you, you will probably be about right. Beware of being assailed by one, and praised by the other. Yours truly

A. Lincoln

The President saw how Grant must be helped. Rosecrans promised: "I will attend to it."

Washington D. C.
May 28. 1863

Major General Rosecrans
Murfreesboro, Tenn.

I would not push you to any rashness; but I am very anxious that you do your utmost, short of rashness, to keep Bragg from getting off to help Johnston against Grant.

A. Lincoln.

543

The Living Lincoln

June 5 brought a telegram from Hooker that across the Rappahannock the Confederates were breaking camp. Lincoln no longer could be called an amateur at war. He had yet to find a general who could use effectively the fine fighting organization that the Army of the Potomac represented, but by now he had begun to understand Lee's methods. Few textbooks on the art of war could have given Hooker better advice than Lincoln offered.

Washington, D. C.,
June 5. 1863

Major General Hooker

Yours of today was received an hour ago. So much of professional military skill is requisite to answer it, that I have turned the task over to Gen. Halleck. He promises to perform it with his utmost care. I have but one idea which I think worth suggesting to you, and that is in case you find Lee coming to the north of the Rappahannock, I would by no means cross to the south of it. If he should leave a rear force at Fredericksburg, tempting you to fall upon it, it would fight in intrenchments, and have you at disadvantage, and so, man for man, worst you at that point, while his main force would in some way be getting an advantage of you northward. In one word, I would not take any risk of being entangled upon the river, like an ox jumped half over a fence, and liable to be torn by dogs, front and rear, without a fair chance to gore one way or kick the other. If Lee would come to my side of the river, I would keep on the same side & fight him, or act on the defence, according as might be my estimate of his strength relatively to my own. But these are mere suggestions which I desire to be controlled by the judgment of yourself and Gen. Halleck.

A. Lincoln

Greatly disturbed, Lincoln sends a telegram.

Executive Mansion,
Washington, June 9. 1863.

Mrs. Lincoln
Philadelphia, Pa.

Think you better put "Tad's" pistol away. I had an ugly dream about him.

A. Lincoln

From Antietam to Vicksburg

Again the President gave Hooker a sound lesson in strategy.

United States Military Telegraph
War Department. Washington DC.
June 10. 1863. [6:40 P.M.]

"CYPHER"
Major General Hooker

Your long despatch of today is just received. If left to me, I would not go south of the Rappahannock, upon Lee's moving north of it. If you had Richmond invested today, you would not be able to take it in twenty days; meanwhile, your communications, and with them, your army would be ruined. I think *Lee's* army, and not *Richmond,* is your true objective point. If he comes towards the Upper Potomac, follow on his flank, and on the inside track, shortening your lines, whilst he lengthens his. Fight him when opportunity offers. If he stays where he is, fret him, and fret him.

A Lincoln

As the war dragged on, as the Emancipation Proclamation created dissent in those sections where strong Southern ties were felt, as casualties mounted and war weariness spread, the Democrats capitalized upon dissatisfactions and disaffections. "Peace Democrats" raised the cry that the South was unbeatable, that Lincoln represented a senseless Republican tyranny. In one bitter word these tactics amounted to defeatism. Lincoln, however, was in a fight to the finish—with the Confederacy, and, if necessary, with the Democrats. A public meeting in Albany gave him a chance to answer his critics, both directly and in the press.

Executive Mansion
Washington [June 12] 1863.

Hon. Erastus Corning & others
Gentlemen

Your letter of May 19th. inclosing the resolutions of a public meeting held at Albany, N. Y. on the 16th. of the same month, was received several days ago.

The resolutions, as I understand them, are resolvable into two propositions—first, the expression of a purpose to sustain the cause of the Union, to secure peace through victory, and to support the

545

administration in every constitutional, and lawful measure to suppress the rebellion; and secondly, a declaration of censure upon the administration for supposed unconstitutional action such as the making of military arrests.

And, from the two propositions a third is deduced, which is, that the gentlemen composing the meeting are resolved on doing their part to maintain our common government and country, despite the folly or wickedness, as they may conceive, of any administration. This position is eminently patriotic, and as such, I thank the meeting, and congratulate the nation for it. My own purpose is the same; so that the meeting and myself have a common object, and can have no difference, except in the choice of means or measures, for effecting that object.

And here I ought to close this paper, and would close it, if there were no apprehension that more injurious consequences, than any merely personal to myself, might follow the censures systematically cast upon me for doing what, in my view of duty, I could not forbear. The resolutions promise to support me in every constitutional and lawful measure to suppress the rebellion; and I have not knowingly employed, nor shall knowingly employ, any other. But the meeting, by their resolutions, assert and argue, that certain military arrests and proceedings following them for which I am ultimately responsible, are unconstitutional. I think they are not. The resolutions quote from the constitution, the definition of treason; and also the limiting safeguards and guarantees therein provided for the citizen, on trials for treason, and on his being held to answer for capital or otherwise infamous crimes, and, in criminal prosecutions, his right to a speedy and public trial by an impartial jury. They proceed to resolve "That these safeguards of the rights of the citizen against the pretensions of arbitrary power, were intended more *especially* for his protection in times of civil commotion." And, apparently, to demonstrate the proposition, the resolutions proceed "They were secured substantially to the English people, *after* years of protracted civil war, and were adopted into our Constitution at the *close* of the Revolution." Would not the demonstration have been better, if it could have been truly said that these safeguards had been adopted, and applied *during* the civil wars and *during* our Revolution, instead of *after* the one, and at the *close* of the other. I too am devotedly for them *after* civil war, and *before* civil war, and at all times "except when, in cases of rebellion or invasion, the public safety may require" their suspension.

The resolutions proceed to tell us that these safeguards "have stood the test of seventy-six years of trial, under our republican system, under circumstances which show that while they constitute the foundation of all free government, they are the elements of the enduring stability of the Republic." No one denies that they have so stood the test up to the beginning of the present rebellion if we except a certain matter at New Orleans hereafter to be mentioned; nor does anyone question that they will stand the same test much longer after the rebellion closes. But these provisions of the Constitution have no application to the case we have in hand, because the arrests complained of were not made for treason—that is, not for *the* treason defined in the Constitution, and upon the conviction of which, the punishment is death—; nor yet were they made to hold persons to answer for any capital, or otherwise infamous crimes; nor were the proceedings following, in any constitutional or legal sense, "criminal prosecutions." The arrests were made on totally different grounds, and the proceedings following, accorded with the grounds of the arrests. Let us consider the real case with which we are dealing, and apply to it the parts of the Constitution plainly made for such cases.

Prior to my installation here it had been inculcated that any state had a lawful right to secede from the national Union; and that it would be expedient to exercise the right, whenever the devotees of the doctrine should fail to elect a President to their own liking. I was elected contrary to their liking; and accordingly, so far as it was legally possible, they had taken seven states out of the Union, had seized many of the United States forts, and had fired upon the United States' flag, all before I was inaugurated; and, of course, before I had done any official act whatever. The rebellion, thus began soon ran into the present civil war; and, in certain respects, it began on very unequal terms between the parties. The insurgents had been preparing for it more than thirty years, while the government had taken no steps to resist them. The former had carefully considered all the means which could be turned to their account. It undoubtedly was a well-pondered reliance with them that in their own unrestricted effort to destroy Union, Constitution, and law, all together, the government would, in great degree, be restrained by the same Constitution and law, from arresting their progress. Their sympathizers pervaded all departments of the government, and nearly all communities of the people. From this material, under cover of "Liberty of speech" "Liberty of the press" and *"Habeas corpus"* they hoped to keep on foot amongst us a most efficient corps of spies, informers, suppliers, and aiders and abettors of their cause in a thousand ways. They knew that in times such as they were inaugurating, by the Constitution itself, the "habeas corpus" might be suspended; but they also knew they had friends who would make a question as to *who* was to suspend it; meanwhile their spies and others might remain at large to help on their cause. Or if, as has happened, the executive should suspend the writ, without ruinous waste of time, instances of arresting innocent persons might occur, as are always likely to occur in such cases; and then a clamor could be raised in regard to this, which might be, at least, of some service to the insurgent cause.

It needed no very keen perception to discover this part of the enemy's programme, so soon as by open hostilities their machinery was fairly put in motion. Yet, thoroughly imbued with a reverence for the guaranteed rights of individuals, I was slow to adopt the strong measures, which by degrees I have been forced to regard as being within the exceptions of the constitution, and as indispensable to the public safety. Nothing is better known to history than that courts of justice are utterly incompetent to such cases. Civil courts are organized chiefly for trials of individuals, or, at most, a few individuals acting in concert; and this in quiet times, and on charges of crimes well defined in the law. Even in times of peace, bands of horsethieves and robbers frequently grow too numerous and powerful for the ordinary courts of justice. But what comparison, in numbers, have such bands ever borne to the insurgent sympathizers even in many of the loyal states? Again, a jury too frequently have at least one member, more ready to hang the panel than to hang the traitor. And yet again, he who dissuades one man from volunteering, or induces one soldier to desert, weakens the Union cause as much as he who kills a Union soldier in battle. Yet this dissuasion, or inducement, may be so conducted as to be no defined crime of which any civil court would take cognizance.

War posed a difficult paradox. In order to preserve civil liberties it sometimes became necessary to curb them. Yet Lincoln had studied the Constitution and defended the ground on which he stood.

From Antietam to Vicksburg

Ours is a case of rebellion—so called by the resolutions before me—in fact, a clear, flagrant, and gigantic case of rebellion; and the provision of the Constitution that "The privilege of the writ of habeas corpus shall not be suspended, unless when in cases of rebellion or invasion, the public safety may require it" is *the* provision which specially applies to our present case. This provision plainly attests the understanding of those who made the Constitution that ordinary courts of justice are inadequate to "cases of rebellion"—attests their purpose that in such cases, men may be held in custody whom the courts acting on ordinary rules, would discharge. Habeas corpus, does not discharge men who are proved to be guilty of defined crime; and its suspension is allowed by the Constitution on purpose that men may be arrested and held, who cannot be proved to be guilty of defined crime, "when, in cases of rebellion or invasion the public safety may require it." This is precisely our present case—a case of rebellion, wherein the public safety does require the suspension. Indeed, arrests by process of courts, and arrests in cases of rebellion, do not proceed altogether upon the same basis. The former is directed at the small per centage of ordinary and continuous perpetration of crime; while the latter is directed at sudden and extensive uprisings against the government, which, at most, will succeed or fail, in no great length of time. In the latter case, arrests are made, not so much for what has been done, as for what probably would be done. The latter is more for the preventive, and less for the vindictive, than the former. In such cases the purposes of men are much more easily understood, than in cases of ordinary crime. The man who stands by and says nothing, when the peril of his government is discussed, cannot be misunderstood. If not hindered, he is sure to help the enemy. Much more, if he talks ambiguously—talks for his country with "buts" and "ifs" and "ands." Of how little value the constitutional provision I have quoted will be rendered, if arrests shall never be made until defined crimes shall have been committed, may be illustrated by a few notable examples. Gen. John C. Breckenridge, Gen. Robert E. Lee, Gen. Joseph E. Johnston, Gen. John B. Magruder, Gen. William B. Preston, Gen. Simon B. Buckner, and Commodore Franklin Buchanan, now occupying the very highest places in the rebel war service, were all within the power of the government since the rebellion began, and were nearly as well known to be traitors then as now. Unquestionably if we had seized and held them, the insurgent cause would be much weaker. But no one of them had then committed any crime defined in the law. Every one of them if arrested would have been discharged on habeas corpus, were the writ allowed to operate. In view of these and similar cases, I think the time not unlikely to come when I shall be blamed for having made too few arrests rather than too many.

By the third resolution the meeting indicate their opinion that military arrests may be constitutional in localities where rebellion actually exists; but that such arrests are unconstitutional in localities where rebellion, or insurrection, does not actually exist. They insist that such arrests shall not be made "outside of the lines of necessary military occupation, and the scenes of insurrection." Inasmuch, however, as the Constitution itself makes no such distinction, I am unable to believe that there is any such constitutional distinction. I concede that the class of arrests complained of, can be constitutional only when, in cases of rebellion or invasion, the public safety may require them; and I insist that in such cases, they are constitutional *wherever* the public safety does require them—as well in places to which they may prevent the rebellion extending, as in those where it may be already prevailing—as well where they may restrain mischievous interference with the raising and supplying of armies, to suppress the rebellion, as where the rebellion may actually be—as well where they may restrain the enticing men out of the army, as where they would prevent mutiny in the army—equally constitutional at all places where they will conduce to the public safety, as against the dangers of rebellion or invasion.

Clement L. Vallandigham, defeated for election to Congress by a Republican gerrymander of his district, had stumped Ohio shouting that the war was a failure, Lincoln a despot. Freemen who submitted to conscription, cried Vallandigham, deserved to lose their liberties. Vallandigham was arrested by Union military authority. Almost waggishly, Lincoln ordered him banished to the Confederate lines. Against this background, Lincoln now spoke of the great dissenter.

Take the particular case mentioned by the meeting. They assert in substance that Mr. Vallandigham was by a military commander, seized and tried "for no other reason than words addressed to a public meeting, in criticism of the course of the administration, and in condemnation of the military orders of that general." Now, if there be no mistake about this—if this assertion is the truth and the whole truth—if there was no other reason for the arrest, then I concede that the arrest was wrong. But the arrest, as I understand, was made for a very different reason. Mr. Vallandigham avows his hostility to the war on the part of the Union; and his arrest was made because he was laboring, with some effect, to prevent the raising of troops, to encourage desertions from the army, and to leave the rebellion without an adequate military force to suppress it. He was not arrested because he was damaging the political prospects of the administration, or the personal interests of the commanding general; but because he was damaging the army, upon the existence, and vigor of which, the life of the nation depends. He was warring upon the military; and this gave the military constitutional jurisdiction to lay hands upon him. If Mr. Vallandigham was not damaging the military power of the country, then his arrest was made on mistake of fact, which I would be glad to correct, on reasonably satisfactory evidence.

I understand the meeting, whose resolutions I am considering, to be in favor of suppressing the rebellion by military force—by armies. Long experience has shown that armies cannot be maintained unless desertion shall be punished by the severe penalty of death. The case requires, and the law and the Constitution, sanction this punishment. Must I shoot a simple-minded soldier boy who deserts, while I must not touch a hair of a wily agitator who induces him to desert? This is none the less injurious when effected by getting a father, or brother, or friend, into a public meeting, and there working upon his feelings, till he is persuaded to write the soldier boy, that he is fighting in a bad cause, for a wicked administration of a contemptible government, too weak to arrest and punish him if he shall desert. I think that in such a case, to silence the agitator, and save the boy, is not only constitutional, but, withal, a great mercy.

If I be wrong on this question of constitutional power, my error lies in believing that certain proceedings are constitutional when, in cases of rebellion or invasion, the public safety requires them, which would not be constitutional when, in absence of rebellion or invasion, the public safety does not require them—in other words, that the Constitution is not in its application in all respects the same, in cases of rebellion or invasion, involving the public safety, as it is in times of profound peace and public security. The Constitution itself makes the distinction; and I can no more be persuaded that the government can constitutionally take no strong measure in time of rebellion, because it can be shown that the same could not be lawfully taken in time of peace, than I can be persuaded that a particular drug is not good medicine for a sick man, because it can be shown to not be good food for a well one. Nor am I able to appreciate the danger, apprehended by the meeting, that the American people will, by means of military arrests during the rebellion, lose the right of public discussion, the liberty of speech and the press, the law of evidence, trial by jury, and habeas corpus, throughout the indefinite peaceful future which I trust lies before them, any more than I am able to believe that a man could contract so strong an appetite for emetics during temporary illness, as to persist in feeding upon them through the remainder of his healthful life.

Scathingly, Lincoln lashed at politics placed above country.

In giving the resolutions that earnest consideration which you request of me, I cannot overlook the fact that the meeting speak as "Democrats." Nor can I, with full respect for their known intelligence, and the fairly presumed deliberation with which they prepared their resolutions, be permitted to suppose that this occurred by accident, or in any way other than that they preferred to designate themselves "Democrats" rather than "American citizens." In this time of national peril I would have preferred to meet you upon a level one step higher than any party platform; because I am sure that from such more elevated position, we could do better battle for the country we all love, than we possibly can from those lower ones, where from the force of habit, the prejudices of the past, and selfish hopes of the future, we are sure to expend much of our ingenuity and strength, in finding fault with, and aiming blows at each other. But since you have denied me this, I will yet be thankful, for the country's sake, that not all Democrats have done so. He on whose discretionary judgment Mr. Vallandigham was arrested and tried, is a Democrat, having no old party affinity with me; and the judge who rejected the constitutional view expressed in these resolutions, by refusing to discharge Mr. V. on habeas corpus, is a Democrat of better days than these, having received his judicial mantle at the hands of President Jackson. And still more, of all those Democrats who are nobly exposing their lives and shedding their blood on the battlefield, I have learned that many approve the course taken with Mr. V. while I have not heard of a single one condemning it. I cannot assert that there are none such.

And the name of President Jackson recalls a bit of pertinent history. After the Battle of New Orleans, and while the fact that the treaty of peace had been concluded, was well known in the city, but before official knowledge of it had arrived, Gen. Jackson still maintained martial, or military law. Now, that it could be said the war was over, the clamor against martial law, which had existed from the first, grew more furious. Among other things a Mr. Louaillier published a denunciatory newspaper article. Gen. Jackson arrested him. A lawyer by the name of Morel procured the U. S. Judge Hall to order a writ of habeas corpus to release Mr. Louaillier. Gen. Jackson arrested both the lawyer and the judge. A Mr. Hollander ventured to say of some part of the matter that "it was a dirty trick." Gen. Jackson arrested him. When the officer undertook to serve the writ of habeas corpus, Gen. Jackson took it from him, and sent him away with a copy. Holding the judge in custody a few days, the general sent him beyond the limits of his encampment, and set him at liberty, with an order to remain till the ratification of peace should be regularly announced, or until the British should have left the southern coast. A day or two more elapsed, the ratification of the treaty of peace was regularly announced, and the judge and others were fully liberated. A few days more, and the judge called Gen. Jackson into court and fined him a thousand dollars, for having arrested him and the others named. The general paid the fine, and there the matter rested for nearly thirty years, when Congress refunded principal and interest. The late Senator Douglas, then in the House of Representatives, took a leading part in the debate, in which the constitutional question was much discussed. I am not prepared to say whom the Journals would show to have voted for the measure.

It may be remarked: First, that we had the same Constitution then, as now. Secondly, that we then had a case of invasion, and that now we have a case of rebellion, and: Thirdly, that the permanent right of the people to public discussion, the liberty of speech and the press, the trial by jury, the law of evidence, and the habeas corpus, suffered no detriment whatever by that conduct of Gen. Jackson, or its subsequent approval by the American Congress.

And yet, let me say that in my own discretion, I do not know whether I would have ordered the arrest of Mr. V. While I cannot shift the responsibility from myself, I hold that, as a general rule, the commander in the field is the better judge of the necessity in any particular case. Of course I must practice a general directory and revisory power in the matter.

One of the resolutions expresses the opinion of the meeting that arbitrary arrests will have the effect to divide and distract those who should be united in suppressing the rebellion; and I am specifically called on to discharge Mr. Vallandigham. I regard this as, at least, a fair appeal to me, on the expediency of exercising a constitutional power which I think exists. In response to such appeal I have to say it gave me pain when I learned that Mr. V. had been arrested, – that is, I was pained that there should have seemed to be a necessity for arresting him – and that it will afford me great pleasure to discharge him so soon as I can, by any means, believe the public safety will not suffer by it. I further say, that as the war progresses, it appears to me, opinion, and action, which were in great confusion at first, take shape, and fall into more regular channels; so that the necessity for arbitrary dealing with them gradually decreases. I have every reason to desire that it would cease altogether; and far from the least is my regard for the opinions and wishes of those who, like the meeting at Albany, declare their purpose to sustain the government in every constitutional and lawful measure to suppress the rebellion. Still, I must continue to do so much as may seem to be required by the public safety.

A. Lincoln.

Sunday, June 14. Washington quaked with an ugly rumor—Lee moved north. In the War Department Lincoln spent the afternoon at the telegraph table. Stanton and Halleck were with him. The second of the telegrams Lincoln sent Hooker again revealed the President adding to his laurels a mastery of war.

From Antietam to Vicksburg

Washington, June 14, 1863 1.14 P.M.

Major-General Hooker:

Do you consider it possible that 15,000 of Ewell's men can now be at Winchester?

A. Lincoln.

Washington, June 14, 1863 — 5.50 P.M.

Major-General Hooker:

So far as we can make out here, the enemy have Milroy surrounded at Winchester, and Tyler at Martinsburg. If they could hold out a few days, could you help them? If the head of Lee's army is at Martinsburg and the tail of it on the plank road between Fredericksburg and Chancellorsville, the animal must be very slim somewhere. Could you not break him?

A. Lincoln.

Executive Mansion, Washington,
June 14. 11.55 P.M. *1863.*

Major General Hooker.

Yours of 11.30 just received. You have nearly all the elements for forming an opinion whether Winchester is surrounded that I have. I really fear — almost believe, it is. No communication has been had with it during the day, either at Martinsburg, or Harper's Ferry. At 7 P.M., we also lost communication with Martinsburg. The enemy had also appeared there some hours before. At 9 P.M. Harper's Ferry said the enemy was reported at Berryville & Smithfield. If I could know that Longstreet and Ewell moved in that direction so long ago as you stated in your last, then I should feel sure that Winchester is strongly invested. It is quite certain that a considerable force of the enemy is thereabout; and I fear it is an overwhelming one, compared with Milroy's. I am unable to give any more certain opinion.

A. Lincoln

Washington,
June 14, 1863 — 1.27 P.M.

Major-General Kelley,
Harper's Ferry:

Are the forces at Winchester and Martinsburg making any effort to get to you?

A. Lincoln.

The Living Lincoln

Washington, D. C.,
June 14 1863

Gen. Schenck
Baltimore

Get Milroy from Winchester to Harper's Ferry if possible. He will be gobbled up, if he remains, if he is not already past salvation.

A. Lincoln

Washington, D. C.,
June 14 1863

Gen. Tyler—
Martinsburg.

Is Milroy invested, so that he cannot fall back to Harper's Ferry?

A. Lincoln

Washington, D. C.,
June 14 1863

Gen. Tyler
Martinsburg.

If you are besieged, how do you despatch me? Why did you not leave, before being besieged?

A. Lincoln

Monday was a difficult day in the White House. The Union force at Winchester had been swept away, Martinsburg isolated, and Lee was loose somewhere in the North although his objective was unknown. Washington, Baltimore, Harrisburg, Philadelphia . . . where might he turn?

With these worries, Lincoln took up a personal problem. Ninian W. Edwards, commissary, and William H. Bailhache, quartermaster, had been charged with using their positions to amass personal fortunes. In late May a number of the President's old friends in Springfield petitioned for the removal of the alleged culprits.*

* A week after this letter both men were replaced.

From Antietam to Vicksburg

Executive Mansion,
Washington, June 15, 1863.

E. L. Baker, Esq
Dear Sir

Not to exceed two hours after you left me I received a letter from Springfield, renewing the pressure upon me in the matter we talked of; and, in fact, leaving me no alternative but to make some change there. I can say but little beyond what I then said to you. The appeal to me in behalf of Mr. Edwards and Mr. Bailhache, for a hearing, does not meet the case. No formal charges are preferred against them, so far as I know; nor do I expect any will be made; or, if made, will be substantiated. I certainly do not suppose Mr. Edwards has, at this time of his life, given up his old habits, and turned dishonest; and while I have not known Mr. Bailhache so long, I have no more affirmative reason to suspect him. The trouble with me is of a different character. Springfield is my home, and there, more than elsewhere, are my lifelong friends. These, for now nearly two years, have been harassing me because of Mr. E. & Mr. B. I think Mr. E. & Mr. B. without dishonesty on the other hand, could have saved me from this, if they had cared to do so. They have seemed to think that if they could keep their official record dryly correct, to say the least, it was not any difference how much they might provoke my friends, and harass me. If this is too strong a statement of the case, still the result has been the same to me; and, as a *misfortune* merely, I think I have already borne a fair share of it.

In what I may do, I shall try to so shape it, as to not seem to mean more than is really intended. Your Obt. Servt.

A. Lincoln.

Lincoln had passed the point where he would tolerate personal animosities that might endanger the Army of the Potomac, and so told Hooker.

(PRIVATE)
Executive Mansion, Washington, D. C., June 16, 1863.
My dear General:

I send you this by the hand of Captain Dahlgren. Your despatch of 11:30 A.M. today is just received. When you say I have long been aware that you do not enjoy the confidence of the major general commanding, you state the case much too strongly.

You do not lack his confidence in any degree to do you any harm. On seeing him, after telegraphing you this morning, I found him more nearly agreeing with you than I was myself. Surely you do not mean to understand that I am withholding my confidence from you when I happen to express an opinion (certainly never discourteously) differing from one of your own.

I believe Halleck is dissatisfied with you to this extent only, that he knows that you write and telegraph ("report," as he calls it) to me. I think he is wrong to find fault with this; but I do not think he withholds any support from you on account of it. If you and he would use the same frankness to one another, and to me, that I use to both of you, there would be no difficulty. I need and must have the professional skill of both, and yet these suspicions tend to deprive me of both.

I believe you are aware that since you took command of the army I have not believed you had any chance to effect anything till now. As it looks to me, Lee's now returning toward Harper's Ferry gives you back the chance that I thought McClellan lost last fall. Quite possibly I was wrong both then and now; but, in the great responsibility resting upon me, I cannot be entirely silent. Now, all I ask is that you will be in such mood that we can get into our action the best cordial judgment of yourself and General Halleck, with my poor mite added, if indeed he and you shall think it entitled to any consideration at all. Yours as ever,

A. Lincoln.

Lincoln chose between Hooker and Halleck.

Executive Mansion, Washington,
June 16. 1863. [10 P.M.]

Major General Hooker.

To remove all misunderstanding, I now place you in the strict military relation to Gen. Halleck, of a commander of one of the armies, to the general-in-chief of all the armies. I have not intended differently; but as it seems to be differently understood, I shall direct him to give you orders, and you to obey them.

A. Lincoln

From Antietam to Vicksburg

To an uneasy wife the President minimized Lee's advance into Pennsylvania.

Washington City, D. C.
June 16. 1863

Mrs. Lincoln
Philadelphia.

It is a matter of choice with yourself whether you come home. There is no reason why you should not, that did not exist when you went away. As bearing on the question of your coming home, I do not think the raid into Pennsylvania amounts to anything at all.

A. Lincoln

At Winchester, Virginia, in the path of Lee's advancing army, General Robert H. Milroy failed to obey an order to pull back to Harper's Ferry, lost the division he commanded, and blamed his misfortune on Halleck and his prejudice against nonprofessional generals. Lincoln had heard the same carping story once too often. Milroy received a sharp reproof.

PRIVATE

Executive Mansion,
Washington, June 29. 1863.

Major General Milroy
My dear Sir:

Your letters to Mr. Blair and to myself, are handed to me by him. I have never doubted your courage and devotion to the cause. But you have just lost a division, and *prima facie* the fault is upon you; and while that remains unchanged, for me to put you in command again, is to justly subject me to the charge of having put you there on purpose to have you lose another. If I knew facts sufficient to satisfy me that you were not in fault, or error, the case would be different. But the facts I do know, while they are not at all conclusive, and I hope they may never prove so, tend the other way.

First, I have scarcely seen anything from you at any time, that did not contain imputations against your superiors, and a chafing against acting the part they had assigned you. You have constantly

559

urged the idea that you were persecuted because you did not come from West Point, and you repeat it in these letters. This, my dear general, is I fear, the rock on which you have split.

In the Winchester case, you were under General Schenck, and he under Gen. Halleck. I know by Gen. Halleck's order book, that he, on the 11th. of June advised Gen. Schenck to call you in from Winchester to Harper's Ferry; and I have been told, but do not know, that Gen. Schenck gave you the order accordingly, on the same day—and I have been told, but do not know, that on receiving it, instead of obeying it, you sent by mail a written protest against obeying it, which did not reach him until you were actually beleaguered at Winchester. I say I do not know this. You hate West Point generally, and General Halleck particularly; but I do know that it is not his fault that you were at Winchester on the 13th. 14th. and morning of the 15th.—the days of your disaster. If Gen. Schenck gave the order on the 11th. as Gen. Halleck advised, it was an easy matter for you to have been off at least on the 12th. The case is inevitably between Gen. Schenck & you. Neither Gen. Halleck, nor anyone else, so far as I know, required you to stay and fight 60,000, with 6,000, as you insinuate. I know Gen. Halleck, through Gen. Schenck required you to get away, & that in abundant time for you to have done it. Gen. Schenck is not a West Pointer & has no prejudice against you on that score. Yours very truly

A. Lincoln

Mrs. Lincoln had fallen from her carriage during a runaway.

Executive Mansion,
Washington, July 3rd. 1863.

Robert T. Lincoln Esq.
Cambridge Mass.

Don't be uneasy. Your mother very slightly hurt by her fall.

A. L.

Please send at once

Through a press release from the War Department, Lincoln gave the country the news of Gettysburg.

From Antietam to Vicksburg

Washington City, July 4, 10. A.M. *1863*
The President announces to the country that news from the Army
of the Potomac, up to 10 P.M. of the 3rd. is such as to cover that
army with the highest honor, to promise a great success to the
cause of the Union, and to claim the condolence of all for the
many gallant fallen. And that for this, he especially desires that
on this day, He whose will, not ours, should ever be done, be
everywhere remembered and reverenced with profoundest gratitude.

Abraham Lincoln

Within hours of the Confederate retreat from Gettysburg, the
Union staggered the South with another smashing blow.

[*July 7, 1863*]

Major-General Halleck:
We have certain information that Vicksburg surrendered to
General Grant on the 4th of July. Now, if General Meade can
complete his work, so gloriously prosecuted thus far, by the literal
or substantial destruction of Lee's army, the rebellion will be over.
Yours, truly,

A. Lincoln.

From Vicksburg continued to come the kind of news that Lincoln
wanted. Grant had bagged 31,600 prisoners at Vicksburg, then added
another 6,000 with the fall of Port Hudson a few days later. To a general who destroyed armies Lincoln wrote a letter of warm congratulations, and made a graceful confession.

Executive Mansion,
Washington, July 13, 1863.

Major General Grant
My dear General
I do not remember that you and I ever met personally. I write
this now as a grateful acknowledgment for the almost inestimable
service you have done the country. I wish to say a word further.
When you first reached the vicinity of Vicksburg, I thought you
should do, what you finally did—march the troops across the neck,
run the batteries with the transports, and thus go below; and I

never had any faith, except a general hope that you knew better than I, that the Yazoo Pass expedition, and the like, could succeed. When you got below, and took Port Gibson, Grand Gulf, and vicinity, I thought you should go down the river and join Gen. Banks; and when you turned northward east of the Big Black, I feared it was a mistake. I now wish to make the personal acknowledgment that you were right, and I was wrong.   Yours very truly

A. Lincoln

XV. "The Signs Look Better"

1863-1864 THE high tide of Lee, beginning with the Seven Days' battles, smashing the Army of the Potomac at Second Manassas, eddying temporarily at Antietam and then surging back with crushing victories at Fredricksburg and Chancellorsville, ended at Gettysburg. A succession of generals had opposed Lee—McClellan, Pope, Burnside, Hooker and Meade—and the Confederate had outwitted and outfought them all, for his had been the initiative at Gettysburg no matter how well Meade had fought once the battle had been forced upon him.

Yet the turning point had been reached. Lincoln now understood Lee. If the Confederate ever was to be beaten decisively overwhelming resources must be accumulated against him. And if Lee failed to understand fully one circumstance that could defeat him it was the fact that though generals changed in the field he was fighting constantly against one mind.

Lincoln's growing knowledge of military science convinced him that once the Army of Northern Virginia had crossed the Mason and Dixon line swift action should make its destruction inevitable. Antietam had given the North its first chance to destroy Lee in this manner. Now at Gettysburg a second chance had been thrown away by the extreme caution of a general. Lincoln spent his anger on a letter he never sent.

Executive Mansion,
Washington, July 14, 1863.

Major General Meade
I have just seen your despatch to Gen. Halleck, asking to be relieved of your command, because of a supposed censure of mine.

563

I am very—*very*—grateful to you for the magnificent success you gave the cause of the country at Gettysburg; and I am sorry now to be the author of the slightest pain to you. But I was in such deep distress myself that I could not restrain some expression of it. I had been oppressed nearly ever since the battles at Gettysburg, by what appeared to be evidences that yourself, and Gen. Couch, and Gen. Smith, were not seeking a collision with the enemy, but were trying to get him across the river without another battle. What these evidences were, if you please, I hope to tell you at some time, when we shall both feel better. The case, summarily stated is this. You fought and beat the enemy at Gettysburg; and, of course, to say the least, his loss was as great as yours. He retreated; and you did not, as it seemed to me, pressingly pursue him; but a flood in the river detained him, till, by slow degrees, you were again upon him. You had at least twenty thousand veteran troops directly with you, and as many more raw ones within supporting distance, all in addition to those who fought with you at Gettysburg; while it was not possible that he had received a single recruit; and yet you stood and let the flood run down, bridges be built, and the enemy move away at his leisure, without attacking him. And Couch and Smith! The latter left Carlisle in time, upon all ordinary calculation, to have aided you in the last battle at Gettysburg; but he did not arrive. At the end of more than ten days, I believe twelve, under constant urging, he reached Hagerstown from Carlisle, which is not an inch over fifty-five miles, if so much. And Couch's movement was very little different.

Again, my dear general, I do not believe you appreciate the magnitude of the misfortune involved in Lee's escape. He was within your easy grasp, and to have closed upon him would, in connection with our other late successes, have ended the war. As it is, the war will be prolonged indefinitely. If you could not safely attack Lee last Monday, how can you possibly do so south of the river, when you can take with you very few more than two-thirds of the force you then had in hand? It would be unreasonable to expect, and I do not expect you can now effect much. Your golden opportunity is gone, and I am distressed immeasureably because of it.

I beg you will not consider this a prosecution, or persecution of yourself. As you had learned that I was dissatisfied, I have thought it best to kindly tell you why.

"The Signs Look Better"

General Oliver O. Howard, who commanded a corps at Gettysburg, was distressed by what he read in the press, and wrote the President in strong support of Meade. By the time Lincoln replied, he had put aside his disappointment.

Executive Mansion,
Washington, July 21. 1863.

My dear General Howard

Your letter of the 18th. is received. I was deeply mortified by the escape of Lee across the Potomac, because the substantial destruction of his army would have ended the war, and because I believed such destruction was perfectly easy—believed that Gen. Meade and his noble army had expended all the skill, and toil, and blood, up to the ripe harvest, and then let the crop go to waste. Perhaps my mortification was heightened because I had always believed—making my belief a hobby possibly—that the main rebel army going north of the Potomac, could never return, if well attended to; and because I was so greatly flattered in this belief, by the operations at Gettysburg. A few days having passed, I am now profoundly grateful for what was done, without criticism for what was not done. Gen. Meade has my confidence as a brave and skillful officer, and a true man. Yours very truly

A. Lincoln

The letter in which Lincoln had written, "as I could not remove Gov. Gamble, I had to remove Gen. Curtis," * found its way into the press. Governor Gamble considered himself insulted. By this time Lincoln had hit upon a device for keeping his temper within bounds.

Executive Mansion,
Washington, July 23, 1863.

His Excellency
H. R. Gamble
Sir

My private secretary has just brought me a letter saying it is a very *"cross"* one from you, about mine to Gen. Schofield, recently published in the Democrat. As I am trying to preserve my own temper, by avoiding irritants, so far as practicable, I have declined to read the cross letter. I think fit to say, however, that when I wrote the letter to Gen. Schofield, I was totally unconscious of any malice, or disrespect towards you, or of using

* See page 543.

565

any expression which should offend you, if seen by you. I have not seen the document in the Democrat, and therefore cannot say whether it is a correct copy. Your Obt. Servt.

A. Lincoln.

Disturbed by the thought that an offense might have been given, Lincoln hastened to send an explanation and an apology.

PRIVATE

Executive Mansion,
Washington, July 23, 1863.

Major General Schenck
My dear Sir:
Returning to the executive room yesterday, I was mortified to find you were gone, leaving no word of explanation. I went down stairs, as I understood, on a perfect understanding with you that you would remain till my return. I got this impression distinctly from "Edward" whom I believe you know. Possibly I misunderstood him. I had been very unwell in the morning, and had scarcely tasted food during the day, till the time you saw me go down. I beg you will not believe I have treated you with intentional discourtesy. Yours as ever

A. Lincoln

Hooker had chafed at inactivity since his removal from command of the Army of the Potomac. Lincoln always sought a place for a general who would fight.

PRIVATE

Executive Mansion,
Washington, July 27, 1863.

Major General Meade:
I have not thrown Gen. Hooker away; and therefore I would like to know whether, it would be agreeable to you, all things considered, for him to take a corps under you, if he himself is willing to do so. Write me, in perfect freedom, with the assurance that I will not subject you to any embarrassment, by making your letter, or its contents, known to any one. I wish to know your wishes before I decide whether to break the subject to him. Do not lean a hair's breadth against your own feelings, or your judg-

ment of the public service, on the idea of gratifying me. Yours truly

> *A. Lincoln*

Lincoln had been sorely tried by men who thought they knew far more than he. In self-defence, he turned to sarcasm. With Alexander, a Texas lawyer who always had been loyal to the Union cause, Lincoln seemed unduly harsh.

> *Executive Mansion,*
> *Washington, July 30, 1863.*

Hon. F. P. Blair
My dear Sir
Yours of today with inclosure is received. Yesterday I commenced trying to get up an expedition for Texas. I shall do the best I can. Meantime I would like to know who is the great man Alexander, that talks so oracularly about "if the President keeps his word" and Banks not having "capacity to run an omnibus on Broadway." How has this Alexander's immense light been obscured hitherto? Yours truly

> *A. Lincoln*

With a deepening confidence in victory, Lincoln expressed for the first time his basic ideas of reconstruction.

> *Executive Mansion, Washington,*
> *August 5, 1863.*

My dear General Banks
Being a poor correspondent is the only apology I offer for not having sooner tendered my thanks for your very successful, and very valuable military operations this year. The final stroke in opening the Mississippi never should, and I think never will, be forgotten.

Recent events in Mexico, I think, render early action in Texas more important than ever. I expect, however, the general-in-chief, will address you more fully upon this subject.

Governor Boutwell read me today that part of your letter to him, which relates to Louisiana affairs. While I very well know what I would be glad for Louisiana to do, it is quite a different thing for me to assume direction of the matter. I would be glad for her to make a new constitution recognizing the Emancipation Proclamation, and adopting emancipation in those parts of the state to which the proclamation does not apply. And while she is at it, I think it would not be objectionable for her to adopt some practical system by which the two races could gradually live themselves out of their old relation to each other, and both come out better prepared for the new. Education for young blacks should be included in the plan. After all, the power, or element, of "contract" may be sufficient for this probationary period; and, by its simplicity, and flexibility, may be the better.

As an anti-slavery man I have a motive to desire emancipation, which pro-slavery men do not have; but even they have strong enough reason to thus place themselves again under the shield of the Union; and to thus perpetually hedge against the recurrence of the scenes through which we are now passing.

Gov. Shepley has informed me that Mr. Durant is now taking a registry, with a view to the election of a constitutional convention in Louisiana. This, to me, appears proper. If such convention were to ask my views, I could present little else than what I now say to you. I think the thing should be pushed forward, so that if possible, its mature work may reach here by the meeting of Congress.

For my own part I think I shall not, in any event, retract the Emancipation Proclamation; nor, as executive, ever return to slavery any person who is free by the terms of that proclamation, or by any of the acts of Congress.

If Louisiana shall send members to Congress, their admission to seats will depend, as you know, upon the respective Houses, and not upon the President.

If these views can be of any advantage in giving shape, and impetus, to action there, I shall be glad for you to use them prudently for that object. Of course you will confer with intelligent and trusty citizens of the state, among whom I would suggest Messrs. Flanders, Hahn, and Durant; and to each of whom I now think I may send copies of this letter. Still it is perhaps better to not make the letter generally public. Yours very truly

A. Lincoln

[*Endorsement*]

Copies sent to Messrs. Flanders, Hahn & Durant, each indorsed as follows.

568

"The Signs Look Better"

The within is a copy of a letter to Gen. Banks. Please observe my directions to him. Do not mention the paragraph about Mexico.

Aug. 6. 1863.

A. Lincoln

To Mrs. Lincoln, on a trip with Tad, the President sent word of a domestic tragedy and passed on news about Kentuckians whom his wife knew.

Executive Mansion, Washington, August 8, 1863.
My dear Wife.

All as well as usual, and no particular trouble any way. I put the money into the Treasury at five per cent, with the privilege of withdrawing it anytime upon thirty days' notice. I suppose you are glad to learn this. Tell dear Tad, poor "Nanny Goat," is lost; and Mrs. Cuthbert & I are in distress about it. The day you left Nanny was found resting herself, and chewing her little cud, on the middle of Tad's bed. But now she's gone! The gardener kept complaining that she destroyed the flowers, till it was concluded to bring her down to the White House. This was done, and the second day she had disappeared, and has not been heard of since. This is the last we know of poor "Nanny."

The weather continues dry, and excessively warm here.

Nothing very important occurring. The election in Kentucky has gone very strongly right. Old Mr. Wickliffe got ugly, as you know, ran for Governor, and is terribly beaten. Upon Mr. Crittenden's death, Brutus Clay, Cassius' brother, was put on the track for Congress, and is largely elected. Mr. Menzies, who, as we thought, behaved very badly last session of Congress, is largely beaten in the district opposite Cincinnati, by Green Clay Smith, Cassius Clay's nephew. But enough. Affectionately

A. Lincoln

Often Lincoln had to cope with generals whose skin was paper-thin. Through late July Halleck had urged Rosecrans to move against the Confederates at Chattanooga before Joseph E. Johnston could re-enforce Bragg. Rosecrans took offense, and complained to Lincoln. In replying, the President demonstrated how practiced he had become in smoothing ruffled feelings without relinquishing his hope for action.

The Living Lincoln

Executive Mansion,
Washington, August 10, 1863.

My Dear General Rosecrans

Yours of the 1st was received two days ago. I think you must have inferred more than Gen Halleck has intended, as to any dissatisfaction of mine with you. I am sure you, as a reasonable man, would not have been wounded, could you have heard all my words and seen all my thoughts, in regard to you. I have not abated in my kind feeling for and confidence in you. I have seen most of your despatches to General Halleck—probably all of them. After Grant invested Vicksburg, I was very anxious lest Johnston should overwhelm him from the outside, and when it appeared certain that part of Bragg's force had gone, and was going to Johnston, it did seem to me, it was the exactly proper time for you to attack Bragg with what force he had left. In all kindness, let me say, it so seems to me yet. Finding from your despatches to General Halleck that your judgment was different, and being very anxious for Grant, I, on one occasion told Gen. Halleck, I thought he should direct you to decide at once, to immediately attack Bragg or to stand on the defensive, and send part of your force to Grant. He replied he had already so directed, in substance. Soon after, despatches from Grant abated my anxiety for him, and in proportion abated my anxiety about any movement of yours. When afterwards, however, I saw a despatch of yours arguing that the right time for you to attack Bragg was not before but would be after the fall of Vicksburg, it impressed me very strangely; and I think I so stated to the Secretary of War and General Halleck. It seemed no other than the proposition that you could better fight Bragg *when* Johnston should be at liberty to return and assist him, than you could *before* he could so return to his assistance.

Since Grant has been entirely relieved by the fall of Vicksburg, by which Johnston is also relieved, it has seemed to me that your chance for a stroke, has been considerably diminished, and I have not been pressing you directly or indirectly. True, I am very anxious for East Tennessee to be occupied by us; but I see and appreciate the difficulties you mention. The question occurs, Can the thing be done at all? Does preparation advance at all? Do you not consume supplies as fast as you get them forward? Have you more animals today than you had at the Battle of Stone River? and yet have not more been furnished you since then than your entire present stock? I ask the same questions as to your mounted force.

Do not misunderstand. I am not casting blame upon you. I rather think, by great exertion, you can get to East Tennessee. But a very important question is, "Can you stay there?" I make no order in the case—that I leave to General Halleck and yourself.

And now, be assured once more, that I think of you in all kindness and confidence: and that I am not watching you with an evil eye. Yours very truly

[No signature]

For justifiable reasons, Grant had relieved McClernand of his command. As gently as possible, Lincoln explained to McClernand why, in this instance, Grant had to be sustained.

Executive Mansion,
Washington, August 12, 1863.

Major General McClernand:
My dear Sir:
Our friend, William G. Greene, has just presented a kind letter in regard to yourself, addressed to me by our other friends, Yates, Hatch, and Dubois. I doubt whether your present position is more painful to you than to myself. Grateful for the patriotic stand so early taken by you in this life-and-death struggle of the nation, I have done whatever has appeared practicable to advance you and the public interest together. No charges, with a view to a trial, have been preferred against you by anyone; nor do I suppose any will be. All there is, so far as I have heard, is Gen. Grant's statement of his reasons for relieving you. And even this I have not seen or sought to see; because it is a case, as appears to me, in which I could do nothing without doing harm. Gen. Grant and yourself have been conspicuous in our most important successes; and for me to interfere, and thus magnify a breach between you, could not but be of evil effect. Better leave it where the law of the case has placed it. For me to force you back upon Gen. Grant, would be forcing him to resign. I cannot give you a new command, because we have no forces except such as already have commanders. I am constantly pressed by those who *scold*

before they *think,* or without thinking at all, to give commands respectively to Fremont, McClellan, Butler, Sigel, Curtis, Hunter, Hooker, and perhaps others; when, all else out of the way, I have no commands to give them. This is now your case, which, as I have before said, pains me, not less than it does you.

My belief is that the permanent estimate of what a general does in the field, is fixed by the "cloud of witnesses" who have been with him in the field; and that relying on these, he who has the right needs not to fear. Your friend as ever

A. Lincoln

To Cousin Lizzie Grimsley, whom Lincoln had not been able to appoint postmistress of Springfield,* the President made a promise.

Executive Mansion, Washington, August 14, 1863.
My dear Cousin Lizzie

I have, by the law, two classes of appointments to make to the Naval School—ten of each, to the year. The first class, according to the law, must be of families of the meritorious naval officers; while the other class does not have such restriction. You see at once that if I have a vacancy in the first class, I cannot appoint Johnny to it; and I have intended for months, and still intend, to appoint him to the very first vacancy I can get in the other class. Yours very truly

A. Lincoln

Delighted that Lincoln had seen him play Falstaff in *King Henry IV,* James H. Hackett sent the President a copy of his recently published *Notes and Comments upon Certain Plays and Actors of Shakespeare, with Criticisms and Correspondence.* Lincoln, whose power of expression was derived in no small measure from Shakespeare, replied with a critical opinion on *Macbeth.*

Executive Mansion,
Washington, August 17, 1863.
My dear Sir:

Months ago I should have acknowledged the receipt of your book, and accompanying kind note; and I now have to beg your pardon for not having done so.

* See page 393.

"The Signs Look Better"

For one of my age, I have seen very little of the drama. The first presentation of Falstaff I ever saw was yours here, last winter or spring. Perhaps the best compliment I can pay is to say, as I truly can, I am very anxious to see it again. Some of Shakspeare's plays I have never read; while others I have gone over perhaps as frequently as any unprofessional reader. Among the latter are Lear, Richard Third, Henry Eighth, Hamlet, and especially Macbeth. I think nothing equals Macbeth. It is wonderful. Unlike you gentlemen of the profession, I think the soliloquy in Hamlet commencing "O, my offence is rank" surpasses that commencing "To be, or not to be." But pardon this small attempt at criticism. I should like to hear you pronounce the opening speech of Richard the Third. Will you not soon visit Washington again? If you do, please call and let me make your personal acquaintance. Yours truly

James H. Hackett, Esq.

A. Lincoln.

General James G. Blunt, commanding Union troops in Kansas, was causing Lincoln anxious moments. The President expressed his unmistakable displeasure.*

Executive Mansion,
Washington, August 1863.

Major General Blunt:

Yours of July 31st is received. Governor Carney did leave some papers with me concerning you; but they made no great impression upon me; and I believe they are not altogether such as you seem to think. As I am not proposing to act upon them, I do not now take the time to re-examine them.

I regret to find you denouncing so many persons as liars, scoundrels, fools, thieves, and persecutors of yourself. Your military position looks critical, but did any body *force* you into it? Have you been *ordered* to confront and fight ten thousand men, with three thousand men? The government cannot make men; and it is very easy, when a man has been given the highest commission, for him to turn on those who gave it and vilify them for not giving him a command according to his rank.

My appointment of you first as a brigadier, and then as a

* Blunt was relieved from command October 19, 1863.

major general, was evidence of my appreciation of your service; and I have not since marked but one thing in connection with you, with which to be dissatisfied. The sending a military order twenty-five miles outside of your lines, and all military lines, to take men charged with no offence against the military, out of the hands of the courts, to be turned over to a mob to be hanged, can find no precedent or principle to justify it. Judge Lynch sometimes takes jurisdiction of cases which prove too strong for the courts; but this is the first case within my knowledge, wherein the court being able to maintain jurisdiction against Judge Lynch, the military has come to the assistance of the latter. I take the facts of this case as you state them yourself, and not from any report of Governor Carney, or other person. Yours truly

A Lincoln

Lincoln made good his promise of ten days earlier.

Washington, D. C.,
August 24 1863

Mrs. Elizabeth J. Grimsley
Springfield, Illinois.

I mail the papers to you today appointing Johnny to the Naval School.

A. Lincoln

In Illinois, war weariness grew. In mid-June, 1863, "Peace" Democrats held a giant rally in the President's home city. The Republicans, at first alarmed and then heartened by the victories of Gettysburg and Vicksburg, decided to hold a demonstration of their own. Lincoln planned to attend, but ended by sending a letter, of which the New York *Times* gloated: "Even the Copperhead gnaws upon it as vainly as a viper upon a file."

Executive Mansion,
Washington, August 26, 1863.

Hon. James C. Conkling
My Dear Sir.

Your letter inviting me to attend a mass meeting of unconditional Union men, to be held at the capital of Illinois, on the 3d day of September, has been received.

"The Signs Look Better"

It would be very agreeable to me, to thus meet my old friends, at my own home; but I cannot, just now, be absent from here, so long as a visit there, would require.

The meeting is to be of all those who maintain unconditional devotion to the Union; and I am sure my old political friends will thank me for tendering, as I do, the nation's gratitude to those other noble men, whom no partizan malice, or partizan hope, can make false to the nation's life.

There are those who are dissatisfied with me. To such I would say: You desire peace; and you blame me that we do not have it. But how can we attain it? There are but three conceivable ways. First, to suppress the rebellion by force of arms. This, I am trying to do. Are you for it? If you are, so far we are agreed. If you are not for it, a second way is, to give up the Union. I am against this. Are you for it? If you are, you should say so plainly. If you are not for *force,* nor yet for *dissolution,* there only remains some imaginable *compromise.* I do not believe any compromise, embracing the maintenance of the Union, is now possible. All I learn, leads to a directly opposite belief. The strength of the rebellion, is its military—its army. That army dominates all the country, and all the people, within its range. Any offer of terms made by any man or men within that range, in opposition to that army, is simply nothing for the present; because such man or men, have no power whatever to enforce their side of a compromise, if one were made with them. To illustrate—Suppose refugees from the South, and peace men of the North, get together in convention, and frame and proclaim a compromise embracing a restoration of the Union; in what way can that compromise be used to keep Lee's army out of Pennsylvania? Meade's army can keep Lee's army out of Pennsylvania; and, I think, can ultimately drive it out of existence. But no paper compromise, to which the controllers of Lee's army are not agreed, can, at all, affect that army. In an effort at such compromise we should waste time, which the enemy would improve to our disadvantage; and that would be all. A compromise, to be effective, must be made either with those who control the rebel army, or with the people first liberated from the domination of that army, by the success of our own army. Now allow me to assure you, that no word or intimation, from that rebel army, or from any of the men controlling it, in relation to any peace compromise, has ever come to my knowledge or be-

575

lief. All charges and insinuations to the contrary, are deceptive and groundless. And I promise you, that if any such proposition shall hereafter come, it shall not be rejected, and kept a secret from you. I freely acknowledge myself the servant of the people, according to the bond of service—the United States Constitution; and that, as such, I am responsible to them.

But, to be plain, you are dissatisfied with me about the Negro. Quite likely there is a difference of opinion between you and myself upon that subject. I certainly wish that all men could be free, while I suppose you do not. Yet I have neither adopted, nor proposed any measure, which is not consistent with even your view, provided you are for the Union. I suggested compensated emancipation; to which you replied you wished not to be taxed to buy Negroes. But I had not asked you to be taxed to buy Negroes, except in such way, as to save you from greater taxation to save the Union exclusively by other means.

You dislike the Emancipation Proclamation; and, perhaps, would have it retracted. You say it is unconstitutional—I think differently. I think the Constitution invests its commander-in-chief, with the law of war, in time of war. The most that can be said, if so much, is, that slaves are property. Is there—has there ever been—any question that by the law of war, property, both of enemies and friends, may be taken when needed? And is it not needed whenever taking it, helps us, or hurts the enemy? Armies, the world over, destroy enemies' property when they cannot use it; and even destroy their own to keep it from the enemy. Civilized belligerents do all in their power to help themselves, or hurt the enemy, except a few things regarded as barbarous or cruel. Among the exceptions are the massacre of vanquished foes, and noncombatants, male and female.

But the proclamation, as law, either is valid, or is not valid. If it is not valid, it needs no retraction. If it is valid, it cannot be retracted, any more than the dead can be brought to life. Some of you profess to think its retraction would operate favorably for the Union. Why better *after* the retraction, than *before* the issue? There was more than a year and a half of trial to suppress the rebellion before the proclamation issued, the last one hundred days of which passed under an explicit notice that it was coming, unless averted by those in revolt, returning to their allegiance. The war has certainly progressed as favorably for us, since the issue of the proclamation as before. I know as fully as one can know the opinions of others, that some of the commanders of our armies in the field who have given us our most important successes, believe the emancipation policy, and the use of colored troops, constitute the heaviest blow yet dealt to the rebellion; and that, at least one of those important successes, could not have been achieved when it was, but for the aid of black soldiers. Among the commanders holding these views are some who have never had any affinity with what is called abolitionism, or with Republican party politics; but who hold them purely as military opinions. I submit these opinions as being entitled to some weight against the objections, often urged, that emancipation, and arming the blacks, are unwise as military measures, and were not adopted, as such, in good faith.

You say you will not fight to free Negroes. Some of them seem willing to fight for you; but, no matter. Fight you, then, exclusively to save the Union. I issued the proclamation on purpose to aid you in saving the Union. Whenever you shall have conquered all resistance to the Union, if I shall urge you to continue fighting, it will be an apt time, then, for you to declare you will not fight to free Negroes.

I thought that in your struggle for the Union, to whatever extent the Negroes should cease helping the enemy, to that extent it weakened the enemy in his resistance to you. Do you think differently? I thought that whatever Negroes can be got to do as soldiers, leaves just so much less for white soldiers to do, in saving the Union. Does it appear otherwise to you? But Negroes, like other people, act upon motives. Why should they do anything for us, if we will do nothing for them? If they stake their lives for us, they must be prompted by the strongest motive—even the promise of freedom. And the promise being made, must be kept.

The signs look better. The Father of Waters again goes unvexed to the sea. Thanks to the great Northwest for it. Nor yet wholly to them. Three hundred miles up, they met New England, Empire, Keystone, and Jersey, hewing their way right and left. The Sunny South too, in more colors than one, also lent a hand. On the spot, their part of the history was jotted down in black and white. The job was a great national one; and let none be banned who bore an honorable part in it. And while those who have cleared the great river may well be proud, even that is not all. It is hard to say that anything has been more bravely, and well done, than at Antietam, Murfreesboro, Gettysburg, and on many fields of lesser note. Nor must Uncle Sam's web-feet be forgotten. At all the watery margins they have been present. Not only on the deep sea, the broad bay, and the rapid river, but also up the narrow muddy bayou, and wherever the ground was a little damp, they have been, and made their tracks. Thanks to all. For the great republic—for the principle it lives by, and keeps alive—for man's vast future,—thanks to all.

Peace does not appear so distant as it did. I hope it will come soon, and come to stay; and so come as to be worth the keeping in all future time. It will then have been proved that, among free men, there can be no successful appeal from the ballot to the bullet; and that they who take such appeal are sure to lose their case, and pay the cost. And then, there will be some black men who can remember that, with silent tongue, and clenched teeth, and steady eye, and well-poised bayonet, they have helped mankind on to this great consummation; while, I fear, there will be some white ones, unable to forget that, with malignant heart, and deceitful speech, they have strove to hinder it.

Still let us not be over-sanguine of a speedy final triumph. Let us be quite sober. Let us diligently apply the means, never doubting that a just God, in His own good time, will give us the rightful result. Yours very truly

A. Lincoln.

Across the narrow Rapidan, the Army of the Potomac was within immediate striking distance of the enemy. Again, that mysterious quality in Lee which seemed to hypnotize Union generals into hesitation and indecision, retained its power. "I am not in condition to follow Lee to Richmond and will be less so after being weakened by a severe battle," Meade wrote Halleck on September 18. Lincoln stirred uneasily. For almost a year he had tried to make his generals reject a military fallacy.

Executive Mansion
Washington, Sept. 19. 1863.

Major General Halleck:
By Gen. Meade's despatch to you of yesterday it appears that he desires your views and those of the government, as to whether

he shall advance upon the enemy. I am not prepared to order, or even advise an advance in this case, wherein I know so little of particulars, and wherein he, in the field, thinks the risk is so great, and the promise of advantage so small. And yet the case presents matter for very serious consideration in another aspect. These two armies confront each other across a small river, substantially midway between the two capitals, each defending its own capital, and menacing the other. Gen. Meade estimates the enemy's infantry in front of him at not less than forty thousand. Suppose we add fifty per cent to this, for cavalry, artillery, and extra-duty men stretching as far as Richmond, making the whole force of the enemy sixty thousand. Gen. Meade, as shown by the returns, has with him, and between him and Washington, of the same classes of well men, over ninety thousand. Neither can bring the whole of his men into a battle; but each can bring as large a percentage in as the other. For a battle, then, Gen. Meade has three men to Gen. Lee's two. Yet, it having been determined that choosing ground, and standing on the defensive, gives so great advantage that the three cannot safely attack the two, the three are left simply standing on the defensive also. If the enemy's sixty thousand are sufficient to keep our ninety thousand away from Richmond, why, by the same rule, may not forty thousand of ours keep their sixty thousand away from Washington, leaving us fifty thousand to put to some other use? Having practically come to the mere defensive, it seems to be no economy at all to employ twice as many men for that object as are needed. With no object, certainly, to mislead myself, I can perceive no fault in this statement, unless we admit we are not the equal of the enemy man for man. I hope you will consider it.

To avoid misunderstanding, let me say that to attempt to fight the enemy slowly back into his intrenchments at Richmond, and there to capture him, is an idea I have been trying to repudiate for quite a year. My judgment is so clear against it, that I would scarcely allow the attempt to be made, if the general in command should desire to make it. My last attempt upon Richmond was to get McClellan, when he was nearer there than the enemy was, to run in ahead of him. Since then I have constantly desired the Army of the Potomac, to make Lee's army, and not Richmond, its objective point. If our army cannot fall upon the enemy and hurt him where he is, it is plain to me it can gain nothing by attempt-

ing to follow him over a succession of intrenched lines into a forti-
fied city. Yours truly

A. Lincoln

Lincoln, a considerate husband, was also a lonely man.

> *Washington, D. C.,*
> *Sep. 20 1863*

Mrs. A. Lincoln
New-York.

I neither see nor hear anything of sickness here now; though
there may be much without my knowing it. I wish you to stay, or
come just as is most agreeable to yourself.

A. Lincoln.

> *Washington, D. C.,*
> *Sept. 21. 1863*

Mrs. A Lincoln
Fifth Avenue Hotel New-York

The air is so clear and cool, and apparently healthy, that I
would be glad for you to come. Nothing very particular, but I
would be glad to see you and Tad.

A Lincoln

From Chattanooga Rosecrans telegraphed: "We have just concluded a terrific day's fighting and have another in prospect for tomorrow." Lincoln sent encouragement and good advice.

> *Washington, D. C.,*
> *Sep 21. 12.35* AM *1863*

Major Gen. Rosecrans
Chattanooga Tenn.

Be of good cheer. We have unabated confidence in you, and in
your soldiers and officers. In the main you must be the judge as to
what is to be done. If I were to suggest, I would say, save your
army, by taking strong positions, until Burnside joins you, when I
hope you can turn the tide. I think you had better send a courier
to Burnside to hurry him up. We can not reach him by telegraph.
We suppose some force is going to you from Corinth, but for want

of communication, we do not know how they are getting along. We shall do our utmost to assist you. Send us your present posting.

A. Lincoln

Mary Lincoln heard from her husband of the outcome of the fighting at Chattanooga (the Battle of Chickamauga). Mrs. Lincoln's brother-in-law was Confederate Brigadier General Ben Hardin Helm.

Washington, D. C.,
Sep. 24 1863

Mrs. A. Lincoln,
Fifth Avenue Hotel New York—
We now have a tolerably accurate summing up of the late battle between Rosecrans and Bragg. The result is that we are worsted, if at all, only in the fact that we, after the main fighting was over, yielded the ground, thus leaving considerable of our artillery and wounded to fall into the enemy's hands, for which we got nothing in turn. We lost, in general officers, one killed, and three or four wounded, all brigadiers; while according to rebel accounts, which we have, they lost six killed, and eight wounded. Of the killed, one major genl. and five brigadiers, including your brother-in-law, Helm; and of the wounded, three major generals, and five brigadiers. This list may be reduced two in number, by correction of confusion in names. At 11/40 A.M. yesterday Gen. Rosecrans telegraphed from Chattanooga "We hold this point, and I cannot be dislodged, except by very superior numbers, and after a great battle." A despatch leaving there after night yesterday says, "No fight today."

A. Lincoln.

On September 29 the Sons of Temperance celebrated their twenty-first anniversary with a march to the White House. "Today came to the Executive Mansion an assembly of cold-water men & cold-water women to make a temperance speech at the Tycoon & receive a response," John Hay recorded in his diary. "They filed into the East Room looking blue & thin in the keen autumnal air. . . . Three blue-skinned damsels did Love, Purity & Fidelity in Red, White & Blue gowns. A few invalid soldiers stumped along in the dismal procession . . . they called Intemperance the cause of our defeats. He could not see it, as the rebels drink more & worse whisky than we do."

The Living Lincoln

September 29, 1863

As a matter of course, it will not be possible for me to make a response co-extensive with the address which you have presented to me. If I were better known than I am, you would not need to be told that in the advocacy of the cause of temperance you have a friend and sympathizer in me.

When I was a young man, long ago, before the Sons of Temperance as an organization, had an existence, I in an humble way, made temperance speeches, and I think I may say that to this day I have never, by my example, belied what I then said.

In regard to the suggestions which you make for the purpose of the advancement of the cause of temperance in the army, I cannot make particular responses to them at this time. To prevent intemperance in the army is even a part of the articles of war. It is part of the law of the land—and was so, I presume, long ago—to dismiss officers for drunkenness. I am not sure that consistently with the public service, more can be done than has been done. All, therefore, that I can promise you is, (if you will be pleased to furnish me with a copy of your address) to have it submitted to the proper department and have it considered, whether it contains any suggestions which will improve the cause of temperance and repress the cause of drunkenness in the army any better than it is already done. I can promise no more than that.

I think that the reasonable men of the world have long since agreed that intemperance is one of the greatest, if not the very greatest of all evils amongst mankind. That is not a matter of dispute, I believe. That the disease exists, and that it is a very great one is agreed upon by all.

The mode of cure is one about which there may be differences of opinion. You have suggested that in an army—our army—drunkenness is a great evil, and one which, while it exists to a very great extent, we cannot expect to overcome so entirely as to leave such successes in our arms as we might have without it. This undoubtedly is true, and while it is, perhaps, rather a bad source to derive comfort from, nevertheless, in a hard struggle, I do not know but what it is some consolation to be aware that there is some intemperance on the other side, too, and that they have no right to beat us in physical combat on that ground.

But I have already said more than I expected to be able to say when I began, and if you please to hand me a copy of your address

582

it shall be considered. I thank you very heartily, gentlemen, for this call, and for bringing with you these very many pretty ladies.

Lincoln still bore the cross of Missouri. A crisis came when a succession of conventions drew up demands upon the President. Lincoln decided that the time had come for a showdown. In his reply he traced the course of events in the unhappy state, weighed evidence with judicial objectivity, passed judgments, and served notice that henceforth he would do his duty as he saw it.

Executive Mansion
Washington D. C. Oct 5. 1863
Hon. Charles D. Drake & others, Committee
Gentlemen

Your original address, presented on the 30th. ultimo, and the four supplementary ones, presented on the 3rd. inst. have been carefully considered.

I hope you will regard the other duties claiming my attention, together with the great length and importance of these documents as constituting a sufficient apology for my not having responded sooner.

These papers, framed for a common object, consist of the things demanded, and the reasons for demanding them. The things demanded are:

First: That General Schofield shall be relieved, and General Butler be appointed, as commander of the Military Department of Missouri.

Second: That the system of enrolled militia in Missouri may be broken up, and national forces be substituted for it, and

Third: That at elections, persons may not be allowed to vote who are not entitled by law to do so.

Among the reasons given, enough of suffering and wrong to Union men is certainly, and I suppose truly stated. Yet the whole case, as presented, fails to convince me, that Gen. Schofield, or the enrolled militia, is responsible for that suffering and wrong. The whole can be explained on a more charitable, and, as I think, a more rational hypothesis. We are in civil war. In such cases there always is a main question; but in this case that question is a perplexing compound—Union and slavery. It thus becomes a question not of two sides merely, but of at least four sides, even among those who are for the Union, saying nothing of those who are against it. Thus, those who are for the Union *with,* but not *without* slavery—those for it *without,* but not *with*—those for it *with* or *without,* but prefer it *with*—and those for it *with* or *without,* but prefer it *without.* Among these again, is a subdivision of those who are for *gradual* but not for *immediate,* and those who are for *immediate,* but not for *gradual* extinction of slavery. It is easy to conceive that all these shades of opinion, and even more, may be sincerely entertained by honest and truthful men. Yet, all being for the Union, by reason of these differences, each will prefer a different way of sustaining the Union. At once sincerity is questioned, and motives are assailed. Actual war coming, blood grows hot, and blood is spilled. Thought is forced from old channels into confusion. Deception breeds and thrives. Confidence dies, and universal suspicion reigns. Each man feels an impulse to kill his neighbor, lest he be first killed by him. Revenge and retaliation follow. And all this, as before said, may be among honest men only. But this is not all. Every foul bird comes abroad, and every dirty reptile rises up. These add crime to confusion. Strong measures, deemed indispensable but harsh at best, such men make worse by maladministration. Murders for old grudges, and murders for pelf, proceed under any cloak that will best cover for the occasion. These causes amply account for what has occurred in Missouri, without ascribing it to the weakness, or wickedness of any general. The newspaper files, those chroniclers of current events, will show that the evils now complained of were quite as prevalent under Fremont, Hunter, Halleck, and Curtis, as under Schofield. If the former had greater force opposed to them, they also had greater force with which to meet it. When the organized rebel army left the state, the main federal force had to go also, leaving the department commander at home relatively no stronger than before. Without disparaging any, I affirm with confidence that no commander of that department has, in proportion to his means, done better than Gen. Schofield.

The first specific charge against Gen. Schofield is that the enrolled militia was placed under his command, whereas it had not been placed under the command of Gen. Curtis. The fact I believe is true; but you do not point out, nor can I conceive, how that did, or could injure loyal men, or the Union cause.

You charge that upon Gen. Curtis being superseded by Gen.

"The Signs Look Better"

Schofield, Franklin A. Dick was superseded by James O. Brod-head, as Provost Marshal General. No very specific showing is made as to how this did, or could injure the Union cause. It recalls, however, the condition of things, as presented to me, which led to a change of commander for that department.

To restrain contraband intelligence and trade, a system of searches, seizures, permits, and passes, had been introduced, I think, by Gen. Fremont. When Gen. Halleck came, he found, and continued this system, and added an order applicable to some parts of the state, to levy and collect contributions from noted rebels, to compensate losses, and relieve destitution caused by the rebellion. The action of Gen. Fremont and Gen. Halleck, as stated, constituted a sort of system, which Gen. Curtis found in full operation when he took command of the department. That there was a necessity for something of the sort was clear; but that it could only be justified by stern necessity, and that it was liable to great abuse in administration, was equally clear. Agents to execute it, contrary to the great prayer, were led into temptation. Some might, while others would not resist that temptation. It was not possible to hold any to a very strict accountability; and those yielding to the temp-tation, would sell permits and passes to those who would pay most, and most readily for them; and would seize property, and collect levies in the aptest way to fill their own pockets. Money being the object, the man having money, whether loyal or disloyal, would be a victim. This practice doubtless existed to some extent, and it was a real additional evil, that it could be and was, plausibly charged to exist in greater extent than it did.

When Gen. Curtis took command of the department, Mr. Dick, against whom I never knew anything to allege, had general charge of this system. A controversy in regard to it rapidly grew into almost unmanageable proportions. One side ignored the *ne-cessity,* and magnified the evils of the system; while the other ig-nored the evils, and magnified the necessity; and each bitterly assailed the motives of the other. I could not fail to see that the controversy enlarged in the same proportion as the professed Union men there distinctly took sides in two opposing political parties. I exhausted my wits, and very nearly my patience also, in efforts to convince both that the evils they charged on each other, were inherent in the case, and could not be cured by giving either party a victory over the other.

Plainly the irritating system was not to be perpetual; and it was plausibly urged that it could be modified at once with advantage. The case could scarcely be worse, and whether it could be made better, could only be determined by a trial. In this view, and not to ban, or brand, Gen. Curtis, or to give a victory to any party, I made the change of commander for the department. I now learn that soon after this change, Mr. Dick was removed, and that Mr. Brodhead, a gentleman of no less good character, was put in the place. The mere fact of this change is more distinctly complained of, than is any conduct of the new officer, or other consequence, of the change.

I gave the new commander no instructions as to the administration of the system mentioned, beyond what is contained in the private letter, afterwards surreptitiously published, in which I directed him to act solely for the public good, and independently of both parties. Neither anything you have presented me, nor anything I have otherwise learned, has convinced me that he has been unfaithful to this charge.

Imbecility is urged as one cause for removing Gen. Schofield; and the late massacre at Lawrence, Kansas, is pressed as evidence of that imbecility. To my mind that fact scarcely tends to prove the proposition. That massacre is only an example, of what Grierson, John Morgan, and many others, might have repeatedly done, on their respective raids, had they chose to incur the personal hazard, and possessed the fiendish hearts to do it.

The charge is made that Gen. Schofield, on purpose to protect the Lawrence murderers, would not allow them to be pursued into Missouri. While no punishment could be too sudden, or too severe for those murderers, I am well satisfied that the preventing of the threatened remedial raid into Missouri, was the only safe way to avoid an indiscriminate massacre there, including probably more innocent than guilty. Instead of condemning, I therefore approve what I understand Gen. Schofield did in that respect.

The charges that Gen. Schofield has purposely withheld protection from loyal people, and purposely facilitated the objects of the disloyal, are altogether beyond my power of belief. I do not arraign the veracity of gentlemen as to the facts complained of; but I do more than question the judgment which would infer that those facts occurred in accordance with the *purposes* of Gen. Schofield.

"The Signs Look Better"

With my present views I must decline to remove Gen. Schofield. In this I decide nothing against Gen. Butler. I sincerely wish it were convenient to assign him a suitable command.

In order to meet some existing evils I have addressed a letter of instructions to Gen. Schofield, a copy of which I inclose to you.

As to the "enrolled militia" I shall endeavor to ascertain, better than I now know, what is its exact value.

Let me say now, however, that your proposal to substitute national force for the "enrolled militia" implies that in your judgment the latter is doing something which needs to be done; and if so, the proposition to throw that force away, and to supply its place by bringing other forces from the field where they are urgently needed seems to me very extraordinary. Whence shall they come? Shall they be withdrawn from Banks, or Grant, or Steele, or Rosecrans? Few things have been so grateful to my anxious feeling as when, in June last, the local force in Missouri aided Gen. Schofield to so promptly send a large general force to the relief of Gen. Grant, then investing Vicksburg, and menaced from without by Gen. Johnston. Was this all wrong? Should the enrolled militia then have been broken up, and Gen. Herron kept from Grant, to police Missouri? So far from finding cause to object, I confess to a sympathy for whatever relieves our general force in Missouri, and allows it to serve elsewhere. I therefore, as at present advised, cannot attempt the destruction of the enrolled militia of Missouri. I may add that the force being under the national military control, it is also within the proclamation in regard to the *Habeas Corpus*.

I concur in the propriety of your request in regard to elections, and have, as you see, directed Gen. Schofield accordingly.

I do not feel justified to enter upon the broad field you present in regard to the political differences between radicals and conservatives. From time to time I have done and said what appeared to me proper to do and say. The public knows it all. It obliges nobody to follow me, and I trust it obliges me to follow nobody. The radicals and conservatives, each agree with me in some things, and disagree in others. I could wish both to agree with me in all things; for then they would agree with each other, and would be too strong for any foe from any quarter. They, however, choose to do otherwise, and I do not question their right. I too shall do what seems to be my duty. I hold whoever commands in Missouri, or elsewhere, responsible to me, and not to either radicals or conservatives. It is my duty to hear all; but at last, I must, within my sphere, judge what to do, and what to forbear. Your Obt. Servt.

A. Lincoln.

Perhaps with surprise, the President sometimes discovered that he was a man deeply loved and respected.

Executive Mansion,
Washington, Oct. 12th. 1863.

Mrs. Alice C. Smith
Boston Mass.

I shall have to acknowledge very briefly your letter informing me of the prosperity of your little boy whom you so kindly named after me. You may rest assured that my little namesake has my best wishes that he may grow to be a good man and a good citizen. Yours Very Truly

A. Lincoln

And a critic, caught unawares, hastily responded: "My 'quarrels' are in no sense *personal*. I have done something in my day towards Electing Presidents and Governors, none of whom have found me an expensive Partizan. . . ."

Executive Mansion,
Washington, Oct. 14, 1863.

Hon. Thurlow Weed
My dear Sir:

I have been brought to fear recently that somehow, by commission or omission, I have caused you some degree of pain. I have never entertained an unkind feeling or a disparaging thought towards you; and if I have said or done anything which has been construed into such unkindness or disparagement, it has been misconstrued. I am sure if we could meet we would not part with any unpleasant impression on either side. Yours as ever

A. Lincoln

Captain James Madison Cutts, Jr., brother of Mrs. Stephen A. Douglas, was in disgrace. A court martial had convicted him of "conduct unbecoming an officer and gentleman"—meaning, specifically, that through keyhole and transom he had watched a lady undress—and of using offensive language to a superior officer and writing derogatory letters. Lincoln's reprimand, delivered before he remitted the sentence, reads like a passage from the Book of Proverbs. Privately, he had quipped that Cutts "should be elevated to the peerage . . . with the title of Count Peeper."

Executive Mansion,
Washington, Oct 26, 1863.

Capt. James M. Cutts.

Although what I am now to say is to be, in form, a reprimand, it is not intended to add a pang to what you have already suffered upon the subject to which it relates. You have too much of life yet before you, and have shown too much of promise as an officer, for your future to be lightly surrendered. You were convicted of two offences. One of them, not of great enormity, and yet greatly to be avoided, I feel sure you are in no danger of repeating. The other you are not so well assured against. The advice of a father to his son "Beware of entrance to a quarrel, but being in, bear it that the opposed may beware of thee," is good, and yet not the best. Quarrel not at all. No man resolved to make the most of himself, can spare time for personal contention. Still less can he afford to take all the consequences, including the vitiating of his temper, and the loss of self-control. Yield larger things to which you can show no more than equal right; and yield lesser ones, though clearly your own. Better give your path to a dog, than be bitten by him in contesting for the right. Even killing the dog would not cure the bite.

In the mood indicated deal henceforth with your fellow-men, and especially with your brother officers; and even the unpleasant events you are passing from will not have been profitless to you.

[*No Signature*]

Hackett, mortified by editorial comments on the letter that Lincoln had written him,* hoped that "such political squibs would probably affect your sensibility about as much as would a charge of mustard seed shot at forty yards distance, fired through a pop-gun barrel at the

---

* See pages 572–73.

naturally armed Alligator." The actor learned that his correspondent had moved beyond the range of sniping critics.

PRIVATE

Executive Mansion,
Washington, Nov. 2. 1863.

James H. Hackett
My dear Sir:

Yours of Oct. 22nd. is received, as also was, in due course, that of Oct. 3rd. I look forward with pleasure to the fulfilment of the promise made in the former.

Give yourself no uneasiness on the subject mentioned in that of the 22nd.

My note to you I certainly did not expect to see in print; yet I have not been much shocked by the newspaper comments upon it. Those comments constitute a fair specimen of what has occurred to me through life. I have endured a great deal of ridicule without much malice; and have received a great deal of kindness, not quite free from ridicule. I am used to it. Yours truly

A. Lincoln

To one of Lincoln's old friends, Stephen T. Logan, went an invitation to a historic occasion.

Executive Mansion,
Washington, Nov. 9, 1863.

Dear Judge

Col. Lamon had made his calculation, as he tells me, to go to Illinois and bring Mrs. L. home this month, when he was called on to act as marshal on the occasion of dedicating the cemetery at Gettysburg Pa on the 19th. He came to me, and I told him I thought that in view of his relation to the government and to me, he could not well decline. Now, why would it not be pleasant for you to come on with Mrs. L. at that time? It will be an interesting ceremony, and I shall be very glad to see you. I know not whether you would care to remain to the meeting of Congress, but that event, as you know, will be very near at hand. Your friend as ever

A. Lincoln.

"The Signs Look Better"

Stanton received an order from the commander-in-chief.

Executive Mansion,
Washington, Nov. 11, 1863.

Hon. Secretary of War.
My dear Sir:

I personally wish Jacob R. Freese, of New Jersey to be appointed a colonel for a colored regiment—and this regardless of whether he can tell the exact shade of Julius Caesar's hair. Yours truly

A. Lincoln

As long as Lincoln is remembered, the words he spoke at Gettysburg can never be forgotten.

Four score and seven years ago our fathers brought forth on this continent, a new nation, conceived in liberty, and dedicated to the proposition that all men are created equal.

Now we are engaged in a great civil war, testing whether that nation, or any nation so conceived and so dedicated, can long endure. We are met on a great battlefield of that war. We have come to dedicate a portion of that field, as a final resting place for those who here gave their lives that that nation might live. It is altogether fitting and proper that we should do this.

But, in a larger sense, we cannot dedicate—we cannot consecrate—we cannot hallow—this ground. The brave men, living and dead, who struggled here, have consecrated it, far above our poor power to add or detract. The world will little note, nor long remember what we say here, but it can never forget what they did here. It is for us the living, rather, to be dedicated here to the unfinished work which they who fought here have thus far so nobly advanced. It is rather for us to be here dedicated to the great task remaining before us—that from these honored dead we take increased devotion to that cause for which they gave the last full measure of devotion—that we here highly resolve that these dead shall not have died in vain—that this nation, under God, shall have a new birth of freedom—and that government of the people, by the people, for the people, shall not perish from the earth.

Abraham Lincoln.

November 19. 1863.

The Living Lincoln

At least one person with Lincoln on the platform that day recognized the immortal quality of the President's remarks. "I should be glad," Edward Everett wrote, "if I could flatter myself that I came as near to the central idea of the occasion, in two hours, as you did in two minutes."

Executive Mansion,
Washington, Nov. 20, 1863.

Hon. Edward Everett.
My dear Sir:

Your kind note of today is received. In our respective parts yesterday, you could not have been excused to make a short address, nor I a long one. I am pleased to know that, in your judgment, the little I did say was not entirely a failure. Of course I knew Mr. Everett would not fail; and yet, while the whole discourse was eminently satisfactory, and will be of great value, there were passages in it which transcended my expectation. The point made against the theory of the general government being only an agency, whose principals are the states, was new to me, and, as I think, is one of the best arguments for the national supremacy. The tribute to our noble women for their angel-ministering to the suffering soldiers, surpasses, in its way, as do the subjects of it, whatever has gone before.

Our sick boy, for whom you kindly inquire, we hope is past the worst. Your Obt. Servt.

A. Lincoln

Lincoln intervened in behalf of a former resident of Springfield, accused of smuggling percussion caps to the enemy.*

"CYPHER"

Executive Mansion
Washington, D. C. Dec. 17. 1863.

Major General Hurlbut
Memphis, Tenn.

I understand you have, under sentence of death, a tall old man, by the name of Henry F. Luckett. I personally knew him, and did not think him a bad man. Please do not let him be exe-

---

* Lincoln pardoned Luckett, March 30, 1864.

cuted, unless upon further order from me, and, in the meantime, send me a transcript of the record.

A. Lincoln

"Henry F Luckett"

Schofield was trying to influence politics in Missouri. Lincoln resolved to change commanders.

Executive Mansion,
Washington, Dec. 18. 1863.

Hon. Sec. of War:
My dear Sir

I believe Gen. Schofield must be relieved from command of the Department of Missouri, otherwise a question of veracity, in relation to his declarations as to his interfering, or not, with the Missouri legislature, will be made with him, which will create an additional amount of trouble, not to be overcome by even a correct decision of the question. The question itself must be avoided. Now for the mode. Senator Henderson, his friend, thinks he can be induced to ask to be relieved, if he shall understand he will be generously treated; and, on this latter point, Gratz Brown will help his nomination, as a major general, through the Senate. In no other way can he be confirmed; and upon his rejection alone, it would be difficult for me to sustain him as commander of the department. Besides, his being relieved from command of the department, and at the same time confirmed as a major general, will be the means of Henderson and Brown leading off together as friends, and will go far to heal the Missouri difficulty.

Another point. I find it is scarcely less than indispensable for me to do something for Gen. Rosecrans; and I find Henderson and Brown will agree to him for the commander of their department.

Again, I have received such evidence and explanations, in regard to the supposed cotton transactions of Gen. Curtis, as fully restores in my mind the fair presumption of his innocence; and, as he is my friend, and, what is more, as I think, the country's friend, I would be glad to relieve him from the impression that I think him dishonest, by giving him a command. Most of the Iowa and Kansas delegations, a large part of that of Missouri, and the delegates from Nebraska, and Colorado, ask this in behalf of Gen. C.

593

and suggest Kansas and other contiguous territory west of Missouri, as a department for him.

In a purely military point of view it may be that none of these things is indispensable, or perhaps, advantageous; but in another aspect, scarcely less important, they would give great relief, while, at the worst, I think they could not injure the military service much. I therefore shall be greatly obliged if yourself and Gen. Halleck can give me your hearty co-operation, in making the arrangement. Perhaps the first thing would be to send Gen. Schofield's nomination to me. Let me hear from you before you take any actual step in the matter. Yours very truly

A. Lincoln

Back on Lincoln's desk came the case of Dr. McPheeters.* Once again the President reiterated fundamental principles.

Executive Mansion,
Washington, Dec. 22. 1863.

O. D. Filley
St. Louis, Mo.

I have just looked over a petition signed by some three dozen citizens of St. Louis, and three accompanying letters, one by yourself, one by a Mr. Nathan Ranney, and one by a Mr. John D. Coalter, the whole relating to the Rev. Dr. McPheeters. The petition prays, in the name of justice and mercy that I will restore Dr. McPheeters to all his ecclesiastical rights.

This gives no intimation as to what ecclesiastical rights are withheld. Your letter states that Provost Marshal Dick, about a year ago, ordered the arrest of Dr. McPheeters, pastor of the Vine Street Church, prohibited him from officiating, and placed the management of the affairs of the church out of the control of its chosen trustees; and near the close you state that a certain course "would insure his release." Mr. Ranney's letter says "Dr. Saml. S. McPheeters is enjoying all the rights of a civilian, but cannot preach the gospel!!!" Mr. Coalter, in his letter, asks "Is it not a strange illustration of the condition of things that the question of who shall be allowed to preach in a church in St. Louis, shall be decided by the *President* of *the United States?*"

Now, all this sounds very strangely; and withal, a little as if

* See pages 527–28.

you gentlemen making the application, do not understand the case alike, one affirming that the Dr. is enjoying all the rights of a civilian, and another pointing out to me what will secure his *release!* On the 2nd. day of January last I wrote Gen. Curtis in relation to Mr. Dick's order upon Dr. McPheeters, and, as I suppose the Dr. is enjoying all the rights of a civilian, I only quote that part of my letter which relates to the church. It is as follows: "But I must add that the U. S. government must not, as by this order, undertake to run the churches. When an individual, in a church or out of it, becomes dangerous to the public interest, he must be checked; but the churches, as such must take care of themselves. It will not do for the U. S. to appoint trustees, supervisors, or other agents for the churches." This letter going to Gen. Curtis, then in command there I supposed of course it was obeyed, especially as I heard no further complaint from Dr. M. or his friends for nearly an entire year.

I have never interfered, nor thought of interfering as to who shall or shall not preach in any church; nor have I knowingly, or believingly, tolerated anyone else to so interfere by my authority. If anyone is so interfering, by color of my authority, I would like to have it specifically made known to me.

If, after all, what is now sought, is to have me put Dr. M. back, over the heads of a majority of his own congregation, that too, will be declined. I will not have control of any church on any side. Yours Respectfully

A. Lincoln

Lincoln's motives could neither be twisted nor doubted from the endorsement which he wrote on the petition requesting that Dr. McPheeters be restored to his pulpit.

December 22, 1863

The assumptions of this paper, so far as I know, or believe are entirely false. I have never deprived Dr. McPheeters of any ecclesiastical right, or authorized, or excused its being done by anyone deriving authority from me. On the contrary, in regard to this very case, I directed, a long time ago, that Dr. McPheeters was to be arrested, or remain at large, upon the same rule as anyone else; and that, in no event, was anyone to interfere by my authority, as to who should, or should not preach in any church. This was done,

I think, in a letter, in the nature of an order, to Mr. Dick. The assumption that I am keeping Dr. M. from preaching in his church is monstrous. If anyone is doing this, by pretense of my authority, I will thank anyone who can, to make out and present me, a specific case against him. If, after all, the Dr. is kept out by the majority of his own parishioners, and my official power is sought to force him in over their heads, I decline that also.

A. Lincoln

Dec. 22. 1863.

A Pittsburgh widow received a note from the President.

Executive Mansion,
Washington [Jany.] 8, 1864.
Mrs. Esther Stockton.
Madam:
Learning that you who have passed the eighty-fourth year of life, have given to the soldiers, some three hundred pairs of stockings, knitted by yourself, I wish to offer you my thanks. Will you also convey my thanks to those young ladies who have done so much in feeding our soldiers while passing through your city? Yours truly,

A. Lincoln

The President stated a tenet by which he lived.

February 5, 1864
Submitted to the Sec. of War. On principle I dislike an oath which requires a man to swear he *has* not done wrong. It rejects the Christian principle of forgiveness on terms of repentance. I think it is enough if the man does no wrong *hereafter*.

A. Lincoln

Over the signature of Samuel C. Pomeroy, a political friend of Lincoln's Secretary of the Treasury, appeared a circular opposing the renomination of the President and favoring Chase as party standard-bearer. Chase denied having any knowledge that the circular was being printed, but others close to the Secretary insisted that the action was taken with his approval. Lincoln accepted the incident quietly.

"The Signs Look Better"

Executive Mansion,
Washington, February 29. 1864.

Hon. Secretary of the Treasury
My dear Sir:

I would have taken time to answer yours of the 22nd. sooner, only that I did not suppose any evil could result from the delay, especially as, by a note, I promptly acknowledged the receipt of yours, and promised a fuller answer. Now, on consideration, I find there is really very little to say. My knowledge of Mr. Pomroy's letter having been made *public* came to me only the day you wrote; but I had, in spite of myself, known of its *existence* several days before. I have not yet read it, and I think I shall not. I was not shocked, or surprised by the appearance of the letter, because I had had knowledge of Mr. Pomroy's committee, and of secret issues which I supposed came from it, and of secret agents who I supposed were sent out by it, for several weeks. I have known just as little of these things as my own friends have allowed me to know. They bring the documents to me, but I do not read them— they tell me what they think fit to tell me, but I do not inquire for more. I fully concur with you that neither of us can be justly held responsible for what our respective friends may do without our instigation or countenance; and I assure you, as you have assured me, that no assault has been made upon you by my instigation, or with my countenance.

Whether you shall remain at the head of the Treasury Department is a question which I will not allow myself to consider from any standpoint other than my judgment of the public service; and, in that view, I do not perceive occasion for a change. Yours truly

A. Lincoln

Lincoln chose between military discipline and human justice.

Executive Mansion,
Washington, March. 1, 1864.

Hon. Sec. of War—
My dear Sir:

A poor widow, by the name of Baird, has a son in the army, that for some offence has been sentenced to serve a long time without pay, or at most, with very little pay. I do not like this punishment of withholding pay—it falls so very hard upon poor families.

After he has been serving in this way for several months, at the tearful appeal of the poor mother, I made a direction that he be allowed to enlist for a new term, on the same conditions as others. She now comes, and says she cannot get it acted upon. Please do it.* Yours truly

A Lincoln

With a constitutional convention soon to be held in Maryland, Lincoln revealed how earnestly he hoped that a slave state would adopt some form of emancipation.

Executive Mansion,
Washington, March 7, 1864.

Hon. John A. J. Creswell
My dear Sir:
I am very anxious for emancipation to be effected in Maryland in some substantial form. I think it probable that my expressions of a preference for *gradual* over *immediate* emancipation, are misunderstood. I had thought the *gradual* would produce less confusion, and destitution, and therefore would be more satisfactory; but if those who are better acquainted with the subject, and are more deeply interested in it, prefer the *immediate,* most certainly I have no objection to their judgment prevailing. My wish is that all who are for emancipation *in any form,* shall co-operate, all treating all respectfully, and all adopting and acting upon the major opinion, when fairly ascertained. What I have dreaded is the danger that by jealousies, rivalries, and consequent ill-blood—driving one another out of meetings and conventions—perchance from the polls—the friends of emancipation themselves may divide, and lose the measure altogether. I wish this letter to not be made public; but no man representing me as I herein represent myself, will be in any danger of contradiction by me. Yours truly

A. Lincoln.

From the beginning of the war Lincoln had needed a general whom he could place at the head of all Union armies. In the West, Grant had risen steadily. In the Vicksburg campaign he had shown brilliant gen-

* On July 19, 1864, Isaac P. Baird was transferred to the 183rd Pennsylvania Volunteers and served until discharged on May 30, 1865.

eralship. Given full command in the West in October, 1863, he had quickly extricated the Army of the Cumberland from a perilous position at Chattanooga. A month later, in the spectacular battles of Lookout Mountain and Missionary Ridge, he drove Bragg's forces from seemingly impregnable positions to defensive intrenchments in Georgia. Thus, under Grant, the Union had seized the initiative and now could destroy the South's ability to resist. Lincoln, as commander-in-chief, rewarded that achievement.

[*March 9, 1864*]

General Grant
    The nation's appreciation of what you have done, and its reliance upon you for what remains to do, in the existing great struggle, are now presented with this commission, constituting you Lieutenant General in the Army of the United States. With this high honor devolves upon you also, a corresponding responsibility. As the country herein trusts you, so, under God, it will sustain you. I scarcely need to add that with what I here speak for the nation goes my own hearty personal concurrence.

    Carl Schurz wanted to take an active part in the approaching presidential campaign. For Lincoln, an old friend posed a ticklish problem.

Executive Mansion,
Washington,
March 13, 1864.

PRIVATE
Major General Schurz
My dear Sir:
    Yours of February 29th, reached me only four days ago; but the delay was of little consequence, because I found, on feeling around, I could not invite you here without a difficulty which at least would be unpleasant, and perhaps would be detrimental to the public service. Allow me to suggest that if you wish to remain in the military service, it is very dangerous for you to get temporarily out of it; because, with a major general once out, it is next to impossible for even the President to get him in again. With my appreciation of your ability, and correct principle, of course I

599

would be very glad to have your service for the country in the approaching political canvass; but I fear we cannot properly have it, without separating you from the military. Yours truly

A. Lincoln

Kentuckians disliked the enlistment of slaves as soldiers. Albert G. Hodges, editor of the Frankfort, Kentucky *Commonwealth,* and Archibald Dixon, who had represented Kentucky in the U. S. Senate from 1852 to 1855, brought their grievances to the White House in late March. Later Hodges asked Lincoln to write down his remarks.

Executive Mansion,
Washington, April 4, 1864.

A. G. Hodges, Esq
Frankfort, Ky.
My dear Sir:

You ask me to put in writing the substance of what I verbally said the other day, in your presence, to Governor Bramlette and Senator Dixon. It was about as follows:

"I am naturally anti-slavery. If slavery is not wrong, nothing is wrong. I cannot remember when I did not so think, and feel. And yet I have never understood that the Presidency conferred upon me an unrestricted right to act officially upon this judgment and feeling. It was in the oath I took that I would, to the best of my ability, preserve, protect, and defend the Constitution of the United States. I could not take the office without taking the oath. Nor was it my view that I might take an oath to get power, and break the oath in using the power. I understood, too, that in ordinary civil administration this oath even forbade me to practically indulge my primary abstract judgment on the moral question of slavery. I had publicly declared this many times, and in many ways. And I aver that, to this day, I have done no official act in mere deference to my abstract judgment and feeling on slavery. I did understand however, that my oath to preserve the Constitution to the best of my ability, imposed upon me the duty of preserving, by every indispensable means, that government—that nation—of which that Constitution was the organic law. Was it possible to lose the nation, and yet preserve the Constitution? By general law life *and* limb must be protected; yet often a limb must be amputated to save a life; but a life is never wisely given to save a limb.

"The Signs Look Better"

I felt that measures, otherwise unconstitutional, might become lawful, by becoming indispensable to the preservation of the Constitution, through the preservation of the nation. Right or wrong, I assumed this ground, and now avow it. I could not feel that, to the best of my ability, I had even tried to preserve the Constitution, if, to save slavery, or any minor matter, I should permit the wreck of government, country, and Constitution all together. When, early in the war, Gen. Fremont attempted military emancipation, I forbade it, because I did not then think it an indispensable necessity. When a little later, Gen. Cameron, then Secretary of War, suggested the arming of the blacks, I objected, because I did not yet think it an indispensable necessity. When, still later, Gen. Hunter attempted military emancipation, I again forbade it, because I did not yet think the indispensable necessity had come. When, in March, and May, and July 1862 I made earnest, and successive appeals to the border states to favor compensated emancipation, I believed the indispensable necessity for military emancipation, and arming the blacks would come, unless averted by that measure. They declined the proposition; and I was, in my best judgment, driven to the alternative of either surrendering the Union, and with it, the Constitution, or of laying strong hand upon the colored element. I chose the latter. In choosing it, I hoped for greater gain than loss; but of this, I was not entirely confident. More than a year of trial now shows no loss by it in our foreign relations, none in our home popular sentiment, none in our white military force, — no loss by it anyhow or anywhere. On the contrary, it shows a gain of quite a hundred and thirty thousand soldiers, seamen, and laborers. These are palpable facts, about which, as facts, there can be no cavilling. We have the men; and we could not have had them without the measure.

"And now let any Union man who complains of the measure, test himself by writing down in one line that he is for subduing the rebellion by force of arms; and in the next, that he is for taking these hundred and thirty thousand men from the Union side, and placing them where they would be but for the measure he condemns. If he cannot face his case so stated, it is only because he cannot face the truth."

I add a word which was not in the verbal conversation. In telling this tale I attempt no compliment to my own sagacity. I claim not to have controlled events, but confess plainly that events have

601

controlled me. Now, at the end of three years' struggle the nation's condition is not what either party, or any man devised, or expected. God alone can claim it. Whither it is tending seems plain. If God now wills the removal of a great wrong, and wills also that we of the North as well as you of the South, shall pay fairly for our complicity in that wrong, impartial history will find therein new cause to attest and revere the justice and goodness of God. Yours truly

A. Lincoln

In an address to the Sanitary Fair in Baltimore Lincoln explored the meaning of a word that was difficult to define.

April 18, 1864

Ladies and Gentlemen—

Calling to mind that we are in Baltimore, we cannot fail to note that the world moves. Looking upon these many people, assembled here, to serve, as they best may, the soldiers of the Union, it occurs at once that three years ago, the same soldiers could not so much as pass through Baltimore. The change from then till now, is both great, and gratifying. Blessings on the brave men who have wrought the change, and the fair women who strive to reward them for it.

But Baltimore suggests more than could happen within Baltimore. The change within Baltimore is part only of a far wider change. When the war began, three years ago, neither party, nor any man, expected it would last till now. Each looked for the end, in some way, long ere today. Neither did any anticipate that domestic slavery would be much affected by the war. But here we are; the war has not ended, and slavery has been much affected—how much needs not now to be recounted. So true is it that man proposes, and God disposes.

But we can see the past, though we may not claim to have directed it; and seeing it, in this case, we feel more hopeful and confident for the future.

The world has never had a good definition of the word liberty, and the American people, just now, are much in want of one. We all declare for liberty; but in using the same *word* we do not all mean the same *thing*. With some the word liberty may mean for each man to do as he pleases with himself, and the product of his

602

labor; while with others the same word may mean for some men to do as they please with other men, and the product of other men's labor. Here are two, not only different, but incompatible things, called by the same name—liberty. And it follows that each of the things is, by the respective parties, called by two different and incompatible names—liberty and tyranny.

The shepherd drives the wolf from the sheep's throat, for which the sheep thanks the shepherd as a *liberator,* while the wolf denounces him for the same act as the destroyer of liberty, especially as the sheep was a black one. Plainly the sheep and the wolf are not agreed upon a definition of the word liberty; and precisely the same difference prevails today among us human creatures, even in the North, and all professing to love liberty. Hence we behold the processes by which thousands are daily passing from under the yoke of bondage, hailed by some as the advance of liberty, and bewailed by others as the destruction of all liberty. Recently, as it seems, the people of Maryland have been doing something to define liberty; and thanks to them that, in what they have done, the wolf's dictionary, has been repudiated.

It is not very becoming for one in my position to make speeches at great length; but there is another subject upon which I feel that I ought to say a word. A painful rumor, true I fear, has reached us of the massacre, by the rebel forces, at Fort Pillow, in the west end of Tennessee, on the Mississippi River, of some three hundred colored soldiers and white officers, who had just been overpowered by their assailants. There seems to be some anxiety in the public mind whether the government is doing its duty to the colored soldier, and to the service, at this point. At the beginning of the war, and for some time, the use of colored troops was not contemplated; and how the change of purpose was wrought, I will not now take time to explain. Upon a clear conviction of duty I resolved to turn that element of strength to account; and I am responsible for it to the American people, to the Christian world, to history, and on my final account to God. Having determined to use the Negro as a soldier, there is no way but to give him all the protection given to any other soldier. The difficulty is not in stating the principle, but in practically applying it. It is a mistake to suppose the government is indifferent to this matter, or is not doing the best it can in regard to it. We do not today *know* that a colored soldier, or white officer commanding colored soldiers, has been massacred by the rebels when made a prisoner. We fear it, believe it, I may say, but we do not *know* it. To take the life of one of their prisoners, on the assumption that they murder ours, when it is short of certainty that they do murder ours, might be too serious, too cruel a mistake. We are having the Fort Pillow affair thoroughly investigated; and such investigation will probably show conclusively how the truth is. If, after all that has been said, it shall turn out that there has been no massacre at Fort Pillow, it will be almost safe to say there has been none, and will be none elsewhere. If there has been the massacre of three hundred there, or even the tenth part of three hundred, it will be conclusively proved; and being so proved, the retribution shall as surely come. It will be matter of grave consideration in what exact course to apply the retribution; but in the supposed case, it must come.

To Tad went a special message.

Executive Mansion,
Washington,
April 28. 1864.

Mrs. A. Lincoln
Metropolitan Hotel
New-York.

The draft will go to you. Tell Tad the goats and father are very well—especially the goats.

A. Lincoln.

To Grant, poised for the great forward movement in which Sherman would strike at Atlanta and Meade at Richmond, Lincoln sent an expression of full confidence. The President would be heartened by Grant's response: "Should my success be less than I desire, and expect, the fault is not with you."

Executive Mansion Washington,
April 30, 1864

Lieutenant General Grant.

Not expecting to see you again before the spring campaign opens, I wish to express, in this way, my entire satisfaction with what you have done up to this time, so far as I understand it. The particulars of your plans I neither know, or seek to know. You are vigilant and self-reliant; and, pleased with this, I wish not to obtrude any constraints or restraints upon you. While I am very anxious that any great disaster, or the capture of our men in great numbers, shall be avoided, I know these points are less likely to escape your attention than they would be mine. If there is anything wanting which is within my power to give, do not fail to let me know it.

And now with a brave army, and a just cause, may God sustain you. Yours very truly

A. Lincoln

Isaac N. Arnold of Chicago, who wanted to be re-elected to Congress, appealed to Lincoln for help. Arnold, who was being blamed for Lincoln's lifting of the ban on the Chicago *Times* in June, 1863, asked Lincoln to state "how far I was responsible for the Burnside order." The President gladly gave a hand to a consistent supporter.

Executive Mansion,
Washington, May 25, 1864.

Hon. I. N. Arnold.
My dear Sir.

In regard to the order of General Burnside suspending the Chicago Times now nearly a year ago, I can only say I was embarrassed with the question between what was due to the military service on the one hand, and the liberty of the press on the other, and I believe it was the despatch of Senator Trumbull and yourself, added to the proceedings of the meeting which it brought me, that turned the scale in favor of my revoking the order. I am far from certain today that the revocation was not right; and I am very sure the small part you took in it, is no just ground to disparage your judgment, much less to impugn your motives. I take it that your devotion to the Union and the administration cannot be questioned by any sincere man. Yours truly

A. Lincoln

When the brother of William Cullen Bryant asked for "remarks" to read to a Lovejoy memorial meeting, Lincoln responded warmly.

The Living Lincoln

Executive Mansion,
Washington, May 30, 1864.

Hon. John H. Bryant
My dear Sir.

Yours of the 14th. inst. inclosing a card of invitation to a pre-liminary meeting contemplating the erection of a monument to the memory of Hon. Owen Lovejoy, was duly received.

As you anticipate, it will be out of my power to attend. Many of you have known Mr. Lovejoy longer than I have, and are better able than I to do his memory complete justice. My personal acquaintance with him commenced only about ten years ago, since when it has been quite intimate; and every step in it has been one of increasing respect and esteem, ending, with his life, in no less than affection on my part. It can be truly said of him that while he was personally ambitious, he bravely endured the obscurity which the unpopularity of his principles imposed, and never accepted official honors, until those honors were ready to admit his principles with him. Throughout my heavy, and perplexing responsibilities here, to the day of his death, it would scarcely wrong any other to say, he was my most generous friend. Let him have the marble monument, along with the well-assured and more enduring one in the hearts of those who love liberty, unselfishly, for all men. Yours truly

A. Lincoln

In replying to resolutions from the Baptists, Lincoln wondered if Christianity was the same North and South.

Executive Mansion,
Washington,
May 30, 1864.

Rev. Dr. Ide ⎫
Hon. J. R. Doolittle ⎬ Committee
& Hon. A. Hubbell ⎭

In response to the preamble and resolutions of the American Baptist Home Mission Society, which you did me the honor to present, I can only thank you for thus adding to the effective and almost unanimous support which the Christian communities are so zealously giving to the country, and to liberty. Indeed it is difficult to conceive how it could be otherwise with any one professing

Christianity, or even having ordinary perceptions of right and wrong. To read in the Bible, as the word of God himself, that "In the sweat of *thy* face shalt thou eat bread," and to preach therefrom that, "In the sweat of *other men's* faces shalt thou eat bread," to my mind can scarcely be reconciled with honest sincerity. When brought to my final reckoning, may I have to answer for robbing no man of his goods; yet more tolerable even this, than for robbing one of himself, and all that was his. When, a year or two ago, those professedly holy men of the South, met in the semblance of prayer and devotion, and, in the name of Him who said "As ye would all men should do unto you, do ye even so unto them" appealed to the Christian world to aid them in doing to a whole race of men, as they would have no man do unto themselves, to my thinking, they contemned and insulted God and His church, far more than did Satan when he tempted the Saviour with the Kingdoms of the earth. The devil's attempt was no more false, and far less hypocritical. But let me forbear, remembering it is also written "Judge not, lest ye be judged."

William Dennison, president of the Baltimore convention, brought Lincoln formal notification of his "unanimous nomination" for a second term as President. Lincoln placed a condition on acceptance.

June 9, 1864

Mr. Chairman and Gentlemen of the Committee:

I will neither conceal my gratification, nor restrain the expression of my gratitude, that the Union people, through their convention, in their continued effort to save, and advance the nation, have deemed me not unworthy to remain in my present position.

I know no reason to doubt that I shall accept the nomination tendered; and yet perhaps I should not declare definitely before reading and considering what is called the platform.

I will say now, however, that I approve the declaration in favor of so amending the Constitution as to prohibit slavery throughout the nation. When the people in revolt, with a hundred days of explicit notice, that they could, within those days, resume their allegiance, without the overthrow of their institution, and that they could not so resume it afterwards, elected to stand out, such an amendment of the Constitution as is now proposed, became a fitting, and necessary conclusion to the final success of the

Union cause. Such alone can meet and cover all cavils. Now, the unconditional Union men, North and South, perceive its importance, and embrace it. In the joint names of Liberty and Union, let us labor to give it legal form, and practical effect.

For five weeks Grant had been battering Lee's slowly retreating army. In a frontal attack at Cold Harbor the Union forces had suffered a costly defeat. Instead of retreating, Grant decided to advance by slipping around Lee's right flank. On June 14 the Union commander wired that his troops were ready to start crossing the James River. Lincoln liked this kind of generalship.

> *United States Military Telegraph,*
> *War Department.*
> *Washington, June 15, 1864*

Lieut. Gen. Grant
Head Qrs. A.P.

Have just read your despatch of 1 P.M. yesterday. I begin to see it. You will succeed. God bless you all.

> *A. Lincoln*

Formally, Lincoln accepted renomination for the Presidency.

> *Executive Mansion,*
> *Washington, June 27, 1864.*

Hon. William Dennison & others, a Committee of the National Union Convention.

Gentlemen:

Your letter of the 14th. inst. formally notifying me that I have been nominated by the convention you represent for the Presidency of the United States for four years from the fourth of March next has been received. The nomination is gratefully accepted, as the resolutions of the convention, called the platform, are heartily approved.

While the resolution in regard to the supplanting of republican government upon the western continent is fully concurred in, there might be misunderstanding were I not to say that the position of the government, in relation to the action of France in Mexico, as assumed through the State Department, and approved and indorsed by the convention, among the measures and acts of the executive, will be faithfully maintained, so long as the state of facts shall leave that position pertinent and applicable.

I am especially gratified that the soldier and the seaman were not forgotten by the convention, as they forever must and will be remembered by the grateful country for whose salvation they devote their lives.

Thanking you for the kind and complimentary terms in which you have communicated the nomination and other proceedings of the convention, I subscribe myself Your Obt. Servt.

Abraham Lincoln

Chilly relations between Chase and Lincoln reached the point where they only communicated by written notes; then, as a result of one of their many quarrels over appointments in the Treasury Department, the President accepted Chase's resignation. To William Pitt Fessenden of Maine, chairman of the Senate Finance Committee, went the cabinet post—and some practical counsel.

Executive Mansion,
Washington, July 4, 1864.

I have today said to Hon. W. P. Fessenden, on his assuming the office of Secretary of the Treasury, that I will keep no person in office in his department, against his express will, so long as I choose to continue him; and he has said to me, that in filling vacancies he will strive to give his willing consent to my wishes in cases when I may let him know that I have such wishes. It is, and will be, my sincere desire, not only to advance the public interest, by giving him complete control of the department, but also to make his position agreeable to him.

In cabinet my view is that in questions affecting the whole country there should be full and frequent consultations, and that nothing should be done particularly affecting any department without consultation with the head of that department.

On July 14, in nearby Maryland, a small Confederate force burned the home of Montgomery Blair. The Postmaster General offended Halleck with some bitter comments about military incompetence in Washington. Lincoln saw an opportunity to let certain members of the cabinet know who headed the government.

The Living Lincoln

Executive Mansion,
Washington, July 14. 1864.

Hon. Secretary of War
Sir.

Your note of today, inclosing Gen. Halleck's letter of yesterday, relative to offensive remarks supposed to have been made by the Postmaster General concerning the military officers on duty about Washington, is received. The general's letter, in substance demands of me that if I approve the remarks, I shall strike the names of those officers from the rolls; and that if I do not approve them, the Postmaster General shall be dismissed from the cabinet. Whether the remarks were really made I do not know; nor do I suppose such knowledge is necessary to a correct response. If they were made I do *not* approve them; and yet, under the circumstances, I would not dismiss a member of the cabinet therefor. I do not consider what may have been hastily said in a moment of vexation at so severe a loss, is sufficient ground for so grave a step. Besides this, *truth* is generally the best vindication against slander. I propose continuing to be myself the judge as to when a member of the cabinet shall be dismissed. Yours truly

A. Lincoln.

With the Democratic National Convention about to assemble in Chicago, Lincoln sketched in a memorandum the danger that was gathering on the political front.

Executive Mansion,
Washington, [*c. July 25*], *1864*

Hon. Clement C. Clay, one of the Confederate gentlemen who recently, at Niagara Falls, in a letter to Mr. Greeley, declared that they were *not* empowered to negotiate for peace, but that they *were,* however, in the confidential employment of their government, has prepared a platform and an address to be adopted by the Democracy at the Chicago Convention, the preparing of these, and conferring with the Democratic leaders in regard to the same, being the confidential employment of their government, in which he, and his confreres are engaged. The following planks are in the platform —

    5. The war to be further prosecuted only to restore the

Union as it was, and only in such manner, that no further detriment to slave property shall be effected.

6. All Negro soldiers and seamen to be at once disarmed and degraded to menial service in the army and navy; and no additional Negroes to be, on any pretence whatever, taken from their masters.

7. All Negroes not having enjoyed actual freedom during the war to be held permanently as slaves; and whether those who shall have enjoyed actual freedom during the war, shall be free to be a legal question.

The following paragraphs are in the address—

"Let all who are in favor of peace; of arresting the slaughter of our countrymen, of saving the country from bankruptcy & ruin, of securing food & raiment & good wages for the laboring classes; of disappointing the enemies of democratic & republican government who are rejoicing in the overthrow of their proudest monuments; of vindicating our capacity for self-government, arouse and maintain these principles, and elect these candidates."

* * * *

"The stupid tyrant who now disgraces the chair of Washington and Jackson could, any day, have peace and restoration of the Union; and would have them, only that he persists in the war merely to free the slaves."

The convention may not literally adopt Mr. Clay's platform and address, but we predict it will do so substantially. We shall see.

Mr. Clay confesses to his Democratic friends that he is for *peace* and *disunion;* but, he says "You cannot elect without a cry of war for the Union; but, once elected, we are friends, and can adjust matters somehow." He also says "You will find some difficulty in proving that Lincoln could, if he would, have peace and reunion, because Davis has not said so, and will not say so; but you must assert it, and re-assert it, and stick to it, and it will pass as at least half-proved."

Lincoln, reading the part of Grant's dispatch that he quoted, must have remembered how often he had tried to instill McClellan, Burnside, Hooker, and Meade with the same military philosophy. Yet he concluded with a warning.

The Living Lincoln

Office U. S. Military Telegraph,
War Department,
Washington, D. C., August 3, 1864.

CYPHER
Lieut. Genl. Grant
City Point, Va.

I have seen your despatch in which you say "I want Sheridan put in command of all the troops in the field, with instructions to put himself south of the enemy, and follow him to the death. Wherever the enemy goes, let our troops go also." This, I think, is exactly right, as to how our forces should move. But please look over the despatches you may have received from here, even since you made that order, and discover, if you can, that there is any idea in the head of any one here, of "putting our army *south* of the enemy," or of following him "to the *death*" in any direction. I repeat to you it will neither be done nor attempted unless you watch it every day, and hour, and force it.

A. Lincoln

In a difficult family situation, Lincoln asked for no special consideration.

Office U. S. Military Telegraph,
War Department,
Washington, D. C., August 8.th. 1864.

Major General Burbridge
Lexington, Ky.

Last December Mrs. Emily T. Helm, half-sister of Mrs. L. and widow of the rebel general Ben. Hardin Helm stopped here on her way from Georgia to Kentucky, and I gave her a paper, as I remember, to protect her against the mere fact of her being Gen. Helm's widow. I hear a rumor today that you recently sought to arrest her, but was prevented by her presenting the paper from me. I do not intend to protect her against the consequences of disloyal words or acts, spoken or done by her since her return to Kentucky, and if the paper given her by me can be construed to give her protection for such words or acts, it is hereby revoked *pro tanto.* Deal with her for current conduct, just as you would with *any other.*

A. Lincoln

"The Signs Look Better"

Halleck feared an uprising in the North to resist the draft. If Lee were to be held on the James, and if Sherman were to take Atlanta, Grant declared that his troops could not be used to do the work of the state militia. Lincoln backed up his general.

> *Executive Mansion,*
> *Washington, August 17. 1864.*

"CYPHER"
Lieut. Gen. Grant
City Point, Va.

I have seen your despatch expressing your unwillingness to break your hold where you are. Neither am I willing. Hold on with a bull-dog grip, and chew & choke, as much as possible.

> *A. Lincoln*

Lincoln sensed that the war had brought irrevocable changes into the pattern of American life. As long as there was honor in government, emancipation could not be an empty promise. This letter, unsigned, may not have been sent, but in it Lincoln had committed himself.

> *Executive Mansion,*
> *Washington, August 17, 1864.*

Hon. Charles D. Robinson
My dear Sir:

Your letter of the 7th. was placed in my hand yesterday by Gov. Randall.

To me it seems plain that saying reunion and abandonment of slavery would be considered, if offered, is not saying that nothing *else* or *less* would be considered, if offered. But I will not stand upon the mere construction of language. It is true, as you remind me, that in the Greeley letter of 1862, I said: "If I could save the Union without freeing any slave I would do it; and if I could save it by freeing all the slaves I would do it; and if I could save it by freeing some, and leaving others alone I would also do that." I continued in the same letter as follows: "What I do about slavery and the colored race, I do because I believe it helps to save the Union; and what I forbear I forbear because I do not believe it would help to save the Union. I shall do less whenever I shall believe what I am doing hurts the cause; and I shall do more when-

613

ever I shall believe doing more will help the cause." All this I said in the utmost sincerity; and I am as true to the whole of it now, as when I first said it. When I afterwards proclaimed emancipation, and employed colored soldiers, I only followed the declaration just quoted from the Greeley letter that "I shall do *more* whenever I shall believe *doing* more will help the cause." The way these measures were to help the cause, was not to be by magic, or miracles, but by inducing the colored people to come bodily over from the rebel side to ours. On this point, nearly a year ago, in a letter to Mr. Conkling, made public at once, I wrote as follows: "But Negroes, like other people, act upon motives. Why should they do anything for us if we will do nothing for them? If they stake their lives for us they must be prompted by the strongest motive—even the promise of freedom. And the promise, being made, must be kept." I am sure you will not, on due reflection, say that the promise being made, must be *broken* at the first opportunity. I am sure you would not desire me to say, or to leave an inference, that I am ready, whenever convenient, to join in re-enslaving those who shall have served us in consideration of our promise. As matter of morals, could such treachery by any possibility, escape the curses of Heaven, or of any good man? As matter of policy, to *announce* such a purpose, would ruin the Union cause itself. All recruiting of colored men would instantly cease, and all colored men now in our service, would instantly desert us. And rightfully too. Why should they give their lives for us, with full notice of our purpose to betray them? Drive back to the support of the rebellion the physical force which the colored people now give, and promise us, and neither the present, nor any coming administration, *can* save the Union. Take from us, and give to the enemy, the hundred and thirty, forty, or fifty thousand colored persons now serving us as soldiers, seamen, and laborers, and we can not longer maintain the contest. The party who could elect a President on a war & slavery restoration platform, would, of necessity, lose the colored force; and that force being lost, would be as powerless to save the Union as to do any other impossible thing. It is not a question of sentiment or taste, but one of physical force, which may be measured, and estimated as horsepower, and steam power, are measured and estimated. And by measurement, it is more than we can lose, and live. Nor can we, by discarding it, get a white force in place of it. There is a witness in every white man's bosom that he would

"The Signs Look Better"

rather go to the war having the Negro to help him, than to help the enemy against him. It is not the giving of one class for another. It is simply giving a large force to the enemy, for *nothing* in return.

In addition to what I have said, allow me to remind you that no one, having control of the rebel armies, or, in fact, having any influence whatever in the rebellion, has offered, or intimated a willingness to, a restoration of the Union, in any event, or on any condition whatever. Let it be constantly borne in mind that no such offer has been made or intimated. Shall we be weak enough to allow the enemy to distract us with an abstract question which he himself refuses to present as a practical one? In the Conkling letter before mentioned, I said: "Whenever you shall have conquered all resistance to the Union, if I shall urge you to continue fighting, it will be an apt time *then* to declare that you will not fight to free Negroes." I repeat this now. If Jefferson Davis wishes, for himself, or for the benefit of his friends at the North, to know what I would do if he were to offer peace and reunion, saying nothing about slavery, let him try me.

Lincoln told the 166th Ohio Regiment why it fought.

August 22, 1864

I suppose you are going home to see your families and friends. For the service you have done in this great struggle in which we are engaged I present you sincere thanks for myself and the country. I almost always feel inclined, when I happen to say anything to soldiers, to impress upon them in a few brief remarks the importance of success in this contest. It is not merely for today, but for all time to come that we should perpetuate for our children's children this great and free government, which we have enjoyed all our lives. I beg you to remember this, not merely for my sake, but for yours. I happen temporarily to occupy this big White House. I am a living witness that any one of your children may look to come here as my father's child has. It is in order that each of you may have through this free government which we have enjoyed, an open field and a fair chance for your industry, enterprise and intelligence; that you may all have equal privileges in the race of life, with all its desirable human aspirations. It is for this the struggle should be maintained, that we may not lose our birthright—not

615

only for one, but for two or three years. The nation is worth fighting for, to secure such an inestimable jewel.

Since May, Grant had suffered cruel losses, but had not taken Richmond; Atlanta still withstood Sherman's forces. Lincoln, who could do no more, faced facts when he wrote the following memorandum, asked his cabinet officers to sign the envelope in which he sealed it, and laid it away for future use.

> *Executive Mansion*
> *Washington, Aug. 23, 1864.*

This morning, as for some days past, it seems exceedingly probable that this administration will not be re-elected. Then it will be my duty to so co-operate with the President-elect, as to save the Union between the election and the inauguration; as he will have secured his election on such ground that he cannot possibly save it afterwards.

> *A. Lincoln*

Thurlow Weed, Henry J. Raymond, and E. D. Morgan—three of the most influential politicians in the country—asked Lincoln to pardon a prisoner. Lincoln replied with a deft proposal that they dared not accept.

> *Executive Mansion,*
> *Washington, August 31. 1864.*

Mr. Louis A. Welton came from the rebel lines into ours with a written contract to furnish large supplies to the rebels, was arrested with the contract in his possession, and has been sentenced to imprisonment for it. He and his friends complain of this, on no substantial evidence whatever, but simply because his word, only given after his arrest, that he only took the contract as a means of escaping from the rebel lines, was not accepted as a full defence. He perceives that if this had been true he would have destroyed the contract so soon as it had served his purpose in getting him across the lines; but not having done this, and being caught with the paper on him, he tells this other absurd story that he kept the paper in the belief that our government would join him in taking the profit of fulfilling the contract.

This is my understanding of the case; and I cannot conceive of a case of a man found in possession of a contract to furnish rebel supplies, who cannot escape, if this be held a sufficient ground of escape. It is simply for the accused to escape by telling a very absurd and improbable story. Now, if Senator Morgan, and Mr. Weed, and Mr. Raymond, will not argue with me that I *ought* to discharge this man, but will, in writing on this sheet, simply request me to do it, I will do it solely in deference to their wishes.

A. Lincoln

As the elections approached, Lincoln had good reason to be grateful for the smashing victory that Sherman gave him.

Executive Mansion,
September 3d, 1864.

The national thanks are herewith tendered by the President to Major General William T. Sherman, and the gallant officers and soldiers of his command before Atlanta, for the distinguished ability, courage, and perseverance displayed in the campaign in Georgia, which, under Divine favor, has resulted in the capture of the city of Atlanta. The marches, battles, sieges, and other military operations that have signalized this campaign must render it famous in the annals of war, and have entitled those who have participated therein to the applause and thanks of the nation.

Abraham Lincoln

Nearly a year had passed since Eliza Gurney had visited the White House. Now from her summer home near Atlantic City, New Jersey, she wrote the President that the influence of the Almighty would strengthen him to accomplish all his "blessed purposes." Lincoln acknowledged his deep indebtedness to the Quaker widow.

Executive Mansion,
Washington, September 4. 1864.

Eliza P. Gurney.
My esteemed friend.

I have not forgotten—probably never shall forget—the very impressive occasion when yourself and friends visited me on a Sabbath forenoon two years ago. Nor has your kind letter, written nearly a year later, ever been forgotten. In all, it has been your purpose to strengthen my reliance on God. I am much indebted to the good Christian people of the country for their constant prayers and consolations; and to no one of them, more than to yourself. The purposes of the Almighty are perfect, and must prevail, though we erring mortals may fail to accurately perceive them in advance. We hoped for a happy termination of this terrible war long before this; but God knows best, and has ruled otherwise. We shall yet acknowledge His wisdom and our own error therein. Meanwhile we must work earnestly in the best light He gives us, trusting that so working still conduces to the great ends He ordains. Surely He intends some great good to follow this mighty convulsion, which no mortal could make, and no mortal could stay.

Your people—the Friends—have had, and are having, a very great trial. On principle, and faith, opposed to both war and oppression, they can only practically oppose oppression by war. In this hard dilemma, some have chosen one horn and some the other. For those appealing to me on conscientious grounds, I have done, and shall do, the best I could and can, in my own conscience, under my oath to the law. That you believe this I doubt not; and believing it, I shall still receive, for our country and myself, your earnest prayers to our Father in Heaven. Your sincere friend

A. Lincoln.

A reply to the loyal colored people of Baltimore upon the presentation of a Bible afforded the President another opportunity of expressing his deepening religious convictions.

September 7, 1864

This occasion would seem fitting for a lengthy response to the address which you have just made. I would make one, if prepared; but I am not. I would promise to respond in writing, had not experience taught me that business will not allow me to do so. I can only now say, as I have often before said, it has always been a sentiment with me that all mankind should be free. So far as able, within my sphere, I have always acted as I believed to be right and just; and I have done all I could for the good of mankind generally. In letters and documents sent from this office I have expressed myself better than I now can. In regard to this Great Book, I have but to say, it is the best gift God has given to man.

"The Signs Look Better"

All the good the Saviour gave to the world was communicated through this book. But for it we could not know right from wrong. All things most desirable for man's welfare, here and hereafter, are to be found portrayed in it. To you I return my most sincere thanks for the very elegant copy of the great Book of God which you present.

News from home for Mrs. Lincoln:

Executive Mansion, Washington,
September 8. 1864.

Mrs. A. Lincoln
Manchester, Vermont

All well, including Tad's pony and the goats. Mrs. Col. Dimmick died night before last. Bob left Sunday afternoon. Said he did not know whether he should see you.

A. Lincoln

Lincoln drafted in pencil an unfinished letter that dealt with the most difficult problem facing a man who wages a war—what sort of peace can he accept?

Executive Mansion,
Washington, Sept. 12. 1864.

Isaac M. Schemerhorn
My dear Sir.

Yours inviting me to attend a Union mass meeting at Buffalo is received. Much is being said about peace; and no man desires peace more ardently than I. Still I am yet unprepared to give up the Union for a peace which, so achieved, could not be of much duration. The preservation of our Union was *not* the sole avowed object for which the war was commenced. It was commenced for precisely the reverse object—*to destroy our Union*. The insurgents commenced it by firing upon the Star of the West, and on Fort Sumter, and by other similar acts. It is true, however, that the administration accepted the war thus commenced, for the sole avowed object of preserving our Union; and it is not true that it has since been, or will be, prosecuted by this administration, for any other object. In declaring this, I only declare what I can know,

619

and do know to be true, and what no other man can know to be false.

In taking the various steps which have led to my present position in relation to the war, the public interest and my private interest, have been perfectly parallel, because in no other way could I serve myself so well, as by truly serving the Union. The whole field has been open to me, where to choose. No place-hunting necessity has been upon me urging me to seek a position of antagonism to some other man, irrespective of whether such position might be favorable or unfavorable to the Union.

Of course I may err in judgment, but my present position in reference to the rebellion is the result of my best judgment, and according to that best judgment, it is the only position upon which any executive can or could save the Union. Any substantial departure from it insures the success of the rebellion. An armistice—a cessation of hostilities—is the end of the struggle, and the insurgents would be in peaceable possession of all that has been struggled for. Any different policy in regard to the colored man, deprives us of his help, and this is more than we can bear. We cannot spare the hundred and forty or fifty thousand now serving us as soldiers, seamen, and laborers. This is not a question of sentiment or taste, but one of physical force which may be measured and estimated as horse-power and steam power are measured and estimated. Keep it and you can save the Union. Throw it away, and the Union goes with it. Nor is it possible for any administration to retain the service of these people with the express or implied understanding that upon the first convenient occasion, they are to be re-inslaved. It *can* not be; and it *ought* not to be.

Lincoln carried an urgent political problem to the victorious Sherman.

Executive Mansion, Washington, D. C.
September 19th, 1864.

Major General Sherman,

The state election of Indiana occurs on the 11th. of October, and the loss of it to the friends of the government would go far towards losing the whole Union cause. The bad effect upon the November election, and especially the giving the state government to those who will oppose the war in every possible way, are too much to risk, if it can possibly be avoided. The draft proceeds, notwithstanding its strong tendency to lose us the state. Indiana is the only important state, voting in October, whose soldiers cannot vote in the field. Anything you can safely do to let her soldiers, or any part of them, go home and vote at the state election, will be greatly in point. They need not remain for the presidential election, but may return to you at once. This is, in no sense, an order, but is merely intended to impress you with the importance, to the army itself, of your doing all you safely can, yourself being the judge of what you can safely do. Yours truly

A. Lincoln

Sheridan, capturing 2,500 rebels and driving Early's corps through Winchester, hears from the President.

Executive Mansion,
Washington,
Sep. 20. 1864.

"CYPHER"
Major General Sheridan
Winchester, Va

Have just heard of your great victory. God bless you all, officers and men. Strongly inclined to come up and see you.

A. Lincoln

To Rosecrans, now commanding the ever-troublesome Department of Missouri, went instructions to allow eligible soldiers to vote, even if they got drunk in the process.

Executive Mansion,
Washington, Sep. 26, 1864

Major General Rosecrans,

One cannot always safely disregard a report, even which one may not believe. I have a report that you incline to deny the soldiers the right of attending the election in Missouri, on the assumed ground that they will get drunk and make disturbance. Last year I sent Gen. Schofield a letter of instruction, dated October 1st, 1863, which I suppose you will find on the files of the department, and which contains, among other things, the following:

"At elections see that those and only those, are allowed to vote, who are entitled to do so by the laws of Missouri, including as of those laws, the restrictions laid by the Missouri convention upon those who may have participated in the rebellion."

This I thought right then, and think right now; and I may add I do not remember that either party complained after the election, of Gen. Schofield's action under it. Wherever the law allows soldiers to vote, their officers must also allow it. Please write me on this subject. Yours truly,

A. Lincoln.

Maryland approached its decision. Calmly Lincoln placed his faith in the logic of events.

Executive Mansion, Washington,
October 10, 1864.

Hon. Henry W. Hoffman
My dear Sir:

A convention of Maryland has framed a new constitution for the state; a public meeting is called for this evening, at Baltimore, to aid in securing its ratification by the people; and you ask a word from me, for the occasion. I presume the only feature of the instrument, about which there is serious controversy, is that which provides for the extinction of slavery. It needs not to be a secret, and I presume it is no secret, that I wish success to this provision. I desire it on every consideration. I wish all men to be free. I wish the material prosperity of the already free which I feel sure the extinction of slavery would bring. I wish to see, in process of disappearing, that only thing which ever could bring this nation to civil war. I attempt no argument. Argument upon the question is already exhausted by the abler, better informed, and more immediately interested sons of Maryland herself. I only add that I shall be gratified exceedingly if the good people of the state shall, by their votes, ratify the new constitution. Yours truly

A. Lincoln

Before October ended, Maryland gave Lincoln a victory as great as the capture of Vicksburg or Atlanta. With satisfaction the President addressed the 42nd Massachusetts Regiment.

October 31, 1864

You have completed a term of service in the cause of your country, and on behalf of the nation and myself I thank you. You are going home; I hope you will find all your friends well. I never see a Massachusetts regiment but it reminds me of the difficulty a regiment from that state met with on its passage through Baltimore; but the world has moved since then, and I congratulate you upon having a better time today in Baltimore than that regiment had.

Tonight, midnight, slavery ceases in Maryland, and this state of things in Maryland is due greatly to the soldiers. Again I thank you for the services you have rendered the country.

Lincoln won re-election with a majority of more than 400,000, and, carrying every state except Kentucky, Delaware and New Jersey, with an electoral vote of 212 to 21. To a serenade on the White House lawn he read a prepared response from a window. "Not very graceful," he told John Hay, "but I am growing old enough not to care much for the manner of doing things."

November 10, 1864

It has long been a grave question whether any government, not *too* strong for the liberties of its people, can be strong *enough* to maintain its own existence, in great emergencies.

On this point the present rebellion brought our republic to a severe test; and a presidential election occurring in regular course during the rebellion added not a little to the strain. If the loyal people, *united,* were put to the utmost of their strength by the rebellion, must they not fail when *divided,* and partially paralyzed, by a political war among themselves?

But the election was a necessity.

We cannot have free government without elections; and if the rebellion could force us to forego, or postpone a national election, it might fairly claim to have already conquered and ruined us. The strife of the election is but human nature practically applied to the facts of the case. What has occurred in this case, must ever recur in similar cases. Human nature will not change. In any future great national trial, compared with the men of this, we shall have as weak, and as strong; as silly and as wise; as bad and good. Let us, therefore, study the incidents of this, as philosophy to learn wisdom from, and none of them as wrongs to be revenged.

But the election, along with its incidental, and undesirable strife, has done good too. It has demonstrated that a people's government can sustain a national election, in the midst of a great civil war. Until now it has not been known to the world that this was a possibility. It shows also how *sound,* and how *strong* we still are. It shows that, even among candidates of the same party, he who is most devoted to the Union, and most opposed to treason, can receive most of the people's votes. It shows also, to the extent yet known, that we have more men now, than we had when the war began. Gold is good in its place; but living, brave, patriotic men, are better than gold.

But the rebellion continues; and now that the election is over, may not all, having a common interest, re-unite in a common effort, to save our common country? For my own part I have striven, and shall strive to avoid placing any obstacle in the way. So long as I have been here I have not willingly planted a thorn in any man's bosom.

While I am deeply sensible to the high compliment of a re-election; and duly grateful, as I trust, to Almighty God for having directed my countrymen to a right conclusion, as I think, for their own good, it adds nothing to my satisfaction that any other man may be disappointed or pained by the result.

May I ask those who have not differed with me, to join with me, in this same spirit towards those who have?

And now, let me close by asking three hearty cheers for our brave soldiers and seamen and their gallant and skilful commanders.

XVI. "With Malice Toward None"

1864-1865   O N E L E C T I O N night, dishing out oysters to those who awaited the returns at the War Department, Lincoln told a story. When in 1860 he knew that he had won the Presidency, he had flung his tired body on a sofa. Nearby, above a bureau, hung a mirror, and in it he seemed to see two images of himself, one paler than the other. Lincoln felt troubled. He arose and faced the mirror squarely. The images disappeared. Then, reclining once more, he glanced at the mirror. The images had returned.

Disturbed and perplexed, Lincoln related the incident to his wife. She wondered if the images might not constitute a sign. Her husband was to be elected President for two terms. The pale face signified that he would not live through the second term.

To the unfinished task of preserving the Union, Lincoln turned his full energies, untroubled by this memory. Louisiana followed Maryland in abolishing slavery and similar action seemed imminent in Arkansas and Missouri. But the transition from military to civil authority produced its own conflicts. Thomas P. May, editor of the New Orleans *Times,* asserted that the delegates to the Louisiana convention were drunk, and the commanding general, S. A. Hurlbut, arrested him. Lincoln moved at once to uphold a fundamental principle of democratic government.

Executive Mansion
Washington, Nov. 14. 1864

PRIVATE
Major General Hurlbut

Few things, since I have been here, have impressed me more painfully than what, for four or five months past, has appeared as

625

bitter military opposition to the new state government of Louisiana. I still indulged some hope that I was mistaken in the fact; but copies of a correspondence on the subject, between Gen. Canby and yourself, and shown me today, dispel that hope. A very fair proportion of the people of Louisiana have inaugurated a new state government, making an excellent new constitution—better for the poor black man than we have in Illinois. This was done under military protection, directed by me, in the belief, still sincerely entertained, that with such a nucleus around which to build, we could get the state into position again sooner than otherwise. In this belief a general promise of protection and support, applicable alike to Louisiana and other states, was given in the last annual message. During the formation of the new government and constitution, they were supported by nearly every loyal person and opposed by every secessionist. And this support, and this opposition, from the respective standpoints of the parties, was perfectly consistent and logical. Every Unionist ought to wish the new government to succeed; and every disunionist must desire it to fail. Its failure would gladden the heart of Slidell in Europe, and of every enemy of the old flag in the world. Every advocate of slavery naturally desires to see blasted, and crushed, the liberty promised the black man by the new constitution. But why Gen. Canby and Gen. Hurlbut should join on the same side is to me incomprehensible.

Of course, in the condition of things at New Orleans, the military must not be thwarted by the civil authority; but when the constitutional convention, for what it deems a breach of privilege, arrests an editor, in no way connected with the military, the military necessity for insulting the convention, and forcibly discharging the editor, is difficult to perceive. Neither is the military necessity for protecting the people against paying large salaries, fixed by a legislature of their own choosing, very apparent. Equally difficult to perceive is the military necessity for forcibly interposing to prevent a bank from loaning its own money to the state. These things, if they have occurred, are, at the best, no better than gratuitous hostility. I wish I could hope that they may be shown to not have occurred. To make assurance against misunderstanding, I repeat that in the existing condition of things in Louisiana, the military must not be thwarted by the civil authority; and I add that on points of difference the commanding general must be judge and

"With Malice Toward None"

master. But I also add that in the exercise of this judgment and control, a purpose, obvious, and scarcely unavowed, to transcend all military necessity, in order to crush out the civil government, will not be overlooked. Yours truly

A. Lincoln

Superbly eloquent was the letter that Lincoln wrote to Mrs. Lydia Bixby of Boston. This message, published in the Boston *Transcript*, appealed to the heart of the nation.

Executive Mansion,
Washington, Nov. 21, 1864.

Dear Madam,—
I have been shown in the files of the War Department a statement of the Adjutant General of Massachusetts, that you are the mother of five sons who have died gloriously on the field of battle.*

I feel how weak and fruitless must be any words of mine which should attempt to beguile you from the grief of a loss so overwhelming. But I cannot refrain from tendering to you the consolation that may be found in the thanks of the Republic they died to save.

I pray that our Heavenly Father may assuage the anguish of your bereavement, and leave you only the cherished memory of the loved and lost, and the solemn pride that must be yours, to have laid so costly a sacrifice upon the altar of freedom. Yours, very sincerely and respectfully,

A. Lincoln.

Mrs. Bixby.

Once Lincoln had determined on a course, he was not easily budged. Banks learned of this trait through experience.

Executive Mansion, Washington,
Dec. 2. 1864.

Major General Banks.
I know you are dissatisfied, which pains me very much; but I wish not to be argued with further. I entertain no abatement of confidence, or friendship for you. I have told you why I cannot order Gen. Canby from the Department of the Gulf—that he

* Actually two, and not five, of Mrs. Bixby's sons were killed.

whom I must hold responsible for military results, is not agreed. Yet I do believe that you, of all men, can best perform the part of advancing the new state government of Louisiana; and therefore I have wished you to go and try, leaving it to yourself to give up the trial at the end of a month, if you find it impracticable, or personally too disagreeable. This is certainly meant in no unkindness; but I wish to avoid further struggle about it. Yours truly

A Lincoln

"Again the blessings of health and abundant harvests claim our profoundest gratitude to Almighty God," Lincoln wrote, opening his annual message to Congress. One paragraph revealed a determination to fight slavery wherever he could.

December 6, 1864

. . . I solicit your authority to furnish to the republic [of Liberia] a gunboat at moderate cost, to be reimbursed to the United States by instalments. Such a vessel is needed for the safety of that state against the native African races; and in Liberian hands it would be more effective in arresting the African slave trade than a squadron in our own hands. The possession of the least organized naval force would stimulate a generous ambition in the republic, and the confidence which we should manifest by furnishing it would win forbearance and favor towards the colony from all civilized nations. . . .

Another paragraph sought to protect the liberty of still one more group.

The act passed at the last session for the encouragement of emigration has, so far as was possible, been put into operation. It seems to need amendment which will enable the officers of the government to prevent the practice of frauds against the immigrants while on their way and on their arrival in the ports, so as to secure them here a free choice of avocations and places of settlement. A liberal disposition towards this great national policy is manifested by most of the European states, and ought to be reciprocated on our part by giving the immigrants effective national protection. I regard our emigrants as one of the principal replenishing streams which are appointed by Providence to repair the ravages of internal war, and its wastes of national strength and health. All that is necessary is to secure the flow of that stream in its present fullness, and to that end the government must, in every way, make it manifest that it neither needs nor designs to impose involuntary military service upon those who come from other lands to cast their lot in our country.

Lincoln faced the problem of the public debt produced by three years of war and offered a solution.

The public debt on the first day of July last, as appears by the books of the Treasury, amounted to $1,740,690,489.49. Probably, should the war continue for another year, that amount may be increased by not far from five hundred millions. Held as it is, for the most part, by our own people, it has become a substantial branch of national, though private, property. For obvious reasons, the more nearly this property can be distributed among all the people the better. To favor such general distribution, greater inducements to become owners might, perhaps, with good effect, and without injury, be presented to persons of limited means. With this view, I suggest whether it might not be both competent and expedient for Congress to provide that a limited amount of some future issue of public securities might be held by any bona fide purchaser exempt from taxation, and from seizure for debt, under such restrictions and limitations as might be necessary to guard against abuse of so important a privilege. This would enable every prudent person to set aside a small annuity against a possible day of want.

Privileges like these would render the possession of such securities, to the amount limited, most desirable to every person of small means who might be able to save enough for the purpose. The great advantage of citizens being creditors as well as debtors, with relation to the public debt, is obvious. Men readily perceive that they cannot be much oppressed by a debt which they owe to themselves.

The public debt on the first day of July last, although somewhat exceeding the estimate of the Secretary of the Treasury made to Congress at the commencement of the last session, falls short of the estimate of that officer made in the preceding December, as to is probable amount at the beginning of this year, by the sum of $3,995,097.31. This fact exhibits a satisfactory condition and conduct of the operations of the Treasury. . . .

The Living Lincoln

In the recent elections Lincoln found a great resource. The nation was young and strong.

At the last session of Congress a proposed amendment of the Constitution abolishing slavery throughout the United States, passed the Senate, but failed for lack of the requisite two-thirds vote in the House of Representatives. Although the present is the same Congress, and nearly the same Members, and without questioning the wisdom or patriotism of those who stood in opposition, I venture to recommend the reconsideration and passage of the measure at the present session. Of course the abstract question is not changed; but an intervening election shows, almost certainly, that the next Congress will pass the measure if this does not. Hence there is only a question of *time* as to when the proposed amendment will go to the states for their action. And as it is to so go, at all events, may we not agree that the sooner the better? It is not claimed that the election has imposed a duty on Members to change their views or their votes, any further than, as an additional element to be considered, their judgment may be affected by it. It is the voice of the people now, for the first time, heard upon the question. In a great national crisis, like ours, unanimity of action among those seeking a common end is very desirable—almost indispensable. And yet no approach to such unanimity is attainable, unless some deference shall be paid to the will of the majority, simply because it is the will of the majority. In this case the common end is the maintenance of the Union; and, among the means to secure that end, such will, through the election, is most clearly declared in favor of such constitutional amendment.

The most reliable indication of public purpose in this country is derived through our popular elections. Judging by the recent canvass and its result, the purpose of the people, within the loyal states, to maintain the integrity of the Union, was never more firm, nor more nearly unanimous, than now. The extraordinary calmness and good order with which the millions of voters met and mingled at the polls, give strong assurance of this. Not only all those who supported the Union ticket, so-called, but a great majority of the opposing party also, may be fairly claimed to entertain, and to be actuated by, the same purpose. It is an unanswerable argument to this effect, that no candidate for any office whatever, high or low, has ventured to seek votes on the avowal that he was for giving up the Union. There have been much impugning of motives, and much heated controversy as to the proper means and best mode of advancing the Union cause; but on the distinct issue of Union or no Union, the politicians have shown their instinctive knowledge that there is no diversity among the people. In affording the people the fair opportunity of showing, one to another and to the world, this firmness and unanimity of purpose, the election has been of vast value to the national cause.

The election has exhibited another fact not less valuable to be known—the fact that we do not approach exhaustion in the most important branch of national resources—that of living men. While it is melancholy to reflect that the war has filled so many graves, and carried mourning to so many hearts, it is some relief to know that, compared with the surviving, the fallen have been so few. While corps, and divisions, and brigades, and regiments have formed, and fought, and dwindled, and gone out of existence, a great majority of the men who composed them are still living. The same is true of the naval service. The election returns prove this. So many voters could not else be found. The states regularly holding elections, both now and four years ago, to wit, California, Connecticut, Delaware, Illinois, Indiana, Iowa, Kentucky, Maine, Maryland, Massachusetts, Michigan, Minnesota, Missouri, New Hampshire, New Jersey, New York, Ohio, Oregon, Pennsylvania, Rhode Island, Vermont, West Virginia, and Wisconsin cast 3,982,011 votes now, against 3,870,222 cast then, showing an aggregate now of 3,982,011. To this is to be added 33,762 cast now in the new states of Kansas and Nevada, which states did not vote in 1860, thus swelling the aggregate to 4,015,773 and the net increase during the three years and a half of war to 145,551. A table is appended showing particulars. To this again should be added the number of all soldiers in the field from Massachusetts, Rhode Island, New Jersey, Delaware, Indiana, Illinois, and California, who, by the laws of those states, could not vote away from their homes, and which number cannot be less than 90,000. Nor yet is this all. The number in organized territories is triple now what it was four years ago, while thousands, white and black, join us as the national arms press back the insurgent lines. So much is shown, affirmatively and negatively, by the election. It is not material to inquire *how* the increase has been produced, or to show that it would have been *greater* but for the war, which is probably true. The important fact remains demonstrated, that we have *more* men *now* than we had when the war *began;* that we are not exhausted, nor in process of exhaustion; that we are *gaining* strength, and may, if need be, maintain the contest indefinitely. This as to men. Material resources are now more complete and abundant than ever.

The national resources, then, are unexhausted, and, as we believe, inexhaustible. The public purpose to re-establish and maintain the national authority is unchanged, and, as we believe, unchangeable. The manner of continuing the effort remains to choose. On careful consideration of all the evidence accessible it seems to me that no attempt at negotiation with the insurgent leader could result in any good. He would accept nothing short of severance of the Union—precisely what we will not and cannot give. His declarations to this effect are explicit and oft-repeated. He does not attempt to deceive us. He affords us no excuse to deceive ourselves. He cannot voluntarily re-accept the Union; we cannot voluntarily yield it. Between him and us the issue is distinct, simple, and inflexible. It is an issue which can only be tried by war, and decided by victory. If we yield, we are beaten; if the Southern people fail him, he is beaten. Either way, it would be the victory and defeat following war. What is true, however, of him who heads the insurgent cause, is not necessarily true of those who follow. Although he cannot re-accept the Union, they can. Some of them, we know, already desire peace and reunion. The number of such may increase. They can, at any moment, have peace simply by laying down their arms and submitting to the national authority under the Constitution. After so much, the government could not, if it would, maintain war against them. The loyal people would not sustain or allow it. If questions should remain, we would adjust them by the peaceful means of legislation, conference, courts, and votes, operating only in constitutional and lawful channels. Some certain, and other possible, questions are, and would be, beyond the executive power to adjust; as, for instance, the admission of members into Congress, and whatever might require the appropriation of money. The executive power itself would be greatly diminished by the cessation of actual war. Pardons and remissions of forfeitures, however, would still be within executive control. In what spirit and temper this control would be exercised can be fairly judged of by the past.

"With Malice Toward None"

A year ago general pardon and amnesty, upon specified terms, were offered to all, except certain designated classes; and, it was, at the same time, made known that the excepted classes were still within contemplation of special clemency. During the year many availed themselves of the general provision, and many more would, only that the signs of bad faith in some led to such precautionary measures as rendered the practical process less easy and certain. During the same time also special pardons have been granted to individuals of the excepted classes, and no voluntary application has been denied. Thus, practically, the door has been, for a full year, open to all, except such as were not in condition to make free choice—that is, such as were in custody or under constraint. It is still so open to all. But the time may come—probably will come—when public duty shall demand that it be closed; and that, in lieu, more rigorous measures than heretofore shall be adopted.

In presenting the abandonment of armed resistance to the national authority on the part of the insurgents, as the only indispensable condition to ending the war on the part of the government, I retract nothing heretofore said as to slavery. I repeat the declaration made a year ago, that "while I remain in my present position I shall not attempt to retract or modify the Emancipation Proclamation, nor shall I return to slavery any person who is free by the terms of that proclamation, or by any of the acts of Congress." If the people should, by whatever mode or means, make it an executive duty to re-enslave such persons, another, and not I, must be their instrument to perform it.

In stating a single condition of peace, I mean simply to say that the war will cease on the part of the government, whenever it shall have ceased on the part of those who began it.

Abraham Lincoln

December 6. 1864.

One day Noah Brooks found the President writing with pencil on a piece of cardboard. "Here," he said after he had finished, "is one speech of mine which has never been printed, and I think it worth printing." Later Lincoln signed his name, "by way of joke," and affixed the title the story now bears. It was published in the Washington *Daily Chronicle* on December 7, 1864.

The Living Lincoln

THE PRESIDENT'S LAST, SHORTEST,
AND BEST SPEECH.

On Thursday of last week two ladies from Tennessee came before the President asking the release of their husbands held as prisoners of war at Johnson's Island. They were put off till Friday, when they came again; and were again put off to Saturday. At each of the interviews one of the ladies urged that her husband was a religious man. On Saturday the President ordered the release of the prisoners, and then said to this lady "You say your husband is a religious man; tell him when you meet him, that I say I am not much of a judge of religion, but that, in my opinion, the religion that sets men to rebel and fight against their government, because, as they think, that government does not sufficiently help *some* men to eat their bread on the sweat of *other* men's faces, is not the sort of religion upon which people can get to heaven!"

A. Lincoln.

In November, Sherman started on his great march to the sea. "Sherman's army," Grant said, "is now somewhat in the condition of a ground-mole when he disappears under a lawn. You can here and there trace his track, but you are not quite certain where he will come out till you see his head." Then on December 22 Sherman telegraphed the President: "I beg to present you as a Christmas gift the city of Savannah with 150 heavy guns & plenty of ammunition & also about 25,000 bales of cotton." Lincoln responded in warm spirit.

Executive Mansion, Washington,
Dec. 26, 1864.

My dear General Sherman.

Many, many, thanks for your Christmas gift—the capture of Savannah.

When you were about leaving Atlanta for the Atlantic coast, I was *anxious,* if not fearful; but feeling that you were the better judge, and remembering that "nothing risked, nothing gained" I did not interfere. Now, the undertaking being a success, the honor is all yours; for I believe none of us went farther than to acquiesce. And, taking the work of Gen. Thomas into the count, as it should be taken, it is indeed a great success. Not only does it afford the obvious and immediate military advantages; but, in showing to the world that your army could be divided, putting the stronger part to an important new service, and yet leaving enough to vanquish the old opposing force of the whole—Hood's army—it brings those who sat in darkness, to see a great light. But what next? I suppose it will be safer if I leave Gen. Grant and yourself to decide.

Please make my grateful acknowledgments to your whole army, officers and men. Yours very truly

A. Lincoln.

The ways of soldiers in trouble awakened in the President the compassion of a man who was also a husband and a father.

Sentences in these three cases commuted to imprisonment in the penitentiary at hard labor during the war.

A. Lincoln

Jan. 11, 1865

Office U. S. Military Telegraph,
War Department,
Washington, D. C., January 11 1865

Officer in command at
Nashville, Tenn.
 Postpone the execution of S. W. Elliott and C. E. Peacher until the third day of February 1865.

A. Lincoln

Executive Mansion,
Washington,
Jan'y 12th, 1865.

Officer in command at
Lexington,
Kentucky
 Suspend execution of sentence of death in case of Solomon Spiegel 9th Michigan Cavalry until further orders, and forward record of trial for examination.

A. Lincoln.

Maj. Eckert
 Please send the above telegram. *Jno. G. Nicolay*

The Living Lincoln

Executive Mansion,
Washington, Jan. 12. 1865.

Lieut. Gen. Grant
City-Point, Va.

If Henry Stork of 5th. Pa. Cavalry has been convicted of desertion, and is not yet executed, please stay till further order & send record.

A. Lincoln

January 12, 1865

If David Levy shall enlist and serve faithfully for one year or until otherwise honorably discharged I will pardon him for the past.

A. Lincoln.

Jan. 12, 1865.

The President writes a difficult letter in behalf of Robert Todd Lincoln.

Executive Mansion, Washington,
Jan. 19, 1865.

Lieut. General Grant:

Please read and answer this letter as though I was not President, but only a friend. My son, now in his twenty-second year, having graduated at Harvard, wishes to see something of the war before it ends. I do not wish to put him in the ranks, nor yet to give him a commission, to which those who have already served long, are better entitled, and better qualified to hold. Could he, without embarrassment to you, or detriment to the service, go into your military family with some nominal rank, I, and not the public, furnishing his necessary means? If no, say so without the least hesitation, because I am as anxious, and as deeply interested, that you shall not be encumbered as you can be yourself. Yours truly

A. Lincoln

Lincoln thought of lives that could be made useful in the years after the war.

"With Malice Toward None"

Executive Mansion,
Washington, 15 February, 1865.

Major Genl. Sheridan
    &*c*   &*c*

Suspend execution in case of Luther T. Palmer 5th N. Y. Artillery for fourteen (14) days and send record to me for examination.

A. Lincoln

John Hay   A.A.G.

Executive Mansion,
Washington, Feb'y 15, 1865.

Major General Sheridan

Suspend execution of death sentence of William Randall, at Harper's Ferry, of 5th N. Y. Heavy Artillery, until further orders, and forward record of trial for examination.

A. Lincoln.

Maj: Eckert
    Please send the above telegram   *Jno. G. Nicolay*

Executive Mansion,
Washington, Feb'y 16, 1865.

Lieutenant General Grant

Suspend execution of death sentence of George W. Brown, Company A Fifteenth New York Engineers, now at City Point, until further orders, and forward record for examination.

A. Lincoln.

Maj. Eckert
    Please send the above telegram   *Jno. G. Nicolay*

Executive Mansion,
Washington, Feb'y 16, 1865.

Lieutenant General Grant:

Suspend execution of death sentence of Charles Love, Seventh New Hampshire Vols. at City Point until further orders, and forward record for examination.

A. Lincoln

Major Eckert
    Please send the above telegram   *Jno. G. Nicolay*

The Living Lincoln

Officer in command
at Harper's Ferry

Chaplain Fitzgibbon yesterday sent me a dispatch invoking clemency for Jackson Stewart and Randall who are to be shot to-day. The dispatch is so vague that there is no means here of ascertaining, whether or not the execution of sentence of one or more of them may not already have been ordered. If not suspend execution of sentence in their cases until further orders and forward records of trials for examination.

A. Lincoln

Maj. Eckert
Please send above telegram   *Jno. G. Nicolay*

Executive Mansion,
Washington, February 17, 1865.

Officer in command at
Davenport Iowa.

Suspend execution of death sentence of Wm A. Craven for four weeks, and forward record for examination.

A. Lincoln

Maj. Eckert
Please send above telegram   *Jno. G. Nicolay*

March 4, 1865 in Washington was a bleak day. Low clouds hung in the sky, the wind blew in heavy gusts, and carriage wheels sank in the mud of Pennsylvania Avenue. On the portico of the capitol Lincoln arose to deliver his Second Inaugural Address. In a quiet voice he read these immortal words.

March 4, 1865

Fellow-Countrymen:

At this second appearing to take the oath of the presidential office, there is less occasion for an extended address than there was at the first. Then a statement, somewhat in detail, of a course to be pursued, seemed fitting and proper. Now, at the expiration of four years, during which public declarations have been constantly called forth on every point and phase of the great contest which still absorbs the attention, and engrosses the energies of the nation, little that is new could be presented. The progress of our arms, upon which all else chiefly depends, is as well known to the public as to myself; and it is, I trust, reasonably satisfactory and encouraging to all. With high hope for the future, no prediction in regard to it is ventured.

On the occasion corresponding to this four years ago, all thoughts were anxiously directed to an impending civil war. All dreaded it—all sought to avert it. While the inaugural address was being delivered from this place, devoted altogether to *saving* the Union without war, insurgent agents were in the city seeking to *destroy* it without war—seeking to dissolve the Union, and divide effects, by negotiation. Both parties deprecated war; but one of them would *make* war rather than let the nation survive; and the other would *accept* war rather than let it perish. And the war came.

One eighth of the whole population were colored slaves, not distributed generally over the Union, but localized in the southern part of it. These slaves constituted a peculiar and powerful interest. All knew that this interest was, somehow, the cause of the war. To strengthen, perpetuate, and extend this interest was the object for which the insurgents would rend the Union, even by war; while the government claimed no right to do more than to restrict the territorial enlargement of it. Neither party expected for the war, the magnitude, or the duration, which it has already attained. Neither anticipated that the *cause* of the conflict might cease with, or even before, the conflict itself should cease. Each looked for an easier triumph, and a result less fundamental and astounding. Both read the same Bible, and pray to the same God; and each invokes His aid against the other. It may seem strange that any men should dare to ask a just God's assistance in wringing their bread from the sweat of other men's faces; but let us judge not that we be not judged. The prayers of both could not be answered; that of neither has been answered fully. The Almighty has His own purposes. "Woe unto the world because of offences! for it must needs be that offences come; but woe to that man by whom the offence cometh!" If we shall suppose that American slavery is one of those offences which, in the providence of God, must needs come, but which, having continued through His appointed time, He now wills to remove, and that He gives to both North and South, this terrible war, as the woe due to those by whom the offence came, shall we discern therein any departure from those divine attributes which the believers in a Living God always ascribe to Him? Fondly do we hope—fervently do we pray —that this mighty scourge of war may speedily pass away. Yet, if God wills that it continue, until all the wealth piled by the bondman's two hundred and fifty years of unrequited toil shall be sunk, and until every drop of blood drawn with the lash, shall be paid by another drawn with the sword, as was said three thousand years ago, so still it must be said "the judgments of the Lord, are true and righteous altogether."

With malice toward none; with charity for all; with firmness in the right, as God gives us to see the right, let us strive on to finish the work we are in; to bind up the nation's wounds; to care for him who shall have borne the battle, and for his widow, and his orphan—to do all which may achieve and cherish a just, and a lasting peace, among ourselves, and with all nations.

Lincoln evaluated the place his address would occupy in history.

Executive Mansion,
Washington, March 15, 1865.

Thurlow Weed, Esq
My dear Sir.

Every one likes a compliment. Thank you for yours on my little notification speech, and on the recent inaugural address. I expect the latter to wear as well as—perhaps better than—anything I have produced; but I believe it is not immediately popular. Men are not flattered by being shown that there has been a difference of purpose between the Almighty and them. To deny it, however, in this case, is to deny that there is a God governing the world. It is a truth which I thought needed to be told; and as whatever of humiliation there is in it, falls most directly on myself, I thought others might afford for me to tell it. Yours truly

A. Lincoln

Desperately pressed, the Confederacy considered arming slaves to fight the North. In stinging words, Lincoln told the 140th Indiana Regiment what he thought of such a course.

"With Malice Toward None"

March 17, 1865

Fellow-Citizens.

A few words only. I was born in Kentucky, raised in Indiana, reside in Illinois, and now here, it is my duty to care equally for the good people of all the states. I am today glad of seeing it in the power of an Indiana regiment to present this captured flag to the good governor of their state. And yet I would not wish to compliment Indiana above other states, remembering that all have done so well. There are but few aspects of this great war on which I have not already expressed my views by speaking or writing. There is one—the recent effort of our erring brethren, sometimes so-called, to employ the slaves in their armies. The great question with them has been; "will the Negro fight for them?" They ought to know better than we; and, doubtless, do know better than we. I may incidentally remark, however, that having, in my life, heard many arguments,—or strings of words meant to pass for arguments,—intended to show that the Negro ought to be a slave, that if he shall now really fight to keep himself a slave, it will be a far better argument why he should remain a slave than I have ever before heard. He, perhaps, ought to be a slave, if he desires it ardently enough to fight for it. Or, if one out of four will, for his own freedom, fight to keep the other three in slavery, he ought to be a slave for his selfish meanness. I have always thought that all men should be free; but if any should be slaves it should be first those who desire it for *themselves,* and secondly those who *desire* it for *others.* Whenever I hear anyone arguing for slavery I feel a strong impulse to see it tried on him personally.

There is one thing about the Negroes fighting for the rebels which we can know as well as they can; and that is that they cannot, at the same time fight in their armies, and stay at home and make bread for them. And this being known and remembered we can have but little concern whether they become soldiers or not. I am rather in favor of the measure; and would at anytime if I could, have loaned them a vote to carry it. We have to reach the bottom of the insurgent resources; and that they employ, or seriously think of employing, the slaves as soldiers, gives us glimpses of the bottom. Therefore I am glad of what we learn on this subject.

In late March at City Point, Virginia, Lincoln met with Grant and Sherman. The cares of long months of war had left their marks upon the President; his face, one observer said, looked "care-ploughed, tempest-tossed and weatherbeaten." One more bloody battle must be fought to win the war, Grant and Sherman agreed; which of them would need to fight it remained a question. Lincoln remained at City Point. He seemed to sense an impending climax.

City Point, Va., March 30, 1865–7.30 P.M.

Hon. Secretary of War:

I begin to feel that I ought to be at home, and yet I dislike to leave without seeing nearer to the end of General Grant's present movement. He has now been out since yesterday morning, and although he has not been diverted from his programme, no considerable effect has yet been produced, so far as we know here. Last night at 10.15, when it was dark as a rainy night without a moon could be, a furious cannonade, soon joined in by a heavy musketry fire, opened near Petersburg and lasted about two hours. The sound was very distinct here, as also were the flashes of the guns upon the clouds. It seemed to me a great battle, but the older hands here scarcely noticed it, and, sure enough, this morning it was found that very little had been done.

A. Lincoln.

In Washington, Stanton replied, there was nothing to do "but petty private ends that you should not be annoyed with." The Secretary of War believed that "a pause by the army now would do harm; if you are on the ground there will be no pause." Lincoln's next message to Stanton revealed that the pressure had not slackened.

City Point, Va.,

March 31, 1865–8.30 P.M.

Hon. Edwin M. Stanton,

Secretary of War:

At 12.30 P.M. today General Grant telegraphed me as follows:

"There has been much hard fighting this morning. The enemy drove our left from near Dabney's house back well toward the Boydton plank road. We are now about to take the offensive at that point, and I hope will more than recover the lost ground."

Later he telegraphed again as follows:

"Our troops, after being driven back on the Boydton plank

"With Malice Toward None"

road, turned and drove the enemy in turn and took the White
Oak road, which we now have. This gives us the ground occupied
by the enemy this morning. I will send you a rebel flag captured
by our troops in driving the enemy back. There have been four
flags captured today."

Judging by the two points from which General Grant telegraphs, I infer that he moved his headquarters about one mile
since he sent the first of the two dispatches.

A. Lincoln.

April brought rain. Grant's cannon opened on Petersburg. Lincoln
telegraphed Mrs. Lincoln of the victory that could be taking shape as
Sheridan began to press the enemy.

Head Quarters Armies of the United States,
City Point,
April 2. 7/45 [A.M.] *1865*

Mrs. A. Lincoln,
Washington, D. C.

Last night Gen. Grant telegraphed that Sheridan with his cavalry and the 5th. Corps had captured three brigades of infantry, a
train of wagons, and several batteries, prisoners amounting to
several thousands. This morning Gen. Grant, having ordered an
attack along the whole line telegraphs as follows:

"Both Wright and Parke got through the enemy's lines. The
battle now rages furiously. Sheridan with his cavalry, the 5th.
Corps, & Miles Division of the 2nd. Corps, which was sent to him
since 1. this A.M. is now sweeping down from the west. All now
looks highly favorable. Ord is engaged, but I have not yet heard
the result in his front."

Robert yesterday wrote a little cheerful note to Capt. Penrose,
which is all I have heard of him since you left. Copy to Secretary
of War.

A. Lincoln

Lincoln showed a reporter a captured rebel flag. "This means victory," he said. "This *is* victory." Three dispatches that day traced Lincoln's insight into the last bloody battle.

The Living Lincoln

City Point, Va.,
April 2, 1865 — 11 A.M.

Hon. Edwin M. Stanton,
Secretary of War:

Dispatches frequently coming in. All going finely. Parke, Wright, and Ord, extending from the Appomattox to Hatcher's Run, have all broken through the enemy's intrenched lines, taking some forts, guns, and prisoners. Sheridan, with his own cavalry, Fifth Corps, and part of the Second, is coming in from the west on the enemy's flank, and Wright is already tearing up the South Side Railroad.

A. Lincoln.

City Point, Va.,
April 2, 1865 — 2 P.M.

Hon. Edwin M. Stanton,
Secretary of War:

At 10.45 A.M. General Grant telegraphed as follows:

"Everything has been carried from the left of the Ninth Corps. The Sixth Corps alone captured more than 3,000 prisoners. The Second and Twenty-fourth Corps both captured forts, guns, and prisoners from the enemy, but I cannot tell the number. We are now closing around the works of the line immediately enveloping Petersburg. All looks remarkably well. I have not yet heard from Sheridan."

His headquarters have been moved up to T. Banks' house, near the Boydton road, about three miles southwest of Petersburg.

A. Lincoln.

Head Quarters Armies of the United States,
City Point,
April. 2. 8/15 P.M. *1865.*

Lieut. General Grant.

Allow me to tender to you, and all with you, the nation's grateful thanks for this additional, and magnificent success. At your kind suggestion, I think I will visit you tomorrow.

A. Lincoln

"With Malice Toward None"

City Point, Va., April 2, 1865.

Mrs. Lincoln:

At 4:30 P.M. today General Grant telegraphs that he has Petersburg completely enveloped from river below to river above, and has captured, since he started last Wednesday, about 12,000 prisoners and 50 guns. He suggests that I shall go out and see him in the morning, which I think I will do. Tad and I are both well, and will be glad to see you and your party here at the time you name.

A. Lincoln.

The final moment approached.

Head Quarters Armies of the United States.
City-Point,
April 3. 8/00 A.M. *1865*

Hon. Sec. of War
Washington D. C.

This morning Gen. Grant reports Petersburg evacuated; and he is confident Richmond also is. He is pushing forward to cut off if possible, the retreating army. I start to him in a few minutes.

A. Lincoln

Head Quarters Armies of the United States,
City-Point,
April 3. 5. P.M. *1865*

Hon. Sec. of War
Washington, D. C.

Yours received. Thanks for your caution; but I have already been to Petersburg, staid with Gen. Grant an hour & a half and returned here. It is certain now that Richmond is in our hands, and I think I will go there tomorrow. I will take care of myself.

Wherever Lee turned he found Sheridan. Lincoln offered his advice.

Head Quarters Armies of the United States,
City-Point,
April 7. 11 A.M. *1865*

Lieut Gen. Grant.

Gen. Sheridan says "If the thing is pressed I think that Lee will surrender." Let the *thing* be pressed.

A Lincoln

The Living Lincoln

Lee surrendered. A crowd marched to the White House. The *National Intelligencer* reported: ". . . The bands played, the howitzers belched forth their thunder, and the people cheered. Call after call was made for the President, and his failure to appear only made the people cry out louder." Lincoln could not deny the persistent clamor, and, appearing, spoke words that recaptured the youthful joviality of the prairie years.

April 10, 1865

Fellow-Citizens:

I am very greatly rejoiced to find that an occasion has occurred so pleasurable that the people cannot restrain themselves. [Cheers.] I suppose that arrangements are being made for some sort of a formal demonstration, this, or perhaps, tomorrow night. [Cries of "We can't wait," "We want it now," &c.] If there should be such a demonstration, I, of course, will be called upon to respond, and I shall have nothing to say if you dribble it all out of me before. [Laughter and applause.] I see you have a band of music with you. [Voices, "We have two or three."] I propose closing up this interview by the band performing a particular tune which I will name. Before this is done, however, I wish to mention one or two little circumstances connected with it. I have always thought "Dixie" one of the best tunes I have ever heard. Our adversaries over the way attempted to appropriate it, but I insisted yesterday that we fairly captured it. [Applause.] I presented the question to the Attorney General, and he gave it as his legal opinion that it is our lawful prize. [Laughter and applause.] I now request the band to favor me with its performance.

Lincoln's heart retained no feeling of giddy exultation. Until he could bind up the nation's wounds there was no victory. Next day he delivered his last public address. Its theme was reconstruction.

April 11, 1865

We meet this evening, not in sorrow, but in gladness of heart. The evacuation of Petersburg and Richmond, and the surrender of the principal insurgent army, give hope of a righteous and speedy peace whose joyous expression cannot be restrained. In the midst of this, however, He, from Whom all blessings flow, must not be forgotten. A call for a national thanksgiving is being prepared, and will be duly promulgated. Nor must those whose harder part gives us the cause of rejoicing, be overlooked. Their honors must not be parcelled out with others. I myself, was near the front, and had the high pleasure of transmitting much of the good news to you; but no part of the honor, for plan or execution, is mine. To Gen. Grant, his skilful officers, and brave men, all belongs. The gallant navy stoody ready, but was not in reach to take active part.

By these recent successes the re-inauguration of the national authority—reconstruction—which has had a large share of thought from the first, is pressed much more closely upon our attention. It is fraught with great difficulty. Unlike the case of a war between independent nations, there is no authorized organ for us to treat with. No one man has authority to give up the rebellion for any other man. We simply must begin with, and mould from, disorganized and discordant elements. Nor is it a small additional embarrassment that we, the loyal people, differ among ourselves as to the mode, manner, and means of reconstruction.

As a general rule, I abstain from reading the reports of attacks upon myself, wishing not to be provoked by that to which I cannot properly offer an answer. In spite of this precaution, however, it comes to my knowledge that I am much censured for some supposed agency in setting up, and seeking to sustain, the new state government of Louisiana. In this I have done just so much as, and no more than, the public knows. In the annual message of Dec. 1863 and accompanying proclamation, I presented *a* plan of reconstruction (as the phrase goes) which, I promised, if adopted by any state, should be acceptable to, and sustained by, the executive government of the nation. I distinctly stated that this was not the only plan which might possibly be acceptable; and I also distinctly protested that the executive claimed no right to say when, or whether members should be admitted to seats in Congress from such states. This plan was, in advance, submitted to the then Cabinet, and distinctly approved by every member of it. One of them suggested that I should then, and in that connection, apply the Emancipation Proclamation to the theretofore excepted parts of Virginia and Louisiana; that I should drop the suggestion about apprenticeship for freed people, and that I should omit the protest against my own power, in regard to the admission of members to Congress; but even he approved every part and parcel of the plan which has since been employed or touched by the action of Louisiana. The new constitution of Louisiana, declaring emancipation for the whole state, practically applies the proclamation to the part previously excepted. It does not adopt apprenticeship for freed people; and it is silent, as it could not well be otherwise, about the admission of members to Congress. So that, as it applies to Louisiana, every member of the Cabinet fully approved the plan. The message went to Congress, and I received many commendations of the plan, written and verbal; and not a single objection to it, from any professed emancipationist, came to my knowledge, until after the news reached Washington that the people of Louisiana had begun to move in accordance with it. From about July 1862, I had corresponded with different persons, supposed to be interested, seeking a reconstruction of a state government for Louisiana. When the message of 1863, with the plan before mentioned, reached New Orleans, Gen. Banks wrote me that he was confident the people, with his military co-operation, would reconstruct, substantially on that plan. I wrote him, and some of them to try it; they tried it, and the result is known. Such only has been my agency in getting up the Louisiana government. As to sustaining it, my promise is out, as before stated. But, as bad promises are better broken than kept, I shall treat this as a bad promise, and break it, whenever I shall be convinced that keeping it is adverse to the public interest. But I have not yet been so convinced.

I have been shown a letter on this subject, supposed to be an able one, in which the writer expresses regret that my mind has not seemed to be definitely fixed on the question whether the seceded states, so-called, are in the Union or out of it. It would perhaps, add astonishment to his regret, were he to learn that since I have found professed Union men endeavoring to make that question, I have *purposely* forborne any public expression upon it. As appears to me that question has not been, nor yet is, a practically material one, and that any discussion of it, while it thus remains practically immaterial, could have no effect other than the mischievous one of dividing our friends. As yet, whatever it may hereafter become, that question is bad, as the basis of a controversy, and good for nothing at all—a merely pernicious abstraction.

We all agree that the seceded states, so-called, are out of their proper practical relation with the Union; and that the sole object of the government, civil and military, in regard to those states is to again get them into that proper practical relation. I believe it is not only possible, but in fact, easier, to do this, without deciding, or even considering, whether these states have ever been out of the Union, than with it. Finding themselves safely at home, it would be utterly immaterial whether they had ever been abroad. Let us all join in doing the acts necessary to restoring the proper practical relations between these states and the Union; and each forever after, innocently indulge his own opinion whether, in doing the acts, he brought the states from without, into the Union, or only gave them proper assistance, they never having been out of it.

The amount of constituency, so to speak, on which the new Louisiana government rests, would be more satisfactory to all, if it contained fifty, thirty, or even twenty thousand, instead of only about twelve thousand, as it does. It is also unsatisfactory to some that the elective franchise is not given to the colored man. I would myself prefer that it were now conferred on the very intelligent, and on those who serve our cause as soldiers. Still the question is not whether the Louisiana government, as it stands, is quite all that is desirable. The question is "Will it be wiser to take it as it is, and help to improve it; or to reject, and disperse it?" "Can Louisiana be brought into proper practical relation with the Union *sooner* by *sustaining,* or by *discarding* her new state government?"

Some twelve thousand voters in the heretofore slave state of Louisiana have sworn allegiance to the Union, assumed to be the rightful political power of the state, held elections, organized a state government, adopted a free-state constitution, giving the benefit of public schools equally to black and white, and empowering the legislature to confer the elective franchise upon the colored man. Their legislature has already voted to ratify the constitutional amendment recently passed by Congress, abolishing slavery throughout the nation. These twelve thousand persons are thus fully committed to the Union, and to perpetual freedom in the state—committed to the very things, and nearly all the things the nation wants—and they ask the nation's recognition, and its assistance to make good their committal. Now, if we reject, and spurn them, we do our utmost to disorganize and disperse them. We in effect say to the white men "You are worthless, or worse— we will neither help you, nor be helped by you." To the blacks we say "This cup of liberty which these, your old masters, hold to your lips, we will dash from you, and leave you to the chances of gathering the spilled and scattered contents in some vague and undefined when, where, and how." If this course, discouraging and paralyzing both white and black, has any tendency to bring Louisiana into proper practical relations with the Union, I have, so far, been unable to perceive it. If, on the contrary, we recognize, and sustain the new government of Louisiana the converse of all this is made true. We encourage the hearts, and nerve the arms of the twelve thousand to adhere to their work, and argue for it, and proselyte for it, and fight for it, and feed it, and grow it, and ripen it to a complete success. The colored man too, in seeing all united for him, is inspired with vigilance, and energy, and daring, to the same end. Grant that he desires the elective franchise, will he not attain it sooner by saving the already advanced steps toward it, than by running backward over them? Concede that the new government of Louisiana is only to what it should be as the egg is to the fowl, we shall sooner have the fowl by hatching the egg than by smashing it? Again, if we reject Louisiana, we also reject one vote in favor of the proposed amendment to the national constitution. To meet this proposition, it has been argued that no more than three-fourths of those states which have not attempted secession are necessary to validly ratify the amendment. I do not commit myself against this, further than to say that such a ratification would be questionable, and sure to be persistently questioned; while a ratification by three-fourths of all the states would be unquestioned and unquestionable.

I repeat the question. "Can Louisiana be brought into proper practical relation with the Union *sooner* by *sustaining* or by *discarding* her new state government?"

What has been said of Louisiana will apply generally to other states. And yet so great peculiarities pertain to each state; and such important and sudden changes occur in the same state; and, withal, so new and unprecedented is the whole case, that no exclusive, and inflexible plan can safely be prescribed as to details and collaterals. Such exclusive, and inflexible plan, would surely become a new entanglement. Important principles may, and must, be inflexible.

In the present *"situation"* as the phrase goes, it may be my duty to make some new announcement to the people of the South.

"With Malice Toward None"

I am considering, and shall not fail to act, when satisfied that action will be proper.

The story of one man's life in Washington on Good Friday, 1865, is told in the notes that follow. Grant, attending the cabinet meeting, asked to be excused that evening since Mrs. Grant and he were anxious to visit their children in Long Branch, New Jersey. The short letter was addressed to James H. Van Allen, who reportedly had written Lincoln to guard his life and not expose it to assassination. Leaving for the theater with Mrs. Lincoln that evening, the President handed George Ashmun a card of admission.

April 14, 1865

No pass is necessary now to authorize any one to go to & return from Petersburg & Richmond. People go & return just as they did before the war.

A Lincoln

Executive Mansion, Washington,
April 14. 1865

Lieut. Genl. Grant

Please call at 11. A.M. today instead of 9. as agreed last evening. Yours truly

A. Lincoln

Let Thomas Geary be discharged from the service on refunding any bounty received.

A. Lincoln.

April 14, 1865.

Executive Mansion,
Washington, April 14, 1865.

Hon. Sec. of State
Sir:

Please assemble the Cabinet at 11. A.M. today.
Gen. Grant will meet with us. Yours truly

A. Lincoln

The Living Lincoln

My dear Sir:

I intend to adopt the advice of my friends and use due pre-caution. . . . I thank you for the assurance you give me that I shall be supported by conservative men like yourself, in the efforts I may make to restore the Union, so as to make it, to use your language, a Union of hearts and hands as well as of states. Yours truly,

A. Lincoln.

Allow Mr. Ashmun & friend to come in at 9 A.M. to-morrow.

A. Lincoln

April 14. 1865.

A beautiful sunny day had given way to patches of fog. Less than a block away from Ford's Theater, in the Herndon House, John Wilkes Booth sat with three comrades at a table. . . .

INDEX

Index

Index

Index

Index

Index

Index

Index

Index

Index

Index

Index

McClernand, John A., letters to, 444–45, 531–32, 534–35, 571–72

McClure, Alexander K., 370

McCullough, Fanny, letter to, 523–24

McCullough, William, 523

McDowell, Irvin, 460, 470, 471, 477

McDowell, James, 113

McGaughey, Edward W., 132

McLean, John, proposed for presidency, 193; and Dred Scott decision, 217; presidential prospects, 323, 326; death, 447

McNab (McKnabb), John, 427

McNeill, Cornelius F., letter to, 324

McPheeters, Samuel B., 527–28, 594–95

Macomb (Ill.), 264

Macon County (Ill.), 306, 336–37

Macy, Daniel, 217

Madison, James, 412

Madison (Wis.), speech at, 297–303

Magoffin, Beriah, letter to, 430–31

Magruder, John B., 549

Mails, to continue, 384

Mallory, Egbert M., 40

Manassas, first battle, 424–25, 460; second battle, 496–99. *See also* Bull Run

Manchester (Eng.), workingmen, letter to, 532–33

Mansfield, Joseph K. F., 514

Marshall, James F. B., 466

Marshall, John, letter to, 154–55

Marshall, Samuel D., letter to, 70

Marshall, Sarah, 154

Maryland, rebellion in, 398–400; legislature free to meet, 400–01; endangered by Fremont, 436; stays in Union, 451; emancipation in, 598, 622–23

Massachusetts, Lincoln in, 124; naturalization law, 291–94; 42nd

Regiment, address to, 622–23; 6th Regiment, attacked, 399

Matheny, Charles W., 118

Matheny, Noah W., letter to, 179–80

Matteson, Joel A., 183–85

Matthews, James L., 529

May, Thomas P., 625

May, William L., 39

Maynard, Horace, 458

Maxcy (Maxey), James, 38, 40

Meade, George G., 565, 578–79; letters to, 563–64, 566

Mechanicsville, Battle of, 483

Medill, Joseph, 522; letters to, 221–22, 354

Meigs, Montgomery, 409

Melancholy, Lincoln's, 134. *See also* Hypochondria

Memphis (Tenn.), 425

Menard County (Ill.), 73

Menzies, John W., 569

Meredosia (Ill.), 283

Merrimack (ironclad), 467

Merryman, Elias H., 38, 39, 68; duel instructions for, 67–68

Messages to Congress, 412–23, 447–54, 516–22, 628–33

Mexican War, Whig position, 96–97; origin of, Lincoln on, 98–109, 119; Lincoln defends stand, 221–22, 339–40

Meyers, John C., 398

Middleport Press, 324

Miller, William, 353

Milroy, Robert H., letter to, 559–60

Minnesota, Indian troubles, 517–18

Missionary Ridge, Battle of, 599

Mississippi, secession, 395, 412

Missouri, divided loyalties, 405; Fremont in, 424, 432–37; endangered by Fremont, 436; stays in Union, 451; factional troubles, 527–30, 541, 543, 583–88, 593–94; election in, 621–22

665

Index

Missouri Compromise, repeal proposed, 157; repealed, 159–60; history of, 161; repeal not sought, 163–66; moral issue, 167–68; repeal, effect on Lincoln, 340; Lincoln urges restoration, 175–76, 190; held unconstitutional, 200

Mob violence, Lincoln deplores, 19–23

Money, in politics, 322

Monitor (floating battery), 467–68

Monroe, James, 320

Moral issue. *See* Slavery, morality of

Morgan, Edwin D., 616; letters to, 407, 486

Morgan County (Ill.), Whigs, 74–75

Mormons, 34–35

Morris, Martin S., letter to, 72–74

"Mortality" (poem), 86–87

Morton, Oliver P., 476

Morrison, James L. D. ("Don"), seeks Land Office, 131, 134–35, 140; in senatorial election, 184; joins Democrats, 193

Motley, John L., 475

Motley, Mary, letter to, 475

"Mud-sill" theory of labor, 299–301

"My childhood's home" (poem), 87–88

Myer (Myers), William H., 40

National Intelligencer, 646

National Union Party, 607–09

Naturalization, Lincoln on, 291–92

Navy, Secretary of. *See* Welles, Gideon

Nebraska Bill, passed, 158; quoted, 159–60; Lincoln's parable, 160; Lincoln and Douglas on, 161–79; and popular sovereignty, 170–73, 213; Lincoln condemns, 190; in Illinois legislature, 191; political effect, 203

Negroes, humanity of, 168–70; equal rights of, 201–04, 237–38, 297; amalgamation, 203, 206; status of, Douglas on, 237, 258–59, 268–70; status of, Lincoln on, 265–70; colonization, 516–17; use of, as soldiers, 532, 537–38, 577, 614–15, 641; massacre of, 603–04; present Bible, 618–19

Nelson, Samuel, 217

New England, Lincoln in, 319–21

New Haven (Conn.), 319–21

New Haven *Palladium,* 325

New Jersey, and Negro franchise, 202; legislature of, Lincoln speaks to, 378–79

New Orleans, Lincoln visits, 5, 6, 336, 337; in Union hands, 490; situation in, 626

New Orleans *Times,* 625

New Salem (Ill.), Lincoln in, 6, 7, 10, 17, 306

New York (state), and Negro franchise, 202

New York *Herald,* 351

New York *Times,* 363, 367, 467, 574

New York *Tribune,* 207, 469, 495

Nevada, Territory, 450

Newton, Thomas W., 120

Niagara Falls, 125–26

Nicolay, John G., 331

Nolin Creek (Ky.), 342

North Carolina, and Negro franchise, 202

Norton, Jesse O., 182

Old Soldier (newspaper), 34

Office-seekers, 396–98. *See also* Patronage

Offutt, Denton, 6, 337

Ohio, 166th Regiment, address to, 615–16

Ohio, Republicans of, 322–23

Ohio River, 5

Opdyke, George, 406

Index

Index

Index

ing, 630–31; *See also* Emancipation, Emancipation Proclamation
Smith, Mrs. Alice C., letter to, 588
Smith, Caleb B., letter to, 333
Smith, Green Clay, 569
Smith, Joseph, 34–35
Smith, William F., 428, 564
Smith, Edwards & Co., 374
"Some Thoughts for the President's Consideration," 393–94
Sons of Temperance, address to, 581–83
South, people of, refusal to condemn, 161–62; Lincoln addresses, 310–17; assurances to, 369, 381–82
South Carolina, secedes, 368, 395, 412
Sovereignty, Lincoln defines, 419
Spears, George, letter to, 10
Speed, Joshua F., Lincoln lives with, 17; mentioned, 35; Lincoln visits, 41; marriage, 46; Unionist, 404; letters to: on Trailor murder, 37–41; on courtship and marriage, 43–47, 56–59; on duelling, 68–69; on congressional nomination, 72; on Lincoln family, 94; on land office, 131–32; on slavery, 188–92; on visiting Chicago, 362
Speed, Mrs. Joshua F. *See* Henning, Fanny
Speed, Mrs. Lucy, 43
Speed, Mary, letter to, 41–43
Spencer County (Ind.), 335
Spiegel, Solomon, 635
Sprigg, Mrs. Benjamin, 96
Springfield (Ill.), prospective capital, 13; Lincoln settles at, 17; life in, 17–18; excited over murder, 37–41; duelling fever, 68–69; Douglas speaks at, 230; "House Divided" speech, 230–39; Lincoln speaks at, 282; Farewell address, 375–76; postoffice, 393

Springfield Marine and Fire Insurance Co., 374
"Squatter sovereignty." *See* Popular sovereignty
Stanton, Edwin M., appointed Secretary of War, 460; order to McClellan, 468; visits Fortress Monroe, 473; Lincoln defends, 475; letters and telegrams to: on personal guard, 461; on William Kellogg, Jr., 479; on Pomroy, 490; about old lady, 527; on Freese appointment, 591; on Missouri, 593–94; on withholding pay, 597–98; on dismissing Cabinet members, 610; on progress of war, 642–45
State Bank of Illinois, 13–15, 33
State sovereignty, 377, 418–21
Stephens, Alexander H., 96
Stephens, James L., 529
Stevens, Isaac I., 514
Stevens, Thaddeus, letter to, 124–25
Stewart, Jackson, 638
Stockton, Mrs. Esther, letter to, 596
Stone, Dan, slavery protest, 16, 339
Stone River, Battle of, 530
Stoneman, George H., 428, 538–39
Strasburg (Va.), 425
Strategy, Lincoln's, 424–25, 437–38, 446–47, 460, 484, 505–07, 544, 545, 579
Strike, right to, 320–21
Stringfellow, Benjamin F., 191
Stringfellow, John H., 191
Strong, William, 115, 116
Strunk, John, 182, 184
Stuart, Bettie, 33
Stuart, John T., partnership with Lincoln, 17, 338–39; defeats Douglas, 31; re-election assured, 36–37; joins Democrats, 193; letters to, 32–37, 393
Stuart, Mrs. John T., 32, 33
Sturtevant, Julian M., letter to, 196–97

Index

Index

Y. M. C. A., Lincoln's reply to, 399
Yates, Richard, 158, 341, 571
Yorktown (Va.), 470, 472
Young, Ammi B., 403
Young Men's Lyceum, speech before, 20–27

Young Men's Republican Union, speech before, 309–19

Zollicoffer, Felix K., 437
Zwisler, Louis, 118